D0225652

About the Cover Images

Detail, *Crossing the River, Burma,* by Ernest Procter, 1920s

This painting by the English artist Ernest Procter depicts a river crossing in Burma during the 1920s, when that country (now Myanmar) was under British colonial rule. The image illustrates the continuation of older ways of living, even as changes introduced by European rule were taking shape. It also highlights the important role of waterways for transportation in Southeast Asia during a period when these watershed ecosystems were being heavily altered by human settlement and development.

Crossing the River, Burma (oil on canvas)/Ernest Procter (1886–1935)/CHRISTIES IMAGES/Private Collection/Bridgeman Images

Decorative Tile, Darb-I Imam Mausoleum, Isfahan, Iran, 17th century

This seventeenth-century ceramic tile is an exquisite example of a form of Islamic art used in the decoration of major public buildings—mosques, minarets, palaces, or in this case a mausoleum in Isfahan, Iran. Many decorative tiles depict nature, including trees, birds, and here a flower. Others incorporate intricate geometric designs or inscriptions from the Quran.

The Darb-i Imam Mausoleum, decorative tilework of the iwan, detail of a flower (photo)/GERARD DEGEORGE/Darb-e Emam Mausoleum, Isfahan, Iran/Bridgeman Images

Ways of the World

A Brief Global History with Sources

VOLUME 2

Since the Fifteenth Century

Ways of the World

A Brief Global History with Sources

FIFTH EDITION

Robert W. Strayer
The College at Brockport: State University of New York

Eric W. Nelson
Missouri State University

bedford/st.martin's
Macmillan Learning
Boston | New York

FOR EVELYN RHIANNON WITH LOVE

Vice President: Leasa Burton
Senior Program Director: Erika Gutierrez
Senior Executive Program Manager: William J. Lombardo
Director of Content Development: Jane Knetzger
Senior Development Editor: Heidi Hood
Associate Development Editor: Stephanie Sosa
Assistant Editor: Carly Lewis
Director of Media Editorial: Adam Whitehurst
Media Editor: Mollie Chandler
Senior Marketing Manager: Melissa Rodriguez
Senior Director, Content Management Enhancement: Tracey Kuehn
Senior Managing Editor: Michael Granger
Executive Content Project Manager: Christina M. Horn
Senior Workflow Project Manager: Lisa McDowell
Production Supervisor: Robin Besofsky / Lawrence Guerra
Director of Design, Content Management: Diana Blume
Interior Design: Lisa Buckley
Cover Design: William Boardman
Cartographer: Mapping Specialists, Ltd.
Text Permissions Editor: Michael McCarty
Text Permissions Researcher: Elaine Kosta, Lumina Datamatics, Inc.
Executive Permissions Editor: Cecilia Varas
Photo Researchers: Bruce Carson / Cheryl Du Bois, Lumina Datamatics, Inc.
Director of Digital Production: Keri deManigold
Executive Media Project Manager: Michelle Camisa
Copyeditor: Susan Zorn
Indexer: Rebecca McCorkle
Composition: Lumina Datamatics, Inc.
Cover Images: top, *Crossing the River, Burma* (oil on canvas)/Ernest Procter (1886–1935)/CHRISTIES IMAGES/Private Collection/Bridgeman Images; bottom, The Darb-i Imam Mausoleum, decorative tilework of the iwan, detail of a flower (photo)/GERARD DEGEORGE/Darb-e Emam Mausoleum, Isfahan, Iran/Bridgeman Images
Printing and Binding: LSC Communications

Library of Congress Control Number: 2021934943

ISBN 978-1-319-24443-9 (Combined Edition)
ISBN 978-1-319-33111-5 (Volume 1)
ISBN 978-1-319-33114-6 (Volume 2)

Printed in the United States of America.

4 5 6 7 26 25 24 23

ACKNOWLEDGMENTS
Text acknowledgments and copyrights appear at the back of the book on page 1073, which constitutes an extension of the copyright page. Art acknowledgments and copyrights appear on the same page as the art selections they cover.

For information, write: Bedford/St. Martin's, 75 Arlington Street, Boston, MA 02116

Preface

Ways of the World is an intentionally brief global history of the human experience that focuses on the **big pictures of world history**, using examples selectively rather than cluttering the narrative with endless details. It repeatedly highlights major transformations in global history, makes frequent comparisons, and spotlights interactions among culturally different peoples. These elements appear in the narrative text, in the book's innovative primary and secondary source features, and now for the first time in **Achieve**, Macmillan Learning's innovative new learning platform. Built with instructors and students in mind, **Achieve for *Ways of the World*** comes loaded with the full-color e-book plus **LearningCurve**, an adaptive quizzing tool that spurs students to read the text before class. It also contains the popular companion source reader ***Thinking through Sources for Ways of the World***, along with a wealth of **assessment options**, including an autograded **exercise for building and supporting a thesis statement, chapter summative quizzes**, robust **reporting and insight tools**, and more. All of this is built around a book that has been revised to further promote **historical thinking skills**, such as chronological reasoning, empathy, analysis and interpretation, and awareness of historical controversies.

A Distinctive Approach to World History

The main title of the book, *Ways of the World*, evokes three dimensions of its distinctive approach, all of them based on our experience as teachers and scholars. The first is **diversity** or **variation**, for the "ways of the world," or the ways of being human in the world, have been many and constantly changing. This book seeks to embrace the global experience of humankind, both in its common features and in its vast diversity, while noticing the changing location of particular centers of innovation and wider influence.

Second, the title *Ways of the World* invokes major **panoramas**, **patterns**, or **pathways** in world history rather than a highly detailed narrative, which can often overwhelm students. Thus most chapters are organized in terms of broad global or transregional themes, illustrated by a limited number of specific examples.

A third implication of the book's title lies in a certain **reflective quality** that appears in the Big Picture essays that introduce each part, in the Conclusions and Reflections section at the end of each chapter, and periodically in the narrative itself. This dimension of the book offers many opportunities for pondering larger questions about how historians operate, about the dilemmas they face in reconstructing the human journey, and about the relationship of the past to the present.

These elements of *Ways of the World* find expression repeatedly in what we call the **four Cs** of world history: context, change, comparison, and connection. The first "C," **context**, refers to the larger frameworks within which particular historical figures, events, societies, and civilizations take shape. In our telling of the human past, context is central, for in world history nothing stands alone. Like Russian nesting dolls, every story finds a place in some more inclusive narrative. European empires in the Americas, for example, take on new meaning when they are understood as part of a global process of imperial expansion that also included the growth of the Inca, Russian, Chinese, and Ottoman empires.

The second "C," large-scale **change**, both within and especially across major regions of the world, represents another prominent emphasis in *Ways of the World*. Examples include the peopling of the planet, the emergence of "civilization," the linking of Eastern and Western hemispheres in the wake of Columbus's voyages, the Industrial Revolution, and many other significant changes during the course of human history. The flip side of change, of course, is continuity, implying a focus on what persists over long periods of time. And so *Ways of the World* seeks to juxtapose these contrasting elements of human experience. While civilizations have changed dramatically over time, some of their essential features—cities, states, patriarchy, and class inequality, for example—have long endured.

A third "C" involves frequent **comparison**, bringing several regions or cultures into our field of vision at the same time. It means constantly asking "what's the difference?" Thus this book makes comparisons between the Agricultural Revolution in the Eastern and Western hemispheres; between the beginnings of Buddhism and the early history of Christianity and Islam; between the Russian and Chinese revolutions; and between feminism in the Global North and the Global South. These and many more comparisons frequently punctuate our account of the global past.

The final "C" emphasizes **connections**, networks of communication and exchange that increasingly shaped the character of the societies that participated in them. In our account of the human story, world history is less about what happened within particular civilizations or cultures than about the processes and outcomes of their meetings with one another. Cross-cultural encounters then become one of the major motors of historical transformation. Examples include the clash of the ancient Greeks and the Persians, the long-distance commercial networks that linked the Afro-Eurasian world, the numerous cross-cultural interactions spawned by the spread of Islam, the trans-hemispheric Columbian exchange of the early modern era, and the more recent growth of a thoroughly entangled global economy.

These emphases have remained at the heart of *Ways of the World* since its initial publication in 2008. As the book matured, it also began to combine a brief narrative text with thematically based sets of primary sources followed by paired secondary sources at the end of each chapter. What has emerged is a new kind of book for the world history course, one that enables students to "do history," using the kind of evidence that historians work with. Each of the **Working with Evidence** primary source collections includes both documents and images and is organized around a particular theme, issue, or question that derives from the chapter narrative. As the title of these features suggests, they enable students to "work with evidence" and thus begin to understand the craft of historians as well as historians' conclusions. They include brief headnotes that provide context for the sources, and they are accompanied by a series of probing Doing History questions appropriate for in-class discussion and writing assignments. Furthermore, Working with Evidence is followed by a **Historians' Voices** secondary source feature that presents two brief extracts from scholarly works, aligned with the theme of the Working with Evidence feature. Thus it can be used in conjunction with that feature or assigned on its own. *Ways of the World*, then, has become a textbook and a sourcebook in one book.

How Has the Content Changed in the Fifth Edition?

History books are always works in progress rather than finished products. The changes in this fifth edition of *Ways of the World* have been driven by two major goals. Our primary goal has been to strengthen the book's support for developing historical thinking skills, because those skills—such as chronological reasoning, empathy, analysis and interpretation, and identification of historical issues and problems—will last long after particular pieces of information have been forgotten. But since high-quality content is central to all historical study and to the development of historical thinking skills, we have also updated the book with new **scholarship** and new **points of view**.

In terms of both content and skill development, this edition addresses our students' ability to make connections between the past and their own lives in the present even as they develop analytical skills and historical empathy. Thus a new feature called **Then and Now** examines a particular theme, one for each part of the book, in both historical and contemporary settings. Themes include patriarchy, slavery, science, China's role on the global stage, and more. The skill of connecting with the past is also reinforced at the beginning of each chapter through updated vignettes called **Connecting Past and Present** that illustrate the continuing relevance of the chapter's material in our world today.

As a part of content updating, four new Working with Evidence primary source features and three new Historians' Voices secondary sources features provide fresh, rich material to engage students and hone their historical comprehension, empathy, analysis, interpretation, and research skills. In Chapter 8, the new Working with Evidence feature, "Society during China's Golden Age," explores the complex social world in Tang and Song China. Likewise, a new "Cultural Encounters in Muslim Spain" feature in Chapter 9 explores the long period of cultural interaction between Muslims, Christians, and Jews in Spain from the eighth century to the sixteenth century. And Chapter 14's new primary source feature, "Consumption and Culture in the Early Modern World," examines the cultural implications of consumption during the several centuries after 1500, using clothing, tea, porcelain, and coffee as examples. Finally, the new Working with Evidence feature entitled "The Socialist Vision and Its Enemies" in Chapter 17 incorporates documents that illustrate some of the ways that socialism was expressed and contested as it took root in modern Europe. Three new Historians' Voices illustrate diverse views on China's economy (Chapter 8), on religious tolerance in Muslim Spain (Chapter 9), and on consumer culture in the early modern world (Chapter 14).

Further content changes in the book have derived from new scholarship in the rapidly expanding field of world history. The **earliest history of our species** has been thoroughly updated to take into account important recent research such as new dating for the first emergence of *Homo sapiens*, new evidence of early failed migrations out of Africa and interactions with other hominid species, new thinking on migration into the Americas, and new discoveries of cave paintings in Indonesia and bone flutes in Germany. Examination of Paleolithic and Neolithic societies now includes new scholarship on the practice of slavery among gatherers and hunters in Alaska, new evidence of the fragility of many early agricultural communities, and updated population estimates for the Neolithic period. Coverage of First Civilizations has also been updated to incorporate new archeological evidence of early trade patterns and recent revisions in the dating of the Indus Valley, Chinese, Oxus, and Nubian civilizations. The revised Part 2 opening now explores the reasons that First Civilizations collapsed, with special emphasis on climate change, environmental degradation, and migrations.

We have also systematically revised our coverage of **modern science** for the fifth edition. Thus the section on the **Scientific Revolution in Chapter 15** has been heavily reworked to incorporate recent scholarship on earlier Chinese and Islamic influences on European science and to discuss how the vast and unprecedented flow of knowledge from across the globe into Europe impacted the Scientific Revolution during the early modern period. This revision is complemented by a new Chapter 15 Then and Now feature entitled "Science" that explores the relationship between the advances of the initial Scientific Revolution and science today. A new section entitled **"A Second Scientific Revolution" in Chapter 22** examines how scientific breakthroughs in the twentieth century profoundly changed our understanding of the cosmos with important cultural implications and laid the groundwork for technological innovations that have transformed modern life.

Coverage of the environment and disease has provided a third focus of revision. In Chapter 11, we expand our analysis of the **long-term impact of the plague** on European society, especially the shift toward laborsaving technologies and the revival of slavery in Europe. In Chapter 13, we update our account of the **Little Ice Age** to reflect recent research, and in Chapter 17 we explore the links between the **Industrial Revolution and our current climate crisis**. Finally, we have revised the section "Microbes in Motion" in Chapter 23 to discuss the **COVID-19 pandemic** in the context of other modern pandemics, and we incorporate a new Then and Now feature on the relationship between humankind and the natural environment today and in the past.

A further focus of revision has involved reworking and expanding our coverage of the **Indian Ocean world** in Chapters 7 and 9 to more fully discuss the spread of Islam in that region. In Chapter 7, we discuss the arrival of Islam in Southeast Asia, with expanded coverage of Melaka, among the first globalized cities in world history. In Chapter 9, we focus on Islam's establishment in southern India, especially in the Hindu Vijayanagar empire, adding another dimension to the theme of Muslim cultural encounter in India. In addition to these major revisions, we have fully updated Part 6 to take into account recent developments in the early twenty-first century.

These changes remind us that textbooks are not fixed and finished compilations of what happened in the past. Rather, such books develop as they respond to new technologies, to new historical research, and to the evolving political, social, and economic conditions of the contemporary world. As authors, we are acutely aware of how much debate and controversy lie behind many of the issues that are explored in *Ways of the World*. This book, then, is a snapshot of our current understanding of world history, shaped by the particular time (the early twenty-first century) and place (the United States) in which it was composed. Such a book written fifty years ago, or in contemporary China, Nigeria, Iran, or Brazil, or in the mid-twenty-first century, would surely be very different. Thus *Ways of the World* can and should be criticized, assessed, and argued with, not simply accepted as a definitive account of the global past.

Enhancements for Nurturing Skill Development

Obviously, the study of history requires some assimilation of information, data, or "facts." But instructors also want to enable their students to manipulate the information in their textbooks, using its ideas and data to answer questions, to make comparisons, to draw conclusions, to criticize assumptions, and to infer implications that are not explicitly disclosed in the text itself. This kind of skill development occurs most effectively as students directly and actively engage with the material in the text.

Ways of the World is designed to promote skill development in various ways. Most obviously, the source-based features in the book itself (Working with Evidence and Historians' Voices) and those in the companion reader (*Thinking through Sources for Ways of the World*, also available in Achieve) invite students to engage actively with documents and images alike, assisted by abundant questions to guide that engagement. New **Then and Now features** and updated **Connecting Past and Present chapter-opening vignettes** encourage students to examine the links between the past and present. **Zooming In** essays, which call attention to particular people, places, and events, offer opportunities to develop the skill of contextualization, situating particulars in a larger framework. Appearing once in each chapter, Zooming In addresses topics such as Göbekli Tepe and monumental construction before agriculture (specially updated for this edition), Trung Trac and female-led resistance to the Chinese empire, gunpowder, the end of the Byzantine Empire, feminism and nationalism in Java, the Cuban Revolution, and many more.

The **Controversies** feature, which appears in one chapter of each part, develops skills in identifying and analyzing historical issues through the exploration of important debates: the origins of major religious traditions, the idea of the Atlantic world, why the Industrial Revolution began in Europe, the concept of globalization, and more. These features counteract the notion of a textbook as an authoritative, encyclopedia-like tome to be assimilated, while conveying an understanding of world history as a frequently contested conversation.

Skills-based active learning also means approaching the text through questions to explore, rather than simply dutifully completing the reading. *Ways of the World* provides such questions in abundance, offering students something to look for as they read. New to this edition, each part-opening Big Picture essay includes **First Reflections** questions that set the stage for actively reading the part ahead but also can help students reflect on the part as a whole after they have read it. A **Seeking the Main Point** question at the start of each chapter helps students focus on the chapter's central theme. **Mapping History** exercises invite students to read maps carefully and to interpret their implications. **Skills-based questions** accompany the narrative text, and the most important of these questions, labeled "Core Ideas," are repeated in the **Revisiting Core Ideas** section in the chapter review to ensure that students absorb the chapter's most important takeaways. **A Wider View** questions at the end of each chapter deal with matters not directly addressed in the text. Instead, they provide opportunities for integration, comparison, analysis, and sometimes speculation.

Skill development is also encouraged by providing frequent contextual markers. Student readers need to know where they are going and where they have been. Thus part-opening **Big Picture essays** preview what follows in the subsequent chapters, while a **chapter outline** suggests what is coming in each chapter. A **Landmarks** visual timeline, providing a chronological overview of major events and processes, appears at the beginning of each part and each chapter. **Snapshot boxes** present succinct glimpses of particular themes, regions, or time periods, adding some trees to the forest of world history. A **list of key terms** at the end of each chapter invites students to check their grasp of the material. As usual with books published by Bedford/St. Martin's, a **rich illustration and map program** provides striking visual markers that enhance the narrative.

In addition, whenever an instructor assigns the **Achieve e-book** (with the option of bundling in the print book for a small additional fee), students have at their disposal all the resources of the print text, including its special features and its primary and secondary sources. But they also gain access to **LearningCurve**, an online adaptive learning tool that helps students actively rehearse what they have read and achieve a deeper understanding and retention of the material. With this adaptive quizzing, students accumulate points toward a target score as they go, giving the interaction a game-like feel. Feedback for incorrect responses explains why the answer is incorrect and directs students back to the text to review before they attempt to answer the question again. The end result is a better understanding of the key elements of the text. Instructors who assign LearningCurve report that their students come to class prepared for discussion and enjoy using it. In addition, LearningCurve's reporting feature allows instructors to quickly diagnose which concepts students are struggling with so they can adjust lectures and activities accordingly.

Further opportunities for skill development are available through the special activities provided in Achieve, many of which are available for the first time with the fifth edition of *Ways of the World*. These easy-to-use assignments include new **journaling reflection activities** that invite students to reflect on what they have read in each chapter, **instructor activity guides** that instructors can use for either remote or in-person collaborative learning, **source and feature quizzes**, **research and writing tutorials**, and more. Most notably, Achieve offers six new **Building a Historical Argument** activities. Provided once per part, these autograded activities enable students to hone their skills in constructing a thesis and identifying evidence to sustain historical arguments. By offering students the opportunity to compose a conclusion to the argument they have constructed, these activities also support the development of writing skills. When required by instructors, the wrap-around pedagogy provided in Achieve virtually ensures active learning. Achieve is a rich asset for instructors who want to support students however they encounter them, whether teaching in a face-to-face, hybrid, or fully remote setting. Thus *Ways of the World* combines an engaging narrative with a rich set of digital and print features that promote the comprehension of content, active learning, and skill development. It seems to us an impressive package. (To learn more about the benefits of LearningCurve, Achieve, and the different versions to package with these digital tools, see the Versions and Supplements section on page xvii.)

"It Takes a Village"

In any enterprise of significance, "it takes a village," as they say. Bringing *Ways of the World* to life in this new edition, it seems, has occupied the energies of several villages. Among the privileges and delights of writing and revising this book has been the opportunity to interact with our fellow villagers.

We are grateful to the community of fellow historians who contributed their expertise to this revision. We especially thank our colleagues Bryan Brinkman, Tonia E. Tinsley, and John F. Chuchiak IV for their translations for our primary source features. We also thank the following reviewers of this edition: Dorian Borbonus, University of Dayton; Matthew Conn, Eastern Michigan University; Adrianna L. Ernstberger, Marian University; Andrei Gandila, University of Alabama at Huntsville; MayaLisa Holzman, Oregon State University; Toby Huff, Harvard University; Jeremy LaBuff, Northern Arizona University; Susan Maneck, Jackson State University; Dean Pavlakis, Carroll College; Charles V. Reed, Elizabeth City State University; Kimberly B. Sherman, Cape Fear Community College; Ira Spar, Ramapo College of New Jersey; Bianka Rhodes Stumpf, Central Carolina Community College; Jeanne M. Vloyanetes, Brookdale Community College; Erin Warford, Hilbert College; and Tara S. Wood, Ball State University.

We also offer our gratitude to reviewers of earlier editions: Andreas Agocs, University of the Pacific; Tonio Andrade, Emory University; Maria S. Arbelaez, University of Nebraska–Omaha; Monty Armstrong, Cerritos High School; Melanie Bailey, Piedmont Virginia Community College; Djene Bajalan, Missouri State University; Veronica L. Bale, Mira Costa College; Anthony Barbieri-Low, University of California, Santa Barbara; Christopher Bellitto, Kean University; Christine Bond, Edmond Memorial High School; Monica Bord-Lamberty, Northwood High School; Mike Burns, Concordia International School, Hanoi; Stanley Burstein, California State University–Los Angeles; Elizabeth Campbell, Daemen College; Theodore Cohen, Lindenwood University; Ralph Croizier, University of Victoria; Gregory Cushman, the University of Kansas; Edward Dandrow, University of Central Florida; Bradley Davis, Eastern Connecticut State University; Peter L. de Rosa, Bridgewater State University; Carter Findley, Ohio State University; Amy Forss, Metropolitan Community College; Denis Gainty, Georgia State University; Duane Galloway, Rowan-Cabarrus Community College; Steven A. Glazer, Graceland University; Sue Gronewald, Kean University; Andrew Hamilton, Viterbo University; J. Laurence Hare, University of Arkansas; Jay Harmon, Houston Christian High School; Michael Hinckley, Northern Kentucky University; Bram Hubbell, Friends Seminary; Ronald Huch, Eastern Kentucky University; Michael Hunt, University of North Carolina at Chapel Hill; Elizabeth Hyde, Kean University; Mark Lentz, University of Louisiana–Lafayette; Ane Lintvedt, McDonogh School; Aran MacKinnon, Georgia College and State University; Harold Marcuse, University of California, Santa Barbara; Kate McGrath, Central Connecticut State University; Merritt McKinney, Volunteer State Community College; C. Brid Nicholson, Kean University; Erin O'Donnell, East Stroudsburg University; Sarah Panzer, Missouri State University; Donna Patch, Westside High School; Charmayne Patterson, Clark Atlanta University; Dean

Pavlakis, Carroll College; Chris Peek, Bellaire High School; Tracie Provost, Middle Georgia State University; Masako Racel, Kennesaw State University; Jonathan T. Reynolds, Northern Kentucky University; James Sabathne, Hononegah High School; Christopher Sleeper, Mira Costa College; Ira Spar, Ramapo College and Metropolitan Museum of Art; Kristen Strobel, Lexington High School; Eddie Supratman, Arkansas State University–Beebe; Michael Vann, Sacramento State University; Peter Winn, Tufts University; and Judith Zinsser, Miami University of Ohio.

The fine people at Bedford/St. Martin's (Macmillan Learning) have provided a second community sustaining this enterprise and the one most directly responsible for the book's fifth edition. It would be difficult for any author to imagine a more supportive and professional publishing team. Our chief point of contact with the Bedford village has been Heidi Hood, our development editor. She has coordinated the immensely complex task of assembling a new edition of the book and has done so with great professional care, with timely responses to our many queries, and with sensitivity to the needs and feelings of authors, even when she found it necessary to decline our suggestions.

Others on the team have also exhibited that lovely combination of personal kindness and professional competence that is so characteristic of the Bedford way. Vice president Leasa Burton, program director Erika Gutierrez, and program manager William Lombardo have kept an eye on the project amid many duties. Christina Horn, our content project manager, managed the process of turning a manuscript into a published book and did so with both grace and efficiency. Assistant editor Carly Lewis has efficiently and thoughtfully prepared manuscript, reviewed e-book pages, and handled countless other project details. Operating behind the scenes in the Bedford village, a series of highly competent and always supportive people have shepherded this revised edition along its way. Photo researcher Bruce Carson identified and acquired the many images that grace this new edition of *Ways of the World* and did so with a keen eye and courtesy. Copy editor Susan Zorn polished the prose and sorted out our many inconsistent usages with a seasoned and perceptive eye. Melissa Rodriguez has overseen the marketing process, while Bedford's sales representatives have reintroduced the book to the academic world. Associate development editor Stephanie Sosa and media editor Mollie Chandler supervised the development and preparation of supplements and media products to support the book, and William Boardman ably coordinated research for the lovely covers that mark *Ways of the World.*

A final and much smaller community sustained this project and its authors. It is that most intimate of villages that we know as a marriage. Sharing that village with me (Robert Strayer) is my wife, Suzanne Sturn. It is her work to bring ideas and people to life onstage, even as I try to do so between these covers. She knows how I feel about her love and support, and no one else needs to. And across the street, I (Eric Nelson) would also like to thank two other residents of this village: my wife,

Alice Victoria, and our daughter, Evelyn Rhiannon, to whom this new edition is dedicated. Without their patience and support, I could not have become part of such an interesting journey.

To all of our fellow villagers, we offer deep thanks for an immensely rewarding experience. We are grateful beyond measure.

Robert Strayer, La Selva Beach, California
Eric Nelson, Springfield, Missouri

Versions and Supplements

Adopters of *Ways of the World* and their students have access to abundant digital and print resources and tools, including documents, assessment and presentation materials, the acclaimed *Bedford Series in History and Culture* volumes, and much more. *Ways of the World* is now available for the first time in Achieve, Macmillan's new complete course platform, which provides access to the narrative as well as a wealth of primary sources and other features, along with assessments and robust insight reports at the ready, all in one affordably priced product. Achieve also includes a downloadable e-book for reading offline. See the following text for more information, visit the book's catalog site at **macmillanlearning.com**, or contact your local Bedford/St. Martin's sales representative.

Get the Right Version and Volume for Your Course—Digital, Print, and Value Options

Whether it's a digital course platform, e-book, print book, value option, or package combining digital and print products, *Ways of the World* is available in a variety of volumes and formats so you can choose what works best for your course. The **comprehensive *Ways of the World*** includes a full-color art and map program and a rich set of features and primary and secondary sources. Digital options for the comprehensive version include the full course platform of Achieve for *Ways of the World* (see below for the description of Achieve's benefits), as well as e-books. The comprehensive version is also available in print in three volume options. For great value in a streamlined product, ***Ways of the World*, Value Edition**, offers the unabridged narrative and selected two-color art and maps—without special features or primary or secondary sources—at a steep discount. The Value Edition is available in e-book format as well as print in three volume options, with loose-leaf format available for the least expensive print option. For the best value, purchase Achieve on its own or package it with the print version of your choice for a small add-on cost. *Ways of the World* is available in the following volume configurations:

- **Combined Volume** (Chapters 1–23): available in Achieve (1- and 2-term subscriptions), e-books, and print volumes for the comprehensive and Value editions
- **Volume 1: Through the Fifteenth Century** (Chapters 1–12): available in Achieve (1- and 2-term subscriptions), e-books, and print volumes for the

comprehensive and Value editions, including loose-leaf format for the Value Edition

- **Volume 2: Since the Fifteenth Century** (Chapters 12–23): available in Achieve (1- and 2-term subscriptions), e-books, and print volumes for the comprehensive and Value editions, including loose-leaf format for the Value Edition

As noted below, any of these volumes can be packaged with additional titles for a discount. To get ISBNs for discount packages, visit **macmillanlearning.com** or contact your Bedford/St. Martin's representative.

Achieve

Assign Achieve—A Comprehensive Course Platform with E-book, Skill-Building Assessments, and Analytics for Instructors

Affordably priced, intuitive, and easy to use, Achieve is a breakthrough solution for building students' skills and confidence in history courses. Achieve for *Ways of the World* includes the rich resources and skill-building content of the e-books for the complete comprehensive text and companion reader, *Thinking through Sources for Ways of the World*, alongside a robust set of summative and formative assessments—many autograded—that help students build confidence in their mastery of the material, reflect on their learning, and build critical, higher-level thinking skills. Achieve for *Ways of the World* includes LearningCurve adaptive quizzing that—when assigned—helps ensure that students do the reading before class; autograded exercises that teach students how to build a thesis and support an argument; quizzes that check student comprehension of primary sources and boxed features; chapter summative quizzes that test student knowledge after they've completed the reading; tutorials with quizzing that build skills such as working with primary sources and avoiding plagiarism; assignable chapter reflections questions that encourage students to engage with their learning; active reading activities that help students read actively for key concepts; class activity guides that can be used in synchronous and asynchronous courses; and iClicker polling questions that engage students during class. These features, plus additional primary source documents, map quizzes, customizable test banks, and detailed reports on student progress, make Achieve an invaluable asset for any instructor.

Achieve easily integrates with course management systems, and, with fast ways to build assignments and organize content, it lets teachers build the courses they want to teach while holding students accountable. For more information, or to arrange a demo or class test, contact us at **historymktg@macmillan.com**.

LearningCurve
macmillan learning

Assign LearningCurve So Your Students Come to Class Prepared

Students using Achieve receive access to LearningCurve for *Ways of the World*. Assigning LearningCurve in place of reading quizzes is easy for instructors, and the reporting features help instructors track overall class trends and spot topics that are giving students trouble so they can adjust their lectures and class activities. This online learning tool is popular with students because it was designed to help them rehearse content at their own pace in a nonthreatening, game-like environment. The feedback for wrong answers provides instructional coaching and sends students back to the book for review. Students answer as many questions as necessary to reach a target score, with repeated chances to revisit material they haven't mastered. When LearningCurve is assigned, students come to class better prepared.

iClicker

iClicker, Active Learning Simplified

iClicker offers simple, flexible tools to help you give students a voice and facilitate active learning in the classroom. Students can participate with the devices they bring to class using our iClicker student app (which work with smartphones, tablets, or laptops) or iClicker remotes. We've now integrated iClicker with Macmillan's Achieve to make it easier than ever to synchronize grades and promote engagement—both in and out of class. iClicker can be used synchronously through its polling feature, or asynchronously for assignments. To learn more, talk to your Macmillan Learning representative or visit us at **www.iclicker.com**.

Take Advantage of Instructor Resources

Bedford/St. Martin's has developed a rich array of teaching resources for this book and for this course. They range from lecture and presentation materials and assessment tools to course management options. Most can be found in Achieve or can be downloaded or ordered at **macmillanlearning.com**.

Instructor's Resource Manual. The instructor's manual offers both experienced and first-time instructors tools for presenting textbook material in engaging ways. It includes content learning objectives, annotated chapter outlines, and strategies for teaching with the textbook, plus suggestions on how to get the most out of LearningCurve and a survival guide for first-time teaching assistants.

Guide to Changing Editions. Designed to facilitate an instructor's transition from the previous edition of *Ways of the World* to this new edition, this guide presents an overview of major changes across the book and of changes in each chapter.

Online Test Bank. The test bank includes a mix of fresh, carefully crafted multiple-choice, short-answer, and essay questions for each chapter. Some of the multiple-choice questions feature a map as the prompt. All questions appear in an easy-to-use test bank software that allows instructors to add, edit, re-sequence, filter by question type, and print questions and answers. Instructors can also export questions into a variety of course management systems.

The Bedford Lecture Kit: *Lecture Outlines, Maps, and Images.* Look good and save time with *The Bedford Lecture Kit*. This resource includes fully customizable multimedia presentations built around chapter outlines that are embedded with maps, figures, and images from the textbook and are supplemented by more detailed instructor notes on key points and concepts.

Print, Digital, and Custom Options for More Choice and Value

For information on free packages and discounts up to 50%, visit **macmillanlearning.com**, or contact your local Bedford/St. Martin's sales representative.

***Thinking through Sources for Ways of the World,* Fourth Edition.** Designed to accompany *Ways of the World*, each chapter of this reader contains approximately five to eight written and visual primary sources organized around a particular theme, issue, or question. Each of these projects is followed by a related Historians' Voices secondary source feature that pairs two brief excerpts from historians who comment on some aspect of the topics covered in the primary sources. *Thinking through Sources for Ways of the World* provides a broad selection of over 140 primary source documents and images as well as editorial apparatus to help students understand the sources. This companion reader is an exceptional value for students and offers plenty of assignment options for instructors, and it is included in Achieve with autograded quizzes for each source. *Thinking through Sources for Ways of the World* is also available on its own as a downloadable e-book.

Bedford Document Collections. These affordable, brief document projects provide 5 to 7 primary sources, an introduction, historical background, and other pedagogical features. Each curated project—designed for use in a single class period and written by a historian about a favorite topic—poses a historical question and guides students through analysis of the sources. Examples include "The Silk Road: Travel and Trade in Pre-Modern Inner Asia," "The Spread of Christianity in the Sixteenth and Early Seventeenth Centuries," "The Singapore Mutiny of

1915: Understanding World War I from a Global Perspective," and "Living through Perestroika: The Soviet Union in Upheaval, 1985–1991." These primary source projects are available in a low-cost, easy-to-use digital format or can be combined with other course materials in Bedford Select to create an affordable, personalized print product. For more information on using Bedford Select to customize your course materials with these and other resources, visit **macmillanlearning.com/bedfordselect**.

Bedford Tutorials for History. Designed to provide resources relevant to individual courses, this collection of over a dozen brief units, each 16 pages long and loaded with examples, guides students through basic skills such as using historical evidence effectively, working with primary sources, taking effective notes, avoiding plagiarism and citing sources, and more. For more information, visit **macmillanlearning.com/historytutorials**.

The Bedford Series in History and Culture. Now also available in low-cost e-books as well as print volumes, the more than 100 titles in this highly praised series combine first-rate scholarship, historical narrative, and important primary documents for undergraduate courses. Each title is brief, inexpensive, and focused on a specific topic or period. Recent titles in the series include *The First World War: Brief History with Documents*, Second Edition, by Susan R. Grayzel; *Spartacus and the Slave Wars: A Brief History with Documents*, Second Edition, by Brent D. Shaw; *Apartheid in South Africa: A Brief History with Documents* by David M. Gordon; *Politics and Society in Japan's Meiji Restoration: A Brief History with Documents* by Anne Walthall and M. William Stele; and *The Congo Free State and the New Imperialism: A Brief History with Documents* by Kevin Grant. For a complete list of titles, visit **macmillanlearning.com**. Package discounts are available.

Trade Books. History titles published by sister companies Hill and Wang; Farrar, Straus and Giroux; Henry Holt and Company; St. Martin's Press; Picador; and Palgrave Macmillan are available at a 50% discount when packaged with Bedford/St. Martin's textbooks. For more information, visit **macmillanlearning.com/tradeup**.

A Pocket Guide to Writing in History. Available in a low-cost e-book as well as in print and updated to reflect changes made in the 2017 *Chicago Manual of Style* revision, this portable and affordable reference tool by Mary Lynn Rampolla provides reading, writing, and research advice useful to students in all history courses. Concise yet comprehensive advice on approaching typical history assignments, developing critical reading skills, writing effective history papers, conducting research, using and documenting sources, and avoiding plagiarism—enhanced with practical tips and examples throughout—has made this slim reference a best seller. Deep discounts are available when bundled with a survey textbook.

A Student's Guide to History. Available in a low-cost e-book as well as in print and updated to reflect changes made in the 2017 *Chicago Manual of Style* revision, this complete guide to success in any history course provides the practical help students need to be successful. In addition to introducing students to the nature of the discipline, author Jules Benjamin teaches a wide range of skills, from preparing for exams to approaching common writing assignments, and explains the research and documentation process with plentiful examples. Deep discounts are available when bundled with a survey textbook.

Brief Contents

Contents

photo: Bridgeman Images

14 Economic Transformations: Commerce and Consequence 1450–1750 592

photo: © Archives Charmet/ Bridgeman Images

photo: Gianni Dagli Orti/Shutterstock

photo: Photo Josse/Leemage/Getty Images

photo: Gianni Dagli Orti/Shutterstock

photo: TopFoto

photo: Bridgeman Images

photo: PhotoQuest/Getty Images

21 A Changing Global Landscape

photo: © Look and Learn/Bridgeman Images

photo: SIMON MAINA/AFP/Getty Images

photo: Image created by Reto Stockli, Nazmi El Saleous, and Marit Jentoft-Nilsen, NASA GSFC

Maps

Features

CONTROVERSIES

HISTORIANS' VOICES

MAPPING HISTORY

SNAPSHOT

THEN AND NOW

WORKING WITH EVIDENCE

ZOOMING IN

Working with Primary Sources

Two sets of primary sources accompany each chapter of *Ways of the World*. **Working with Evidence** collections appear at the end of each chapter in the book, while *Thinking through Sources* sets are available either as a print supplement or in Achieve—the interactive course platform for this text. Both collections typically feature written sources, such as inscriptions, letters, diaries, law codes, official records, and sacred texts, alongside visual sources—paintings, sculptures, engravings, photographs, posters, cartoons, buildings, and artifacts. Both collections are followed by a pair of secondary sources—short extracts from the writings of modern historians, archeologists, and other scholars. Collectively these sources provide an opportunity for you to practice the work of historians in a kind of guided "history laboratory." In working with this evidence, you are "doing history," much as students conducting lab experiments in chemistry or biology courses are "doing science."

Since each feature explores a theme of a particular chapter, the chapter narrative itself provides a broad context for analyzing these sources. Furthermore, brief introductions to each feature and to each document or image offer more specific context or background information, while questions provide things to look for as you examine each source. Other more integrative questions offer a focus for using those sources together to probe larger historical issues. What follows are a few more specific suggestions for assessing these raw materials of history.

Working with Documents

Written sources or documents are the most common type of primary source that historians use. For example, a number of ancient Buddhist texts are sampled in the Working with Evidence feature of Chapter 4, while the documents in Chapter 13 present ideas about political authority in Mughal India, France, and the Inca Empire.

Analysis of such documents usually begins with the basics:

- Who wrote the document?
- When and where was it written?
- What type of document is it (for example, a letter to a friend, a political decree, an exposition of a religious teaching)?

Sometimes the document itself will provide answers to these questions. On other occasions, you may need to rely on the introductions.

Once these basics have been established, a historian is then likely to consider several further questions that situate the document in its particular historical context:

- Why was the document written, for what audience, and under what circumstances?
- What point of view does it reflect? What other views or opinions is the document arguing against? Can you get a sense of the larger conversation in which this document is participating?

Inspiration and intention are crucial factors that shape the form and content of a source. For instance, one might examine a document differently depending on whether it was composed for a private or a public readership, or whether it was intended to be read by a small elite or a wider audience.

Still another level of analysis seeks to elicit useful information from the document.

- What material in the document is believable, and what is not?
- What might historians learn from this document?
- What can the document tell us about the individual who produced it and the society from which he or she came?

In all of this, historical imagination is essential. Informed by knowledge of the context and the content of the document, your imagination will help you read it through the eyes of its author and its audience. You should ask yourself: how might this document have been understood at the time it was written? But in using your imagination, you must take care not to read into the documents your own assumptions and understandings. It is a delicate balance, a kind of dance that historians constantly undertake. Even documents that contain material that historians find unbelievable can be useful, for we seek not only to know what actually happened in the past but also to grasp the world as the people who lived that past understood it. And so historians sometimes speak about reading documents "against the grain," looking for meanings that the author might not have intended to convey.

Working with Images

Visual sources derive from the material culture of the past—religious icons or paintings that add to our understanding of belief systems, a family portrait that provides insight into presentations of self in a particular time and place, a building or sculpture that reveals how power and authority were displayed in a specific empire. These kinds of evidence represent another category of primary source material that historians can use to re-create and understand the past. But such visual sources can be even more difficult to interpret than written documents. The ideas that animated the creators of particular images or artifacts are often not obvious. Nor are the meanings they conveyed to those who viewed or used them. The lovely images from the ancient Indus River valley civilization contained in the Working with Evidence feature for Chapter 2, for example, remain enigmatic although still engaging to twenty-first-century viewers. Propaganda posters, frequently used in the source features for Volume 2, convey vividly how various groups or governments understood their own times. Despite the difficulties of interpretation, visual sources can provide insights not offered by written documents.

To use visual sources, we must try as best we can to see these pieces of evidence through the eyes of the societies that produced them and to decode the symbols and other features that imbue them with meaning. Thus context is, if anything, even more crucial for analyzing visual evidence than it is for documents. For example, understanding European depictions of the Muslim world, featured in Chapter 12, depends heavily on some knowledge of both European and Islamic history and culture. A set of basic questions, similar to those you would ask about a written document, provides a starting point for analyzing visual sources:

- When and where was the image or artifact created?
- Who made the image or artifact? Who paid for or commissioned it? For what audience(s) was it intended?
- Where was the image or artifact originally displayed or used?

Having established this basic information about the image or artifact, you may simply want to describe it, as if to someone who had never seen it before.

- If the source is an image, who or what is depicted? What activities are shown? How might you describe the positioning of figures, their clothing, hairstyles, and other visual cues?
- If the source is an object or building, how would you describe its major features?

Finally, you will want to take a stab at more interpretive issues, making use of what you know about the context in which the visual source was created.

- What likely purpose or function did the image or artifact serve?
- What message(s) does it seek to convey?
- How could it be interpreted differently depending on who viewed or used it?
- What are the meanings of any symbols or other abstract features in the visual source?
- What can the image or artifact tell us about the society that produced it and the time period in which it was created?

Beyond analyzing particular sources, you will be invited to draw conclusions from sets of related sources—both visual and written—that address a central theme in the chapter. What can you learn, for example, about the life of Chinese commoners and elites from the sources in Chapter 8? And what do the images and documents in the Working with Evidence feature of Chapter 15 disclose about the reception of Christianity in various cultural settings?

Alongside these primary sources, the **Historians' Voices** features offer you the opportunity to consider how contemporary scholars make historical arguments and draw sound conclusions. While primary sources—documentary and visual alike—are the foundation for all historical accounts, students and scholars gain further perspective from reading the analysis of modern experts who use their deep knowledge of the sources to examine and explain the past. Immersing yourself in documents, images, and the writings of modern scholars allows you to catch a glimpse of the messiness, the ambiguity, the heartaches, and the achievements of history as it was lived and as it has been recorded.

Using these sources effectively, however, is no easy task. In fact, the work of historians might well be compared with that of Sisyphus, the ancient Greek king who, having offended the gods, was condemned to eternally roll a large rock up a mountain, only to have it ceaselessly fall back down. Like Sisyphus, historians work at a mission that can never be completely successful—to recapture the past before it is lost forever in the mists of time and fading memory. The evidence available is always partial and fragmentary. Historians and students of history alike are limited and fallible, for we operate often at a great distance—in both time and culture—from those we are studying. And we rarely agree on important matters, divided as we are by sex, nationality, religion, race, and values, all of which shape our understandings of the past.

Despite these challenges, scholars and students have long found their revisiting of the past a compelling project—intensely interesting, personally meaningful, and even fun—particularly when working with "primary" or "original" sources, which are the building blocks of all historical accounts. Such sources are windows into the lives of our ancestors, though these windows are often smudged and foggy. We hope that working with the evidence contained in these sources will enrich your own life as you listen in on multiple conversations from the past, eavesdropping, as it were, on our ancestors.

Prologue

From Cosmic History to Human History

History books in general, and world history textbooks in particular, share something in common with those Russian nested dolls in which a series of carved figures fit inside one another. In much the same fashion, all historical accounts take place within some larger context, as stories within stories unfold. Individual biographies and histories of local communities, particularly modern ones, occur within the context of one nation or another. Nations often find a place in some more encompassing civilization, such as the Islamic world or the West, or in a regional or continental context such as Southeast Asia, Latin America, or Africa. And those civilizational or regional histories in turn take on richer meaning when they are understood within the even broader story of world history, which embraces humankind as a whole.

In recent decades, some world historians have begun to situate that remarkable story of the human journey in the much larger framework of both cosmic and planetary history, an approach that has come to be called "big history." It is really the "history of everything" from the big bang to the present, and it extends over the enormous, almost unimaginable timescale of some 13.8 billion years, the current rough estimate of the age of the universe.[1]

The History of the Universe

To make this vast expanse of time even remotely comprehensible, some scholars have depicted the history of the cosmos as if it were a single calendar year (see Snapshot). On that cosmic calendar, most of the action took place in the first few milliseconds of January 1. As astronomers, physicists, and chemists tell it, the universe that we know began in an eruption of inconceivable power and heat. Out of that explosion of creation emerged matter, energy, gravity, electromagnetism, and the "strong" and "weak" forces that govern the behavior of atomic nuclei. As gravity pulled the rapidly expanding cosmic gases into increasingly dense masses, stars formed, with the first ones lighting up around 600 million years after the big bang or toward the end of January on the cosmic calendar.

Hundreds of billions of stars followed, each with its own history, though following common patterns. They emerged, flourished for a time, and then collapsed and died. In their final stages, they sometimes generated supernovae, black holes,

SNAPSHOT The History of the Universe as a Cosmic Calendar

Big bang	January 1	13.8 billion years ago
Stars and galaxies begin to form	End of January	13.2? billion years ago
Milky Way galaxy forms	March / early April	10 billion years ago
Origin of the solar system and earth	September 9	4.5 billion years ago
Earliest life on earth	Late September	3.8 billion years ago
Oxygen forms on earth	December 1	1.3 billion years ago
First worms	December 16	658 million years ago
First fish, first vertebrates	December 19	534 million years ago
First reptiles, first trees	December 23	370 million years ago
Age of dinosaurs	December 24–28	66 to 240 million years ago
First human-like creatures	December 31 (late evening)	2.7 million years ago
First agriculture	December 31: 11:59:35	12,000 years ago
Birth of the Buddha / Greek civilization	December 31: 11:59:55	2,500 years ago
Birth of Jesus	December 31: 11:59:56	2,000 years ago

Source: Information from Carl Sagan, *The Dragons of Eden* (New York: Random House, 1977), 13–17; David Christian, *Origin Story: A Big History of Everything* (New York: Little, Brown, 2018), 13–14.

and pulsars—phenomena at least as fantastic as the most exotic of earlier creation stories. Within the stars, enormous nuclear reactions gave rise to the elements that are reflected in the periodic table known to all students of chemistry. Over eons, these stars came together in galaxies, such as our own Milky Way, which probably emerged in March or early April, and in even larger structures called groups, clusters, and superclusters. Adding to the strangeness of our picture of the cosmos is the recent and controversial notion that perhaps 90 percent or more of the total mass of the universe is invisible to us, consisting of a mysterious and mathematically predicted substance known to scholars only as "dark matter."

The contemplation of cosmic history has prompted profound religious or philosophical questions about the meaning of human life. For some, it has engendered a sense of great insignificance in the face of cosmic vastness. In disputing the earth- and human-centered view of the cosmos, long held by the Catholic Church, the eighteenth-century French thinker Voltaire wrote: "This little globe, nothing more than a point, rolls in space like so many other globes; we are lost in this immensity."[2] Nonetheless, human consciousness and our awareness of the mystery of this immeasurable universe render us unique and generate for many people feelings of awe, gratitude, and humility that are almost religious. As tiny but knowing observers of this majestic cosmos, we have found ourselves living in a grander home than ever we knew before.

The History of a Planet

For most of us, one star, our own sun, is far more important than all the others, despite its quite ordinary standing among the billions of stars in the universe and its somewhat remote location on the outer edge of the Milky Way galaxy. Circling that star is a series of planets, formed of leftover materials from the sun's birth. One of those planets, the third from the sun and the fifth largest, is home to all of us. Human history—our history—takes place not only on the earth but also as part of the planet's history.

That history began with the emergence of the entire solar system, including the earth, about two-thirds of the way through the history of the universe, some 4.5 billion years ago, or early September on the cosmic calendar. Geologists have learned a great deal about the history of the earth: the formation of its rocks and atmosphere; the movement of its continents; the collision of the tectonic plates that make up its crust; and the constant changes of its landscape as mountains formed, volcanoes erupted, and erosion transformed the surface of the planet. All of this has been happening for more than 4 billion years and continues still.

The most remarkable feature of the earth's history—and so far as we know unrepeated elsewhere—was the emergence of life from the chemical soup of the early planet. It happened rather quickly, only about 700 million years after the earth itself took shape, or late September on the cosmic calendar. Then for some 3 billion years, life remained at the level of microscopic single-celled organisms. According to biologists, the many species of larger multicelled creatures—all of the flowers, shrubs, and trees as well as all of the animals of land, sea, and air—have evolved in an explosive proliferation of life-forms over the past 600 million years, or since mid-December on the cosmic calendar. The history of life on earth has, however, been periodically punctuated by massive die-offs, at least five of them, in which very large numbers of animal or plant species have perished. The most widespread of these "extinction events," known to scholars as the Permian mass extinction, occurred around 250 million years ago and eliminated some 90 percent of living species on the planet. That catastrophic diminution of life-forms on the earth has been associated with massive volcanic eruptions, the release of huge quantities of carbon dioxide and methane into the atmosphere, and a degree of global warming that came close to extinguishing all life on the planet. Much later, around 66 million years ago, another such extinction event decimated about 75 percent of plant and animal species, including what was left of the dinosaurs. Most scientists now believe that it was caused primarily by the impact of a huge asteroid that landed near the Yucatán Peninsula off the coast of southern Mexico, generating enormous earthquakes, tsunamis, fireballs, and a cloud of toxic dust and debris. Many scholars believe we are currently in the midst of a sixth extinction event, driven, like the others, by major climate change, but which, unlike the others, is the product of human actions.

So life on earth has been and remains both fragile and resilient. Within these conditions, every species has had a history as its members struggled to find resources, cope with changing environments, and deal with competitors. Egocentric creatures that we are, however, human beings have usually focused their history books and history courses entirely on a single species—our own, *Homo sapiens*, humankind. On the cosmic calendar, *Homo sapiens* is an upstart primate whose entire history occurred in the last few minutes of December 31. Almost all of what we normally study in history courses—agriculture, writing, civilizations, empires, industrialization—took place in the very last minute of that cosmic year. The entire history of the United States occurred in the last second.

Yet during that very brief time, humankind has had a career more remarkable and arguably more consequential for the planet than any other species. At the heart of human uniqueness lies our amazing capacity for accumulating knowledge and skills. Other animals learn, of course, but for the most part they learn the same things over and over again. Twenty-first-century chimpanzees in the wild master much the same set of skills as their ancestors did a million years ago. But the exceptional communication abilities provided by human language allow us to learn from one another, to express that learning in abstract symbols, and then to pass it on, cumulatively, to future generations. Thus we have moved from stone axes to lasers, from spears to nuclear weapons, from "talking drums" to the Internet, from grass huts to the pyramids of Egypt, the Taj Mahal of India, and the skyscrapers of modern cities.

This extraordinary ability has translated into a human impact on the earth that is unprecedented among all living species.[3] Human populations have multiplied far more extensively and have come to occupy a far greater range of environments than has any other large animal. Through our ingenious technologies, we have appropriated for ourselves, according to recent calculations, some 25 to 40 percent of the solar energy that enters the food chain. We have recently gained access to the stored solar energy of coal, gas, and oil, all of which have been many millions of years in the making, and we have the capacity to deplete these resources in a few hundred or a few thousand years. Other forms of life have felt the impact of human activity, as numerous extinct or threatened species testify. Human beings have even affected the atmosphere and the oceans as carbon dioxide and other emissions of the industrial age have warmed the climate of the planet in ways that broadly resemble the conditions that triggered earlier extinction events. Thus human history has been, and remains, of great significance, not for ourselves alone, but also for the earth itself and for the many other living creatures with which we share it.

The History of the Human Species . . . in a Single Paragraph

The history of our species has occurred during roughly the last 250,000–350,000 years, conventionally divided into three major phases, based on the kind of technology that was most widely practiced. The enormously long Paleolithic age, with its gathering and hunting way of life, accounts for 95 percent or more of the time that humans have occupied the planet. People utilizing a stone-age Paleolithic technology initially settled every major landmass on the earth and constructed the first human societies (see Chapter 1). Then beginning about 12,000 years ago with the first Agricultural Revolution, the domestication of plants and animals increasingly became the primary means of sustaining human life and societies. In giving rise to agricultural villages and chiefdoms, to pastoral communities depending on their herds of animals, and to state- and city-based civilizations, this agrarian way of life changed virtually everything and fundamentally reshaped human societies and their relationship to the natural order. Finally, around 1750 a quite sudden spurt in the rate of technological change, which we know as the Industrial Revolution, began to take hold. That vast increase in productivity, wealth, and human control over nature once again transformed almost every aspect of human life and gave rise to new kinds of societies that we call "modern."

Here then, in a single paragraph, is the history of humankind—the Paleolithic era, the agricultural era, and, most recently and briefly, the modern industrial era. Clearly this is a big picture perspective, based on the notion that the human species as a whole has a history that transcends any of its particular and distinctive cultures. That perspective—known variously as planetary, global, or world history—has become increasingly prominent among those who study the past. Why should this be so?

Why World History?

Not long ago—in the mid-twentieth century, for example—virtually all college-level history courses were organized in terms of particular civilizations or nations. In the United States, courses such as Western Civilization or some version of American History served to introduce students to the study of the past. Since then, however, a set of profound changes has pushed much of the historical profession in a different direction.

The world wars of the twentieth century, revealing as they did the horrendous consequences of unchecked nationalism, persuaded some historians that a broader view of the past might contribute to a sense of global citizenship. Economic and cultural globalization has highlighted both the interdependence of the world's peoples and their very unequal positions within that world. Moreover, we are aware as never before that our problems—whether they involve economic well-being, global warming, disease, or terrorism—respect no national boundaries. To many thoughtful people, a global present seemed to call for a global past. Furthermore, as colonial empires shrank and new nations asserted themselves on the world stage, these peoples also insisted that their histories be accorded equivalent treatment with those of Europe and North America. An explosion of new knowledge about the histories of Asia, Africa, and pre-Columbian America erupted from the research of scholars around the world. All of this has generated a "world history movement," reflected in college and high school curricula, in numerous conferences and specialized studies, and in a proliferation of textbooks, of which this is one.

This world history movement has attempted to create a global understanding of the human past that highlights broad patterns cutting across particular civilizations and countries, while acknowledging in an inclusive fashion the distinctive histories of its many peoples. This is, to put it mildly, a tall order. How is it possible to encompass within a single book or course the separate stories of the world's various peoples? Surely it must be something more than just recounting the history of one civilization or culture after another. How can we distill a common history of humankind as a whole from the distinct trajectories of particular peoples? Because no world history book or course can cover everything, what criteria should we use for deciding what to include and what to leave out? Such questions have ensured no end of controversy among students, teachers, and scholars of world history, making it one of the most exciting fields of historical inquiry.

Context, Change, Comparison, and Connection: The Four Cs of World History

Despite much debate and argument, most scholars and teachers of world history would probably agree on four major emphases of this remarkable field of study. The first lies in the observation that in world history, nothing stands alone. Every event, every historical figure, every culture, society, or civilization gains significance from its inclusion in some larger framework. This means that **context** is central to world history and that contextual thinking is the essential skill that world history teaches. And so we ask the same question about every particular occurrence: where does it fit in the larger scheme of things?

A second common theme in world history involves **change** over time. Most often, it is the "big picture" changes—those that affect large segments of humankind—that are of greatest interest. How did the transition from a gathering and hunting economy to one based on agriculture take place? How did cities, empires, and civilizations take shape in various parts of the world? What impact did the growing prominence of Europe have on the rest of the world in recent centuries? A focus on change provides an antidote to a persistent tendency of human thinking that historians call "essentialism." A more common term is "stereotyping." It refers to our inclination to define particular groups of people with an unchanging or essential set of characteristics. Women are nurturing; peasants are conservative; Americans are aggressive; Hindus are religious. Serious students of history soon become aware that every significant category of people contains endless variations and conflicts and that those human communities are constantly in flux. Peasants may often accept the status quo, except of course when they rebel, as they frequently have. Americans have experienced periods of isolationism and withdrawal from the world as well as times of aggressive engagement with it. Things change.

But some things persist, even if they also change. We should not allow an emphasis on change to blind us to the continuities of human experience. A recognizably Chinese state has operated for more than 2,000 years. Slavery and patriarchy persisted as human institutions for thousands of years until they were challenged in recent centuries, and in various forms they exist still. The teachings of Buddhism, Christianity, and Islam have endured for centuries, though with endless variations and transformations.

A third element that operates constantly in world history books and courses is that of **comparison**. Whatever else it may be, world history is a comparative discipline, seeking to identify similarities and differences in the experience of the world's peoples. What is the difference between the development of agriculture in the Middle East and in Mesoamerica? Was the experience of women largely the same in all patriarchal societies? Why did the Industrial Revolution and a modern way of life evolve first in Western Europe rather than somewhere else? What distinguished the French, Russian, and Chinese revolutions from one another? Describing and, if possible, explaining such similarities and differences are among the major tasks of world history. Comparison has proven an effective tool in efforts to counteract Eurocentrism, the notion that Europeans or people of European descent have long been the primary movers and shakers of the historical process. That notion arose in recent centuries when Europeans were in fact the major source of innovation in the world and did for a time exercise something close to world domination. But comparative world history sets this recent European prominence in a global and historical context, helping us to sort out what was distinctive about the development of Europe and what similarities it bore to other major regions of the world. Puncturing the pretensions of Eurocentrism has been high on the agenda of world history.

A fourth emphasis within world history, and in this book, involves the interactions, encounters, and **connections** among different and often distant peoples. Focusing on cross-cultural connections—whether those of conflict or more peaceful exchange—represents an effort to counteract a habit of thinking about particular peoples, states, or cultures as self-contained or isolated communities. Despite the historical emergence of many separate and distinct societies, none of them developed alone. Each was embedded in a network of relationships with both near and more distant peoples.

Moreover, these cross-cultural connections did not begin with Columbus. The Chinese, for example, interacted continuously with the nomadic peoples on their northern border; generated technologies that diffused across all of Eurasia; transmitted elements of their culture to Japan, Korea, and Vietnam; and assimilated a foreign religious tradition, Buddhism, that had originated in India. Though clearly distinctive, China was not a self-contained or isolated civilization. Thus world history remains always alert to the networks, webs, and encounters in which particular civilizations or peoples were enmeshed.

Context, change, comparison, and connection—all of them operating on a global scale—represent various ways of bringing some coherence to the multiple and complex stories of world history. They will recur repeatedly in the pages that follow.

A final observation about this account of world history: *Ways of the World*, like all other world history textbooks, is radically unbalanced in terms of coverage. Chapter 1, for example, takes on some 95 percent of the human story, well over 200,000 years of our history. By contrast, the last century alone occupies four entire chapters. In fact, the six major sections of the book deal with progressively shorter time periods, in progressively greater detail. This imbalance owes much to the relative scarcity of information about earlier periods of our history. But it also reflects a certain "present mindedness," for we look to history, always, to make sense of our current needs and circumstances. And in doing so, we often assume that more recent events have a greater significance for our own lives in the here and now than those that occurred in more distant times. Whether you agree with this assumption or not, you will have occasion to ponder it as you consider the many and various "ways of the world" that have emerged in the course of the human journey and as you contemplate their relevance for your own journey.

Ways of the World

A Brief Global History with Sources

Bridgeman Images

CHAPTER 12

The Worlds of the Fifteenth Century

CONNECTING PAST AND PRESENT

"For many people in our community, the statue [of Christopher Columbus] represents patriarchy, oppression and divisiveness," declared Andrew Ginther, mayor of Columbus, Ohio, in June of 2020. "We will no longer live in the shadow of our ugly past. . . . Now is the right time to replace this statue with artwork that demonstrates our enduring fight to end racism and celebrate the themes of diversity and inclusion."[1] One of many such removals all across the country in the summer of 2020, the city council's action occurred in the context of a nationwide eruption of protest against police killings of African Americans under the slogan "Black Lives Matter."

The statue, which had stood in a prominent place in front of city hall since 1955, was a gift from Genoa, Italy, Columbus's sister city and birthplace of the famous explorer. According to its dedication plaque, it was intended to celebrate his "values and virtues" and the connection between these two distant cities that embraced him. But by 2020 it had become a local focus of a wider and growing debate about the significance and legacy of Columbus. Was he, as one prominent activist for indigenous rights put it, "a perpetrator of genocide . . . , a slave trader, a thief, a pirate, and most certainly not a hero"?[2] Or should Americans celebrate Columbus because he was, as one public commentator claimed, "a man ahead of his time whose vision and discovery changed the course of world history by connecting the peoples of the world for the first time"?[3]

« **The Meeting of Two Worlds** This nineteenth-century painting shows Columbus on his first voyage to the New World. He is reassuring his anxious sailors by pointing to the first sight of land. In light of its long-range consequences, this voyage represents a major turning point in world history.

This sharp debate about Columbus reminds us that the past is endlessly contested and that it continues to resonate in the present. But it also reflects a broad agreement that the voyages of Columbus marked a decisive turning point, for better or worse, in world history and represent arguably the most important event of the fifteenth century.

It was not, however, the only globally significant development of that century. If Columbus launched a European empire-building process in the Americas, other empires were also in the making during the fifteenth century. In 1383, a Central Asian Turkic warrior named Timur launched the last major pastoral invasion of adjacent civilizations. In 1405, an enormous Chinese fleet set out across the entire Indian Ocean basin, only to voluntarily withdraw twenty-eight years later, thus forgoing an empire in Asia. Four new empires gave the Islamic world a distinct political and cultural shape. One of them, the Ottoman Empire, put a final end to Christian Byzantium with the conquest of Constantinople in 1453, even as Spanish Christians completed the "reconquest" of the Iberian Peninsula from the Muslims in 1492. And in the Americas, the Aztec and Inca empires gave a final and spectacular expression to Mesoamerican and Andean civilizations before they were both swallowed up in the burst of European imperialism that followed the arrival of Columbus.

SEEKING THE MAIN POINT

What elements of fifteenth-century world history represented a continuation of earlier patterns, and what elements signaled a break with the past?

Because the fifteenth century was an era of transition on many fronts, it provides an occasion for a bird's-eye view of the world through an imaginary global tour. This excursion around the world will briefly review the human saga thus far and establish a baseline from which the enormous transformations of the centuries that followed might be measured. How, then, might we describe the world, and the worlds, of the fifteenth century?

Societies and Cultures of the Fifteenth Century

One way to describe the world of the fifteenth century is to identify the various types of human communities that it contained. Bands of gatherers and hunters, villages of agricultural peoples, newly emerging chiefdoms or small states, pastoral communities, established civilizations and empires—all of these social or political forms would have been apparent to a widely traveled visitor in the fifteenth century. Representing alternative ways of organizing human life, all of them were long established by the fifteenth century, but the balance among them in 1500 was quite different than it had been a thousand years earlier.

Paleolithic Persistence: Australia and North America

Despite millennia of agricultural advance, substantial areas of the world still hosted gathering and hunting societies, known to historians as Paleolithic (Old Stone Age) peoples. All of Australia, much of Siberia, the arctic coastlands, and parts of Africa and the Americas fell into this category. These peoples were not simply relics of a bygone age, for they too had a history and a sizable presence in the world during

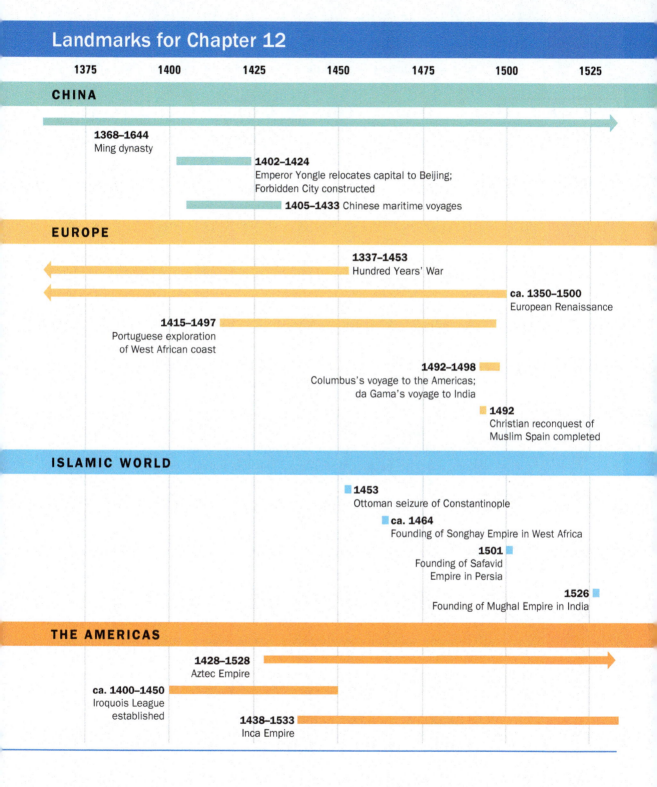

Landmarks for Chapter 12

1375 | 1400 | 1425 | 1450 | 1475 | 1500 | 1525

CHINA

1368–1644
Ming dynasty

1402–1424
Emperor Yongle relocates capital to Beijing; Forbidden City constructed

1405–1433 Chinese maritime voyages

EUROPE

1337–1453
Hundred Years' War

ca. 1350–1500
European Renaissance

1415–1497
Portuguese exploration of West African coast

1492–1498
Columbus's voyage to the Americas; da Gama's voyage to India

1492
Christian reconquest of Muslim Spain completed

ISLAMIC WORLD

1453
Ottoman seizure of Constantinople

ca. 1464
Founding of Songhay Empire in West Africa

1501
Founding of Safavid Empire in Persia

1526
Founding of Mughal Empire in India

THE AMERICAS

1428–1528
Aztec Empire

ca. 1400–1450
Iroquois League established

1438–1533
Inca Empire

the fifteenth century, although most history books largely ignore them after the age of agriculture arrived.

CORE IDEA

■ Identifying Alternatives to Civilizations
What alternatives to the cities, states, and empires of established civilizations persisted in the world of the fifteenth century?

Consider, for example, Australia. That continent's many separate groups, some 250 of them, still practiced a gathering and hunting way of life in the fifteenth century, a pattern that continued well after Europeans arrived in the late eighteenth century. Over many thousands of years, these people had assimilated various material items or cultural practices from outsiders—outrigger canoes, fishhooks, complex netting techniques, artistic styles, rituals, and mythological ideas—but despite the presence of farmers in nearby New Guinea, no agricultural practices penetrated the Australian mainland. Was it because large areas of Australia were unsuited for the kind of agriculture practiced in New Guinea? Or did the peoples of Australia, enjoying an environment of sufficient resources, simply see no need to change their way of life?

Despite the absence of agriculture, Australia's peoples had mastered and manipulated their environment, in part through "firestick farming," the practice of deliberately setting fires, which they described as "cleaning up the country." These controlled burns cleared the underbrush, thus making hunting easier and encouraging the growth of certain plant and animal species. In addition, native Australians exchanged goods among themselves over distances of hundreds of miles, created elaborate mythologies and ritual practices, and developed sophisticated traditions of sculpture and rock painting. They accomplished all of this with an economy and technology rooted in the distant Paleolithic past.

A very different kind of gathering and hunting society flourished in the fifteenth century along the northwest coast of North America among the Chinookan, Tulalip, Skagit, and other peoples. With some 300 edible animal species and an abundance of salmon and other fish, this extraordinarily bounteous environment provided the foundation for what scholars sometimes call "complex" or "affluent" gathering and hunting cultures. What distinguished the northwest coast peoples from those of Australia were permanent village settlements with large and sturdy houses, considerable economic specialization, ranked societies that sometimes included slavery, chiefdoms dominated by powerful clan leaders or "big men," and extensive storage of food.

Although these and other gathering and hunting peoples persisted in the fifteenth century, both their numbers (an estimated 1 percent of the world's population by 1500) and the area they inhabited had contracted greatly as the Agricultural Revolution unfolded across the planet. That relentless advance of the farming frontier continued in the centuries ahead as the Russian, Chinese, and European empires encompassed the lands of the remaining Paleolithic peoples.

Agricultural Village Societies: The Igbo and the Iroquois

Far more numerous than gatherers and hunters but still a small percentage of the total world population were those many peoples who, though fully agricultural, had avoided incorporation into larger empires or civilizations and had not developed their own city- or state-based societies. Living usually in small village-based communities and organized in terms of kinship relations, such people predominated during the fifteenth century in much of North America; in most of the tropical lowlands of South America and the Caribbean; in parts of the Amazon River basin, Southeast Asia, and Africa south of the equator; and throughout Pacific Oceania. Historians have often treated them as marginal to the cities, states, and large-scale civilizations that predominate in most accounts of the global past. Viewed from within their own circles, though, these societies were at the center of things, each with its own history of migration, cultural transformation, social conflict, incorporation of new people, political rise and fall, and interaction with strangers.

East of the Niger River in the heavily forested region of West Africa lay the lands of the **Igbo** (EE-boh) peoples. By the fifteenth century, their neighbors, the Yoruba and Bini, had begun to develop small states and urban centers. But the Igbo, whose dense population and extensive trading networks might well have given rise to states, declined to follow suit. The deliberate Igbo preference was to reject the kingship and state-building efforts of their neighbors. They boasted on occasion that "the Igbo have no kings." Instead, they relied on other institutions to maintain social cohesion beyond the level of the village: title societies in which wealthy men received a series of prestigious ranks, women's associations, hereditary ritual experts serving as mediators, and a balance of power among kinship groups. It was a "stateless society," famously described in Chinua Achebe's *Things Fall Apart*, the most widely read novel to emerge from twentieth-century Africa.

■ **Identifying Change**
What changes were transforming the societies of the West African Igbo and the North American Iroquois as the fifteenth century unfolded?

But the Igbo peoples and their neighbors did not live in isolated, self-contained societies. They traded actively among themselves and with more distant peoples, such as the large African kingdom of Songhay (sahn-GEYE) far to the north. Cotton cloth, fish, copper and iron goods, decorative objects, and more drew neighboring peoples into networks of exchange. Common artistic traditions reflected a measure of cultural unity in a politically fragmented region, and all of these peoples seem to have changed from a matrilineal to a patrilineal system of tracing their descent. Little of this registered in the larger civilizations of the Afro-Eurasian world, but to the peoples of the West African forest during the fifteenth century, these processes were central to their history and their daily lives. Soon, however, all of them would be caught up in the transatlantic slave trade and would be changed substantially in the process.

Across the Atlantic in what is now central New York State, other agricultural village societies were also undergoing major change during the several centuries preceding their incorporation into European trading networks and empires. The Iroquois-speaking peoples of that region had only recently become fully agricultural, adopting maize- and bean-farming techniques that had originated centuries earlier in Mesoamerica. As this productive agriculture took hold by 1300 or so, the population grew, the size of settlements increased, and distinct peoples emerged. Frequent warfare also erupted among them. Some scholars have speculated that as agriculture, largely seen as women's work, became the primary economic activity, "warfare replaced successful food getting as the avenue to male prestige."[4]

Whatever caused it, this increased level of conflict among **Iroquois** peoples triggered a remarkable political innovation around the fifteenth century: a loose alliance or confederation among five Iroquois-speaking peoples—the Mohawk,

Iroquois Women This seventeenth-century French engraving depicts two Iroquois women preparing a meal. Among the Iroquois, women controlled both agriculture and property and had a significant voice in public affairs. (De Agostini Picture Library/M. Seemuller/Bridgeman Images)

Oneida, Onondaga, Cayuga, and Seneca (see Map 12.5, page 518). Based on an agreement known as the Great Law of Peace, the Five Nations, as they called themselves, agreed to settle their differences peacefully through a confederation council of clan leaders, some fifty of them altogether, who had the authority to adjudicate disputes and set reparation payments. Operating by consensus, the Iroquois League of Five Nations effectively suppressed the blood feuds and tribal conflicts that had only recently been so widespread. It also coordinated its peoples' relationship with outsiders, including the Europeans, who arrived in growing numbers in the centuries after 1500.

The Iroquois League gave expression to values of limited government, social equality, and personal freedom, concepts that some European colonists found highly attractive. One British colonial administrator declared in 1749 that the Iroquois had "such absolute Notions of Liberty that they allow no Kind of Superiority of one over another, and banish all Servitude from their Territories."[5] Such equality extended to gender relationships, for among the Iroquois, descent was matrilineal (reckoned through the woman's line), married couples lived with the wife's family, and women controlled agriculture and property. While men were hunters, warriors, and the primary political officeholders, women selected and could depose those leaders.

Wherever they lived in 1500, over the next several centuries independent agricultural peoples such as the Iroquois and Igbo, like many other such peoples before them, were increasingly encompassed by expanding economic networks and conquest empires based in Western Europe, Russia, China, or India.

Pastoral Peoples: Central Asia and West Africa

Pastoral peoples had long impinged more directly and dramatically on civilizations than did gathering and hunting or agricultural village societies. The Mongol incursion, along with the enormous empire to which it gave rise, was one in a long series of challenges from the steppes, but it was not quite the last. As the Mongol

Empire disintegrated, a brief attempt to restore it occurred in the late fourteenth and early fifteenth centuries under the leadership of a Turkic warrior named **Timur**, born in what is now Uzbekistan and known in the West as Tamerlane (see Map 12.1, page 505).

With a ferocity that matched or exceeded that of his model, Chinggis Khan, Timur's army of pastoralists brought immense devastation yet again to Russia and Persia, and also to India. Timur himself died in 1405, while preparing for an invasion of China. Conflicts among his successors prevented any lasting empire, although his descendants retained control of the area between Persia and Afghanistan for the rest of the fifteenth century. That state hosted a sophisticated elite culture combining Turkic and Persian elements, particularly at its splendid capital of Samarkand, as its rulers patronized artists, poets, traders, and craftsmen. Timur's conquest proved to be the last great military success of pastoral peoples from Central Asia. In the centuries that followed, their homelands were swallowed up in the expanding Russian and Chinese empires, as the balance of power between steppe pastoralists of inner Eurasia and the civilizations of outer Eurasia turned decisively in favor of the latter.

■ Assessing Significance
What role did Central Asian and West African pastoralists play in their respective regions?

In Africa, pastoral peoples stayed independent of established empires several centuries longer than those of Inner Asia, for not until the late nineteenth century were they incorporated into European colonial states. The experience of the **Fulbe** (fulb), West Africa's largest pastoral society, provides an example of an African herding people with a highly significant role in the fifteenth century and beyond. From their homeland in the western fringe of the Sahara along the upper Senegal River, the Fulbe had migrated gradually eastward in the centuries after 1000 C.E. (see Map 12.3, page 509). Unlike the pastoral peoples of Inner Asia, they generally lived in small communities among agricultural peoples and paid various grazing fees and taxes for the privilege of pasturing their cattle. Relations with their farming hosts often were tense because the Fulbe resented their subordination to agricultural peoples, whose way of life they despised. That sense of cultural superiority became even more pronounced as the Fulbe, in the course of their eastward movement, slowly adopted Islam. Some of them in fact dropped out of a pastoral life and settled in towns, where they became highly respected religious leaders. In the eighteenth and nineteenth centuries, the Fulbe were at the center of a wave of religiously based uprisings, or jihads, that greatly expanded the practice of Islam and gave rise to a series of new states ruled by the Fulbe themselves.

Modern Fulbe Herdsmen This photo shows modern Fulbe herdsmen from Nigeria tending to perhaps their most distinctive animal, long-horned cattle. Wealth in many pastoralist groups is reckoned through the size of cattle herds. (Eye Ubiquitous/Newscom)

Civilizations of the Fifteenth Century: Comparing China and Europe

Beyond the foraging, farming, and pastoral societies of the fifteenth-century world were its civilizations, those city-centered and state-based societies that were far larger and more densely populated, more powerful and innovative, and much more unequal in terms of class and gender than other forms of human community. Since the First Civilizations had emerged between 3500 and 1000 B.C.E., both the geographic space they encompassed and the number of people they embraced had grown substantially. By the fifteenth century, about 30 percent of the world's land was controlled by states and a considerable majority of the world's population lived within one or another of these civilizations. But most of these people, no doubt, identified more with local communities than with a larger civilization. What might an imaginary global traveler notice about the world's major civilizations in the fifteenth century?

Ming Dynasty China

Assessing Significance What was the significance of the Ming dynasty in Chinese history?

Such a traveler might well begin his or her journey in China. That civilization had been greatly disrupted by a century of Mongol rule, and its population had been sharply reduced by the plague. During the **Ming dynasty** (1368–1644), however, China recovered (see Map 12.1). In the early decades of that dynasty, the Chinese attempted to eliminate all signs of foreign rule, discouraging the use of Mongol names and dress while promoting Confucian learning and orthodox gender roles based on earlier models from the Han, Tang, and Song dynasties. Emperor Yongle (YAHNG-leh) (r. 1402–1424) sponsored an enormous *Encyclopedia* of some 11,000 volumes. With contributions from more than 2,000 scholars, this work sought to summarize or compile all previous writing on history, geography, philosophy, ethics, government, and more. Yongle also relocated the capital to Beijing, ordered the building of a magnificent imperial residence known as the Forbidden City, and constructed the Temple of Heaven, where subsequent rulers performed Confucian-based rituals to ensure the well-being of Chinese society. Two empresses wrote instructions for female behavior, emphasizing traditional expectations after the disruptions of the previous century. Culturally speaking, China was looking to its past.

Politically, the Ming dynasty reestablished the civil service examination system that had been neglected under Mongol rule and went on to create a highly centralized government. Power was concentrated in the hands of the emperor himself, while a cadre of eunuchs (castrated men) personally loyal to the emperor exercised great authority, much to the dismay of the official bureaucrats. The state acted vigorously to repair the damage of the Mongol years by restoring millions of acres to cultivation; rebuilding canals, reservoirs, and irrigation works; and planting, according to some estimates, a billion trees in an effort to reforest China. As a result, the economy rebounded, both international and domestic trade flourished, and the population grew. During the fifteenth century, China had recovered and was perhaps the best governed and most prosperous of the world's major civilizations.

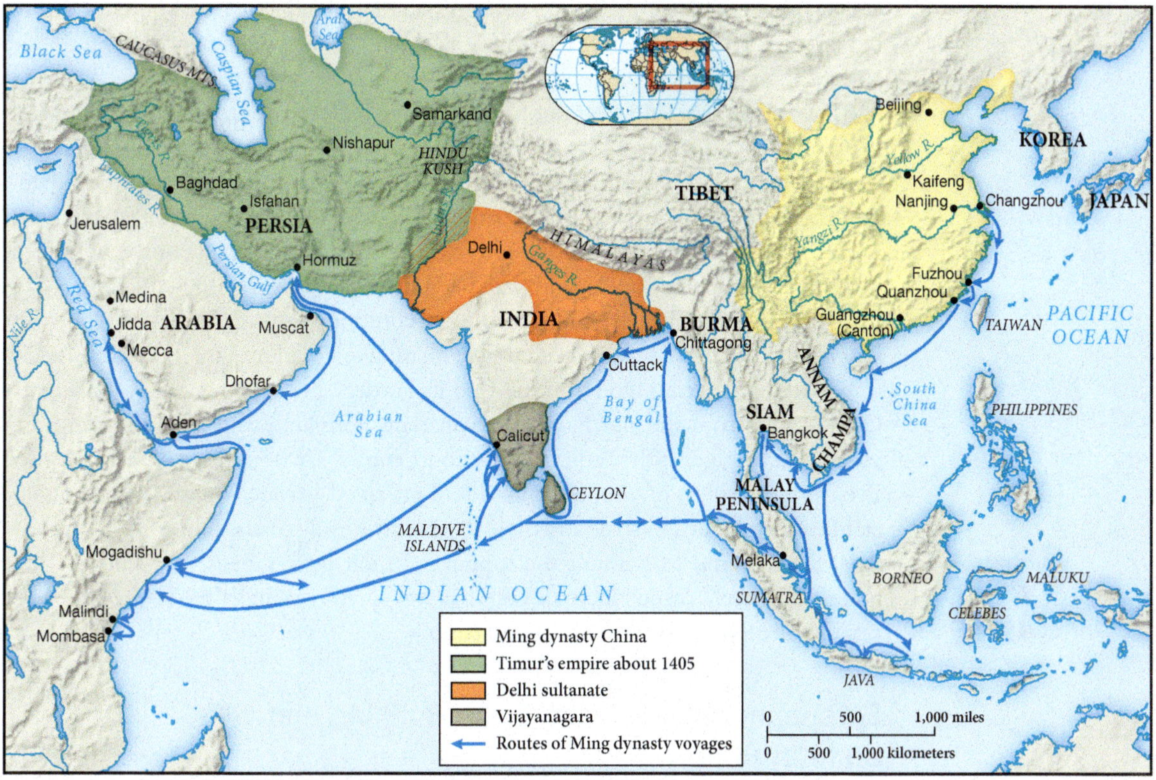

Map 12.1 Asia in the Fifteenth Century
The fifteenth century in Asia witnessed the massive Ming dynasty voyages into the Indian Ocean, the last major eruption of pastoral power in Timur's empire, and the flourishing of the maritime city of Melaka.

China also undertook the largest and most impressive maritime expeditions the world had ever seen. Since the eleventh century, Chinese sailors and traders had been a major presence in the South China Sea and in Southeast Asian port cities, with much of this activity in private hands. But now, after decades of preparation, an enormous fleet, commissioned by Emperor Yongle himself, was launched in 1405, followed over the next twenty-eight years by six more such expeditions. On board more than 300 ships of the first voyage was a crew of some 27,000, including 180 physicians, hundreds of government officials, 5 astrologers, 7 high-ranking or grand eunuchs, carpenters, tailors, accountants, merchants, translators, cooks, and thousands of soldiers and sailors. Visiting many ports in Southeast Asia, Indonesia, India, Arabia, and East Africa, these fleets, captained by the Muslim eunuch **Zheng He** (JUHNG-huh), sought to enroll distant peoples and states in the Chinese tribute system (see Map 12.1). Dozens of rulers accompanied the fleets back to China, where they presented tribute, performed the required rituals of submission, and received in return abundant gifts, titles, and trading opportunities. Officially described as "bringing order to the world," Zheng He's expeditions served to establish Chinese power and prestige in the Indian Ocean and to exert Chinese control over foreign trade in the region. The Chinese, however, did not seek to conquer new territories, establish Chinese settlements, or spread their culture, though they did intervene in a number of local disputes.

The most surprising feature of these voyages was how abruptly and deliberately they were ended. After 1433, Chinese authorities simply stopped such expeditions and allowed this enormous and expensive fleet to deteriorate in port. "In less than a hundred years," wrote a recent historian of these voyages, "the greatest navy the world had ever known had ordered itself into extinction."[6] Part of the reason involved the death of the emperor Yongle, who had been the chief patron of the enterprise. Many high-ranking officials had long seen the expeditions as a waste of resources because China, they believed, was the self-sufficient "middle kingdom," the center of the civilized world, requiring little from beyond its borders. In their eyes, the real danger to China came from the north, where barbarians constantly threatened. Finally, they viewed the voyages as the project of the court eunuchs, whom these officials despised. Even as these voices of Chinese officialdom prevailed, private Chinese merchants and craftsmen continued to settle and trade in Japan, the Philippines, Taiwan, and Southeast Asia, but they did so without the support of their government. The Chinese state quite deliberately turned its back on what was surely within its reach—a large-scale maritime empire in the Indian Ocean basin.

European Comparisons: State Building and Cultural Renewal

CORE IDEA

Comparing China and Europe
What major differences stand out in the histories of fifteenth-century China and Western Europe? What similarities are apparent?

At the other end of the Eurasian continent, similar processes of demographic recovery, political consolidation, cultural flowering, and overseas expansion were under way. Western Europe, having escaped Mongol conquest but devastated by the plague, began to regrow its population during the second half of the fifteenth century. As in China, the infrastructure of civilization proved a durable foundation for demographic and economic revival.

Politically too, Europe joined China in continuing earlier patterns of state building. In China, however, this meant a unitary and centralized government that encompassed almost the whole of its civilization, while in Europe a decidedly fragmented system of many separate, independent, and highly competitive states made for a sharply divided Western civilization (see Map 12.2). Many of these states—Spain, Portugal, France, England, the city-states of Italy (Milan, Venice, and Florence), various German principalities—learned to tax their citizens more efficiently, to create more effective administrative structures, and to raise standing armies. A small Russian state centered on the city of Moscow also emerged in the fifteenth century as Mongol rule faded away. Much of this state building was driven by the needs of war, a frequent occurrence in such a fragmented and competitive political environment. England and France, for example, fought intermittently for more than a century in the Hundred Years' War (1337–1453) over rival claims to territory in France. Nothing remotely similar disturbed the internal life of Ming dynasty China.

Map 12.2 Europe in 1500
By the end of the fifteenth century, Christian Europe had assumed its early modern political shape as a system of competing states threatened by an expanding Muslim Ottoman Empire.

■ **Defining Change**
What was new about the Renaissance?

A renewed cultural blossoming, the **European Renaissance**, likewise paralleled the revival of all things Confucian in Ming dynasty China. In Europe, however, that blossoming celebrated and reclaimed a classical Greco-Roman tradition that earlier had been lost or obscured. Beginning in the vibrant commercial cities of Italy between roughly 1350 and 1500, the Renaissance reflected the belief of the wealthy male elite that they were living in a wholly new era, far removed from the confined religious world of feudal Europe. Educated citizens of these cities sought inspiration in the art and literature of ancient Greece and Rome; they were "returning to the sources," as they put it. Their purpose was not so much to reconcile these works with the ideas of Christianity, as the twelfth- and thirteenth-century university scholars had done, but to use them as a cultural standard to imitate and then to surpass. The elite patronized great Renaissance artists such as Leonardo da Vinci, Michelangelo, and Raphael, whose paintings and sculptures were far more naturalistic, particularly in portraying the human body, than those of their medieval counterparts. Some of these artists looked to the Islamic world for standards of excellence, sophistication, and abundance. (See Working with Evidence: Islam and Renaissance Europe, page 530.)

Although religious themes remained prominent, Renaissance artists now included portraits and busts of well-known contemporary figures and scenes from ancient mythology. In the work of those scholars known as humanists, reflections on secular topics such as grammar, history, politics, poetry, rhetoric, and ethics complemented more religious matters. For example, Niccolò Machiavelli's (1469–1527) famous work *The Prince* was a prescription for political success based on the way politics actually operated in a highly competitive Italy of rival city-states rather than on idealistic and religiously based principles. His slim volume was filled with ruthless advice, including the observation that "the ends justify the means" when ruling a state and that it was safer for a sovereign to be feared than loved by his subjects. But the teachings in *The Prince* were controversial, with many critics at the time rejecting its amoral analysis of political life and its assertion that rulers should—indeed must—set aside moral concerns to rule effectively.

While the great majority of Renaissance writers and artists were men, among the remarkable exceptions to that rule was Christine de Pizan (1363–1430), the daughter of a Venetian official who lived mostly in Paris. Her writings pushed against the misogyny of many European thinkers of the time. In her *City of Ladies*, she mobilized numerous women from history, Christian and pagan alike, to demonstrate that women too could be active members of society and deserved an education equal to that of men. "No matter which way I looked at it," she wrote, "I could find no evidence from my own experience to bear out such a negative view of female nature and habits. Even so . . . I could scarcely find a moral work by any author which didn't devote some chapter or paragraph to attacking the female sex."[7]

Heavily influenced by classical models, Renaissance figures were more interested in capturing the unique qualities of particular individuals and in describing the world as it was than in portraying or exploring eternal religious truths. In its focus on the affairs of this world, Renaissance culture reflected the urban bustle and commercial preoccupations of Italian cities. Its secular elements challenged the otherworldliness of Christian culture, and its individualism signaled the dawning of a more capitalist economy of private entrepreneurs. A new Europe was in the making, one more different from its own recent past than Ming dynasty China was from its pre-Mongol glory.

European Comparisons: Maritime Voyaging

A global traveler during the fifteenth century might be surprised to find that Europeans, like the Chinese, were also launching outward-bound maritime expeditions. Initiated in 1415 by the small country of Portugal, those voyages sailed ever farther down the west coast of Africa, supported by the state and blessed by the pope (see Map 12.3). As the century ended, two expeditions marked major breakthroughs, although few

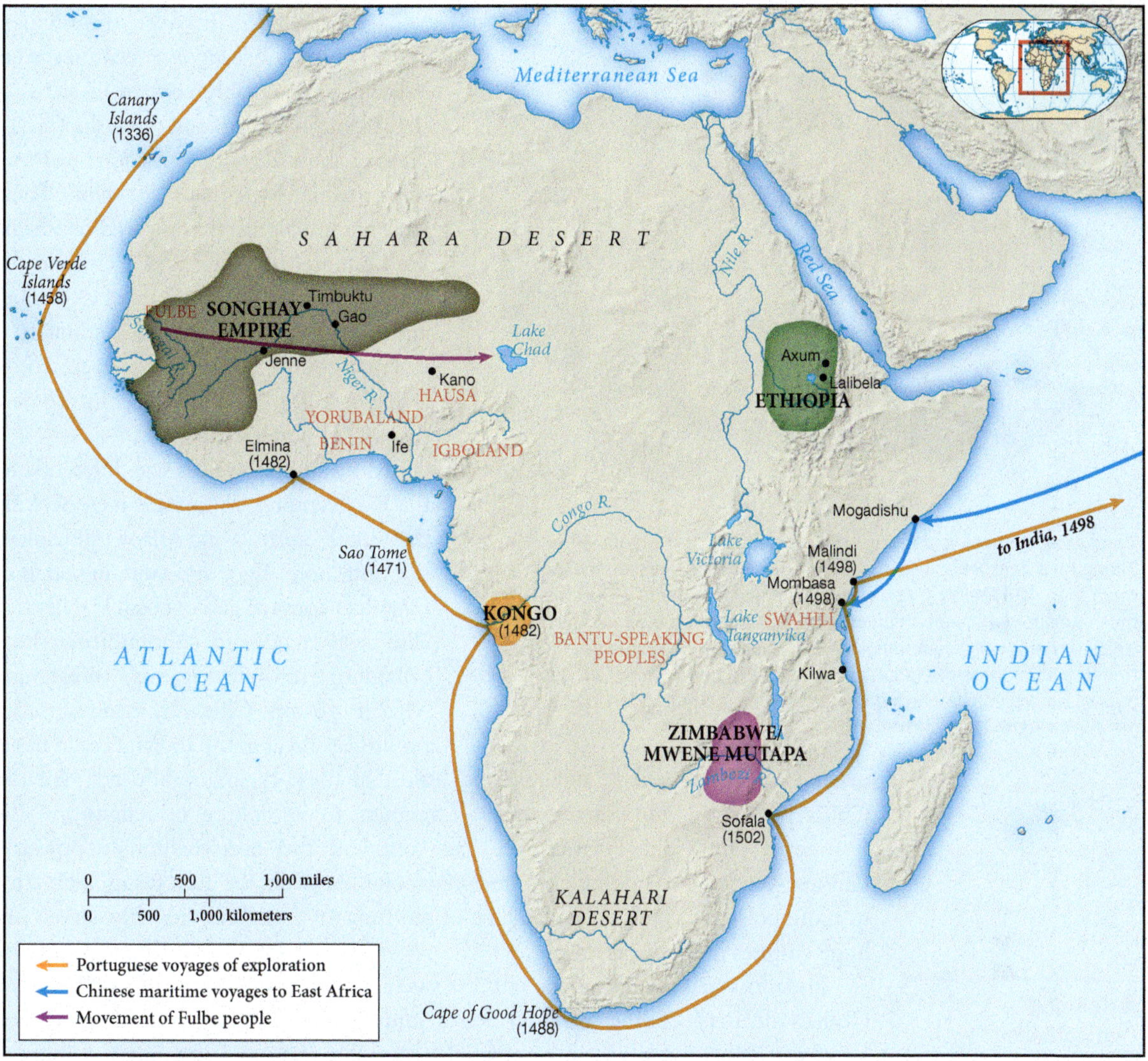

Map 12.3 Africa in the Fifteenth Century

By the fifteenth century, Africa was a panorama of political and cultural diversity, encompassing large empires, such as Songhay; smaller kingdoms, such as Kongo; city-states among the Yoruba, Hausa, and Swahili peoples; village-based societies without states at all, as among the Igbo; and pastoral peoples, such as the Fulbe. Both European and Chinese maritime expeditions touched on Africa during that century, even as Islam continued to find acceptance in the northern half of the continent.

suspected it at the time. In 1492, Christopher Columbus, funded by Spain, Portugal's neighbor and rival, made his way west across the Atlantic hoping to arrive in the East and, in one of history's most consequential mistakes, ran into the Americas. Five years later, in 1497, Vasco da Gama launched a voyage that took him around the tip of South Africa, along the East African coast, and, with the help of a Muslim pilot, across the Indian Ocean to Calicut in southern India.

Comparing Chinese and European Ships Among the largest vessels in Zheng He's fleet were "treasure ships" such as this vessel, measuring more than 400 feet long and carrying a crew of perhaps 1,000 men. The much smaller European ship next to it is similar to the *Santa Maria* on which Christopher Columbus made his voyage to the Americas. Chinese treasure ships were the largest vessels of the period, with four decks, nine masts, watertight compartments, and sophisticated rudders. (Gregory A. Harlin/National Geographic Image Collection/Bridgeman Images)

The differences between the Chinese and European oceangoing ventures were striking, most notably perhaps in terms of size. Columbus captained three ships and a crew of about 90, while da Gama had four ships, manned by perhaps 170 sailors. These were minuscule fleets compared to Zheng He's hundreds of ships and a crew in the many thousands. "All the ships of Columbus and da Gama combined," according to a recent account, "could have been stored on a single deck of a single vessel in the fleet that set sail under Zheng He."[8]

Motivation as well as size differentiated the two ventures. Europeans were seeking the wealth of Africa and Asia—gold, spices, silk, and more. They also were in search of Christian converts and of possible Christian allies with whom to continue their long crusading struggle against threatening Muslim powers. China, by contrast, faced no similar threat in the Indian Ocean basin, needed no military allies, and required little that these regions produced. Nor did China possess an impulse to convert foreigners to its culture or religion, as the Europeans surely did. Furthermore, the confident and overwhelmingly powerful Chinese fleet sought neither conquests nor colonies, while the Europeans soon tried to monopolize by force the commerce of the Indian Ocean and violently carved out huge empires in the Americas.

■ Making Comparisons
How did European maritime voyages in the fifteenth century differ from the Chinese voyages of Zheng He? What accounts for those differences?

The most striking difference in these two cases lay in the sharp contrast between China's decisive ending of its voyages and the continuing, indeed escalating, European effort, which soon brought the world's oceans and growing numbers of the world's people under its control. This is why Zheng He's voyages were so long neglected in China's historical memory. They led nowhere, whereas the initial European expeditions, so much smaller and less promising, were but the first steps on a journey to world power. But why did the Europeans continue a process that the Chinese had deliberately abandoned?

In the first place, Europe had no unified political authority with the power to order an end to its maritime outreach. Its system of competing states, so unlike China's single state, ensured that once begun, rivalry alone would drive the Europeans to the ends of the earth. Beyond this, much of Europe's elite had an interest in overseas expansion. Its budding merchant communities saw opportunity for profit; its competing monarchs eyed the revenue from taxing overseas trade or from seizing overseas resources; the Church foresaw the possibility of widespread conversion; and impoverished nobles might imagine fame and fortune abroad. In China, by contrast, support for Zheng He's voyages was very shallow in official circles, and when the emperor Yongle passed from the scene, those opposed to the voyages prevailed within the politics of the court.

Finally, the Chinese were very much aware of their own antiquity, believed strongly in the absolute superiority of their culture, and felt with good reason that, should they desire something from abroad, others would bring it to them. Europeans too believed themselves unique, particularly in religious terms as the possessors of Christianity, the "one true religion." In material terms, though, they were seeking out the greater riches of the East, and they were highly conscious that Muslim power blocked easy access to these treasures and posed a military and religious threat to Europe itself. All of this propelled continuing European expansion in the centuries that followed.

The Chinese withdrawal from the Indian Ocean facilitated the European entry. It cleared the way for the Portuguese to penetrate the region, where they faced only the eventual naval power of the Ottomans. Had Vasco da Gama encountered Zheng He's massive fleet as his four small ships sailed into Asian waters in 1498, world history may well have taken quite a different turn. As it was, however, China's abandonment of oceanic voyaging and Europe's embrace of the seas marked different responses to a common problem that both civilizations shared—growing populations and land shortage. In the centuries that followed, China's rice-based agriculture was able to expand production internally by more intensive use of the land, while the country's territorial expansion was inland toward Central Asia. By contrast, Europe's agriculture, based on wheat and livestock, expanded primarily by acquiring new lands in overseas possessions, which were gained as a consequence of a commitment to oceanic expansion.

Civilizations of the Fifteenth Century: The Islamic World

Beyond the domains of Chinese and European civilization, our fifteenth-century global traveler would surely have been impressed with the transformations of the Islamic world. Stretching across much of Afro-Eurasia, the enormous realm of Islam experienced a set of remarkable changes during the fifteenth and early sixteenth centuries, as well as the continuation of earlier patterns. The most notable change lay in the political realm, for an Islamic civilization that had been severely fragmented since at least 900 now crystallized into four major states or empires (see Map 12.4). At the same time, a long-term process of conversion to Islam continued the cultural transformation of Afro-Eurasian societies both within and beyond these new states.

CORE IDEA

Noticing Change
What new departures can you identify in the Islamic world of the fifteenth and sixteenth centuries?

In the Islamic Heartland: The Ottoman and Safavid Empires

The most impressive and enduring of the new Islamic states was the **Ottoman Empire**, which lasted in one form or another from the fourteenth to the early twentieth century. It was the creation of one of the many Turkic warrior groups that had

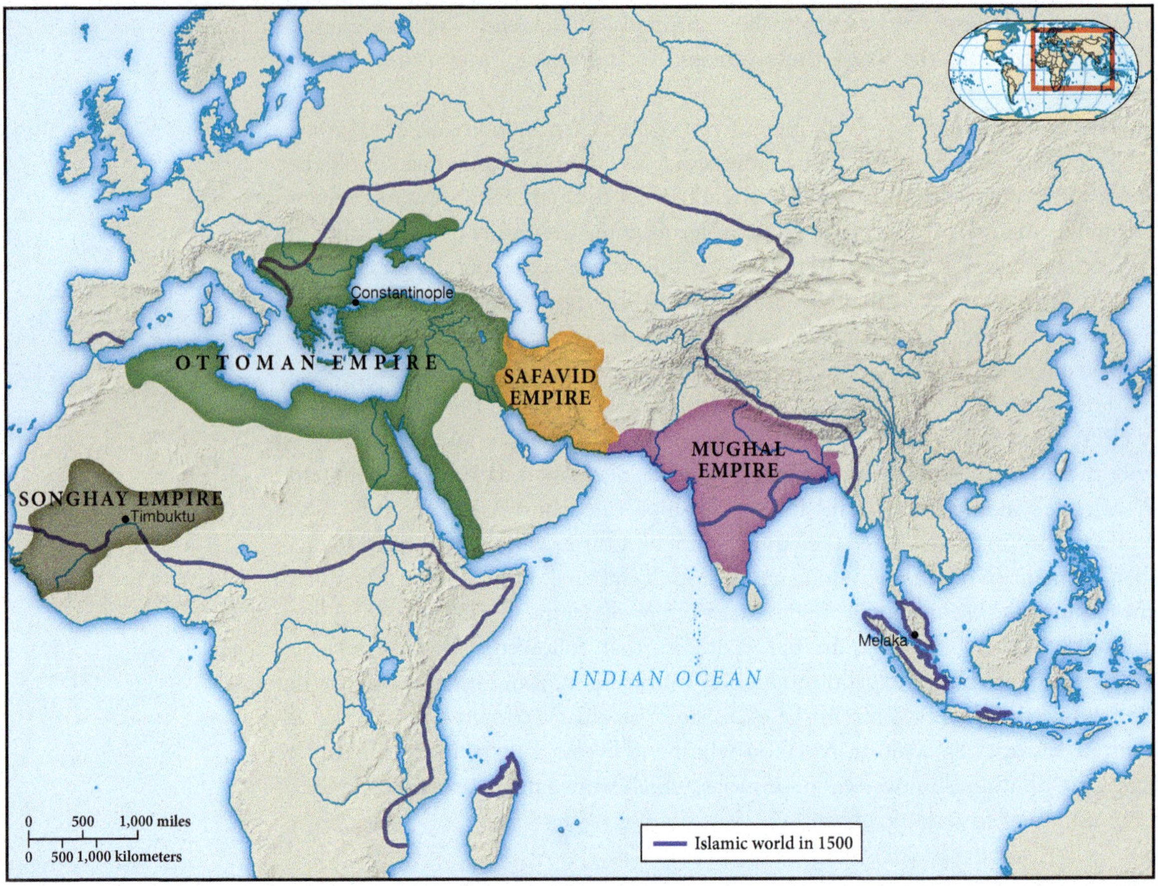

Map 12.4 Empires of the Islamic World
The most prominent political features of the vast Islamic world in the fifteenth and sixteenth centuries were four large states: the Songhay, Ottoman, Safavid, and Mughal empires.

migrated into Anatolia, slowly and sporadically, in the several centuries following 1000 C.E. By the mid-fifteenth century, these Ottoman Turks had already carved out a state that encompassed much of the Anatolian peninsula and had pushed deep into southeastern Europe (the Balkans), acquiring in the process a substantial Christian population. During the sixteenth century, the Ottoman Empire extended its control to much of the Middle East, coastal North Africa, the lands surrounding the Black Sea, and even farther into Eastern Europe.

The Ottoman Empire was a state of enormous significance in the world of the fifteenth century and beyond. In its huge territory, long duration, incorporation of many diverse peoples, and economic and cultural sophistication, it was one of the great empires of world history. In the fifteenth century, only Ming dynasty China and the Incas matched it in terms of wealth, power, and splendor. The empire represented the emergence of the Turks as the dominant people of the Islamic world, ruling now over many Arabs, who had initiated this new faith more than 800 years before. In adding "caliph" (successor to the Prophet) to their other titles, Ottoman sultans claimed the legacy of the earlier Abbasid Empire. They sought to bring a renewed unity to the Islamic world, while also serving as protector of the faith, the "strong sword of Islam."

The Ottoman Empire also represented a new phase in the long encounter between Christendom and the world of Islam. In the Crusades, Europeans had taken the aggressive initiative in that encounter, but the rise of the Ottoman Empire reversed their roles. The **Ottoman seizure of Constantinople** in 1453 marked the final demise of Christian Byzantium and allowed Ottoman rulers to see themselves as successors to the Roman Empire. (See Zooming In: 1453 in Constantinople, page 514.) It also opened the way to further expansion, and in 1529 a rapidly expanding Ottoman Empire laid siege to Vienna in the heart of Central Europe. The political and military expansion of Islam, at the expense of Christendom, seemed clearly under way. Many Europeans spoke fearfully of the "terror of the Turk."

In the neighboring Persian lands to the east of the Ottoman Empire, another Islamic state was also taking shape in the late fifteenth and early sixteenth centuries—the Safavid (SAH-fah-vihd) Empire. Its leadership was also Turkic, but in this case it had emerged from a Sufi religious order founded several centuries earlier by Safi al-Din (1252–1334). The long-term significance of the **Safavid Empire**, which was established in the decade following 1500, was its decision to forcibly impose a Shia version of Islam as the official religion of the state. Over time, this form of Islam gained popular support and came to define the unique identity of Persian (Iranian) culture.

This Shia empire also introduced a sharp divide into the political and religious life of heartland Islam, for almost all of Persia's neighbors practiced a Sunni form of the faith. For a century (1534–1639), periodic military conflict erupted between the Ottoman and Safavid empires, reflecting both territorial rivalry and sharp religious differences. In 1514, the Ottoman sultan wrote to the Safavid ruler in the most bitter of terms:

> You have denied the sanctity of divine law . . . you have deserted the path of salvation and the sacred commandments . . . you have opened to Muslims the gates of tyranny and oppression . . . you have raised the standard of irreligion and heresy. . . . [Therefore] the *ulama* and our doctors have pronounced a sentence of death against you, perjurer and blasphemer.[9]

This Sunni/Shia hostility has continued to divide the Islamic world into the twenty-first century.

On the Frontiers of Islam: The Songhay and Mughal Empires

While the Ottoman and Safavid empires brought both a new political unity and a sharp division to the heartland of Islam, two other states performed a similar role on the expanding African and Asian frontiers of the faith. In the West African savannas,

ZOOMING IN

1453 in Constantinople

On May 29, 1453, forces of the Muslim Ottoman sultan Mehmed II seized control of the great Christian city of Constantinople, an event that marked the final end of the Roman/Byzantine Empire and the ascendancy of the Ottoman Empire. In retrospect, this event acquired a certain air of inevitability about it, for the Byzantine Empire had been retreating for almost two centuries before the steady advance of the Ottomans. By 1453, that once-great empire, heir to all things Roman, had shrunk to little more than the city itself, with only some 50,000 inhabitants and 8,000 active defenders compared to a vast Ottoman army of 60,000 soldiers. And little was left of the fabled wealth of the city. But what later observers see as inevitable generally occurs only with great human effort and amid vast uncertainty about the outcome. So it was in Constantinople in 1453.

Ottoman Turks storm the walls of Constantinople in 1453.

Constantine XI, the last Byzantine emperor, was well aware of the odds he faced. Yet his great city, protected by water on two sides and a great wall on a third, had repeatedly withstood many attacks and sieges. Furthermore, until the very end, he had hoped for assistance from Western Christians, even promising union with the Roman Church to obtain it. But no such help arrived, at least not in sufficient quantities to make a difference, though rumors of a fleet from Venice persisted. The internal problems of the Western powers as well as the long-standing hostility between Eastern Orthodoxy and Roman Catholicism ensured that Constantinople would meet its end alone.

On the Ottoman side, enormous effort was expended with no assurance of success. In 1451, a new sultan came to the throne of the Ottoman Empire, Mehmed II, only nineteen years old and widely regarded as not very promising. Furthermore, some among the court officials had reservations about an attack on Constantinople. But the young sultan seemed determined to gain the honor promised in Islamic prophesies, going back to Muhammad himself, to the one who conquered the city. Doing so could also rid him of a potential rival

photo: ullstein bild Dtl./Getty Images

the **Songhay Empire** rose in the second half of the fifteenth century. It was the most recent and the largest in a series of impressive states that operated at a crucial intersection of the trans-Saharan trade routes and that derived much of their revenue from taxing that commerce. Islam was a growing faith in Songhay but was limited largely to urban elites. This cultural divide within Songhay largely accounts for the religious behavior of its fifteenth-century monarch Sonni Ali (r. 1464?–1492), who gave alms and fasted during Ramadan in proper Islamic style but also enjoyed a reputation as a magician and possessed a charm thought to render his soldiers invisible to their enemies. Nonetheless, Songhay had become a major center of Islamic learning and commerce by the early sixteenth century. A North African traveler known as Leo Africanus remarked on the city of **Timbuktu**:

> Here are great numbers of [Muslim] religious teachers, judges, scholars, and other learned persons who are bountifully maintained at the king's expense.

to the Ottoman throne, who had taken refuge in Constantinople.

And so preparations began for an assault on the once-great city. The Ottomans assembled a huge fleet, gathered men and materials, and constructed a fortress to control access to Constantinople by water. In late 1452, Mehmed secured the services of a Hungarian master cannon builder named Orban, who constructed a number of huge cannons, one of which could hurl a 600-pound stone ball over a mile. These weapons later had a devastating effect on the walls surrounding Constantinople. Interestingly enough, Orban had first offered his services to the Byzantine emperor, who simply could not afford to pay for this very expensive project.

In early April of 1453, the siege began, and it lasted for fifty-seven days. As required by Islamic law, Mehmed offered three times to spare the emperor and his people if they surrendered. Constantine apparently considered the offer seriously, but he finally refused, declaring, "We have all decided to die with our own free will." After weeks of furious bombardment, an ominous silence descended on May 28. Mehmed had declared a day of rest and prayer before the final assault the next day. That evening, the Byzantine emperor ordered a procession of icons and relics about the city and then entered the ancient Christian church of Hagia Sophia, seeking forgiveness for his sins and receiving Holy Communion.

And then, early the next day, the final assault began. Ottoman forces breached Constantinople's great walls despite the brave efforts of the defenders. Constantine discarded his royal regalia and died fighting like a common soldier. A later legend suggested that angels turned Constantine into marble and buried him in a nearby cave, from which he would eventually reappear to retake the city for Christendom.

Islamic law required that soldiers be permitted three days of plundering the spoils, but Mehmed was reluctant, eager to spare the city he longed for as his capital. So he limited plundering to one day. Even so, the aftermath was terrible. According to a Christian eyewitness, "The enraged Turkish soldiers . . . gave no quarter. When they had massacred and there was no longer any resistance, they were intent on pillage and roamed through the town stealing, disrobing, pillaging, killing, raping, taking captive men, women, children, monks, priests."[10] When Mehmed himself entered the city, praying at the Christian altar of Hagia Sophia, he reportedly wept at seeing the destruction that had occurred.

Constantinople was now a Muslim city, capital of the Ottoman Empire, and Hagia Sophia became a mosque. A momentous change had occurred in the relationship between the world of Islam and that of Christendom.

QUESTIONS

What factors contributed to Mehmed's victory? Under what circumstances might a different outcome have been possible?

> Here too are brought various manuscripts or written books from Barbary [North Africa] which are sold for more money than any other merchandise. . . . It is a wonder to see the quality of merchandise that is daily brought here and how costly and sumptuous everything is.[11]

The Mughal (MOO-guhl) Empire in India bore similarities to Songhay, for both governed largely non-Muslim populations. Much as the Ottoman Empire initiated a new phase in the interaction of Islam and Christendom, so too did the **Mughal Empire** continue an ongoing encounter between Islamic and Hindu civilizations. Established in the early sixteenth century, the Mughal Empire was the creation of yet another Islamized Turkic group that invaded India in 1526. Over the next century, the Mughals (a Persian term for Mongols) established unified control over most of the Indian peninsula, giving it a rare period of political unity. During its first 150 years, the Mughal Empire, a land of great wealth and imperial splendor,

Ottoman Janissaries Originating in the fourteenth century, the Janissaries became the elite infantry force of the Ottoman Empire. Complete with uniforms, cash salaries, and marching music, they were the first standing army in the region since the days of the Roman Empire. When gunpowder technology became available, Janissary forces soon were armed with muskets, grenades, and handheld cannons. This Turkish miniature painting dates from the sixteenth century. (Topkapi Palace Museum, Istanbul, Turkey/Album/Art Resource, NY)

undertook a remarkable effort to blend many Hindu groups and a variety of Muslims into an effective partnership. The inclusive policies of the early Mughal emperors showed that Muslim rulers could accommodate their overwhelmingly Hindu subjects.

Together these four Muslim empires—Ottoman, Safavid, Songhay, and Mughal—brought to the Islamic world a greater measure of political coherence, military power, economic prosperity, and cultural brilliance than it had known since the early centuries of Islam. This new energy, sometimes called a "second flowering of Islam," impelled the continuing spread of the faith to yet new regions.

The most prominent of these was oceanic Southeast Asia, which for centuries had been intimately bound up in the world of Indian Ocean commerce, while borrowing elements of both Hindu and Buddhist traditions. By the fifteenth century, that trading network was largely in Muslim hands, and the demand for Southeast Asian spices was mounting as the Eurasian world recovered from the devastation of Mongol conquest and the plague. Growing numbers of Muslim traders settled along the Malay Peninsula and in Java and Sumatra, bringing their faith with them. Eager to attract those traders to their port cities, some rulers in the region converted to Islam, transforming themselves into Muslim sultans and imposing Islamic law. Thus, unlike in the Middle East and India, where Islam was established in the wake of Arab or Turkic conquest, in Southeast Asia, as in West Africa, it was introduced by traveling merchants and solidified through the activities of Sufi holy men.

The rise of **Melaka**, strategically located on the waterway between Sumatra and Malaya, was a sign of the times (see Map 12.1). During the fifteenth century, it was transformed from a small fishing village to a major Muslim port city (see "Sea Roads as a Catalyst for Change: Southeast Asia" in Chapter 7). A Portuguese visitor in 1512 observed that Melaka had "no equal in the world. . . . Commerce between different nations for a thousand leagues on every hand must come to Malacca."[12] The city also became a springboard for the spread of Islam throughout the region. In the eclectic style of Southeast Asian religious history, the Islam of Melaka demonstrated much blending with local and Hindu/Buddhist traditions, while the city itself, like many port towns, had a reputation for "rough behavior." An Arab Muslim pilot in the 1480s commented critically: "They have no culture at all. . . . You do not know whether they are Muslim or not."[13] Nonetheless, Melaka, like Timbuktu on the West African frontier of an expanding Islamic world, became a center for Islamic learning, attracting students from elsewhere in Southeast Asia in the fifteenth century. As the core regions of Islam were consolidating politically, the frontier of the faith continued to move steadily outward.

CORE IDEA

Comparing Civilizations

In what ways did the civilizations of China, Europe, and the Islamic world seem to be moving in the same direction, and in what respects were they diverging from one another?

Civilizations of the Fifteenth Century: The Americas

Across the Atlantic, centers of civilization had long flourished in Mesoamerica and in the Andes. The fifteenth century witnessed new, larger, and more politically unified expressions of those civilizations, embodied in the Aztec and Inca empires. Both were the work of previously marginal peoples who had forcibly taken over and absorbed older cultures, giving them new energy, and both were decimated in the sixteenth century at the hands of Spanish conquistadores and their diseases (see Map 12.5).

The Aztec Empire

The state known to history as the **Aztec Empire** was largely the work of the Mexica (meh-SHEEH-kah) people, a semi-nomadic group from northern Mexico who had migrated southward and by 1325 had established themselves on a small island in Lake Texcoco. Over the next century, the Mexica developed their military capacity, served as mercenaries for more powerful people, negotiated elite marriage alliances with those people, and built up their own capital city of Tenochtitlán (te-nawch-tee-tlahn). In 1428, a Triple Alliance between the Mexica and two nearby city-states launched a highly aggressive program of military conquest that in

Map 12.5 The Americas in the Fifteenth Century

The Americas before Columbus represented a world almost completely separate from Afro-Eurasia. The Americas featured societies similar to those found in the Eastern Hemisphere, though with a different balance among them and with pastoral peoples nearly absent.

less than 100 years brought more of Mesoamerica within a single political framework than ever before. Aztec authorities, eager to shed their rather undistinguished past, now claimed descent from earlier Mesoamerican peoples such as the Toltecs and Teotihuacán.

With a core population recently estimated at 5 to 6 million people, the Aztec Empire was a loosely structured and unstable conquest state that witnessed frequent rebellions by its subject peoples. Conquered peoples and cities were required to provide labor for Aztec projects and to regularly deliver to their Aztec rulers impressive quantities of textiles and clothing, military supplies, jewelry and other luxuries, various foodstuffs, animal products, building materials, rubber balls, paper, and more. The process was overseen by local imperial tribute collectors, who sent the required goods on to Tenochtitlán, a metropolis of 150,000 to 200,000 people, where they were meticulously recorded.

That city featured numerous canals, dikes, causeways, and bridges. A central walled area of palaces and temples included a pyramid almost 200 feet high. Surrounding the city were "floating gardens," artificial islands created from swamplands that supported a highly productive agriculture. Vast marketplaces reflected the commercialization of the economy. A young Spanish soldier who beheld the city in 1519 declared, "Gazing on such wonderful sights, we did not know what to say, or whether what appeared before us was real."[14]

Beyond tribute from conquered peoples, ordinary trade, both local and long-distance, permeated Aztec domains. The extent of empire and rapid population growth stimulated the development of markets and the production of craft goods, particularly in the fifteenth century. Virtually every settlement, from the capital city to the smallest village, had a marketplace that hummed with activity during weekly market days. The largest was that of Tlatelolco, near the capital city, which stunned the Spanish with its huge size, its good order, and the immense range of goods available. Hernán Cortés, the Spanish conquistador who defeated the Aztecs, wrote that "every kind of merchandise such as can be met with in every land is for sale there, whether of food and victuals, or ornaments of gold and silver, or lead, brass, copper, tin, precious stones, bones, shells, snails and feathers."[15] Professional merchants, known as *pochteca*, were legally commoners, but their wealth, often exceeding that of the nobility, allowed them to rise in society and become "magnates of the land."

Among the "goods" that the pochteca obtained were enslaved people, many of whom were destined for sacrifice in the bloody rituals so central to Aztec religious life. Long a part of Mesoamerican and many other world cultures, human sacrifice assumed an unusually prominent role in Aztec public life and thought during the fifteenth century. Tlacaelel (1398–1480), who was for more than half a century a prominent official of the Aztec Empire, is often credited with crystallizing the ideology of state that gave human sacrifice such great importance.

■ Assess the Role of Religion
How did Aztec religious thinking support the empire?

In this cyclical understanding of the world, the sun, central to all life and identified with the Aztec patron deity Huitzilopochtli (wee-tsee-loh-pockt-lee), tended to lose its energy in a constant battle against encroaching darkness. Thus the Aztec

Aztec Double-Headed Serpent Sixteen inches long and composed of around 2,000 pieces of blue-green turquoise for the body and rare red and white shells for its nostrils, gums, and terrifying fangs, this remarkable sculpture of a snake with one body and two heads was likely for ritual use. The important Aztec god Quetzalcóatl is often depicted as a serpent, and some scholars have argued that this sculpture represents him. (Werner Forman/Getty Images)

world hovered always on the edge of catastrophe. To replenish its energy and thus postpone the descent into endless darkness, the sun required the life-giving force found in human blood. Because the gods had shed their blood ages ago in creating humankind, it was wholly proper for people to offer their own blood to nourish the gods in the present. The high calling of the Aztec state was to supply this blood, largely through its wars of expansion and from prisoners of war, who were destined for sacrifice. The victims were "those who have died for the god." The growth of the Aztec Empire therefore became the means for maintaining cosmic order and avoiding utter catastrophe. This ideology also shaped the techniques of Aztec warfare, which put a premium on capturing prisoners rather than on killing the enemy. As the empire grew, priests and rulers became mutually dependent, and "human sacrifices were carried out in the service of politics."[16] Massive sacrificial rituals, together with a display of great wealth, served to impress enemies, allies, and subjects alike with the immense power of the Aztecs and their gods.

Alongside these sacrificial rituals was a philosophical and poetic tradition of great beauty, much of which mused on the fragility and brevity of human life. Such an outlook characterized the work of Nezahualcoyotl (1402–1472), a poet and king of the city-state of Texcoco, which was part of the Aztec Empire:

> Truly do we live on Earth?
> Not forever on earth; only a little while here.
> Although it be jade, it will be broken.
> Although it be gold, it is crushed.
> Although it be a quetzal feather, it is torn asunder.
> Not forever on earth; only a little while here.[17]

The Inca Empire

CORE IDEA

Comparing Empires
What distinguished the Aztec and Inca empires from each other?

While the Mexica were constructing an empire in Mesoamerica, a relatively small community of Quechua-speaking people, known to us as the Incas, was building the Western Hemisphere's largest imperial state along the entire spine of the Andes Mountains. Much as the Aztecs drew on the traditions of the Toltecs and Teotihuacán, the Incas incorporated the lands and cultures of earlier Andean civilizations: Chavín, Moche, Wari, and Tiwanaku. The **Inca Empire**, however, was much larger than the Aztec state; it stretched some 2,500 miles along the Andes and contained perhaps 10 million subjects. Whereas the Aztec Empire controlled only part of the Mesoamerican cultural region, the Inca state encompassed practically the whole of Andean civilization during its short life in the fifteenth and early sixteenth centuries. In the speed of its creation and the extent of its territory, the Inca Empire bears some similarity to that of the Mongols.

Both the Aztec and Inca empires represent rags-to-riches stories in which quite modest and remotely located people very quickly created by military conquest the largest states ever witnessed in their respective regions, but the empires themselves were quite different. In the Aztec realm, the Mexica rulers largely left their conquered people alone, if the required tribute was forthcoming. No elaborate administrative system arose to integrate the conquered territories or to assimilate their people to Aztec culture.

The Incas, on the other hand, erected a rather more bureaucratic empire. At the top reigned the emperor, an absolute ruler regarded as divine, a descendant of the creator god Viracocha and the son of the sun god Inti. Each of the some eighty provinces in the empire had an Inca governor. In theory, the state owned all land and resources, though in practice state lands, known as "lands of the sun," existed alongside properties owned by temples, elites, and traditional communities. At least in the central regions of the empire, subjects were grouped into hierarchical units of 10, 50, 100, 500, 1,000, 5,000, and 10,000 people, each headed by local officials, who were appointed and supervised by an Inca governor or the emperor. A separate set of "inspectors" provided the imperial center with an independent check on provincial officials.

Births, deaths, marriages, and other population data were carefully recorded on *quipus*, the knotted cords that served as an accounting device. A resettlement program moved one-quarter or more of the population to new locations, in part to disperse conquered and no doubt resentful people and sometimes to reward loyal followers with promising opportunities. Efforts at cultural integration required the leaders of conquered peoples to learn Quechua (keh-choo-wah). Their sons were removed to the capital of Cuzco for instruction in Inca culture and language. Even now, millions of people from Ecuador to Chile still speak Quechua, and it is the official second language of Peru after Spanish.

■ Describing Policies
In what ways did Inca authorities seek to integrate their vast domains?

But the sheer human variety of the Incas' enormous empire required great flexibility. In some places Inca rulers encountered bitter resistance; in others local elites were willing to accommodate Incas and thus benefit from their inclusion in the empire. Where centralized political systems already existed, Inca overlords could delegate control to native authorities. Elsewhere they had to construct an administrative system from scratch. Everywhere they sought to incorporate local people into the lower levels of the administrative hierarchy. While the Incas required their subject peoples to acknowledge major Inca deities, these peoples were then largely free to carry on their own religious traditions. The Inca Empire was a fluid system that varied greatly from place to place and over time. It depended as much on the posture of conquered peoples as on the demands and desires of Inca authorities.

Machu Picchu Machu Picchu, high in the Andes Mountains, was constructed by the Incas in the fifteenth century on a spot long held sacred by local people. Its 200 buildings stand at some 8,000 feet above sea level, making it a "city in the sky." It was probably a royal retreat or religious center, rather than a location serving administrative, commercial, or military purposes. The outside world became aware of Machu Picchu only in 1911, when it was popularized by a Yale University archeologist. (fStop/Superstock)

Like the Aztec Empire, the Inca state represented an especially dense and extended network of economic relationships within the "American web," but these relationships took shape in quite a different fashion. Inca demands on their conquered people were expressed, not so much in terms of tribute, but as labor service, known as *mita*, which was required periodically of every household. What people produced at home usually stayed at home, but almost everyone also had to work for the state. Some labored on large state farms or on "sun farms," which supported temples and religious institutions; others herded, mined, served in the military, or toiled on state-directed construction projects.

Those with particular skills were put to work manufacturing textiles, metal goods, ceramics, and stonework. The most well known of these specialists were the "chosen women," who were removed from their homes as young girls, trained in Inca ideology, and set to producing corn beer and cloth at state centers. Later they were given as wives to men of distinction or sent to serve as priestesses in various temples, where they were known as "wives of the Sun." In return for such labor services, Inca ideology, expressed in terms of family relationships, required the state to arrange elaborate feasts at which large quantities of food and drink were consumed and to provide food and other necessities when disaster struck. Thus the authority of the state penetrated and directed Inca society and economy far more than did that of the Aztecs.

If the Inca and Aztec civilizations differed sharply in their political and economic arrangements, they resembled each other more closely in their gender systems. Both societies practiced what scholars call "gender parallelism," in which "women and men operate in two separate but equivalent spheres, each gender enjoying autonomy in its own sphere."[18] In both Mesoamerican and Andean societies, such systems had emerged long before their incorporation into the Aztec and Inca empires. In the Andes, men reckoned their descent from their fathers and women from their mothers, while Mesoamericans had long viewed children as belonging equally to their mothers and fathers. Parallel religious cults for women and men likewise flourished in both societies. Inca men venerated the sun, while women worshipped the moon, with matching religious officials. In Aztec temples, both male and female priests presided over rituals dedicated to deities of both sexes. Particularly among the Incas, parallel hierarchies of male and female political officials governed the empire, while in Aztec society, women officials exercised local authority under a title that meant "female person in charge of people." Social roles were clearly defined and different for men and women, but the domestic concerns of women—childbirth, cooking, weaving, cleaning—were not regarded as inferior to the activities of men. Among the Aztecs, for example, sweeping was a powerful and sacred act with symbolic significance as "an act of purification and a preventative against evil elements penetrating the center of the Aztec universe, the home."[19] In the Andes, men broke the ground, women sowed, and both took part in the harvest.

This was gender complementarity, not gender equality. Men occupied the top positions in both political and religious life, and male infidelity was treated more lightly than women's unfaithfulness. As the Inca and Aztec empires expanded, military life, limited to men, grew in prestige, perhaps skewing an earlier gender parallelism. The Incas in particular imposed a more rigidly patriarchal order on their subject peoples. In other ways, the new Aztec and Inca rulers adapted to the gender systems of the people they had conquered. Among the Aztecs, the tools of women's work, the broom and the weaving spindle, were ritualized as weapons; sweeping the home was believed to assist men at war; and childbirth was regarded by women as "our

Inca Agricultural Practice This sixteenth-century drawing by Felipe Guaman Poma, an Inca nobleman, illustrates the cooperation of Inca men and women in agriculture. The men are loosening the soil with a "foot-plow," while the women plant the seeds. (Werner Forman/Getty Images)

kind of war."[20] Inca rulers replicated the gender parallelism of their subjects at a higher level, as the *sapay Inca* (the Inca ruler) and the *coya* (his female consort) governed jointly, claiming descent respectively from the sun and the moon.

Webs of Connection

Few people in the fifteenth century lived in entirely separate and self-contained communities. Almost all were caught up, to one degree or another, in various and overlapping webs of influence, communication, and exchange.[21] Perhaps most obvious were the webs of empire, large-scale political systems that brought together a variety of culturally different people. Christians and Muslims encountered each other directly in the Ottoman Empire, as did Hindus and Muslims in the Mughal Empire. And no empire tried more diligently to integrate its diverse peoples than the fifteenth-century Incas.

Religion too linked far-flung peoples, and divided them as well. Christianity provided a common religious culture for peoples from England to Russia, although the great divide between Roman Catholicism and Eastern Orthodoxy endured, and in the sixteenth century the Protestant Reformation would shatter permanently the Christian unity of the Latin West. Although Buddhism had largely vanished from its South Asian homeland, it remained a link among China, Korea, Tibet, Japan, and parts of Southeast Asia, even as it splintered into a variety of sects and practices. More than either of these, Islam actively brought together its many peoples. In the hajj, the pilgrimage to Mecca, Africans, Arabs, Persians, Turks, Indians, and many others joined as one people as they rehearsed together the events that gave birth to their common faith. And yet divisions and conflicts persisted within the vast realm of Islam, as the violent hostility between the Sunni Ottoman Empire and the Shia Safavid Empire so vividly illustrates.

CORE IDEA

Describing Connections
In what different ways did the peoples of the fifteenth century interact with one another?

Long-established patterns of trade among peoples occupying different environments and producing different goods were certainly much in evidence during the fifteenth century, as they had been for millennia. Hunting societies of Siberia funneled furs and other products of the forest into the Silk Road trading network traversing the civilizations of Eurasia. In the fifteenth century, some of the agricultural peoples in southern Nigeria were receiving horses brought overland from the drier regions of Africa to the north, where those animals flourished better. The Mississippi River in North America and the Orinoco and Amazon rivers in South America facilitated a canoe-borne commerce along those waterways. Coastal shipping in large seagoing canoes operated in the Caribbean and along the Pacific coast between Mexico and Peru. In Pacific Polynesia, the great voyaging networks across vast oceanic distances that had flourished especially since 1000 were in decline by 1500 or earlier, leading to the abandonment of a number of islands.

The great long-distance trading patterns of the Afro-Eurasian world, in operation for a thousand years or more, continued in the fifteenth century, although the balance among them was changing (see Map 12.6). The Silk Road overland network, which had flourished under Mongol control in the thirteenth and fourteenth centuries,

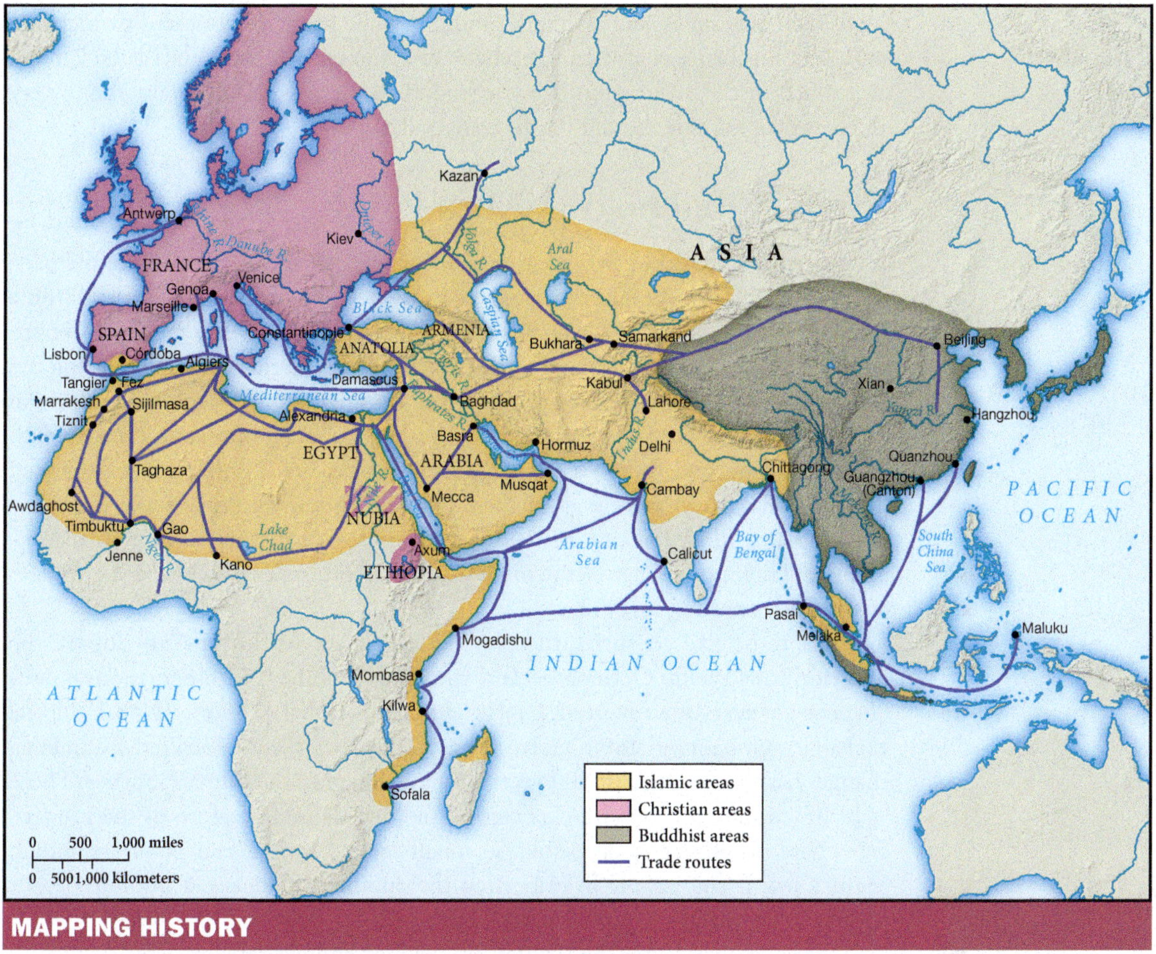

Map 12.6 Religion and Commerce in the Afro-Eurasian World

By the fifteenth century, the many distinct peoples and societies of the Eastern Hemisphere were linked to one another by ties of religion and commerce. Of course, most people were not directly involved in long-distance trade, and many people in areas shown as Buddhist or Islamic on the map practiced other religions. While much of India, for example, was ruled by Muslims, the majority of its people followed some form of Hinduism. And although Islam had spread to West Africa, that religion had not penetrated much beyond the urban centers of the region.

READING THE MAP Where were Buddhists concentrated in the Indian Ocean region? In which areas were Muslims most prominent? What can this map tell us about Christianity in the Indian Ocean world?

INTERPRETING THE MAP What does this map suggest about the places where cross-cultural contacts and interactions among the three major faiths during the fifteenth century might most likely have occurred?

contracted in the fifteenth century as the Mongol Empire broke up and the devastation of the plague reduced demand for its products. The rise of the Ottoman Empire also blocked direct commercial contact between Europe and China, but oceanic trade from Japan, Korea, and China through the islands of Southeast Asia and across the Indian Ocean picked up considerably. Larger ships made it possible to trade in bulk goods such as grain as well as luxury products, while more sophisticated partnerships and credit mechanisms greased the wheels of commerce. A common Islamic culture over much of this vast region likewise smoothed the passage of goods among very different peoples, as it also did for the trans-Saharan trade.

After 1500: Looking Ahead to the Modern Era

While ties of empire, culture, commerce, and disease surely linked many of the peoples in the world of the fifteenth century, none of those connections operated on a genuinely global scale. Although the densest webs of connection had been woven within the Afro-Eurasian zone of interaction, this huge region had no enduring ties with the Americas, and neither of them had sustained contact with the peoples of Pacific Oceania. That situation was about to change as Europeans in the sixteenth century and beyond forged a set of genuinely global relationships that generated sustained interaction among all of these regions. That huge process and the many outcomes that flowed from it marked the beginning of what world historians commonly call the modern age—the more than five centuries that followed the voyages of Columbus starting in 1492.

Over those five centuries, the previously separate worlds of Afro-Eurasia, the Americas, and Pacific Oceania became inextricably linked, with enormous consequences for everyone involved. Global empires, a global economy, global cultural exchanges, global migrations, global disease, global wars, and global environmental changes have made the past 500 years a unique phase in the human journey. Those webs of communication and exchange—the first defining feature of the modern era—have progressively deepened, so much so that by the end of the twentieth century few if any people lived beyond the cultural influences, economic ties, or political relationships of a globalized world.

Several centuries after the Columbian voyages, and clearly connected to them, a second distinctive feature of the modern era took shape: the emergence of a radically new kind of human society, first in Europe during the nineteenth century and then in various forms elsewhere in the world. The core feature of such societies was industrialization. That revolutionary economic process was accompanied by a host of other transformations: accelerating technological innovation; the massive consumption of energy and raw materials; a scientific outlook on the world; an unprecedented increase in human population (see the Snapshot, page 527); rapid urbanization; widespread commercialization; more powerful and intrusive states; the growing prominence and dominance of Europeans on the world stage; and a very different balance of global power.

This was the revolution of modernity, comparable in its pervasive consequences only to the Agricultural Revolution of some 10,000 years ago. It usually meant a self-conscious and often uneasy awareness of living and thinking in new ways that deliberately departed from tradition. Sorting out what was gained and what was lost during the modern transformation has been a persistent and highly controversial

SNAPSHOT **World Population Growth, 1000–2000**

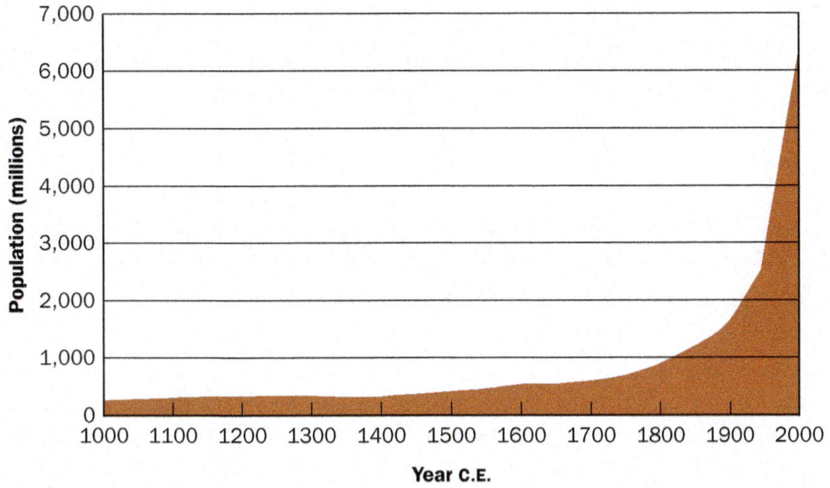

Source: Data from David Christian, *Map of Time* (Berkeley: University of California Press, 2004), 343; https://www.worldometers.info/world-population/world-population-by-year/.

thread of human thought over the past several centuries. And it is a central concern of historians who trace the contours of the human journey in the centuries after 1500.

CONCLUSIONS AND REFLECTIONS

Perspectives on Turning Points

In our endless efforts to discover meaning in our lives, we are inclined to find "turning points," times when something seems to shift, when new directions or possibilities arise. In personal life, birthdays, graduations, marriages, divorces, and losing or gaining a job are among the events that mark turning points for individuals. Historians too seek to identify turning points, both globally and for particular civilizations, cultures, and peoples. In this chapter, such turning points abound.

For many historians, the fifteenth century in general marks the beginning of a modern era of global entanglement, symbolized by "1492" and the voyages of Columbus and to a lesser extent by "1498," when the Portuguese explorer Vasco da Gama arrived in India. At the time, of course, few people understood that they had experienced a major turning point and were now living in a new era. In just a few decades, however, Spanish conquest and rampant disease made it crystal clear to the people of the Aztec and Inca empires that their world had changed forever.

Within European or Western civilization, the cultural flowering known as the Renaissance convinced many of its intellectuals and artists that they had entered a new era of creativity and enlightenment that would recover and even surpass the accomplishments of the ancient Greeks and Romans. Thus the Renaissance became for many at the time and later a "turning point" toward modernity and progress that moved decisively beyond the "Dark Ages" of earlier centuries. More recently scholars have disputed the notion that it was a sharp break with what came before. The Dark Ages no longer seem so dark, nor does the Renaissance appear so enlightened. Turning points are often in the eye of the beholder.

China in the early fifteenth century provides an example of a turning point that did not turn. Its massive maritime voyages in the Indian Ocean world created the possibility of a Chinese maritime empire and perhaps even contact with the Americas. In abruptly ending those voyages, China presented historians with a fascinating "what if" or counterfactual question. Was it the absence of Chinese naval power in the Indian Ocean that allowed Europeans to penetrate that region of the world? History perhaps turns on what did not happen as well as on what did.

The fifteenth century also represented a turning point in the Islamic world as four major Muslim empires took shape, thus ending, or at least diminishing, a long period of intense political fragmentation. The most important of those new states was the Ottoman Empire. Its conquest of Constantinople in 1453 marked a decisive turning point that was instantly recognizable to all. The Christian Byzantine Empire was dead; the world of European Christendom faced a formidable threat both militarily and religiously; and the Ottoman Empire was one of the great powers of the Mediterranean world. In the long relationship between the Christian and Islamic worlds, things had changed.

In the Americas as well the emergence of new empires represented a turning point in the history of the region, for the Aztec and Inca empires were the largest and most powerful states ever to take shape in the Western Hemisphere. And yet they also represented a continuation of earlier traditions of civilization in both Mesoamerica and the Andes. So while turning points imply a break with the past, they can also call attention to striking continuities with it.

Globally too, "turning points" and continuities intersect. The world of the fifteenth century was increasingly dominated by civilizations and empires, but other kinds of human societies persisted from the more distant past. All of Australia and parts of North America continued to support Paleolithic peoples practicing a gathering and hunting way of life. And the Igbo of West Africa and the Iroquois of North America represent the persistence of agricultural village societies operating without the cities, states, and empires characteristic of civilizations.

The notion of "turning points" can be useful for highlighting important changes in the lives of individuals and in human history. But the complexity or messiness of personal life and of the historical process, as well as the constant interplay of persistence and change, suggest that we treat this notion with caution. Neither individual lives nor historical processes can be adequately captured by any list of "turning points."

Revisiting Chapter 12

Revisiting Specifics

Revisiting Core Ideas

1. **Identifying Alternatives to Civilizations** What alternatives to the cities, states, and empires of established civilizations persisted in the world of the fifteenth century?
2. **Comparing China and Europe** What major differences stand out in the histories of fifteenth-century China and Western Europe? What similarities are apparent?
3. **Noticing Change** What new departures can you identify in the Islamic world of the fifteenth and sixteenth centuries?
4. **Comparing Civilizations** In what ways did the civilizations of China, Europe, and the Islamic world seem to be moving in the same direction, and in what respects were they diverging from one another?
5. **Comparing Empires** What distinguished the Aztec and Inca empires from each other?
6. **Describing Connections** In what different ways did the peoples of the fifteenth century interact with one another?

A Wider View

1. Assume for the moment that the Chinese had not ended their maritime voyages in 1433. How might the subsequent development of world history have been different? What value is there in asking this kind of "what if" or counterfactual question?
2. How does this chapter distinguish among the various kinds of societies contained in the world of the fifteenth century? What other ways of categorizing the world's peoples might work as well or better?
3. What common patterns might you notice across the world of the fifteenth century? And what variations in the historical trajectories of various regions can you identify?
4. **Looking Back** What would surprise a knowledgeable observer from 500 or 1000 C.E., were he or she to make a global tour in the fifteenth century? What features of that earlier world might still be recognizable?

To learn more about the topics in this chapter, see **For Further Study** at the end of this book.

WORKING WITH EVIDENCE

Islam and Renaissance Europe

The Renaissance era in Europe, roughly 1350 to 1500, represented the crystallization of a new third-wave civilization at the western end of Eurasia. In cultural terms, its writers and artists sought to link themselves to the legacy of the pre-Christian Greeks and Romans. But if Europeans were reaching back to their classical past, they were also reaching out—westward to the wholly new world of the Americas, southward to Africa, and eastward to Asia generally and the Islamic world in particular. The European Renaissance, in short, was shaped not only from within but also by its encounters with a wider world.

Interaction with the world of Islam was, of course, nothing new. Centuries of Muslim rule in Spain, the Crusades, and the expansion of the Ottoman Empire were markers in the long relationship of conflict, cooperation, and mutual influence between Christendom and the realm of Islam. Politically, that relationship was changing in the fifteenth century. The Christian reconquest of Spain from Muslim rule was completed by 1492. At the other end of the Mediterranean Sea, the Turkish Ottoman Empire was expanding into the Christian regions of southeastern Europe, while becoming a major player in European international politics.

Despite such conflicts, commerce flourished across political and religious divides. European bulk goods such as wool, timber, and glassware, along with silver and gold, were exchanged for high-value luxury goods from the Islamic world or funneled through it from farther east—spices, silks, carpets, tapestries, precious stones, gold, dyes, and pigments. Along with goods, Arab and Muslim learning—in medicine, astronomy, philosophy, architecture, mathematics, business practices, and more—also flowed into the Christian West. These various engagements with the Islamic world found expression in Renaissance Italy, as the sources that follow illustrate.

SOURCE 12.1 Portrait of Mehmed II ▶

The year 1453 marked a watershed in the long relationship between Christendom and the Islamic world, for it was in that year that the Ottoman sultan Mehmed II decisively conquered the great Christian city of Constantinople, bringing the thousand-year history of Byzantium to an inglorious end. To many Europeans, that event was a catastrophe and Mehmed was the "terror of the world." Others, however, saw opportunity. Less than a year after that event, the northern Italian city of Venice signed a peace treaty with the Ottoman sultan, declaring, "It is our intention to live in peace and friendship with the Turkish emperor."[22] Some even expressed admiration for the conquering Muslim ruler, described by George of Trebizond, a leading Renaissance scholar, as "a wise king and one who philosophizes about the greatest matters."[23]

For his part, Mehmed admired both classical and contemporary European culture, even as his armies threatened European powers. This cosmopolitan emperor stocked his library with Western texts and decorated the walls of his palace with Renaissance-style frescoes. Seeing himself as heir to Roman imperial authority, he now added "Caesar" to his other titles. And in 1480, he had his portrait painted by the leading artist of Venice, Gentile Bellini, who had been sent to the Ottoman court as a cultural ambassador of his city.

Source 12.1 shows Bellini's portrait of the emperor sitting under a marble arch, a symbol of triumph that evokes his dramatic conquest of Constantinople. The three golden crowns on the upper left and right likely represent the lands recently acquired for the Ottoman Empire, and the inscription at the bottom describes Mehmed as "Conqueror of the World."

- What overall impression of the sultan does this portrait convey?
- Why might this Muslim ruler want his portrait painted by a Christian artist from Venice?
- Why might Bellini and the city government of Venice be willing—even eager—to undertake the assignment, less than thirty years after the Muslim conquest of Constantinople?

GENTILE BELLINI | *Portrait of Mehmed II* | 1480

Bridgeman Images

SOURCE 12.2 Machiavelli on the Turkish State

The increasing power of the Ottoman Empire inspired fear and admiration among Christian observers, along with a growing interest in how the Turkish sultan governed his state. Niccolò Machiavelli (1469–1527), the diplomat, historian, and political theorist from Florence, offered his assessment of Ottoman government in his most famous treatise, *The Prince*, when he compared the Turkish state to that of France, one of the most powerful kingdoms in Western Europe.

- How would you characterize Machiavelli's view of the Ottoman state? Does he see it clearly as superior or inferior to that of France, or just different?
- Does religion enter into Machiavelli's analysis?
- Many at the time criticized Machiavelli's *Prince* for its amoral analysis of political life and its assertion that rulers must set aside concerns about morality to rule effectively. Is there anything in this passage that supports this interpretation of Machiavelli's thought?

NICCOLÒ MACHIAVELLI | *The Prince* | 1513

Examples of these two kinds of government in our own time are the Turk and the King of France. All the Turkish monarchy is governed by one ruler, the others are his servants, and dividing his kingdom into "sangiascates" [administrative units], he sends to them various administrators, and charges or recalls them at his pleasure. But the King of France is surrounded by a large number of ancient nobles, recognized as such by their subjects, and loved by them; they have their prerogatives, which the king cannot deprive them of without danger to himself. Whoever now considers these two states will see that it would be difficult to acquire the state of the Turk; but having conquered it, it would be very easy to hold it.

The causes of the difficulty of occupying the Turkish kingdom are, that the invader could not be invited by princes of that kingdom, nor hope to facilitate his enterprise by the rebellion of those around [the Turkish sultan], as will be evident from reasons given above. Because, being all slaves, and bound, it will be more difficult to corrupt them, and even if they were corrupted, little effect could be hoped for, as they would not be able to carry the people with them for the reasons mentioned. Therefore, whoever assaults the Turk must be prepared to meet his united forces, and must rely more on his own strength than on the disorders of others [i.e., rebellious subjects of the Turkish ruler]; but having once conquered him, and beaten him in battle so that he can no longer raise armies, nothing else is to be feared except the family of the prince, and if this is extinguished [i.e., if all members of the Turkish ruler's family are killed], there is no longer any one to be feared, the others having no credit with the people; and as the victor before the victory could place no hope in them, so he need not fear them afterwards. The contrary is the case in the kingdoms governed like that of France, because it is easy to enter them by winning over some baron of the kingdom, there being always some malcontents, and those desiring innovations. These can, for the reasons stated, open the way to you and facilitate victory; but afterwards, if you wish to keep possession, infinite difficulties arise, both from those who have aided you and from those you have oppressed. Nor is it sufficient to extinguish the family of the prince, for there remain those nobles who will make themselves the head of new changes, and being neither able to content them nor exterminate them, you will lose the state whenever an occasion arises.

Source: Niccolò Machiavelli, *The Prince*, translated by Luigi Ricci (London: Grant Richards, 1903), 15–16.

SOURCE 12.3 Venetian Trade in the Middle East

Venice had long been the primary point of commercial contact between Europe and the East and the source of the much-desired luxury goods that its merchants obtained from Alexandria in Egypt. At that time, Egypt was ruled by the Mamluks, Muslims who had driven the last of the European Crusaders out of the Middle East in 1291. Venetian traders, however, were more interested in commerce than in religion, and by the fifteenth century they enjoyed a highly profitable relationship with the Mamluk rulers of Egypt and Syria, despite the periodic opposition of the pope and threats of excommunication. Thus it is not surprising that the Renaissance artists of Venice were prominent among those who reflected the influence of the Islamic world in their work. By the late fifteenth century, something of a fad for oriental themes surfaced in Venetian pictorial art.

Source 12.3, painted by an anonymous Venetian artist in 1511, expresses this intense interest in the Islamic world. The setting is Damascus in Syria, then ruled by the Mamluk regime. The local Mamluk governor of the city, seated on a low platform with an elaborate headdress, is receiving an ambassador from Venice, shown in a red robe and standing in front of the governor. Behind him in black robes are other members of the Venetian delegation, while in the foreground various members of Damascus society—both officials and merchants—are distinguished from one another by variations in their turbans. Behind the wall lies the city of Damascus with its famous Umayyad mosque, formerly a Roman temple to Jupiter and later a Christian church, together with its three minarets. The city's lush gardens and its homes with wooden balconies and rooftop terraces complete the picture of urban Islam.

- What impressions of the city and its relationship with Venice does the artist seek to convey?
- How are the various social groups of Damascus distinguished from one another in this painting? What does the very precise visual description of these differences suggest about Venetian understanding of urban Mamluk society?
- What does the total absence of women suggest about their role in the public life of Damascus?
- How would you know that this is a Muslim city? What role, if any, does religion play in this depiction of the relationship between Christian Venice and Islamic Damascus?

The Venetian Ambassador Visits Damascus | **1511**

Bridgeman Images

SOURCE 12.4 Greek and Islamic Philosophers in Renaissance Art

Beyond political and commercial relationships, Europeans had long engaged with the Islamic world intellectually as well. Source 12.4 illustrates that engagement in a work by Girolamo da Cremona, a fifteenth-century Italian painter known for his "illuminations" of early printed books. Created in 1483 (only some forty years after the invention of the printing press in Europe), it served as the frontispiece for one of the first printed versions of Aristotle's writings, translated into Latin, along with commentaries by the twelfth-century Muslim scholar Ibn Rushd (1126–1198), better known in the West as Averroes.

Aristotle, of course, was the great Greek philosopher of the fourth century B.C.E. whose writings presented a systematic and rational view of the world, while commenting on practically every branch of knowledge. The legacy of Greek thought in general and Aristotle in particular passed into both the Christian and Islamic worlds. Ibn Rushd, who wrote voluminous commentaries on Aristotle's works and much else as well, lived in Muslim Spain, where he argued for the compatibility of Aristotelian philosophy and the religious perspectives of Islam. While that outlook faced growing opposition in the Islamic world, Aristotle's writings found more fertile ground among European scholars in the new universities of the twelfth and thirteenth centuries, where they became the foundation of university curricula and nourished the growth of "natural philosophy." In large measure it was through translations of Ibn Rushd's Arabic commentaries on Aristotle that Europeans regained access to the thinking of that ancient philosopher. A long line of European scholars defined themselves as "Averroists."

The painting in Source 12.4 is presented as a parchment leaf, torn to disclose two worlds behind Aristotle's text. At the top in a rural setting, Aristotle, dressed in a blue robe, is speaking to Ibn Rushd, clad in a yellow robe with a round white turban. The bottom of the painting depicts the world of classical Greek mythology. The painted jewels, gems, and pearls testify to the great value placed on such illuminated and printed texts.

- What overall impression of Renaissance thinking about the classical world and the world of Islam does this painting convey?
- Notice the gestures of the two men at the top, as well as the pen in Ibn Rushd's hand and the book at his feet. How might you describe the relationship between the men?
- What made it possible for at least some European Christians of the Renaissance era to embrace both the pagan Aristotle and the Islamic Ibn Rushd?

GIROLAMO DA CREMONA | *Aristotle and Averroes* | 1483

SOURCE 12.5 A Papal Call for Crusade

Violent conflict was also a feature of Christian/Muslim relations during the Renaissance, particularly on the Iberian Peninsula, where Christian forces had triumphed by the 1490s. In the eastern Mediterranean, the growing power of the Turks led to less successful military campaigns or Crusades by Christian powers, several of which were organized by the papacy. In this selection dating from 1343, Pope Clement VI seeks support to send a fleet to counter Turkish naval raids against Christian communities in what are now Greece and the Aegean Islands.

- What specific strategies does Clement pursue to recruit the faithful to his cause?
- How might you describe Clement's posture toward Islam?
- How does this call to crusade compare to earlier Crusader movements to seize the Holy Lands?

POPE CLEMENT VI | *Call for Crusade* | September 30, 1343

Those who launch themselves against the Catholic faith and strive to destroy the Christian religion must be resisted by the faithful with valour and steadfastness. The faithful themselves, fired by ardour for the orthodox faith, and armed to the fullest extent by its virtues, must oppose their hateful design with a rampart of determination, and forbid their evil undertakings with a firm defence. In this way, arrayed in mental and bodily armour, and directed by the light of faith, they may, with the assistance of God for whom they fight, cast down the insurgents, who lack [such] spiritual protection and are blinded by the shadows of unbelief.

To our sorrow, recent proof has confirmed what we have been hearing for some time now about groups of those unbelieving pagans, called . . . the Turks, who thirst for blood of Christian people and seek the destruction of the Catholic faith. For some time past they have mobilised the strength of their nation and used a great number of armed vessels to invade by sea Christian territories in the region of *Romania* [Greece and the Aegean Islands], and other neighbouring places in the hands of the faithful. Raging atrociously against the Christians and their lands and islands, they have taken to roaming the seas, as they are doing at present, despoiling and depopulating the settlements . . . and what is worse, seizing the Christians themselves as booty and subjecting them to horrible and perpetual slavery, selling them like animals and forcing them to deny their Catholic faith.

[The pope then declares his plan to create a fleet to counter the Turks.]

And so that the faithful may respond the more willingly, in so far as they know that they will receive the greater grace for their labours . . . we grant to those faithful who proceed with the flotilla or in another fashion in support of the Christians . . . and who remain on campaign for a year . . . and also those who die while engaged on this matter, or receive wounds in the field . . . forgiveness of their sins, for which they are truthfully contrite and which they have confessed orally. . . .

We grant the same indulgence of their sins to those who do not take part in person, but who send suitable soldiers at their own expense in accordance with their means and standing . . . and also to those who offer as much from their own goods for the matter, as they would have spent going there, staying there for a year, and coming back. . . .

Source: Norman Housley, *Documents on the Later Crusades 1274–1580* (New York: St. Martin's Press, 1996), 79–81.

DOING HISTORY

1. **Making Comparisons** What range of postures toward the Islamic world do these sources convey? How might you account for the differences among them?
2. **Imagining Reactions** How might Clement VI in Source 12.5 react to the other four sources in this feature?
3. **Analyzing Sources** While all of these sources deal with the Islamic world, with what different aspects of that world are they concerned?
4. **Considering European Identity** What role did the Islamic world play in the emerging identity of European civilization?

Christian/Muslim Relations during the Renaissance

The relationship between Christian and Islamic civilizations during the Middle Ages and Renaissance has been the subject of considerable attention from historians, who have emphasized both hostility and competition as well as peaceful cross-cultural contacts and exchanges between the two faiths. In Voice 12.1, Jerry Brotton, a specialist on the Renaissance, explores how trade and cultural exchange between Christians and Muslims profoundly shaped the European Renaissance. In Voice 12.2, Bernard Lewis, an expert in Islamic history, examines the reasons behind Christians' and Muslims' hostility toward one another during their first millennium of interaction.

- What reasons do these two sources identify for the intense cultural interaction between Christian and Islamic societies during the Renaissance?
- What do Brotton and Lewis agree on? And on what matters do they disagree?
- **Integrating Primary and Secondary Sources** Which sources in this collection might Brotton and Lewis draw upon to support their assertions?

VOICE 12.1

Jerry Brotton on the Role of Cross-cultural Exchange in the European Renaissance | 2002

The Renaissance Bazaar [Brotton's book] describes the historical period starting in the early 15th century when eastern and western societies vigorously traded art, ideas, and luxury goods in a competitive but amicable exchange that shaped what we now call the European Renaissance. The eastern bazaar is a fitting metaphor for the fluid transactions that occurred throughout the 15th and 16th centuries, when Europe began to define itself by purchasing and emulating the opulence and cultured sophistication of the cities, merchants, scholars and empires of the Ottomans, the Persians, and the Egyptian Mamluks. The flow of spices, silks, carpets, porcelain, majolica, porphyry, glassware, lacquer, dyes, and pigments from the eastern bazaars of Muslim Spain, Mamluk Egypt, Ottoman Turkey, Persia, and the Silk Road between China and Europe provided the inspiration and materials for the [Renaissance] art and architecture of Bellini, van Eyck, Dürer, and Alberti. The transmission of Arabic understanding of astronomy, philosophy, and medicine also profoundly influenced thinkers and scientists like Leonardo da Vinci, Copernicus, Vesalius, and Montaigne, whose insights into the workings of the human mind and body, as well as the individual's relationship to the wider world, are often still seen as the foundation of modern science and philosophy. It was the complex impact of these exchanges between east and west that created the culture, art, and scholarship that have been popularly associated with the Renaissance.

Source: Jerry Brotton, *The Renaissance Bazaar: From the Silk Road to Michelangelo* (Oxford: Oxford University Press, 2002), 1.

VOICE 12.2

Bernard Lewis on Hostility between Christians and Muslims | 1995

Between Islam and Christendom there was inevitably great and continuing hostility, but it was not due, in accordance with currently fashionable notions, to misperception and misunderstanding. On the contrary, the two understood each other very well, far better than either of them, in their other encounters could understand the more remote civilizations of Asia and, later, pre-Columbian America. As well as a shared or, rather, disputed mission and domain, Islam and Christendom had a great shared inheritance, which drew on common sources: the science and philosophy of Greece, the law and government of Rome, the ethical monotheism of Judaea, and beyond all of them, the deeply rooted cultures of the ancient Middle East. Christians and Muslims around the Mediterranean could find a common language in both the figurative and the literal senses. They could communicate, they could argue, if only to disagree; they could translate, as they did, both ways. All of this would have been difficult, if not impossible, between Christians or Muslims, on the one hand, and exponents of the civilizations of India or China, on the other.

Source: Bernard Lewis, *Cultures in Conflict: Christians, Muslims and Jews in the Age of Discovery* (Oxford: Oxford University Press, 1995), 14.

PART 4

The Early Modern World

1450–1750

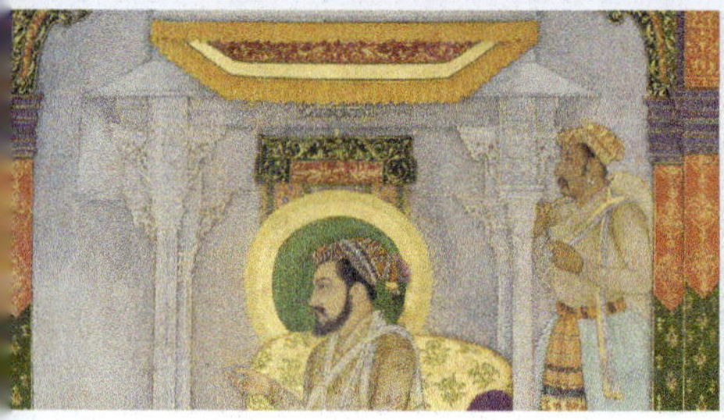

THE BIG PICTURE

Toward Modernity . . . or Not?

For the sake of clarity and coherence, historians often characterize a particular period of time in a brief phrase such as "the age of First Civilizations" or "the era of revolutions." Though useful and even necessary, such capsule descriptions vastly oversimplify what actually happened. Historical reality is always more messy, more complicated, and more uncertain than any shorthand label can convey. Such is surely the case when we examine the three centuries spanning the years from roughly 1450 to 1750, commonly labeled the "early modern era."

Sprouts of Modernity?

In defining those centuries as "the early modern era," historians are suggesting that during this period of time we can find some initial signs, markers, or sprouts of what became the modern world. Such indicators of a new era in human history include the beginnings of genuine globalization; new demographic, economic, and intellectual patterns; and a growing European presence in world affairs.

The most obvious expression of globalization lay in the oceanic journeys of European explorers, the European conquest and colonial settlement of the Americas, and all that followed from these events. The Atlantic slave trade linked Africa permanently to Europe and the Western Hemisphere, while the global silver trade allowed Europeans to buy their way into ancient Asian markets. The massive exchange of plants, animals, diseases, and people, known to historians as the Columbian exchange, created wholly new networks of interaction across both the Atlantic and Pacific oceans, with enormous global implications. Furthermore, missionaries carried Christianity far beyond Europe, making it a genuinely global religion with a presence in the Americas, China, Japan, the Philippine Islands, Siberia, and south-central Africa.

But Western Europeans were not alone in weaving this emerging global web. Russians marched across Siberia to the Pacific, creating the world's largest territorial state. China expanded deep into Inner Asia, bringing Mongolia, Xinjiang, and Tibet into a much-enlarged Chinese empire. The Turkish Ottoman Empire brought much of the Middle East, North Africa, and southeastern Europe into the Islamic world's largest and most powerful state. Japanese merchants moved aggressively to open up commercial opportunities in Southeast Asia even as Indian traders penetrated the markets of Central Asia, Persia, and Russia.

Scattered signs of what later generations thought of as "modern life" likewise appeared in various places around the world. One obviously modern cultural development took place in Europe, where the Scientific Revolution transformed, at least for a few people, their view of the world, their approach to seeking knowledge, and their understanding of traditional Christianity. Subsequently, a scientific outlook spread globally, becoming perhaps the most potent marker of modern life.

Demographically, China, Japan, India, and Europe experienced the beginnings of modern population growth. Human numbers more than doubled between 1400 and 1800 (from about 374 million to 968 million), even as the globalization of disease produced a demographic catastrophe in the Americas and the slave trade limited African population growth.

Yet another indication of modern life lay in more highly commercialized economies centered in large cities that developed in various parts of Eurasia and the Americas. By the early eighteenth century, for example, Japan was one of the most urbanized societies in the world. In China, Southeast Asia, India, and across the Atlantic basin, more and more people found themselves, sometimes willingly and at other times involuntarily, producing for distant markets rather than for the use of their local communities.

Stronger and more cohesive states represented yet another modern global pattern as they incorporated various local societies into larger units while actively promoting trade, manufacturing, and a common culture within their borders. France, the Dutch Republic, Russia, Morocco, the Mughal Empire, Vietnam, Burma, Siam, and Japan all represent this kind of state. Their military power likewise soared as the "gunpowder revolution" kicked in around the world. Thus large-scale empires proliferated across Asia and the Middle East, while various European powers carved out new domains in the Americas. Within these empires, human pressures on the land intensified as forests were felled, marshes were drained, and the hunting grounds of foragers and the grazing lands of pastoralists were confiscated for farming or ranching.

Continuing Older Patterns?

But all of this may be misleading if it suggests that European world domination and more fully modern societies were a sure thing, an inevitable outgrowth of early modern developments. In fact, that future was far from clear in 1750. Although Europeans ruled the Americas and controlled the world's sea routes, their political and military power in mainland Asia and Africa was very limited, and they certainly did not hold all the leading roles in the global drama of these three centuries.

Furthermore, Islam, not Christianity, was the most rapidly spreading faith in much of Asia and Africa. And in 1750 Europe, India, and China were roughly comparable in their manufacturing output. It was not obvious that Europeans would soon dominate the planet. Moreover, populations and economies had surged at various points in the past, only to fall back again in a cyclical pattern. Nothing guaranteed that the early modern surge would be any more lasting than the others.

Nor was there much to suggest that anything approaching modern industrial society was on the horizon. Animal and human muscles, wind, wood, and water still provided almost all of the energy that powered human economies. Handicraft techniques of manufacturing had nowhere been displaced by factory-based production, steam power, or electricity. Long-established elites, not middle-class upstarts, everywhere provided leadership and enjoyed the greatest privileges, while rural peasants, not urban workers, represented the primary social group in the lower classes. Kings and nobles, not parliaments and parties, governed. Female subordination was assumed to be natural almost everywhere, for nowhere had ideas of gender equality taken root.

Thus modern society, with its promise of liberation from ancient inequalities and from mass poverty, hardly seemed around the corner. Kings ruled most of Europe, and male landowning aristocrats remained at the top of the social hierarchy. A change in ruling dynasties occurred in China that brought with it a reaffirmation of Confucian values and the social structure that privileged landowning and office-holding elites, all of them men. Most Indians practiced some form of Hinduism and owed their most fundamental loyalty to local castes. The realm of Islam maintained its central role in the Eastern Hemisphere as the Ottoman Empire revived the political fortunes of Islam and the religion sustained its long-term expansion into Africa and Southeast Asia. In short, for the majority of people, the three centuries between 1450 and 1750 marked less an entry into the modern era than the continuation of older patterns.

From this mixture of what was new and what was old during the early modern era, the three chapters that follow highlight the changes. Chapter 13 discusses the new empires of those three centuries—European, Middle Eastern, and Asian. New global patterns of long-distance commerce in spices, sugar, silver, fur, and enslaved people represent the themes of Chapter 14. New cultural trends—both within the major religious traditions of the world and in the emergence of modern science—come together in Chapter 15. With the benefit of hindsight, we may see various "sprouts of modernity" as harbingers of things to come, but from the viewpoint of 1700 or so, the future was open and uncertain, as it almost always is.

FIRST REFLECTIONS

1. **Questioning Chronology** How might you support the authors' decision to describe the centuries from 1450 to 1750 as an "early modern era"? How might you criticize that decision?
2. **Questioning a Concept** The idea of an "early modern era" has sometimes been criticized as Eurocentric. How do the authors seek to avoid this criticism while continuing to use the term?
3. **Thinking Like a Historian** The authors say that they chose to emphasize what was new during these three centuries rather than what persisted from earlier times. What is potentially lost in making this choice?

Landmarks in World History (ca. 1450–ca. 1750)

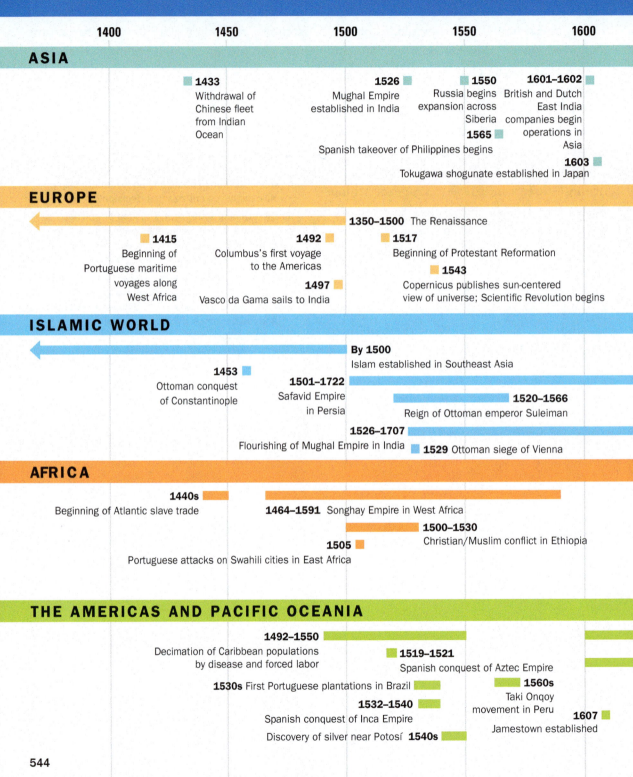

1400 | 1450 | 1500 | 1550 | 1600

ASIA

1433 Withdrawal of Chinese fleet from Indian Ocean

1526 Mughal Empire established in India

1550 Russia begins expansion across Siberia

1565 Spanish takeover of Philippines begins

1601–1602 British and Dutch East India companies begin operations in Asia

1603 Tokugawa shogunate established in Japan

EUROPE

1350–1500 The Renaissance

1415 Beginning of Portuguese maritime voyages along West Africa

1492 Columbus's first voyage to the Americas

1497 Vasco da Gama sails to India

1517 Beginning of Protestant Reformation

1543 Copernicus publishes sun-centered view of universe; Scientific Revolution begins

ISLAMIC WORLD

By 1500 Islam established in Southeast Asia

1453 Ottoman conquest of Constantinople

1501–1722 Safavid Empire in Persia

1520–1566 Reign of Ottoman emperor Suleiman

1526–1707 Flourishing of Mughal Empire in India

1529 Ottoman siege of Vienna

AFRICA

1440s Beginning of Atlantic slave trade

1464–1591 Songhay Empire in West Africa

1500–1530 Christian/Muslim conflict in Ethiopia

1505 Portuguese attacks on Swahili cities in East Africa

THE AMERICAS AND PACIFIC OCEANIA

1492–1550 Decimation of Caribbean populations by disease and forced labor

1519–1521 Spanish conquest of Aztec Empire

1530s First Portuguese plantations in Brazil

1532–1540 Spanish conquest of Inca Empire

1540s Discovery of silver near Potosí

1560s Taki Onqoy movement in Peru

1607 Jamestown established

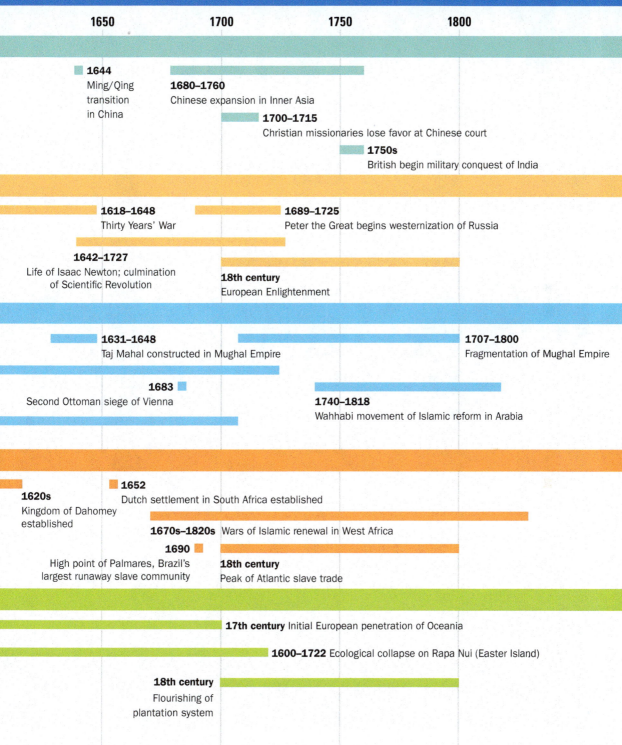

1650 1700 1750 1800

1644 Ming/Qing transition in China

1680–1760 Chinese expansion in Inner Asia

1700–1715 Christian missionaries lose favor at Chinese court

1750s British begin military conquest of India

1618–1648 Thirty Years' War

1689–1725 Peter the Great begins westernization of Russia

1642–1727 Life of Isaac Newton; culmination of Scientific Revolution

18th century European Enlightenment

1631–1648 Taj Mahal constructed in Mughal Empire

1707–1800 Fragmentation of Mughal Empire

1683 Second Ottoman siege of Vienna

1740–1818 Wahhabi movement of Islamic reform in Arabia

1620s Kingdom of Dahomey established

1652 Dutch settlement in South Africa established

1670s–1820s Wars of Islamic renewal in West Africa

1690 High point of Palmares, Brazil's largest runaway slave community

18th century Peak of Atlantic slave trade

17th century Initial European penetration of Oceania

1600–1722 Ecological collapse on Rapa Nui (Easter Island)

18th century Flourishing of plantation system

CHAPTER 13

Political Transformations

Empires and Encounters

1450–1750

CONNECTING PAST AND PRESENT

"Putin [president of Russia] wants the old Russian Empire back. . . . As Russian tsar, which is how he sees himself, his empire cannot work without Ukraine. He sees us as a colony."[1] This was the view of Ukrainian president Petro Poroshenko in 2018, as he resisted persistent Russian incursions into the affairs of his country. In a similar vein, critics of Turkey's intervention in Libya's civil war in 2020 claimed that Turkey's president Erdogan embraced "expansionist visions of reviving the Ottoman Empire, with—naturally—himself as the supreme sultan."[2] Thus memories of the Russian and Ottoman empires, initially constructed in the early modern era, continue to shape understandings of current events and perhaps to inspire actions in the present as well.

Underlying these comments is a sharply critical posture toward any revival of these earlier empires. Indeed, empire building has been largely discredited during the twentieth and twenty-first centuries, and "imperialist" has become a term of insult rather than a source of pride. How very different were the three centuries (1450–1750) of the early modern era, when empire building was a global process! In the Americas, the Aztec and Inca empires flourished before they, along with nearly all of the Western Hemisphere, were incorporated into the rival empires of the Spanish, Portuguese, British, French, and Dutch. Within those European imperial systems, vast transformations took place: old

« **The Mughal Empire** Among the most magnificent of the early modern empires was that of the Mughals in India. In this painting by an unknown Mughal artist, the seventeenth-century emperor Shah Jahan is holding a *durbar*, or ceremonial assembly, in the audience hall of his palace. The material splendor of the setting shows the immense wealth of the court, while the halo around Shah Jahan's head indicates the special spiritual grace or enlightenment associated with emperors.

societies were destroyed, and new societies arose as Native Americans, Europeans, and Africans came into sustained contact with one another for the first time in world history. It was an encounter with revolutionary implications that extended far beyond the Americas themselves.

But European empires in the Americas were not alone on the imperial stage of the early modern era. Across the immense expanse of Siberia, the Russians constructed what was then the world's largest territorial empire, making Russia an Asian as well as a European power. Qing (chihng) dynasty China penetrated deep into Inner Asia, doubling the size of the country while incorporating millions of non-Chinese people who practiced Islam, Buddhism, or animistic religions. On the South Asian peninsula, the Islamic Mughal Empire brought Hindus and Muslims into a closer relationship than ever before, sometimes quite peacefully and at other times with great conflict. In the Middle East, the Turkish Ottoman Empire reestablished something of the earlier political unity of heartland Islam and posed a serious military and religious threat to European Christendom. Thus the early modern era was an age of empire.

SEEKING THE MAIN POINT

What was the significance of empire in the early modern era? What was more pronounced among these empires—their similarities or their differences?

European Empires in the Americas

Among the early modern empires, those of Western Europe were distinctive because the conquered territories lay an ocean away from the imperial heartland, rather than adjacent to it. Following the breakthrough voyages of Columbus, the Spanish focused their empire-building efforts in the Caribbean and then, in the early sixteenth century, turned to the mainland, making stunning conquests of the powerful but fragile Aztec and Inca empires. Meanwhile, the Portuguese established themselves along the coast of present-day Brazil. In the early seventeenth century, the British, French, and Dutch launched colonial settlements along the eastern coast of North America. From these beginnings, Europeans extended their empires to encompass most of the Americas, at least nominally, by the mid-eighteenth century (see Map 13.1). It was a remarkable achievement. What had made it possible?

The European Advantage

Geography provides a starting point for explaining Europe's American empires. Countries on the Atlantic rim of Europe (Portugal, Spain, Britain, and France) were simply closer to the Americas than were any potential Asian competitors. Moreover, the enormously rich markets of the Indian Ocean world provided little incentive for its Chinese, Indian, or Muslim participants to venture much beyond their own waters. Europeans, however, were powerfully motivated to do so.

After 1200 or so, European elites were increasingly aware of their region's marginal position in the rich world of Eurasian commerce and were determined to

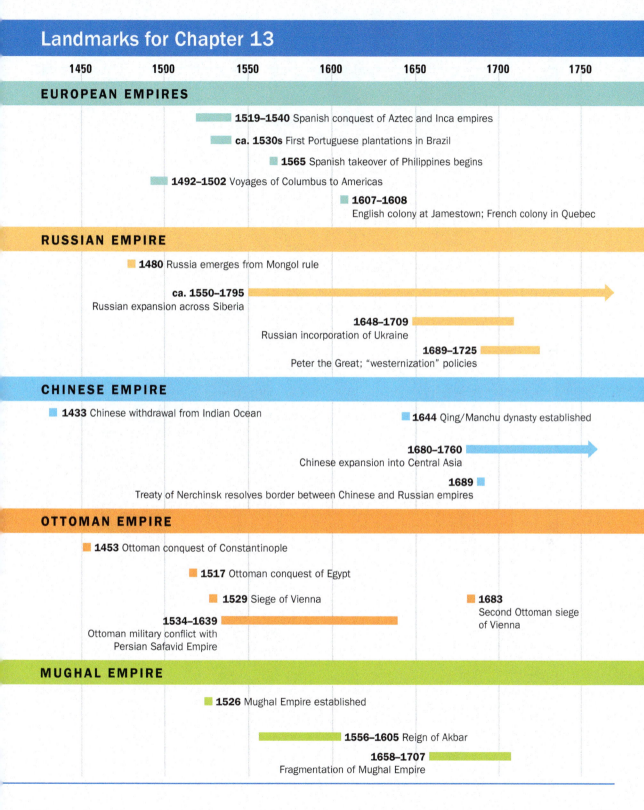

Landmarks for Chapter 13

1450 1500 1550 1600 1650 1700 1750

EUROPEAN EMPIRES

1519–1540 Spanish conquest of Aztec and Inca empires

ca. 1530s First Portuguese plantations in Brazil

1565 Spanish takeover of Philippines begins

1492–1502 Voyages of Columbus to Americas

1607–1608 English colony at Jamestown; French colony in Quebec

RUSSIAN EMPIRE

1480 Russia emerges from Mongol rule

ca. 1550–1795 Russian expansion across Siberia

1648–1709 Russian incorporation of Ukraine

1689–1725 Peter the Great; "westernization" policies

CHINESE EMPIRE

1433 Chinese withdrawal from Indian Ocean

1644 Qing/Manchu dynasty established

1680–1760 Chinese expansion into Central Asia

1689 Treaty of Nerchinsk resolves border between Chinese and Russian empires

OTTOMAN EMPIRE

1453 Ottoman conquest of Constantinople

1517 Ottoman conquest of Egypt

1529 Siege of Vienna

1683 Second Ottoman siege of Vienna

1534–1639 Ottoman military conflict with Persian Safavid Empire

MUGHAL EMPIRE

1526 Mughal Empire established

1556–1605 Reign of Akbar

1658–1707 Fragmentation of Mughal Empire

Map 13.1 European Colonial Empires in the Americas

By the beginning of the eighteenth century, European powers had laid claim to most of the Western Hemisphere. Their wars and rivalries during that century led to an expansion of Spanish and English claims, at the expense of the French.

gain access to that world. Once the Americas were discovered, windfalls of natural resources, including highly productive agricultural lands, drove further expansion, ultimately underpinning the long-term growth of the European economy into the nineteenth and twentieth centuries. The drive to expand beyond Europe was also motivated by the enduring rivalries of competing European states. At the same time, the growing and relatively independent merchant class sought direct access to Asian wealth to avoid the reliance on Muslim intermediaries that they found so distasteful. Impoverished nobles and commoners alike found opportunity for gaining wealth and status in the colonies. Missionaries and others were inspired by crusading zeal to enlarge the realm of Christendom. Persecuted minorities were in search of a new start in life. All of these compelling motives drove the relentlessly expanding imperial frontier in the Americas. Summarizing their intentions, one Spanish conquistador declared: "We came here to serve God and the King, and also to get rich."[3]

In carving out these empires, often against great odds and with great difficulty, Europeans nonetheless had certain advantages, despite their distance from home. Their states and trading companies effectively mobilized both human and material resources. European innovations in mapmaking, navigation, sailing techniques, and ship design—building on earlier models from the Mediterranean, Indian Ocean, and Chinese regions—likewise enabled Europeans to penetrate the Atlantic Ocean. Their ironworking technology, gunpowder weapons, and horses initially had no parallel in the Americas, although many peoples later acquired them.

Identifying Contingency
What enabled Europeans to carve out huge empires an ocean away from their homelands?

Divisions within and between local societies provided allies for the determined European invaders. Various subject peoples of the Aztec Empire, for example, resented Mexica domination and willingly joined conquistador **Hernán Cortés** in the Spanish assault on that empire. In the final attack on the Aztec capital of Tenochtitlán, Cortés's forces contained fewer than 1,000 Spaniards and many times that number of Tlaxcalans, former subjects of the Aztecs. After their defeat, tens of thousands of Aztecs themselves joined Cortés as he carved out a Spanish Mesoamerican empire far larger than that of the Aztecs. (See Zooming In: Doña Marina, page 552.) Much of the Inca elite, according to a recent study, "actually welcomed the Spanish invaders as liberators and willingly settled down with them to share rule of Andean farmers and miners."[4] A violent dispute between two rival contenders for the Inca throne, the brothers Atahualpa and Huáscar, certainly helped the European invaders recruit allies to augment their own minimal forces. In short, Spanish military victories were not solely of their own making, but the product of alliances with local peoples, who supplied the bulk of the Europeans' conquering armies.

Perhaps the most significant of European advantages lay in their germs and diseases, with which Native Americans had no familiarity. Those diseases decimated society after society, sometimes in advance of the Europeans' actual arrival. In particular regions such as the Caribbean, Virginia, and New England, the rapid buildup of immigrant populations, coupled with the sharply diminished native numbers, allowed Europeans to actually outnumber local peoples within a few decades.

ZOOMING IN

Doña Marina: Between Two Worlds

In her brief life, she was known variously as Malinal, Doña Marina, and La Malinche. By whatever name, she was a woman who experienced the encounter of the Old World and the New in particularly intimate ways, even as she became a bridge between them. Born around 1505, Malinal was the daughter of an elite and cultured family in the borderlands between the Maya and Aztec cultures in what is now southern Mexico. Two dramatic events decisively shaped her life. The first occurred when her father died and her mother remarried, bearing a son to her new husband. To protect this boy's inheritance, Malinal's family sold her into slavery. Eventually, she came into the possession of a Maya chieftain in Tabasco on the Gulf of Mexico.

Doña Marina (left) translating for Cortés.

Here her second life-changing event took place in March 1519, when the Spanish conquistador Hernán Cortés landed his troops and inflicted a sharp military defeat on Tabasco. In the negotiations that followed, Tabasco authorities gave lavish gifts to the Spanish, including twenty women, one of whom was Malinal. Described by Bernal Díaz, one of Cortés's associates, as "good-looking, intelligent, and self-assured," the teenage Malinal soon found herself in service to Cortés himself. Since Spanish men were not supposed to touch non-Christian women, these newcomers were distributed among his officers, quickly baptized, and given Christian names. Thus Malinal became Doña Marina.

With a ready ear for languages and already fluent in Mayan and Nahuatl, the language of the Aztecs, Doña Marina soon picked up Spanish and quickly became indispensable to Cortés as an interpreter, cross-cultural broker, and strategist. She accompanied him on his march inland to the Aztec capital, Tenochtitlán, and on several occasions her language skills and cultural awareness allowed her to uncover spies and plots. Díaz reported that "Doña Marina, who understood full well what was

photo: Bridgeman Images

The Great Dying and the Little Ice Age

However Europeans acquired American empires, their global significance is apparent. Chief among the consequences was the demographic collapse of Native American societies. Although precise figures are debated, scholars generally agree that the pre-Columbian population of the Western Hemisphere was substantial, perhaps 60 to 80 million. The greatest concentrations of people lived in the Mesoamerican and Andean zones, which were dominated by the Aztec and Inca empires. Long isolation from the Afro-Eurasian world and the lack of most domesticated animals meant the absence of acquired immunities to Old World diseases such as smallpox, measles, typhus, influenza, malaria, and, later, yellow fever.

CORE IDEA

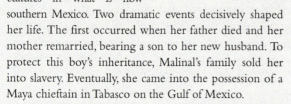

Describing Change
What large-scale transformations did European empires generate in the Americas, in Europe, and globally?

Therefore, when Native American peoples came into contact with these European and African diseases, they died in appalling numbers, in many cases losing up to 90 percent of the population. The densely settled peoples of Caribbean islands virtually vanished within fifty years of Columbus's arrival. Central Mexico, with a happening, told [Cortés] what was going on." In the Aztec capital, where Cortés took the emperor Moctezuma captive, it fell to Doña Marina to persuade him to accept this humiliating position and surrender his wealth to the Spanish. Even Cortés, who was never very gracious with his praise for her, acknowledged that "after God, we owe this conquest of New Spain to Doña Marina." Aztecs soon came to see this young woman as the voice of Cortés, referring to her as La Malinche, a Spanish approximation of her original name. So paired did Cortés and La Malinche become in Aztec thinking that Cortés himself was often called Malinche.

More than an interpreter for Cortés, Doña Marina also became his mistress and bore him a son. But after the initial conquest of Mexico was complete and he no longer needed her skills, Cortés married Doña Marina off to another Spanish conquistador, Juan Jaramillo, with whom she lived until her death, probably around 1530. Cortés did provide her with several pieces of land, one of which, ironically, had belonged to Moctezuma. Her son, however, was taken from her and raised in Spain.

In 1523, Doña Marina performed one final service for Cortés, accompanying him on a mission to Honduras to suppress a rebellion. There her personal life seemed to come full circle, for near her hometown she encountered her mother, who had sold her into slavery, and her half-brother. Díaz reported that they "were very much afraid of Doña Marina," thinking that they would surely be put to death by their now-powerful and well-connected relative. But in a replay of the biblical story of Joseph and his brothers, Doña Marina quickly reassured and forgave them, while granting them "many golden jewels and some clothes."

In the centuries since her death, Doña Marina has been highly controversial. For much of the colonial era, she was viewed positively as an ally of the Spanish. But after independence, some came to see her as a traitor to her own people, shunning her heritage and siding with the invaders. Still others have considered her as the mother of Mexico's multiracial, or mestizo, culture. Should she be understood primarily as a victim or as a skillful survivor negotiating hard choices under difficult circumstances?

Whatever the judgments of later generations, Doña Marina herself seems to have made a clear choice to cast her lot with the Europeans. Even when Cortés had given her to another man, Doña Marina expressed no regret. According to Díaz, she declared, "Even if they were to make me mistress of all the provinces of New Spain, I would refuse the honor, for I would rather serve my husband and Cortés than anything else in the world."

QUESTIONS

How might you define the significance of Doña Marina's life? In what larger contexts might her life find a place?

population estimated at some 10 to 20 million before the Spanish conquest, declined to about 1 million by 1650. A native Nahuatl (nah-watl) account depicted the social breakdown that accompanied the smallpox pandemic: "A great many died from this plague, and many others died of hunger. They could not get up to search for food, and everyone else was too sick to care for them, so they starved to death in their beds."[5]

The situation was similar in Dutch and British territories of North America. A Dutch observer in New Netherland (later New York) reported in 1656 that he had been told by local people that disease had "melted down" their numbers by 90 percent since the coming of the Europeans.[6] To Governor Bradford of Plymouth colony (in present-day Massachusetts), such conditions represented the "good hand of God" at work, "sweeping away great multitudes of the natives . . . that he might make room for us."[7] Not until the late seventeenth century did native numbers begin to recuperate somewhat from this catastrophe, and even then, not everywhere.

As the **Great Dying** took hold in the Americas, it interacted with another natural phenomenon, this time one of genuinely global proportions. Known as the **Little Ice Age**, it was a period from the thirteenth to nineteenth centuries of unusually cool temperatures that spanned much of the early modern period, most prominently in the Northern Hemisphere. Its causes were complex and multifaceted. Several natural processes contributed to global cooling, including a low point in sunspot activity, slight changes in the earth's orbit around the sun, and an unusually large number of volcanic eruptions in the tropics whose ash and gases blocked the sun's warming energy. But human actions also contributed to climate change. As many millions died, large areas of Native American farmland were deserted and the traditional practice of using burning to manage forests also stopped in many regions. These changes sparked a resurgence of plant life, which in turn took large amounts of carbon dioxide, a greenhouse gas, out of the atmosphere, contributing to global cooling. These factors combined with natural medium- and short-term climate fluctuations to bring shorter growing seasons and less hospitable weather conditions that adversely affected food production across the globe.

While the onset, duration, and effects of the Little Ice Age varied from region to region, the impact of a cooler climate reached its peak in many areas in the mid-seventeenth century, helping to spark what scholars term the **General Crisis**. Much of China, Europe, and North America experienced record or near-record cold winters during this period. Regions near the equator in the tropics and Southern Hemisphere also experienced extreme conditions and irregular rainfall, resulting, for instance, in the growth of the Sahara Desert. Wet, cold summers reduced harvests dramatically in Europe, while severe droughts ruined crops in many other regions, especially China, which suffered terrible drought between 1637 and 1641. Difficult weather conditions accentuated other stresses in societies, leading to widespread famines, epidemics, uprisings, and wars in which millions perished. Eurasia did not escape lightly from these stresses: the collapse of the Ming dynasty in China, nearly constant warfare in Europe, and civil war in Mughal India all occurred in the context of the General Crisis, which only fully subsided when more favorable weather patterns took hold starting in the eighteenth century.

Nor were the Americas, already devastated by the Great Dying, spared the suffering that accompanied the Little Ice Age and the General Crisis of the seventeenth century. In central Mexico, heartland of the Aztec Empire and the center of Spanish colonial rule in the area, severe drought in the five years after 1639 sent the price of maize skyrocketing, left granaries empty and many people without water, and prompted an unsuccessful plot to declare Mexico's independence from Spain. Continuing drought years in the decades that followed witnessed repeated public processions of the statue of Our Lady of Guadalupe, who had gained a reputation for producing rain. The Caribbean region during the 1640s experienced the opposite condition—torrential rains that accompanied more frequent El Niño weather patterns—which provided ideal conditions for the breeding of mosquitoes that carried both yellow fever and malaria. A Maya chronicle for 1648 noted, "There was bloody vomit and we began to die."[8]

Like the Great Dying, the General Crisis reminds us that climate often plays an important role in shaping human history. But it also reminds us that human activity—the importation of deadly diseases to the Americas, in this case—also helped shape the climate, and that this has been true long before our current climate crisis.

The Columbian Exchange

In sharply diminishing the population of the Americas, the Great Dying, together with the impact of the Little Ice Age, created an acute labor shortage and certainly did make room for immigrant newcomers, both colonizing Europeans and enslaved Africans. Over the several centuries of the colonial era and beyond, various combinations of indigenous, European, and African peoples created entirely new societies in the Americas, largely replacing the many and varied cultures that had flourished before 1492. To those colonial societies, Europeans and Africans brought not only their germs and their people but also their plants and animals. Wheat, rice, sugarcane, grapes, and many garden vegetables and fruits, as well as numerous weeds, took hold in the Americas, where they transformed the landscape and made possible a recognizably European diet and way of life. In what is now the continental United States, for example, the centuries since 1600 have witnessed the destruction of some 90 percent of the old-growth forests as the land has been burned, logged, and turned into fields and pastures. Even more revolutionary were the newcomers' animals—horses, pigs, cattle, goats, sheep—all of which were new to the Americas and multiplied spectacularly in an environment largely free of natural predators. These domesticated animals made possible the ranching economies and cowboy cultures of both North and South America. Horses also transformed many Native American societies, particularly in the North American West, as settled farming peoples such as the Pawnee abandoned their fields to hunt bison from horseback. As a male-dominated hunting and warrior culture emerged, women lost much of their earlier role as food producers. Both environmentally and socially, these changes were revolutionary.

In the other direction, American food crops such as corn, potatoes, and cassava spread widely in the Eastern Hemisphere, where they provided the nutritional foundation for the population growth that became everywhere a hallmark of the modern era. In Europe, calories derived from corn and potatoes helped push human numbers from some 60 million in 1400 to 390 million in 1900. Those Amerindian crops later provided cheap and reasonably nutritious food for millions of industrial workers. Potatoes, especially, allowed Ireland's population to grow enormously and then condemned many of the Irish to starvation or emigration when an airborne fungus, also from the Americas, destroyed the crop in the mid-nineteenth century. In China, corn, peanuts, and especially sweet potatoes supplemented the traditional rice and wheat to sustain China's modern population explosion. By the early twentieth century, food plants of American origin represented about 20 percent of total Chinese food production. In Africa, corn took hold quickly and was used as a cheap

■ Describing a Process
In what ways was the Columbian exchange a global phenomenon?

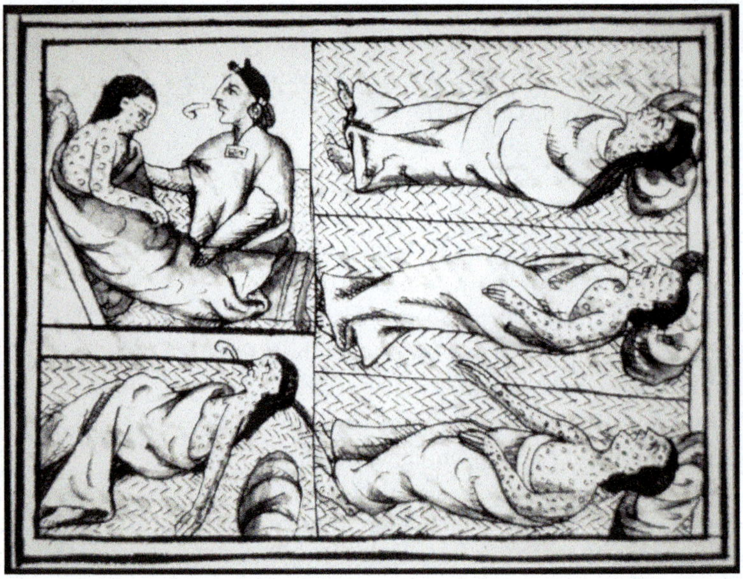

Disease and Death among the Aztecs Smallpox, which accompanied the Spanish to the Americas, devastated native populations. This image, drawn by an Aztec artist and contained in the sixteenth-century Florentine Codex, illustrates the impact of the disease in Mesoamerica. (Peter Newark American Pictures/Bridgeman Images)

food for the human cargoes of the transatlantic trade. Beyond food crops, American stimulants such as tobacco and chocolate were soon used around the world. By the seventeenth century, how-to manuals instructed Chinese users on smoking techniques, and tobacco had become, in the words of one enamored Chinese poet, "the gentleman's companion, it warms my heart and leaves my mouth feeling like a divine furnace."[9] Tea from China and coffee from the Islamic world also spread globally, contributing to this worldwide biological exchange. Never before in human history had such a large-scale and consequential diffusion of plants and animals operated to remake the biological environment of the planet.

This enormous network of communication, migration, trade, disease, and the transfer of plants and animals, all generated by European colonial empires in the Americas, has been dubbed the "**Columbian exchange**." It gave rise to something wholly new in world history: an interacting Atlantic world that permanently connected Europe, Africa, and North and South America. But the long-term benefits of this Atlantic network were very unequally distributed. The peoples of Africa and the Americas experienced social disruption, slavery, disease, and death on an almost unimaginable scale, while Western Europeans reaped the greatest rewards. Mountains of new information flooded into Europe, shaking up conventional understandings of the world and contributing to a revolutionary new way of thinking known as the Scientific Revolution. The wealth of the colonies—precious metals, natural resources, new food crops, slave labor, financial profits, colonial markets—provided one of the foundations on which Europe's Industrial Revolution was built. The colonies also provided an outlet for the rapidly growing population of European societies and represented an enormous extension of European civilization. In short, the colonial empires of the Americas greatly facilitated a changing global balance of power, which now thrust the previously marginal Western Europeans into an increasingly central and commanding role on the world stage. "Without a New World to deliver economic balance in the Old," concluded a prominent world historian, "Europe would have remained inferior, as ever, in wealth and power, to the great civilizations of Asia."[10]

Comparing Colonial Societies in the Americas

European colonial empires—Spanish, Portuguese, British, and French alike—did not simply conquer and govern established societies, but rather generated wholly new societies, born of the decimation of Native American populations and the introduction of European and African peoples, cultures, plants, and animals. European colonial strategies were based on an economic theory known as **mercantilism**, which held that governments served their countries' economic interests best by encouraging exports and accumulating bullion (precious metals such as silver and gold). In this scheme of things, colonies provided closed markets for the manufactured goods of the "mother country" and, if they were lucky, supplied great quantities of bullion as well. Such an outlook fueled European wars and colonial rivalries around the world in the early modern era.

Meanwhile, in the colonies themselves, empire took shape in various ways. Some differences derived from the contrasting societies of the colonizing powers, such as a semi-feudal and Catholic Spain and a more rapidly changing Protestant England. The kind of economy established in particular regions—settler-dominated agriculture, plantations based on slave labor, ranching, or mining—likewise influenced the colonies' development. So too did the character of the Native American cultures—the more densely populated and urbanized Mesoamerican and Andean civilizations differed greatly from the more sparsely populated rural villages of North America.

CORE IDEA

■ Comparing Empire Building
In what different ways did European empire building take shape in the Americas?

Furthermore, women and men often experienced colonial intrusion in quite distinct ways. Beyond the common burdens of violent conquest, epidemic disease, and coerced labor, both Native American and enslaved African women had to cope with the additional demands made on them as females. Conquest was often accompanied by the transfer of women to the new colonial rulers. Cortés, for example, commanded the Aztec ruler: "You are to deliver women with light skins, corn, chicken, eggs, and tortillas."[11] Soon after conquest, many Spanish men married elite native women. It was a long-standing practice in Amerindian societies and was encouraged by both Spanish and indigenous male authorities as a means of cementing their new relationship. It was also advantageous for some of the women involved. One of Aztec emperor Moctezuma's daughters, who was mistress to Cortés and eventually married several other Spaniards, wound up with the largest landed estate in the Valley of Mexico. Below this elite level of interaction, however, far more women experienced sexual violence and abuse. Rape accompanied conquest in many places, and dependent or enslaved women working under the control of European men frequently found themselves required to perform sexual services. This was a tragedy and humiliation for native and enslaved men as well, for they were unable to protect their women from such abuse.

Such variations in culture, policy, economy, and gender generated quite different colonial societies in several major regions of the Americas.

In the Lands of the Aztecs and the Incas

The Spanish conquest of the Aztec and Inca empires in the early sixteenth century gave Spain access to the most wealthy, urbanized, and densely populated regions of the Western Hemisphere. Within a century and well before the British had even begun their colonizing efforts in North America, the Spanish in Mexico and Peru had established nearly a dozen major cities; several impressive universities; hundreds of cathedrals, churches, and missions; an elaborate administrative bureaucracy; and a network of regulated international commerce.

■ Connecting Economy and Society
What was the economic foundation of colonial rule in Mexico and Peru? How did it shape the kinds of societies that developed there?

The economic foundation for this emerging colonial society lay in commercial agriculture, much of it on large rural estates, and in silver and gold mining. In both cases, native peoples, rather than enslaved Africans or European workers, provided most of the labor, despite their much diminished numbers. Almost everywhere that labor was coerced, often directly required by colonial authorities under a legal regime known as *encomienda*. It was, in fact, a forced labor system not far removed from slavery. By the seventeenth century, the *hacienda* system had taken shape, by which the private owners of large estates directly employed native workers. With low wages, high taxes, and large debts to the landowners, the *peons* who worked these estates enjoyed little control over their lives or their livelihood.

On this economic base, a distinctive social order grew up, replicating something of Spanish class and gender hierarchies while accommodating the racially and culturally different Indians and Africans as well as growing numbers of multiracial people. At the top of this colonial society were the male Spanish settlers, who were politically and economically dominant and seeking to become a landed aristocracy. One Spanish official commented in 1619: "The Spaniards, from the able and rich to the humble and poor, all hold themselves to be lords and will not serve [do manual labor]."[12] Politically, they increasingly saw themselves not as colonials, but as residents of a Spanish kingdom, subject to the Spanish monarch yet separate and distinct from Spain itself and deserving of a large measure of self-government. Therefore, they chafed under the heavy bureaucratic restrictions imposed by the Crown. "I obey but I do not enforce" was a slogan that reflected local authorities' resistance to orders from Spain. But the Spanish minority, never more than 20 percent of the population, was itself a divided community. Descendants of the original conquistadores sought to protect their privileges against immigrant newcomers; Spaniards born in the Americas (*creoles*) resented the pretensions to superiority of those born in Spain (*peninsulares*); landowning Spaniards felt threatened by the growing wealth of commercial and mercantile groups practicing less prestigious occupations. Spanish missionaries and church authorities were often sharply critical of how these settlers treated native peoples.

While Spanish women shared the racial privileges of their husbands, they were clearly subordinate in gender terms, unable to hold public office and viewed as weak and in need of male protection. But they were also regarded as the "bearers of civilization," and through their capacity to produce legitimate children, they were the essential link for transmitting male wealth, honor, and status to future generations.

This required strict control of their sexuality and a continuation of the Iberian obsession with "purity of blood." In Spain, that concern had focused on potential liaisons with Jews and Muslims; in the colonies, the alleged threat to female virtue derived from Native American and African men.

From a male viewpoint, the problem with Spanish women was that there were very few of them. This demographic fact led to the most distinctive feature of these new colonial societies in Mexico and Peru—the emergence of a ***mestizo*** (mehs-TEE-zoh), or multiracial, population, initially the product of unions between Spanish men and Indian women. Rooted in the sexual imbalance among Spanish immigrants (seven men to one woman in early colonial Peru, for example), the emergence of a mestizo population was facilitated by the desire of many surviving indigenous women for the relative security of life in a Spanish household, where they and their children would not be subject to the abuse and harsh demands made on native peoples. Over the 300 years of the colonial era, mestizo numbers grew substantially, becoming the majority of the population in Mexico sometime during the nineteenth century. Such multiracial people were divided into dozens of separate groups known as *castas* (castes), based on their precise racial heritage and skin color.

Mestizos were largely Hispanic in culture, but Spaniards looked down on them during much of the colonial era, regarding them as illegitimate, for many were not born of "proper" marriages. Despite this attitude, their growing numbers and the economic usefulness of their men as artisans, clerks, supervisors of labor gangs, and lower-level officials in both church and state bureaucracies led to their recognition as a distinct social group. *Mestizas*, women of various racial backgrounds, worked as domestic servants or in their husbands' shops, wove cloth, and manufactured candles and cigars, in addition to performing domestic duties. A few became quite wealthy. An illiterate mestiza named Mencia Perez married successively two reasonably well-to-do Spanish men and upon their deaths took over their businesses, becoming in her own right a very rich woman by the 1590s. At that point, no one would have referred to her as a mestiza.

Interracial Marriage in Colonial Mexico This eighteenth-century painting by the famous Zapotec artist Miguel Cabrera shows a Spanish man, a *mestiza* woman, and their child, who was labeled as *castiza*. By the twentieth century, such multiracial people represented the majority of the population of Mexico, and cultural blending had become a central feature of the country's identity. (Bridgeman Images)

Particularly in Mexico, mestizo identity blurred the sense of sharp racial difference between Spanish and Indian peoples and became a major element in the identity of modern Mexico. More recently, however, the use of the term "mestizo" has been criticized for being associated with colonialism, for privileging lighter-skinned people, and for distancing individuals from those of African background.

At the bottom of Mexican and Peruvian colonial societies were the indigenous peoples, known to Europeans as "Indians." Traumatized by the Great Dying, they were subject to gross abuse and exploitation as the primary labor force for the mines and estates of the Spanish Empire and were required to render tribute payments to their Spanish overlords. Their empires dismantled by Spanish conquest, their religions attacked by Spanish missionaries, and their diminished numbers forcibly relocated into larger settlements, many Indians gravitated toward the world of their conquerors. Many learned Spanish; converted to Christianity; moved to cities to work for wages; ate the meat of cows, chickens, and pigs; used plows and draft animals rather than traditional digging sticks; and took their many grievances to Spanish courts. Indian women endured some distinctive conditions because Spanish legal codes generally defined them as minors rather than responsible adults. As those codes took hold, Indian women were increasingly excluded from the courts or represented by their menfolk. This made it more difficult to maintain female property rights. In 1804, for example, a Maya legal petition identified eight men and ten women from a particular family as owners of a piece of land, but the Spanish translation omitted the women's names altogether.

But much that was indigenous persisted. At the local level, Indian male authorities retained a measure of autonomy, and traditional markets operated regularly. Both Andean and Maya women continued to leave personal property to their female descendants. Maize, beans, and squash persisted as the major elements of Indian diets in Mexico. Christian saints in many places blended easily with specialized indigenous gods, while belief in magic, folk medicine, and communion with the dead remained strong. Memories of the past also endured. The Tupac Amaru revolt in Peru during 1780–1781 was made in the name of the last independent Inca emperor. In that revolt, the wife of the leader, Micaela Bastidas, was referred to as La Coya, the female Inca, evoking the parallel hierarchies of male and female officials who had earlier governed the Inca Empire (see "The Inca Empire" in Chapter 12).

Thus Spaniards, mestizos, and Indians represented the major social categories in the colonial lands of what had been the Inca and Aztec empires, while enslaved Africans and freemen were less numerous than elsewhere in the Americas. Despite the sharp divisions among these groups, some movement was possible. Indians who acquired an education, wealth, and some European culture might "pass" as mestizo. Likewise, more fortunate mestizo families might be accepted as Spaniards over time. Colonial Spanish America was a vast laboratory of ethnic variety and cultural change. It was dominated by Europeans, to be sure, but was a rather more fluid and culturally blended society than the racially rigid colonies of British North America.

Colonies of Sugar

Another and quite different kind of colonial society emerged in the lowland areas of Brazil, ruled by Portugal, and in the Spanish, British, French, and Dutch colonies in the Caribbean. These regions lacked the great civilizations of Mexico and Peru. Nor did they provide much mineral wealth until the Brazilian gold rush of the 1690s and the discovery of diamonds a little later. Still, Europeans found a very profitable substitute in sugar, which was much in demand in Europe, where it was used as a medicine, a spice, a sweetener, a preservative, and in sculptured forms as a decoration that indicated high status. Whereas commercial agriculture in the Spanish Empire served a domestic market in its towns and mining camps, these sugar-based colonies produced almost exclusively for export, while importing their food and other necessities.

Large-scale sugar production had been pioneered by Arabs, who had introduced it in the Mediterranean. Europeans learned the technique and transferred it to their Atlantic island possessions and then to the Americas. For a century (1570–1670), Portuguese planters along the northeast coast of Brazil dominated the world market for sugar. Then the British, French, and Dutch turned their Caribbean territories into highly productive sugar-producing colonies, breaking the Portuguese and Brazilian monopoly.

■ Comparing Societies
How did the plantation societies of Brazil and the Caribbean differ from those in the southern colonies of North America?

Sugar decisively transformed Brazil and the Caribbean. Its production, which involved both growing the sugarcane and processing it into usable sugar, was very labor-intensive and could most profitably occur in a large-scale, almost industrial setting. It was perhaps the first modern industry in that it produced for an international and mass market, using capital and expertise from Europe, with production facilities located in the Americas. However, its most characteristic feature—the massive use of slave labor—was an ancient practice. In the absence of a Native American population, which had been almost totally wiped out in the Caribbean or had fled inland in Brazil, European sugarcane planters turned to Africa and the Atlantic slave trade for an alternative workforce. The vast majority of the African captives transported across the Atlantic, some 80 percent or more, ended up in Brazil and the Caribbean. (See "Commerce in People: The Transatlantic Slave System" in Chapter 14.)

Enslaved people worked on sugar-producing estates in horrendous conditions. The heat and fire from the cauldrons, which turned raw sugarcane into crystallized sugar, reminded many visitors of scenes from Hell. These conditions, combined with disease, generated a high death rate, perhaps 5 to 10 percent per year, which required plantation owners to constantly import more enslaved people. A Jesuit observer in 1580 aptly summarized the situation: "The work is great and many die."[13]

More males than females were imported from Africa into the sugar economies of the Americas, leading to major and persistent gender imbalances. Nonetheless, enslaved women did play distinctive roles in these societies. Women made up about half of the field gangs that did the heavy work of planting and harvesting sugarcane. They were subject to the same brutal punishments and received the same rations as their male counterparts, though they were seldom permitted to undertake the more

Plantation Life in the Caribbean This painting from 1823 shows the use of slave labor on a plantation in Antigua, a British-ruled island in the Caribbean. Notice the overseer with a whip supervising the tilling and planting of the field. (© British Library Board. All Rights Reserved/Bridgeman Images)

skilled labor inside the sugar mills. Women who worked in urban areas, mostly for white female owners, did domestic chores and were often hired out as laborers in various homes, shops, laundries, inns, and brothels. Discouraged from establishing stable families, women had to endure, often alone, the wrenching separation from their children that occurred when they were sold. Mary Prince, an enslaved Caribbean woman who wrote a brief account of her life, recalled the pain of families torn apart: "The great God above alone knows the thoughts of the poor slave's heart, and the bitter pains which follow such separations as these. All that we love taken away from us—oh, it is sad, sad! and sore to be borne!"[14]

The extensive use of African slave labor gave these plantation colonies a very different ethnic and racial makeup than that of highland Spanish America, as indicated by the Snapshot: Ethnic Composition of Colonial Societies in Latin America (1825), page 563. Thus, after three centuries of colonial rule, a substantial majority of Brazil's population was either partially or wholly of African descent. In the French Caribbean colony of Haiti in 1790, the corresponding figure was 93 percent.

SNAPSHOT Ethnic Composition of Colonial Societies in Latin America (1825)

	Highland Spanish America	Portuguese America (Brazil)
Europeans	18.2 percent	23.4 percent
Multiracial	28.3 percent	17.8 percent
Africans	11.9 percent	49.8 percent
Native Americans	41.7 percent	9.1 percent

Source: Data from Thomas E. Skidmore and Peter H. Smith, *Modern Latin America* (New York: Oxford University Press, 2001), 25.

As in Spanish America, interracial unions were common in colonial Brazil. Cross-racial unions accounted for only about 10 percent of all marriages, but the use of concubines and informal liaisons among Indians, Africans, and Portuguese produced a substantial multiracial population. From their ranks derived much of the urban skilled workforce and many of the supervisors in the sugar industry. As many as forty separate and named groups, each indicating a different racial mixture, emerged in colonial Brazil. The largest group at the time were the product of European-African unions, which the Portuguese called ***mulattoes***, a highly derogatory term widely used in the eighteenth century but offensive to many people then and now.

The plantation complex of the Americas, based on African slavery, extended beyond the Caribbean and Brazil to encompass the southern colonies of British North America, where tobacco, cotton, rice, and indigo were major crops, but the social outcomes of these plantation colonies were quite different from those farther south. Because European women had joined the colonial migration to North America at an early date, these colonies experienced less racial variety and certainly demonstrated less willingness to recognize the offspring of multiracial unions and accord them a place in society. A sharply defined racial system (with black Africans, "red" Native Americans, and white Europeans) evolved in North America, whereas both Portuguese and Spanish colonies acknowledged a wide variety of multiracial groups.

Slavery too was different in North America than in the sugar colonies. By 1750 or so, enslaved people in what became the United States proved able to reproduce themselves, and by the time of the Civil War almost all enslaved North Americans had been born in the New World. That was never the case in Latin America, where large-scale importation of new enslaved people continued well into the nineteenth century. Nonetheless, many more enslaved people were voluntarily set free by their owners in Brazil than in North America, and free blacks and biracial or multiracial people in Brazil had more economic opportunities than did their counterparts in the United States. At least a few among them found positions as political leaders, scholars, musicians, writers, and artists. Some were even hired as slave catchers.

Does this mean, then, that racism was absent in colonial Brazil? Certainly not, but it was different from racism in North America. For one thing, in North America, any African ancestry, no matter how small or distant, made a person "black"; in Brazil, a person of African and non-African ancestry was considered not black, but some other biracial or multiracial category. Racial prejudice surely persisted, for European characteristics were prized more highly than African features, and people regarded as white had enormously greater privileges and opportunities than others. Nevertheless, skin color in Brazil, and in Latin America generally, was only one criterion of class status, and the perception of color changed with the educational or economic standing of individuals. A light-skinned person of biracial or multiracial background who had acquired some wealth or education might well pass as a white. One curious visitor to Brazil was surprised to find a darker-skinned man serving as a local official. "Isn't the governor a mulatto?" inquired the visitor. "He was, but he isn't any more," was the reply. "How can a governor be a mulatto?"[15]

Settler Colonies in North America

Yet another distinctive type of colonial society emerged in the northern British colonies of New England, New York, and Pennsylvania. The lands the British acquired were widely regarded in Europe as the unpromising leftovers of the New World, lacking the obvious wealth and sophisticated cultures of the Spanish possessions. Until at least the eighteenth century, these British colonies remained far less prominent on the world stage than those of Spain or Portugal.

■ **Comparing Colonies**
What distinguished the British settler colonies of North America from their Spanish or Portuguese counterparts in Latin America?

The British settlers came from a more rapidly changing society than did those from an ardently Catholic, semi-feudal, authoritarian Spain. When Britain launched its colonial ventures in the seventeenth century, it had already experienced considerable conflict between Catholics and Protestants, the rise of a merchant capitalist class distinct from the nobility, and the emergence of Parliament as a check on the authority of kings. Although they brought much of their English culture with them, many of the British settlers—Puritans in Massachusetts and Quakers in Pennsylvania, for example—sought to escape aspects of an old European society rather than to re-create it, as was the case for most Spanish and Portuguese colonists. The easy availability of land and the outsider status of many British settlers made it even more difficult to follow the Spanish or Portuguese colonial pattern of sharp class hierarchies, large rural estates, and dependent laborers.

Thus men in Puritan New England became independent heads of family farms, a world away from Old England, where most land was owned by nobles and gentry and worked by servants, tenants, and paid laborers. But if men escaped the class restrictions of the old country, women were less able to avoid its gender limitations. While Puritan Christianity extolled the family and a woman's role as wife and mother, it reinforced largely unlimited male authority. "Since he is thy Husband," declared Boston minister Benjamin Wadsworth in 1712 to the colony's women, "God has made him the Head and set him above thee."[16]

Furthermore, British settlers were far more numerous than their Spanish counterparts, outnumbering them five to one by 1750. By the time of the American Revolution, some 90 percent or more of the population in the New England and middle Atlantic colonies were Europeans. Devastating diseases and a highly aggressive military policy had largely cleared the colonies of Native Americans, and their numbers, which were far smaller to start with, did not rebound in subsequent centuries as they did in the lands of the Aztecs and the Incas. Moreover, slave labor was not needed in an agricultural economy dominated by numerous small-scale independent farmers working their own land, although elite families, especially in urban areas, sometimes employed enslaved people as household servants. These were almost pure European **settler colonies**, for they lacked the substantial presence of indigenous, African, and multiracial people who were so prominent elsewhere.

Other differences likewise emerged. A largely Protestant England was far less interested in spreading Christianity among the remaining native peoples than were the large and well-funded missionary societies of Catholic Spain. Although religion loomed large in the North American colonies, the church and colonial state were not so intimately connected as they were in Latin America. The Protestant emphasis on reading the Bible for oneself led to a much greater mass literacy than in Latin America, where three centuries of church education still left some 95 percent of the population illiterate at independence. By contrast, well over 75 percent of white males in British North America were literate by the 1770s, although women's

Settler Farms In this eighteenth-century engraving, men work clearing the land for agriculture while a woman in the foreground collects water from a well. Unlike other regions of the Americas, the New England and middle Atlantic colonies were dominated by European immigrants who created small family farms. (Sarin Images/Granger, NYC—All rights reserved)

literacy rates were somewhat lower. Furthermore, British settler colonies evolved traditions of local self-government more extensively than in Latin America. Preferring to rely on joint stock companies or wealthy individuals operating under a royal charter, Britain had nothing resembling the elaborate imperial bureaucracy that governed Spanish colonies. For much of the seventeenth century, a prolonged power struggle between the English king and Parliament meant that the British government paid little attention to the internal affairs of the colonies. Therefore, elected colonial assemblies, seeing themselves as little parliaments defending "the rights of Englishmen," vigorously contested the prerogatives of royal governors sent to administer their affairs.

The grand irony of the modern history of the Americas lay in the reversal of long-established relationships between the northern and southern continents. For thousands of years, the major centers of wealth, power, commerce, and innovation lay in Mesoamerica and the Andes. That pattern continued for much of the colonial era, as the Spanish and Portuguese colonies seemed far more prosperous and successful than their British or French counterparts in North America. In the nineteenth and twentieth centuries, however, the balance shifted. What had once been the "dregs" of the colonial world became the United States, more politically stable, more democratic, more economically successful, and more internationally powerful than a divided, unstable, and much less prosperous Latin America.

The Steppes and Siberia: The Making of a Russian Empire

At the same time that Western Europeans were building their empires in the Americas, the **Russian Empire**, which subsequently became the world's largest state, was taking shape. By 1480, a small Russian state centered on the city of Moscow was emerging from two centuries of Mongol rule. That state soon conquered a number of neighboring Russian-speaking cities and incorporated them into its expanding territory. Located on the remote, cold, and heavily forested eastern fringe of Christendom, it was perhaps an unlikely candidate for constructing one of the great empires of the modern era. And yet, over the next three centuries, it did precisely that, extending Russian domination over the vast tundra, forests, and grasslands of northern Asia that lay to the south and east of Moscow, all the way to the Pacific Ocean. Russians also expanded westward, bringing numerous Poles, Germans, Ukrainians, Belorussians, and Baltic peoples into the Russian Empire.

■ **Describing Motives**
What motivated Russian empire building?

It was security concerns that drew Russian attention to the grasslands south and east of the Russian heartland, where pastoral peoples, like the Mongols before them, frequently raided their agricultural Russian neighbors and sold many into slavery. Across the vast expanse of Siberia, Russian motives were quite different, for the scattered peoples of its endless forests and tundra posed no threat to Russia. Numbering only some 220,000 in the seventeenth century and speaking more than 100 languages, they were mostly hunting, gathering, and herding people, living in small-scale societies and largely without access to gunpowder weapons. What drew the Russians across Siberia was opportunity—primarily the "soft gold" of fur-bearing animals, whose pelts were in great demand on the world market, especially as the world cooled during the Little Ice Age.

Whatever motives drove it, this enormous Russian Empire took shape in the three centuries between 1500 and 1800 (see Map 13.2). A growing line of wooden forts offered protection to frontier towns and trading centers as well as to mounting numbers of Russian farmers. Empire building was an extended process, involving the Russian state and its officials as well as a variety of private interests—merchants, hunters, peasants, churchmen, exiles, criminals, and adventurers. For the Russian

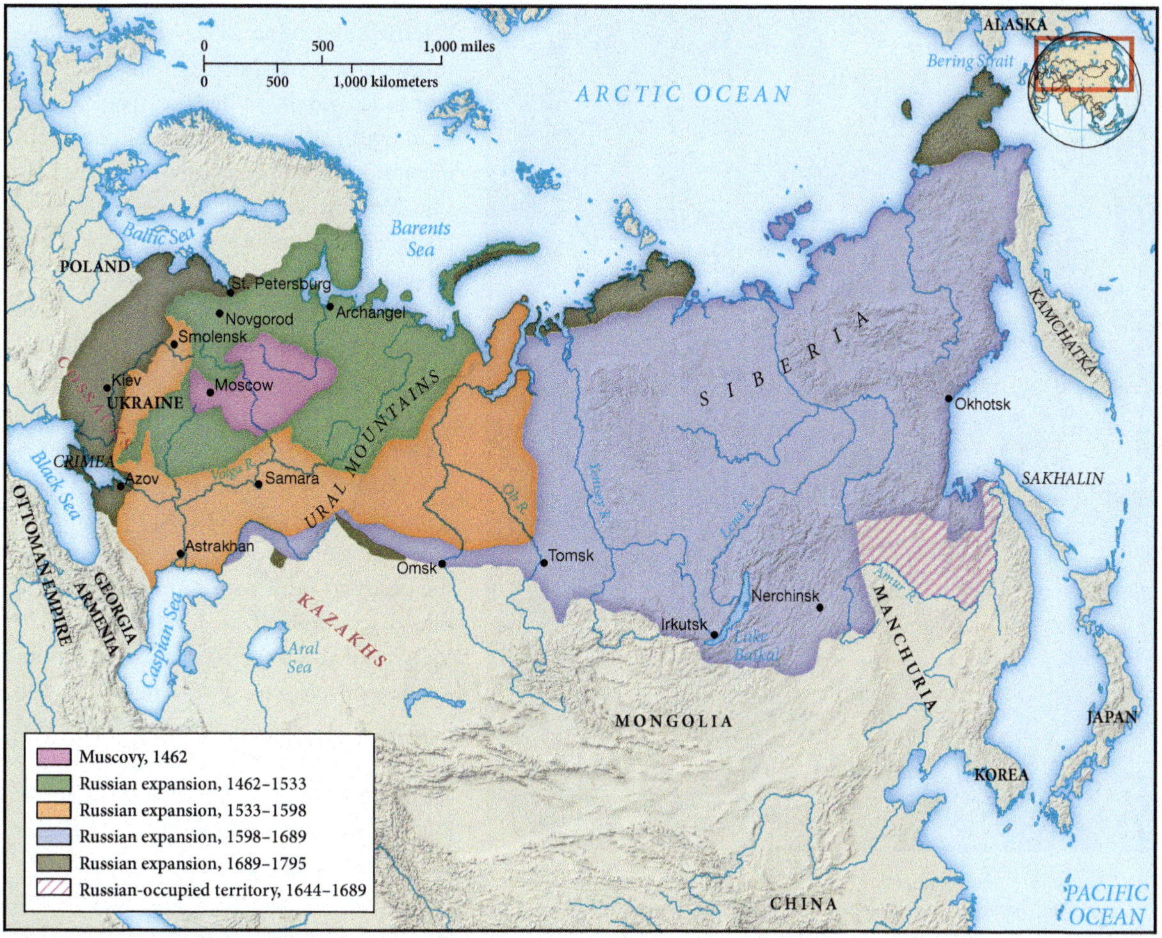

Map 13.2 The Russian Empire

From its beginnings as a small principality under Mongol control, Moscow became the center of a vast Russian Empire during the early modern era.

migrants to these new eastern lands, the empire offered "economic and social improvements over what they had known at home—from more and better land to fewer lords and officials."[17] Political leaders and educated Russians generally defined the empire in grander terms: defending Russian frontiers; enhancing the power of the Russian state; and bringing Christianity, civilization, and enlightenment to savages. But what did that empire mean to those on its receiving end?

Experiencing the Russian Empire

First, of course, empire meant conquest. Although resistance was frequent, in the long run Russian military might, based in modern weaponry and the organizational capacity of a state, brought both the steppes and Siberia under Russian control. Everywhere Russian authorities demanded an oath of allegiance by which native peoples swore "eternal submission to the grand tsar," the monarch of the Russian Empire. They also demanded ***yasak***, or "tribute," paid in cash or in kind. In Siberia, this meant enormous quantities of furs, especially the extremely valuable sable, which Siberian peoples were compelled to produce. As in the Americas, devastating epidemics accompanied conquest, particularly in the more remote regions of Siberia, where local people had little immunity to smallpox or measles. Also accompanying conquest was an intermittent pressure to convert to Christianity. Tax breaks, exemptions from paying tribute, and the promise of land or cash provided incentives for conversion, while the destruction of many mosques and the forced resettlement of Muslims added to the pressures. Yet the Russian state did not pursue conversion with the single-minded intensity that Spanish authorities exercised in Latin America, particularly if missionary activity threatened political and social stability. The empress Catherine the Great, for example, established religious tolerance for Muslims in the late eighteenth century and created a state agency to oversee Muslim affairs.

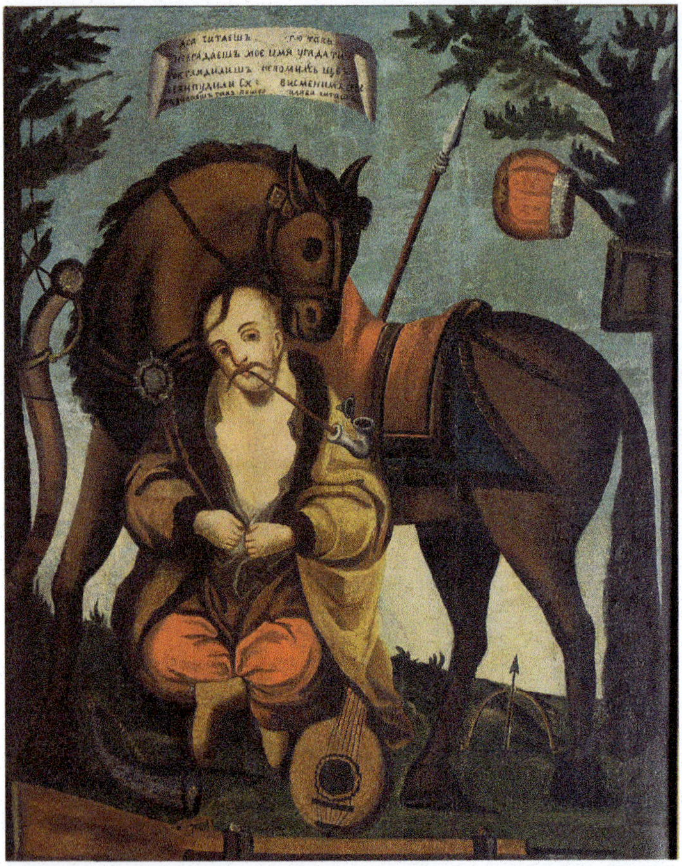

The Cossacks In the vanguard of Russian expansion across Siberia were the Cossacks, bands of fiercely independent warriors consisting of peasants who had escaped serfdom as well as criminals and other adventurers. In this eighteenth-century painting, a Cossack is depicted preparing to depart from an encampment and surrounded by the items of everyday Cossack life, including his horse, spear, bow, hunting horn, lyre, and pipe. Note also his red hat hanging from a tree branch. (Bridgeman Images)

The most profoundly transforming feature of the Russian Empire was the influx of Russian settlers, whose numbers by the end of the eighteenth century had overwhelmed native peoples, giving their lands a distinctively Russian character. By 1720, some 700,000 Russians lived in Siberia, thus reducing the native Siberians to 30 percent of the total population, a proportion that dropped to 14 percent in the nineteenth century. The loss of hunting grounds and pasturelands to Russian agricultural settlers undermined long-standing economies and rendered local people dependent on Russian markets for grain, sugar, tea, tobacco, and alcohol. Pressures to encourage pastoralists to abandon their nomadic ways included the requirement to pay fees and to obtain permission to cross agricultural lands. Kazakh herders responded with outrage: "The grass and the water belong to Heaven, and why should we pay any fees?"[18] Intermarriage, prostitution, and sexual abuse resulted in some multiracial offspring, but these were generally absorbed as Russians rather than identified as distinctive communities, as in Latin America.

Over the course of three centuries, both Siberia and the steppes were incorporated into the Russian state. Their native peoples were not driven into reservations or eradicated as in the Americas. Many of them, though, were Russified, adopting the Russian language and converting to Christianity, even as their traditional ways of life—hunting and herding—were much disrupted. The Russian Empire represented the final triumph of an agrarian civilization over the hunting societies of Siberia and over the pastoral peoples of the grasslands. The wealth of empire—rich agricultural lands, valuable furs, mineral deposits—played a major role in making Russia one of the great powers of Europe by the eighteenth century, and it has enjoyed that position ever since.

CORE IDEA

Assessing Cause and Effect

How did the Russian Empire transform the life of its conquered peoples and of the Russian homeland itself?

Russians and Empire

If the empire transformed the conquered peoples, it also fundamentally changed Russia itself. Within an increasingly multiethnic empire, Russians declined as a proportion of the overall population, although they remained politically dominant. Among the growing number of non-Russians in the empire, Slavic-speaking Ukrainians and Belorussians predominated, while the vast territories of Siberia and the steppes housed numerous separate peoples, but with quite small populations.

Unlike its expansion to the east, Russia's westward movement occurred in the context of military rivalries with the major powers of the region—the Ottoman Empire, Poland, Sweden, Lithuania, Prussia, and Austria. During the late seventeenth and eighteenth centuries, Russia acquired substantial territories in the Baltic region, Poland, and Ukraine. This contact with Europe also fostered an awareness of Russia's backwardness relative to Europe and prompted an extensive program of westernization, particularly under the leadership of Peter the Great (r. 1689–1725). His massive efforts included vast administrative changes, the enlargement and modernization of Russian military forces, a new educational system for the sons of noblemen, and dozens of manufacturing enterprises. Russian nobles were instructed to dress in European styles and to shave their sacred and much-revered beards. The newly created capital city of St. Petersburg was to be Russia's "window on the West."

One of Peter's successors, Catherine the Great (r. 1762–1796), followed up with further efforts to Europeanize Russian cultural and intellectual life, viewing herself as part of the European Enlightenment. Thus Russians were the first of many peoples to measure themselves against the West and to mount major "catch-up" efforts.

But this European-oriented and Christian state had also become an Asian power, bumping up against China, India, Persia, and the Ottoman Empire. It was on the front lines of the encounter between Christendom and the world of Islam. This straddling of Asia and Europe was the source of a long-standing identity problem that has troubled educated Russians for 300 years. Was Russia a backward European country, destined to follow the lead of more highly developed Western European societies? Or was it different, uniquely Slavic or even Asian, shaped by its Mongol legacy and its status as an Asian power? It is a question that Russians have not completely answered even in the twenty-first century. Either way, the very size of that empire, bordering on virtually all of the great agrarian civilizations of outer Eurasia, turned Russia, like many empires before it, into a highly militarized state, "a society organized for continuous war," according to one scholar.[19] It also reinforced the highly autocratic character of the Russian Empire because such a huge state arguably required a powerful monarchy to hold its vast domains and highly diverse peoples together.

Clearly, the Russians had created an empire, similar to those of Western Europe in terms of conquest, settlement, exploitation, religious conversion, and feelings of superiority. Nonetheless, the Russians had acquired their empire under different circumstances than did the Western Europeans. The Spanish and the British had conquered and colonized the New World, an ocean away and wholly unknown to them before 1492. They acquired those empires only after establishing themselves as distinct European states. The Russians, on the other hand, absorbed adjacent territories, and they did so at the same time that a modern Russian state was taking shape. "The British had an empire," wrote historian Geoffrey Hosking. "Russia *was* an empire."[20] Perhaps this helps explain the unique longevity of the Russian Empire. Whereas the Spanish, Portuguese, and British colonies in the Americas long ago achieved independence, the Russian Empire remained intact until the collapse of the Soviet Union in 1991. So thorough was Russian colonization that Siberia and much of the steppes remain still an integral part of the Russian state.

Asian Empires

Even as Western Europeans were building their empires in the Americas and the Russians were expanding across Siberia, other imperial projects were likewise under way. The Chinese pushed deep into central Eurasia; Turko-Mongol invaders from Central Asia created the Mughal Empire, bringing much of Hindu South Asia within a single Muslim-ruled political system; and the Ottoman Empire brought Muslim rule to a largely Christian population in southeastern Europe and Turkish rule to largely Arab populations in North Africa and the Middle East. None of these empires had the global reach or worldwide impact of Europe's American colonies; they were regional rather than global in scope. Nor did they have the same devastating and transforming impact on their conquered peoples, for those peoples were not being exposed to new diseases. Nothing remotely approaching the catastrophic population collapse of Native American peoples occurred in these Asian empires. Moreover, the process of building these empires did not transform the imperial homeland as fundamentally as the wealth of the Americas transformed European imperial powers and to a lesser extent Siberia transformed Russia. Nonetheless, these expanding Asian empires reflected the energies and vitality of their respective civilizations in the early modern era, and they gave rise to profoundly important cross-cultural encounters, with legacies that echoed for many centuries.

Making China an Empire

In the fifteenth century, China had declined an opportunity to construct a maritime empire in the Indian Ocean, as Zheng He's massive fleet was withdrawn after 1433 and left to wither away (see "Ming Dynasty China" in Chapter 12). In the seventeenth and eighteenth centuries, however, China built another kind of empire on its northern and western frontiers that vastly enlarged the territorial size of the country and incorporated a number of non-Chinese peoples. Undertaking this enormous project of imperial expansion was China's Qing, or Manchu, dynasty (1644–1912). Strangely enough, the Qing dynasty was itself of foreign and nomadic origin, hailing from Manchuria, north of the Great Wall. The violent Manchu takeover of China, part of the General Crisis of the seventeenth century, was facilitated by a widespread famine and peasant rebellions associated with the Little Ice Age. But having conquered China, the Qing rulers sought to maintain their ethnic distinctiveness by forbidding intermarriage between themselves and the Chinese. Nonetheless, their ruling elites also mastered the Chinese language and Confucian teachings and used Chinese bureaucratic techniques to govern the empire.

For many centuries, the Chinese had interacted with the nomadic peoples who inhabited the dry and lightly populated regions now known as Mongolia, Xinjiang, and Tibet. Trade, tribute, and warfare ensured that these ecologically and culturally different worlds were well known to the Chinese, quite unlike the New World "discoveries" of the Europeans. Chinese authority in the area had been intermittent and actively resisted. Then, in the early modern era, the Qing dynasty undertook an eighty-year military effort (1680–1760) that brought these huge regions solidly under its control. It was largely security concerns, rather than economic need, that motivated this aggressive posture. During the late seventeenth century, the creation of a substantial state among the western Mongols, known as the Zunghars, revived Chinese memories of an earlier Mongol conquest. As in so many other cases, expansion was viewed as a defensive necessity. The eastward movement of the Russian Empire likewise appeared potentially threatening, but after increasing tensions and a number of skirmishes and battles, this danger was resolved diplomatically, rather than militarily, in the Treaty of Nerchinsk (1689), which marked the boundary between Russia and China.

Qing Conquests in Central Asia Painted by the Chinese artist Jin Tingbiao in the mid-eighteenth century, this image portrays Machang, a leading warrior involved in the westward extension of the Qing Empire. The painting was commissioned by the emperor himself and served to honor the bravery of Machang. (Pictures from History/CPA Media)

CORE IDEA

Describing a Process

What were the distinctive features of Chinese empire building in the early modern era?

Although undertaken by the non-Chinese Manchus, the Qing dynasty campaigns against the Zunghar Mongols marked the evolution of China into a Central Asian empire. The Chinese, however, have seldom thought of themselves as an imperial power. Rather, they spoke of the "unification" of the peoples of central Eurasia within a Chinese state. Nonetheless, historians have seen many similarities between **Qing expansion** and other cases of early modern empire building, while noting some clear differences as well.

Clearly the Qing dynasty takeover of central Eurasia was a conquest, making use of China's more powerful military technology and greater resources. Furthermore, the area was ruled separately from the rest of China through a new office called the Court of Colonial Affairs. Like other colonial powers, the Qing made active use of local notables—Mongol aristocrats, Muslim officials, Buddhist leaders—as they attempted to govern the region as inexpensively as possible. Sometimes these native officials abused their authority, demanding extra taxes or labor service from local people and thus earning their hostility. In places, those officials imitated Chinese ways by wearing peacock feathers, decorating their hats with gold buttons, or adopting a Manchu hairstyle that was much resented by many Chinese who were forced to wear it.

More generally, however, Qing officials did not seek to assimilate local people into Chinese culture and showed considerable respect for the Mongolian, Tibetan, and Muslim cultures of the region. People of noble rank, Buddhist monks, and those associated with monasteries were excused from the taxes and labor service required of ordinary people. Nor was the area flooded with Chinese settlers. In parts of Mongolia, for example, Qing authorities sharply restricted the entry of Chinese merchants and other immigrants in an effort to preserve the area as a source of recruitment for the Chinese military. They feared that the "soft" and civilized Chinese ways might erode the fighting spirit of the Mongols.

The long-term significance of this new Qing imperial state was tremendous. It greatly expanded the territory of China and added a small but important minority of non-Chinese people to the empire's vast population (see Map 13.3). The borders of contemporary China are essentially those created during the Qing dynasty. Some of those peoples, particularly those in Tibet and Xinjiang, have retained their older identities and in recent decades have actively sought greater autonomy or even independence from China.

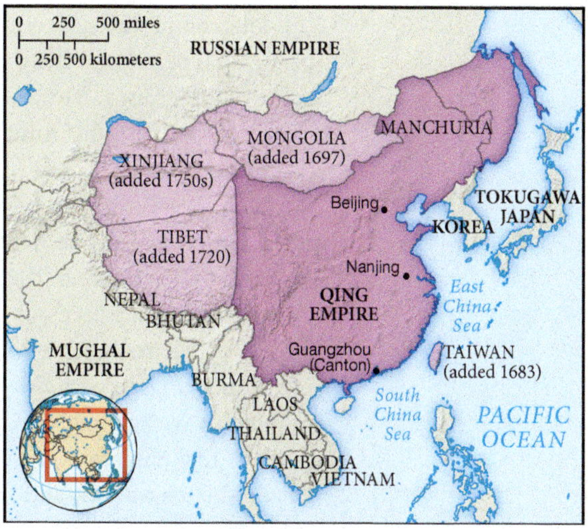

Map 13.3 China's Qing Dynasty Empire
After many centuries of intermittent expansion into Central Asia, the Qing dynasty brought this vast region firmly under its control.

Even more important, Qing conquests, together with the expansion of the Russian Empire, utterly transformed Central Asia. For centuries, that region had been the cosmopolitan crossroads of Eurasia, hosting the Silk Road trading network, welcoming all the major world religions, and generating an enduring encounter between the nomads of the steppes and the farmers of settled agricultural regions. Now under Russian or Qing rule, it became the backward and impoverished region known to nineteenth- and twentieth-century observers. Land-based commerce across Eurasia increasingly took a backseat to oceanic trade. Indebted Mongolian nobles lost their land to Chinese merchants, while nomads, no longer able to herd their animals freely, fled to urban areas, where many were reduced to begging. The incorporation of inner Eurasia into the Russian and Qing empires "eliminated permanently as a major actor on the historical stage the nomadic pastoralists, who had been the strongest alternative to settled agricultural society since the second millennium [B.C.E.]."[21] It was the end of a long era.

Muslims and Hindus in the Mughal Empire

If the creation of a Qing imperial state in the early modern era provoked a final clash of nomadic pastoralists and settled farmers, India's **Mughal Empire** hosted a different kind of encounter—a further phase in the long interaction of Islamic and Hindu cultures in South Asia. That empire was the product of Central Asian warriors who were Muslims in religion and Turkic in culture and who claimed descent from Chinggis Khan and Timur. Their brutal conquests in the sixteenth century provided India with a rare period of relative political unity (1526–1707), as Mughal emperors exercised a fragile control over a diverse and fragmented subcontinent that had long been divided into a bewildering variety of small states, principalities, tribes, castes, sects, and ethno-linguistic groups.

The central division within Mughal India was religious. The ruling dynasty and perhaps 20 percent of the population were Muslims; most of the rest practiced some form of Hinduism. Mughal India's most famous emperor, **Akbar** (r. 1556–1605), clearly recognized this fundamental reality and acted deliberately to accommodate the Hindu majority. After conquering the warrior-based and Hindu Rajputs of northwestern India, Akbar married several of their princesses but did not require them to convert to Islam. He incorporated a substantial number of Hindus into the political-military elite of the empire and supported the building of Hindu temples as well as mosques, palaces, and forts. (See Working with Evidence, Source 13.1, page 582.) But Akbar also acted to soften some Hindu restrictions on women, encouraging the remarriage of widows and discouraging child marriages and *sati* (the practice in which a widow followed her husband to death by throwing herself on his funeral pyre). A few elite women were also able to exercise political power, including Nur Jahan, the twentieth and favorite wife of Akbar's successor Emperor Jahangir (r. 1605–1627). She was widely regarded as the power behind the throne of her alcohol- and opium-addicted husband, giving audiences to visiting dignitaries, consulting with ministers, and even having a coin issued in her name.

CORE IDEA

Assessing Change
How did Mughal attitudes and policies toward Hindus change from the time of Akbar to that of Aurangzeb?

In directly religious matters, Akbar imposed a policy of toleration, deliberately restraining the more militantly Islamic *ulama* (religious scholars) and removing the special tax (*jizya*) on non-Muslims. He constructed a special House of Worship where he presided over intellectual discussion with representatives of many religions—Muslim, Hindu, Christian, Buddhist, Jewish, Jain, and Zoroastrian. Akbar went so far as to create his own state cult, a religious faith aimed at the Mughal elite that drew on Islam, Hinduism, and Zoroastrianism and emphasized loyalty to the emperor himself. The overall style of the Mughal Empire was that of a blended elite culture in which both Hindus and various Muslim groups could feel comfortable. Thus Persian artists and writers were welcomed into the empire, and the Hindu epic *Ramayana* was translated into Persian, while various Persian classics appeared in Hindi and Sanskrit. In short, Akbar and his immediate successors downplayed a distinctly Islamic identity for the Mughal Empire in favor of a cosmopolitan and hybrid Indian-Persian-Turkic culture.

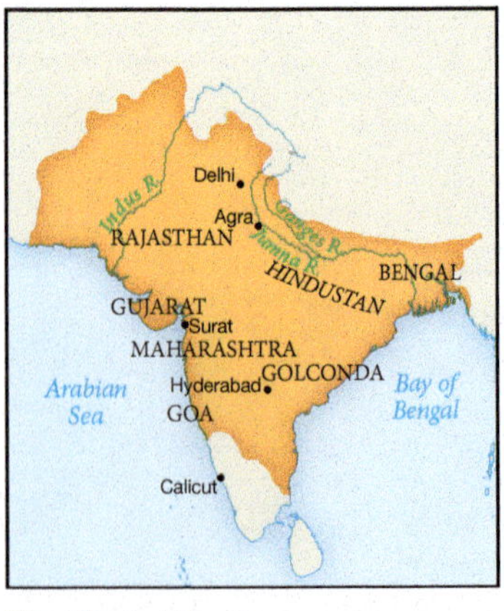

The Mughal Empire

Such policies fostered sharp opposition among some Muslims. The philosopher Shaykh Ahmad Sirhindi (1564–1624), claiming to be a "renewer" of authentic Islam in his time, strongly objected to this cultural synthesis. The worship of saints, the sacrifice of animals, and support for Hindu religious festivals all represented impure intrusions of Sufi Islam or Hinduism that needed to be rooted out. In Sirhindi's view, it was primarily women who had introduced these deviations: "Because of their utter stupidity [Muslim] women pray to stones and idols and ask for their help. . . . Women participate in the holidays of Hindus and Jews. They celebrate Diwali [a major Hindu festival] and send their sisters and daughters presents similar to those exchanged by the infidels."[22] It was therefore the duty of

Muslim rulers to impose the sharia (Islamic law), to enforce the jizya, and to remove non-Muslims from high office.

This strain of Muslim thinking found a champion in the emperor **Aurangzeb** (ow-rang-ZEHB) (r. 1658–1707), who reversed Akbar's policy of accommodation and sought to impose Islamic supremacy. While Akbar had discouraged the Hindu practice of sati, Aurangzeb forbade it outright. Music and dance were now banned at court, and previously tolerated vices such as gambling, drinking, prostitution, and narcotics were actively suppressed. Dancing girls were ordered to get married or leave the empire altogether. Some Hindu temples were destroyed, and the jizya was reimposed. "Censors of public morals," posted to large cities, enforced Islamic law.

Aurangzeb's religious policies, combined with intolerable demands for taxes to support his many wars of expansion, antagonized Hindus and prompted various movements of opposition to the Mughals. "Your subjects are trampled underfoot," wrote one anonymous protester. "Every province of your empire is impoverished. . . . God is the God of all mankind, not the God of Mussalmans [Muslims] alone."[23] These opposition movements, some of them self-consciously Hindu, fatally fractured the Mughal Empire, especially after Aurangzeb's death in 1707, and opened the way for a British takeover in the second half of the eighteenth century.

Thus the Mughal Empire was the site of a highly significant encounter between two of the world's great religious traditions. It began with an experiment in multicultural empire building and ended in growing antagonism between Hindus and Muslims. In the centuries that followed, both elements of the Mughal experience would be repeated.

Muslims and Christians in the Ottoman Empire

Like the Mughal state, the **Ottoman Empire** was also the creation of Turkic warrior groups, whose aggressive raiding of agricultural civilizations was sometimes legitimized in Islamic terms as *jihad*, religiously sanctioned warfare against infidels. Beginning around 1300 from a base area in northwestern Anatolia, these Ottoman Turks over the next three centuries swept over much of the Middle East, North Africa, and southeastern Europe to create the Islamic world's most significant empire (see Map 13.4). During those centuries, the Ottoman state was transformed from a small frontier principality to a prosperous, powerful, cosmopolitan empire, heir both to the Byzantine Empire and to leadership within the Islamic world. Its sultan combined the roles of a Turkic warrior prince, a Muslim caliph, and a conquering emperor, bearing the "strong sword of Islam" and serving as chief defender of the faith.

Gaining such an empire transformed Turkish social life as well. The relative independence of Central Asian pastoral women, their open association with men, and their political influence in society all diminished as the Turks adopted Islam, beginning in the tenth century, and later acquired an empire in the heartland of ancient and patriarchal Mediterranean civilizations. Now elite Turkish women found themselves secluded and often veiled; enslaved women from the Caucasus Mountains and the

MAPPING HISTORY

Map 13.4 The Ottoman Empire

At its high point in the mid-sixteenth century, the Ottoman Empire encompassed a vast diversity of peoples; straddled Europe, Africa, and Asia; and battled both the Austrian and Safavid empires.

READING THE MAP What specific territorial disputes with the Persian Safavid Empire were likely to cause conflicts between the Ottomans and their powerful neighbor? What geographical features and political realities were barriers to further expansion of the Ottoman Empire?

MAKING CONNECTIONS Compare this map with Map 13.2: The Russian Empire. What happened to the Ottoman Empire's tributary states north of the Black Sea after 1689? Where were the likely points of tension or conflict between the Ottoman and Russian empires during the early modern period?

Sudan grew more numerous; official imperial censuses did not count women; and orthodox Muslim reformers sought to restrict women's religious gatherings.

And yet within the new constraints of a settled Islamic empire, Turkish women retained something of the social power they had enjoyed in pastoral societies. From around 1550 to 1650, women of the royal court had such an influence in political matters that their critics referred to the "sultanate of women." Islamic law permitted women important property rights, which enabled some to become quite wealthy, endowing religious and charitable institutions. Many women actively used the Ottoman courts to protect their legal rights in matters of marriage, divorce, and inheritance, sometimes representing themselves or acting as agents for female relatives. In 1717, the wife of an English ambassador to the Ottoman Empire compared the lives of Turkish and European women, declaring, "'Tis very easy to see that they have more liberty than we have."[24]

Within the Islamic world, the Ottoman Empire represented the growing prominence of Turkic people, for their empire now incorporated a large number of Arabs, among whom the religion had been born. The responsibility and the prestige of protecting Mecca, Medina, and Jerusalem—the holy cities of Islam—now fell to the Ottoman Empire. A century-long conflict (1534–1639) between the Ottoman Empire, espousing the Sunni version of Islam, and the Persian Safavid Empire, holding fast to the Shia form of the faith, expressed a deep and enduring division within the Islamic world. Nonetheless, Persian culture, especially its poetry, painting, and traditions of imperial splendor, occupied a prominent position among the Ottoman elite.

The Ottoman Empire, like its Mughal counterpart, was the site of a highly significant cross-cultural encounter in the early modern era, adding yet another chapter to the long-running story of interaction between the Islamic world and Christendom. As the Ottoman Empire expanded across Anatolia, and as the Byzantine state visibly weakened and large numbers of Turks settled in the region, the empire's mostly Christian population converted in large numbers to Islam. By 1500, some 90 percent of Anatolia's inhabitants were Muslims and Turkic speakers. The climax of this Turkic assault on the Christian world of Byzantium occurred in the 1453 conquest of Constantinople, when the city fell to Muslim invaders. (See Zooming In: 1453 in Constantinople, Chapter 12, page 514.) Renamed Istanbul, that splendid Christian city became the capital of the Ottoman Empire. Byzantium, heir to the glory of Rome and the guardian of Orthodox Christianity, was no more.

CORE IDEA

■ Assessing Significance
How might you describe the significance of the Ottoman Empire during the early modern era?

In the empire's southeastern European domains, known as the Balkans, the Ottoman encounter with Christian peoples unfolded quite differently than it had in Anatolia. In the Balkans, Muslims ruled over a large Christian population, but the scarcity of Turkish settlers and the willingness of the Ottoman authorities to accommodate the region's Christian churches led to far fewer conversions. By the early sixteenth century, only about 19 percent of the area's people were Muslims, and 81 percent were Christians.

The Ottoman Siege of Vienna, 1683 This anonymous late seventeenth-century painting captures the crucial moment in the siege of Vienna when a last Ottoman attack is pushed back by Austrian, French, and Polish forces. The siege marked the end of a serious Muslim threat to Christian Europe. (akg-images/Newscom)

Many of these Christians had welcomed Ottoman conquest because taxes were lighter and oppression less pronounced than under their former Christian rulers. Christian communities such as the Eastern Orthodox and Armenian churches were granted considerable autonomy in regulating their internal social, religious, educational, and charitable affairs. Nonetheless, many Christian and Jewish women appealed legal cases dealing with marriage and inheritance to Muslim courts, where their property rights were greater. A substantial number of Christian men—Balkan landlords, Greek merchants, government officials, and high-ranking clergy—became part of the Ottoman elite, sometimes without converting to Islam. Jewish refugees fleeing Christian persecution in a Spain recently "liberated" from Islamic rule likewise found greater opportunity in the Ottoman Empire, where they became prominent in trade and banking circles. In these ways, Ottoman dealings with the Christian and Jewish populations of the empire broadly resembled Akbar's policies toward the Hindu majority of Mughal India. In another way, however, Turkish rule bore heavily on Christians. Through a process known as the ***devshirme*** (devv-shirr-MEH) (the collecting or gathering),

Ottoman authorities siphoned off many thousands of young boys from Christian families into the service of the state. Removed from their families and required to learn Turkish, these boys usually converted to Islam and were trained for either the civil administration or military service in elite Janissary units. Although it was a terrible blow for families who lost their children, the *devshirme* also represented a means of upward mobility within the Ottoman Empire. But this social gain occurred at a high price.

If Ottoman authorities were relatively tolerant toward Christians within their borders, the empire itself represented an enormous threat to Christendom generally. The seizure of Constantinople, the conquest of the Balkans, Ottoman naval power in the Mediterranean, and the siege of Vienna in 1529 and again in 1683 raised anew "the specter of a Muslim takeover of all of Europe."[25] One European ambassador reported fearfully in 1555 from the court of the Turkish ruler Suleiman: "He tramples the soil of Hungary with 200,000 horses, he is at the very gates of Austria, threatens the rest of Germany, and brings in his train all the nations that extend from our borders to those of Persia.[26] Indeed, the "terror of the Turk" inspired fear across much of Europe and placed Christendom on the defensive, even as Western Europeans were expanding aggressively across the Atlantic and into the Indian Ocean.

But the Ottoman encounter with Christian Europe spawned admiration and cooperation as well as fear and trembling. Italian Renaissance artists portrayed the splendor of the Islamic world. (See Working with Evidence, Chapter 12.) The sixteenth-century French philosopher Jean Bodin praised the religious tolerance of the Ottoman sultan in contrast to Christian intolerance: "The King of the Turks who rules over a great part of Europe safeguards the rites of religion as well as any prince in this world. Yet he constrains no-one, but on the contrary permits everyone to live as his conscience dictates."[27] The French government on occasion found it useful to ally with the Ottoman Empire against its common enemy of Habsburg Austria, while European merchants willingly violated a papal ban on selling firearms to the Turks. Cultural encounter involved more than conflict.

CONCLUSIONS AND REFLECTIONS

The Importance of Context

World history is, to put it mildly, a big subject. To teachers and students alike, it can easily seem overwhelming in its detail. And yet the central task of world history is *not* the inclusion of endless facts or particular cases. It is rather to establish contexts or frameworks within which carefully selected facts and cases take on new meaning. In world history, every event, every process, every historical figure, and every culture, society, or civilization gains significance from its incorporation into some larger context or framework.

The usefulness of this kind of thinking becomes apparent as we seek to place European empire building in the Americas in some larger frame of reference. The broad outlines of European colonization in the Western Hemisphere are familiar to most American and European students. The voyages of Columbus; the initial military conquests by European forces; the Great Dying as European and African diseases decimated Native American societies; the vast exchange of plants and animals that colonization generated; large-scale European settlement; enslaved Africans and plantation agriculture—all of this marks these empires as enormously significant on a global scale. Studied alone, as they often are, these imperial projects seem to portray Europeans as the major agents of change in the early modern era. They were, apparently, in the driver's seat.

And yet, juxtaposing European empires in the Americas with other patterns of empire building of the same time puts the role of Europeans in a wider context. Such contextualization reminds us that Western Europe was not the only center of vitality and expansion in the early modern age and that culturally different peoples interacted in multiple empires. As it expanded, the Russian Empire incorporated dozens of nationalities (Ukrainian, Georgian, Lithuanian, Polish, for example) as well as Siberian hunters and Central Asian pastoralists. Mongolians, Tibetans, and Uighurs were forcibly brought into the Chinese empire. In the Mughal Empire, a Muslim minority governed a Hindu majority. And the Ottoman Empire brought numerous Christian Europeans in the Balkans under Muslim rule, even as other Europeans were creating empires across the Atlantic. In short, Europeans were not alone in the driver's seat of world history during the early modern era.

Contextualizing also allows us to see more clearly the distinctive features of European empires in the Americas by viewing them in the mirror of other imperial creations. The Chinese, Mughal, and Ottoman empires continued older patterns of cultural interaction, while those of Europe represented something wholly new in human history—an interacting Atlantic world of Europe, Africa, and the Americas. Furthermore, the European empires had a far greater impact on the peoples they incorporated than did other empires. Nowhere else did empire building generate such a catastrophic population collapse as in the Americas, although disease and the violence of Russian rule in Siberia brought death and devastation to many of its indigenous peoples. Nor did Asian empires foster slave-based societies and transcontinental trade in enslaved people, as did Europe's American colonies.

Finally, Europe was enriched and transformed by its American possessions far more than China and the Ottomans were by their territorial acquisitions. Europeans gained enormous new biological resources from their empires—corn, potatoes, tomatoes, chocolate, tobacco, timber, furs, and much more—as well as great wealth in the form of gold, silver, and land. The wealth of empire propelled Europe to a dominant position in the world by the nineteenth century. Here again Russia's experience paralleled that of Western Europe, though to a lesser extent, as its empire enabled the country to emerge as one of the Great Powers of Europe by the eighteenth century.

Thus the outlook of world history is relational, comparative, and contextual. Like Russian nested dolls, every story finds a place within a larger story. Nothing stands alone.

Revisiting Chapter 13

Revisiting Specifics

Hernán Cortés, 551
Great Dying, 554
Little Ice Age, 554
General Crisis, 554
Columbian exchange, 556
mercantilism, 557
mestizo, 559
mulattoes, 563
settler colonies, 565
Russian Empire, 566
yasak, 568
Qing expansion, 572
Mughal Empire, 573
Akbar, 574
Aurangzeb, 575
Ottoman Empire, 575
devshirme, 578

Revisiting Core Ideas

1. **Describing Change** What large-scale transformations did European empires generate in the Americas, in Europe, and globally?
2. **Comparing Empire Building** In what different ways did European empire building take shape in the Americas?
3. **Assessing Cause and Effect** How did the Russian Empire transform the life of its conquered peoples and of the Russian homeland itself?
4. **Describing a Process** What were the distinctive features of Chinese empire building in the early modern era?
5. **Assessing Change** How did Mughal attitudes and policies toward Hindus change from the time of Akbar to that of Aurangzeb?
6. **Assessing Significance** How might you describe the significance of the Ottoman Empire during the early modern era?

A Wider View

1. The experience of empire for conquered peoples was broadly similar whoever their rulers were. Does the material in this chapter support or challenge this idea?
2. In thinking about the similarities and differences among the empires of the early modern era, what categories of comparison might be most useful to consider?
3. In the chapter maps, notice areas of the world not included in a major empire. Pick an area and research what was happening there in the early modern era.
4. In what ways is the legacy of these early modern empires still visible in the early twenty-first century?
5. **Looking Back** Compared to the world of the fifteenth century, what new patterns of development are visible in the empire-building projects of the following centuries?

To learn more about the topics in this chapter, see **For Further Study** at the end of this book.

WORKING WITH EVIDENCE

State Building in the Early Modern Era

The empires of the early modern era were the projects of states, though these states often made use of various private groups—missionaries, settlers, merchants, mercenaries—to achieve the goals of empire. Such imperial states—Mughal India, the Ottoman Empire, France, the Inca Empire, and Ming dynasty China, for example—were invariably headed by kings or emperors who were the source of ultimate political authority in their lands. Each of those rulers sought to govern societies divided by religion, region, ethnicity, or class. During the three centuries between 1450 and 1750, all of these states, and a number of non-imperial states as well, moved toward greater political integration through more assertive monarchs and more effective central bureaucracies, which curtailed, though never eliminated, entrenched local interests. The growth of empire accompanied this process of political integration, and perhaps helped cause it. The sources that follow allow us to catch a glimpse of this state-building effort in several distinct settings.

SOURCE 13.1 The Memoirs of Emperor Jahangir

The diverse peoples of India had seldom experienced a political system that encompassed most of the subcontinent. But in the early modern era, the Mughal Empire gave to South Asia a rare period of substantial political unity. Source 13.1 offers excerpts from the memoirs of Jahangir, who ruled the Mughal state from 1605 to 1627, following the reign of his more famous father, Akbar. Written in Persian, the literary language of the eastern Islamic world, Jahangir's account reflects on the events of his coronation and of the policies that he subsequently put in place.

- Why do you think Jahangir mounted such an elaborate coronation celebration for himself?
- In what ways did Jahangir seek to ensure the effective authority of the state he led?
- In what ways was Jahangir a distinctly Muslim ruler? In what respects did he and his father depart from Islamic principles?
- Based on these selections, what concrete problems of governance can you infer were facing Jahangir?

JAHANGIR | *Memoirs* | 1605–1627

At the age of thirty-eight, I became Emperor. . . . Hence I assumed the titles of . . . the world-subduing emperor, the world-subduing king.

On this occasion I made use of the throne prepared by my father, and enriched at an expense without parallel for the celebration of the festival of the new year. . . . I caused also the imperial crown, which my father had caused to be made after the manner of that which was worn by the great kings of Persia, to be . . . placed . . . on my brows, as an omen auspicious to the stability and happiness of my reign. . . .

For forty days and forty nights I caused the . . . great imperial state drum, to strike up, without ceasing, the strains of joy and triumph; and . . . the ground was spread by my directions with the most costly brocades and gold embroidered carpets. Censers [containers for burning incense] of gold and silver were disposed in different directions for the purpose of burning odoriferous drugs, and nearly three thousand camphorated wax lights . . . illuminated the scene. . . . And finally, the Emirs of the empire . . . covered from head to foot in gold and jewels, and shoulder to shoulder, stood round in brilliant array, also waiting for the commands of their sovereign. . . .

I instituted . . . special regulations . . . as rules of conduct, never to be deviated from in their respective stations.

1. I remitted [canceled] altogether to my subjects three sources of revenue taxes or duties. . . .
2. I directed, when the district lay waste or destitute of inhabitants, that towns should be built.
3. Merchants traveling through the country were not to have their bales or packages of any kind opened without their consent. . . .
5. No person was permitted either to make or sell either wine or any other kind of intoxicating liquor. I undertook to institute this regulation, although it is sufficiently notorious that I have myself the strongest inclination for wine. . . .
7. No person was to suffer, for any offense, the loss of a nose or ear. If the crime were theft, the offender was to be scourged with thorns, or deterred from further transgression by an attestation on the Koran.
8. [High officials] were prohibited from possessing themselves by violence of the lands of the subject, or from cultivating them on their own account. . . .
10. The governors in all the principal cities were directed to establish infirmaries or hospitals, with competent medical aid for the relief of the sick. . . .

[H]aving on one occasion asked my father [Akbar] the reason why he had forbidden any one to prevent or interfere with the building of these haunts of idolatry [Hindu temples], his reply was in the following terms: "My dear child," said he, "I find myself a powerful monarch, the shadow of God upon earth. I have seen that he bestows the blessings of his gracious providence upon all his creatures without distinction. Ill should I discharge the duties of my exalted station, were I to withhold my compassion and indulgence from any of those entrusted to my charge. With all of the human race, with all of God's creatures, I am at peace: why then should I permit myself, under any consideration, to be the cause of molestation or aggression to any one? Besides, are not five parts in six of mankind either Hindus or aliens to the faith; and were I to be governed by motives of the kind suggested in your inquiry, what alternative can I have but to put them all to death! I have thought it therefore my wisest plan to let these men alone. Neither is it to be forgotten, that the class of whom we are speaking . . . are usefully engaged, either in the pursuits of science or the arts, or of improvements for the benefit of mankind, and have in numerous instances arrived at the highest distinctions in the state, there being, indeed, to be found in this city men of every description, and of every religion on the face of the earth."

Source: *The Memoirs of the Emperor Jahangir*, translated from the Persian by Major David Price (London: Oriental Translation Committee, 1829), 1–3, 5–8, 15.

SOURCE 13.2 The Palace of an Ottoman Emperor

Begun in 1465 and finished in 1478, the Topkapi Palace in Constantinople was organized around a series of courtyards and served for centuries as the main residence of the Ottoman emperors. At the height of Ottoman power, around 4,000 family members, servants, eunuchs, officials, and soldiers of the imperial entourage resided in the complex.

Topkapi also served as a ceremonial space where important state occasions and religious celebrations took place. This late eighteenth-century painting depicts the second courtyard and the Felicity Gate, which guarded the entrance to the inner court, where no one aside from the ruler's relatives and closest advisers was granted access. Here, at the principal ceremonial site in the palace, emperors observed religious ceremonies, received foreign ambassadors, celebrated accessions to the throne, and at times of war handed the banner of the Prophet Muhammad to their military leaders. In this image, Sultan Selim III (r. 1789–1807) sits on his throne with his chief advisers around him. Ottoman officials and court dignitaries pay homage to their ruler. Participants are arrayed in hierarchical order according to their relative social or political importance, signaled by their clothing—note their increasingly tall and elaborate headgear—and their proximity to the sultan.

- What can this image tell us about the size and form of Ottoman imperial ceremonies? What types of people are missing from this image, and what can their absence tell us about Ottoman imperial life?
- Why might Ottoman rulers have chosen this space to stage important ceremonies?
- How might ceremonies like this one strengthen the sultan's rule?

A Reception at the Court of Selim III | **late 18th century**

Bridgeman Images

SOURCE 13.3 French State Building and Louis XIV ▶

Like their counterparts in the Middle East and Asia, a number of European states in the early modern era also pursued the twin projects of imperial expansion abroad and political integration at home. Perhaps the most well-known example of such European state-building efforts is that of France under the rule of Louis XIV (r. 1643–1715). Louis and other European monarchs, such as those in Spain and Russia, operated under a set of assumptions known as absolutism, which held that kings ruled by "divine right" and could legitimately claim sole and uncontested authority in their realms. Louis's famous dictum *"L'état, c'est moi"* ("I am the state") summed up the absolutist ideal.

Source 13.3A illustrates one way in which Louis attempted to realize this ideal. Written by Louis himself, this document focuses on the importance of "spectacle" and public display in solidifying the exalted role of the monarch. The "carousel" described here was an extravagant pageant held in Paris in June 1662. It featured various exotic animals, princes, and nobles arrayed in fantastic costumes representing distant lands, as well as many equestrian competitions. Unifying this disparate assembly was King Louis himself, dressed as a Roman emperor, while on the shields of the nobles was that grand symbol of the monarchy, the sun.

Source 13.3B is a depiction of Louis XIV's costume for a 1653 ballet entitled *La Nuit* (The Night) in which he played the rising sun. Louis represents Apollo, the god of light and the sun, a deity that viewers of the opera would have associated with the Roman emperor Augustus, who considered Apollo his patron. Note the elaborate costume, which includes a magnificent gold wig and sun imagery on his chest and footwear. The images of the sun on this costume were similar to those that Louis adopted as his personal symbol at the 1662 carousel.

- What posture does Louis take toward his subjects in Source 13.3A?
- What does the image of Louis as Apollo in Source 13.3B tell us about the nature of royal spectacle? How does this image shape how you envision the carousel described in Source 13.3A?
- How does Louis understand the role of spectacle in general and the carousel in particular?
- What does the choice of the sun as a royal symbol suggest about Louis's conception of his role in the French state and empire?

SOURCE 13.3A
LOUIS XIV | *Memoirs* | 1670

The more I moved away from all the excesses towards gentler pursuits, the more I had to preserve and cultivate carefully everything that connected me through affection to my peoples and especially people of noble carriage, without diminishing my authority or the respect that was owed me, to make them see in so doing that it was in no way by aversion to them nor an assumed strictness nor crudeness of spirit, but simply reason and duty that made me in other ways more reserved and exacting towards them. The society of pleasures [shared public activities], which gives to people of the Court [powerful aristocrats who interacted with Louis] a moral closeness with us, touches and charms them more than one can express. The common people, on the other hand, delight in the spectacle, by which in the end we always seek to please them. . . . By this, we hold their minds and their hearts, sometimes more tightly maybe than through rewards and charitable gestures. With regards to foreigners, in a state seen as otherwise flourishing and well-ordered, whatever is consumed in these expenses potentially viewed as superfluous, makes on them a very favorable impression of magnificence, power, riches, and greatness. . . .

The carousel . . . had only been envisaged as a simple celebration at the beginning, but we discussed it with passion, and it became a sufficiently large and magnificent spectacle, either by the number of movements, or by the novelty of the dress, or from the variety of emblems.

It was from this day that I started to adopt the emblem I have had ever since, and that you see so many places. I believed that, without stopping at something particular and lesser, it had to represent somehow the duties of a prince, and inspire me personally to fulfill them. We chose as the body, the sun, which is the noblest in all the rules of this art form, and which by its singular quality, by the brilliance surrounding it, by the light that it sends to the other stars making up a sort of Court for it, by the equal and fair sharing of this same light to all the climates of the world that it accomplishes, by the good that it does in all places, incessantly producing from all sides, life, joy, and action, by its endless motion in which it nonetheless seems ever peaceful, by this constant and unchanging path from which it never waivers or wanders, is certainly the brightest and most beautiful image of a great monarch.

Those who saw me rule easily enough without being obstructed or disturbed by anything, in the amount of attention that royalty demands, persuaded me to add the shape of the world, and as a soul [a motto in Latin] *nec pluribus impar* (not unequal to many things): by which they understood what pleasantly flattered a young king's ambition, that sufficing alone in so many things, I would undoubtedly suffice again to govern other empires, as would the sun to light up other worlds, if they were also exposed to its rays.

Source: *Mémoires de Louis XIV,* edited by Jean Longonon (Paris: Éditions Jules Tallandier, 1927), 122–24. Translated by Tonia E. Tinsley.

SOURCE 13.3B

Louis XIV in Costume | 1653

Apic/Getty Images

SOURCE 13.4 An Outsider's View of the Inca Empire

Pedro de Cieza de León (1520–1554), a Spanish chronicler of the Inca Empire of the early sixteenth century, came to the Americas as a boy at the age of thirteen. For the next seventeen years, Cieza took part as a soldier in a number of expeditions that established Spanish rule in various parts of South America. Along the way, he collected a great deal of information, especially about the Inca Empire, which he began to publish on his return to Spain in 1550. Despite a very limited education, Cieza wrote a series of works that have become a major source for historians about the workings of the Inca Empire and about the Spanish conquest of that land. The selection that follows focuses on the techniques that the Incas used to govern their huge empire.

- How would you describe Cieza's posture toward the Inca Empire? What in particular did he seem to appreciate about it?
- Based on this account, what difficulties did the Inca rulers face in governing their realm?
- What policies or practices did the Inca authorities follow in seeking to integrate their empire?

PEDRO DE CIEZA DE LEÓN | *Chronicles of the Incas* | ca. 1550

The Incas had the seat of their empire in the city of Cuzco, where the laws were given and the captains set out to make war. . . . As soon as one of these large provinces was conquered, ten or twelve thousand of the men and their wives . . . . were ordered to leave and remove themselves from it. These were transferred to another town or province of the same climate and nature as that which they left. . . .

One of the things most to be envied in these rulers is how well they knew to conquer such vast lands. . . .

[T]hey entered many lands without war, and the soldiers who accompanied the Inca were ordered to do no damage or harm, robbery or violence. If there was a shortage of food in the province, he ordered supplies brought in from other regions so that those newly won to his service would not find his rule and acquaintance irksome. . . .

In many others, where they entered by war and force of arms, they ordered that the crops and houses of the enemy be spared. . . . But in the end the Incas always came out victorious, and when they had vanquished the others, they did not do them further harm, but released those they had taken prisoner . . . and put them back in possession of their property and rule, exhorting them not to be foolish and try to compete with his royal majesty nor abandon his friendship, but to be his friends as their neighbors were. And saying this, he gave them a number of beautiful women and fine pieces of wool or gold. . . .

They never deprived the native chieftains of their rule. They were all ordered to worship the sun as God, but they were not prohibited from observing their own religions and customs. . . .

[T]hey [the Incas] had their representatives in the capitals of all the provinces. . . . They served as head of the provinces or regions, and from every so many leagues around the tributes were brought to one of these capitals. . . . [W]hen they came from the city of Cuzco to go over the accounts, or they were ordered to go to Cuzco to give an accounting . . . everything had to come out right. Few years went by in which an accounting of all these things was not made. . . .

When the Incas set out to visit their kingdom, it is told that they traveled with great pomp, riding in rich litters set upon smooth, long poles of the finest wood and adorned with gold and silver. . . .

So many people came to see his [the Inca's] passing that all the hills and slopes seemed covered with them, and all called down blessings upon him. . . .

[The Inca] . . . . stopped wherever he liked to inquire into the state of his kingdom; he willingly listened to those who came to him with complaints, righting wrongs and punishing those who had committed an injustice. . . .

[T]hese rulers, as the best measure, ordered and decreed, with severe punishment for failure to obey, that all the natives of their empire should know and understand the language of Cuzco, both they and their women. . . .

The Incas took such care to see that justice was meted out that nobody ventured to commit a felony or theft. . . .

[I]n each of the many provinces there were many storehouses filled with supplies and other needful things; thus, in times of war, wherever the armies went they drew upon the contents of these storehouses, without ever touching the supplies of their confederates or laying a finger on what they had in their settlements. And when there was no war, all this stock of supplies and food was divided up among the poor and the widows. . . . If there came a lean year, the storehouses were opened and the provinces were lent what they needed in the way of supplies; then, in a year of abundance, they paid back all they had received.

Source: *The Incas of Pedro de Cieza de León,* translated by Harriet de Onis (Norman: University of Oklahoma Press, 1959), 56–57, 158–60, 165–73, 177–78.

SOURCE 13.5 The Temple of Heaven: Beijing, China ►

The largest sacred site in the world in the fifteenth century lay in China. Known as the Temple of Heaven, it was constructed early in the century in the Ming dynasty capital of Beijing by the ambitious emperor Yongle (r. 1402–1424), who likewise ordered the building of the Forbidden City, a magnificent imperial residence.

Set in a forest of more than 650 acres, the Temple of Heaven was in Chinese thinking the primary place where Heaven and Earth met. From their residence in the Forbidden City, Chinese emperors of the Ming and Qing dynasties led a procession of thousands twice a year to this sacred site, where they offered sacrifices, implored the gods for a good harvest, and performed those rituals that maintained the cosmic balance. These sacred ceremonies, which commoners were barred even from watching, demonstrated the emperor's respect for the age-old source of his imperial authority, the Mandate of Heaven, from which Chinese emperors derived their legitimate right to rule. As the emperor bowed to Heaven, he was modeling in good Confucian fashion the respect required of all subordinates to their social superiors and especially to the emperor himself.

The temple complex and its various buildings were laced with ancient symbolism. The southern part of the wall that enclosed the complex was square, symbolizing the Earth, while the northern wall was rounded or semi-circular, suggesting Heaven in Daoist thinking. Major buildings were likewise built in the round while being situated within a square enclosure, also symbolizing the intersection of Heaven and Earth. The most prominent building was the Hall of Prayer for Good Harvest (Source 13.5), constructed by 1420. There the emperor prayed and conducted rituals to ensure a successful agricultural season, on which the country's well-being and his own legitimacy depended. The emperor and others approached the hall from the south on a gradually ascending 360-meter walkway symbolizing progression from Earth to Heaven. The walkway divides into three parallel paths: the center one for the gods; the left for the emperor; and the right for the empress and court officials.

- Which of these symbolic features can you identify in Source 13.5?
- What impressions or understandings might those who observed the ceremonies or learned about them take away from the experience?
- What does this ceremonial space have in common with that of the Felicity Gate in Topkapi Palace (Source 13.2)? What differentiates the two?

The Hall of Prayer for Good Harvest | ca. 1420

Dorling Kindersley/UIG/Bridgeman Images

DOING HISTORY

1. **Making Comparisons** To what extent did these five early modern states face similar problems and devise similar solutions? How did they differ? In particular, how did the rulers of these states deal with subordinates?
2. **Assessing Spectacle** In what different ways was spectacle, royal splendor, or public display evident in the sources? How would you define the purpose of such display? How effective has spectacle been in consolidating state authority?
3. **Distinguishing Power and Authority** Some scholars have made a distinction between "power," the ability of a state to coerce its subjects into some required behavior, and "authority," the ability of a state to persuade its subjects to do its bidding voluntarily by convincing them that it is proper, right, or natural to do so. What examples of power and authority can you find in these sources? How were power and authority related?
4. **Comparing Past and Present** Early modern states differed in many ways from states today. How would you define those differences? Consider the personal role of the ruler, the use of violence, the means of establishing authority, and the extent to which the state could shape the lives of its citizens.

Early Modern Rulers

The following two voices provide recent descriptions of how early modern rulers defined and displayed their authority and power. In Voice 13.1, Charles Parker compares Emperor Kangxi of China and Louis XIV of France and finds them "cut from the same cloth." In Voice 13.2, John Darwin examines the many cultural influences that shaped the royal government of the Mughal emperor Akbar.

- According to Parker, what attributes of a powerful ruler did Kangxi and Louis XIV share?
- According to Darwin, what cultural and political traditions did Akbar draw upon to rule over the Mughal Empire? Which did he reject, abandon, or modify?
- **Integrating Primary and Secondary Sources** What elements of kingship described by Parker and Darwin are evident in the primary sources preceding this feature? To what extent are these elements specific to certain rulers or states?

VOICE 13.1

Charles Parker on Emperor Kangxi of China and Louis XIV of France | 2010

For Europe's most powerful monarch [Louis XIV], the Qing dynasty under Kangxi emperor (r. 1661–1722) represented an ideal political order. The emperor wielded absolute power and enjoyed divine blessing; he employed an army of civil servants to govern his dominions; he possessed authority over a vast domain stretching from the eastern coastline to Outer Mongolia and Tibet; and he resided in a magnificent palace that exuded majestic order and power. In many respects Louis's reign (1643–1715) also embodied these characteristics, though on a less grand scale. Casting himself in the image of Apollo (the Greek god of light and sun), Louis promoted himself as the Sun King and he professed to rule by divine right; he dominated Europe and pushed France's borders to the farthest point; and he too presided over an elaborate court life at Versailles that reflected his prestige and authority. The Kangxi emperor and the Sun King, on opposite ends of Eurasia, were cut from the same cloth.

Source: Charles H. Parker, *Global Interactions in the Early Modern Age, 1400–1800* (Cambridge: Cambridge University Press, 2010), 13–14.

VOICE 13.2

John Darwin on Emperor Akbar's Public Image | 2008

Akbar projected himself not as a Muslim warrior-king, but as the absolute monarch of a diverse subject population. His official genealogy laid claim to descent from both Tamerlane and Genghis Khan, and thus to their legacy as "world conquerors." Mughal court ritual—especially Akbar's daily appearance on an elevated platform—emphasized the *padshah*'s [an elevated Persian royal title referring to the monarch] supreme authority over even the greatest and wealthiest of his subjects. The court was the centre of lavish literary patronage. It promoted the study of the Muslim "rational sciences" and the writing of poetry, the main literary medium of the Islamic world. But Mughal court culture looked to Persian or Central Asian models for its art and literature. Persian was the language of intellectual life as well as of government. The life and landscape of Iran (not that of India) inspired the Mughal poets, who evoked a world far away "from the polluting influences of the subject peoples." . . . Akbar's regime was cosmopolitan and eclectic, a tribute to Central Asia's influence as a great cultural entrepôt. It is even possible that his abortive attempt to impose a more centralized government in the 1570s and '80s (which led to the great revolt of 1580–82) was remotely inspired by the Chinese system of meritocratic bureaucracy. . . . Famously, Akbar rejected the classic Islamic distinction between the Muslim faithful (the *umma*) and the unbelievers. He abolished the *jizya* (poll-tax on non-Muslims) in 1579, and flirted with propagating a new religious synthesis of Islam and Hinduism.

Source: John Darwin, *After Tamerlane: The Rise and Fall of Global Empires 1400–2000* (London: Bloomsbury, 2008), 85–86.

CHAPTER 14

Economic Transformations

Commerce and Consequence

1450–1750

CONNECTING PAST AND PRESENT

"In the bowels of the Cape Coast Castle in Ghana, there's a dungeon built beneath the church chapel, where kidnapped and enslaved Africans could hear the devils above worshipping their god, while those below languished in misery until the slave ships arrived. I stood there, in that place, and inhaled deeply, swallowing mouthfuls of last breaths, and I almost choked. I could taste every bead of sweat and pain and blood and loss. I ran my fingers across the jagged walls and could feel their scarred flesh and bowed spines."[1] Such were the reflections of a young African American man, one of hundreds who journeyed to Ghana in 2019 as a part of the Year of Return, marking the 400th anniversary of the arrival in Virginia of the first enslaved Africans.

This visitor's emotional encounter with the legacy of the transatlantic slave system reminds us of the enormous significance of this commerce in human beings for the early modern world and of its continuing resonance even in the twenty-first century. Commerce in enslaved people, however, was only one component of those international networks of exchange that shaped human interactions during the centuries between 1450 and 1750. Europeans now smashed their way into the ancient spice trade of the Indian Ocean, developing new relationships with Asian societies. Silver, obtained from mines in Spanish America, enriched Western Europe, even as much of it made its way to China, where it allowed Europeans to participate more fully in the rich commerce of East Asia. Furs from North America and

« **The Atlantic Slave Trade** This eighteenth-century French engraving shows the sale of enslaved Africans at Gorée, a major slave-trading port in what is now Dakar in Senegal. A European merchant and an African authority figure negotiate the arrangement, while the shackled victims wait for their fate to be decided.

Siberia found a ready market in Europe and China, while the hunting and trapping of those fur-bearing animals transformed both natural environments and human societies. And despite their growing prominence in long-distance exchange, Europeans were far from the only actors in early modern commerce. Southeast Asians, Chinese, Indians, Armenians, Arabs, Africans, and Native Americans likewise played major roles in the making of the world economy during the early modern era.

Thus commerce joined empire as the twin creators of interlocking global networks during these centuries. Together they gave rise to new relationships, disrupted old patterns, brought distant peoples into contact with one another, enriched some, and impoverished or enslaved others. What was gained and what was lost in the transformations born of global commerce have been the subject of great controversy ever since.

SEEKING THE MAIN POINT

In what different ways did global commerce transform human societies and the lives of individuals during the early modern era?

Europeans and Asian Commerce

European empires in the Western Hemisphere grew out of an accident—Columbus's unknowing encounter with the Americas. In Asia, it was a very different story. The voyage (1497–1499) of the Portuguese mariner Vasco da Gama, in which Europeans sailed to India for the first time, was certainly no accident. It was the outcome of a deliberate, systematic, century-long Portuguese effort to explore a sea route to the East, by creeping slowly down the West African coast, around the tip of South Africa, up the East African coast, and finally across the Indian Ocean to India. There Europeans encountered an ancient and rich network of commerce that stretched from East Africa to China. They were certainly aware of the wealth of that commercial network, but largely ignorant of its workings.

■ Identifying Motives
What drove European involvement in the world of Asian commerce?

The most immediate motivation for this massive effort was the desire for tropical spices—cinnamon, nutmeg, mace, cloves, and, above all, pepper—which were widely used as condiments, preservatives, medicines, and aphrodisiacs. A fifteenth-century English book declared: "Pepper [from Java] is black and has a good smack, And every man doth buy it."[2] Other products of the East, such as Chinese silk, Indian cottons, rhubarb for medicinal purposes, emeralds, rubies, and sapphires, were also in great demand.

Underlying this growing interest in Asia was the more general recovery of European civilization following the disaster of the Black Death in the early fourteenth century. During the fifteenth century, Europe's population was growing again, and its national monarchies—in Spain, Portugal, England, and France—were learning how to tax their subjects more effectively and to build substantial military forces equipped with gunpowder weapons. Its cities were growing too. Some of them—in England, the Netherlands, and northern Italy, for example—were becoming centers of international commerce, giving birth to economies based on market exchange, private ownership, and the accumulation of capital for further investment.

For many centuries, Eastern goods had trickled into the Mediterranean through the Middle East from the Indian Ocean commercial network. From the viewpoint of an increasingly dynamic Europe, several major problems accompanied this pattern

Landmarks for Chapter 14

1450 | 1500 | 1550 | 1600 | 1650 | 1700 | 1750

EUROPEAN AND ASIAN COMMERCE

- **1498** Portuguese explorer Vasco da Gama reaches India
- **1505** Portuguese assault on Mombasa in East Africa
- **ca. 1565–ca. 1665** Spanish takeover of Philippine Islands
- **1601–1602** British and Dutch East India companies established
- **1635** Japanese seclusion from the West begins; persecution of Christians

SILVER TRADE

- **ca. 1550** Silver discoveries in Bolivia and Japan
- **1570s** Silver shipments from Mexico to Manila begin
- **1570s** Chinese require tax payment in silver
- **ca. 1750** Decline of Spain as an imperial power

FUR TRADE

- **1600–1700** Growing European demand for furs; Little Ice Age at its peak
- **1600–1700** Peak of Russian fur trade in Siberia
- **1630s–1640s** Hurons decimated by European diseases
- **1664–1763** British-French rivalry for North America

ATLANTIC SLAVE TRADE

- **1440s** First European export of enslaved persons from West Africa
- **1526** King Afonso of Kongo protests impact of slave trade
- **1605–1694** Palmares: community of the formerly enslaved in Brazil
- **1700–1850** Peak of transatlantic slave system
- **1700–1800** Rise of Dahomey kingdom, based on slave trade

of trade. First, of course, the source of supply for these much-desired goods lay solidly in Muslim hands, most immediately in Egypt. The Italian commercial city of Venice largely monopolized the European trade in Eastern goods, annually sending convoys of ships to Alexandria in Egypt. Venetians resented the Muslim monopoly on Indian Ocean trade, and other European powers disliked relying on Venice as well as on Muslims. Circumventing these monopolies provided both religious and political motivations for the Portuguese to attempt a sea route to India that bypassed both Venetian and Muslim intermediaries. In addition, many Europeans of the time were persuaded that a mysterious Christian monarch, known as Prester John, ruled somewhere in Asia or Africa. Joining with his mythical kingdom to continue the Crusades and combat a common Islamic enemy was likewise a goal of the Portuguese voyages.

A further problem for Europeans lay in paying for Eastern goods. Few products of an economically less developed Europe were attractive in Eastern markets. Thus Europeans were required to pay cash—gold or silver—for Asian spices or textiles. This persistent trade deficit contributed much to the intense desire for precious metals that attracted early modern European explorers, traders, and conquerors. Portuguese voyages along the West African coast, for example, were seeking direct access to African goldfields. The enormously rich silver deposits of Mexico and Bolivia provided at least a temporary solution to this persistent European problem.

First the Portuguese and then the Spanish, French, Dutch, and British found their way into the ancient Asian world of Indian Ocean commerce (see Map 14.1). How they behaved in that world and what they created there differed considerably among the various European countries, but collectively they contributed much to the new regime of globalized trade.

A Portuguese Empire of Commerce

The **Indian Ocean commercial network** into which Vasco da Gama and his Portuguese successors sailed was a world away from anything they had known. It was vast, both in geographic extent and in the diversity of those who participated in it. East Africans, Arabs, Persians, Indians, Malays, Chinese, and others traded freely. Most of them were Muslims, though hailing from many separate communities, but Hindus, Buddhists, Christians, Jews, and Chinese likewise had a role in this commercial network. Had the Portuguese sought simply to participate in peaceful trading, they certainly could have done so, but it was quickly apparent that European trade goods were crude and unattractive in Asian markets and that Europeans would be unable to compete effectively. Moreover, the Portuguese soon learned that most Indian Ocean merchant ships were not heavily armed and certainly lacked the onboard cannons that Portuguese ships carried. Since the withdrawal of the Chinese fleet from the Indian Ocean early in the fifteenth century, no major power was in a position to dominate the sea lanes, and many smaller-scale merchants generally traded openly, although piracy was sometimes a problem.

Given these conditions, the Portuguese saw an opening, for their ships could outgun and outmaneuver competing naval forces, while their onboard cannons

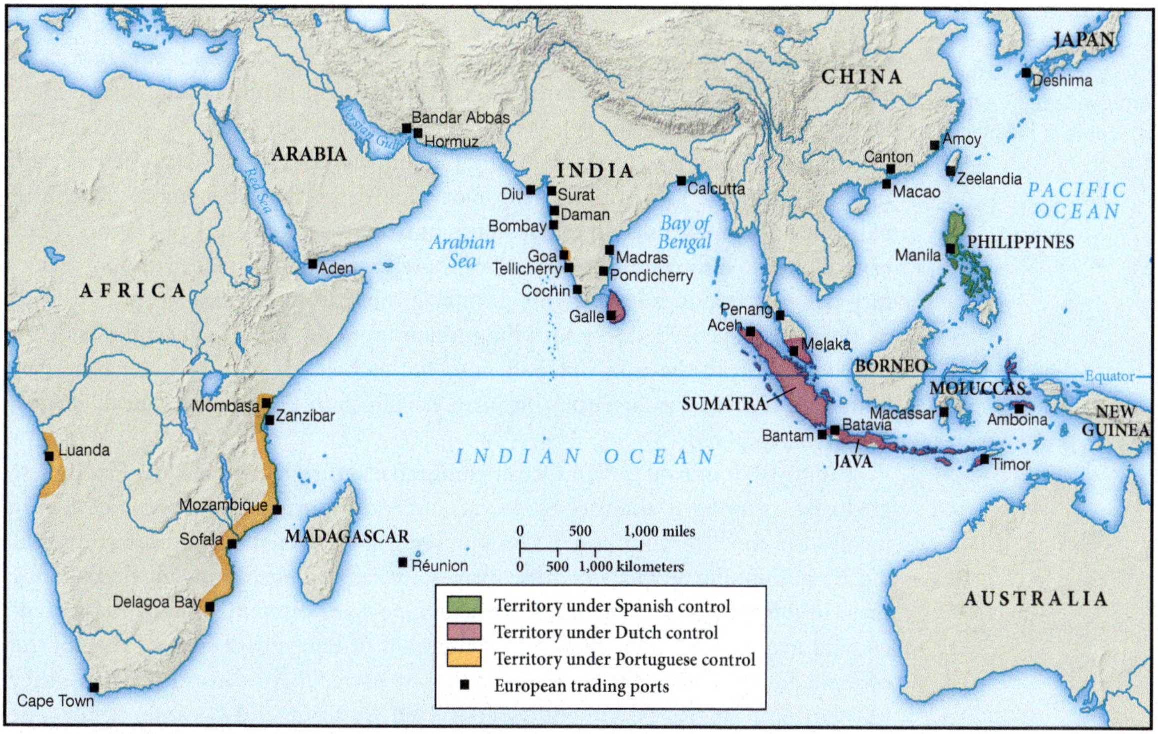

Map 14.1 Europeans in Asia in the Early Modern Era
The early modern era witnessed only very limited territorial control by Europeans in Asia. Trade, rather than empire, was the chief concern of the Western newcomers, who were not, in any event, a serious military threat to major Asian states.

could devastate coastal fortifications. Although their overall economy lagged behind that of Asian producers, this military advantage enabled the Portuguese to quickly establish fortified bases at several key locations within the Indian Ocean world—Mombasa in East Africa, Hormuz at the entrance to the Persian Gulf, Goa on the west coast of India, Melaka in Southeast Asia, and Macao on the south coast of China. With the exception of Macao, which had been obtained through bribery and negotiations with Chinese authorities, these Portuguese bases were obtained forcibly against small and weak states. In Mombasa, for example, the commander of a Portuguese fleet responded to local resistance in 1505 by burning and sacking the city, killing some 1,500 people, and seizing large quantities of cotton and silk textiles and carpets. The king of Mombasa wrote a warning to a neighboring city:

> This is to inform you that a great lord has passed through the town, burning it and laying it waste. He came to the town in such strength and was of such a cruelty that he spared neither man nor woman, or old nor young—nay, not even the smallest child. . . . Nor can I ascertain nor estimate what wealth they have taken from the town.[3]

Assessing Goals To what extent did the Portuguese realize their own goals in the Indian Ocean?

What the Portuguese created in the Indian Ocean is commonly known as a **trading post empire**, for they aimed to control commerce, not large territories or populations, and to do so by force of arms rather than by economic competition. Seeking to monopolize the spice trade, the Portuguese king grandly titled himself "Lord of the Conquest, Navigation, and Commerce of Ethiopia, Arabia, Persia, and India." Portuguese authorities in the East tried to require all merchant vessels to purchase a *cartaz*, or pass, and to pay duties of 6 to 10 percent on their cargoes. They partially blocked the traditional Red Sea route to the Mediterranean and for a century or so monopolized the highly profitable route around Africa to Europe. Even so, they never succeeded in controlling much more than half of the spice trade to Europe, and from the mid-sixteenth into the eighteenth century older routes by both land and sea through the Ottoman Empire into the Mediterranean revived and even prospered.

Failing to dominate Indian Ocean commerce as they had hoped, the Portuguese gradually assimilated themselves to its ancient patterns. They became heavily involved in the "carrying trade," transporting Asian goods to Asian ports, thus selling their shipping services because they were largely unable to sell their goods. Even in their major settlements, the Portuguese were outnumbered by Asian traders, and many married Asian women. Hundreds of Portuguese escaped the control of their government altogether and settled in Asian or African ports, where they learned local languages, sometimes converted to Islam, and became simply one more group in the diverse trading culture of the East.

By 1600, the Portuguese trading post empire was in steep decline. This small European country was overextended, and rising Asian states such as Japan, Burma, Mughal India, Persia, and the sultanate of Oman actively resisted Portuguese commercial

The Spice Trade For thousands of years, spices were a major trade item in the Indian Ocean commercial network, as this fifteenth-century French depiction of the gathering of pepper in southern India illustrates. In the early modern era, Europeans gained direct access to this ancient network for the first time. (© Archives Charmet/Bridgeman Images)

control. Unwilling to accept a dominant Portuguese role in the Indian Ocean, other European countries also gradually contested Portugal's efforts to monopolize the rich spice trade to Europe.

Spain and the Philippines

The Spanish were the first to challenge Portugal's position as they established themselves on what became the Philippine Islands, named after the Spanish king Philip II. There they found an archipelago of islands, thousands of them, occupied by culturally diverse peoples and organized in small and highly competitive chiefdoms. One of the local chiefs later told the Spanish: "There is no king and no sole authority in this land; but everyone holds his own view and opinion, and does as he prefers."[4] Some of these chiefdoms were involved in tribute trade with China, and a small number of Chinese settlers lived in the port towns. Nonetheless, the region was of little interest to the governments of China and Japan, the major powers in the area.

These conditions—proximity to China and the Spice Islands, small and militarily weak societies, the absence of competing claims—encouraged the Spanish to establish outright colonial rule on the islands of the **Philippines**, rather than to imitate a Portuguese-style trading post empire. Accomplished largely from Spanish Mexico, conquest and colonization involved small-scale military operations, gunpowder weapons, local alliances, gifts and favors to chiefs, and the pageantry of Catholic ritual, all of which contributed to a relatively easy and often bloodless Spanish takeover of the islands in the century or so after 1565. Accompanying Spanish rule was a major missionary effort that turned Filipino society into the only major outpost of Christianity in Asia. That effort also opened up a new front in the long encounter of Christendom and Islam, for on the southern island of Mindanao, Islam was gaining strength and provided an ideology of resistance to Spanish encroachment for 300 years. Indeed, Mindanao remains a contested part of the Philippines into the twenty-first century.

Beyond the missionary enterprise, other features of Spanish colonial practice in the Americas found expression in the Philippines. People living in scattered settlements were persuaded or forced to relocate into more concentrated Christian communities. Tribute, taxes, and unpaid labor became part of ordinary life. Large landed estates emerged, owned by Spanish settlers, Catholic religious orders, or prominent Filipinos. Women who had played major roles as ritual specialists, healers, and midwives were now displaced by male Spanish priests, and the ceremonial instruments of these women were deliberately defiled and disgraced. Short-lived revolts and flight to interior mountains were among the Filipino responses to colonial oppression.

CORE IDEA

Comparing Asian Colonies
How did the Portuguese, Spanish, Dutch, and British initiatives in Asia differ from one another?

Yet others fled to **Manila**, the new capital of the colonial Philippines. By 1600, it had become a flourishing and culturally diverse city of more than 40,000 inhabitants and was home to many Spanish settlers and officials and growing numbers of Filipino migrants. Its rising prosperity also attracted some 3,000 Japanese and more than 20,000 Chinese. Serving as traders, artisans, and sailors, the Chinese in particular became an essential element in the Spanish colony's growing economic relationship with China; however, their economic prominence and their resistance to conversion earned them Spanish hostility and clearly discriminatory treatment. Periodic Chinese revolts, followed by expulsions and massacres, were the result. On one occasion in 1603, the Spanish killed about 20,000 people, nearly the entire Chinese population of the island.

The East India Companies

Far more important than the Spanish as European competitors for the spice trade were the Dutch and English, both of whom entered Indian Ocean commerce in the early seventeenth century. Together these rising North European powers quickly overtook and displaced the Portuguese, often by force, even as they competed vigorously with each other as well. During the sixteenth century, the Dutch had become a highly commercialized and urbanized society, and their business skills and maritime shipping operations were the envy of Europe. Around 1600, both the British and the Dutch, unlike the Portuguese, organized their Indian Ocean ventures through private companies that were able to raise money and share risks among a substantial number of merchant investors. Both the **British East India Company** and the **Dutch East India Company** received charters from their respective governments granting them trading monopolies and the power to make war and to govern conquered peoples. Thus they established their own parallel and competing trading post empires, with the Dutch focused on the islands of Indonesia and the English on India. A similar French company also established a presence in the Indian Ocean basin, beginning in 1664.

A European View of Asian Commerce The various East India companies (British, French, and Dutch) represented the major vehicle for European commerce in Asia during the early modern era. This wall painting, dating from 1778 and titled *The East Offering Its Riches to Britannia*, hung in the main offices of the British East India Company. (© British Library Board. All Rights Reserved/Bridgeman Images)

Operating in a region of fragmented and weak political authority, the Dutch acted to control not only the shipping of cloves, cinnamon, nutmeg, and mace but also their production. With much bloodshed, the Dutch seized control of a number of small spice-producing islands, forcing their people to sell only to the Dutch and destroying the crops of those who refused. On the Banda Islands, famous for their nutmeg, the Dutch killed, enslaved, or left to starve virtually the entire population of some 15,000 people and then replaced them with Dutch planters, using a slave labor force, mostly from other parts of Asia, to produce the nutmeg crop. One Indonesian sultan asked a Dutch commander, "Do you believe that God has preserved for your trade alone islands which lie so far from your homeland?"[5] Apparently the Dutch did. And for a time in the seventeenth century, they were able to monopolize the trade in nutmeg, mace, and cloves and to sell these spices in Europe and India at fourteen to seventeen times the price they paid in Indonesia.[6] While Dutch profits soared, the local economy of the Spice Islands was shattered and their people were impoverished.

The British East India Company operated differently from its Dutch counterpart. Less well financed and less commercially sophisticated, the British were largely excluded from the rich Spice Islands by the Dutch monopoly. Thus they fell back on India, where they established three major trading settlements during the seventeenth century: Bombay (now Mumbai), on India's west coast, and Calcutta and Madras, on the east coast. Although British naval forces soon gained control of the Arabian Sea and the Persian Gulf, largely replacing the Portuguese, on land they were no match for the powerful Mughal Empire, which ruled most of the Indian subcontinent.

■ Making Comparisons
What was similar and what was different in how the Dutch and British behaved in the Indian Ocean world?

Therefore, the British were unable to practice "trade by warfare," as the Dutch did in Indonesia.[7] Rather, they secured their trading bases with the permission of Mughal authorities or local rulers, with substantial payments and bribes as the price of admission to the Indian market. When some independent English traders plundered a Mughal ship in 1636, local authorities detained British East India Company officials for two months and forced them to pay a whopping fine. Although pepper and other spices remained important in British trade, British merchants came to focus much more heavily on Indian cotton textiles, which were becoming widely popular in England and its American colonies. Hundreds of villages in the interior of southern India became specialized producers for this British market.

Like the Portuguese before them, both the Dutch and English became heavily involved in trade within Asia. The profits from this "carrying trade" enabled them to purchase Asian goods without paying for them in gold or silver from Europe. Dutch and English traders also began to deal in bulk goods for a mass market—pepper, textiles, and later, tea and coffee—rather than just luxury goods for an elite market. In the second half of the eighteenth century, both the Dutch and British trading post empires slowly evolved into a more conventional form of colonial domination, in which the British came to rule India and the Dutch controlled Indonesia.

Asians and Asian Commerce

The European presence was far less significant in Asia than it was in the Americas or Africa during these centuries. European political control was limited to the Philippines, parts of Java, and a few of the Spice Islands. The small Southeast Asian state of Siam was able to expel the French in 1688, outraged by their aggressive religious efforts at conversion and their plotting to extend French influence. To the great powers of Asia—Mughal India, China, and Japan—Europeans represented no real military threat and played minor roles in their large and prosperous economies. Japan provides a fascinating case study in the ability of major Asian powers to control the European intruders.

■ Defining Roles
What role did Asian political authorities and merchants play in Indian Ocean commerce in the face of European intrusion?

When Portuguese traders and missionaries first arrived in that island nation in the mid-sixteenth century, soon followed by Spanish, Dutch, and English merchants, Japan was plagued by endemic conflict among numerous feudal lords, known as *daimyo*, each with his own cadre of *samurai* warriors. In these circumstances, the European newcomers found a hospitable welcome; their military technology, shipbuilding skills, geographic knowledge, commercial opportunities, and even religious ideas proved useful or attractive to various elements in Japan's fractious and competitive society. The second half of the sixteenth century, for example, witnessed the growth of a substantial Christian movement, with some 300,000 converts and a Japanese-led church organization.

By the early seventeenth century, however, a series of remarkable military figures had unified Japan politically, under the leadership of a supreme military commander known as the *shogun*, who hailed from the Tokugawa clan. With the end of Japan's civil wars, successive shoguns came to view Europeans as a threat to the country's newly established unity rather than as an opportunity. They therefore expelled Christian missionaries and violently suppressed the practice of Christianity. This policy included the execution, often under torture, of some sixty-two missionaries and thousands of Japanese converts. Shogunate authorities also forbade Japanese from traveling abroad and banned most European traders altogether, permitting only the Dutch, who appeared less interested in spreading Christianity, to trade at a single site. Thus, for two centuries (1650–1850), Japanese authorities of the Tokugawa shogunate largely closed their country off from the emerging world of European commerce, although they maintained their trading ties to China, Korea, and Southeast Asia.

In the early seventeenth century, a large number of Japanese traders began to operate in Southeast Asia, where they behaved much like the newly arriving Europeans, frequently using force in support of their commercial interests. But unlike European states, the Japanese government of the Tokugawa shogunate explicitly disavowed any responsibility for or connection with these Japanese merchants. In one of many letters to rulers of Southeast Asian states, the Tokugawa shogun wrote to officials in Cambodia in 1610:

> Merchants from my country [Japan] go to several places in your country [Cambodia] as well as Cochinchina and Champa [Vietnam]. There they become cruel and ferocious. . . . These men cause terrible damage. . . . They commit crimes and cause suffering. . . . Their offenses are extremely serious. Please punish them immediately according to the laws of your country. It is not necessary to have any reservations in this regard.[8]

Thus Japanese merchants lacked the kind of support from their government that European merchants consistently received, but they did not refrain from trading in Southeast Asia.

Nor did other Asian merchants disappear from the Indian Ocean, despite European naval dominance. Arab, Indian, Chinese, Javanese, Malay, Vietnamese, and other traders benefited from the upsurge in seaborne commerce. A long-term movement of Chinese merchants into Southeast Asian port cities continued in the early modern era, enabling the Chinese to dominate the growing spice trade between that region and China. Southeast Asian merchants, many of them women, continued a long tradition of involvement in international trade. Malay proverbs from the sixteenth century, for example, encouraged "teaching daughters how to calculate and make a profit."[9] Overland trade within Asia remained wholly in Asian hands and grew considerably. Based in New Julfa near the capital of the Safavid Empire, Christian merchants originally from Armenia were particularly active in the commerce linking Europe, the Middle East, Central Asia, and India, with a few traveling as far as the Philippines and Mexico in pursuit of trading opportunities. Tens of thousands of Indian merchants and moneylenders, mostly Hindus representing sophisticated family firms, lived throughout Central Asia, Persia, and Russia, thus connecting this vast region to markets in India. These international Asian commercial networks, equivalent in their commercial sophistication to those of Europe, continued to operate successfully even as Europeans militarized the seaborne commerce of the Indian Ocean.

Within India, large and wealthy family firms, such as the one headed by Virji Vora during the seventeenth century, were able to monopolize the buying and selling of particular products, such as pepper or coral, and thus dictate terms and prices to the European trading companies. "He knoweth that wee must sell," complained one English trader about Vora, "and so beats us downe till we come to his owne rates." Furthermore, Vora was often the only source of loans for the cash-strapped Europeans, forcing them to pay interest rates as high as 12 to 18 percent annually. Despite their resentments, Europeans had little choice, because "none but Virji Vora hath moneye to lend or will lend."[10]

Silver and Global Commerce

Even more than the spice trade of Eurasia, it was the silver trade that gave birth to a genuinely global network of exchange (see Map 14.2). As one historian put it, silver "went round the world and made the world go round."[11] The mid-sixteenth-century discovery of enormously rich silver deposits in Bolivia, and simultaneously in Japan, suddenly provided a vastly increased supply of that precious metal. Spanish America alone produced perhaps 85 percent of the world's silver during the early modern era. Spain's sole Asian colony, the Philippines, provided a critical link in this emerging network of global commerce. Manila, the colonial capital of the Philippines, was the destination of annual Spanish shipments of silver, which were drawn from the rich mines of Bolivia, transported initially to Acapulco in Mexico, and from there shipped across the Pacific to the Philippines. This trade was the first direct and sustained link between the Americas and Asia, and it initiated a web of trans-Pacific commerce that grew steadily over the centuries.

Map 14.2 The Global Silver Trade
Silver was one of the first major commodities to be exchanged on a genuinely global scale.

CORE IDEA

■ Assessing Significance
What was the significance of the silver trade in the early modern era of world history?

At the heart of that Pacific web, and of early modern global commerce generally, was China's huge economy, especially its growing demand for silver. In the 1570s, Chinese authorities consolidated a variety of tax levies into a single tax, which its huge population was now required to pay in silver. This sudden new demand for the white metal caused its value to skyrocket. It meant that foreigners with silver could now purchase far more of China's silks and porcelains than before.

This demand set silver in motion around the world, with the bulk of the world's silver supply winding up in China and much of the rest elsewhere in Asia. The routes by which this **"silver drain"** operated were numerous. Chinese, Portuguese, and Dutch traders flocked to Manila to sell Chinese goods in exchange for silver. European ships carried Japanese silver to China. Much of the silver shipped across the Atlantic to Spain was spent in Europe generally and then used to pay for the Asian goods that the French, British, and Dutch so greatly desired. Silver paid for some enslaved Africans and for spices in Southeast Asia. The standard Spanish silver coin, known as a **piece of eight**, was used by merchants in North America, Europe, India, Russia, and West Africa as a medium of exchange. By 1600, it circulated widely in southern China. A Portuguese merchant in 1621 noted that silver "wanders throughout all the world . . . before flocking to China, where it remains as if at its natural center."[12]

A Silver Mine of Potosí This colonial-era painting shows the enormously rich silver mines of Potosí, then a major global source of the precious metal and the largest city in the Americas. Brutally hard work and poisonous exposure to the mercury used in the refining process led to the deaths of many thousands of workers, even as the silver transformed the world economy in the early modern era. (Granger, NYC—All rights reserved)

In its global journeys, silver transformed much that it touched. At the world's largest silver mine in what is now Bolivia, the city of **Potosí** arose from a barren landscape high in the Andes, ten-weeks' journey by mule from Lima. "New people arrive by the hour, attracted by the smell of silver," commented a Spanish observer in the 1570s.[13] With 160,000 people, Potosí became the largest city in the Americas and equivalent in size to London, Amsterdam, or Seville. Its wealthy European elite lived in luxury, with all the goods of Europe and Asia at their disposal. Meanwhile, the city's Native American miners worked in conditions so horrendous that some families held funeral services for men drafted to work in the mines. A Spanish priest observed, "Once inside they spend the whole week in there without emerging. . . . If 20 healthy Indians enter on Monday, half may emerge crippled on Saturday."[14] The environment too suffered, as highly intensive mining techniques caused severe deforestation, soil erosion, and flooding.

But the silver-fueled economy of Potosí also offered opportunity, not least to women. Spanish women might rent out buildings they owned for commercial purposes or send their often enslaved servants into the streets as small-scale traders, earning a few pesos for the household. Those less well-to-do often ran stores, pawnshops, bakeries, and taverns. Indian and *mestiza* women likewise opened businesses that provided the city with beverages, food, clothing, and credit.

In Spain itself, which was the initial destination for much of Latin America's silver, the precious metal vastly enriched the Crown, making Spain the envy of its European rivals during the sixteenth century. Spanish rulers could now pursue military and political ambitions in both Europe and the Americas far beyond the country's own resource base. "New World mines," concluded several prominent historians, "supported the Spanish empire."[15] Nonetheless, this vast infusion of wealth did not fundamentally transform the Spanish economy, because it generated inflation of prices more than real economic growth. A rigid economy laced with monopolies and regulations, an aristocratic class that preferred leisure to enterprise, and a crusading insistence on religious uniformity all prevented the Spanish from using their silver windfall in a productive fashion. When the value of silver dropped in the early seventeenth century, Spain lost its earlier position as the dominant Western European power. More generally, the flood of American silver that circulated in Europe drove prices higher, further impoverished many, stimulated uprisings across the continent, and, together with the Little Ice Age of global cooling, contributed to what historians sometimes call a General Crisis of upheaval and instability in the seventeenth century. (See "The Great Dying and the Little Ice Age" in Chapter 13.)

Japan, another major source of silver production in the sixteenth century, did better. Its military rulers, the Tokugawa shoguns, used silver-generated profits to defeat hundreds of rival feudal lords and unify the country. Unlike their Spanish counterparts, the shoguns allied with the country's vigorous domestic merchant class to develop a market-based economy and to invest heavily in agricultural and industrial enterprises. Japanese state and local authorities alike acted vigorously to protect and renew Japan's dwindling forests, while millions of families in the eighteenth century took steps to have fewer children by practicing late marriages, contraception, abortion, and infanticide. The outcome was the dramatic slowing of Japan's population growth, the easing of an impending ecological crisis, and a flourishing, highly commercialized economy. These were the foundations for Japan's remarkable nineteenth-century Industrial Revolution.

In China, silver deepened the already substantial commercialization of the country's economy. To obtain the silver needed to pay their taxes, more and more people had to sell something—either their labor or their products. Communities that devoted themselves to growing mulberry trees, on which silkworms fed, had to buy their rice from other regions. Thus the Chinese economy became more regionally specialized. Particularly in southern China, this surging economic growth resulted in the loss of about half the area's forest cover as more and more land was devoted to cash crops. No Japanese-style conservation program emerged to address this growing problem. An eighteenth-century Chinese poet, Wang Dayue, gave voice to the fears that this ecological transformation generated, writing that "the hills resembled heads now shaven clean of hair."[16]

China's role in the silver trade is a useful reminder of Asian centrality in the world economy of the early modern era. Its large and prosperous population, increasingly operating within a silver-based economy, fueled global commerce, vastly increasing the quantity of goods exchanged and the geographic range of world trade. Despite their obvious physical presence in the Americas, Africa, and Asia, economically speaking Europeans were essentially middlemen, funneling American silver to Asia and competing with one another for a place in the rich markets of the East. The productivity of the Chinese economy was evident in Spanish America, where cheap and well-made Chinese goods easily outsold those of Spain. In 1594, the Spanish viceroy of Peru observed that "a man can clothe his wife in Chinese silks for [25 pesos], whereas he could not provide her with clothing of Spanish silks with 200 pesos."[17] Indian cotton textiles likewise outsold European woolen or linen textiles in the seventeenth century to such an extent that French laws in 1717 prohibited the wearing of Indian cotton or Chinese silk clothing as a means of protecting French industry.

"The World Hunt": Fur in Global Commerce

In the early modern era, furs joined silver, textiles, and spices as major items of global commerce.[18] Their harvesting had an important environmental impact as well as serious implications for the human societies that generated and consumed them. Furs, of course, had long provided warmth and conveyed status in colder regions of the world, but the integration of North America and of northern Asia (Siberia) into a larger world economy vastly increased their significance in global trade.

By 1500, European population growth and agricultural expansion had sharply diminished the supply of fur-bearing animals, such as beaver, rabbits, sable, marten, and deer. Furthermore, much of the early modern era witnessed a period of cooling temperatures and harsh winters, known as the Little Ice Age, which may well have increased the demand for furs. "The weather is bitterly cold and everyone is in furs although we are almost in July," observed a surprised visitor from Venice while in London in 1604.[19] These conditions pushed prices higher, providing strong economic incentives for European traders to tap the immense wealth of fur-bearing animals found in North America.

The **fur trade** was a highly competitive enterprise. The French were most prominent in the St. Lawrence valley, around the Great Lakes, and later along the Mississippi River; British traders pushed into the Hudson Bay region; and the Dutch focused their attention along the Hudson River in what is now New York. They were frequently rivals for the great prize of North American furs. In the southern colonies of British North America, deerskins by the hundreds of thousands found a ready market in England's leather industry (see Map 14.3).

Only a few Europeans directly engaged in commercial trapping or hunting. They usually waited for Native Americans to bring the furs or skins initially to their coastal settlements and later to their fortified trading posts in the interior of North America.

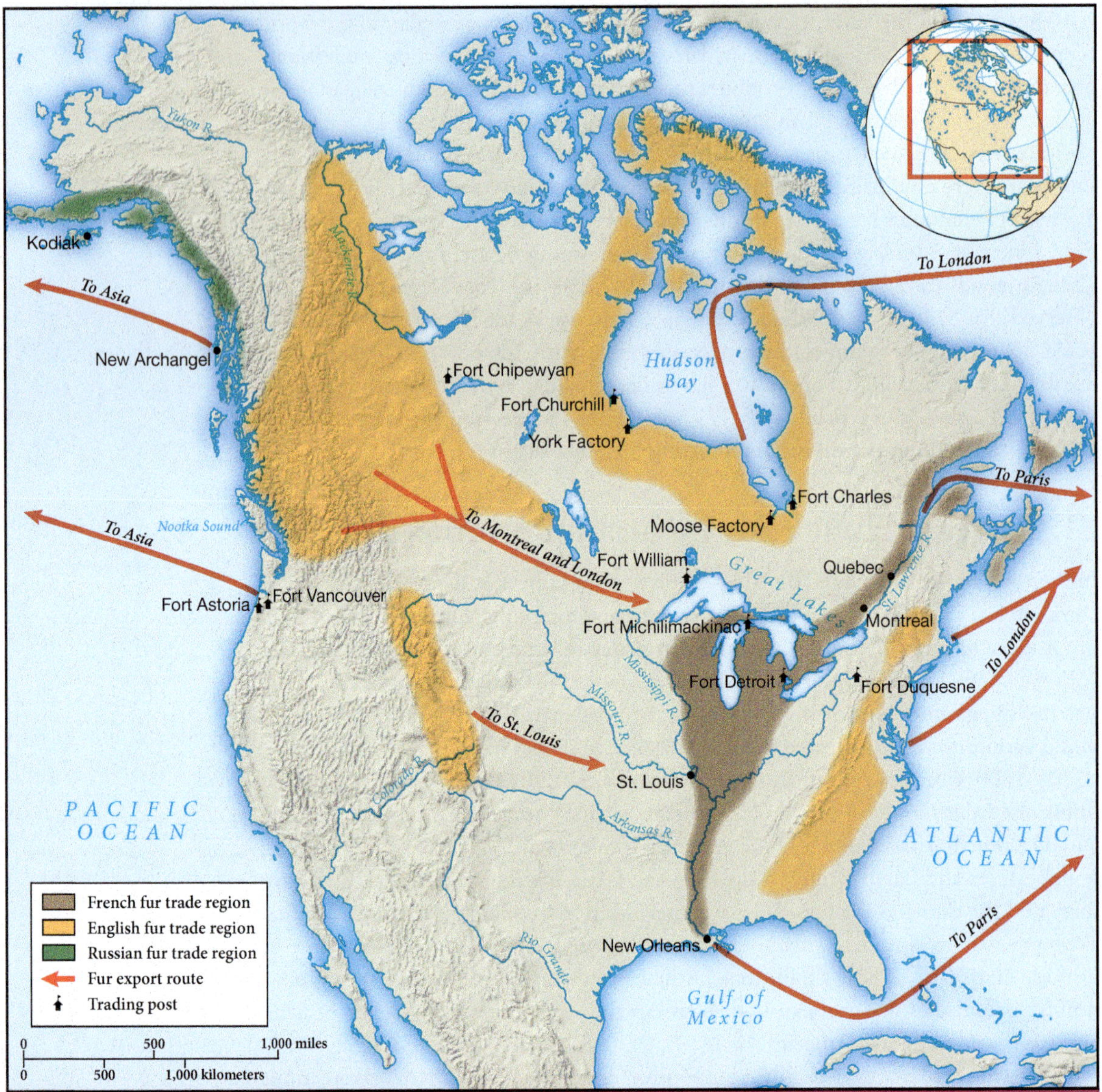

MAPPING HISTORY

Map 14.3 The North American Fur Trade

North America, as well as Russian Siberia, funneled an apparently endless supply of furs into the circuits of global trade during the early modern era.

READING THE MAP Which overseas markets were American furs shipped to? Did the trading networks originally established by the French and English remain completely separate, or did they interact with each other in some regions to funnel furs to overseas markets?

INTERPRETING THE MAP How might waterways have facilitated the movement of furs from the interior of the Americas to overseas markets?

European merchants paid for the furs with a variety of trade goods, including guns, blankets, metal tools, rum, and brandy, amid much ceremony, haggling over prices, and ritualized gift giving. Native Americans represented a cheap labor force in this international commercial effort, but they were not a directly coerced labor force.

Over the three centuries of the early modern era, enormous quantities of furs and deerskins found their way to Europe, where they considerably enhanced the standard of living in those cold climates. The environmental price was paid in the Americas, and it was high. A consistent demand for beaver hats led to the near extinction of that industrious animal in much of North America by the early nineteenth century and with it the degradation or loss of many wetland habitats. By the 1760s, hunters in southeastern British colonies took about 500,000 deer every year, seriously diminishing the deer population of the region. As early as 1642, Miantonomo, a chief of the New England Narragansett people, spoke of the environmental consequences of English colonialism:

> You know our fathers had plenty of deer and skins and our plains were full of game and turkeys, and our coves and rivers were full of fish. But, brothers, since these Englishmen have seized our country, they have cut down the grass with scythes, and the trees with axes. Their cows and horses eat up the grass, and their hogs spoil our bed of clams; and finally we shall all starve to death.[20]

For the Native American peoples who hunted, trapped, processed, and transported these products, the fur trade bore various benefits, particularly at the beginning. One Native American trapper told a French missionary, "The beaver does everything perfectly well. It makes kettles, hatchets, swords, knives, bread; and, in short, it makes everything."[21] The Hurons, who lived on the northern shores of Lakes Erie and Ontario in the early seventeenth century, annually exchanged some 20,000 to 30,000 pelts, mostly beaver, for trade items, some of which they used to strengthen their relationships with neighboring peoples. These goods also enhanced the authority of Huron chiefs by providing them with gifts to distribute among their followers. At least initially, competition among Europeans ensured that Native American leaders could negotiate reasonable prices for their goods. Furthermore, their important role in the lucrative fur trade protected them for a time from the kind of extermination, enslavement, or displacement that was the fate of native peoples in Portuguese Brazil.

CORE IDEA

Assessing Change
What impact did the fur trade have on the indigenous peoples of North America?

Nothing, however, protected them against the diseases carried by Europeans. In the 1630s and 1640s, to cite only one example of many, about half of the Hurons perished from influenza, smallpox, and other European-borne diseases. Furthermore, the fur trade generated warfare beyond anything previously known. Competition among Native American societies became more intense as the economic stakes grew higher. Catastrophic population declines owing to disease stimulated "mourning wars," designed to capture people who could be assimilated into much-diminished societies. A century of French-British rivalry for North America (1664–1763) forced Native American societies to take sides, to fight, and to die in these European imperial conflicts. Firearms, of course, made warfare far more deadly than before.

Beyond the fur trade, many Native American peoples actively sought to take advantage of the new commercial economy now impinging upon them. The Iroquois, for example, began to sell new products such as ginseng root, much in demand in China as a medicine. They also rented land to Europeans, worked for wages in various European enterprises, and started to use currency when barter was ineffective. But as they became enmeshed in these commercial relationships, Native Americans grew dependent on European trade goods. Among the Algonquians, for example, iron tools and cooking pots replaced those of stone, wood, or bone; gunpowder weapons took the place of bows and arrows; European textiles proved more attractive than traditional beaver and deerskin clothing; and flint and steel were found to be more effective for starting fires than wooden drills. A wide range of traditional crafts were thus lost, while the native peoples did not gain a corresponding ability to manufacture the new items for themselves. Enthusiasm for these imported goods and continued European demands for furs and skins frequently eroded the customary restraint that characterized traditional hunting practices, resulting in the depletion of many species. One European observer wrote of the Creek Indians: "[They] wage eternal war against deer and bear . . . which is indeed carried to an unreasonable and perhaps criminal excess, since the white people have dazzled their senses with foreign superfluities."[22]

Alongside germs and guns, yet another highly destructive European import was alcohol—rum and brandy, in particular. Whiskey, a locally produced grain-based alcohol, only added to the problem. With little prior experience of alcohol and little time to adjust to its easy availability, these drinks "hit Indian societies with explosive force."[23] Binge drinking, violence among young men, promiscuity, and addiction followed in many places. In 1753, Iroquois leaders complained bitterly to European authorities in Pennsylvania: "These wicked Whiskey Sellers, when they have once got the Indians in liquor, make them sell their very clothes from their backs. . . . If this practice be continued, we must be inevitably ruined."[24] In short, it was not so much the fur trade itself that decimated Native American societies, but all that accompanied it—disease, dependence, guns, alcohol, and the growing encroachment of European colonial empires.

All of this had particular implications for women. A substantial number of native women married European traders according to the "custom of the country"—with no sanction from civil or church authorities. Such marriages eased the difficulties of this cross-cultural exchange, providing traders with guides, interpreters, and negotiators. But sometimes these women were left abandoned when their husbands returned to Europe. More generally, the fur trade enhanced the position of men in their societies because hunting or trapping animals was normally a male occupation. Among the Ojibwa, a gathering and hunting people in the northern Great Lakes region, women had traditionally acquired economic power by creating food, utensils, clothing, and decorations from the hides and flesh of the animals that their husbands caught. With the fur trade in full operation, women spent more time processing those furs for sale than in producing household items, some of which were now available for purchase from Europeans. And so, as one scholar put it, "women lost authority and prestige." At the same time, however, women generated and controlled the trade in wild rice and maple syrup, both essential to the livelihood of European traders.[25] Thus the fur trade offered women a mix of opportunities and liabilities.

Paralleling the North American fur trade was the one simultaneously taking shape within a rapidly expanding Russian Empire, which became a major source of furs for Western Europe, China, and the Ottoman Empire. The profitability of that trade in furs was the chief incentive for Russia's rapid expansion during the sixteenth and seventeenth centuries across Siberia, where the **"soft gold"** of fur-bearing animals was abundant. The international sale of furs greatly enriched the Russian state as well as many private merchants, trappers, and hunters. Here the silver trade and the fur trade intersected, as Europeans paid for Russian furs largely with American gold and silver. The consequences for native Siberians were similar to those in North America, as disease took its toll, as indigenous people became dependent on Russian goods, as the settler frontier encroached on native lands, and as many species of fur-bearing mammals were seriously depleted. In several ways, however, the Russian fur trade was unique. Whereas several European nations competed in North America and generally obtained their furs through commercial negotiations with Indian societies, no such competition accompanied Russian expansion across Siberia. Russian authorities imposed a tax or tribute, payable in furs, on every able-bodied Siberian male between eighteen and fifty years of age. To enforce the payment, they took hostages from Siberian societies, with death as a possible outcome if the required furs were not forthcoming. A further difference lay in the large-scale presence of private Russian hunters and trappers, who competed directly with their Siberian counterparts.

The Fur Trade in Russia Russian authorities demanded tribute paid in furs from every able-bodied native Siberian male between eighteen and fifty years of age. This early eighteenth-century engraving depicts a fur-clad Siberian holding in one hand his hunting bow and trident and in the other two mink or ermine. The thick, soft fur of both these animals was much in demand on world markets. (Science & Society Picture Library/Getty Images)

CORE IDEA

■ Comparing Trading Networks
What differences can you identify in the operation and impact of the spice, silver, and fur trades?

Commerce in People: The Transatlantic Slave System

Of all the commercial ties that linked the early modern world into a global network of exchange, none had more profound or enduring human consequences than the **transatlantic slave system**. (See Controversies: Debating the Atlantic World, page 612.)

CONTROVERSIES

Debating the Atlantic World

Beginning in the 1970s, the notion of an "Atlantic world" increasingly swept the historical profession like a storm. It referred to the creation of a network of communication, interaction, and exchange all around the Atlantic basin among the peoples of Europe, Africa, and North and South America, often known as the Columbian exchange. This Atlantic world sensibility reflected the international politics of the post–World War II era, in which the North Atlantic Treaty Organization (NATO), an anticommunist alliance of North American and Western European states, played an important role. Studies of the Atlantic world in earlier centuries resonated with this transatlantic Cold War–era political partnership.

For historians, the "Atlantic world" idea held many attractions. It helped to free historical study from the rigid framework of the nation-state, allowing scholars and students to examine "flows" or "circulations"—such as the Columbian exchange—processes that operated beyond particular states and within larger spaces. In this respect, Atlantic world thinking paralleled historical investigation of the Mediterranean world or the Indian Ocean world, other sea-based zones of interaction.

The "Atlantic world" idea also encouraged comparison, particularly attractive to world historians. How similar or different were the various European empires—Spanish, Portuguese, British, French, Dutch—constructed in the Americas? Students in the United States are often surprised to learn that fewer than 5 percent of the enslaved Africans transported across the Atlantic wound up in North America and that the vast majority landed in Brazil or the Caribbean region.

Moreover, the Atlantic world provided a larger context in which to situate the history of particular societies or nations. The modern history of the Caribbean region, for example, is inexplicable without some grasp of its connection to Africa, the source of enslaved people; to Europe, the source of settlers, disease, and empires; and to North America, the source of valuable trade.

For some historians, however, the Atlantic world idea distorted our understanding of the early modern era. There never was a single cohesive Atlantic world, some have argued. Instead there were British, Spanish, French, and Dutch Atlantic worlds, each different and often in conflict. There were Catholic, Protestant, Islamic, and Jewish Atlantic worlds, and a black Atlantic world as well.

Furthermore, the Atlantic region was never a self-contained unit, but interacted with other regions of the world. Asian tea was dumped in Boston harbor during the American "tea party." Silver from the Americas fueled trade with Asia, with some 75 percent of it winding up in China. Textiles from India and cowrie shells from the Maldives, a group of islands in the Indian Ocean, served as currency in the transatlantic slave trade. And in the mid-eighteenth century, the value of British and Dutch imports from Asia was greater than the value of those from the Americas.

Critics also argued that an overly enthusiastic or exclusive focus on the Atlantic world exaggerates its significance in early modern world history. But placing the Atlantic world in a larger global framework corrects any such exaggeration and raises many fascinating questions. Why were Europeans able to construct major empires in the Americas but not in Africa or Asia? Why did European empires in the Americas feature large-scale European settlement, while the Chinese and Ottoman empires in Asia and the Middle East did not involve much Chinese or Turkish migration? How does the transatlantic slave system look when it is compared to the trans-Saharan and Indian Ocean slave trades, both of which were much older? And how does the transatlantic commerce in the early modern era compare with earlier Afro-Eurasian patterns of long-distance trade that had a much longer history? In short, the Atlantic world becomes a more meaningful concept when it is framed in genuinely global contexts.

Between 1500 and 1866, this trade in human beings took an estimated 12.5 million people from African societies, shipped them across the Atlantic in the infamous Middle Passage, and deposited some 10.7 million of them in the Americas, where they lived out their often brief lives as enslaved people. About 1.8 million (14.4 percent) died during the transatlantic crossing, while countless others perished in the process of

Beyond these controversies about the usefulness and limitations of the Atlantic world concept, historians have also debated the operation of this transoceanic network, with particular focus on questions of "agency" and "impact." "Agency" refers to the ability of individuals or groups to take action, to make things happen, and to affect the outcome of historical processes. So who created the Atlantic world? The earliest and most obvious answer to this question claimed that the Atlantic world was the product of European rulers, explorers, armies, settlers, merchants, and missionaries. But taking a closer look, historians have discovered agency in other places as well. Unknown to their European carriers, pathogens "acted" independently to generate the Great Dying in the Americas, largely beyond the intention or control of any human agent. Many indigenous rulers, acting in their own interests, joined their larger military forces to the small armies of the Spanish conquistadores to defeat the powerful Aztec and Inca empires. African rulers and commercial elites violently procured the human cargoes of the slave trade and sold them to European merchants waiting on Africa's western coast.

Agency was also expressed in numerous acts of resistance against Europeans, such as the Great Pueblo Rebellion of 1680, the creation of runaway slave communities in Brazil, and the Haitian Revolution, all of which shaped the contours of the Atlantic world. Culturally too, conquered and enslaved people retained their human capacity to act and create, even in enormously repressive conditions. For example, they adapted Christianity to their own needs, often blending it with elements of traditional beliefs and practices. A famous book about slavery in the American south by Eugene Genovese bore the pointed subtitle *The World the Slaves Made*. Agency, in short, was not limited to Europeans, and the Atlantic world was not wholly a European creation.

The multiple interactions of the Atlantic world have also stimulated debate about "impact" or the consequences of inclusion in this transoceanic network. For millions of enslaved individuals and millions more who perished in the Great Dying, the impact was tragic and painful almost beyond description. About this there is little debate. More controversial questions arise about the impact of Atlantic world encounters on broader regions and their peoples. Were indigenous societies of the Western Hemisphere destroyed or decimated by conquest, disease, labor demands, and loss of land? Or were they, as historian John Kicze describes them, remarkably "resilient cultures"? How did the demand for enslaved people affect African population growth, economic development, the role of women, and state formation? Did the wealth derived from the Atlantic world of empire, commerce, and slavery enable Britain's Industrial Revolution, or was it only a minor factor?

Finally, the intersection of questions about agency and impact in the Atlantic world has raised contentious issues about moral responsibility. If Europeans or Euro-Americans were the primary agents of the slave trade, the Great Dying, and the exploitation of native peoples, do they owe an apology and compensation to the descendants of their victims? How does the well-documented role of African political and economic elites in the transatlantic slave system complicate our thinking about such issues?

About all of this, debate continues.

QUESTIONS TO CONSIDER

1. With what questions about the Atlantic world do you feel most engaged? Why?
2. What makes the Atlantic world a compelling concept for historians?
3. How does the treatment of early modern empires in Chapter 13 and commerce in Chapter 14 respond to the questions raised in this essay?

capture and transport to the African coast.[26] (See Map 14.4.) Despite the language of commerce and exchange with which it is often described, this transatlantic slave system was steeped in violence, coercion, and brutality. It involved forcible capture and repeated sale, beatings and brandings, chains and imprisonment, rebellions and escapes, lives of enforced and unpaid labor, broken families, and humans treated as property.

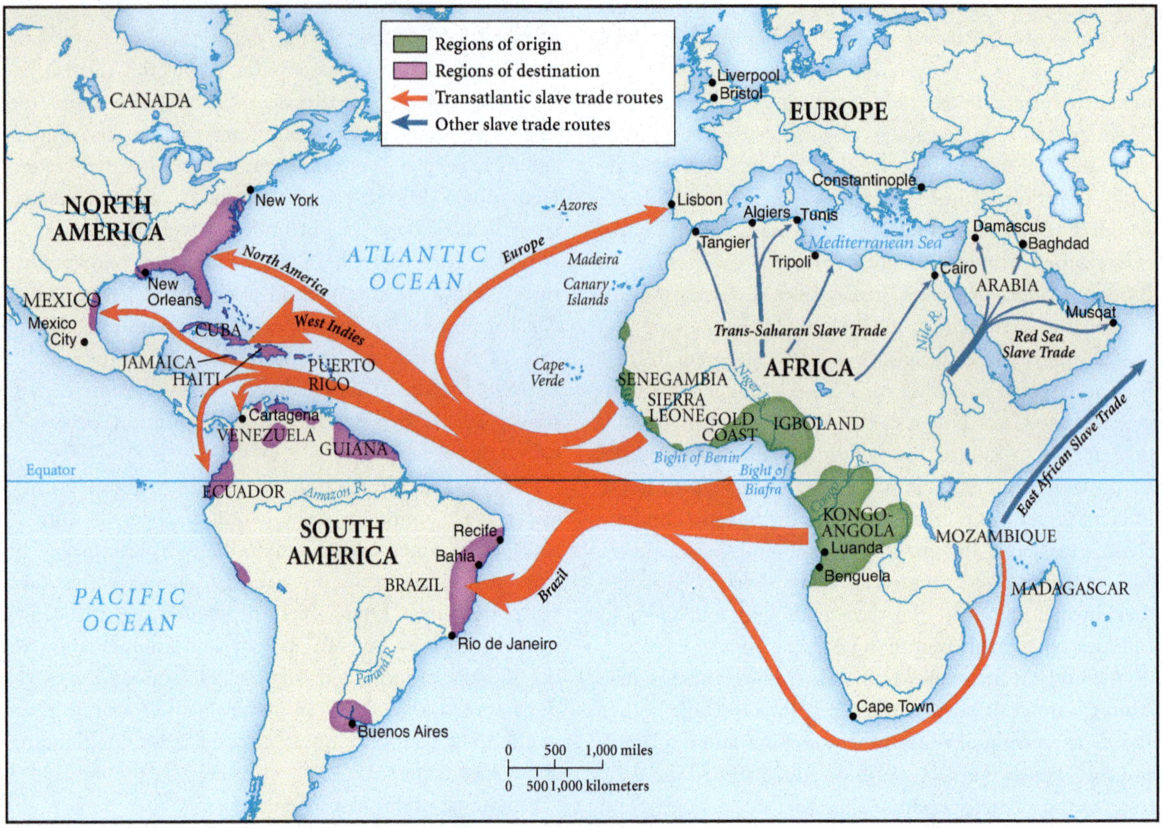

Map 14.4 The Transatlantic Slave System
Stimulated by the plantation complex of the Americas, the transatlantic slave system represented an enormous extension of the ancient practice of people owning and selling other people.

Beyond the multitude of individual tragedies that it spawned, the transatlantic slave system transformed entire societies. Within Africa itself, that commerce thoroughly disrupted some societies, strengthened others, and corrupted many. Elites often enriched themselves, while the enslaved Africans, of course, were victimized almost beyond imagination.

In the Americas, this transatlantic network added a substantial African presence to the mix of European and Native American peoples. This **African diaspora** (the global spread of African peoples) injected into these new societies issues of race that endure still in the twenty-first century. It also introduced elements of African culture, such as religious ideas, musical and artistic traditions, and cuisine, into the making of American cultures. The profits from the slave trade and the labor of enslaved Africans certainly enriched European and Euro-American societies, even as the practice of slavery contributed to European racial stereotypes of other peoples. Finally, slavery became a metaphor for many kinds of social oppression, quite different from plantation slavery, in the centuries that followed. Workers protested the slavery of wage labor, colonized people rejected the slavery of imperial domination, and feminists sometimes defined patriarchy as a form of slavery.

Slavery in the Islamic World This eighteenth-century image of an enslaved woman accompanying her upper-class Turkish owner to the public baths highlights the slave trade in the Ottoman and Indian Ocean worlds and serves as a reminder that slavery was not limited to the Atlantic world in the early modern era. Unlike in the Americas, most enslaved people in North Africa and Southwest Asia served as domestic servants, with enslaved women generally preferred to males. (Bridgeman Images)

The Slave Trade in Context

The transatlantic slave system represented the most recent large-scale expression of a very widespread human practice—the owning and exchange of human beings. Before 1500, the Mediterranean and Indian Ocean basins were the major arenas of Old World slave systems, and southern Russia was a major source of its victims. Many African societies likewise both practiced slavery themselves and sold enslaved people into these international commercial networks. A trans-Saharan slave trade had long funneled African captives into Mediterranean slavery, and an East African slave trade from at least the seventh century C.E. brought Africans into the Middle East and the Indian Ocean basin. Both operated largely within the Islamic world and initiated the movement of African peoples beyond the continent itself.

Furthermore, slavery came in many forms. In the Indian Ocean world, for example, enslaved Africans were often assimilated into the societies of their owners and lost the sense of a distinctive identity that was so prominent in North America. In some places, children inherited the slave status of their parents; elsewhere those children were free persons. Within the Islamic world, where most enslaved people worked in domestic settings, the preference was for enslaved women and girls by a two-to-one margin, while the later transatlantic slave system, which funneled captives into plantation labor, favored males by a similar margin. Not all enslaved people, however, occupied degraded positions. Some in the Islamic world acquired prominent military or political status. Most enslaved people in the premodern world worked in their owners' households, farms, or shops, with smaller numbers laboring in large-scale agricultural or industrial enterprises.

■ Establishing Context
In what larger contexts can the Atlantic slave system be understood?

The slave system that emerged in the Americas was distinctive in several ways. One was simply the immense size of that system and its centrality to the economies of colonial America, which featured a great deal of plantation agriculture. Furthermore, slave status throughout the Americas was inherited across generations, and there was little hope of eventual freedom for the vast majority. Nowhere else, with the possible exception of ancient Greece, was the contradiction between slavery and the social values affirming human freedom and equality quite so sharp. Perhaps most distinctive was the racial dimension: Atlantic slavery came to be identified wholly with Africa and with "blackness."

The origins of Atlantic slavery clearly lie in the Mediterranean world and with that now-common sweetener known as sugar. Until the Crusades, Europeans knew nothing of sugar and relied on honey and fruits to sweeten their bland diets. However, as they learned from the Arabs about sugarcane and the laborious techniques for producing usable sugar, Europeans established sugar-producing plantations within the Mediterranean and later on various islands off the coast of West Africa. It was a "modern" industry, perhaps the first one, in that it required huge capital investment, substantial technology, an almost factory-like discipline among workers, and a mass market of consumers. The immense difficulty and danger of the work, the limitations attached to serf labor, and the general absence of wageworkers all pointed to slavery as a source of labor for sugar plantations.

■ Analyzing Causation
What explains the rise of the Atlantic slave trade?

Initially, Slavic-speaking communities from the Black Sea region furnished the bulk of the enslaved people for Mediterranean plantations, so much so that "Slav" became the basis for the word "slave" in many European languages. In 1453, however, when the Ottoman Turks seized Constantinople, the supply of Slavs was effectively cut off. At the same time, Portuguese mariners were exploring the coast of West Africa; they were looking primarily for gold, but they also found there an alternative source of enslaved people available for sale. Thus, when sugar, and later tobacco and cotton, plantations took hold in the Americas, Europeans had already established links to a West African source of supply. They also now had religious justification for their actions, for in 1452 the pope formally granted to the kings of Spain and Portugal "full and free permission to invade, search out, capture, and subjugate the Saracens [Muslims] and pagans and any other unbelievers . . . and to reduce their persons into perpetual slavery."[27] Largely through a process of elimination, Africa became the primary source of slave labor for the plantation economies of the Americas. Slavic peoples were no longer available; Native Americans quickly perished from European diseases; even marginal Europeans such as poor people and criminals were Christians and therefore supposedly exempt from slavery; and European indentured servants, who agreed to work for a fixed period in return for transportation, food, and shelter, were expensive and temporary. Africans, on the other hand, were skilled farmers; they had some immunity to both tropical and European diseases; they were not Christians; they were, relatively speaking, close at hand; and they were readily available in substantial numbers through African-operated commercial networks.

Moreover, Africans were black. The precise relationship between slavery and European racism has long been a much-debated subject. Historian David Brion Davis has suggested the controversial view that "racial stereotypes were transmitted, along with black slavery itself, from Muslims to Christians."[28] For many centuries, Muslims had drawn on sub-Saharan Africa as one source of enslaved people and in the process had developed a form of racism. The fourteenth-century Tunisian scholar Ibn Khaldun wrote that black people were "submissive to slavery, because Negroes have little that is essentially human and have attributes that are quite similar to those of dumb animals."[29]

Other scholars find the origins of racism within European culture itself. For the English, argues historian Audrey Smedley, the process of conquering Ireland had generated by the sixteenth century a view of the Irish as "rude, beastly, ignorant, cruel, and unruly infidels," perceptions that were then transferred to Africans enslaved on English sugar plantations of the West Indies.[30] Whether Europeans borrowed such images of Africans from their Muslim neighbors or developed them independently, slavery and racism soon went hand in hand. "Europeans were better able to tolerate their brutal exploitation of Africans," writes a prominent world historian, "by imagining that these Africans were an inferior race, or better still, not even human."[31]

The Slave Trade in Practice

The European demand for enslaved people was clearly the chief cause of this tragic commerce, and from the point of sale on the African coast to the massive use of slave labor on American plantations, the entire enterprise was in European hands. Within Africa itself, however, a different picture emerges, for over the four centuries of the Atlantic slave trade, European demand elicited an African supply. The slave trade quickly came to operate largely with Europeans waiting on the coast, either on their ships or in fortified settlements, to purchase enslaved people from African merchants and political elites. Certainly, Europeans tried to exploit African rivalries to obtain enslaved people at the lowest possible cost, and the firearms they funneled into West Africa may well have increased the warfare from which so many enslaved people were derived. But from the point of initial capture to sale on the coast, the entire enterprise was normally in African hands. Almost nowhere did Europeans attempt outright military conquest; instead they generally dealt as equals with local African authorities.

CORE IDEA

■ Defining Roles
What roles did Europeans and Africans play in the unfolding of the Atlantic slave trade?

An arrogant agent of the British Royal Africa Company in the 1680s learned the hard way who was in control when he spoke improperly to the king of Niumi, a small state in what is now Gambia. The company's records describe what happened next:

> [O]ne of the grandees [of the king], by name Sambalama, taught him better manners by reaching him a box on the ears, which beat off his hat, and a few thumps on the back, and seizing him . . . and several others, who together with the agent were taken and put into the king's pound and stayed there three or four days till their ransom was brought, value five hundred bars.[32]

In exchange for enslaved persons, African sellers sought both European and Indian textiles, cowrie shells (widely used as money in West Africa), European metal goods, firearms and gunpowder, tobacco and alcohol, and various decorative items such as beads. Europeans purchased some of these items—cowrie shells and Indian textiles, for

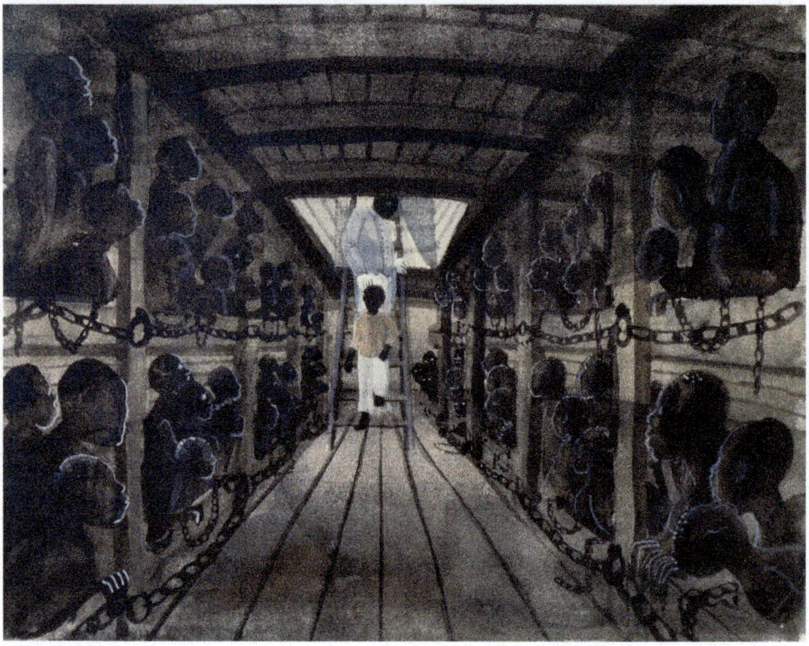

The Middle Passage This nineteenth-century painting of enslaved people held below decks illustrates the horrendous crowded conditions and the use of chains to restrain the enslaved during the transatlantic voyage, a journey experienced by many millions of captured Africans. (DEA/G. DAGLI ORTI/Getty Images)

example—with silver mined in the Americas. Thus the transatlantic slave system connected with commerce in silver and textiles as it became part of an emerging worldwide network of exchange. Issues about the precise mix of goods that African authorities desired, about the number and quality of enslaved people to be purchased, and always about the price of everything were settled in endless negotiation. Most of the time, a leading historian concluded, the slave trade took place "not unlike international trade anywhere in the world of the period."[33]

For the enslaved individuals themselves—seized in the interior, often sold several times on the harrowing journey to the coast, sometimes branded, and held in squalid dungeons while awaiting transportation to the New World—it was anything but a normal commercial transaction. One European engaged in the trade noted that "the negroes are so willful and loath to leave their own country, that they have often leap'd out of the canoes, boat, and ship, into the sea, and kept under water till they were drowned, to avoid being taken up and saved by our boats."[34]

Over the four centuries of the slave trade, millions of Africans underwent such experiences, but their numbers varied considerably over time. During the sixteenth century, slave exports from Africa averaged fewer than 3,000 annually. In those years, the Portuguese were at least as much interested in African gold, spices, and textiles. Furthermore, as in Asia, they became involved in transporting African goods, including enslaved people, from one African port to another, thus becoming the "truck drivers" of coastal West African commerce.[35] In the seventeenth century, the pace picked up as the slave trade became highly competitive, with the British, Dutch, and French contesting the earlier Portuguese monopoly. The century and a half between 1700 and 1850 marked the high point of the slave trade as the plantation economies of the Americas boomed. (See Snapshot: The Slave Trade in Numbers, page 619.)

Geographically, the slave system drew mainly on the societies of West and South-Central Africa, from present-day Mauritania in the north to Angola in the south.

SNAPSHOT The Slave Trade in Numbers (1501–1866)

The Rise and Decline of the Slave Trade

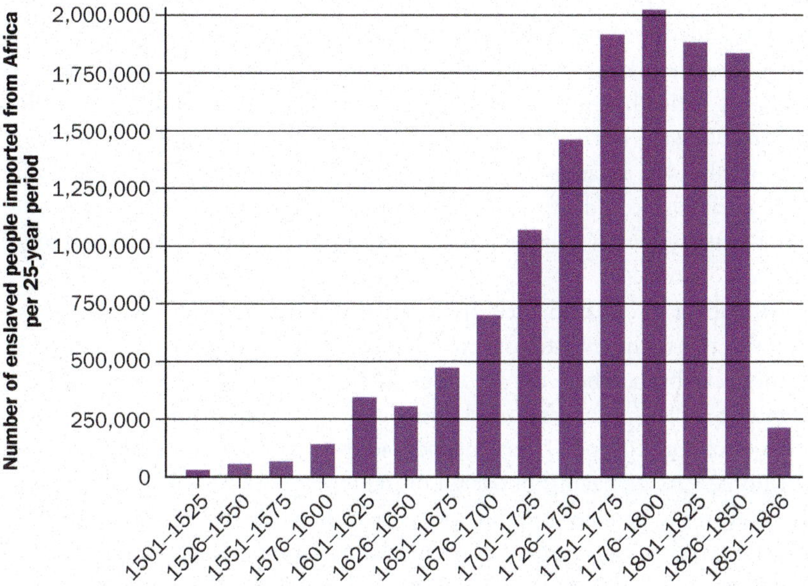

The Destination of Enslaved People

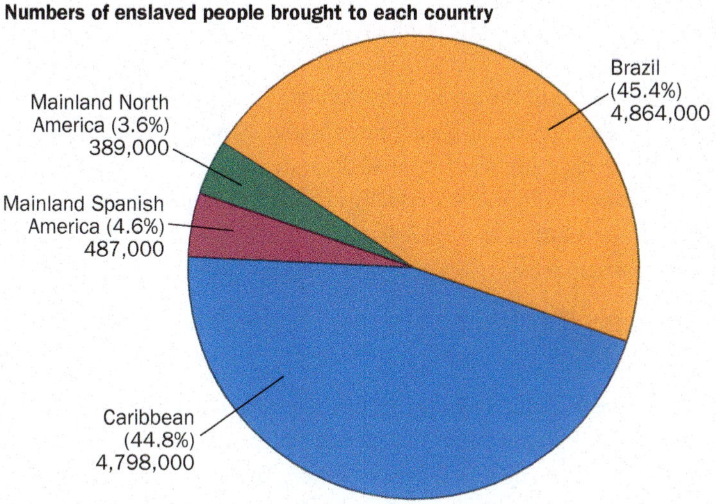

Source: Data from Trans-Atlantic Slave Trade Database, accessed December 26, 2017, http://www.slavevoyages.org/assessment/estimates.

Initially focused on the coastal regions, the slave raiding progressively penetrated into the interior as the demand for enslaved people picked up. Socially, these enslaved people were mostly drawn from various marginal groups in African societies—prisoners of war, criminals, debtors, people who had been "pawned" during times of difficulty. Thus Africans did not generally sell "their own people" into slavery. Divided into hundreds of separate, usually small-scale, and often rival communities—cities, kingdoms, microstates, clans, and villages—the various peoples of West Africa had no concept of an "African" identity. Those whom they captured and sold were normally outsiders, vulnerable people who lacked the protection of membership in an established community. When short-term economic or political advantage could be gained, such people were sold. In this respect, the transatlantic slave system was little different from the experience of enslavement elsewhere in the world.

The destination of enslaved Africans, half a world away in the Americas, however, made the transatlantic system very different. The vast majority wound up in Brazil or the Caribbean, where the labor demands of the plantation economy were most intense. Smaller numbers found themselves in North America, mainland Spanish America, or Europe. Their journey across the Atlantic was horrendous, with the Middle Passage having an overall mortality rate of more than 14 percent.

Enslaved Africans frequently resisted their fates in a variety of ways. About 10 percent of the transatlantic voyages experienced a major rebellion by desperate captives, and resistance continued in the Americas, taking a range of forms from surreptitious slowdowns of work to outright rebellion. One common act was to flee. Many who escaped joined free communities of formerly enslaved people known as **maroon societies**, which were founded in remote regions, especially in South America and the Caribbean. The largest such settlement was **Palmares** in Brazil, which endured for most of the seventeenth century, housing 10,000 or more people, mostly of African descent but also including Native Americans, mestizos, and renegade whites. While slave owners feared wide-scale slave rebellions, these were rare, and even small-scale rebellions were usually crushed with great brutality. It was only with the Haitian Revolution of the 1790s that a full-scale slave revolt brought lasting freedom for its participants.

Consequences: The Impact of the Slave Trade in Africa

From the viewpoint of world history, the chief outcome of the transatlantic slave system lay in the new global linkages that it generated as Africa became a permanent part of an interacting Atlantic world. Millions of its people were now compelled to make their lives in the Americas, where they made an enormous impact both demographically and economically. Until the nineteenth century, they outnumbered European immigrants to the Americas by three or four to one, and West African societies were increasingly connected to an emerging European-centered world economy. These vast processes set in motion a chain of consequences that have transformed the lives and societies of people on both sides of the Atlantic.

Although the slave trade did not produce in Africa the kind of population collapse that occurred in the Americas, it certainly slowed Africa's growth at a time when Europe, China, and other regions were expanding demographically. Beyond the loss of millions of people over four centuries, the demand for enslaved Africans produced economic stagnation and social disruption. Economically, the slave trade stimulated little positive change in Africa because those Africans who benefited most from the traffic in people were not investing in the productive capacities of their societies. Although European imports generally did not displace traditional artisan manufacturing, no technological breakthroughs in agriculture or industry increased the wealth available to these societies. Maize and manioc (cassava), introduced from the Americas, added a new source of calories to African diets, but the international demand was for Africa's people, not its agricultural products.

Socially too, the slave trade shaped African societies. It surely fostered moral corruption, particularly as judicial proceedings were manipulated to generate victims for export. A West African legend tells of cowrie shells, a major currency of the slave trade, growing on corpses of decomposing enslaved people, a symbolic recognition of the corrupting effects of this commerce in human beings.

CORE IDEA

Describing Change
What changes did the Atlantic slave system bring to African societies?

African women felt the impact of the slave trade in various ways, beyond those who numbered among its transatlantic victims. Since far more men than women were shipped to the Americas, the labor demands on those women who remained increased substantially, compounded by the growing use of cassava, a labor-intensive import from the New World. Unbalanced sex ratios also meant that far more men than before could marry multiple women. Furthermore, the use of enslaved women and girls within West African societies grew as the export trade in enslaved men expanded. Retaining women and girls for their own use allowed warriors and nobles in the Senegambia region to distinguish themselves more clearly from ordinary peasants. In the Kongo, enslaved women provided a source of dependent laborers for the plantations that sustained the lifestyle of urban elites. A European merchant on the Gold Coast in the late eighteenth century observed that every free man owned at least one or two enslaved people.

A *Signare* of Senegal While many women suffered greatly because of the Atlantic slave trade, a few grew quite wealthy and powerful. Known as *signares*, they married European merchants and built their own trading networks. The *signare* in this eighteenth-century French image is shown at the slave port of Saint Louis Island in Senegal. She is dressed in the fashionable and imported textiles that display her status. (Florilegius/Alamy Stock Photo)

For much smaller numbers of women, the slave trade provided an opportunity to exercise power and accumulate wealth. In the Senegambia region, where women had long been involved in politics and commerce, marriage to European

ZOOMING IN

Ayuba Suleiman Diallo: To Slavery and Back

February 1730 found Ayuba Suleiman Diallo, less than thirty years of age, living between the Gambia and Senegal rivers in West Africa among the Fulbe-speaking people.[36] Like his father, a prominent Islamic scholar and teacher, Ayuba was a Muslim who was literate in Arabic, a prayer leader in the local mosque, and a *hafiz*, someone who had memorized the entire Quran. He was also husband to two wives and father to four children. Now his father sent the young man on an errand. He was to take several of their many enslaved people to a location some 200 miles away, where an English trading ship had anchored, and exchange them for paper and other goods. The paper was especially important, for his father's income depended on inscribing passages from the Quran on small slips of paper and selling them as protective charms.

Ayuba Suleiman Diallo.

To put it mildly, things did not go as planned. Unable to reach an agreement with the English merchant Captain Stephen Pike, Ayuba traveled to the lands of the Mandinka, where he traded the people that his father had entrusted him with for a number of cows. Well beyond the safety of his own country, he was in dangerous territory. As he and his companions stopped to rest on the journey home, they were seized, their heads were shaved, and they were sold to the very same Captain Pike. Although Ayuba was able to send a message to his father asking to be ransomed, the ship sailed before a reply was received. And so Ayuba, along with 168 others, both men and women, headed for the British American colony of Maryland, where 150 of them arrived alive.

Sold to a local planter, Ayuba was immediately sent to the tobacco fields, but when he became ill from this heavy and unaccustomed work, his owner assigned him the less arduous and more familiar task of tending cattle. Alone

traders offered advantage to both partners. For European male merchants, as for fur traders in North America, such marriages afforded access to African-operated commercial networks as well as the comforts of domestic life. Some of the women involved in these cross-cultural marriages, known as ***signares***, became quite wealthy, operating their own trading empires, employing large numbers of enslaved women, and acquiring elaborate houses, jewelry, and fashionable clothing.

Furthermore, the state-building enterprises that often accompanied the sale of enslaved people in West Africa offered yet other opportunities to a few women. As the Kingdom of **Dahomey** (deh-HOH-mee) expanded during the eighteenth century, the royal palace, housing thousands of women and presided over by a powerful Queen Mother, served to integrate the diverse regions of the state. Each lineage was required to send a daughter to the palace even as well-to-do families sent additional girls to increase their influence at court. In the Kingdom of Kongo, women held lower-level administrative positions, the head wife of a nobleman exercised authority over hundreds of junior wives and enslaved people, and women served on the council with the cattle, Ayuba was able to withdraw into a nearby forest to pray, but he was spotted by a young white boy who mocked him and threw dirt in his face. Sometime later, no doubt in despair, Ayuba ran away, but he was soon captured and housed in the county jail, located in the back room of a tavern. There he became something of a local curiosity and attracted the attention of a lawyer named Thomas Bluett. When Ayuba refused wine, wrote a few lines in Arabic, and mentioned "Allah" and "Muhammad," Bluett realized that he was "no common slave." Bluett became fascinated by Ayuba's story, and he initiated a process that took both of them to England in 1733, where philanthropists purchased Ayuba's freedom.

Ayuba's reception in England was amazing. Now fluent in English, Ayuba was received by the English royal family and various members of the nobility, hosted by leading scholars, and entertained by wealthy merchants, eager to tap his knowledge of economic conditions in West Africa. The prominent artist William Hoare painted his portrait, complete with a small Quran hanging from his neck.

In 1734, he finally set off for home, loaded with gifts from his English friends. There he encountered, quite by chance, the same Mandinka men who had sold him only a few years before. Francis Moore, a European trader accompanying Ayuba, wrote that he "fell into a most terrible passion and was for killing them" and was restrained from doing so only with difficulty. He arrived in his hometown to find that his father had recently died. His wives and children, however, were all alive and welcomed him warmly. One of his wives had remarried, believing him gone forever, but her new husband readily gave way, and Ayuba resumed his place of prominence in his own community until his death in 1773.

He also resumed his life as a slave owner. Selling some of the gifts he had acquired in England, he purchased an enslaved woman and two horses soon after his arrival back in West Africa. According to Moore, he "spoke always very handsomely of the English," and he continued his association with the Royal African Company, the primary English trading firm in West Africa, in its rivalry with French traders.[37] The last mention of Ayuba in the records of that company noted that he was seeking compensation for the loss of two enslaved people and a watch, probably the one given him in England by Queen Caroline.

QUESTIONS

What might you infer about Ayuba's own view of slavery and the slave trade? What insights or questions about the slave trade does his remarkable story suggest?

that advised the monarch. The neighboring region of Matamba was known for its female rulers, most notably the powerful Queen Nzinga (1626–1663), who guided the state amid the complexities and intrigues of various European and African rivalries and gained a reputation for her resistance to Portuguese imperialism.

Within particular African societies, the impact of the transatlantic slave system differed considerably from place to place and over time. Many small-scale kinship-based societies, lacking the protection of a strong state, were thoroughly disrupted by raids from more powerful neighbors, and insecurity was pervasive. Oral traditions in southern Ghana, for example, reported that "there was no rest in the land," that people went about in groups rather than alone, and that mothers kept their children inside when European ships appeared.[38] Some larger kingdoms such as Kongo and Oyo slowly disintegrated as access to trading opportunities and firearms enabled outlying regions to establish their independence. (For an account of one young man's journey to slavery and back, see Zooming In: Ayuba Suleiman Diallo.)

However, African authorities also sought to take advantage of the new commercial opportunities and to manage the slave trade in their own interests. The Kingdom of **Benin**, in the forest area of present-day Nigeria, successfully avoided a deep involvement in the trade while diversifying the exports with which it purchased European firearms and other goods. As early as 1516, its ruler began to restrict the slave trade and soon forbade the export of enslaved men altogether, a ban that lasted until the early eighteenth century. By then, the ruler's authority over outlying areas had declined, and the country's major exports of pepper and cotton cloth had lost out to Asian and then European competition. In these circumstances, Benin felt compelled to resume limited participation in the slave trade. The neighboring Kingdom of Dahomey, on the other hand, turned to a vigorous involvement in the slave trade in the early eighteenth century under strict royal control. The army conducted annual slave raids, and the government soon came to depend on the trade for its essential revenues. The slave trade in Dahomey became the chief business of the state and remained so until well into the nineteenth century.

CONCLUSIONS AND REFLECTIONS

Global Trade and Moral Complexity

"Trade Makes the World Go Round" was the title of an article in the *Wall Street Journal* in 2005. It was certainly an appropriate description for the commercially entangled world of the early twenty-first century. But long-distance or transregional trade has long propelled human societies, though at various speeds and in various directions. For millennia the Silk Road commerce across northern Eurasia and the Sea Road trade in the Indian Ocean basin generated substantial change in the societies that they linked, as did the Sand Road exchange across the Sahara Desert that emerged after 300 C.E. (See Chapter 7.)

In the early modern era, however, major changes in patterns of world trade made the world go round even faster. One was the growing prominence of Western Europeans. Previously marginal players in global commerce, now they established a major presence in the ancient exchange networks of the Indian Ocean, initially through a Portuguese "trading post empire" and later through the British and Dutch East India companies. By far the most significant European initiative was the creation of economic networks of trade in furs, silver, sugar, enslaved people, and more across both the Atlantic and Pacific oceans.

These new and unprecedented patterns of world trade were enormously consequential. They permanently linked the Eastern and Western hemispheres for the first time in human history, thus laying the foundations of the genuinely global economy of modern times. Exploring this complex historical process raises an endlessly debated question about trade: Who benefits? Answering that question raises still other issues: Was the trade genuinely voluntary or coerced? What differences in political or military power existed among the participants? How equivalent were the economies of the trading partners? Who produced the goods that were exchanged and in what circumstances? And how were traded products distributed within the receiving societies?

In the Dutch trade with the Spice Islands, military power enabled merchants to control both production and shipping, thus generating enormous profits while reducing native growers to slavery, poverty, or starvation. By contrast, British merchants in India had to operate under the control of the powerful Mughal Empire and were often dependent on wealthy Indian lenders. Meanwhile, British demand for highly popular cotton textiles transformed many Indian villagers into specialized producers for the European market.

The silver trade enabled many Europeans to purchase valued Chinese goods and also enabled Spain to become a major power for a time. But the miners who produced silver in colonial Potosí were subjected to horrendous conditions that made their lives miserable and brief, while their wealthy Spanish rulers lived in luxury.

The North American fur trade obviously benefited those Europeans who were able to purchase warm clothing. And indigenous North American peoples, who generated those furs, gained access to useful European products and were not directly coerced. The byproducts of that trade, however, decimated many Native American societies as it introduced devastating diseases, alcoholic beverages, and firearms. And many animal species, such as beaver and deer, also paid the price for this trade.

The commerce in enslaved Africans raises an even more complex moral equation. Clearly both African and European merchants benefited economically from this commerce, as did their rulers. So too did American plantation owners and all those who now had access to cheap sugar, cotton, tobacco, and other goods produced by enslaved people. The enslaved Africans themselves, however, deported from their homeland and treated as commodities, were subject to abuse and exploitation almost beyond description. Who is most responsible for what we now see as a moral calamity—African sellers, European buyers, or perhaps all those who purchased commodities produced by enslaved people and the products made from them? And to complicate matters even further, commerce in enslaved persons was widespread and considered "natural" in early modern times in many parts of the world, including Africa. To what extent should prevailing cultural norms at the time shape our assessment?

To put it mildly, the costs and benefits of early modern global trade were not borne equally by its many participants. The question of "who benefits?" is both complex and sometimes morally ambiguous. Such are the unsettling issues that arise as we contemplate how "trade made the world go round."

Revisiting Chapter 14

Revisiting Specifics

Indian Ocean commercial network, 596
trading post empire, 598
Philippines (Spanish), 599
Manila, 599
British East India Company, 600
Dutch East India Company, 600
"silver drain," 604
piece of eight, 604
Potosí, 605
fur trade, 607
"soft gold," 611
transatlantic slave system, 611
African diaspora, 614
maroon societies / Palmares, 620
signares, 622
Dahomey, 622
Benin, 624

Revisiting Core Ideas

1. **Comparing Asian Colonies** How did the Portuguese, Spanish, Dutch, and British initiatives in Asia differ from one another?
2. **Assessing Significance** What was the significance of the silver trade in the early modern era of world history?
3. **Assessing Change** What impact did the fur trade have on the indigenous peoples of North America?
4. **Comparing Trading Networks** What differences can you identify in the operation and impact of the spice, silver, and fur trades?
5. **Defining Roles** What roles did Europeans and Africans play in the unfolding of the Atlantic slave trade?
6. **Describing Change** What changes did the Atlantic slave system bring to African societies?

A Wider View

1. To what extent did Europeans transform earlier patterns of commerce, and in what ways did they assimilate into those older patterns?
2. What lasting legacies of early modern trading networks are evident today? And what aspects of those networks are no longer in operation?
3. Who should be assigned the moral responsibility for the transatlantic slave system? Is this an appropriate task for historians?
4. **Looking Back** Asians, Africans, and Native Americans experienced early modern European expansion in quite different ways. Based on Chapters 13 and 14, how might you describe and explain those differences? In what ways were they active agents in the historical process rather than simply victims of European actions?

To learn more about the topics in this chapter, see **For Further Study** at the end of this book.

WORKING WITH EVIDENCE

Consumption and Culture in the Early Modern World

As global commerce expanded in the early modern era, growing numbers of people around the world gained increased access to goods from far away, and some of these products—sugar, pepper, tobacco, tea, and cotton textiles, for example—gradually dropped in price, becoming more widely available. Widespread consumption of these formerly exclusive goods brought cultural change. Increased access to products threatened their use as signifiers of elite status, and profits generated by their trade created commercial classes of traders and merchants that were often more wealthy than traditional elites. The consumption of some products, including tea, coffee, chocolate, and tobacco, also created new arenas for social interaction. The sources that follow illustrate the relationship between consumption and culture during the several centuries after 1500, using clothing, tea, porcelain, and coffee as examples.

SOURCE 14.1 Clothing and Status in the Americas ▶

Clothing has long been an important means of displaying status in public settings, and the growing availability of imported fabrics and garments increased the fashion and dress options of people from many different social backgrounds. Source 14.1 shows a woman of Native American ancestry (*India*) and a man of African/Indian descent (*Chino combujo*) as well as their child, who is categorized as a *loba*, or "wolf." The image comes from a series of paintings created in eighteenth-century Mexico by the well-known Zapotec artist Miguel Cabrera to depict some eighteen or more multiracial couples and their children, each with a distinct designation. The woman in this image is wearing a *huipil*, a traditional Maya tunic or blouse, while the man is dressed in a European-style waistcoat, vest, and lace shirt, while holding a black tricorne hat, widely popular in Europe during the seventeenth and eighteenth centuries. While this system slotted people into a hierarchical social order defined by race and heritage, it did allow for some social mobility. If individuals managed to acquire some education, land, or money, they might gain in social prestige and even pass as members of a more highly favored category. Adopting the dress and lifestyle of higher-ranking groups could facilitate this process.

- What role does clothing play in establishing the status of the people depicted in the image?
- Why do you think the woman is shown in more traditional costume, while the man is portrayed in European dress?
- What indications of status ambition or upward mobility can you identify in Source 14.1? How might individuals in Mexico of multiracial origin like those depicted in this image use clothing to challenge their perceived status?

MIGUEL CABRERA | ***Detail from a Series on Multiracial Marriages in Mexico*** | **1763**

Index Fototeca/Bridgeman Images

SOURCE 14.2 Regulating Dress in Europe and Japan

Moralists and government authorities everywhere worried that the growing availability of textiles, furs, and other products would lead to overspending by members of all social classes and might undermine the social order by allowing people to dress beyond their station. In Europe governments frequently promulgated laws regulating dress, perhaps nowhere more so than in the great trading city of Venice, which for centuries was a leading emporium for exotic fabrics and other precious items from the East. Source 14.2A is extracted from a law passed in February 1511 that laid out detailed provisions limiting the extravagance of dress in the city. As the law was reiterated in the following decades, its rules were probably not followed.

In Japan as well, the emergence of a vibrant urban culture based on commerce and consumption challenged traditional distinctions between social classes and caused the government to issue ever more detailed laws regulating dress. Source 14.2B is taken from *The Japanese Family Storehouse* (1688), a book about how merchants made and squandered their fortunes in the seventeenth century. It was written by Ihara Saikaku, a prominent poet and novelist.

- What reasons do Venetian authorities give for issuing their law? Why do you think that the law declares that "all new fashions are banned"?
- For what reasons does Ihara support government regulation on dress? What concerns does Ihara share with Venetian authorities?
- What can you infer about the specific elements of dress that signified social standing in Europe and Japan?
- What can Sources 14.1 and 14.2 tell us about the relationship between clothing and status in the early modern world?

SOURCE 14.2A

Venetian Law Regulating Dress | **1511**

It is announced to all. . . to correct, modify, and take steps against the unusually high expenditures that have been made, and that are being made, in this city and in its territory by men and women of all kinds and stations. . . .

First: Concerning ornaments to the head, it is permissible to wear gold or silver work, both spun continuously and pieced, as long as its value does not exceed fifteen ducats. No pearls or jewels of any kind or type may be worn on the head or on the neck or on any other part of the body, except one strand of pearls at the neckline, which may be worth no more than fifty ducats. . . .

Robes truly must be plain and simple and of one same color and cloth with no ornamentation at the neckline nor a border at the hem. No ornament can be worn over robes, except for a jeweled collar, which may not be worth more than 500 ducats, on those robes that do not have a veil. They may be made with thirty-two *braccia* of silk cloth, whether they have open sleeves or ducal sleeves. Those that have open sleeves may not have more than a quarter of a train; the same holds for those of woolen cloth, which may be made of twenty-eight *braccia* of cloth and no more, of the width of serge. Totally prohibited are chains in place of belts, hoop-belts, sashes, both decorated and plain pockets, and ribbons or cords of gold or silver net and heavy cords. The only thing[s] that may be worn are woven belts with their silver fittings, the total value of which may not exceed fifteen ducats. The total value of all rings for the fingers may not exceed 400 ducats. Be it also declared that all new fashions are banned, which is to say that from now on, no one may wear any new fashion that may be described or imagined.

Source: Marin Sanudo, *Venice Città Excelentissima: Selections from the Diaries of Marin Sanudo*, edited by Patricia H. Labalme and Laura Sanguineti White, translated by Linda Carroll (Baltimore: Johns Hopkins University Press, 2008), 305–6.

SOURCE 14.2B

IHARA SAIKAKU | *The Japanese Family Storehouse* | 1688

Fashions have changed from those of the past and have become increasingly ostentatious. In everything people have a liking for finery above their station. Women's clothes in particular go to extremes. Because they forget their proper place, extravagant women should be in fear of divine punishment. Even the robes of the awesome high-ranking families used to be of nothing finer than Kyoto habutae [a smooth strong silk]. . . . But in recent years, certain shrewd Kyoto [the imperial capital of Japan] people have started to lavish every manner of magnificence on men's and women's clothes and to put out design books in color. With modish fine-figured patterns, palace style hundred-color prints, and bled dapple tie-dye, they go [to] the limit for unusual designs to suit any taste. Such behavior by wives and the marriages of daughters have drained the household finances and impaired the family business of countless merchants. . . .

When we look at these garments [for sale in a shop], we see that the outer material of white figured silk gauze has been folded over and used as the lining as well, with a layer of crimson silk crepe between, making a three-layered summer kimono [a traditional Japanese garment]. Sleeves and collar are padded with silk wadding. There was nothing like this in olden times. To go further than this, they would have to use various materials of Chinese-style weaving as everyday clothes. The recent clothing laws were for all the provinces and all the people. If we give this some thought we realize that we can be grateful for them. It is distressing to see a merchant wearing good silks. Pongee suits him better and looks better on him. But fine clothes are essential to a samurai's status, and therefore even a samurai who is without attendants should not dress like an ordinary person.

Source: Donald Shively, "Sumptuary Regulation and Status in Early Tokugawa Japan," *Harvard Journal of Asiatic Studies* 25 (1964–1965): 124–25.

SOURCE 14.3 Tea and Porcelain in Europe ▶

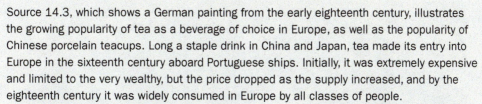

Source 14.3, which shows a German painting from the early eighteenth century, illustrates the growing popularity of tea as a beverage of choice in Europe, as well as the popularity of Chinese porcelain teacups. Long a staple drink in China and Japan, tea made its entry into Europe in the sixteenth century aboard Portuguese ships. Initially, it was extremely expensive and limited to the very wealthy, but the price dropped as the supply increased, and by the eighteenth century it was widely consumed in Europe by all classes of people.

Chinese teacups without handles also became popular and arrived packed in tea or rice via European merchant vessels. By the seventeenth century, the demand for Chinese porcelain in Europe was so large that Chinese artisans created styles and patterns specifically for a European market. Unlike tea, fine Chinese porcelain remained an expensive luxury item and sign of status, but the widespread demand for teacups caused European manufacturers to mass-produce cheaper alternatives that often mimicked Chinese porcelain. The teacups sitting on the table in the foreground of the image are of the finest quality and were manufactured in China between 1662 and 1722. The image also depicts the practice of pouring the tea into the saucer to cool it.

- What is the likely status of the woman in this image, and what evidence would you point to in support of your assessment? What specific cultural practices associated with the consumption of tea can you identify in the image?
- Note the European house on the teacup at the bottom left. What does this indicate about the willingness of the Chinese to cater to European tastes?
- How do you think the cups in this image might have been used to denote status even after tea drinking became common in Europe? In what ways might fine Chinese porcelain have shaped the culture of tea consumption among elites?

Tea Drinking and Chinese Porcelain Cups | **18th century**

■ ■ ■

SOURCE 14.4 A Critical View of Coffeehouses in the Ottoman Empire

During the early modern period, coffee, like tea, became a popular beverage for the first time in many regions around the globe. As coffee entered the Ottoman Empire in the sixteenth century from its place of origin in Ethiopia and Yemen, it encountered considerable opposition, partly because it was consumed in the new social arena of the coffeehouse. Authorities suspected, sometimes quite rightly, that coffeehouses were places of moral decadence and political intrigue. Moralists in the Islamic world labeled the coffeehouse a "refuge of Satan" that drew people away from the mosques even as it brought together all different classes. In Source 14.4, Mustafa bin Ahmed (1541–1600), an Ottoman official and writer better known by his pen name Mustafa Ali, offers a largely negative assessment of Cairo's coffeehouses in his description of a visit to the city in 1599.

- What is it about coffeehouses that Ali criticizes? Does he see any positive role for coffeehouses in society?
- How might Ali's role as an Ottoman official have shaped his view of coffeehouses?
- How might one of the "veteran soldiers" or "aged officers" that Ali identifies react to his description?

MUSTAFA ALI | *Description of Cairo* | 1599

Also [remarkable] is the multitude of coffee-houses in the city of Cairo, the concentration of coffee-houses at every step, and of perfect places where people can assemble. Early rising worshippers and pious men get up and go [there], drink a cup of coffee adding life to their life. They feel, in a way, that its slight exhilaration strengthens them for their religious observance and worship. From that point of view their coffee-houses are commended and praised. But if one considers the ignorant people that assemble in them it is questionable whether they deserve praise. . . .

To make it short, the coffee-houses of Egypt are filled mostly with dissolute persons and opium-eaters. Many are occupied by veteran soldiers, aged officers. When they arrive early in the morning rags and rush mats are spread out, and they stay until evening. . . . [These former military men] are a bunch of parasites . . . whose work consists of presiding over the coffee-house, of drinking coffee on credit, talking of frugality, when the matter comes up, and, having told certain matters with all sorts of distortions. . . . In other words, their talk is mostly lies, their nonsensical speeches are either gossip and backbiting or slander and calumny. . . .

Source: Mustafa Ali, *Mustafa Ali's Description of Cairo of 1599*, translated by Andreas Tietze (Vienna: Verlag der Österreichischen Akademie Der Wissenschaften, 1975), 37.

SOURCE 14.5 An Ottoman Coffeehouse

Critics like Ali failed to stop the spread of coffee in the Ottoman Empire, where it came to embody a new "public culture of fun" as it wore away at earlier religious restrictions on the enjoyment of life.[39] Source 14.5 depicts the new social space of the Turkish coffeehouse, including the numerous activities that accompanied coffee drinking.

- What specific activities can you identify in this painting?
- Would you read this painting as critical of the coffeehouse, as celebrating it, or as a neutral description? Note that the musicians and those playing board games at the bottom are engaged in activities that were considered rather disreputable. How would you describe the general demeanor of the men in the coffeehouse?
- How do you think that Ali in Source 14.4 might react to this image?

A Gathering of Turkish Men at an Ottoman Coffeehouse | **16th century**

Bridgeman Images

SOURCE 14.6 Coffeehouse Culture in England

Coffee spread from the Ottoman Empire to Europe, where authorities worried that coffee and coffeehouses encouraged both laziness and disorder, as King Charles II of England proclaimed in a short-lived effort to ban coffeehouses in his kingdom: "Many Tradesmen and others, do herein misspend much of their time, which might and probably would be employed in and about their Lawful Calling and Affairs; but also, for that in such Houses . . . divers false, malitious and scandalous reports are devised and spread abroad to the Defamation of His Majestie's Government, and to the Disturbance of the Peace and Quiet of the Realm."[40] But European authorities had even less success than their Ottoman counterparts in restraining coffee consumption and suppressing coffeehouse culture. "News from the Coffee-house," a song published in 1667 by the actor and poet Thomas Jordan, conveys the types of conversation that one might expect at a coffeehouse in seventeenth-century London.

- What impression does this song give you of the type of atmosphere one would find in a seventeenth-century English coffeehouse? What sorts of topics were discussed at a coffeehouse?
- Does "News from the Coffee-house" support the case made by Charles II when he issued his ban just a few years after Jordan penned this song?
- How might Jordan respond to the criticism leveled against coffeehouses by Ali in Source 14.4 or by Charles II?

THOMAS JORDAN | *News from the Coffee-house* | 1667

You that delight in Wit and Mirth,
And long to hear such News,
As comes from all parts of the Earth,
Dutch, Danes, and Turks and Jews,
I'll send you a Rendezvous,
Where it is smoking new;
Go hear it at a *Coffee-house*;
It cannot but be true.

There battles and sea-fights are fought,
And bloody plots displayed;
They know more things that ere was thought,
Or ever was betrayed:
No money in the Minting-house
Is half so bright and new;
And coming from the coffee-house,
It cannot but be true. . . .

The drinking there of chocolate
Can make a fool a Sophy [wise man];
'Tis thought the Turkish Mahomet
[Muhammad]
Was first inspired with coffee,
By which his powers did overflow
The land of Palestine;
Then let us to the coffee-house go,
'Tis cheaper far than wine.

You shall know there what fashions are,
How periwiggs are curl'd,
And for a penny you shall heare
All novells in the world;
Both old and young, and great and small,
And rich and poore, you'll see;
Therefore let's to the coffee all,
Come all away with me.

Source: R. Chambers, ed., *The Book of Days: A Miscellany of Popular Antiquities in Connection with the Calendar* (London: W. & R. Chambers, 1879), 1:172–73.

DOING HISTORY

1. **Connecting Consumption and Culture** In what different ways did the growing availability of goods change the cultures that consumed them?
2. **Thinking about the Social Implications of Consumption** How did consumption of new products create new social environments?
3. **Raising Questions about Cultural Borrowing** What do these sources suggest about the problems and opportunities caused by cross-cultural borrowing?
4. **Making Connections** In our own time, consumption of goods from around the world continues to have cultural implications. What examples of cultural change linked to the consumption of new or imported goods can you identify in the highly globalized world of the twenty-first century?

HISTORIANS' VOICES

On Consumer Culture in the Early Modern World

Here two historians assess the development of consumer culture during the early modern period. Frank Trentmann, a leading expert on the emergence of modern consumer culture, examines in Voice 14.1 what made the cultures of consumption in the Netherlands and Britain during the seventeenth and eighteenth centuries distinct from earlier consumer cultures in Renaissance Europe and Ming China. In Voice 14.2, Anne Gerritsen, a professor of Chinese history, and Giorgio Riello, a historian of global history and culture, assess the varied impacts of increased global exchange on the production and consumption of goods across the globe in the early modern period.

- According to Trentmann, what specific factors made the culture of consumption distinctly dynamic and innovative in the Netherlands and Britain during the early modern period?
- In what ways did consumption spurred by global exchange transform the early modern world according to Gerritsen and Riello?
- **Integrating Primary and Secondary Sources** How might you construct an essay about early modern consumer culture using the two voices and the various sources in this feature?

VOICE 14.1

Frank Trentmann on Consumer Culture in the Netherlands and Britain | 2016

It was in the north-west of Europe, in the Netherlands and Britain, that a more dynamic, innovative culture of consumption came to take hold in the seventeenth and eighteenth centuries. The growth in shops, markets and personal belongings was well under way in Renaissance Europe and Ming China, but their further expansion in the Netherlands and Britain was only in part a continuation of this earlier trend. For the two countries separated by the North Sea changed after 1600 in ways that, together, created a new kind of consumer culture. The exponential rise in [the amount of] stuff went hand in hand with a rise in novelty, variety and availability, and this was connected to a more general openness to the world of goods and its contribution to the individual self [individual identity and well-being], to social order and economic development. What distinguished the basket of goods in the eighteenth century was the combination of novelty, variety and the speed of change. Tobacco, tea and porcelain were new things that spawned new forms of consuming, socializing and self-representation. Equally important was the jump in variety. The manufacturer Matthew Boulton, who sold tea kettles, buckles, buttons and toothpick cases, had 1,500 designs on his books.

Source: Frank Trentmann, *Empire of Things: How We Became a World of Consumers, from the Fifteenth Century to the Twenty-First* (New York: Harper, 2016), 53.

VOICE 14.2

Anne Gerritsen and Giorgio Riello on the Impacts of Global Consumption and Exchange | 2018

Between 1500 and 1800 the exchange of goods became global, and European consumers could buy goods from all over the world. At the beginning of the period, goods from Asia were seen as exotic luxuries for kings and noblemen; by the end of the period silks and porcelains had come within the reach of orphans in Amsterdam or the descendants of slaves in New Spain. The impact of this development was huge: the African slave trade and the sugar and cotton plantations throughout the Americas were closely related to the almost insatiable desire for global goods. In early modern Europe, the demand for Asian goods vastly outstripped supply, and new commodities were manufactured to make up for this shortfall. Arguably the textile manufacturers and potteries of Central and Northern England that drove the Industrial Revolution did so because of the competition with Asian goods. In sum, global goods transformed the early modern world.

Source: Beat Kümin, ed., *The European World 1500–1800: An Introduction to Early Modern History*, 3rd ed. (London: Routledge, 2018), 212–13.

Gianni Dagli Orti/Shutterstock

CHAPTER

15

Cultural Transformations

Religion and Science

1450–1750

CONNECTING PAST AND PRESENT

"Britain brought the gospel to us in the past. Now, by God's providence we are here when Christianity is very much challenged and the UK churches are really declining."[1] This was the view expressed in 2017 by Girma Bishaw, a London-based Ethiopian-British pastor, referring to a growing movement among African Christian organizations who sought to bring the Gospel back to an increasingly secular West. These "reverse missionaries" represented a remarkable shift from earlier efforts by European and North American missionaries to bring Christianity to Africa and Asia, beginning in the early modern era. One reason for the empty churches in the West lay in another cultural change—the spread of modern scientific and secular thinking, which for some people undermined religious belief. That enormous transformation likewise took shape in the early modern era.

And so, alongside new empires and new patterns of commerce, the early modern centuries also witnessed novel cultural and religious transformations that likewise connected distant peoples. Riding the currents of European empire building and commercial expansion, Christianity was established solidly in the Americas and the Philippines and, though far more modestly, in Siberia, China, Japan, and India. A cultural tradition largely limited to Europe in 1500 was now becoming a genuine world religion, spawning a multitude of cultural encounters—though it spread hardly at all within the vast and still-growing domains of Islam. This globalization of Christianity persisted in the nineteenth and twentieth centuries. But while Christianity

« **The Virgin of Guadalupe** According to Mexican tradition, a dark-skinned Virgin Mary appeared to an indigenous peasant named Juan Diego in 1531, an apparition reflected in this Mexican painting from 1720. Belief in the Virgin of Guadalupe represented the incorporation of European Catholicism into the emerging culture and identity of Mexico.

was spreading globally, a new understanding of the universe and a new approach to knowledge were taking shape among European thinkers of the Scientific Revolution, giving rise to another kind of cultural encounter—that between science and religion. Science was a new and competing worldview, and for some it became almost a new religion. In time, it grew into a defining feature of global modernity, achieving a worldwide acceptance that exceeded that of Christianity or any other religious tradition.

Although Europeans were central players in the globalization of Christianity and the emergence of modern science, they were not alone in shaping the cultural transformations of the early modern era. Asian, African, and Native American peoples largely determined how Christianity would be accepted, rejected, or transformed as it entered new cultural environments. Science emerged within an international and not simply a European context, and it met varying receptions in different parts of the world. Islam continued a long pattern of religious expansion and renewal, even as Christianity began to compete with it as a world religion. Buddhism maintained its hold in much of East Asia, as did Hinduism in South Asia and numerous smaller-scale religious traditions in Africa. And Europeans themselves were certainly affected by the many "new worlds" that they now encountered. The cultural interactions of the early modern era, in short, did not take place on a one-way street.

SEEKING THE MAIN POINT

To what extent did the cultural changes of the early modern world derive from cross-cultural interactions rather than from developments within societies and civilizations?

The Globalization of Christianity

Despite its Middle Eastern origins and its earlier presence in many parts of the Afro-Asian world, Christianity was largely limited to Europe at the beginning of the early modern era. In 1500, the world of Christendom stretched from the Iberian Peninsula in the west to Russia in the east, with small and beleaguered communities of various kinds in Egypt, Ethiopia, southern India, and Central Asia. Internally, the Christian world was seriously divided between the Roman Catholics of Western and Central Europe and the Eastern Orthodox of Eastern Europe and Russia. Externally, it was very much on the defensive against an expansive Islam. Muslims had ousted Christian Crusaders from their toeholds in the Holy Land by 1300, and with the Ottoman seizure of Constantinople in 1453, they had captured the prestigious capital of Eastern Orthodoxy. The Ottoman siege of Vienna in 1529, and again in 1683, marked a Muslim advance into the heart of Central Europe. Except in Spain and Sicily, which had recently been reclaimed for Christendom after centuries of Muslim rule, the future, it must have seemed, lay with Islam rather than Christianity.

Western Christendom Fragmented: The Protestant Reformation

As if these were not troubles enough, in the early sixteenth century the **Protestant Reformation** shattered the unity of Roman Catholic Christianity, which for the

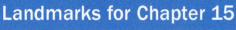

Landmarks for Chapter 15

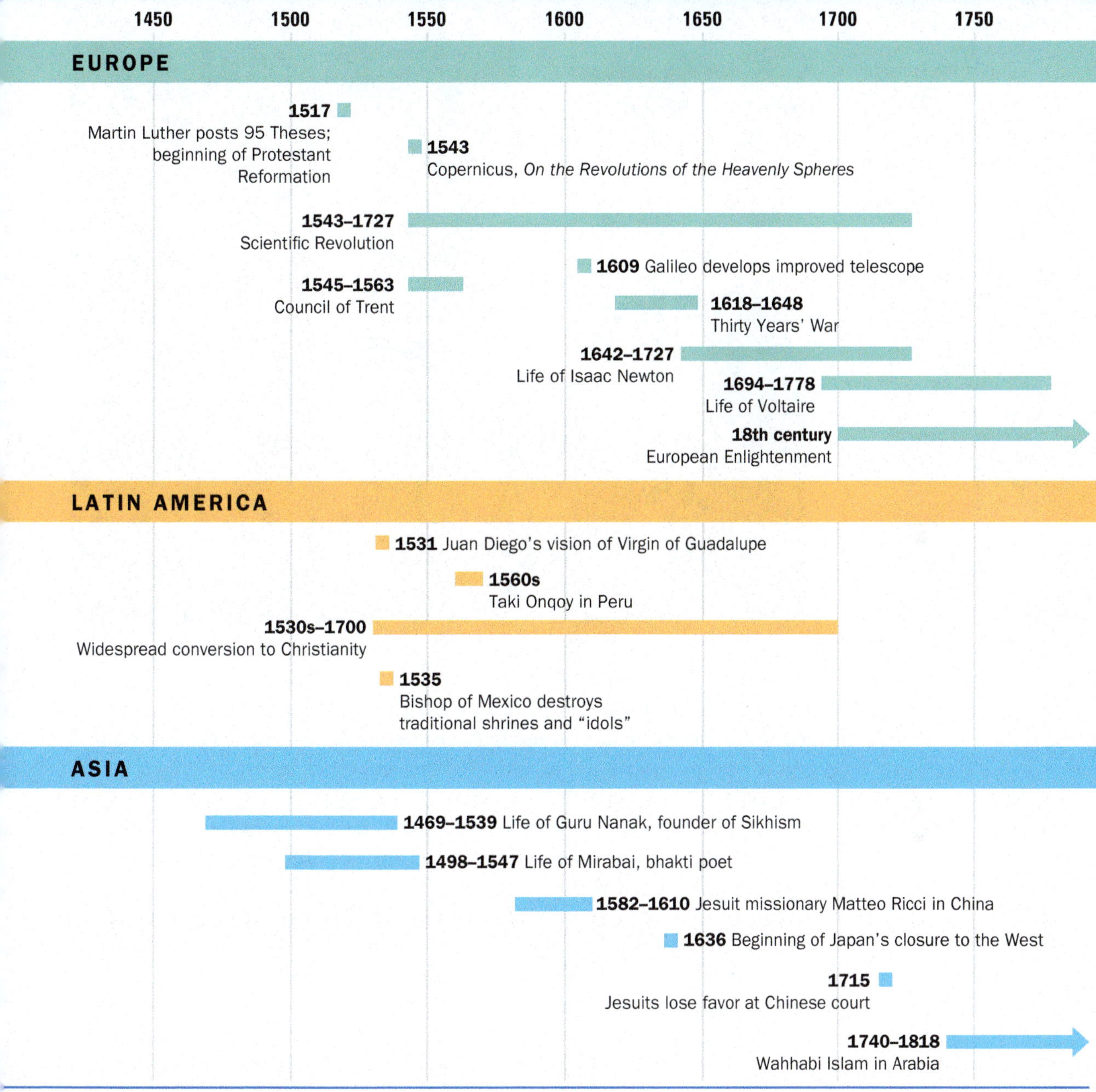
1450
1500
1550
1600
1650
1700
1750
EUROPE
1517 Martin Luther posts 95 Theses; beginning of Protestant Reformation
1543 Copernicus, *On the Revolutions of the Heavenly Spheres*
1543–1727 Scientific Revolution
1609 Galileo develops improved telescope
1545–1563 Council of Trent
1618–1648 Thirty Years' War
1642–1727 Life of Isaac Newton
1694–1778 Life of Voltaire
18th century European Enlightenment
LATIN AMERICA
1531 Juan Diego's vision of Virgin of Guadalupe
1560s Taki Onqoy in Peru
1530s–1700 Widespread conversion to Christianity
1535 Bishop of Mexico destroys traditional shrines and "idols"
ASIA
1469–1539 Life of Guru Nanak, founder of Sikhism
1498–1547 Life of Mirabai, bhakti poet
1582–1610 Jesuit missionary Matteo Ricci in China
1636 Beginning of Japan's closure to the West
1715 Jesuits lose favor at Chinese court
1740–1818 Wahhabi Islam in Arabia

previous 1,000 years had provided the cultural and organizational foundation of an emerging Western European civilization. The Reformation began in 1517 when a German priest, **Martin Luther** (1483–1546), publicly invited debate about various abuses within the Roman Catholic Church by issuing a document, known as the Ninety-Five Theses, allegedly nailing it to the door of a church in Wittenberg. In itself,

The Protestant Reformation This woodcut by the Protestant artist Lucas Cranach the Younger, entitled *The True and False Churches*, depicts Martin Luther at its center preaching the pure word of God from his pulpit. On the left and below Luther, Cranach depicts an orderly and godly Protestant congregation at worship. To the right the open flaming mouth of a demon consumes bishops, monks, and the pope, who physically embody for Cranach the false and disorderly Catholic Church. (akg-images/Newscom)

this was nothing new, for many had long been critical of the luxurious life of the popes, the corruption and immorality of some clergy, the Church's selling of indulgences (said to remove the penalties for sin), and other aspects of church life and practice.

What made Luther's protest potentially revolutionary, however, was its theological basis. A troubled and brooding man anxious about his relationship with God, Luther had recently come to a new understanding of salvation, which, he believed, came through faith alone. Neither the good works of the sinner nor the sacraments of the Church had any bearing on the eternal destiny of the soul. To Luther, the source of these beliefs, and of religious authority in general, was not the teaching of the Church, but the Bible alone, interpreted according to the individual's conscience. All of this challenged the authority of the Church and called into question the special position of the clerical hierarchy and the pope. In sixteenth-century Europe, this was the stuff of revolution. (See Snapshot: Catholic/Protestant Differences in the Sixteenth Century, page 643.)

Contrary to Luther's original intentions, his ideas provoked a massive schism within the world of Catholic Christendom, for they came to express a variety of political, economic, and social tensions as well as religious differences. Some

SNAPSHOT Catholic/Protestant Differences in the Sixteenth Century

	Catholic	Protestant
Religious authority	The Bible and church tradition as defined by pope and church councils	The Bible alone
Role of the pope	Leader of church	Authority of the pope denied
Ordination of clergy	Apostolic succession: direct line between original apostles and all subsequently ordained clergy	Apostolic succession denied; ordination by individual congregations or denominations
Role of clergy	Priests are generally celibate; sharp distinction between priests and laypeople; priests are mediators between God and humankind	Ministers may marry; priesthood of all believers; clergy have different functions (to preach, administer sacraments) but no distinct spiritual status
Salvation	Importance of church sacraments as channels of God's grace	Importance of faith alone; God's grace is freely and directly granted to believers
Status of Mary	Highly prominent, ranking just below Jesus; provides constant intercession for believers	Less prominent; Mary's intercession on behalf of the faithful denied
Role of saints	Prominent spiritual exemplars and intermediaries between God and humankind	Generally disdained as a source of idolatry; saints refer to all Christians
Prayer	To God, but often through or with Mary and saints	To God alone; no role for Mary and saints

kings and princes, many of whom had long disputed the political authority of the pope, found in these ideas a justification for their own independence and an opportunity to gain the lands and revenues previously held by the Church. In the Protestant idea that all vocations were of equal merit, middle-class urban dwellers found a new religious legitimacy for their growing role in society. For common people, who were offended by the corruption and luxurious living of some churchmen, the new religious ideas served to express their opposition to the entire social order, particularly in a series of German peasant revolts in the 1520s.

Although large numbers of women were attracted to Protestantism, Reformation teachings and practices did not offer them a substantially greater role in the Church or society. Protestant opposition to celibacy and monastic life closed the convents,

CORE IDEA

Analyzing Change
In what ways did the Protestant Reformation transform European society, culture, and politics?

which had offered some women an alternative to marriage. Nor were Protestants (except the Quakers) any more willing than Catholics to offer women an official role within their churches. The importance that Protestants gave to reading the Bible for oneself stimulated education and literacy for women, but given the emphasis on women as wives and mothers subject to male supervision, they had little opportunity to use that education outside of the family.

Reformation thinking spread quickly both within and beyond Germany, thanks in large measure to the recent invention of the printing press. Luther's many pamphlets and his translation of the New Testament into German were soon widely available. "God has appointed the [printing] Press to preach, whose voice the pope is never able to stop," declared the English Protestant writer John Foxe in 1563.[2] As the movement spread to France, Switzerland, England, and elsewhere, it also divided, amoeba-like, into a variety of competing Protestant churches—Lutheran, Calvinist, Anglican, Quaker, Anabaptist—many of which subsequently subdivided, producing a bewildering array of Protestant denominations. Each was distinctive, but none gave allegiance to Rome or the pope.

Thus to the sharp class divisions and the fractured political system of Europe was now added the potent brew of religious difference, operating both within and between states (see Map 15.1). For more than thirty years (1562–1598), French society was torn by violence between Catholics and the Protestant minority known as Huguenots (HYOO-guh-noh). The culmination of European religious conflict took shape in the **Thirty Years' War** (1618–1648), a Catholic–Protestant struggle that began in the Holy Roman Empire but eventually engulfed most of Europe. It was a horrendously destructive war, during which, scholars estimate, between 15 and 30 percent of the German population perished from violence, famine, or disease. Finally, the Peace of Westphalia (1648) brought the conflict to an end, with some reshuffling of boundaries and an agreement that each state was sovereign, authorized to control religious affairs within its own territory. Whatever religious unity Catholic Europe had once enjoyed was now permanently splintered.

The Protestant breakaway, combined with reformist tendencies within the Catholic Church itself, provoked a Catholic Reformation, or **Counter-Reformation**. In the Council of Trent (1545–1563), Catholics clarified and reaffirmed their unique doctrines, sacraments, and practices, such as the authority of the pope, priestly celibacy, the veneration of saints and relics, and the importance of church tradition and good works, all of which Protestants had rejected. Moreover, they set about correcting the abuses and corruption that had stimulated the Protestant movement by placing a new emphasis on the education of priests and their supervision by bishops. New religious orders, such as the Society of Jesus (Jesuits), provided a dedicated brotherhood of priests committed to the revival of the Catholic Church and its extension abroad. Renewed efforts to foster individual spirituality and personal piety were accompanied by crackdowns on dissidents and the censorship of books.

MAPPING HISTORY

Map 15.1 Reformation Europe in the Sixteenth Century

The rise of Protestantism added yet another set of religious divisions, both within and between states, to the world of Christendom, which was already sharply divided between the Roman Catholic Church and the Eastern Orthodox Church. Note that France and much of Eastern Europe returned firmly to the Catholic faith during the seventeenth century.

READING THE MAP What parts of Western Europe were predominantly Protestant by the end of the sixteenth century? Which regions remained predominantly Catholic? How would you describe the religious situation in the Holy Roman Empire?

MAKING CONNECTIONS Compare this map with Map 15.2: The Globalization of Christianity. Did Catholic or Protestant states control the largest overseas colonies?

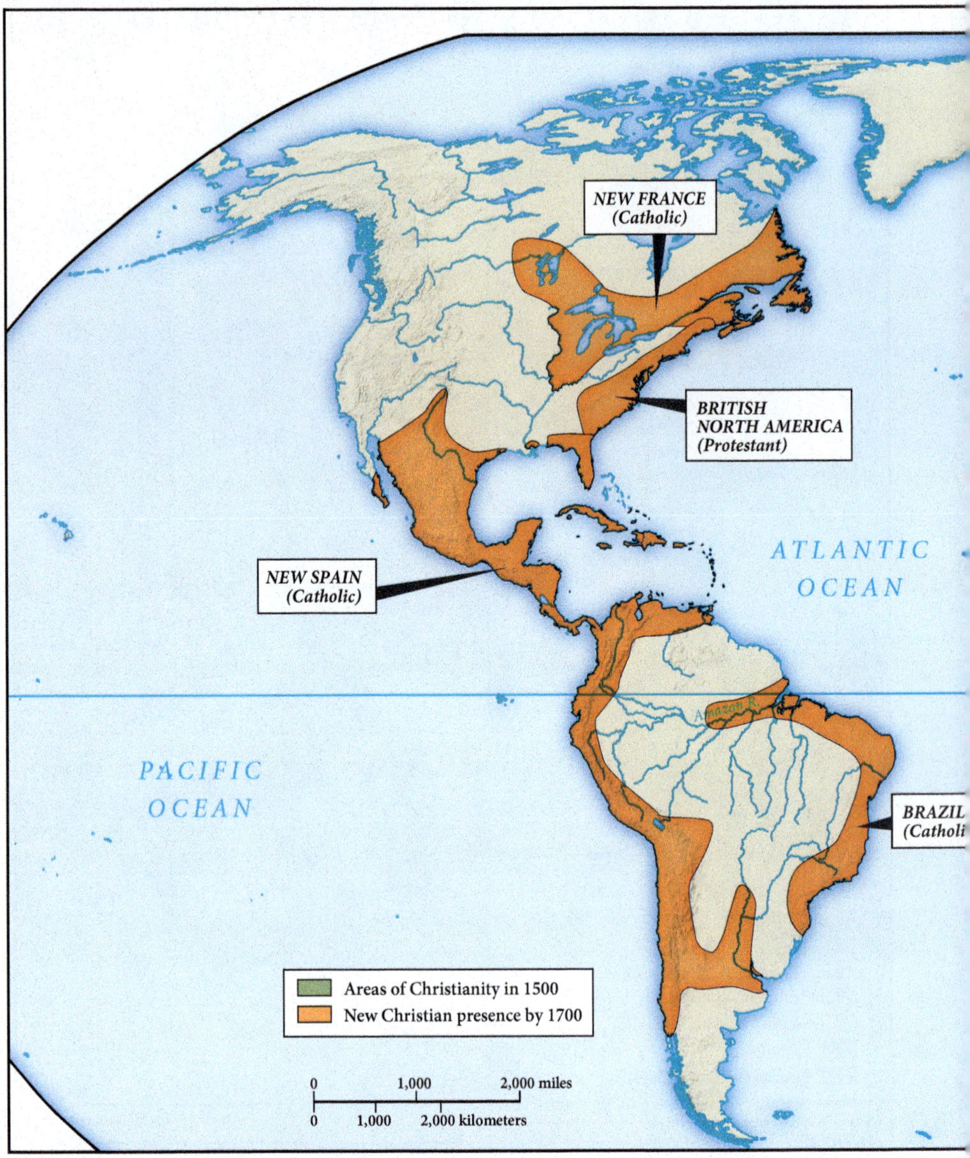

Map 15.2 The Globalization of Christianity
The growing Christian presence in Asia, Africa, and especially the Americas, combined with older centers of that faith, gave the religion derived from Jesus a global dimension during the early modern era.

Although the Reformation was profoundly religious, it encouraged a skeptical attitude toward authority and tradition, for it had, after all, successfully challenged the immense prestige and power of the established Church. Protestant reformers fostered religious individualism, as people now read and interpreted the scriptures for themselves and sought salvation without the mediation of the Church. In the

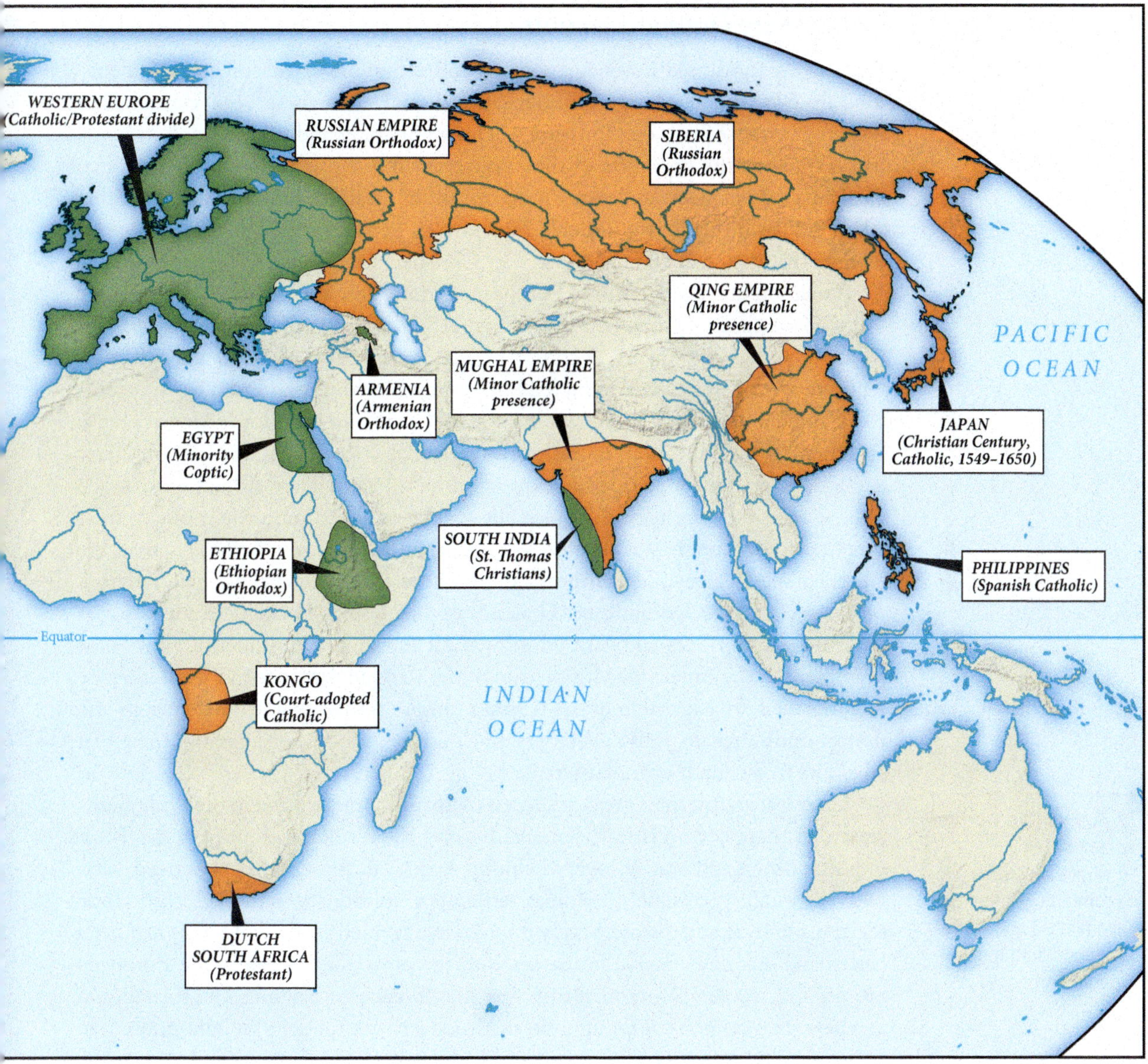

centuries that followed, some people turned that skepticism and the habit of thinking independently against all conventional religion. Thus the Protestant Reformation opened some space for new directions in European intellectual life.

In short, it was a more highly fragmented but also a renewed and revitalized Christianity that established itself around the world in the several centuries after 1500 (see Map 15.2).

Christianity Outward Bound

Christianity motivated European political and economic expansion and also benefited from it. The resolutely Catholic Spanish and Portuguese both viewed their movement overseas as a continuation of a long crusading tradition that only recently had completed the liberation of their countries from Muslim control. When Vasco da Gama's small fleet landed in India in 1498, local authorities understandably asked, "What brought you hither?" The travelers replied, with no sense of contradiction, that they had come "in search of Christians and of spices."[3]

If religion drove and justified European ventures abroad, it is difficult to imagine the globalization of Christianity (see Map 15.2) without the support of empire. Colonial settlers and traders, of course, brought their faith with them and sought to replicate it in their newly conquered homelands. New England Puritans, for example, planted a distinctive Protestant version of Christianity in North America, with an emphasis on education, moral purity, personal conversion, civic responsibility, and little tolerance for competing expressions of the faith. They did not show much interest in converting native peoples but sought rather to push them out of their ancestral territories. It was missionaries, mostly Catholic, who actively spread the Christian message beyond European communities. Organized primarily in religious orders such as the Dominicans, Franciscans, and Jesuits, Portuguese missionaries took the lead in Africa and Asia, while Spanish and French missionaries were most prominent in the Americas. Missionaries of the Russian Orthodox Church likewise accompanied the expansion of the Russian Empire across Siberia, where priests and monks ministered to Russian settlers and trappers, who often donated their first sable furs to a church or monastery.

■ Assessing Cultural Interaction
In what ways was European Christianity assimilated into Native American cultures of Spanish America?

Missionaries had their greatest success in Spanish America and in the Philippines, areas that shared two critical elements beyond their colonization by Spain. Most important, perhaps, was an overwhelming European presence, experienced variously as military conquest, colonial settlement, missionary activity, forced labor, social disruption, and disease. Surely it must have seemed as if the old gods had been bested and that any possible future lay with the powerful religion of the European invaders. A second common factor was the absence of a literate world religion in these two regions. Throughout the modern era, peoples solidly rooted in Confucian, Buddhist, Hindu, or Islamic traditions proved far more resistant to the Christian message than those who practiced more localized, small-scale, orally based religions. (See Working with Evidence, page 674, for sources illustrating the global spread of Christianity.) Spanish America and China illustrate the difference between those societies in which Christianity became widely practiced and those that largely rejected it.

Conversion and Adaptation in Spanish America

The decisive conquest of the Aztec and Inca empires and all that followed from it—disease, population collapse, loss of land to Europeans, forced labor, resettlement—created a setting in which the religion of the victors took hold in

Spanish American colonies. Europeans saw their political and military success as a demonstration of the power of the Christian God. Native American peoples generally agreed, and by 1700 or earlier the vast majority had been baptized and saw themselves in some respects as Christians. After all, other conquerors such as the Aztecs and the Incas had always imposed their gods in some fashion on defeated peoples. So it made sense, both practically and spiritually, for many millions of indigenous people to accept baptism, contribute to the construction of village churches, attend services, and embrace images of saints.

CORE IDEA

Assessing Differences

Why were missionary efforts to spread Christianity so much less successful in China than in Spanish America?

Despite the prominence of the Virgin Mary as a religious figure across Latin America, the cost of conversion was high, especially for women. Many women who had long served as priests, shamans, or ritual specialists had no corresponding role in a Catholic church, led by an all-male clergy. And convent life, which had provided some outlet for female authority and education in Catholic Europe, was reserved largely for Spanish women in the Americas.

Earlier conquerors had made no attempt to eradicate local deities and religious practices. The flexibility and inclusiveness of Mesoamerican and Andean religions had made it possible for subject people to accommodate the gods of their new rulers while maintaining their own traditions. But Europeans were different. They claimed an exclusive religious truth and sought the utter destruction of local gods and everything associated with them. Operating within a Spanish colonial regime that actively encouraged conversion, missionaries often proceeded by persuasion and patient teaching. At times, though, their frustration with the persistence of "idolatry, superstition, and error" boiled over into violent campaigns designed to uproot old religions once and for all. In 1535, the bishop of Mexico proudly claimed that he had destroyed 500 pagan shrines and 20,000 idols. During the seventeenth and early eighteenth centuries, church authorities in the Andean region periodically launched movements of "extirpation," designed to fatally undermine native religion. They destroyed religious images and ritual objects, publicly urinated on native "idols," desecrated the remains of ancestors, flogged "idolaters," and held religious trials and "processions of shame" aimed at humiliating offenders.

Such aggressive action generated resistance. Writing around 1600, the native Peruvian nobleman Guaman Poma de Ayala commented on the posture of native women toward Christianity: "They do not confess …

Andean Christianity Religious syncretism in the Andes emerged during the early modern era and continues to play an important role in the religious life of the region today. This modern image shows Peruvians, at an altitude of 16,000 feet, participating in a pilgrimage that combines ancient Andean celebrations of the approaching harvest and new year with a Catholic festival. (Hughes Hervé/AGE Fotostock)

nor do they go to mass. . . . And resuming their ancient customs and idolatry, they do not want to serve God or the crown."[4] Occasionally, overt resistance erupted. One such example was the religious revivalist movement in central Peru in the 1560s, known as **Taki Onqoy** (dancing sickness). Possessed by the spirits of local gods, or *huacas*, traveling dancers and teachers predicted that an alliance of Andean deities would soon overcome the Christian God, inflict the intruding Europeans with the same diseases that they had brought to the Americas, and restore the world of the Andes to an imagined earlier harmony. "The world has turned about," one member declared, "and this time God and the Spaniards [will be] defeated and all the Spaniards killed and their cities drowned . . . so that there will remain no memory of them."[5]

More common than such frontal attacks on Christianity, which colonial authorities quickly smashed, were efforts at blending religious traditions by reinterpreting Christian practices within an Andean framework and incorporating local elements into an emerging Andean Christianity. Women, for instance, might offer the blood of a llama to strengthen a village church or make a cloth covering for the Virgin Mary and a shirt for an image of a huaca with the same material. Some Andeans continued to venerate local huacas even as they engaged with Christian missionaries who sought to destroy images and holy sites. "Father, are you tired of taking our idols from us?" asked one resilient Andean resident of a Jesuit missionary. "Take away that mountain if you can, since that is the God I worship."[6]

In Mexico as well, an immigrant Christianity was assimilated into patterns of local culture. Churches built on or near the sites of old temples became the focus of community identity. *Cofradias*, church-based associations of laypeople, organized community processions and festivals and made provisions for proper funerals and burials for their members. Central to an emerging Mexican Christianity were the saints who closely paralleled the functions of precolonial gods. Saints were imagined as parents of the local community and the true owners of its land, and their images were paraded through the streets on the occasion of great feasts and were collected by individual households. Mexico's Virgin of Guadalupe neatly combined both Mesoamerican and Spanish notions of Divine Motherhood (see the chapter-opening photo and Historians' Voice 15.1, page 682). Although parish priests were almost always Spanish, the *fiscal*, or leader of the church staff, was a native Christian of great local prestige who carried on the traditions and role of earlier religious specialists.

Throughout the colonial period and beyond, many Mexican Christians also took part in rituals derived from the past, with little sense of incompatibility with Christian practice. Incantations to various gods for good fortune in hunting, farming, or healing and sacrifices involving self-bleeding provided spiritual assistance in those areas of everyday life not directly addressed by Christian rites. Conversely, these practices also showed signs of Christian influence. Wax candles, normally used in Christian services, might now appear in front of a stone image of a precolonial god. The anger of a neglected saint, rather than that of a traditional god, might explain someone's illness and require offerings, celebration, or a new covering to regain his or her favor. In such ways did Christianity take root in the new cultural environments of Spanish America, but it was a distinctly Andean or Mexican Christianity, not merely a copy of the Spanish version.

An Asian Comparison: China and the Jesuits

Analyzing Cultural Interaction
In what different ways did Chinese authorities respond to Christian missionaries?

The Chinese encounter with Christianity was very different from that of Native Americans in Spain's New World empire. At no point was China's political independence or cultural integrity threatened by the handful of European missionaries and traders working there during the early modern period. A strong, independent, confident China required a different missionary strategy, for Europeans needed the permission of Chinese authorities to operate in the country. Whereas Spanish missionaries working in a colonial setting sought to convert the masses, the **Jesuits in China**, the leading missionary order there, took deliberate aim at the official Chinese elite. Following the example of their most famous missionary, Matteo Ricci (in China 1582–1610), many Jesuits learned Chinese, became thoroughly acquainted with classical Confucian texts, and dressed like Chinese scholars. Initially, they downplayed their mission to convert and instead emphasized their interest in exchanging ideas and learning from China's ancient culture. For a time in the seventeenth and early eighteenth centuries, the Jesuits found favor at the Chinese imperial court. Their Western mathematical, astronomical, technological, and mapmaking skills rendered them useful, and the emperor appointed a series of Jesuits to head the Chinese Bureau of Astronomy.

In presenting Christian teachings, Jesuits were at pains to be respectful of Chinese culture, pointing out parallels between Confucianism and Christianity rather than portraying Christianity as something new and foreign. They chose to define Chinese rituals honoring the emperor or venerating ancestors as secular or civil observances rather than as religious practices that had to be abandoned. Such efforts to accommodate Chinese culture contrast sharply with the frontal attacks on Native American religions in the Spanish Empire.

The religious and cultural outcomes of the missionary enterprise likewise differed greatly in the two regions. Nothing approaching mass conversion to Christianity took place in China, as it had in Latin America. During the sixteenth and seventeenth centuries, a modest number of Chinese scholars and officials did become Christians, attracted by the personal lives of the missionaries, by their interest in Western science, and by the moral certainty that Christianity offered. Among ordinary people, Christianity spread very modestly amid tales of miracles attributed to the Christian God, while missionary teachings about "eternal life" sounded to some like Daoist prescriptions for immortality. At most, though, missionary efforts over the course of some 250 years (1550–1800) resulted in 200,000 to 300,000 converts, a minuscule number in a Chinese population approaching 300 million by 1800. What explains the very limited acceptance of Christianity in early modern China?

Fundamentally, the missionaries offered little that the Chinese really wanted. Confucianism for the elites and Buddhism, Daoism, and a multitude of Chinese gods and spirits at the local level adequately supplied the spiritual needs of most Chinese.

Jesuits in China In this seventeenth-century engraving, two Jesuit missionaries stand before a Christian altar in China dressed in the clothing of imperial officials. The Jesuits were initially welcomed among the educated elite of the country because of their Western learning, particularly in the fields of astronomy and mapmaking, even if their Christian missionary endeavors were less warmly received. (Bridgeman Art Library/Image Partner/Getty Images)

Furthermore, it became increasingly clear that Christianity was an all-or-nothing faith that required converts to abandon much of traditional Chinese culture. Christian monogamy, for example, seemed to require Chinese men to put away their concubines. What would happen to these deserted women? Finally, despite all their efforts, Christian missionaries remained outsiders in China. From the mid-seventeenth century on, this status was only reinforced in the minds of many Chinese elites by the growing numbers of Europeans in East Asia, most of whom did not try to assimilate into Chinese culture, and the Jesuits' willingness to work under what many saw as the foreign and uncivilized Manchus after the Qing dynasty seized power in 1644. (For more on the Manchus, see "Making China an Empire" in Chapter 13.) By the early eighteenth century, the papacy and competing missionary orders came to oppose the Jesuit policy of accommodation. The pope claimed authority over Chinese Christians and declared that sacrifices to Confucius and the veneration of ancestors were "idolatry" and thus forbidden to Christians. The pope's pronouncements represented an unacceptable challenge to the authority of the emperor and an affront to Chinese culture. In 1715, an outraged Emperor Kangxi prohibited Westerners from spreading Christian doctrine in his kingdom (see Working with Evidence, Source 15.4B, page 680). This represented a major turning point in the relationship between Christian missionaries and Chinese society. Many were subsequently expelled, and missionaries lost favor at court.

Persistence and Change in Afro-Asian Cultural Traditions

Although Europeans were central players in the globalization of Christianity, theirs was not the only expanding or transformed culture of the early modern era. African religious ideas and practices, for example, accompanied enslaved people to the

Americas. Common African forms of religious revelation—divination, dream interpretation, visions, spirit possession—found a place in the Africanized versions of Christianity that emerged in the New World. Europeans frequently perceived these practices as evidence of sorcery, witchcraft, or even devil worship and tried to suppress them. Nonetheless, syncretic (blended) religions such as Vodou in Haiti, Santeria in Cuba, and Candomblé and Macumba in Brazil persisted. They derived from various West African traditions and featured drumming, ritual dancing, animal sacrifice, and spirit possession. Over time, they incorporated Christian beliefs and practices such as church attendance, the search for salvation, and the use of candles and crucifixes and often identified their various spirits or deities with Catholic saints.

Expansion and Renewal in the Islamic World

CORE IDEA

■ Identifying What Is New

What new departures in cultural life are apparent in the Islamic world, China, and India during the early modern era?

The early modern era likewise witnessed the continuation of the "long march of Islam" across the Afro-Asian world. In sub-Saharan Africa, in the eastern and western wings of India, and in Central and Southeast Asia, the expansion of the Islamic frontier, a process already a thousand years in the making, extended farther still. Conversion to Islam generally did not mean a sudden abandonment of old religious practices in favor of the new. Rather, it was more often a matter of "assimilating Islamic rituals, cosmologies, and literatures into . . . local religious systems."[7]

Continued Islamization was not usually the product of conquering armies and expanding empires. It depended instead on wandering Muslim holy men or Sufis, Islamic scholars, and itinerant traders, none of whom posed a threat to local rulers. In fact, such people often were useful to those rulers and their communities. They offered literacy in Arabic, established informal schools, provided protective charms containing passages from the Quran, served as advisers to local authorities and healers to the sick, often intermarried with local people, and generally did not insist that new converts give up their older practices. What they offered, in short, was connection to the wider, prestigious, prosperous world of Islam. Islamization extended modestly even to the Americas, particularly in Brazil, where Muslims led a number of slave revolts in the early nineteenth century.

The islands of Southeast Asia illustrate the diversity of belief and practice that accompanied the spread of Islam in the early modern era. During the seventeenth century in Aceh, a Muslim sultanate on the northern tip of Sumatra, authorities sought to enforce the dietary codes and almsgiving practices of Islamic law. After four successive women ruled the area in the late seventeenth century, women were forbidden from exercising political power. On Muslim Java, however, numerous women served in royal courts, and women throughout Indonesia continued their longtime role as buyers and sellers in local markets. Among ordinary Javanese, traditional animistic practices of spirit worship coexisted easily with a tolerant and accommodating Islam, while merchants often embraced a more orthodox version of the religion in line with Middle Eastern traditions.

Explaining Change
What accounts for the rise of Islamic reform or renewal movements?

To such orthodox Muslims, religious syncretism, which accompanied Islamization almost everywhere, became increasingly offensive, even heretical. Such sentiments played an important role in movements of religious renewal and reform that emerged throughout the vast Islamic world of the eighteenth century. The leaders of such movements sharply criticized those practices that departed from earlier patterns established by Muhammad and from the authority of the Quran. For example, in India, governed by the Muslim Mughal Empire, religious resistance to official policies that accommodated Hindus found concrete expression during the reign of the emperor Aurangzeb (r. 1658–1707) (see "Muslims and Hindus in the Mughal Empire" in Chapter 13). A series of religious wars in West Africa during the eighteenth and early nineteenth centuries took aim at corrupt Islamic practices and the rulers, Muslim and non-Muslim alike, who permitted them. In Southeast and Central Asia, tension grew between practitioners of localized and blended versions of Islam and those who sought to purify such practices in the name of a more authentic and universal faith.

The most well known and widely visible of these Islamic renewal movements took place during the mid-eighteenth century in Arabia, the original homeland of the faith, where they found expression in the teachings of the Islamic scholar Muhammad Ibn Abd al-Wahhab (1703–1792). The growing difficulties of the Islamic world, such as the weakening of the Ottoman Empire, were directly related, he argued, to deviations from the pure faith of early Islam. Al-Wahhab was particularly upset by common religious practices in central Arabia that seemed to him idolatry—the widespread veneration of Sufi saints and their tombs, the adoration of natural sites, and even the respect paid to Muhammad's tomb at Medina. All of this was a dilution of the absolute monotheism of authentic Islam.

The Wahhabi movement took a new turn in the 1740s when it received the political backing of Muhammad Ibn Saud, a local ruler who found al-Wahhab's ideas compelling. With Ibn Saud's support, the religious movement became an expansive state in central Arabia. Within that state, offending tombs were razed; "idols" were eliminated; books on logic were destroyed; the use of tobacco, hashish, and musical instruments was forbidden; and certain taxes not authorized by religious teaching were abolished.

Although **Wahhabi Islam** has long been identified with sharp restrictions on women, al-Wahhab himself generally emphasized the rights of women within a patriarchal Islamic framework. These included a woman's right to consent to and stipulate conditions for a marriage, to control her dowry, to divorce, and to engage in commerce. Such rights, long embedded in Islamic law, had apparently been forgotten or ignored in eighteenth-century Arabia. Furthermore, al-Wahhab did not insist on head-to-toe covering of women in public and allowed for the mixing of unrelated men and women for business or medical purposes.

By the early nineteenth century, this new reformist state encompassed much of central Arabia, with Mecca itself coming under Wahhabi control in 1803 (see Map 15.3). Although an Egyptian army broke the power of the Wahhabis in 1818, the movement's influence continued to spread across the Islamic world. Together with the ongoing expansion of the religion, these movements of reform and renewal signaled the continuing cultural vitality of the Islamic world even as the European presence on the world stage assumed larger dimensions.

Map 15.3 The Expansion of Wahhabi Islam
From its base in central Arabia, the Wahhabi movement represented a challenge to the Ottoman Empire, while its ideas subsequently spread widely within the Islamic world.

China: New Directions in an Old Tradition

Neither China nor India experienced cultural or religious change as dramatic as that of the Reformation in Europe or the Wahhabi movement in Arabia. Nor did Confucian or Hindu cultures during the early modern era spread widely, as did Christianity and Islam. Nonetheless, neither of these traditions remained static. As in Christian Europe, challenges to established orthodoxies in China and India emerged as commercial and urban life, as well as political change, fostered new thinking.

China during the Ming and Qing dynasties continued to operate broadly within a Confucian framework, enriched now by the insights of Buddhism and Daoism to generate a system of thought called Neo-Confucianism. Chinese Ming dynasty rulers, in their aversion to the despised Mongols, embraced and actively supported this native Confucian tradition, whereas the foreign Qing rulers did so to woo Chinese intellectuals to support the new dynasty. Within this context, a considerable amount of controversy, debate, and new thinking emerged during the early modern era.

During late Ming times, for example, the influential thinker **Wang Yangming** (1472–1529) argued that "intuitive moral knowledge exists in people . . . even robbers know that they should not rob."[8] Thus anyone could achieve a virtuous life by introspection and contemplation, without the extended education, study of classical texts, and constant striving for improvement that traditional Confucianism prescribed for an elite class of "gentlemen." Such ideas figured prominently among Confucian scholars of the sixteenth century, although critics contended that such thinking promoted an excessive individualism. They also argued that Wang Yangming's ideas had undermined the Ming dynasty and contributed to China's conquest by the foreign Qing. Some Chinese Buddhists as well sought to make their religion more accessible to ordinary people by suggesting that laypeople at home could undertake practices similar to those performed by monks in monasteries. Withdrawal from the world was not necessary for enlightenment. This kind of moral or religious individualism bore some similarity to the thinking of

Dream of the Red Chamber This mid-eighteenth-century image depicts a garden scene from *The Dream of the Red Chamber,* a wildly popular epic novel that found a wide readership in Qing China and is now considered one of China's "Four Great Classical Novels." (Pictures from History/Bridgeman Images)

Martin Luther, who argued that individuals could seek salvation by "faith alone," without the assistance of a priestly hierarchy.

While such matters occupied the intellectual elite of China, in the cities a lively popular culture emerged among the less educated. For city-dwellers, plays, paintings, short stories, and especially novels provided diversion and entertainment that were a step up from what could be found in teahouses and wineshops. Numerous "how-to" painting manuals allowed a larger public to participate in this favorite Chinese art form. Even though Confucian scholars disdained popular fiction, a vigorous printing industry responded to the growing demand for exciting novels. The most famous was Cao Xueqin's mid-eighteenth-century novel ***The Dream of the Red Chamber***, a huge book that contained 120 chapters and some 400 characters, most of them women. It explored the social life of an eighteenth-century elite family with connections to the Chinese court.

India: Bridging the Hindu/Muslim Divide

In a largely Hindu India, ruled by the Muslim Mughal Empire, several significant cultural departures took shape in the early modern era that brought Hindus and Muslims together in new forms of religious expression. At the level of elite culture, the Mughal ruler Akbar formulated a state cult that combined elements of Islam, Hinduism, and Zoroastrianism (see "Muslims and Hindus in the Mughal Empire" in Chapter 13). The Mughal court also embraced Renaissance Christian art, and soon murals featuring Jesus, Mary, and Christian saints appeared on the walls of palaces, garden pavilions, and harems. The court also commissioned a prominent Sufi spiritual master to compose an illustrated book describing various Hindu yoga postures. Intended to bring this Hindu tradition into Islamic Sufi practice, the book, known as the *Ocean of Life*, portrayed some of the yogis in a Christ-like fashion.

Within popular culture, the flourishing of a devotional form of Hinduism known as *bhakti* also bridged the gulf separating Hindu and Muslim. Through songs, prayers, dances, poetry, and rituals, devotees sought to achieve union with one or another of India's many deities. Appealing especially to women, the bhakti movement provided an avenue for social criticism. Its practitioners often set aside caste distinctions and disregarded the detailed rituals of the Brahmin priests in favor of personal religious experience. Among the most beloved of bhakti poets was **Mirabai** (1498–1547), a high-caste woman from northern India who upon her husband's death abandoned her upper-class family and conventional Hindu practice. Much of her poetry deals with her yearning for union with Krishna, a Hindu deity she regarded as her husband, lover, and lord. This mystical dimension of the bhakti movement had much in common with Sufi forms of Islam, which also emphasized direct experience of the Divine. Such similarities helped blur the distinction between Hinduism and Islam in India, as both bhaktis and Sufis honored spiritual sages and all those seeking after God.

Guru Nanak This painting shows a seated Guru Nanak, the founder of Sikhism, disputing with four kneeling Hindu holy men. (© British Library Board. All Rights Reserved /Bridgeman Images)

Yet another major cultural change that blended Islam and Hinduism emerged with the growth of **Sikhism** as a new and distinctive religious tradition in the Punjab region of northern India. Its founder, Guru Nanak (1469–1539), had been involved in the bhakti movement but came to believe that "there is no Hindu; there is no Muslim; only God." His teachings and those of subsequent gurus also generally ignored caste distinctions and untouchability and ended the seclusion of women, while proclaiming the "brotherhood of all mankind" as well as the essential equality of men and women. Drawing converts from Punjabi peasants and merchants, both Muslim and Hindu, the Sikhs gradually became a separate religious community. They developed their own sacred book, known as the Guru Granth (teacher book); created a central place of worship and pilgrimage in the Golden Temple of Amritsar; and prescribed certain dress requirements for men, including keeping hair and beards uncut, wearing a turban, and carrying a short sword. During the seventeenth century, Sikhs encountered hostility from both the Mughal Empire and some of their Hindu neighbors. In response, Sikhism evolved from a peaceful religious movement, blending Hindu and Muslim elements, into a militant community whose military skills were highly valued by the British when they took over India in the late eighteenth century.

■ **Making Comparisons**
In what ways did religious changes in Asia and the Middle East parallel those in Europe, and how did they differ?

A New Way of Thinking: The Birth of Modern Science

While some Europeans were actively attempting to spread the Christian faith to distant corners of the world, others were developing an understanding of the cosmos at least partially at odds with Christian teaching. These were the makers of the

Scientific Revolution, a vast intellectual and cultural transformation that took place between the mid-sixteenth and early eighteenth centuries. It was sparked in part by the vast and unprecedented flow of new knowledge into Europe from across the globe that led many to question older ways of thinking. These new scientists no longer relied on the external authority of the Bible, the Church, the speculations of ancient philosophers, or the received wisdom of cultural tradition. For them, knowledge was acquired through rational inquiry based on evidence, the product of human minds alone. Many who created this revolution saw themselves as departing radically from older ways of thinking. "The old rubbish must be thrown away," wrote a seventeenth-century English scientist. "These are the days that must lay a new Foundation of a more magnificent Philosophy."[9]

The long-term significance of the Scientific Revolution was enormous. Within early modern Europe, it fundamentally altered ideas about the place of humankind within the cosmos and sharply challenged both the teachings and the authority of the Church. When applied to the affairs of human society, scientific ways of thinking challenged ancient social hierarchies and political systems and played a role in the revolutionary upheavals of the modern era. But science was also used to legitimize gender and racial inequalities, giving new support to old ideas about the natural inferiority of women and enslaved people. When married to the technological innovations of the Industrial Revolution, science fostered both the marvels of modern production and the horrors of modern means of destruction. By the twentieth century, science had become so widespread that it largely lost its association with European culture and became the chief marker of global modernity. Like Buddhism, Christianity, and Islam, modern science became a universal worldview, open to all who could accept its premises and its techniques. Over the past several centuries, it has substantially eroded religious belief and practice, particularly among the well educated in the West.

The Question of Origins

CORE IDEA

Explaining Origins
What factors help to explain the birth of modern science in Europe?

Why did Europeans take a leading role in the Scientific Revolution, and why did it occur during the early modern period? One critical factor was Europe's ability to draw on technological and scientific advances made elsewhere in Afro-Eurasia. China's technological accomplishments, based on practical knowledge of the natural world, were unmatched anywhere in the several centuries after 1000, and many of its innovations flowed to Europe in the centuries before the Scientific Revolution. There they inspired further practical discoveries. Speaking of the development of printing, gunpowder, and the magnetic compass, a prominent seventeenth-century English scientist, Francis Bacon, declared that "no empire, no sect, no star, seems to have exerted greater power and influence in human affairs than these mechanical discoveries."[10] While Bacon described the origins of these technologies as "obscure and inglorious," we now know that all three appeared first in China.

From the realm of Islam, Europeans accessed both ancient Greek learning and the remarkable achievements of Muslim scholars. After the late 1000s, this learning entered Christian Europe in an explosion of translations from Greek and Arabic into Latin, primarily accomplished in regions of southern Spain and Sicily where Christian states came to rule over formerly Muslim territories. The prolific Aristotle, with his logical approach and "scientific temperament," made the deepest impression, helping to fuel a growing interest in rational thought and confidence in human reason. But European thinkers also learned from scholars in the Islamic world. Muslim thinkers had brought together ancient Greek and Persian learning, Indian mathematics, and the Muslim belief in a single all-powerful creator God to achieve significant breakthroughs in optics, astronomy, medicine, pharmacology, and much more. Muslim scholars pioneered new approaches to systematic observation, experimental science, and the application of mathematics to the study of the natural world, all of which were similar to approaches later taken up by European scientists.

Then, starting in the fifteenth century, Europeans found themselves at the center of a massive new exchange of information created by their expanding overseas empires, commercial networks, and missionary initiatives. As they became aware of lands, peoples, plants, animals, societies, and religions from around the world, this unprecedented tidal wave of new knowledge, uniquely available to Europeans, shook up older ways of thinking. It also stoked curiosity, fueled discoveries and inventions, and sparked the development of new tools to manage knowledge, including natural history collections, botanical gardens, and classification systems. The sixteenth-century Italian doctor, mathematician, and writer Girolamo Cardano (1501–1576) expressed a sense of wonderment at these developments: "The most unusual [circumstance of my life] is that I was born in this century in which the whole world became known; whereas the ancients were familiar with but a little more than a third part of it." He worried, however, that amid this explosion of knowledge, "certainties will be exchanged for uncertainties."[11] It was precisely those uncertainties—skepticism about established views—that provided such a fertile cultural ground for the emergence of modern science. The Reformation too contributed to that cultural climate in its challenge to authority, its encouragement of mass literacy, and its affirmation of secular professions.

The needs of new overseas empires and commerce also drove scientific and technological advances. Europeans focused considerable resources on improving navigation, cartography, and shipbuilding to facilitate their long-distance voyages; ballistics and artillery to maintain their superiority in naval warfare; and mining techniques to produce the precious metals that they used to trade in Asian markets. Some innovations occurred overseas. In the Spanish empire, shipbuilders discovered new types of timber and tree resins in the forests of the Americas and the Philippines, while entrepreneurs developed new processes for extracting silver from low-grade ores in the mining centers of the Andes and Mexico.

Across the globe, Europeans drew on the knowledge of indigenous peoples as they sought local products, technologies, and natural resources that possessed economic or other potential value. For his botanical catalog of local plants, for instance, one French trading company official in India relied on Hindu holy men and healers with "a lot of wisdom" to identify and describe the uses of native plants.[12] He also employed local artists who drew hundreds of scientifically exact images and indigenous gardeners who traveled sometimes hundreds of miles to secure live specimens.

If growing contact with other regions of the world provided critical impetus for Europe's Scientific Revolution, its historical development as a reinvigorated and fragmented civilization also gave rise to conditions particularly favorable to the scientific enterprise. By the twelfth and thirteenth centuries, Europeans had evolved a legal system that guaranteed a measure of independence for a variety of institutions—the Church, towns and cities, guilds, professional associations, and universities. This legal revolution was based on the idea of the "corporation," a collective group of people that was treated as a unit, a legal person, with certain rights to regulate and control its own members. Most important for the development of science was the emergence of universities as corporations with legal privileges that allowed scholars to pursue their studies in relative freedom from the dictates of church or state authorities. Within them, the study of the natural world began slowly to separate itself from philosophy and theology and to gain a distinct identity. Their curricula featured "a core of readings and lectures that were basically scientific," drawing heavily on the writings of Aristotle, which had only recently become available to Western Europeans.[13] Most of the major European figures in the Scientific Revolution were trained in universities, and after the mid-seventeenth century another type of corporation, the scientific academy, emerged in which science was also disseminated and discussed.

Science as Cultural Revolution

While knowledge flowing along new global networks transformed European understandings of the natural world, it was breakthroughs in the study of the heavens that most directly challenged traditional Christian understandings of the universe. Before the Scientific Revolution, educated Europeans held to an ancient view of the world in which the earth was stationary and at the center of the universe, and around it revolved the sun, moon, and stars embedded in ten spheres of transparent crystal. This understanding coincided well with the religious outlook of the Catholic Church because the attention of the entire universe was centered on the earth and its human inhabitants, among whom God's plan for salvation unfolded. It was a universe of divine purpose, with angels guiding the hierarchically arranged heavenly bodies along their way while God watched over the whole from his realm beyond the spheres. The Scientific Revolution was revolutionary because it fundamentally challenged this understanding of the cosmos.

CORE IDEA

Examining a Concept

What was revolutionary about the Scientific Revolution and all that followed from it?

The initial breakthrough came from the Polish mathematician and astronomer Nicolaus **Copernicus**, whose famous book *On the Revolutions of the Heavenly Spheres* was published in the year of his death, 1543. Its essential argument was that "at the middle of all things lies the sun" and that the earth, like the other planets, revolved around it. Thus, the earth was no longer unique or at the obvious center of God's attention.

But it took more than a century for numerous astronomers, natural philosophers, and mathematicians to empirically prove that Copernicus was correct and to overturn other aspects of the traditional earth-centered cosmos. In the early seventeenth century Johannes Kepler, a German mathematician, showed that the planets followed elliptical orbits, undermining the ancient belief that they moved in perfect circles. In 1609 the Italian **Galileo** (gal-uh-LAY-oh) developed an improved telescope, with which he made many observations that undermined established understandings of celestial bodies (see Zooming In: Galileo and the Telescope: Reflecting on Science and Religion, page 662). Some thinkers began to discuss the notion of an unlimited universe in which humankind occupied a mere speck of dust in an unimaginable vastness. The seventeenth-century French mathematician and philosopher Blaise Pascal perhaps spoke for many when he wrote, "The eternal silence of these infinite spaces frightens me."[14]

The culmination of this new science of the heavens came in the work of Sir Isaac **Newton** (1642–1727), the Englishman who formulated the modern laws of motion and mechanics, which remained unchallenged until the twentieth century. At the core of Newton's thinking was the concept of universal gravitation. "All bodies whatsoever," Newton declared, "are endowed with a principle of mutual gravitation."[15] Here was the grand unifying idea of early modern astronomy and physics. The radical implication of this view was that the heavens and the earth, long regarded as separate and distinct spheres, were not so different after all, for the motion of a cannonball or the falling of an apple obeyed the same natural laws that governed the orbiting planets. While often portrayed as a solitary genius, Newton tested and sometimes revised his thinking in light of data gathered across the globe on such natural phenomena as the motion of pendulums near the equator, tides in Southeast Asia, and the stars of the southern sky.

The Telescope Johannes Hevelius, an astronomer of German Lutheran background living in what is now Poland, constructed extraordinarily long telescopes in the mid-seventeenth century with which he observed sunspots, charted the surface of the moon, and discovered several comets. Such telescopes played a central role in transforming understandings of the universe during the Scientific Revolution. (World History Archive/Alamy)

By the time Newton died, a revolutionary new understanding of the physical universe had emerged among educated Europeans: the universe was no longer propelled by supernatural forces but functioned on its own according to scientific principles that could be described mathematically. Articulating this view, Kepler wrote, "The machine of the universe is not similar to a divine animated being but similar to a clock."[16] Furthermore, it was a machine that regulated itself, requiring neither God nor angels to account for its normal operation.

ZOOMING IN

Galileo and the Telescope: Reflecting on Science and Religion

The Scientific Revolution was predicated on the idea that knowledge of how the universe worked was acquired through a combination of careful observations, controlled experiments, and the formulation of general laws, expressed in mathematical terms. Perhaps no single invention enabled the Scientific Revolution more than telescopes, the first of which were produced in the early seventeenth century by Dutch eyeglass makers.

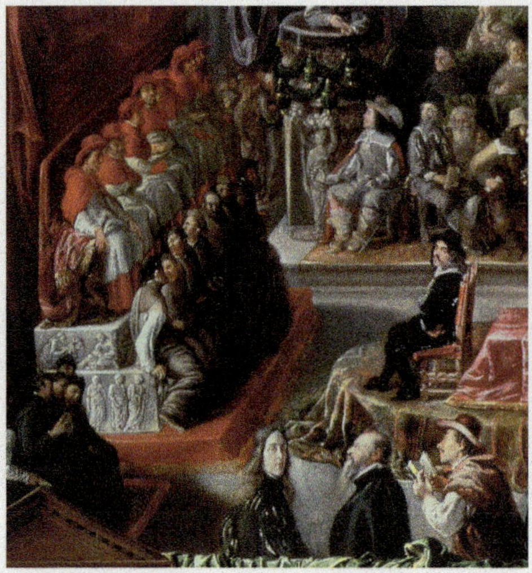

Galileo on trial.

The impact of new instruments depended on how scientists employed them. In the case of the telescope, it was the brilliant Italian mathematician and astronomer Galileo Galilei (1564–1642) who unlocked its potential when he used it to observe the night sky. Within months of creating his own telescope, which improved on earlier designs, Galileo made a series of discoveries that called into question well-established understandings of the cosmos. He observed craters on the moon and sunspots, or blemishes, moving across the face of the sun, which challenged the traditional notion that no imperfection or change marred the heavenly bodies. Moreover, his discovery of the moons of Jupiter and many new stars suggested a cosmos far larger than the finite universe of traditional astronomy. In 1610, Galileo published his remarkable findings in a book titled *The Starry Messenger*, where he emphasized time and again that his precise observations provided irrefutable evidence of a cosmos unlike that described by traditional authorities. "With the aid of the telescope," he argued, "this has been scrutinized so directly and with such ocular certainty that all the disputes which have vexed the philosophers through so many ages have been resolved, and we are at last freed from wordy debates about it."[17]

Galileo's empirical evidence transformed the debate over the nature of the cosmos. His dramatic and unexpected discoveries were readily grasped, and with the aid of a telescope anyone could confirm their veracity. His initial findings were

photo: Bridgeman Images

Knowledge of that universe could be obtained through human reason alone—by observation, deduction, and experimentation—without the aid of ancient authorities or divine revelation.

Like the physical universe, the human body also lost some of its mystery. The careful dissections of cadavers and animals enabled doctors and scientists to describe the human body with much greater accuracy and to understand the circulation of the blood throughout the body. The heart was no longer the mysterious center of the body's heat and the seat of its passions; instead it was just another machine, a complex muscle that functioned as a pump.

Much of this scientific thinking developed in the face of strenuous opposition from the Catholic Church, for both its teachings and its authority were under attack. The Italian philosopher Giordano Bruno, proclaiming an infinite universe and many worlds, was burned at the stake in 1600, and Galileo was compelled by heralded by many in the scientific community, including Christoph Clavius, the Church's leading astronomer in Rome. Galileo's findings led him to conclude that Copernicus (1473–1543), an earlier astronomer and mathematician, had been correct when he had advanced the theory that the sun rather than the earth was at the center of the solar system. But Galileo's evidence could not definitively prove Copernicus's theory to the satisfaction of critics, leading Galileo to study other phenomena, such as the tides, that could provide further evidence that the earth was in motion.

When the Church condemned Copernicus's theory in 1616, it remained silent on Galileo's astronomical observations, instead warning him to refrain from teaching or promoting Copernicus's ideas. Ultimately, though, Galileo came into conflict with church authorities when in 1629 he published, with what he thought was the consent of the Church, the *Dialogue Concerning the Two Chief World Systems*, a work sympathetic to Copernicus's sun-centric system. In 1632, Galileo was tried by the Roman Inquisition, an ecclesiastical court charged with maintaining orthodoxy, and convicted of teaching doctrines against the express orders of the Church. He recanted his beliefs and at the age of sixty-nine was sentenced to house arrest.

Although Galileo was formally convicted of disobeying the Church's order to remain silent on the issue of Copernicus's theory, the question most fundamentally at stake in the trial was "What does it mean, 'to know something'?"[18] This question of the relationship between scientific knowledge, primarily concerned with how the universe works, and other forms of "knowledge," derived from divine revelation or mystical experience, has persisted in the West. Over 350 years after the trial, Pope John Paul II spoke of Galileo's conviction in a public speech in 1992, declaring it a "sad misunderstanding" that belongs to the past, but one with ongoing resonance because "the underlying problems of this case concern both the nature of science and the message of faith." Then the pope declared scientific and religious knowledge to be compatible: "There exist two realms of knowledge, one which has its source in Revelation and one which reason can discover by its own power. . . . The distinction between the two realms of knowledge ought not to be understood as opposition. . . . The methodologies proper to each make it possible to bring out different aspects of reality."[19]

Galileo himself had expressed something similar centuries earlier. "Nor is God," he wrote, "any less excellently revealed in Nature's actions than in the sacred statements of the Bible."[20] Finding a place for new scientific knowledge in a constellation of older wisdom traditions proved a fraught but highly significant development in the emergence of the modern world.

QUESTION

What can Galileo's discoveries with his telescope and his conviction by the Inquisition tell us about the Scientific Revolution?

the Church to publicly renounce his belief that the earth orbited around the sun and rotated on its axis.

But scholars have sometimes exaggerated the conflict of science and religion, casting it in military terms as an almost unbroken war. Many of the leaders of the early movement saw themselves as natural philosophers studying natural theology, the idea that God could be known through the study of his creation. Newton, a serious biblical scholar, proclaimed, "This most beautiful system of the sun, planets, and comets could only proceed from the counsel and dominion of an intelligent Being."[21] In such ways the scientists sought to accommodate religion. Over time, scientists and church leaders learned to coexist through a kind of compartmentalization. Science might prevail in its limited sphere of describing the physical universe, but religion was still the arbiter of truth about those ultimate questions concerning human salvation, righteous behavior, and the larger purposes of life.

Science and Enlightenment

Initially limited to a small handful of scholars, the ideas of the Scientific Revolution spread to a wider European public during the eighteenth century, aided by novel techniques of printing and bookmaking, by a popular press, by growing literacy, and by a host of scientific societies. Moreover, the new approach to knowledge—rooted in human reason, skeptical of authority, expressed in natural laws—was now applied to human affairs, not just to the physical universe. The Scottish professor Adam Smith (1723–1790), for example, formulated laws that accounted for the operation of the economy and that, if followed, he believed, would generate inevitably favorable results for society. Growing numbers of people believed that the long-term outcome of scientific development would be "enlightenment," a term that has come to define the eighteenth century in European history. If human reason could discover the laws that governed the universe, surely it could uncover ways in which humankind might govern itself more effectively.

■ **Assessing Cultural Conflict**
In what ways did the Enlightenment challenge older patterns of European thinking?

"What is Enlightenment?" asked the prominent German intellectual Immanuel Kant (1724–1804). "It is man's emergence from his self-imposed . . . inability to use one's own understanding without another's guidance. . . . Dare to know! 'Have the courage to use your own understanding' is therefore the motto of the enlightenment."[22] Although they often disagreed sharply with one another, **European Enlightenment** thinkers shared this belief in the power of knowledge to transform human society. They also shared a satirical, critical style, a commitment to open-mindedness and inquiry, and in various degrees a hostility to established political and religious authority. Many took aim at arbitrary governments, the "divine right of kings," and the aristocratic privileges of European society. The English philosopher John Locke (1632–1704) offered principles for constructing a constitutional government, a contract between rulers and ruled that was created by human ingenuity rather than divinely prescribed. Much of Enlightenment thinking was directed against the superstition, ignorance, and corruption of established religion. In his *Treatise on Toleration*, the French writer **Voltaire** (1694–1778) reflected the outlook of the Scientific Revolution as he commented sarcastically on religious intolerance:

> This little globe, nothing more than a point, rolls in space like so many other globes; we are lost in its immensity. Man, some five feet tall, is surely a very small part of the universe. One of these imperceptible beings says to some of his neighbors in Arabia or Africa: "Listen to me, for the God of all these worlds has enlightened me; there are nine hundred million little ants like us on the earth, but only my anthill is beloved of God; He will hold all others in horror through all eternity."[23]

Voltaire's own faith, like that of many others among the "enlightened," was deism. Deists believed in a rather abstract and remote Deity, sometimes compared to a clockmaker, who had created the world and set it in motion, but not in a personal God who intervened in history or tampered with natural law. Others became

The Philosophers of the Enlightenment This painting shows the French philosopher Voltaire with a group of intellectual luminaries at the summer palace of the Prussian king Frederick II. Such literary gatherings, sometimes called salons, were places of lively conversation among mostly male participants and came to be seen as emblematic of the European Enlightenment. (Balfore Archive Images/Alamy)

pantheists, who believed that God and nature were identical. Here were conceptions of religion shaped by the outlook of science. Sometimes called "natural religion," it was devoid of mystery, revelation, ritual, and spiritual practice, while proclaiming a God that could be "proven" by human rationality, logic, and the techniques of scientific inquiry. In this view, all else was superstition. Among the most radical of such thinkers were the several Dutchmen who wrote the *Treatise of Three Imposters*, which claimed that Moses, Jesus, and Muhammad were fraudulent deceivers who based their teachings on "the ignorance of Peoples [and] resolved to keep them in it."[24]

Prominent among the debates spawned by the Enlightenment was the question of women's nature, their role in society, and the education most appropriate for them. Although well-to-do Parisian women hosted in their elegant salons many gatherings of the largely male Enlightenment figures, most of those men were anything but ardent feminists. The male editors of the famous *Encyclopédie*, a vast compendium of Enlightenment thought, included very few essays by women. One of the male authors expressed a common view: "[Women] constitute the principal ornament of the world. . . . May they, through submissive discretion and . . . artless cleverness, spur us [men] on to virtue."[25] In his treatise *Emile*, Jean-Jacques Rousseau described women as fundamentally different from and inferior to men and urged that "the whole education of women ought to be relative to men."[26]

Such views were sharply contested by any number of other Enlightenment figures—men and women alike. The *Journal des Dames* (Ladies Journal), founded in Paris in 1759, aggressively defended women. "If we have not been raised up in the sciences as you have," declared Madame Beaulmer, the *Journal*'s first editor, "it is you [men] who are the guilty ones; for have you not always abused . . . the bodily strength that nature has given you?"[27] The philosopher Marquis de **Condorcet** (1743–1794) looked forward to the "complete destruction of those prejudices that have established an inequality of rights between the sexes."[28] And in 1792, the British writer Mary Wollstonecraft directly confronted Rousseau's view of women and their education: "What nonsense! . . . till women are more rationally educated, the progress of human virtue and improvement in knowledge must receive continual checks."[29] Thus was initiated a debate that echoed throughout the centuries that followed.

Though solidly rooted in Europe, Enlightenment thought was influenced by the growing global awareness of its major thinkers. Voltaire, for example, idealized China as an empire governed by an elite of secular scholars selected for their talent, which stood in sharp contrast to continental Europe, where aristocratic birth and military prowess were far more important. The example of Confucianism—supposedly secular, moral, rational, and tolerant—encouraged Enlightenment thinkers to imagine a future for European civilization without the kind of supernatural religion that they found so offensive in the Christian West.

The central theme of the Enlightenment—and what made it potentially revolutionary—was the idea of progress. Human society was not fixed by tradition or divine command but could be changed, and improved, by human action guided by reason. No one expressed this soaring confidence in human possibility more clearly than the French thinker Condorcet, who boldly declared that "the perfectibility of humanity is indefinite." Belief in progress was a sharp departure from much of premodern social thinking, and it inspired those who later made the great revolutions of the modern era in the Americas, France, Russia, China, and elsewhere. Born of the Scientific Revolution, that was the faith of the Enlightenment. For some, it was virtually a new religion.

The age of the Enlightenment, however, also witnessed a reaction against too much reliance on human reason. Jean-Jacques Rousseau (1712–1778) minimized the importance of book learning for the education of children and prescribed instead an immersion in nature, which taught self-reliance and generosity rather than the greed and envy fostered by "civilization." The Romantic movement in art and literature appealed to emotion, intuition, passion, and imagination rather than cold reason and scientific learning. Religious awakenings—complete with fiery sermons, public repentance, and intense personal experience of sin and redemption—shook Protestant Europe and North America in the eighteenth and early nineteenth centuries. The Methodist movement—with its emphasis on Bible study, confession of sins, fasting, enthusiastic preaching, and resistance to worldly pleasures—was a case in point.

Various forms of "enlightened religion" also arose in the early modern centuries, reflecting the influence of Enlightenment thinking. Quakers, for example, emphasized tolerance, an absence of hierarchy and ostentation, a benevolent God, and an "inner light" available to all people. Unitarians denied the Trinity, original sin, predestination, and the divinity of Jesus, but honored him as a great teacher and a moral prophet. Later, in the nineteenth century, proponents of the "social gospel" saw the essence of Christianity not in personal salvation but in ethical behavior. Science and the Enlightenment surely challenged religion, and for some they eroded religious belief and practice. Just as surely, though, religion persisted, adapted, and revived for many others.

European Science beyond the West

In the long run, the achievements of the Scientific Revolution spread globally, becoming the most widely sought-after product of European culture and far more desired than Christianity, democracy, socialism, or Western literature. In the early modern era, however, interest in European scientific thinking within major Asian societies was both modest and selective.

In the seventeenth century, Chinese scholars developed their own sophisticated approach to studying the natural world known as ***kaozheng***, or "research based on evidence." Intended to "seek truth from facts," kaozheng was critical of the unfounded speculation of conventional Confucian philosophy and instead emphasized the importance of verification, precision, accuracy, and rigorous analysis in all fields of inquiry. It was a genuinely scientific approach to knowledge, but one that was applied more to the study of the past and to practical applications of learning in medicine, farming, and industry than to fields like astronomy, physics, or anatomy, which were more prominent in Europe.

Analyzing Cultural Interaction
How was European science received in the major civilizations of Asia in the early modern era?

European scientific learning arrived in China at about the same time that kaozheng was taking root, and Chinese elites took interest in some of aspects of it. Imperial officials, for instance, were impressed by European techniques for predicting eclipses, reforming the calendar, and making accurate maps of the empire. European mathematics was also of particular interest to Chinese scholars who were exploring the history of Chinese mathematics. To convince their skeptical colleagues that the barbarian Europeans had something to offer in this field, some Chinese scholars argued that European mathematics had in fact grown out of much earlier Chinese ideas and could therefore be adopted with comfort. European medicine, however, had little impact on Chinese physicians before the nineteenth century.

In such ways, early modern Chinese thinkers selectively assimilated Western science into their own studies of history and the natural world on their own terms.

Although Japanese authorities largely closed their country off from the West in the early seventeenth century (see "Asians and Asian Commerce" in Chapter 14), one window remained open. Alone among Europeans, the Dutch were permitted to trade in Japan at a single location near Nagasaki, but not until 1720 did the Japanese lift the ban on importing Western books. Then a number of European texts in medicine, astronomy, geography, mathematics, and other disciplines were translated and studied by a small group of Japanese scholars. They were especially impressed with Western anatomical studies, for in Japan dissection was work fit only for outcasts. Returning from an autopsy conducted by Dutch physicians in the mid-eighteenth century, several Japanese observers reflected on their experience: "We remarked to each other how amazing the autopsy had been, and how inexcusable it had been for us to be ignorant of the anatomical structure of the human body."[30] Nonetheless, this small center of "Dutch learning," as it was called, remained isolated amid a pervasive Confucian-based culture. Not until the mid-nineteenth century, when Japan was forcibly opened to Western penetration, would European-style science assume a prominent place in Japanese culture.

Like China and Japan, the Ottoman Empire in the sixteenth and seventeenth centuries was an independent, powerful, successful society whose intellectual elites saw no need for a wholesale embrace of things European. In the seventeenth century, interest in the fields of logic, dialectic, philosophy, and rational theology among the intellectual elite in the Ottoman Empire was heightened by scholars who fled Safavid Iran and North African scholars who settled mostly in Egypt. Ottoman scholars were also conscious of the rich tradition of Muslim astronomy and chose not to translate the works of major European scientists such as Copernicus, Kepler, or Newton, although they were broadly aware of European scientific achievements by 1650. They valued astronomy mainly for its practical usefulness in making maps and calendars rather than for its larger philosophical implications. In any event, the notion of a sun-centered solar system did not cause the kind of upset in the Ottoman Empire that it did in Europe. As in Japan, the systematic embrace of Western science would have to await the nineteenth century, when the Ottoman Empire was under far more intense pressure from Europeans and reform seemed more necessary.

Looking Ahead: Science in the Nineteenth Century and Beyond

In Europe itself, the impetus of the Scientific Revolution continued to unfold. Modern science, it turned out, was a cumulative and self-critical enterprise, which in the nineteenth century and later was applied to new domains of human inquiry in ways that undermined some of the assumptions of the Enlightenment. This remarkable phenomenon justifies a brief look ahead at several scientific developments in the nineteenth and twentieth centuries. (See Then and Now: Science, page 670.)

In the realm of biology, for example, Charles Darwin (1809–1882) laid out a complex argument that all life was in constant change, that an endless and competitive struggle for survival over millions of years constantly generated new species of plants and animals, while casting others into extinction. Human beings were not excluded from this vast process, for they too were the work of evolution operating through natural selection. Darwin's famous books *The Origin of Species* (1859) and *The Descent of Man* (1871) were threatening to many traditional Christian believers, perhaps more so than Copernicus's ideas about a sun-centered universe had been several centuries earlier.

Describing Change
How did nineteenth- and twentieth-century developments in the sciences challenge Enlightenment ideas and principles?

At the same time, Karl Marx (1818–1883) articulated a view of human history that likewise emphasized change and struggle. Conflicting social classes—enslaved people and their owners, peasants and nobles, workers and capitalists—successively drove the process of historical transformation. Although he was describing the evolution of human civilization, Marx saw himself as a scientist. He based his theories on extensive historical research; like Newton and Darwin, he sought to formulate general laws that would explain events in a rational way. Nor did he believe in heavenly intervention, chance, or the divinely endowed powers of kings. In Marx's view the coming of socialism—a society without classes or class conflict—was not simply a good idea; it was inevitable, inscribed in the laws of historical development. (See "Social Protest" in Chapter 17.) Like the intellectuals of the Enlightenment, Darwin and Marx believed strongly in progress, but in their thinking, conflict and struggle rather than reason and education were the motors of progress. The Enlightenment image of the thoughtful, rational, and independent individual was fading. Individuals—plant, animal, and human alike—were now viewed as enmeshed in vast systems of biological, economic, or social conflict.

The work of the Viennese doctor Sigmund Freud (1856–1939) applied scientific techniques to the operation of the human mind and emotions and in doing so cast further doubt on Enlightenment conceptions of human rationality. At the core of each person, Freud argued, lay primal impulses toward sexuality and aggression, which were only barely held in check by the thin veneer of social conscience derived from civilization. Our neuroses arose from the ceaseless struggle between our irrational drives and the claims of conscience and society. This too was a far cry from the Enlightenment conception of the human condition.

And in the twentieth century, developments in physics, such as relativity and quantum theory, called into question some of the established verities of the Newtonian view of the world, particularly at the subatomic level and at speeds approaching that of light. In this new physics, time is relative to the position of the observer; space can warp and light can bend; matter and energy are equivalent; black holes and dark matter abound; and probability, not certain prediction, is the best that scientists can hope for. None of this was even on the horizon of those who made the original Scientific Revolution in the early modern era.

THEN AND NOW

Science

"Science is not now what it was at its start," reflected the Noble Prize–winning physicist Steven Weinberg in 2015.[31] Each new discovery since the Scientific Revolution has raised further questions and problems, making final answers elusive, tentative, and always open to revision. Moreover, in our own time, science—and the technologies derived from it—shape nearly every aspect of our lives, making our "scientific age" very different from that of the "scientific revolution" now more than four centuries in the past.

Nonetheless, contemporary science still has much in common with the outlook of Copernicus, Galileo, and Newton. Scientists then and now share a method or technique that embraces careful observation, controlled repeatable experiments, and application of evidence to formulate theories or laws. Weinberg observed that science is a method "well tuned to nature" that was "waiting for people to discover it."[32] Strikingly similar in his thinking, Galileo asserted almost four centuries earlier that the universe was like a great book lying open before us, if we could just "understand the language . . . that it was written in."[33] This shared way of thinking and practice links today's scientists to their earliest predecessors.

But over the centuries science has also changed in important ways. Today, the scope of the physical sciences has expanded substantially from the fields of astronomy and physics, where early breakthroughs were made, into fields like chemistry, electromagnetism, and the atomic and subatomic structures of matter. Moreover, whole new fields of science have emerged. Our understanding of living things—cell structures, ecosystems, evolution, and more—has been transformed by the natural sciences and especially by biology. Meanwhile, earth sciences, such as geology, oceanography, and meteorology, have unlocked the secrets of our planet's history, including its changing climate and the movements of its tectonic plates.

The methods of science have also been applied to the study of human societies. Social scientists—sociologists, political scientists, anthropologists, economists—use scientific principles to examine how human societies are structured and evolve. Psychologists too have used scientific techniques to examine the operation of the human mind and emotions. Some historians have embraced "scientific history," including Karl Marx, who formulated general laws of human development. Thus the continuing process of scientific investigation has expanded the scope of inquiry into the mysteries of the physical universe, of life, and of humankind.

As the scope of science has expanded and scientific learning has evolved, modern scientists have challenged and even overturned some of the most important understandings and perspectives of their early modern predecessors. Newton viewed his concept of "universal gravitation" as applicable everywhere, but today contemporary scientists have come to understand that very different laws apply at quantum and subatomic scales. And twentieth- and twenty-first-century scientists have disclosed amazing features of the universe—such as black holes, dark matter, and dark energy—of which Newton and his contemporaries were wholly unaware.

Early modern scientists focused on the earth and its place in the solar system. Their modern counterparts, however, have ventured far beyond this limited sphere, disclosing an ever-expanding universe with billions of galaxies containing an uncountable number of stars, some of which contain planetary systems. In line with the religious thinking of his time, Newton believed that the earth was created about 4000 B.C.E. Modern scientists have dated its formation to about 4.5 billion years ago.

Modern scientists have also replaced the certainty that Newton's laws provided with a sense of the limitations of what science can know—especially at the quantum or subatomic

CONCLUSIONS AND REFLECTIONS

What's New?

"What's new?" It is a common greeting, but it is also a profound historical question, especially when applied to human culture, religion, and ways of thinking about the world. Yet the answers are not always obvious or clear-cut.

level. It turns out that knowing the precise position of a particle makes it impossible to know its precise velocity at the same time. All of this reminds us that science—like the study of history—is a continuing process of discovery, revision, and the formulation of new questions.

In undertaking their work, current scientists have many advantages. They receive enormous financial support from governments and corporations, while their early modern counterparts funded their own work or received support from wealthy patrons. And scientists today have at their disposal an enormous array of technological aids—particle accelerators and powerful computers, for example—while Galileo and Newton were assisted only by modest telescopes.

Galileo could not have imagined the telescopes available to modern scientists. (European Southern Observatory/Science Source)

In the sixteenth and seventeenth centuries, science was almost exclusively an elite European phenomenon, and, aside from medicine, its discoveries were largely theoretical in nature with few practical applications. In contrast, today's science is a global phenomenon, an important driver of technological innovation, and for many a defining feature of modernity. It has also transformed almost every part of the world economy—medicine, manufacturing, communication, transportation, and the military. Thus science plays a much greater role in the everyday lives of people today. This accelerating pace of scientific breakthroughs has encouraged many to view science as a powerful source of human progress.

Others, however, have pushed back against science. Religious teachings on occasion continue to elicit opposition to science as they did in the early modern period, when the Church felt challenged by scientific views that left little place for God. Some Christians, for instance, still reject Darwin's theory of evolution because it contradicts their literal understanding of biblical teachings about the creation of life.

Much modern criticism of science focuses on the horrendous outcomes that it has generated: nuclear weapons, capable of obliterating a sizable city in an instant, and environmental devastation, including an emerging climate crisis, deriving from industrialization. While generating much human progress, some have argued, science has also given us the means of our own destruction.

Still others have criticized the use by authoritarian governments of scientifically based technologies, from surveillance cameras to artificial intelligence, to control or oppress their citizens. Social critics abhor the references to alleged scientific findings to perpetuate racism and ideas of female inferiority. And significant numbers of people have rejected the scientific consensus about the human causes of global warming, in part because they associate those ideas with a political ideology they find offensive. Thus, while science has triumphed as an essential element of modern life, it has also provoked controversy in both its earlier and its more recent expressions.

QUESTIONS

In what ways is science today similar to science in the sixteenth and seventeenth centuries? In what ways is it different? How does modern science shape your understanding of the Scientific Revolution?

At one level, the early modern era, culturally speaking, witnessed much that was new. The Protestant Reformation was a new departure within the Christian tradition, as was the spread of Christianity to the Americas, the Philippine Islands, and Siberia. The emergence of the bhakti tradition within Hinduism and of the separate religious tradition of Sikhism likewise represented something new in South Asian cultural life. For leading scientists and churchmen of Europe, the ideas of the Scientific Revolution were certainly novel and for some immensely threatening.

And yet some cultural transformations that appeared new within particular times and places were part of longer-term historical processes. As Islam increasingly took hold in Southeast Asia and parts of Africa, it was certainly something new to recent converts. But the "long march of Islam" across the Afro-Eurasian world had been in the making for 1,000 years. And while Luther's formal break with the Catholic Church marked a decisive change in Latin Christendom, it drew on long-standing criticisms of the wealth of popes, clerical immorality, and the selling of indulgences. What is "new" in one context may be "old" in another.

Furthermore, what appears as an innovation was often the product of cultural borrowing and the blending of old and new. Conversion to Christianity or Islam, for example, did not usually mean the wholesale abandonment of established religions, but the assimilation of new elements within older patterns of belief and practice. Thus as Latin American Christianity evolved, it was not a mere copy of what European missionaries sought to impose. Haitian Vodou and Brazilian Candomblé incorporated both European Christian and traditional West African elements. Sikhism in north India drew on both Islam and Hinduism. Even the Scientific Revolution, so apparently a Western innovation, was facilitated by European access to ancient Greek learning, Islamic science, Indian mathematics, and the knowledge of indigenous peoples.

So cultural borrowing was often selective rather than wholesale. Many peoples who appropriated Christianity or Islam in the Americas, sub-Saharan Africa, and Southeast Asia certainly did not accept the rigid exclusivity and ardent monotheism of more orthodox versions of those faiths. Elite Chinese were far more interested in European mapmaking and mathematics than in Western medicine, while Japanese scholars became fascinated with the anatomical work of the Dutch. Neither, however, adopted Christianity in a widespread manner.

Cultural borrowing was also frequently contested. Some objected to much borrowing at all. Thus members of the Taki Onqoy movement in Peru sought to wipe out Spanish influence and control, while Chinese and Japanese authorities clamped down firmly on European missionaries, even as they maintained some interest in European technological and scientific skills. European missionaries in Latin America and Muslim reformers in Wahhabi Arabia both objected strenuously to cultural borrowing from other traditions, which they understood as "idolatry" and the dilution of the pure faith.

To ease the tensions of cultural borrowing, efforts to "domesticate" foreign ideas and practices proliferated. Thus the Jesuits in China tried to point out similarities between Christianity and Confucianism, and Native American converts identified Christian saints with their own gods and spirits. Various Europeans, including Galileo, Newton, deists, Quakers, and Unitarians, sought to accommodate the perspectives of modern science while retaining a religious outlook on life. Such efforts did not always succeed, with some in Europe, for instance, denying, at least for a time, discoveries such as a sun-centered universe and biological evolution.

Cultural borrowing complicates our understanding of "what's new" in history. How much of what appears "new" in human cultural evolution is altogether novel? And how much is a rearrangement of existing patterns, a gradual change over time, or a blending of borrowed elements?

Revisiting Chapter 15

Revisiting Specifics

Protestant Reformation, 640
Martin Luther, 641
Thirty Years' War, 644
Counter-Reformation, 644
Taki Onqoy, 650
Jesuits in China, 651
Wahhabi Islam, 654
Wang Yangming, 655
The Dream of the Red Chamber, 656
Mirabai, 656
Sikhism, 657
Scientific Revolution, 658
Copernicus, 660
Galileo, 661
Newton, 661
European Enlightenment, 664
Voltaire, 664
Condorcet, 666
kaozheng, 667

Revisiting Core Ideas

1. **Analyzing Change** In what ways did the Protestant Reformation transform European society, culture, and politics?
2. **Assessing Differences** Why were missionary efforts to spread Christianity so much less successful in China than in Spanish America?
3. **Identifying What Is New** What new departures in cultural life are apparent in the Islamic world, China, and India during the early modern era?
4. **Explaining Origins** What factors help to explain the birth of modern science in Europe?
5. **Examining a Concept** What was revolutionary about the Scientific Revolution and all that followed from it?

A Wider View

1. What factors drive cultural change?
2. Which of the cultural changes described in this chapter seemed to affect small elite groups, and which had a wider impact? Does this difference affect your judgment about their historical significance?
3. In what ways were the cultural changes of the early modern era associated with sharp social or political conflicts?
4. **Looking Back** Based on Chapters 13 through 15, how might you challenge a Eurocentric understanding of the early modern era while acknowledging the growing role of Europeans on the global stage?

To learn more about the topics in this chapter, see **For Further Study** at the end of this book.

WORKING WITH EVIDENCE

Christianity: Becoming a Global Religion

During the early modern centuries, missionaries—mostly Roman Catholic—rode the tide of European expansion to establish Christianity in the Americas and parts of Africa and Asia. In those places, native converts sometimes imitated European patterns and at other times adapted the new religion to their own cultural traditions. Thus the Christian world of the early modern era was far more globalized than before 1500. The sources that follow illustrate the variety of receptions that Christianity received in different places and the cultural blending or mixing that occurred when new peoples embraced the faith.

SOURCE 15.1 Cultural Blending in Andean Christianity ▶

Throughout Latin America, Christianity was established in the context of European conquest and colonial rule. As the new faith took hold across the region, it incorporated much that was of European origin, as the construction of many large and ornate churches illustrates. But local communities also sought to blend this European Catholic Christianity with religious symbols and concepts drawn from their own traditions in a process that historians call syncretism. In the Andes, for example, Inca religion featured a supreme creator god (Viracocha); a sun god (Inti), regarded as the creator of the Inca people; a moon goddess (Killa), who was the wife of Inti; and an earth mother goddess (Pachamama), associated with mountain peaks and fertility. Those religious figures found their way into Andean understanding of Christianity, as Source 15.1 illustrates.

Painted around 1740 by an unknown artist, this striking image shows the Virgin Mary placed within the "rich mountain" of Potosí in Bolivia, from which the Spanish had extracted so much silver (see "Silver and Global Commerce" in Chapter 14). Thus Christianity was visually expressed in an Andean tradition that viewed mountains as the embodiment of the gods. Native miners whose labor enriched their colonial rulers are depicted as smaller figures on the mountainside. A somewhat larger figure at the bottom of the mountain is an Inca ruler dressed in royal garb receiving tribute from his people. At the bottom left are the pope and a cardinal, while on the right stand the Habsburg emperor Charles V and perhaps his wife.

- What is Mary's relationship to the heavenly beings standing above her (God the Father on the right; the dove, symbolizing the Holy Spirit, in the center; and Jesus on the left), as well as to the miners at work in the mountain? What is the significance of the crown above her head and her outstretched arms?
- The European figures at the bottom are shown in a posture of prayer or thanksgiving. What might the artist have been trying to convey? How would you interpret the relative size of the European and Andean figures?

- Why do you think the artist placed Mary inside the mountain rather than on it, while depicting her dress in a mountain-like form?
- What marks this painting as an example of syncretism?
- Do you read this image as subversive of the colonial order or as supportive of it? Do you think the artist who painted Source 15.1 was a European or a Native American Christian?

La Virgen del Cerro (Virgin Mary of the Mountains) | **ca. 1740**

Museo de la Casa de la Moneda, Potosí, Bolivia/Gilles Mermet/akg-images

■ ■ ■

SOURCE 15.2 Christianity through Maya Eyes

European missionaries, clergy, inquisitors, and government officials wrote most of the surviving sources about the conversion of Mesoamerica, but the *Books of the Chilam Balam* offer a rare indigenous perspective. Written in the seventeenth and eighteenth centuries, their Maya authors recorded local rituals, medical knowledge, history, myths, prophecies, and Christian instruction in the Yucatec Mayan language using the European Latin alphabet. The passages that follow come from the *Chilam Balam of Chumayel*, a town on the Yucatán Peninsula of modern Mexico. They reveal how Christian concepts were integrated into an existing Maya worldview and cosmology.

- How is the exploitation of the Maya in the Spanish colonial system reflected in these passages? How do these conditions affect Maya understandings of Christianity and the relationship of indigenous people to the Christian God?
- In what specific ways have Christian beliefs and practices been blended with their Maya counterparts? In the passage concerned with Christ's life and crucifixion, the four cardinal directions and arrow-stones are ritual elements drawn from pre-Christian Maya ceremonial practices that involved the ritual slaying of a human being. How does this information shape your understanding of this Maya description of the crucifixion and resurrection of Christ?
- Compare the elements of religious blending or syncretism in these passages and those in Source 15.1. What similarities and differences can you identify?

The Chilam Balam of Chumayel | 18th century

[On the Fate of the Maya Gods]

Nevertheless, the first gods were perishable gods. Their worship came to its inevitable end. They lost their efficacy by the benediction of the Lord of Heaven, after the redemption of the world was accomplished, after the resurrection of the true God, the true Dios, when he blessed heaven and earth. Then was your worship abolished, Maya men. Turn away your hearts from your [old] religion.

[A Maya Account of Jesus' Birth, Crucifixion, and Resurrection]

In the middle of the town of Tihoo [Mérida] is the cathedral, the fiery house, the mountainous house, the dark house, for the benefit of God the Father, God the Son and God the Holy Spirit.

Who enters into the house of God? Father, it is the one named Ix-Kalem [the Holy One].

What day did the Virgin conceive? Father, 4 Oc [a specific day in the Maya calendar] . . . when she conceived.

What day did he come forth [from the womb]? On 3 Oc [a specific day in the Maya calendar] he came forth.

What day did he die? On 1 Cimi [a specific day in the Maya calendar] he died. Then he entered the tomb on 1 Cimi.

What entered his tomb? Father, a coffer of stone entered his tomb.

What entered into his thigh? Father, it was the red arrow-stone. It entered into the precious stone of the world, there in heaven.

And his arm? Father, the arrow-stone; and that it might be commemorated it entered into the red living rock in the east. Then it came to the north and entered into the white living rock. After that it entered the black living rock in the west. Thus also [it entered] the yellow living rock in the south. . . .

[On the Coming of Christianity and Prophecy for Future Divine Intervention]

Then with the true God, the true Dios [God], came the beginning of our misery. It was the beginning of tribute, the beginning of church dues, the beginning of strife with purse-snatching, the beginning of strife with blow-guns, the beginning of strife by trampling on the people, the beginning of robbery with violence, the beginning of forced debts. . . . This was the origin of service to the Spaniards and priests, of service to the local chiefs. . . . It was by Antichrist on earth, the kinkajous [a small rainforest mammal] of the towns, the foxes of the towns, the blood-sucking insects of the town, those who drained the poverty of the working people [who made working people poor]. But it shall still come to pass that tears shall come to the eyes of our Lord God. The justice of our Lord God shall descend upon every part of the world, straight from God upon . . . the avaricious hagglers of the world.

[Prophecy on the End Times]

Then, I tell you, justice shall descend to the end that Christianity and salvation may arise. Then the rulers of the towns shall be asked for their proofs and titles of ownership, if they know of them. Then they shall come forth from the forests and from among the rocks and live like men; then towns shall be established [again]. There shall be no fox to bite them. . . . Five years shall run until the end of my prophecy, and then shall come the time for the tribute to come down. Then there shall be an end to the paying for the wars which our fathers raised [against the Spaniards]. You shall not call the *katun* [a twenty-year period] which is to come a hostile one, when Jesus Christ, the guardian of our souls shall come. Just as [we are saved] here on earth, so shall he bear our souls to his holy heaven also. You are sons of the true God. Amen.

Source: *The Book of Chilam Balam of Chumayel*, translated by Ralph L. Roys (Norman: University of Oklahoma Press, 1967), 79, 98, 124–27.

SOURCE 15.3 Making Christianity Chinese

In China, unlike in Latin America, Christian missionaries operated in a setting wholly outside of European political control and with far fewer converts. Nonetheless, in China too the tendency toward syncretism was evident. Jesuit missionaries sought to present the Christian message within a Chinese cultural context, and Chinese Christians often transposed the new religion into more familiar cultural concepts.

Source 15.3 provides an example of Christianity becoming Chinese. In the early seventeenth century, the Jesuits published several books in the Chinese language describing the life of Christ and illustrated them with a series of woodblock prints created by Chinese artists. Although they were clearly modeled on European images, those prints cast Christian figures into an altogether Chinese setting. The print in Source 15.3 portrays the familiar biblical story of the Annunciation, when an angel informs Mary that she will be the mother of Jesus. The house and furniture shown in the print suggest the dwelling of a wealthy Chinese scholar. The view from the window shows a seascape, mountains in the distance, a lone tree, and a "scholar's rock"—all of which were common features in Chinese landscape painting. The clouds that appear at the angel's feet and around the shaft of light shining on Mary are identical to those associated with sacred Buddhist and Daoist figures. To Chinese eyes, the angel might well appear as a Buddhist bodhisattva, while Mary may resemble a Ming dynasty noblewoman or perhaps Kuanyin, the Chinese Buddhist goddess of mercy and compassion.

- What specifically Chinese elements can you identify in this image?
- How might educated Chinese have responded to this image?
- The European engraving on which this Chinese print was modeled included in the background the scene of Jesus' crucifixion. Why might the Chinese artist have chosen to omit that scene from his image?

Illustration of the Annunciation | **ca. 17th century**

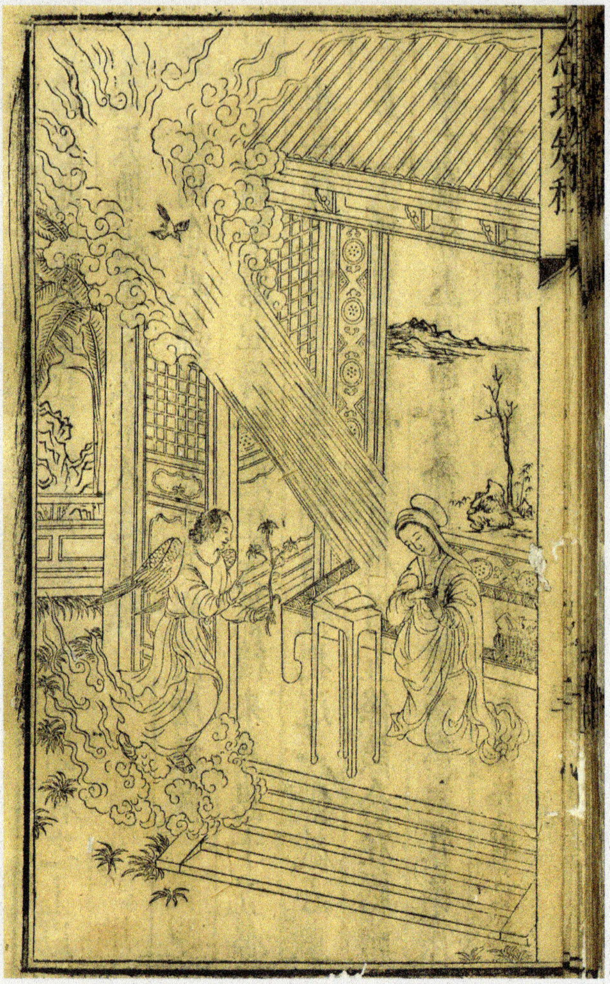

SOURCE 15.4 The Chinese Rites Controversy

Religious syncretism on occasion provoked heated debate, as the Chinese Rites Controversy illustrates. European opponents of the Jesuits raised objections to Jesuit acceptance of some Chinese customs, including the honoring of ancestors (what their critics called ancestor worship) and devotion to Confucius. The Jesuits viewed ancestor reverence as compatible with Christianity and Confucian ceremonies as civil rites rather than religious observances, but many European opponents understood these Chinese practices as religious in nature and therefore incompatible with orthodox Christian teachings. Ultimately the Jesuits lost this debate when Pope Clement XI issued a decree banning these "Chinese rites" in 1715. Source 15.4A is the pope's decree, and Source 15.4B records the Chinese emperor's response to the pope's pronouncement.

- What specific practices did Clement prohibit, and what reasons did he offer for his ban? How would the pope's prohibitions make it more difficult for a Chinese convert to Christianity to maintain his or her place in Chinese society?
- Why did the emperor ban the teaching of Christianity in his realm? What can his reaction tell us about the Jesuit approach to conversion in China?
- Do you think that Source 15.3 contravenes Clement's decree, or would the pope approve of the continued dissemination of such images in China?

SOURCE 15.4A

***Papal Decree Banning Chinese Rites* | 1715**

I. The West calls *Deus* [God] the creator of Heaven, Earth, and everything in the universe. Since the word *Deus* does not sound right in the Chinese language, the Westerners in China and Chinese converts to Catholicism have used the term "Heavenly Lord" for many years. From now on such terms as "Heaven" and "Shangti" should not be used: *Deus* should be addressed as the Lord of Heaven, Earth, and everything in the universe. . . .

II. The spring and autumn worship of Confucius, together with the worship of ancestors, is not allowed among Catholic converts. It is not allowed even though the converts appear in the ritual as bystanders, because to be a bystander in this ritual is as pagan as to participate in it actively.

III. Chinese officials and successful candidates in the metropolitan, provincial, or prefectural examinations, if they have been converted to Roman Catholicism, are not allowed to worship in Confucian temples on the first and fifteenth days of each month. . . .

IV. No Chinese Catholics are allowed to worship ancestors in their familial temples.

V. Whether at home, in the cemetery, or during the time of a funeral, a Chinese Catholic is not allowed to perform the ritual of ancestor worship. . . .

Despite the above decisions, I have made it clear that other Chinese customs and traditions that can in no way be interpreted as heathen in nature should be allowed to continue among Chinese converts. The way the Chinese manage their households or govern their country should by no means be interfered with.

Source: Dun J. Li, *China in Transition, 1517–1911* (New York: Van Nostrand Reinhold, 1969), 22–24.

SOURCE 15.4B

Decree of Emperor Kangxi | 1721

Reading this proclamation, I have concluded that the Westerners are petty indeed. It is impossible to reason with them because they do not understand larger issues as we understand them in China. There is not a single Westerner versed in Chinese works, and their remarks are often incredible and ridiculous. To judge from this proclamation, their religion is no different from other small, bigoted sects of Buddhism or Taoism. I have never seen a document which contains so much nonsense. From now on, Westerners should not be allowed to preach in China, to avoid further trouble.

Source: Dun J. Li, *China in Transition, 1517–1911* (New York: Van Nostrand Reinhold, 1969), 22.

SOURCE 15.5 Christian Art in the Mughal Empire

The rulers of Mughal India during the time of Akbar (r. 1556–1605) and Jahangir (r. 1605–1627) also invited Jesuit missionaries to their court. But while Chinese elite circles received the Jesuits for their scientific skills, especially in astronomy, the Mughal court seemed more interested in the religious and artistic achievements of European civilization. Akbar invited the Jesuits to take part in cross-religious discussions that included Muslim, Hindu, Jain, and Zoroastrian scholars. Furthermore, the Mughal emperors eagerly embraced European art, which the Jesuits provided to them, much of it devotional and distinctly Christian. Mughal artists quickly learned to paint in the European style, and soon murals featuring Jesus, Mary, and Christian saints appeared on the walls of Mughal palaces, while miniature paintings adorned books and jewelry.

In religious terms, however, the Jesuit efforts were "a fantastic and extravagant failure,"[34] for these Muslim rulers of India were not in the least interested in abandoning Islam for the Christian faith, and few conversions of any kind occurred. Akbar and Jahangir, however, were cosmopolitan connoisseurs of art, which they collected, reproduced, and displayed. European religious art also had propaganda value in enhancing their status. Jesus and Mary, after all, had a prominent place within Islam. Jesus was seen both as an earlier prophet and as a mystical figure, similar to the Sufi masters who were so important in Indian Islam. Mughal paintings pairing the adult Jesus and Mary side by side were placed above the imperial throne as well as on the emperor's jewelry and his official seal, suggesting an identification of Jesus and a semi-divine emperor. That the mothers of both Akbar and Jahangir were named Mary only added to the appeal. Thus Akbar and Jahangir sought to incorporate European-style Christian art into their efforts to create a blended and tolerant religious culture for the elites of their vast and diverse realm.

But as Catholic devotional art was reworked by Mughal artists, it was also subtly changed. Source 15.5 shows an early seventeenth-century depiction of the Holy Family painted by an Indian artist.

- Why do you think that this Mughal painter portrayed Joseph and Mary as distinguished and educated persons rather than as the humble carpenter and his peasant wife, as in so many European images? Why might he have placed the family in rather palatial surroundings instead of a stable?
- How do you imagine European missionaries responded to this representation of the Holy Family?

- How might more orthodox Muslims have reacted to the larger project of creating a blended religion making use of elements from many traditions?
- What similarities can you identify between this Indian image and the Chinese print in Source 15.3? Pay attention to the setting, the clothing, the class status of the human figures, and the scenes outside the windows.

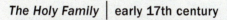

The Holy Family | **early 17th century**

Bridgeman Images

DOING HISTORY

1. **Making Comparisons** What common Christian elements do you find in these sources? What differences in the expression of Christianity can you define?
2. **Considering Mary** The Catholic Christian tradition as it developed in Latin America, China, and India as well as Europe assigned a very important role to representations of the Virgin Mary. Why might such images of Mary have been so widely appealing? In what ways does the image of the Holy Mother differ in Sources 15.1, 15.3, and 15.5? In what ways were those images adapted to the distinctive cultures in which they were created?
3. **Pondering Syncretism** From a missionary viewpoint, develop arguments for and against religious syncretism using these sources as points of reference.

HISTORIANS' VOICES

Missions in Mesoamerica and China

Missionary efforts to win new converts and strengthen the devotion of new Christians took many different forms during the early modern period. These voices examine specific missionary efforts in sixteenth-century Mesoamerica and seventeenth- and eighteenth-century China. In Voice 15.1, Merry Wiesner-Hanks explores two alternative foundation narratives for the Virgin of Guadalupe shrine in Mexico (see the image at the beginning of this chapter). In Voice 15.2, Diarmaid MacCulloch describes Jesuit missionary strategies in China.

- How does your understanding of the Virgin of Guadalupe shrine and the way that Mexico was Christianized change depending on which interpretation of its foundation you accept?
- What challenges did the Jesuit mission in China face, and how did the Jesuits seek to overcome them?
- What strategies for strengthening the devotion of new converts are highlighted in these two voices?
- **Integrating Primary and Secondary Sources** How do these voices help you to better understand the Working with Evidence sources?

VOICE 15.1

Merry Wiesner-Hanks on the Virgin of Guadalupe | 2015

[T]he Virgin of Guadalupe can serve as a good example [of syncretism]. . . . In the seventeenth century, published texts in Spanish and Nahuatl [an indigenous Mexican language] told of the appearance of the Virgin Mary in 1531 to Juan Diego Cuauhtlatoatzin, an indigenous farmer and Christian convert, on a hill near Tenochtitlan (now within Mexico City). Speaking in Nahuatl, the apparition told Juan Diego that a church should be built at the site, and her image miraculously appeared on his cloak. Shortly afterward a church dedicated to the Virgin of Guadalupe was begun. . . . Preachers and teachers interpreted her appearance as a sign of the Virgin's special protection of indigenous people and those of mixed ancestry . . . , and pilgrims from all over Mexico began to make the trek to her shrine. . . .

In the twentieth century, however, many scholars, including some members of the Mexican clergy, came to doubt whether the apparition had ever happened or Juan Diego himself had even existed. They pointed out that written accounts were not published until over a century later, and that church officials and missionaries active in central Mexico in 1531 made no mention of the event. . . . Specialists in Nahuatl culture note that the hill where the apparition was reported was originally the site of a shrine to Coatlicue, the mother of the most powerful Aztec God Huitzilopochtli, and that aspects of the veneration of the Virgin of Guadalupe were also part of honoring Coatlicue or other Aztec mother goddesses. In their view, the colonial Catholic Church had simply invented the story as part of its efforts to strip Aztec Holy sites of their original meaning.

Source: Merry E. Wiesner-Hanks, *A Concise History of the World* (Cambridge: Cambridge University Press, 2015), 267.

VOICE 15.2

Diarmaid MacCulloch on Jesuit Missionary Strategies in China | 2009

The Jesuits quickly decided that missionaries must adapt themselves to Chinese customs. This involved much rapid self-education. Their first great missionary, the Italian Matteo Ricci, on his arrival in 1582 adopted the dress of a Buddhist monk (*bonze*), without realizing that *bonzes* were despised by the people who mattered. When his mistake was pointed out, he and his fellow Jesuits began dressing as Confucian scholars, complete with long beards; they were determined to show that their learning was worthy of respect in a culture with a deep reverence for scholarship. . . . The Chinese upper class was indeed impressed by the Jesuits' knowledge of mathematics, astronomy and geography, and the Society gained an honoured place at the emperor's court through its specialist use of these skills. . . .

The Jesuit emphasis on their honoured place at Court was always something of a diversion from the real reasons for the growth of adherents, who were very different in their social profile from the exalted figures around the emperor. At the peak of the Chinese mission's success at the end of the seventeenth century, it was serving perhaps around a quarter of a million people. . . . Yet at that time there were only seventy-five priests to serve this number, laboring under enormous difficulties with language. . . . What the Jesuits did very effectively in this situation was to inspire a local leadership which was not clerical, both catechists [teachers of the basic tenets of the faith] and a particular Chinese phenomenon . . . , "Chinese virgins": laywomen consecrated to singleness but still living with their families, teaching women and children.

Source: Diarmaid MacCulloch, *Christianity: The First Three Thousand Years* (New York: Penguin, 2009), 706–7.

PART 5

The European Moment in World History

1750–1900

THE BIG PICTURE

European Centrality and the Problem of Eurocentrism

During the century and a half between 1750 and 1900, sometimes referred to as the "long nineteenth century," two new and related phenomena held center stage in the global history of humankind and represent the major themes of the four chapters that follow. The first of these, explored in Chapters 16 and 17, was the creation of a new kind of human society, commonly called "modern," emerging from the intersection of the Scientific, French, and Industrial Revolutions, all of which took shape initially in Western Europe. The second theme of this long nineteenth century, which is addressed in Chapters 18 and 19, was

PHOTOS: left, Gianni Dagli Orti/Shutterstock; center, TopFoto; right, Bridgeman Images the growing ability of these modern societies to exercise enormous power and influence over the rest of humankind through their empires, economic penetration, military intervention, diplomatic pressure, and missionary activity.

These developments marked a major turning point in world history in several ways. Western Europeans and their North American offspring now assumed a new and far more prominent role in the world than ever before. Furthermore, this "European moment" in world history established a new phase of human connectedness or entanglement that later generations labeled as "globalization." Finally, Europeans were also leading a human intervention in the natural order of unprecedented dimensions, largely the product of industrialization. Thus the long nineteenth century represents the starting point of the Anthropocene era, or the "age of man," a concept that points to the many ways in which humankind itself has become an active agent of change in the physical and biological evolution of the planet. It marks an epic transformation in the relationship of humanity to the earth, equivalent perhaps to the early stages of the Agricultural Revolution.

Europe's global centrality during the nineteenth century generated understandings of both geography and history that centered the entire human story on Europe. Thus flat maps placed Europe at the center of the world, while dividing Asia in half. Europe was granted continental status, even though it was more accurately only the western peninsula of Asia, much as India was its southern peninsula. Other regions of the world, such as the Far East or the Near (Middle) East, were defined in terms of their distance from Europe. History textbooks often portrayed people of European extraction at the center of human progress. Other peoples and civilizations, by contrast, were long believed to be static or stagnant, thus largely lacking any real history. Most Europeans assumed that these "backward" peoples and regions must either imitate the Western model or face further decline and possible extinction. Until the mid-twentieth century, such ideas went largely unchallenged in the Western world.

The rise of the academic discipline of world history in the decades following World War II represented a sharp challenge to such Eurocentric understandings of the human past. But in dealing with recent centuries, historians have confronted a distinct problem: how to avoid Eurocentrism when considering a phase of world history in which Europeans were in fact central.

At least five responses to this dilemma are reflected in the chapters that follow. First, the "European moment" has been recent and perhaps brief. Other peoples too had times of "cultural flowering" that granted them a period of primacy or influence—for example, the Arabs (600–1000), Chinese (1000–1500), Mongols (1200–1350), and Incas and Aztecs (fifteenth century)—but all of these were limited to particular regions of Afro-Eurasia or the Americas.[1] Even though the European moment operated on a genuinely global scale, Western peoples enjoyed their worldwide primacy for two centuries at most. The events of the late twentieth and early twenty-first centuries—the dissolution of colonial empires, the rise of India and especially China, and the assertion of Islam—suggest the end, or at least the erosion, of the age of European predominance.

Second, we need to remember that the rise of Europe occurred within an international context. It was the withdrawal of the Chinese naval fleet that allowed Europeans to enter the Indian Ocean in the sixteenth century, while Native Americans' lack of immunity to European diseases and their own divisions and conflicts greatly assisted the European takeover of the Western Hemisphere. The Industrial Revolution, explored in Chapter 17, benefited from New World resources and markets and from the stimulus of superior Asian textile and pottery production. Chapters 18 and 19 make clear that European control of other regions everywhere depended on the cooperation of local elites. Europeans, like everyone else, were embedded in a web of relationships that shaped their own histories.

A third reminder is that the rise of Europe to a position of global dominance was not an easy or automatic process. Frequently it occurred in the face of ferocious resistance and rebellion, which often required Europeans to modify their policies and practices. The so-called Indian mutiny in mid-nineteenth-century South Asia, a massive uprising against British colonial rule, did not end British control, but it substantially transformed the character of the colonial experience. Even when Europeans exercised political power, they could not do precisely as they pleased. Empire, formal and informal alike, was always in some ways a negotiated arrangement.

Fourth, peoples the world over made active use of Europeans and European ideas for their own purposes, seeking to gain advantage over local rivals or to benefit themselves in light of new conditions. During the Haitian Revolution, examined in Chapter 16, enslaved Africans made use of radical French ideas about "the rights of man" in ways that most Europeans never intended. Later in Southeast Asia, a number of highland minority groups, long oppressed by the dominant lowland Vietnamese, viewed the French invaders as liberators and assisted in their takeover of Vietnam. Recognizing that Asian and African peoples remained active agents, pursuing their own interests even in oppressive conditions, is another way of countering residual Eurocentrism.

Moreover, what was borrowed from Europe was always adapted to local circumstances. Thus Japanese or Russian industrial development did not wholly follow the pattern of England's Industrial Revolution. The Christianity that took root in the Americas or later in Africa evolved in culturally distinctive ways. Ideas of nationalism, born in Europe, were used to oppose European imperialism throughout Asia and Africa. The most interesting stories of modern world history are not simply those of European triumph or the imposition of Western ideas and practices but those of encounters, though highly unequal, among culturally different peoples.

Finally, despite Europeans' unprecedented prominence on the world stage, they were not the only game in town, nor were they the sole preoccupation of Asian, African, and Middle Eastern peoples. While China confronted Western aggression in the nineteenth century, it was also absorbing a huge population increase and experiencing massive peasant rebellions that grew out of distinctly Chinese conditions. Furthermore, cultural influence moved in many directions as European and American intellectuals began to absorb the spiritual traditions of India and as Japanese art became highly fashionable in the West.

None of this diminishes the significance of the European moment in world history, but it sets that moment in a larger context of continuing patterns of historical development and of interaction and exchange with other peoples.

FIRST REFLECTIONS

1. **Questioning Chronology** What marks 1750–1900 as a distinct period of world history?
2. **Applying Historical Perspective** As the authors note, other civilizations have also experienced periods of primacy or greater influence in the past. How does this fact shape your understanding of growing European dominance in world affairs between 1750 and 1900?
3. **Thinking about Bias** How do the authors seek to avoid Eurocentrism while acknowledging the growing prominence of Europeans on the world stage during this period of time (1750–1900)?
4. **Thinking Like a Historian** How might historians from China, Africa, or the Islamic world view these centuries differently from historians in the Western world?

Landmarks in World History (ca. 1750–ca. 1900)

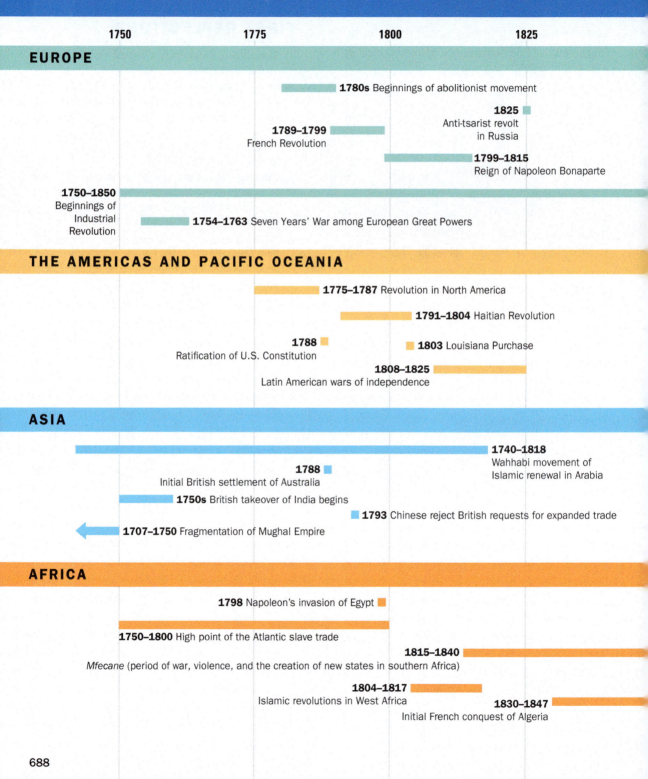

1750 | 1775 | 1800 | 1825

EUROPE

1780s Beginnings of abolitionist movement

1825 Anti-tsarist revolt in Russia

1789–1799 French Revolution

1799–1815 Reign of Napoleon Bonaparte

1750–1850 Beginnings of Industrial Revolution

1754–1763 Seven Years' War among European Great Powers

THE AMERICAS AND PACIFIC OCEANIA

1775–1787 Revolution in North America

1791–1804 Haitian Revolution

1788 Ratification of U.S. Constitution

1803 Louisiana Purchase

1808–1825 Latin American wars of independence

ASIA

1740–1818 Wahhabi movement of Islamic renewal in Arabia

1788 Initial British settlement of Australia

1750s British takeover of India begins

1793 Chinese reject British requests for expanded trade

1707–1750 Fragmentation of Mughal Empire

AFRICA

1798 Napoleon's invasion of Egypt

1750–1800 High point of the Atlantic slave trade

1815–1840 *Mfecane* (period of war, violence, and the creation of new states in southern Africa)

1804–1817 Islamic revolutions in West Africa

1830–1847 Initial French conquest of Algeria

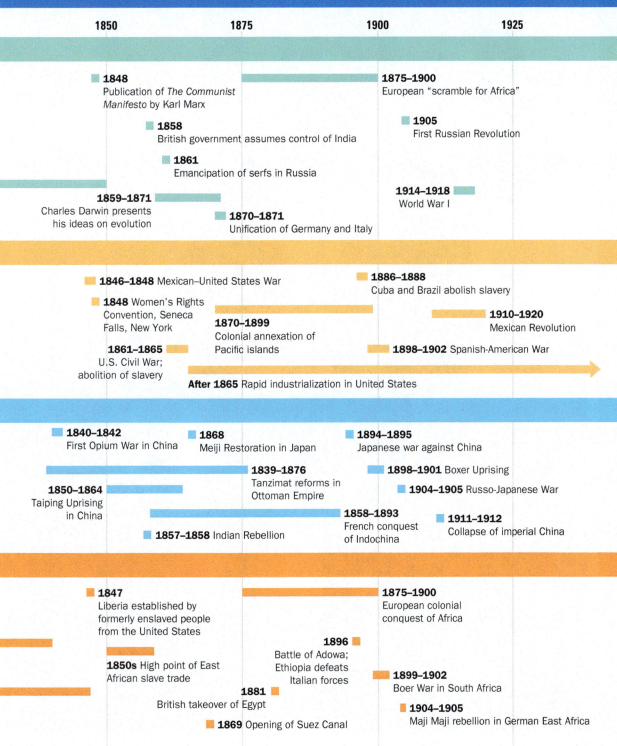

1850 | 1875 | 1900 | 1925

1848 Publication of *The Communist Manifesto* by Karl Marx

1858 British government assumes control of India

1861 Emancipation of serfs in Russia

1859–1871 Charles Darwin presents his ideas on evolution

1870–1871 Unification of Germany and Italy

1875–1900 European "scramble for Africa"

1905 First Russian Revolution

1914–1918 World War I

1846–1848 Mexican–United States War

1848 Women's Rights Convention, Seneca Falls, New York

1861–1865 U.S. Civil War; abolition of slavery

1870–1899 Colonial annexation of Pacific islands

After 1865 Rapid industrialization in United States

1886–1888 Cuba and Brazil abolish slavery

1910–1920 Mexican Revolution

1898–1902 Spanish-American War

1840–1842 First Opium War in China

1850–1864 Taiping Uprising in China

1868 Meiji Restoration in Japan

1839–1876 Tanzimat reforms in Ottoman Empire

1857–1858 Indian Rebellion

1858–1893 French conquest of Indochina

1894–1895 Japanese war against China

1898–1901 Boxer Uprising

1904–1905 Russo-Japanese War

1911–1912 Collapse of imperial China

1847 Liberia established by formerly enslaved people from the United States

1850s High point of East African slave trade

1881 British takeover of Egypt

1869 Opening of Suez Canal

1875–1900 European colonial conquest of Africa

1896 Battle of Adowa; Ethiopia defeats Italian forces

1899–1902 Boer War in South Africa

1904–1905 Maji Maji rebellion in German East Africa

Photo Josse/Leemage/Getty Images

CHAPTER 16

Atlantic Revolutions, Global Echoes

1750–1900

- **Atlantic Revolutions in a Global Context**
- **Comparing Atlantic Revolutions**
  - The North American Revolution, 1775–1787
  - The French Revolution, 1789–1815
  - The Haitian Revolution, 1791–1804
  - Latin American Revolutions, 1808–1825
- **Echoes of Revolution**
  - The Abolition of Slavery
  - Nations and Nationalism
  - Feminist Beginnings
- **Conclusions and Reflections: Pondering the Outcomes of Revolutions**

CONNECTING PAST AND PRESENT

"Two hundred and thirty years after it first erupted, the French Revolution hovers over current events in France."[1] So wrote one analyst of the widespread protests and riots that exploded in France in late 2018 and continued intermittently into 2020. These protests began with popular opposition to a projected rise in fuel prices and came to encompass a range of other issues, including police brutality, economic insecurity and inequality, and widespread distrust of the government and the "establishment." Dubbed the Yellow Vest Movement for the bright yellow vests they wore, the protesters lacked a clear hierarchical organization, but they marched, most often peacefully, sometimes blocked roads and public spaces, and on occasion set fires and engaged in violence. Their demands evoked the values of fairness and equality that have figured prominently in French public life since the French Revolution of 1789.

That upheaval was the centerpiece of a much larger set of revolutions that shook both sides of the Atlantic world between 1775 and 1825. It was preceded by the American Revolution, which gained independence for thirteen British colonies along the eastern coast of North America. And it was followed by a massive slave rebellion in Haiti that ended both slavery and French colonialism in that country even as it helped to shape the revolutions in Latin America that threw off Spanish and Portuguese colonial

« **Revolutionaries** Few participants in the Atlantic revolutions were more active than Jean-Baptiste Belley-Mars (ca. 1746–1805). Kidnapped from West Africa, he was sold into slavery on Saint-Domingue (modern Haiti). After purchasing his freedom, he fought in the American Revolution. During the French Revolution he helped persuade the National Convention to outlaw slavery. As a French officer sent to crush the Haitian Revolution, he opposed the brutal tactics used and was imprisoned. Here Belley-Mars is depicted next to a bust of Guillaume Raynal, an opponent of slavery.

rule. These four closely related upheavals reflected the new connections among Europe, Africa, North America, and South America that took shape in the wake of Columbus's voyages and the subsequent European conquests. Together, they launched a new chapter in the history of the Atlantic world, while the echoes of those revolutions reverberated in the larger world, as chattel slavery was attacked, nationalism was nurtured, and feminism found its first major public expression.

SEEKING THE MAIN POINT

What might be the most important outcomes of the Atlantic revolutions, both immediately and in the century that followed?

Atlantic Revolutions in a Global Context

Writing to a friend in 1772, before any of the Atlantic revolutions had occurred, the French intellectual Voltaire asked, "My dear philosopher, doesn't this appear to you to be the century of revolutions?"[2] He was certainly on target, and not only for Europe. From the early eighteenth century to the mid-nineteenth, many parts of the world witnessed political and social upheaval, leading some historians to think in terms of a "world crisis" or "converging revolutions." By the 1730s, the Safavid dynasty that had ruled Persia (now Iran) for several centuries had completely collapsed, even as the powerful Mughal Empire governing India also fragmented. About the same time, the Wahhabi movement in Arabia seriously threatened the Ottoman Empire, and its religious ideals informed major political upheavals in Central Asia and elsewhere (see "Expansion and Renewal in the Islamic World" in Chapter 15). The Russian Empire under Catherine the Great experienced a series of peasant uprisings, most notably one led by the Cossack commander Pugachev in 1773–1774 that briefly proclaimed the end of serfdom before that rebellion was crushed. China too in the late eighteenth and early nineteenth centuries hosted a number of popular though unsuccessful rebellions, a prelude perhaps to the huge Taiping revolution of 1850–1864. Beginning in the early nineteenth century, a new wave of Islamic revolutions shook West Africa, while in southern Africa a series of wars and migrations known as the *mfecane* (the breaking or crushing) involved widespread and violent disruptions as well as the creation of new states and societies.

Thus the Atlantic revolutions in North America, France, Haiti, and Latin America took place within a larger global framework. Like many of the other upheavals, they too occurred in the context of expensive wars, weakening states, and destabilizing processes of commercialization. But compared to upheavals elsewhere, the Atlantic revolutions were distinctive. The costly wars that strained European imperial states—Britain, France, and Spain in particular—were global rather than regional. In the so-called Seven Years' War (1754–1763), Britain and France joined battle in North America, the Caribbean, West Africa, and South Asia. The expenses of those conflicts prompted the British to levy additional taxes on their North American colonies and the French monarchy to seek new revenue from its landowners. These actions contributed to the launching of the North American and French revolutions, respectively.

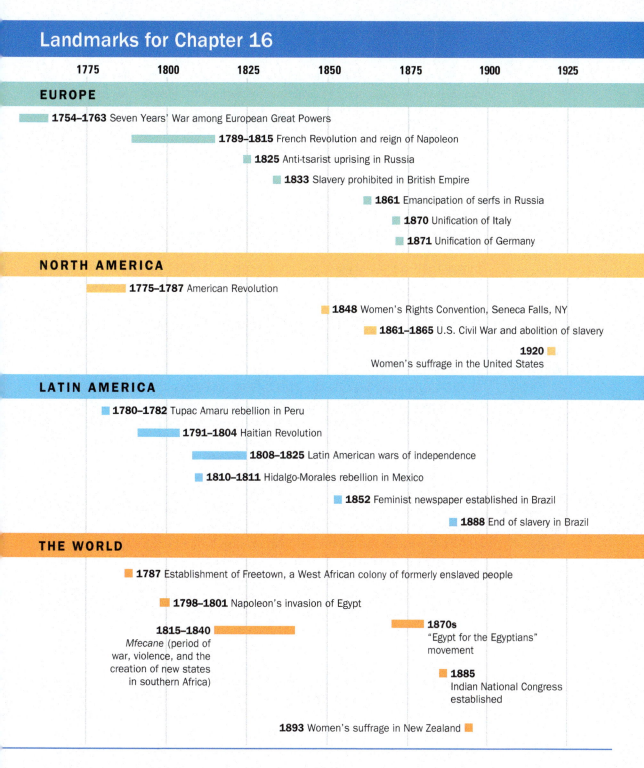

Landmarks for Chapter 16

1775 | 1800 | 1825 | 1850 | 1875 | 1900 | 1925

EUROPE

1754–1763 Seven Years' War among European Great Powers

1789–1815 French Revolution and reign of Napoleon

1825 Anti-tsarist uprising in Russia

1833 Slavery prohibited in British Empire

1861 Emancipation of serfs in Russia

1870 Unification of Italy

1871 Unification of Germany

NORTH AMERICA

1775–1787 American Revolution

1848 Women's Rights Convention, Seneca Falls, NY

1861–1865 U.S. Civil War and abolition of slavery

1920 Women's suffrage in the United States

LATIN AMERICA

1780–1782 Tupac Amaru rebellion in Peru

1791–1804 Haitian Revolution

1808–1825 Latin American wars of independence

1810–1811 Hidalgo-Morales rebellion in Mexico

1852 Feminist newspaper established in Brazil

1888 End of slavery in Brazil

THE WORLD

1787 Establishment of Freetown, a West African colony of formerly enslaved people

1798–1801 Napoleon's invasion of Egypt

1815–1840 *Mfecane* (period of war, violence, and the creation of new states in southern Africa)

1870s "Egypt for the Egyptians" movement

1885 Indian National Congress established

1893 Women's suffrage in New Zealand

Furthermore, the Atlantic revolutions were distinctive in that they were closely connected to one another. The American revolutionary leader Thomas Jefferson was the U.S. ambassador to France on the eve of the French Revolution, providing advice and encouragement to French reformers and revolutionaries. Simón Bolívar, a leading figure in Spanish American struggles for independence, twice visited Haiti, where he received military aid from the first black government in the Americas.

CORE IDEA

Assessing the Role of Ideas
In what ways did the ideas of the Enlightenment contribute to the Atlantic revolutions?

Beyond such direct connections, the various Atlantic revolutionaries shared a set of common ideas, as the Atlantic basin became a world of intellectual and cultural exchange. The ideas that animated the Atlantic revolutions derived from the European Enlightenment and were shared across the ocean in newspapers, books, and pamphlets. At the heart of these ideas was the radical notion that human political and social arrangements could be engineered, and improved, by human action. Thus conventional and long-established ways of living and thinking—the divine right of kings, state control of trade, aristocratic privilege, the authority of a single church—were no longer sacrosanct and came under repeated attack. New ideas of liberty, equality, free trade, religious tolerance, republicanism, and human rationality were in the air. Politically, the core notion was "popular sovereignty," which meant that the authority to govern derived from the people rather than from God or from established tradition. As the Englishman John Locke (1632–1704) had argued, the "social contract" between ruler and ruled should last only as long as it served the people well. In short, it was both possible and desirable to start over in the construction of human communities. In the late eighteenth and early nineteenth centuries, these ideas were largely limited to the Atlantic world. While all of the Atlantic revolutions involved the elimination of monarchs, at least temporarily, across Asia and the Middle East such republican political systems (those operating with elected representatives of the people rather than a monarch) were virtually inconceivable until much later. There the only solution to a bad monarch was a new and better one.

In the world of the Atlantic revolutions, ideas born of the Enlightenment generated endless controversy. Were liberty and equality compatible? What kind of government—unitary and centralized or federal and decentralized—best ensured freedom? And how far should liberty be extended? Except in Haiti, the chief beneficiaries of these revolutions were propertied white men of the "middling classes." Although women, enslaved people, Native Americans, and men without property did not gain much from these revolutions, the ideas that accompanied those upheavals gave them ammunition for the future. Because their overall thrust was to extend political rights further than ever before, these Atlantic movements have often been referred to as "democratic revolutions."

A final distinctive feature of the Atlantic revolutions lies in their immense global impact, extending well beyond the Atlantic world. The armies of revolutionary France, for example, invaded Egypt, Germany, Poland, and Russia, carrying seeds of change. The ideals that animated these Atlantic revolutions inspired efforts in many countries to abolish slavery, to extend the right to vote, to develop constitutions, and to secure greater equality for women. Nationalism, perhaps the most potent ideology of the modern era, was nurtured in the Atlantic revolutions and shaped much of nineteenth- and twentieth-century world history. The ideas of human equality articulated in these revolutions later found expression in feminist, socialist, and communist movements. The Universal Declaration of Human Rights, adopted by the United Nations in 1948, echoed and amplified those principles while providing the basis for any number of subsequent protests against oppression, tyranny, and deprivation. In 1989, a number of Chinese students, fleeing the suppression of a democracy movement in their own country, marched at the head of a huge parade in Paris, celebrating the bicentennial of the French Revolution. And in 2011, the Middle Eastern uprisings known as the Arab Spring initially prompted numerous comparisons with the French Revolution. The Atlantic revolutions had a long reach.

Comparing Atlantic Revolutions

Despite their common political vocabulary and a broadly democratic character, the Atlantic revolutions differed substantially from one another. They were triggered by different circumstances, expressed quite different social and political tensions, and varied considerably in their outcomes. Liberty, noted Simón Bolívar, "is a succulent morsel, but one difficult to digest."[3] "Digesting liberty" occurred in quite distinct ways in the various sites of the Atlantic revolutions.

The North American Revolution, 1775–1787

Every schoolchild in the United States learns early that the **American Revolution** was a struggle for independence from oppressive British rule. That struggle began in 1775 and was formalized by the Declaration of Independence in 1776. It resulted in an unlikely military victory by 1781 and generated a federal constitution in 1787, joining thirteen formerly separate colonies into a new nation (see Map 16.1). It was the first in a series of upheavals that rocked the Atlantic world and beyond in the century that followed. But was it a genuine revolution? What, precisely, did it change?

By making a break with Britain, the American Revolution marked a decisive political change, but in other ways it was, strangely enough, a conservative movement because it originated in an effort to preserve the existing liberties of the colonies rather than to create new ones. For much of the seventeenth and eighteenth centuries, the British colonies in North America enjoyed a considerable degree of local autonomy, as the British government was embroiled in its own internal conflicts and various European wars. Furthermore, Britain's West Indian colonies seemed more profitable and of greater significance than those of North America. In these circumstances, local elected assemblies in North America, dominated by the wealthier property-owning settlers, achieved something close to self-government. Colonists came to regard such autonomy as a birthright and part of their English heritage. Thus, until the mid-eighteenth century, almost no one in the colonies thought of breaking away from England because participation in the British Empire provided

CORE IDEA

■ **Dissecting Revolution**
What was revolutionary about the American Revolution, and what was not?

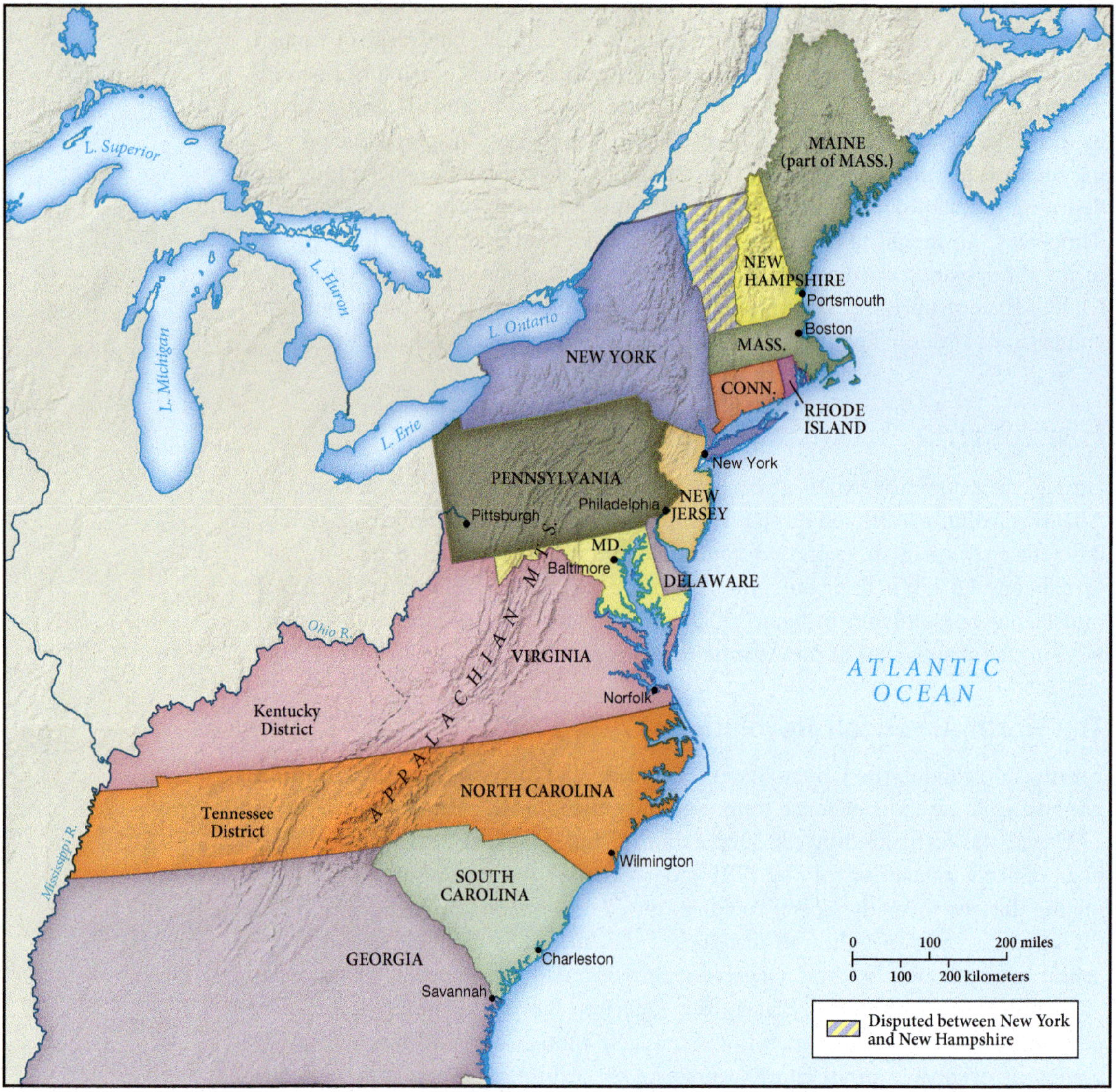

Map 16.1 The United States after the American Revolution
The union of the thirteen British colonies in North America created the embryonic United States, shown here in 1788. Over the past two centuries and more of anticolonial struggles, it was the only example of separate colonies joining together after independence to form a larger and enduring nation.

many advantages—protection in war, access to British markets, and confirmation of the settlers' identity as "Englishmen"—and few drawbacks.

There were, however, real differences between Englishmen in England and those in the North American colonies. Within the colonies, English settlers had developed societies described by a leading historian as "the most radical in the contemporary

Western world." Certainly class distinctions were real and visible, and a small class of wealthy "gentlemen"—the Adamses, Washingtons, Jeffersons, and Hancocks—wore powdered wigs, imitated the latest European styles, were prominent in political life, and were generally accorded deference by ordinary people. But the ready availability of land following the dispossession of Native Americans, the scarcity of people, and the absence of both a titled nobility and a single established church meant that social life was far more open than in Europe. No legal distinctions differentiated clergy, aristocracy, and commoners, as they did in France. All free men enjoyed the same status before the law, but enslaved people and, in some ways, white women did not. These conditions made for less poverty, more economic opportunity, fewer social differences, and easier relationships among the classes than in Europe. The famous economist Adam Smith observed that British colonists were "republican in their manners . . . and their government" well before their independence from England.[4]

Thus the American Revolution grew not from social tensions within the colonies, but from a rather sudden and unexpected effort by the British government to tighten its control over the colonies and to extract more revenue from them. As Britain's global struggle with France drained its treasury and ran up its national debt, British authorities, beginning in the 1760s, looked to America to make good these losses. Abandoning its neglectful oversight of the colonies, Britain began to act like a genuine imperial power, imposing a variety of new taxes and tariffs on the colonies without their consent, for they were not represented in the British Parliament. Many of the colonists were infuriated, because such measures challenged their economic interests, their established traditions of local autonomy, and their identity as true Englishmen. Armed with the ideas of the Enlightenment—popular sovereignty, natural rights, the consent of the governed—they went to war, and by 1781 they had prevailed, with considerable aid from the French, who were only too pleased to harm the interests of their British rivals.

Patriots and Loyalists This English engraving dating from 1775 depicts a club-wielding mob of "Liberty Men" forcing a Virginian loyalist (someone committed to continued British rule) to sign a document, probably endorsing independence for the colonies. The threat of violence toward the loyalist is apparent in the armed crowd, the barrel of tar being used as a table in the foreground, and the sack of feathers hanging from the gallows in the background. Patriots frequently tarred and feathered recalcitrant loyalists during the lead-up to the American Revolution. (Granger, NYC—All rights reserved)

What was revolutionary about the American experience was not so much the revolution itself but the kind of society that had already emerged within the colonies. Independence from Britain was not accompanied by any wholesale social transformation. Rather, the revolution accelerated the established democratic tendencies of the colonial societies. Political authority remained largely in the hands of the existing elites who had led the revolution, although property requirements for voting were lowered and more white men of modest means, such as small farmers and urban artisans, were elected to state legislatures.

This widening of political participation gradually eroded the power of traditional gentlemen, but no women or people of color shared in these gains. Land was not seized from its owners, except in the case of pro-British loyalists who had fled the country. Although slavery was gradually abolished in the northern states, where it counted for little, it remained firmly entrenched in the southern states, where it counted for much. Chief Justice John Marshall later gave voice to this conservative understanding of the American Revolution: "All contracts and rights, respecting property, remained unchanged by the Revolution."[5] In the century that followed independence, the United States did become the world's most democratic country, but this development was less the direct product of the revolution and more the gradual working out in a reformist fashion of earlier practices and the principles of equality announced in the Declaration of Independence.

Nonetheless, many American patriots felt passionately that they were creating "a new order for the ages." James Madison in the *Federalist Papers* made the point clearly: "We pursued a new and more noble course . . . and accomplished a revolution that has no parallel in the annals of human society." Supporters abroad agreed. On the eve of the French Revolution, a Paris newspaper proclaimed that the United States was "the hope and model of the human race."[6] In both cases, they were referring primarily to the political ideas and practices of the new country. The American Revolution, after all, initiated the political dismantling of Europe's New World empires. The "right to revolution," proclaimed in the Declaration of Independence and made effective only in a great struggle, inspired revolutionaries and nationalists from Simón Bolívar in nineteenth-century Latin America to Ho Chi Minh in twentieth-century Vietnam. Moreover, the new U.S. Constitution—with its Bill of Rights, checks and balances, separation of church and state, and federalism—was one of the first sustained efforts to put the political ideas of the Enlightenment into practice. That document, and the ideas that it embraced, echoed repeatedly in the political upheavals of the century that followed.

The French Revolution, 1789–1815

Act Two in the drama of the Atlantic revolutions took place in France, beginning in 1789, although it was closely connected to Act One in North America. Thousands of French soldiers had provided assistance to the American colonists and now returned home full of republican enthusiasm. Thomas Jefferson, the U.S. ambassador in Paris, reported that France "has been awakened by our revolution."[7] More immediately, the French government, which had generously aided the Americans in an effort to undermine its British rivals, was teetering on the brink of bankruptcy and had long sought reforms that would modernize the tax system and make it more equitable. In a desperate effort to raise taxes against the opposition of the privileged classes, the French king, Louis XVI, had called into session an ancient representative body, the Estates General. It consisted of male representatives of the three "estates," or legal orders, of prerevolutionary France: the clergy, the nobility, and the commoners. The first two estates comprised about 2 percent of the population, and the Third Estate included everyone else. When that body convened in 1789, representatives of the Third Estate soon organized themselves as the National Assembly, claiming the sole authority to make laws for the country. A few weeks later, they forthrightly claimed in the **Declaration of the Rights of Man and Citizen** that "men are born and remain free and equal in rights," and this declaration later became the preamble of the 1791 French constitution. These actions, unprecedented and illegal in the *ancien régime* (old regime), launched the **French Revolution** and radicalized many of the participants in the National Assembly.

CORE IDEA

■ Making Comparisons

How did the French Revolution differ from the American Revolution?

The French Revolution was quite different from its North American predecessor. Whereas the American Revolution expressed the tensions of a colonial relationship with a distant imperial power, the French insurrection was driven by sharp conflicts within French society. Members of the titled nobility—privileged, prestigious, and wealthy—resented and resisted the monarchy's efforts to subject them to new taxes. Educated middle-class men such as doctors, lawyers, lower-level officials, and merchants were growing in numbers and sometimes in wealth and were offended by the remaining privileges of the aristocracy, from which they were excluded. Ordinary urban men and women, many of whose incomes had declined for a generation, were hit particularly hard in the late 1780s by the rapidly rising price of bread and widespread unemployment. Peasants in the countryside, though largely free of serfdom, were subject to hated dues imposed by their landlords, taxes from the state, obligations to the Church, and the requirement to work without pay on public roads. As Enlightenment ideas penetrated French society, more and more people, mostly in the Third Estate but also including some priests and nobles, found a language with which to articulate these grievances. The famous French writer Jean-Jacques Rousseau had told them that it was "manifestly contrary to the law of nature . . . that a handful of people should gorge themselves with superfluities while the hungry multitude goes in want of necessities."[8]

These social conflicts gave the French Revolution, especially during its first five years, a much more violent, far-reaching, and radical character than its American counterpart. It was a profound social upheaval, more comparable to the revolutions of Russia and China in the twentieth century than to the earlier American Revolution. Initial efforts to establish a constitutional monarchy and promote harmony among the classes gave way to more radical measures, as internal resistance and foreign opposition produced a fear that the revolution might be overturned. In the process, urban crowds organized insurrections. Some peasants attacked the residences of their lords, burning the documents that recorded their dues and payments. The National

The Execution of Louis XVI The regicide of Louis XVI in January 1793 marked an important moment in the radicalization of the French Revolution and shocked many observers across Europe. In this nineteenth-century engraving of the dramatic event, a large crowd looks on as Louis receives last rites from a priest and his executioners prepare the guillotine. (Private Collection/Photo © The Holborn Archive/ Bridgeman Images)

Assembly decreed the end of all legal privileges and eliminated what remained of feudalism in France. Even slavery was abolished, albeit briefly. Church lands were sold to raise revenue, and priests were put under government authority.

In 1793, King Louis XVI and his queen, Marie Antoinette, were executed, an act of regicide that shocked traditionalists all across Europe and marked a new stage in revolutionary violence. What followed was the Terror of 1793–1794. Under the leadership of Maximilien **Robespierre** (ROHBS-pee-air) and his Committee of Public Safety, tens of thousands deemed enemies of the revolution lost their lives on the guillotine. Shortly thereafter, Robespierre himself was arrested and guillotined, accused of leading France into tyranny and dictatorship. "The revolution," remarked one of its victims, "was devouring its own children."

Accompanying attacks on the old order were efforts to create a wholly new society, symbolized by a new calendar with the Year 1 in 1792, marking a fresh start for France. Unlike the Americans, who sought to restore or build on earlier freedoms, French revolutionaries perceived themselves to be starting from scratch and looked to the future. For the first time in its history, the country became a republic and briefly passed universal male suffrage, although it was never implemented. The old administrative system was rationalized into eighty-three territorial departments, each with a new name. As revolutionary France prepared for war against its threatened and threatening neighbors, it created the world's largest army, with some 800,000 men, and all adult males were required to serve. Led by officers from the middle and even lower classes, this was an army of citizens representing the nation.

Assessing the Impact of Revolution
In what ways did the French Revolution impact various social groups in French society?

In terms of gender roles, the French Revolution did not create a new society, but it did raise the question of female political equality far more explicitly than the American Revolution had done. Partly this was because French women were active in the major events of the revolution. In July 1789, they took part in the famous storming of the Bastille, a large fortress, prison, and armory that had come to symbolize the oppressive old regime. In October of that year, some 7,000 Parisian women, desperate about the shortage of bread, marched on the palace at Versailles, stormed through the royal apartments searching for the despised Queen Marie Antoinette, and forced the royal family to return with them to Paris.

The Women's March on Versailles In the autumn of 1789 rising bread prices and fears of an aristocratic plot to starve the poor caused market women in Paris to lead a march to the royal palace of Versailles. After a tense standoff, Louis XVI agreed to return to Paris escorted by thousands of revolutionaries. This contemporary depiction shows women on their way to Versailles armed with a variety of makeshift weapons and a cannon. (Leemage/Getty Images)

Backed by a few male supporters, women also made serious political demands. They signed petitions detailing their complaints: lack of education, male competition in female trades, the prevalence of prostitution, the rapidly rising price of bread and soap. One petition, reflecting the intersection of class and gender, referred to women as the "Third Estate of the Third Estate." Another demanded the right to bear arms in defense of the revolution. Over sixty women's clubs were established throughout the country. A small group called the *Cercle Social* (Social Circle) campaigned for women's rights, noting that "the laws favor men at the expense of women, because everywhere power is in your [men's] hands."[9] The French playwright and journalist Olympe de Gouges appropriated the language of the Declaration of Rights to insist that "woman is born free and lives equal to man in her rights."

But the assertion of French women in the early years of the revolution seemed wildly inappropriate and threatening to most men, uniting conservatives and revolutionaries alike in defense of male privileges. And so in late 1793, the country's all-male legislative body voted to ban all women's clubs. "Women are ill-suited for elevated thoughts and serious meditation," declared one of the male representatives. "A woman should not leave her family to meddle in affairs of government." Here was a conception of gender that defined masculinity in terms of exercising political power. Women who aspired to do so were, in the words of one revolutionary orator, "denatured *viragos*" (unnatural domineering women), in short, not really women at all.[10] Thus French revolutionaries were distinctly unwilling to offer any political rights to women, even though they had eliminated class restrictions, at least in theory; granted religious freedom to Jews and Protestants; and abolished slavery. Nonetheless, according to a leading historian, "the French Revolution, more than any other event of its time, opened up the question of women's rights for consideration" and thus laid the foundations for modern feminism.[11]

If not in terms of gender, the immediate impact of the revolution was felt in many other ways. Streets got new names; monuments to the royal family were destroyed; titles vanished; people referred to one another as "citizen so-and-so." Real politics in the public sphere emerged for the first time as many people joined political clubs, took part in marches and demonstrations, served on local committees, and ran for public office. Ordinary men and women, who had identified primarily with their local communities, now began to think of themselves as belonging to a nation. The state replaced the Catholic Church as the place for registering births, marriages, and deaths, and revolutionary festivals substituted for church holidays.

More radical revolutionary leaders deliberately sought to convey a sense of new beginnings and endless possibilities. At a Festival of Unity held in 1793 to mark the first anniversary of the end of monarchy, participants burned the crowns and scepters of the royal family in a huge bonfire while releasing a cloud of 3,000 white doves. The Cathedral of Notre Dame was temporarily turned into the Temple of Reason, while a "Hymn to Liberty" combined traditional church music with the explicit message of the Enlightenment:

> Oh Liberty, sacred Liberty / Goddess of an enlightened people
> Rule today within these walls. / Through you this temple is purified.
> Liberty! Before you reason chases out deception, / Error flees, fanaticism is beaten down.
> Our gospel is nature / And our cult is virtue.
> To love one's country and one's brothers, / To serve the Sovereign People
> These are the sacred tenets / And pledge of a Republican.[12]

Elsewhere too the French Revolution evoked images of starting over. Witnessing that revolution in 1790, the young William Wordsworth, later a famous British Romantic poet, imagined "human nature seeming born again." "Bliss it was in that dawn to be alive," he wrote. "But to be young was very heaven."

The French Revolution also differed from the American Revolution in the way its influence spread. At least until the United States became a world power at the end of the nineteenth century, what inspired others was primarily the example of its revolution and its constitution. French influence, by contrast, spread through conquest, largely under the leadership of **Napoleon Bonaparte** (r. 1799–1815). A highly successful general who seized power in 1799, Napoleon is often credited with taming the revolution in the face of growing disenchantment with its more radical features and with the social conflicts it generated. He preserved many of its more moderate elements, such as civil equality, a secular law code, religious freedom, and promotion by merit, while reconciling with the Catholic Church and suppressing the revolution's more democratic elements in a military dictatorship. In short, Napoleon kept the revolution's emphasis on social equality for men but dispensed with liberty.

Like many of the revolution's ardent supporters, Napoleon was intent on spreading its benefits far and wide. In a series of brilliant military campaigns, his forces subdued most of Europe, thus creating the continent's largest empire since the days of the Romans (see Map 16.2). Within that empire, Napoleon imposed such revolutionary practices as ending feudalism, proclaiming equality of rights, insisting on religious toleration, codifying the laws, and rationalizing government administration. In many places, these reforms were welcomed, and seeds of further change were planted. But French domination was also resented and resisted,

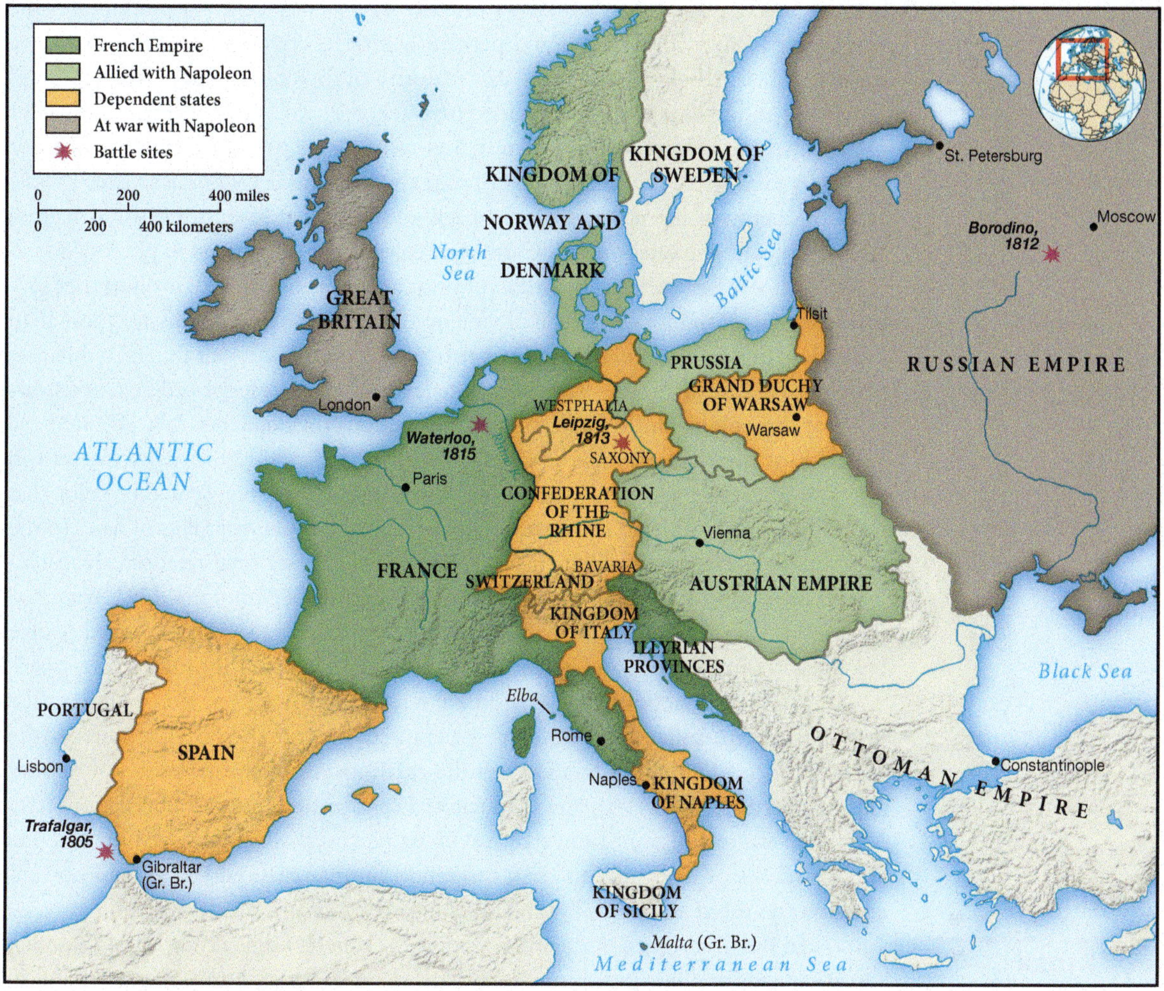

Map 16.2 Napoleon's European Empire
The French Revolution spawned a French Empire, under Napoleon's leadership, that encompassed most of Europe and served to spread the principles of the revolution.

stimulating national consciousness throughout Europe. That too was a seed that bore fruit in the century that followed. More immediately, national resistance, particularly from Russia and Britain, brought down Napoleon and his amazing empire by 1815 and marked an end to the era of the French Revolution, though not to the potency of its ideas.

The Haitian Revolution, 1791–1804

Nowhere did the example of the French Revolution echo more loudly than in the French Caribbean colony of Saint Domingue, later renamed Haiti (see Map 16.3, page 706). Widely regarded as the richest colony in the world, Saint Domingue boasted 8,000 plantations, which in the late eighteenth century produced some 40 percent of the world's sugar and perhaps half of its coffee. A slave labor force of about 500,000 people made up the vast majority of the colony's population. Whites numbered about 40,000, sharply divided between very well-to-do plantation owners, merchants, and lawyers and those known as *petits blancs* (peh-TEE blahnk), or poor whites. A third social group consisted of some 30,000 *gens de couleur libres* (free people of color), many of them of multiracial background. Given its enormous inequalities and its rampant exploitation, this Caribbean colony was primed for explosion.

In such a volatile setting, the ideas and example of the French Revolution lit several fuses and set in motion a spiral of violence that engulfed the colony for more than a decade. The principles of the revolution, however, meant different things to different people. To the *grands blancs*—the rich white landowners—it suggested greater autonomy for the colony and fewer economic restrictions on trade, but they resented the demands of the *petits blancs*, who sought equality of citizenship for all whites. Both white groups were adamantly opposed to the insistence of free people of color that the "rights of man" meant equal treatment for all free people regardless of race. To the enslaved, the promise of the French Revolution was a personal freedom that challenged the entire slave labor system. In a massive revolt beginning in 1791, triggered by rumors that the French king had already declared an end to slavery, enslaved people burned 1,000 plantations and killed hundreds of whites as well as multiracial people.

Soon warring factions of the enslaved, whites, and free people of color battled one another. Spanish and British forces, seeking to enlarge their own empires at the expense of the French, only added to the turmoil. Amid the confusion, brutality, and massacres of the 1790s, power gravitated toward the enslaved population, now led by the astute Toussaint Louverture, who had formerly been enslaved himself. He and his successor overcame internal resistance, outmaneuvered the foreign powers, and even defeated an attempt by Napoleon to reestablish French control.

CORE IDEA

■ Identifying Uniqueness
What was distinctive about the Haitian Revolution, both in world history generally and in the history of Atlantic revolutions?

When the dust settled in the early years of the nineteenth century, it was clear that something remarkable and unprecedented had taken place, a revolution unique in the Atlantic world and in world history. Socially, the last had become first. In the only completely successful slave revolt in world history, "the lowest order of the society—slaves—became equal, free, and independent citizens."[13] Politically, they had thrown off French colonial rule, creating the second independent republic in the Americas and the first non-European state to emerge from Western colonialism. They renamed their country "Haiti," a term meaning "mountainous" or "rugged" in the language of the original Taino people. It was a symbolic break with Europe and represented an effort to connect with the long-deceased native inhabitants of the land. Some, in fact, referred to themselves as "Incas." At the formal declaration of Haiti's independence on January 1, 1804, Jean-Jacques Dessalines, the new country's first head of state, declared: "I have given the French cannibals blood for blood; I have avenged America."[14] In defining all Haitian citizens as "black" and legally equal regardless of color or class, Haiti directly confronted elite preferences for lighter skin even as it disallowed citizenship for most whites. Economically, the country's plantation system, oriented wholly toward the export of sugar and coffee, had been largely destroyed. As whites fled or were killed, both private and state lands were redistributed among formerly enslaved people and free blacks, and Haiti became a nation of small-scale farmers producing mostly for their own needs, with a much smaller export sector.

The Haitian Revolution This early nineteenth-century engraving, titled *Revenge Taken by the Black Army*, shows black Haitian soldiers hanging a large number of French soldiers, thus illustrating both the violence and the racial dimension of the upheaval in Haiti. (Bridgeman Images)

The destructiveness of the **Haitian Revolution**, its bitter internal divisions of race and class, and continuing external opposition contributed much to Haiti's abiding poverty as well as to its authoritarian and unstable politics. So too did the enormous "independence debt" that the French forced on the fledgling republic in 1825, a financial burden that endured for well over a century. "Freedom" in Haiti came to mean primarily the end of slavery rather than the establishment of political rights for all. In the early nineteenth century, however, Haiti was a source of enormous hope and of great fear. Within weeks of the Haitian slave uprising in 1791, enslaved people in Jamaica had composed songs in its honor, and it was not long before slave owners in the Caribbean and North America observed a new "insolence" among those that they enslaved. Certainly, its example inspired other slave rebellions, gave a boost to the dawning abolitionist movement, and has been a source of pride for people of African descent ever since.

To whites throughout the hemisphere, the cautionary saying "Remember Haiti" reflected a sense of horror at what had occurred there and a determination not to allow political change to reproduce that fearful outcome again. Particularly in Latin America, the events in Haiti injected a deep caution and social conservatism in the elites who led their countries to independence in the early nineteenth century. Ironically, though, the Haitian Revolution also led to a temporary expansion of slavery elsewhere. Cuban plantations and their enslaved workers considerably increased their production of sugar as that of Haiti declined. Moreover, Napoleon's defeat in Haiti persuaded him to sell to the United States the French territories known as the Louisiana Purchase, from which a number of "slave states" were carved out. Nor did the example of Haiti lead to successful independence struggles in the rest of the thirty or so Caribbean colonies. Unlike mainland North and South America, Caribbean decolonization had to await the twentieth century. In such contradictory ways did the echoes of the Haitian Revolution reverberate in the Atlantic world.

Latin American Revolutions, 1808–1825

The final act in a half century of Atlantic revolutionary upheaval took place in the Spanish and Portuguese colonies of mainland Latin America (see Map 16.3). These **Latin American revolutions** were shaped by preceding events in North America, France, and Haiti as well as by their own distinctive societies and historical experiences. As in British North America, native-born elites (known as *creoles*) in the Spanish colonies were offended and insulted by the Spanish monarchy's efforts during the eighteenth century to exercise greater power over its colonies and to subject them to heavier taxes and tariffs. Creole intellectuals had also become familiar with ideas of popular sovereignty, republican government, and personal liberty derived from the European Enlightenment. But these conditions, similar to those in North America, led initially only to scattered and uncoordinated protests rather than to outrage, declarations of independence, war, and unity, as had occurred in the British colonies. Why did Spanish colonies win their independence almost fifty years later than those of British North America?

Map 16.3 Latin American Independence
With the exception of Haiti, Latin American revolutions brought independence to new states but offered little social change or political opportunity for the vast majority of people.

Spanish colonies had long been governed in a rather more authoritarian fashion than their British counterparts and were more sharply divided by class. In addition, whites throughout Latin America were vastly outnumbered by Native Americans, people of African ancestry, and those of biracial and multiracial backgrounds. All of this inhibited the growth of a movement for independence, notwithstanding the example of North America and similar provocations.

Despite their growing disenchantment with Spanish rule, creole elites did not so much generate a revolution as have one thrust upon them by events in Europe. In 1808, Napoleon invaded Spain and Portugal, deposing the Spanish king Ferdinand VII and forcing the Portuguese royal family into exile in Brazil. With legitimate royal authority now in disarray, Latin Americans were forced to take action. The outcome, ultimately, was independence for the various states of Latin America, established almost everywhere by 1826. But the way in which independence occurred and the kind of societies it generated differed greatly from the experience of both North America and Haiti.

The process lasted more than twice as long as it did in North America, partly because Latin American societies were so divided by class, race, and region. In North America, violence was directed almost entirely against the British and seldom spilled over into domestic disputes, except for some bloody skirmishes with loyalists. In Mexico, by contrast, the move toward independence began in 1810–1811 in a peasant insurrection, driven by hunger for land and by high food prices and led successively by two priests, Miguel Hidalgo and José Morelos. Alarmed by the social radicalism of the **Hidalgo-Morelos rebellion**, creole landowners, with the support of the Church, raised an army and crushed the insurgency. Later that alliance of clergy and creole elites brought Mexico to a more socially controlled independence in 1821. Such violent conflict among Latin Americans, along lines of race, class, and ideology, accompanied the struggle against Spain in many places.

CORE IDEA

■ Connecting Influences

How were the Latin American revolutions shaped by the American, French, and Haitian revolutions that happened earlier?

The entire independence movement in Latin America took place under the shadow of a great fear—the dread of social rebellion from below—that had little counterpart in North America. The extensive violence of the French and Haitian revolutions was a lesson to Latin American elites that political change could easily get out of hand and was fraught with danger to themselves. An abortive rebellion of Native Americans in Peru in the early 1780s, led by **Tupac Amaru**, a man who claimed direct descent from the last Inca emperor, reminded whites that they sat atop a potentially explosive society, most of whose members were exploited and oppressed people of color. So too did the Hidalgo-Morelos rebellion in Mexico.

And yet the creole sponsors of independence movements, both regional military leaders such as Simón Bolívar and José de San Martín and their civilian counterparts, required the support of "the people," or at least some of them, if they were to prevail against Spanish forces. The answer to this dilemma was found in nativism, which cast all of those born in the Americas—creoles, Indians, multiracial people, free blacks—as Americanos, while the enemy was defined as those born in Spain or Portugal. This was no easy task, because many creole whites and mestizos saw themselves as Spanish and because great differences of race, culture, and wealth divided the Americanos. Nonetheless, nationalist leaders made efforts to mobilize people of color into the struggle with promises of freedom, the end of legal restrictions, and social advancement. Many of these leaders were genuine liberals who had been influenced by the ideals of the Enlightenment, the French Revolution, and Spanish liberalism. In the long run, however, few of those promises were kept. Certainly, the lower classes, Native Americans, and enslaved people benefited little from independence. "The imperial state was destroyed in Spanish America," concluded one historian, "but colonial society was preserved."[15]

Simón Bolívar Among the heroic figures of Spanish American independence movements, none was more significant than Simón Bolívar, shown here in a moment of triumph entering his hometown of Caracas in present-day Venezuela. But Bolívar was immensely disappointed in the outcomes of independence, as his dream of a unified South America perished amid the rivalries of separate countries. (*Bolívar's Victory Parade in Caracas*, chalk lithograph by R. Weibezahl/Sammlung Archiv für Kunst und Geschichte, Berlin, Germany/akg-images)

Nor did women as a group gain much from the independence struggle, though they had participated in it in various ways. Upper-class or wealthy women gave and raised money for the cause and provided safe havens for revolutionary meetings. In Mexico, some women disguised themselves as men to join the struggle, while numerous working-class and peasant women served as cooks and carriers of supplies in a "women's brigade." A considerable number of women were severely punished for their disloyalty to the Crown, with some forty-eight executed in Colombia. Yet, after independence, few social gains rewarded these efforts. General San Martín of Argentina accorded national recognition to a number of women, and modest improvement in educational opportunities for women appeared. But Latin American women continued to be wholly excluded from political life and remained under firm legal control of the men in their families.

A further difference in the Latin American situation lay in the apparent impossibility of uniting the various Spanish colonies, so much larger than the small British territories of North America, despite several failed efforts to do so. Thus no United States of Latin America emerged. Distances among the colonies and geographic obstacles to effective communication were certainly greater than in the Eastern Seaboard colonies of North America, and their longer colonial experience had given rise to distinct and deeply rooted regional identities. Shortly before his death in 1830, the prominent independence leader Simón Bolívar, who so admired George Washington and had so ardently hoped for greater unity, wrote in despair to a friend: "[Latin] America is ungovernable. Those who serve the revolution plough the sea."[16]

The aftermath of independence in Latin America marked a reversal in the earlier relationship of the two American continents. The United States, which began its history as the leftover "dregs" of the New World, grew increasingly wealthy, industrialized, democratic, internationally influential, and generally stable, with the major exception of the Civil War. The Spanish colonies, which took shape in the wealthiest areas and among the most sophisticated cultures of the Americas, were widely regarded as the more promising region compared to England's North American territories, which had a backwater reputation. But in the nineteenth century, as newly independent countries in both regions launched a new phase of their histories, those in Latin America became relatively underdeveloped, impoverished, undemocratic, politically unstable, and dependent on foreign technology and investment. Begun in broadly similar circumstances, the Latin American and North American revolutions occurred in very different societies and gave rise to very different historical trajectories.

Echoes of Revolution

The repercussions of the Atlantic revolutions reverberated far beyond their places of origin and persisted long after those upheavals had been concluded. Britain's loss of its North American colonies, for example, fueled its growing interest and interventions in Asia, contributing to British colonial rule in India and the Opium Wars in China. Napoleon's brief conquest of Egypt (1798–1801) opened the way for a modernizing regime to emerge in that ancient land and stimulated westernizing reforms in the Ottoman Empire (see "The Ottoman Empire and the West in the Nineteenth Century" in Chapter 19). During the nineteenth century, the idea of a "constitution" found advocates in Poland, Russia, the Spanish-ruled Philippines, China, the Ottoman Empire, and British-governed India.

Within Europe, which was generally dominated by conservative governments following Napoleon's final defeat, smaller revolutionary eruptions occurred in 1830, more widely in 1848, and in Paris in 1870. They reflected ideas of republicanism, greater social equality, and national liberation from foreign rule. Such ideas and social pressures pushed the major states of Western Europe, the United States, and Argentina to enlarge their voting publics, generally granting universal male suffrage by 1914. An abortive attempt to establish a constitutional regime even broke out in autocratic Russia in 1825, led by aristocratic military officers influenced by French revolutionary ideas. While it quickly failed, it marked the beginning of a revolutionary tradition in Russia that came to fruition only in 1917. More generally, the American and French revolutions led sympathetic elites in Central Europe and elsewhere to feel that they had fallen behind, that their countries were "sleeping." As early as 1791, a Hungarian poet gave voice to such sentiments: "O you still in the slave's collar . . . And you too! Holy consecrated kings . . . turn your eyes to Paris! Let France set out the fate of both king and shackled slave."[17]

Beyond these echoes of the Atlantic revolutions, three major movements arose to challenge continuing patterns of oppression or exclusion. Abolitionists sought the end of slavery; nationalists hoped to foster unity and independence from foreign rule; and feminists challenged male dominance. Each of these movements bore the marks of the Atlantic revolutions, and although they took root first in Europe and the Americas, each came to have a global significance in the centuries that followed.

The Abolition of Slavery

CORE IDEA

Connecting Historical Legacies
In what ways did the Atlantic revolutions contribute to the abolitionist, nationalist, and feminist movements of the nineteenth century?

In little more than a century, from roughly 1780 to 1890, a remarkable transformation occurred in human affairs as slavery, widely practiced and little condemned since at least the beginning of civilization, lost its legitimacy and was largely ended. In this amazing process, the ideas and practices of the Atlantic revolutions played an important role.

Enlightenment thinkers in eighteenth-century Europe had become increasingly critical of slavery as a violation of the natural rights of every person, and the public pronouncements of the American and French revolutions about liberty and equality likewise focused attention on this obvious breach of those principles. To this secular antislavery thinking was added an increasingly vociferous religious voice, expressed first by Quakers and then by Protestant evangelicals in Britain and the United States. To them, slavery was "repugnant to our religion" and a "crime in the sight of God."[18] What made these moral arguments more widely acceptable was the growing belief that, contrary to much earlier thinking, slavery was not essential for economic progress. After all, England and New England were among the most prosperous regions of the Western world in the early nineteenth century, and both were based on free labor. Slavery in this view was out of date, unnecessary in the new era of industrial technology and capitalism. Thus moral virtue and economic success were joined. It was an attractive argument. The actions of enslaved people themselves likewise hastened the end of slavery. The dramatically successful Haitian Revolution was followed by three major rebellions in the British West Indies, all of which were harshly crushed, in the early nineteenth century. The **Great Jamaica Revolt** of 1831–1832, in which perhaps 60,000 enslaved people attacked several hundred plantations, was particularly important in prompting Britain to abolish slavery throughout its empire in 1833. These revolts demonstrated clearly that enslaved people were hardly "contented," and the brutality with which they were suppressed appalled British public opinion. Growing numbers of the British public came to believe that slavery was "not only morally wrong and economically inefficient, but also politically unwise."[19]

Abolitionism This unusual late eighteenth-century abolitionist image depicts an enslaved African in chains holding a knife on the deck of a ship. Unlike most abolitionist representations of Africans, which show their subjects kneeling, praying, or pleading, the subject of this engraving strikes a defiant pose as he seemingly contemplates suicide, or perhaps resistance, rather than captivity. (*The Dying Negro*... by T. Day and J. Bicknell, Second Edition, with additions [London: John Stockdale, 1793], http://access.bl.uk/item/viewer/ark:/81055/vdc_00000002B740)

These various strands of thinking—secular, religious, economic, and political—came together in an **abolitionist movement**, most powerfully in Britain, which brought growing pressure on governments to close down the trade in enslaved people and then to ban slavery itself. In the late eighteenth century, such a movement gained wide support among middle- and working-class people in Britain. Its techniques included pamphlets with heartrending descriptions of slavery, numerous petitions to Parliament, lawsuits, and boycotts of slave-produced sugar. Frequent public meetings dramatically featured the testimony of Africans who had experienced the horrors of slavery firsthand. In 1807, Britain forbade the sale of enslaved people within its empire and in 1834 emancipated those who remained enslaved. Over the next half century, other nations followed suit, responding to growing international pressure, particularly from Britain, then the world's leading economic and military power. British naval vessels patrolled the Atlantic, intercepted illegal slave ships, and freed their human cargoes in a small West African settlement called Freetown, in present-day Sierra Leone. Following their independence, most Latin American countries abolished slavery by the 1850s. Brazil, in 1888, was the last to do so, bringing more than four centuries of Atlantic slavery to an end. A roughly similar set of conditions—fear of rebellion, economic inefficiency, and moral concerns—persuaded the Russian tsar (zahr) to free the many serfs of that huge country in 1861, although there it occurred by fiat from above rather than from growing public pressure.

■ **Explaining Change** What accounts for the end of Atlantic slavery during the nineteenth century?

None of this happened easily. Even after slavery was outlawed by Britain, it continued to find a place in the British world, with slave-produced cotton from the southern United States supplying its crucial textiles industry and imperial officials often turning a blind eye toward the illegal traffic of women and girls into the sex trade in British Southeast Asia. Slave economies continued to flourish well into the nineteenth century, and plantation owners vigorously resisted the onslaught of abolitionists. So did slave traders, both European and African, who together shipped millions of additional captives, mostly to Cuba and Brazil, long after the British had declared the trade illegal. Osei Bonsu, the powerful king of the West African state of Asante, was puzzled as to why the British would no longer purchase enslaved people from him. "If they think it bad now," he asked a local British representative in 1820, "why did they think it good before?"[20] Nowhere was the persistence of slavery more evident and resistance to abolition more intense than in the southern states of the United States. It was the only slaveholding society in which the end of slavery occurred through a bitter, prolonged, and highly destructive civil war (1861–1865).

The end of Atlantic slavery during the nineteenth century surely marked a major and quite rapid turn in the world's social history and in the moral thinking of humankind. Nonetheless, the outcomes of that process were often surprising and far from the expectations of abolitionists or the formerly enslaved. In most cases, the economic lives of the enslaved people did not improve dramatically upon emancipation. Nowhere in the Atlantic world, except Haiti, did a redistribution of land follow the end of slavery. But freedmen everywhere desperately sought economic autonomy on their own land, and in parts of the Caribbean such as Jamaica, where unoccupied land was available, independent peasant agriculture proved possible for some. Elsewhere, as in the southern United States, various forms of legally free but highly dependent labor, such as sharecropping, emerged to replace slavery and to provide low-paid and often indebted workers for planters. The understandable reluctance of the formerly enslaved to continue working in plantation agriculture created labor shortages and set in motion a huge new wave of global migration. Large numbers of indentured servants from India and China were imported into the Caribbean, Peru, South Africa, Hawaii, Malaya, and elsewhere to work in mines, on plantations, and in construction projects. There they often toiled in conditions not far removed from slavery itself.

Assessing Impact
How did the end of slavery affect the lives of the formerly enslaved?

Newly freed people did not achieve anything close to political equality, except in Haiti. White planters, farmers, and mine owners retained local authority in the Caribbean, where colonial rule persisted until well into the twentieth century. In the southern United States, a brief period of "radical reconstruction," during which newly freed blacks did enjoy full political rights and some power, was followed by harsh segregation laws, denial of voting rights, a wave of lynchings, and a virulent racism that lasted well into the twentieth century. For most formerly enslaved people, emancipation usually meant "nothing but freedom."[21] Unlike the situation in the Americas, the end of serfdom in Russia transferred to the peasants a considerable portion of the nobles' land, but the need to pay for this land with "redemption dues" and the rapid growth of Russia's rural population ensured that most peasants remained impoverished and politically volatile.

In both West and East Africa, the closing of the external slave trade decreased the price of enslaved people and increased their use within African societies to produce the export crops that the world economy now sought. Thus, as Europeans imposed colonial rule on Africa in the late nineteenth century, they loudly proclaimed their commitment to ending slavery in a continent from which they had extracted enslaved people for more than four centuries. This was surely among the more ironic outcomes of the abolitionist process.

In the Islamic world, where slavery had long been practiced and elaborately regulated, the freeing of enslaved people, though not required, was strongly recommended as a mark of piety. Some nineteenth-century Muslim authorities opposed slavery altogether on the grounds that it violated the Quran's ideals of freedom and equality. But unlike Europe and North America, the Islamic world generated no popular grassroots antislavery movements. There slavery was outlawed gradually only in the twentieth century under the pressure of international opinion.

Nations and Nationalism

In addition to contributing to the end of slavery, the Atlantic revolutions also gave new prominence to a relatively recent kind of human community—the nation. By the end of the twentieth century, the idea that humankind was divided into separate nations, each with a distinct culture and territory and deserving an independent political life, was so widespread as to seem natural and timeless. And yet for most of human experience, states did not usually coincide with the culture of a particular people, for all the great empires and many smaller states governed culturally diverse societies. Few people considered rule by foreigners itself a terrible offense because the most important identities and loyalties were local, limited to clan, village, or region, with only modest connection to the larger state or empire that governed them. People might on occasion consider themselves part of larger religious communities (such as Christians or Muslims) or ethno-linguistic groupings such as Greek, Arab, or Maya, but such identities rarely provided the basis for enduring states.

All of that began to change during the era of Atlantic revolutions. Independence movements in both North and South America were made in the name of new nations. The French Revolution declared that sovereignty lay with "the people," and its leaders mobilized this people to defend the "French nation" against its external enemies. In 1793, the revolutionary government of France declared a mass conscription (*levée en masse*) with a stirring call to service:

> Henceforth, until the enemies have been driven from the territory of the Republic, all the French are in permanent requisition for army service. The young men shall go to battle; the married men shall forge arms and transport provisions; the women shall make tents and clothes, and shall serve in the hospitals; the children shall turn old linen into lint; the old men shall repair to the public places, to stimulate the courage of the warriors and preach the unity of the Republic and the hatred of kings.[22]

Napoleon's conquests likewise stimulated national resistance in many parts of Europe. European states had long competed and fought with one another, but increasingly in the nineteenth century, those states were inhabited by people who felt themselves to be citizens of a nation, deeply bound to their fellows by ties of blood, culture, or common experience, not simply common subjects of a ruling dynasty. It was a novel form of political loyalty.

The rise of **nationalism** was also facilitated by Europe's modern transformation, as older identities and loyalties eroded. Science weakened the hold of religion on some. Migration to industrial cities or abroad diminished allegiance to local communities. At the same time, printing and the publishing industry standardized a variety of dialects into a smaller number of European languages, a process that allowed a growing reading public to think of themselves as members of a common linguistic group or nation. All of this encouraged political and cultural leaders to articulate appealing ideas of their particular nations and ensured a growing circle of people receptive to such ideas. Thus the idea of the "nation" was constructed or even invented, but it was often imagined and presented as a reawakening of older linguistic or cultural identities, and it certainly drew on the songs, dances, folktales, historical experiences, and collective memories of earlier cultures (see Map 16.4).

Explaining Change
What accounts for the growth of nationalism as a powerful political and personal identity in the nineteenth century?

Whatever its precise origins, nationalism proved to be an infinitely flexible and enormously powerful idea in nineteenth-century Europe and beyond. It inspired the political unification of both Italy (1870) and Germany (1871), gathering their previously fragmented peoples into new states. It encouraged Greeks and Serbs to assert their independence from the Ottoman Empire; Czechs and Hungarians to

MAPPING HISTORY

Map 16.4 The Nations and Empires of Europe, ca. 1880

By the end of the nineteenth century, the national principle had substantially reshaped the map of Europe, especially in the unification of Germany and Italy. However, several major empires remained, each with numerous subject peoples who likewise sought national independence.

READING THE MAP In which regions of Europe were empires most prominent? Where did nation-states predominate? How might one generalize about the distribution of empires and nation-states in Europe around 1880?

MAKING CONNECTIONS Compare this map with Map 16.2: Napoleon's European Empire. What changed on the political map of Europe after the collapse of Napoleon's empire? What stayed the same?

demand more autonomy within the Austrian Empire; Poles and Ukrainians to become more aware of their oppression within the Russian Empire; and the Irish to seek "home rule" and separation from Great Britain. By the end of the nineteenth century, a small Zionist movement, seeking a homeland in Palestine, had emerged among Europe's frequently persecuted Jews.

Popular nationalism made the normal rivalry among European states even more acute and fueled a highly competitive drive for colonies in Asia and Africa. The immensity of the suffering and sacrifice that nationalism generated in Europe was vividly disclosed during the horrors of World War I. Furthermore, nationalism fueled rivalries among the various European-derived states in the Americas, reflected, for example, in the Mexican–United States War of 1846–1848 and the devastating conflict between Paraguay and the Triple Alliance of Argentina, Brazil, and Uruguay between 1864 and 1870, in which about half of Paraguay's population perished.

Governments throughout the Western world now claimed to act on behalf of their nations and deliberately sought to instill national loyalties in their citizens through schools, public rituals, the mass media, and military service. Russian authorities, for example, imposed the use of the Russian language, even in parts of the country where it was not widely spoken. They succeeded, however, only in producing a greater awareness of Ukrainian, Polish, and Finnish nationalism.

As it became more prominent in the nineteenth century, nationalism took on a variety of political ideologies. Some supporters of liberal democracy and representative government, as in France or the United States, saw nationalism, with its emphasis on "the people," as an aid to their aspirations toward wider involvement in political life. Often called civic nationalism, such a view identified the nation with a particular territory and maintained that people of various cultural backgrounds could assimilate into the dominant culture, as in the process of "becoming American." Other versions of nationalism, in Germany, for example, sometimes defined the nation in racial terms that excluded those who did not share an imagined common ancestry, such as Jews. In the hands of conservatives, nationalism could be used to combat socialism and feminism, for those movements allegedly divided the nation along class or gender lines. Thus nationalism generated endless controversy because it provided no clear answer to the questions of who belonged to the nation or who should speak for it.

Nor was nationalism limited to the Euro-American world in the nineteenth century. An "Egypt for the Egyptians" movement arose in the 1870s as British and French intervention in Egyptian affairs deepened. When Japan likewise confronted European aggression in the second half of the nineteenth century, its long sense of itself as a distinct culture was readily transformed into an assertive modern nationalism. In British-ruled India, small groups of Western-educated men began to think of their enormously diverse country as a single nation. The Indian National Congress, established in 1885, gave expression to this idea. The notion of the Ottoman Empire as a Turkish national state rather than a Muslim or dynastic empire took hold among a few people. By the end of the nineteenth century, some

Nationalism in Poland In the eighteenth century, Poland had been divided among Prussia, Austria, and Russia and disappeared as a separate and independent state. Polish nationalism found expression in the nineteenth century in a series of revolts against Poland's Russian occupiers. This painting shows Russian officers surrendering their standards to Polish insurgents during the November Uprising of 1830. The revolt was subsequently crushed, and Poland regained its independence as a nation-state only in 1918 at the end of World War I. (ullstein bild/Granger, NYC–All rights reserved)

Chinese intellectuals began to think in terms of a Chinese nation beset both by a foreign ruling dynasty and by predatory Europeans. Along the West African coast, the idea of an "African nation" stirred among a handful of the formerly enslaved and missionary-educated men. Although Egyptian and Japanese nationalism gained broad support, elsewhere in Asia and Africa such movements would have to wait until the twentieth century, when they exploded with enormous power on the stage of world history.

Feminist Beginnings

A third echo of the Atlantic revolutions lay in the emergence of a feminist movement. Although scattered voices had earlier challenged patriarchy, never before had an organized and substantial group of women called into question this most fundamental and accepted feature of all preindustrial civilizations—the subordination of women to men. But in the century following the French Revolution, such a challenge took shape, especially in Europe and North America. Then, in the twentieth century, feminist thinking transformed "the way in which women and men work, play, think, dress, worship, vote, reproduce, make love and make war."[23] How did this extraordinary process get launched in the nineteenth century?

Thinkers of the European Enlightenment had challenged many ancient traditions, including on occasion that of women's intrinsic inferiority (see "Science and Enlightenment" in Chapter 15). The French writer Condorcet, for example, called for "the complete destruction of those prejudices that have established an inequality of rights between the sexes." The French Revolution then raised the possibility of re-creating human societies on new foundations. Many women participated in these events, and a few insisted, unsuccessfully, that the revolutionary ideals of liberty and equality must include women. In neighboring England, the French Revolution stimulated the writer Mary Wollstonecraft to pen her famous ***Vindication of the Rights of Woman*** in 1792, one of the earliest expressions of a feminist consciousness. "Who made man the exclusive judge," she asked, "if woman partake with him of the gift of reason?"

■ Assessing Significance
What were the achievements and limitations of nineteenth-century feminism?

Within the growing middle classes of industrializing societies, more women found both educational opportunities and some freedom from household drudgery. Such women increasingly took part in temperance movements, charities, abolitionism, and missionary work, as well as socialist and pacifist organizations. Some of their working-class sisters became active trade unionists. On both sides of the Atlantic, small numbers of these women began to develop a feminist consciousness that viewed women as individuals with rights equal to those of men. The first organized expression of this new feminism took place at the Women's Rights Convention in Seneca Falls, New York, in 1848. At that meeting, **Elizabeth Cady Stanton** drafted a statement that began by paraphrasing the Declaration of Independence: "We hold these truths to be self-evident, that all men and women are created equal."

From the beginning, feminism became a transatlantic movement in which European and American women attended the same conferences, corresponded regularly, and read one another's work. Access to schools, universities, and the professions were among their major concerns as growing numbers of women sought these previously unavailable opportunities. The more radical among them refused to take their husbands' surname or wore trousers under their skirts. Elizabeth Cady Stanton published a Women's Bible, excising the parts she found offensive. As heirs to the French Revolution, feminists ardently believed in progress and insisted that it must now include a radical transformation of the position of women.

By the 1870s, feminist movements in the West were focusing primarily on the issue of suffrage and were gaining a growing constituency. Now many ordinary middle-class housewives and working-class mothers joined their better-educated sisters in the movement. By 1914, some 100,000 women took part in French feminist organizations, while the National American Woman Suffrage Association claimed 2 million members. Most operated through peaceful protest and persuasion, but the British Women's Social and Political Union organized a campaign of violence that included blowing up railroad stations, slashing works of art, and smashing department store windows. One British activist, Emily Davison, threw herself in front of the king's horse during a race in Britain in 1913 and was trampled to death. By the beginning of the twentieth century in the most highly industrialized countries of the West, the women's movement had become a mass movement.

That movement had some effect. By 1900, upper- and middle-class women had gained entrance to universities, though in small numbers, and women's literacy rates were growing steadily. In the United States, a number of states passed legislation allowing women to manage and control their own property and wages, separate from their husbands. Divorce laws were liberalized in some places. Professions such as medicine opened to a few, and teaching beckoned to many more. In Britain, Florence Nightingale professionalized nursing and attracted thousands of women into it, while Jane Addams in the United States virtually invented "social work," which also became a female-dominated profession. Progress was slower in the political domain. In 1893, New Zealand became the first country to give the vote to all adult women; Finland followed in 1906. Elsewhere widespread voting rights for women in national elections were not achieved until after World War I, in 1920 in the United States, and in France not until 1945.

Women's Suffrage Suffragists in Britain frequently faced arrest while promoting their cause. This photograph taken in 1914 documents the arrest of Emmeline Pankhurst, leader of the British suffragists, outside Buckingham Palace in London when she tried to deliver a petition to King George V. Some imprisoned suffragists went on hunger strikes to force the authorities to respond to their demands and were met with brutal efforts at forcible feeding by prison officials. (IWM/Getty Images)

Beyond these concrete accomplishments, the movement prompted an unprecedented discussion about the role of women in modern society. In Henrik Ibsen's play *A Doll's House* (1879), the heroine, Nora, finding herself in a loveless and oppressive marriage, leaves both her husband and her children. European audiences were riveted, and many were outraged. Writers, doctors, and journalists addressed previously taboo sexual topics, including homosexuality and birth control. Socialists too found themselves divided about women's issues. Did the women's movement distract from the class solidarity that Marxism proclaimed, or did it provide added energy to the workers' cause? Feminists themselves disagreed about the proper basis for women's rights. Some took their stand on the modern idea of human equality: "Whatever is right for a man is right for a woman." Others, particularly in France, based their claims more on the distinctive role of women as mothers. "It is above all this holy function of motherhood," wrote one advocate of **maternal feminism**, "which requires that women watch over the futures of their children and gives women the right to intervene not only in all acts of civil life, but also in all acts of political life."[24]

Not surprisingly, feminism provoked bitter opposition. Some academic and medical experts argued that the strains of education and life outside the home would cause serious reproductive damage and as a consequence depopulate the nation. Thus feminists were viewed as selfish, willing to sacrifice the family or even the nation while pursuing their individual goals. Some saw suffragists, like Jews and socialists, as "a foreign body in our national life." Never before in any society had such a passionate and public debate about the position of women erupted. It was a novel feature of Western historical experience in the aftermath of the Atlantic revolutions.

Like nationalism, a concern with women's rights spread beyond Western Europe and North America, though less widely. An overtly feminist newspaper was established in Brazil in 1852, and an independent school for girls was founded in Mexico in 1869. A handful of Japanese women and men, including the empress Haruko, raised issues about marriage, family planning, and especially education as the country began its modernizing process after 1868, but the state soon cracked down firmly, forbidding women from joining political parties or even attending political meetings. In Russia, the most radical feminist activists operated within socialist or anarchist circles, targeting the oppressive tsarist regime. Within the Islamic world and in China, some modernists came to believe that education and a higher status for women strengthened the nation in its struggles for development and independence and therefore deserved support. (See Zooming In: Kartini, page 720, for an example from the Dutch East Indies.) Huda Sharawi, founder of the first feminist organization in Egypt, returned to Cairo in 1923 from an international conference in Italy and threw her veil into the sea. Many upper-class Egyptian women soon followed her example.

Nowhere did nineteenth-century feminism have thoroughly revolutionary consequences. But as an outgrowth of the French and Industrial revolutions, it raised issues that echoed repeatedly and more loudly in the century that followed.

CONCLUSIONS AND REFLECTIONS

Pondering the Outcomes of Revolutions

Revolutions change things, but not always the same things and not always quickly or permanently. Political life, for example, changed in each of the four locations of the Atlantic revolutions. In the United States, Haiti, and Latin America, political ties to a colonial power were broken, while in France the execution of Louis XVI ended the monarchy. Furthermore, all of these revolutions nurtured nationalist sentiments and loyalties both within and outside those nations. In the Americas,

ZOOMING IN

Kartini: Feminism and Nationalism in Java

The ideas of the European Enlightenment and the Atlantic revolutions resonated deeply in the life of a remarkable young Javanese woman named Kartini during the late nineteenth century, when her country was part of the Dutch East Indies (now Indonesia).[25] Born in 1879 into a large aristocratic Javanese family, young Kartini attended a Dutch elementary school, where she learned the Dutch language and observed the relative freedom of her European classmates, in sharp contrast to the constraints and ritualized interactions of her own family. At the age of twelve, in keeping with Javanese Muslim custom, Kartini was abruptly removed from her school. For the next four years, she never left her home.

Kartini.

Through her father, a high official in the Dutch colonial administration who much admired Western education, Kartini still had access to Dutch books, and later she was tutored by several Europeans, including one woman with strong socialist and feminist leanings. She also read widely on her own and began an extensive correspondence, largely with Dutch friends in the Netherlands, that lasted until her death. By the time she was twenty, Kartini had acquired an impressive Western education and a network of relationships with prominent Europeans both in the Netherlands and in Java.

From her letters, we learn something of Kartini's thinking. In light of her exposure to Europeans and European thought, she found the absolute subordination of Javanese women completely unacceptable. The seclusion of girls, the total separation of the sexes, the absence of educational opportunities—all of this drove her almost to despair. "Are fine women of no use to civilization?" she asked. But it was the prospect of a traditional high-class Javanese marriage that she found most appalling. Her husband would be "a stranger, an unknown man, whom my parents would choose for me . . . without my knowledge." During the wedding ceremony, she would be expected to prostrate herself before the bridegroom and kiss his feet as a sign of her future submission. Even then, she would be only one

photo: Royal Tropical Institute

struggles against British, French, Spanish, or Portuguese rule emphasized the distinctive features of particular colonized peoples as they emerged into independent nationhood. The French Revolution roused its people to defend the French nation against its enemies, while French aggression under Napoleon stimulated national resistance in many countries.

The social outcomes of revolution were more varied. French revolutionaries ended what legal privileges remained to the aristocracy, opening opportunities to men of talent from the lower classes. In Haiti a successful slave revolt completely upended the social order, as the last became first. In North and Latin America, however, no such dramatic social changes occurred, although in the United States, the gradual extension of democracy allowed some white men to rise in political and social life.

of several wives. "Do you understand now," she wrote to a Dutch confidant, "the deep aversion I have for marriage?"

Kartini was equally outraged by particular features of Dutch colonial rule, especially its racism. Conscious of her membership in a "despised brown race," she deplored the need for "creeping in the dust" before Europeans. Javanese generally were not supposed to speak Dutch with their colonial masters, as if "Dutch is too beautiful to be spoken by a brown mouth." And yet, for Kartini, it was Dutch education and its universal Enlightenment values—"freedom, equality, fraternity," as she put it, echoing the slogan of the French Revolution—that would lead to Javanese emancipation from both Dutch and Javanese oppression. "Europe will teach us to be truly free," she wrote.

Nonetheless, Kartini openly embraced much of her own culture—its art, music, and poetry; its regard for the dead; its hospitality to the poor; its spiritual depth—and she certainly did not seek to transform Javanese into "half-Europeans." But she did believe that "contact with another civilization" and modern European education in particular would enable Javanese "to develop the fine qualities that are peculiar to their race." "Emancipation is in the air," she declared in early 1901.

Kartini's fondest hope was to contribute to that emancipation by studying in the Netherlands and then opening a school for girls in Java. But these grand dreams were thwarted by opposition from her own family, from Javanese officials, and from much of the Dutch colonial bureaucracy. Java's leading newspaper denounced her intentions as "outrageous," and local gossip had it that she simply wanted to marry a European and become a Europeanized woman. A backup plan to study in the colonial capital of Batavia likewise came to naught with a sudden announcement in mid-1903 that her father had arranged for her to be married to a much older and polygamous man of her social class. Kartini was devastated. "My crown has fallen from my head. My golden illusions of purity and chastity lie shattered in the dust. . . . Now I am nothing more than all the rest."[26]

Although Kartini felt that she was "done with all personal happiness," she determined to make her marriage a model for the future, actually meeting her husband before the wedding and extracting from him a written promise that she could continue with her plans to create a school for girls. But she soon became pregnant, and four days after the birth of her son in 1904, she died at the age of twenty-five. As her writings subsequently became known in Indonesia, Kartini came to be regarded as a pioneer of both feminist and nationalist thinking, and a number of "Kartini schools" were established in her memory.

QUESTION

In what ways was Kartini's life shaped by living at the intersection of Javanese and European worlds?

Almost everywhere, the aftermath of revolutions produced disappointment as they generated unfulfilled expectations. Women were surely among the most disappointed, for nowhere did they benefit substantially from these revolutions. But the ideas of the revolutions—freedom and equality—percolated in society and inspired later feminist movements, which did begin to alter the social life of women. Even the right to vote, however, had to await the twentieth century for most women.

Except in Haiti, these revolutions also bitterly disappointed enslaved people who expected to gain their freedom as a result of these upheavals. The abolitionist movement that drew on the revolutions' ideas of freedom and equality faced fierce opposition from slaveholders. In the United States a bitter and bloody civil war finally put an end to slavery in that country, but even then most formerly enslaved people remained long impoverished, and their descendants long suffered from a deeply rooted racism. Poverty, dependence, and political instability persisted long after the revolution in Haiti as well, which surely led to some disappointment among its people.

In France, revolutionaries expecting the complete eradication of the monarchy were disappointed when Napoleon declared himself "emperor" in 1802. He was just the first in a series of emperors who ruled France on and off until 1870. In Latin America the failure to unite its various regions as the British colonies of North America did was among the chief disappointments.

Were the benefits of revolution worth the cost in blood, treasure, and disruption? Opinions obviously differed. Many revolutionaries acted on the basis of Enlightenment ideas, believing that the structure of human societies was not forever ordained by God or tradition and that it was both possible and necessary to reconstruct those societies. They saw themselves as correcting ancient and enduring injustices. To those who complained about the violence of revolutions, supporters pointed to the violence that maintained the status quo and the unwillingness of favored classes to accommodate changes that threatened those unjust privileges. It was persistent injustice that made revolution necessary and perhaps inevitable.

To their victims, critics, and opponents, revolutions appeared in a quite different light. Conservatives generally viewed human societies not as machines whose parts could be easily rearranged but as organisms that evolved slowly. Efforts at radical and sudden change only invited disaster, as the unrestrained violence of the French Revolution at its height demonstrated. The brutality and bitterness of the Haitian Revolution arguably contributed to the unhappy future of that country. Furthermore, critics charged that revolutions were largely unnecessary because societies were in fact changing. France was becoming a modern society, and feudalism was largely gone well before the revolution exploded. Slavery was ended peacefully in many places, nonviolent protest made many gains for women, and democratic reform proceeded gradually throughout the nineteenth century. Was this not a preferable alternative to revolutionary upheaval?

Such debates persisted into the twentieth century and beyond as revolutions in Mexico, Russia, China, Vietnam, Cuba, and elsewhere raised many of the same questions.

Revisiting Chapter 16

Revisiting Specifics

Great Jamaica Revolt, 710
abolitionist movement, 710
nationalism, 713
Vindication of the Rights of Woman, 717
Elizabeth Cady Stanton, 717
maternal feminism, 719

Revisiting Core Ideas

1. **Assessing the Role of Ideas** In what ways did the ideas of the Enlightenment contribute to the Atlantic revolutions?
2. **Dissecting Revolution** What was revolutionary about the American Revolution, and what was not?
3. **Making Comparisons** How did the French Revolution differ from the American Revolution?
4. **Identifying Uniqueness** What was distinctive about the Haitian Revolution, both in world history generally and in the history of Atlantic revolutions?
5. **Connecting Influences** How were the Latin American revolutions shaped by the American, French, and Haitian revolutions that happened earlier?
6. **Connecting Historical Legacies** In what ways did the Atlantic revolutions contribute to the abolitionist, nationalist, and feminist movements of the nineteenth century?

A Wider View

1. What was the role of oppression and injustice, the weakening of political authorities, new ideas, or the activities of small groups of determined activists in fomenting eighteenth- and nineteenth-century revolutions?
2. "The influence of revolutions endured long after they ended and far beyond where they started." To what extent does this chapter support or undermine this idea?
3. Did the Atlantic revolutions fulfill or betray the goals of those who made them? Consider this question in both short- and long-term perspectives.
4. **Looking Back** To what extent did the Atlantic revolutions reflect the influence of early modern historical developments (1450–1750)?

To learn more about the topics in this chapter, see **For Further Study** at the end of this book.

WORKING WITH EVIDENCE

Opponents of the Atlantic Revolutions

The radical notions that authority to govern derived from the people and that human societies could and should be improved through political and social engineering inspired many in the Atlantic world to overthrow their rulers during the late eighteenth and early nineteenth centuries. But others voiced their opposition to revolution. In doing so they raised concerns about the violence and disorder that often accompanied the overthrow of governments, the disruptive pace of change, the rejection of long-established traditions and institutions, and the social and cultural implications of new conceptions of liberty, equality, and religious freedom. Moreover, once in power, some revolutionaries denied or limited "universal rights" for enslaved people, women, and other groups. The sources that follow give voice to these opponents of the Atlantic revolutions.

SOURCE 16.1 A New York Clergyman's Criticism of the Continental Congress

Samuel Seabury (1729–1796), an Anglican minister and resident of Westchester, New York, was a vocal critic of the American Revolution who published a series of letters under the pseudonym "a Westchester Farmer." In his letters, Seabury frequently criticized the Continental Congress—the convention of delegates that became the governing body for the American revolutionaries—for infringing on the same personal freedoms that it accused the British government of disregarding. In this passage, Seabury expresses his opposition to the Non-Consumption Agreement—a boycott established in late 1774 barring American colonists from engaging in direct trade with Britain.

- Which personal freedoms does Seabury accuse the Continental Congress of infringing upon?
- In what specific ways does Seabury draw on the language of rights and liberties to oppose the Continental Congress?
- Is Seabury a loyalist supporter of British colonial government, a supporter of the American Revolution, or a critic of both? Why?

SAMUEL SEABURY | *Letter of a Westchester Farmer* | 1774

My Friends and Countrymen,

The American Colonies are unhappily involved in a scene of confusion and discord. The bands of civil society are broken; the authority of government weakened, and in some instances taken away: Individuals are deprived of their liberty; their property is frequently invaded by violence. From this distressed situation it was hoped, that the wisdom and prudence of the [Continental] Congress lately assembled at Philadelphia, would have delivered us.... We ardently expected that some prudent scheme of accommodating our unhappy disputes with the Mother-Country, would have been adopted and pursued. But alas! they are broken up without ever attempting it: they have taken no [*sic*] one step that tended to peace . . . and have either ignorantly misunderstood, carelessly neglected, or basely betrayed the interests of all the Colonies....

Let us now attend a little to the Non-Consumption Agreement, which the Congress, in their Association, have imposed upon us.... [W]e are not to purchase or use any East-India Tea whatsoever; nor any goods, wares, or [newly imported] merchandise from Great-Britain or Ireland . . . nor any molasses, syrups, &c. from the British plantations in the West-Indies . . . nor wine from Madeira....

Will you submit to this slavish regulation?—You must.—Our sovereign Lords and Masters, the High and Mighty Delegates, in Grand Continental Congress assembled, have ordered and directed it. They have directed the [Revolutionary] Committees in the respective colonies, to establish such further regulations as they may think proper, for carrying their association, of which this Non-consumption agreement is a part, into execution.... The Committee of New York . . . [will] inspect the conduct of the inhabitants. . . . Among other things, Whether they drink any Tea or wine in their families . . . or wear any British or Irish manufactures; or use any English molasses, &c. . . . If they do, their names are to be published in the Gazette, that they might be *publicly known*, and *universally condemned, as foes to the Rights of British America*, and *enemies of American Liberty*.—And then *the parties of the said Association will respectively break off all dealings with him or her*.—In plain English,—They shall be considered as Out-laws, unworthy of the protection of civil society, and delivered over to the vengeance of a lawless, outrageous mob, to be *tarred, feathered, hanged, drawn, quartered, and burnt*.—O rare American Freedom! . . .

Will you be instrumental in bringing the most abject slavery on yourselves? Will you choose such Committees? Will you submit to them . . . ? Do as you please: but, by HIM that made me, I will not.—No, if I must be enslaved, let it be by a KING at least, and not by a parcel of upstart lawless Committee-men. If I must be devoured, let me be devoured by the jaws of a lion, and not *gnawed* to death by rats and vermin.

Did you choose your supervisors for the purpose of enslaving you? . . . You ought, my friends, to assert your own freedom. Should such another attempt be made upon you, assemble yourselves together: tell your supervisor, that he has exceeded his commission:—That you will have no such Committees:—that you are Englishmen, and will maintain your rights and privileges, and will eat, and drink, and wear, whatever the public laws of your country permit, without asking leave of any illegal, tyrannical Congress or Committee on earth....

. . . If you like it better, choose your Committee, or suffer it to be chosen by half a dozen Fools in your neighbourhood.—open your doors to them,—let them examine your tea-cannisters, and molasses-jugs, and your wives and daughters petty-coats,—bow, and cringe, and tremble, and quake,—fall down and worship our sovereign Lord the Mob.—But I repeat it, by H—n, I will not.—No my house is my castle. . . . Before *I* submit, I will die: live *you*, and be slaves....

November 16, 1774.

A. W. Farmer

Source: Samuel Seabury, *Free Thoughts, on the Proceedings of the Continental Congress, Held at Philadelphia Sept. 5 1774* (New York: James Rivington, 1774), 3, 17–19. Spelling of some words has been modernized.

SOURCE 16.2 A British Conservative's Critique of the Universal Rights of Man

Edmund Burke (1729–1797), a member of the British Parliament and statesman from Ireland, was one of the first and most influential critics of the principles on which the French Revolution was based. In his *Reflections on the Revolution in France*, first published in 1790, Burke accepts that political change can and should occur but argues that successful political reform must happen incrementally and be based on existing political structures and traditions. Political systems founded on statements of universal rights were fatally flawed in Burke's view because they encouraged excessive individualism, selfishness, and personal ambition. At the root of all political communities, Burke identified the sacrifice of natural or universal rights as a positive trade-off that allowed individuals to live in peaceful civil societies. In some ways, Burke's more cautious approach reflected the experiences of his native Britain, which in the previous century had experienced two revolutionary upheavals, one of which included a prolonged and violent civil war that culminated in the execution of the king. Burke, however, was not an opponent of all revolutions. He had supported the American revolutionaries, whom he saw as working within British political traditions rather than abandoning them.

In Source 16.2, Burke rejects the idea that French revolutionaries could found a successful new state based on the principles espoused in the Declaration of the Rights of Man and Citizen. Burke published these objections before war, violence, and the Terror radicalized the French Revolution, so his arguments focus on those principles on which the Atlantic revolutions were based rather than on revulsion with the disorder and violence that often accompanied the overthrow of political regimes.

- What is Burke's understanding of universal human rights and their place in government?
- Which rights does Burke grant to individuals in a civil state?
- How might Burke have reacted to Seabury's objections to revolutionary committees in Source 16.1?

EDMUND BURKE | *Reflections on the Revolution in France* | 1790

[I]t is in vain to talk to them [revolutionaries] of the practice of their ancestors, the fundamental laws of their country, the fixed form of a constitution. . . . They despise experience as the wisdom of unlettered men; and as for the rest, they have wrought underground a mine that will blow up at one grand explosion all examples of antiquity, all precedents, charters, and acts of parliament. They have "the rights of men." Against these there can be no prescription; against these no agreement is binding: these admit no temperament, and no compromise: any thing withheld from their full demand is so much of fraud and injustice. Against these their rights of men let no government look for security in the length of its continuance, or in the justice and lenity of its administration. The objections of these specialists, if its forms do not quadrate [conform] with their theories, are as valid against such an old and beneficent government as against the most violent tyranny, or the greenest usurpation. . . .

In denying their false claims of right, I do not mean to injure those [rights] which are real, and are such as their pretended rights would totally destroy. If civil society be made for the advantage of man, all the advantages for which it is made become his right. It is an institution of beneficence; and law itself is only beneficence acting by a rule. Men have a right to live by that rule; they have a right to justice. . . . They have a right to the fruits of their industry, and to the means of making their industry fruitful. They have a right to the acquisitions of their parents; to the nourishment and improvement of their offspring; to instruction in life, and to consolation in death. Whatever each man can separately do, without trespassing upon others, he has a right to do for himself; and he has a right to a fair portion of all which society, with all its combinations of skill and force, can do in his favour. But as to the share of power, authority, and direction which each individual ought to have in the management of the state, that I must deny to be amongst the direct original rights of man in civil society; for I have in my contemplation the civil social man, and no other. . . .

Government is not made in virtue of natural rights, which may and do exist in total independence of it. . . . By having a right to every thing, they want every thing. . . . Among these wants is to be reckoned the want . . . of a sufficient restraint upon their passions. Society requires not only that the passions of individuals should be subjected, but that even in the mass and body, as well as in the individuals, the inclinations of men should frequently be thwarted, their will controlled, and their passions brought into subjection. This can only be done by a power out[side] of themselves; and not . . . subject to that will and to those passions which is its office to bridle and subdue. In this sense the restraints on men, as well as their liberties, are to be reckoned among their rights. But as the liberties and the restrictions vary with times and circumstances, and admit of infinite modifications, they cannot be settled upon any abstract rule; and nothing is so foolish as to discuss them upon that principle.

Source: Edmund Burke, *Reflections on the Revolution in France* (London: John Sharpe, 1820), 1:80–84.

SOURCE 16.3 An English Cartoon's Reaction to Revolutionary Violence

Over time, the French Revolution became more radical and violent, culminating in the Reign of Terror (1793–1794), during which thousands of political opponents of the revolutionary regime were executed. An important step in this descent into violence was the execution of Louis XVI in January 1793. Source 16.3, a British political cartoon, conveys a highly critical, indeed horrified, outlook on the violence that accompanied the French Revolution. Captioned "Hell Broke Loose," it depicts the execution of Louis XVI and was printed shortly after his death. The flying demonic figures in the image are repeating popular slogans of the revolution: "*Vive la nation*" ("Long live the nation") and "*Ça ira*" ("That will go well," or more loosely, "We will win").

- What is the significance of the demons and dragons in the cartoon? How are the soldiers at the bottom of the image portrayed?
- What meaning would you attribute to the caption, "Hell Broke Loose"? What disasters might critics of the revolution have imagined coming in its wake?
- How do you understand the beam of light from heaven that falls on Louis XVI?
- How might Burke (Source 16.2) react to this cartoon and the execution of Louis XVI? As you examine this image, compare it with the depiction of Louis XVI's execution on page 700.

Hell Broke Loose, or, The Murder of Louis | **1793**

VIVE LA NATION
HELL BROKE LOOSE, OR, THE MURDER OF LOUIS.

Library of Congress, Prints and Photographs Division, LC-DIG-ppmsca-10742

SOURCE 16.4 The French National Assembly and Slavery

Victory in 1789 left revolutionaries in control of France and faced with the task of reconciling their idealistic slogans and principles with the competing demands of government. Few debates were more contentious than that surrounding the status of free men of color and enslaved people in the French colonies and especially the sugar islands of the Caribbean. Some revolutionary voices pressed for the outlawing of slavery as incompatible with a new state based on universal rights and liberties. Others pressed for free men of color to be embraced as full citizens while maintaining slavery, which, they argued, was too important for the colonial and French economies to be abandoned. Meanwhile, many white plantation owners and people in France whose livelihoods depended on colonial trade argued forcefully against granting any rights to peoples of color because this could lead to the emancipation of enslaved people in the future. In 1791 the lawmaking body in France known as the National Assembly opted for a compromise, rejecting freedom for enslaved people while granting citizenship to free men of color. Source 16.4 reproduces the text of this decree and an explanation offered by the Assembly for its decision. The law of 1791 set the stage for the Haitian Revolution. Only after the successful slave uprising in Haiti did the French revolutionary government finally pass a law abolishing slavery in 1794. But this law was short-lived; Napoleon rescinded it in 1802.

- How did the National Assembly justify its decision to maintain slavery in French colonies?
- What does the decision to grant the rights of citizenship to free men of color but not to enslaved people tell us about the reasoning of the Assembly?
- What does this source reveal about the thinking of French revolutionaries concerning race, property rights, and personal freedom?

Decree and Explanation of the French National Assembly | May 15 and 29, 1791

Decree of May 15. The National Assembly decrees that the legislature will never deliberate on the political status of people of color who were not born of free fathers and mothers without the previous free, and unprompted request of the colonies; that the presently existing Colonial Assemblies will admit the people of color born of free fathers and mothers if they otherwise have the required status.

Explanation of May 29. The National Assembly, attentive to all means of assuring prosperity in the colonies, to ensure that the citizens living there enjoy the advantages of the constitution . . . , recognizes that local circumstances and the kind of agriculture that brings colonial prosperity appear to require introducing into the colonial constitution several exceptions to the [French Revolution's] general principles.

. . . [On March 28, 1790] The National Assembly declared that the legislature would discuss the status of nonfree persons only on the unprompted request of the Colonial Assemblies.

The National Assembly was able to make this commitment because it only involved individuals [this paragraph refers to enslaved people] of a foreign land who, by their profound ignorance, the misfortune of their exile, the consideration of their own interest, and the urgent law of necessity, can only hope that in time the progress of public opinion and enlightenment will produce a change of conditions that, in the present state of things, would be contrary to the general good and might become equally dangerous for them.

Source: Laurent Dubois and John D. Garrigus, *Slave Revolution in the Caribbean 1789–1804: A Brief History with Documents*, 2nd ed. (Boston: Bedford/St. Martin's, 2017), 70–71.

SOURCE 16.5 Imagining Women's Suffrage

Echoes of the Atlantic revolutions, including abolitionism and feminism, also had their opponents. Critics frequently made their cases against these movements by imagining a world that might be created if groups like the suffragists won the rights that they sought. In this 1897 cartoon entitled "An Inauguration of the Future," the artist offers a vision of what America would become if women were granted the right to vote. It depicts the inauguration of a female president, who is surrounded on the stage by other women in positions of power. To the bottom right on the sidelines of the inauguration, a man is depicted in a distinctly domestic role holding a crying baby.

- Note the women in military uniforms on the stage and in the crowd. Why do you think that the artist included these figures in the image?
- What potential implications of granting women the right to vote does this artist want the viewer to consider?
- While not so far-fetched today, how might this image have been viewed during the late nineteenth century?

***An Inauguration of the Future* | 1897**

Stock Montage/Getty Images

DOING HISTORY

1. **Considering Universal Rights** In what ways do these sources criticize the idea of universal human rights as the basis for government? Do they reject the concept of human rights altogether?
2. **Making Comparisons** In what different ways do opponents argue against the Atlantic revolutions and their echoes? Consider issues of rights, social stability, race, and gender.
3. **Identifying Opponents of the Revolutions** Based on these sources and the text narrative, which groups of people opposed the Atlantic revolutions? Why?

HISTORIANS' VOICES

How the French Revolution Went Wrong

Criticism of the French Revolution continued into the nineteenth century as historians and others in France sought to explain why a movement based on universal rights and democratic principles became one defined by terror and later dictatorship. Voice 16.1 is from Alexis de Tocqueville (1805–1859), a nobleman, diplomat, historian, and social critic who is best known for his books *Democracy in America* (1830) and *The Old Regime and the French Revolution* (1856). Sympathetic to republican forms of government, he wrote about the French Revolution in the mid-nineteenth century during a period of political turmoil that saw a French republican government replaced by the monarchical rule of Napoleon III. In the passage reproduced here, Tocqueville lays out the broad contours of a proposed future book about the revolution. The historian and literary critic Hippolyte Taine (1828–1893) provides our second voice. Writing in the 1870s when the collapse of Napoleon III's government once again shook the French polity, Taine was an outspoken critic of the Jacobins, who led France during the most radical phase of the French Revolution. But in the passage reproduced here he also takes aim at the failures of leadership during the early years of the revolution, which he sees as opening the door to the Jacobins.

- What do Tocqueville and Taine agree on? Where do they disagree?
- Do Tocqueville and Taine offer any sense as to how the outcome of the revolution might have been different?
- To what extent should a historian today take into account the historical contexts in which Tocqueville and Taine wrote when assessing their interpretations of the revolution?
- **Integrating Primary and Secondary Sources** To what extent do Tocqueville's and Taine's assessments agree with the criticisms of the French Revolution found in Sources 16.2 and 16.3?

VOICE 16.1

Tocqueville on the Course of the French Revolution | 1856

I shall first go over the period of 1789, when their affections were divided between the love of freedom and the love of equality; when they desired to establish free as well as democratic institutions, and to acknowledge and confirm rights as well as to destroy privileges. This was an era of youth, enthusiasm, of pride, of generous and heartfelt passions; despite its errors, men will remember it long, and for many a day to come it will disturb the slumbers of those who seek to corrupt or enslave the French.

In the course of a hasty sketch of the Revolution, I shall endeavour to show what errors, what faults, what disappointments led the French to abandon their first aim, to forget liberty, and to aspire to become the equal servants of the master of the world [Napoleon]; how a far stronger and more absolute government than the one the Revolution overthrew then seized and monopolized all political power, suppressed all the liberties which had been so dearly bought, and set up in their stead empty shams; deprived electors of all means of obtaining information, of the right of assemblage, and of the faculty of exercising a choice, yet talked of popular sovereignty; . . . and while stripping the nation of every vestige of self-government, of constitutional guarantees, and of liberty of thought, speech, and the press—that is to say, of the most precious and the noblest conquests of 1789—still dared to claim descent from that great era.

Source: Alexis de Tocqueville, *The Old Regime and the Revolution*, translated by John Bonner (New York: Harper and Brothers, 1856), v–vi.

VOICE 16.2

Hippolyte Taine on the Failure of the Early Years of the Revolution and the Rise of the Radical Revolution | 1881

So far, the weakness of the legal government is extreme. For four years [from the start of the revolution in 1789 to the beginning of the Terror in 1793], whatever its kind, everywhere and constantly, it [the revolutionary government] has been disobeyed, for four years, whatever its kind, it has never dared enforce obedience. Recruited among the cultivated and refined class, the rulers of the country have brought with them into power the prejudices and sensibilities of the epoch; . . . they have deferred to the will of the multitude and, with too much faith in the rights of man, they have had too little in the rights of the magistrate; moreover, through humanity, they have abhorred bloodshed and, unwilling to repress, they have allowed themselves to be repressed. Thus . . . they have carried on the administration, or legislated, athwart innumerable insurrections, almost all of them going unpunished; while their constitutions . . . have done no more than transform spontaneous anarchy into legal anarchy. Willfully and through distrust of authority they have undermined the principle of command, reduced the King to the post of a decorative puppet, and almost annihilated the central power: from the top to the bottom of the hierarchy the superior has lost his hold on the inferior. . . . [T]he Declaration of Rights [of Man and Citizen], proclaiming "the jurisdiction of constituents over their clerks," has invited the assistants to make the assault. . . . [O]n the first attack, often at the first summons, all have surrendered, and now the citadel, with every other public fortress is in the hands of the Jacobins [the radicals who brought forth the Terror in France].

Source: Hippolyte Taine, *The French Revolution*, translated by John Durand (New York: Peter Smith, 1931), 3:2–4.

SARGENT. SC

CHAPTER 17

Revolutions of Industrialization

1750–1900

CONNECTING PAST AND PRESENT

In mid-2017, Erik Solheim, the Norwegian head of the UN Environment Program, argued that "humanity's advancement in science, technology and industrialization [is] harming the planet, hence the need to reverse course."[1] At the same time, Dr. Lloyd G. Adu Amoah, a prominent professor at the University of Ghana in West Africa, declared: "We [Africans] need to industrialize, because if we don't, we are not adding value to what the African continent has."[2]

Taken together, these two statements—from a European and an African—represent perhaps the most compelling dilemma facing humankind in the twenty-first century. How can we embrace the wealth and improvement in human life universally associated with industrialization, while coping with the terrible environmental threat to our fragile planet that industrialized economies have generated? That profound dilemma has its origins in the enormously transformative process of the Industrial Revolution, which took place initially in Europe during the century and a half between 1750 and 1900. Not since the Agricultural Revolution some 12,000 years ago have our ways of living and our relationship to the natural world been so fundamentally altered.

Industrialization started in Britain, but it spread quickly to continental Western Europe, the United States, Russia, and Japan. Everywhere that it took root, the Industrial Revolution transformed economies and created distinctive industrial societies with new working environments, social classes, values, conflict, protests, and patterns of migration. It also had profound

« **Industrial Britain** To the modern eye this engraving of one of the first and largest copper works in Wales vividly conveys a sense of the dirt, smoke, and pollution of early industrial societies. However, at the time of its publication in 1862, many viewers would have seen in this image a celebration of modern industry and humankind's growing productivity centered on factories.

effects on regions like Latin America that did not industrialize but increasingly supplied the insatiable demands of industrialized economies for raw materials and markets. By 1900 a global revolution was well under way.

In any long-term reckoning, the history of industrialization is very much an unfinished story. Are we at the beginning of a movement leading to worldwide industrialization, stuck in the middle of a world permanently divided into rich and poor countries, or approaching the end of an environmentally unsustainable industrial era? Whatever the future holds, this chapter focuses on the early stages of an immense transformation in the global condition of humankind.

SEEKING THE MAIN POINT

How revolutionary was the Industrial Revolution?

Industrialization: The Global Context

The epic economic transformation of the Industrial Revolution took shape as a very substantial increase in human numbers unfolded—from about 375 million people in 1400 to about 1 billion in the early nineteenth century. Accompanying this growth in population was an emerging energy crisis, most pronounced in Western Europe, China, and Japan, as wood and charcoal, the major industrial fuels, became more scarce and more costly. In short, "global energy demands began to push against the existing local and regional ecological limits."[3] In broad terms, the Industrial Revolution marked a human response to those limits. It was a twofold revolution—drawing on new sources of energy and new technologies—that combined to utterly transform economic and social life on the planet.

In terms of energy, the Industrial Revolution came to rely on fossil fuels such as coal, oil, and natural gas, which supplemented and largely replaced the earlier energy sources of wind, water, wood, and the muscle power of people and animals that had long sustained humankind. It was a breakthrough of unprecedented proportions that made available for human use, at least temporarily, immensely greater quantities of energy. During the nineteenth century, yet another fuel became widely available as Europeans learned to exploit guano, or seabird excrement, found on the islands off the coast of Peru. Used as a potent fertilizer, guano enabled highly productive input-intensive farming practices. In much of Western Europe, North America, Australia, and New Zealand, it sustained the production of crops that fed both the draft animals and the growing human populations of the industrializing world.[4]

The technological dimension of the Industrial Revolution has been equally significant. Early signs of the technological creativity that spawned the Industrial Revolution appeared in eighteenth-century Britain, where a variety of innovations transformed cotton textile production. It was only in the nineteenth century, though, that Europeans in general and the British in particular clearly forged ahead of the rest of the world. (See Controversies: Debating "Why Europe?") The great breakthrough was the coal-fired **steam engine**, which provided an inanimate and

Landmarks for Chapter 17

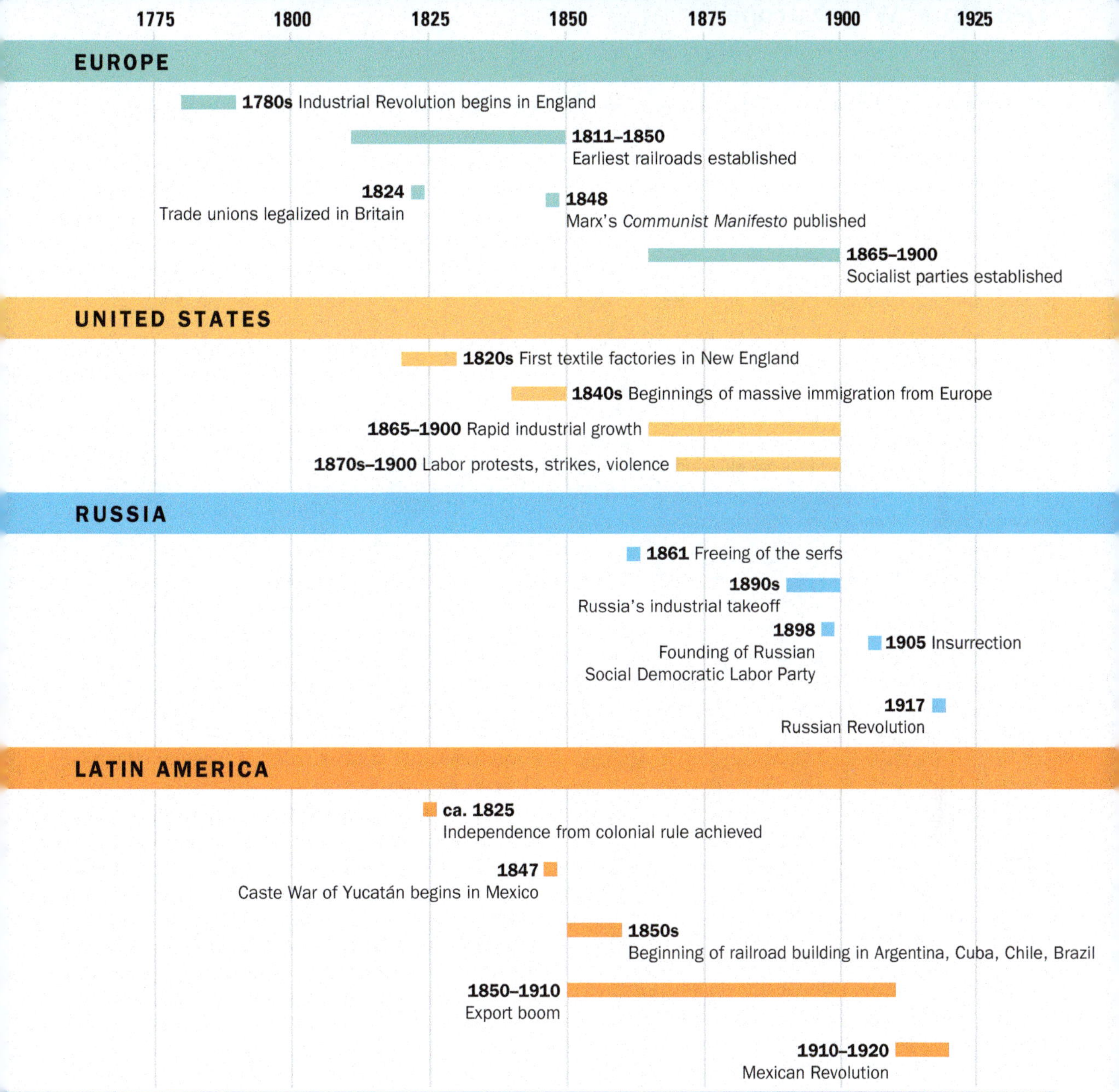
1775
1800
1825
1850
1875
1900
1925
EUROPE
1780s Industrial Revolution begins in England
1811–1850 Earliest railroads established
1824 Trade unions legalized in Britain
1848 Marx's Communist Manifesto published
1865–1900 Socialist parties established
UNITED STATES
1820s First textile factories in New England
1840s Beginnings of massive immigration from Europe
1865–1900 Rapid industrial growth
1870s–1900 Labor protests, strikes, violence
RUSSIA
1861 Freeing of the serfs
1890s Russia's industrial takeoff
1898 Founding of Russian Social Democratic Labor Party
1905 Insurrection
1917 Russian Revolution
LATIN AMERICA
ca. 1825 Independence from colonial rule achieved
1847 Caste War of Yucatán begins in Mexico
1850s Beginning of railroad building in Argentina, Cuba, Chile, Brazil
1850–1910 Export boom
1910–1920 Mexican Revolution

almost limitless source of power that could be used to drive any number of machines as well as locomotives and oceangoing ships. Soon the Industrial Revolution spread beyond the textile industry to iron and steel production, railroads and steamships, food processing, and construction. Later in the nineteenth century, a so-called second Industrial Revolution focused on chemicals, electricity, precision machinery,

CONTROVERSIES

Debating "Why Europe?"

The Industrial Revolution marked a dramatic change in the trajectory of human history. But why did that breakthrough occur first in Europe? This question has long been a source of great controversy among scholars.

A "European Miracle"

Does the answer lie in some unique or "miraculous" feature of European history, culture, or society? Perhaps, as one scholar recently suggested, Europeans have been distinguished for several thousand years by a restless, creative, and freedom-loving culture with its roots in the aristocratic warlike societies of early Indo-European invaders, which rendered them uniquely open to change and development.[5] But critics have questioned both the claims to European cultural uniqueness and causal links between industrialization and developments of the distant past.

Or should we focus more narrowly on the period between about 1400 and 1800 for the origins of this "European miracle"?[6] During those centuries distinctive new forms of landowning and farming practices emerged, especially in Britain, which made land and labor available for capitalist agriculture and enabled the accumulation of wealth in the hands of a few. Was this "agricultural revolution" a prelude to the subsequent "industrial revolution"?

Or perhaps it was the Scientific Revolution, a distinctly European event that generated a new view of the cosmos, that stimulated industrialization. It turns out, however, that early industrial technologies derived from the workshops of artisans and craftsmen rather than from the laboratories of scientists. And so by the early twenty-first century, many historians were thinking in terms of a broader cultural pattern, an eighteenth-century "Industrial Enlightenment" in which scientific methods and a general belief in an ordered universe mixed with commitment to the ideas of "progress" and human improvement to foster technological innovation.

And what about Europe's many relatively small and highly competitive states? Perhaps their rivalries stimulated innovation and provided an "insurance against economic and technological stagnation," which the larger Chinese, Ottoman, or Mughal empires lacked. In their struggles with other states, European governments desperately needed revenue, and to get it, European authorities developed an unusual alliance with their merchant classes. Merchant capitalists were granted special privileges, monopolies, or even tax-collecting responsibilities in exchange for much-needed loans or payments to the state. Governments granted charters and monopolies to private trading companies, and states founded scientific societies and offered prizes to promote innovation. European merchants and other innovators after the fifteenth century became more independent from state control and enjoyed a higher social status than their counterparts in more established civilizations. Such internally competitive semi-capitalist economies, coupled with a highly competitive system of rival states, arguably fostered innovation in the new civilization taking shape in Western Europe. But at the same time, nearly constant war and the destruction that accompanied it also served as a long-term drain on European resources.

Britain especially benefited from several advantages of the "European miracle," including a spirit of innovation, a lot of easily accessible coal, a growing consumer market, plentiful cheap capital accumulated in agriculture and trade, and its island geography, which frequently shielded it from the worst effects of Europe's wars. It also had a relatively high-wage workforce, which gave British businesses an extraordinary incentive to invent laborsaving technologies.

the telegraph and telephone, rubber, printing, and much more. Agriculture too was affected as mechanical reapers, chemical fertilizers, pesticides, and refrigeration transformed this most ancient of industries. Sustaining this explosion of technological innovation was a "culture of innovation," a widespread and almost obsessive belief that things could be endlessly improved.

The "Great Divergence"

But was Europe alone destined to lead the way to modern economic life? To many world historians, such views are both Eurocentric and deterministic; they also fly in the face of much recent research. Historians now know that India, the Islamic world, and especially China had experienced times of great technological and scientific flourishing. For reasons much debated, all of these flowerings of creativity had slowed down considerably or stagnated by the early modern era, when the pace of technological change in Europe began to pick up. But these earlier achievements certainly suggest that Europe was not alone in its capacity for technological innovation.

Nor did Europe enjoy any overall economic advantage as late as 1750. Recent scholars have found rather "a world of surprising resemblances" among major Eurasian societies during the eighteenth century. Economic indicators such as life expectancies, patterns of consumption and nutrition, wage levels, general living standards, widespread free markets, and prosperous merchant communities suggest "a global economic parity" across the major civilizations of Europe and Asia.[7] Thus Europe had no obvious economic lead, even on the eve of the Industrial Revolution. So much for the "European miracle"!

Trade and Empire

But if there was little that was economically distinctive within Europe itself, perhaps it was the spoils of empire and the benefits of global trade after 1500 that allowed Europeans to accumulate the wealth that funded industrial enterprises back home. Far more than their early modern counterparts, European empires provided access to an abundance of raw materials—timber, fish, maize, potatoes—along with products like sugar and cotton produced by enslaved labor. Moreover, these empires generated a global economy that funneled the trade of the world through Europe. Demand for Asian goods, including porcelain and especially cotton cloth, spurred manufacturers in Europe to produce similar items, while production for overseas markets further sparked industry in Europe. The new wealth spawned a growing middle class in Europe whose members bought the products of the Industrial Revolution. As one scholar has put it, "The industrial revolution . . . emerged from the exploitive advantages Europe was already gaining in the world's markets."[8] So rather than something distinctive about European society, perhaps it was Europe's increasing engagement with the wider world that sparked industrialization.

Many or most of these factors likely played some role in Europe's industrialization. But in considering the "Why Europe?" question, historians confront the relative importance of internal and external factors in explaining historical change. Was industrialization primarily spurred by some special combination of elements peculiar to Western Europe, or were broader global relationships of greater significance? Arguments giving great weight to internal features of European life seem to congratulate Europeans on their good fortune or wisdom, while those that contextualize it globally and point to the unique character of European imperial trade and exploitation are rather more critical. Furthermore, the former seem to imply a certain long-term inevitability to European prominence, while the latter see the Industrial Revolution as more of a surprise, the outcome of a unique conjuncture of events . . . in short, luck.

QUESTIONS TO CONSIDER

1. How might your understanding of the Industrial Revolution change if you subscribed to the "European miracle," the "Great Divergence," or the "Trade and Empire" school of thought?
2. How does this overview of the "Why Europe?" debate shape your understanding of the Industrial Revolution?

CORE IDEA

Establishing Context What is the significance of the Industrial Revolution in the larger framework of world history?

Together, these new sources of energy and new technologies gave rise to an enormously increased output of goods and services. In Britain, where the Industrial Revolution began, industrial output increased some fiftyfold between 1750 and 1900. It was a wholly unprecedented and previously unimaginable jump in the capacity of human societies to produce wealth, to extend life expectancies, and to increase human

Producing Gas from Coal Coal was central to the Industrial Revolution. An early industrial process in Britain involved the burning of coal to produce "coal gas," used for public lighting. This image from 1822 shows that process in action at one such production facility in London. Those who stoked the furnaces often developed various lung diseases and died early. (Print Collector/Getty Images)

numbers. Furthermore, industrialization soon spread beyond Britain to continental Western Europe and then in the second half of the nineteenth century to the United States, Russia, and Japan. In the twentieth century it became a genuinely global process. More than anything else, industrialization marks the past 250 years as a distinct phase of human history.

In the long run, the Industrial Revolution unarguably improved the material conditions of life for much of humankind. But it also unarguably wrought a mounting impact on the environment. At first the worst effects were primarily local or regional, concentrated in places where mines or factories were located. The extraction of raw materials—coal, iron ore, petroleum—altered landscapes and polluted local groundwater. The factory waste and human sewage generated by industrial towns emptied into rivers, turning them into poisonous cesspools. In 1858 the Thames River running through London smelled so bad that the British House of Commons had to suspend its session. Smoke from coal-fired industries and domestic use polluted the air in urban areas and sharply increased the incidence of respiratory illness. The British novelist Charles Dickens, who witnessed the impact of industrialization firsthand, described a typical factory town in one of his novels:

> It was a town of red brick, or of brick that would have been red if the smoke and ashes had allowed it; . . . It was a town of machinery and tall chimneys, out of which interminable serpents of smoke trailed themselves for ever and ever, and never got uncoiled. It had a black canal in it, and a river that ran purple with ill-smelling dye.[9]

As the Industrial Revolution grew and spread, the impact of pollution and environmental degradation became increasingly global in scale. In 1900 the world consumed fifty-five times as much coal per year as it had in 1800. This growing use of fossil fuels began a gradual increase in greenhouse gas levels in the atmosphere, a trend that sharply accelerated only in the second half of the twentieth century, when its impact on climate change became increasingly well known. In the early industrial era, however, only a few scientists even suspected such a connection.

The Industrial Revolution also allowed humankind to reengineer ever-larger parts of the planet that in the past had been only lightly populated and exploited. Beginning in the 1850s, grasslands in relatively arid regions across the globe, from Argentina and Australia to the steppes of Central Asia and the Great Plains of North America, were put under the plow for the first time. This enormous expansion of tilled lands was made possible by innovations in farm machinery, irrigation pumps, and especially the railroads and steamships that brought fertilizer from distant lands and transported crops grown in remote, often landlocked regions to world markets. These new agricultural lands—alongside new pasturelands as well—fed a growing population that was also living longer thanks to advances in public health and medicine, setting in motion a historic rise in the human population. World population doubled between 1800 and 1900 and then quadrupled in the twentieth century.

Thus for many historians, the Industrial Revolution marked a new era in both human history and the history of the planet that scientists increasingly call the Anthropocene era, or the "age of man." More and more, human industrial activity left a mark not only on human society but also on the ecological, atmospheric, and geological history of the earth, with enormous implication for all life.

The First Industrial Society

Wherever it took hold, the Industrial Revolution generated, within a century or less, an economic miracle, at least in comparison with earlier technologies. The **British textile industry**, which used 52 million pounds of cotton in 1800, consumed 588 million pounds in 1850, as multiple technological innovations and factory-based production vastly increased output. Britain's production of coal likewise soared from 5.23 million tons in 1750 to 68.4 million tons a century later.[10] Railroads crisscrossed Britain and much of Europe like a giant spider web (see Map 17.1). Most of this dramatic increase in production occurred in mining, manufacturing, and services. Thus agriculture, for millennia the overwhelmingly dominant economic sector in every civilization, shrank in relative importance. In Britain, for example, agriculture generated only 8 percent of national income in 1891 and employed fewer than 8 percent of working Britons in 1914. Accompanying this vast economic change was an epic transformation of social life. "In two centuries," wrote one prominent historian, "daily life changed more than it had in the 7,000 years before."[11] Nowhere were the revolutionary dimensions of industrialization more apparent than in Great Britain, the world's first industrial society.

The social transformation of the Industrial Revolution both destroyed and created. Referring to the impact of the Industrial Revolution on British society, historian Eric Hobsbawm wrote: "In its initial stages it destroyed their old ways of living and left them free to discover or make for themselves new ones, if they could and knew how. But it rarely told them how to set about it."[12] For many people, it was an enormously painful, even traumatic process, full of social conflict, insecurity, and false starts even as it offered new opportunities, an eventually higher standard of

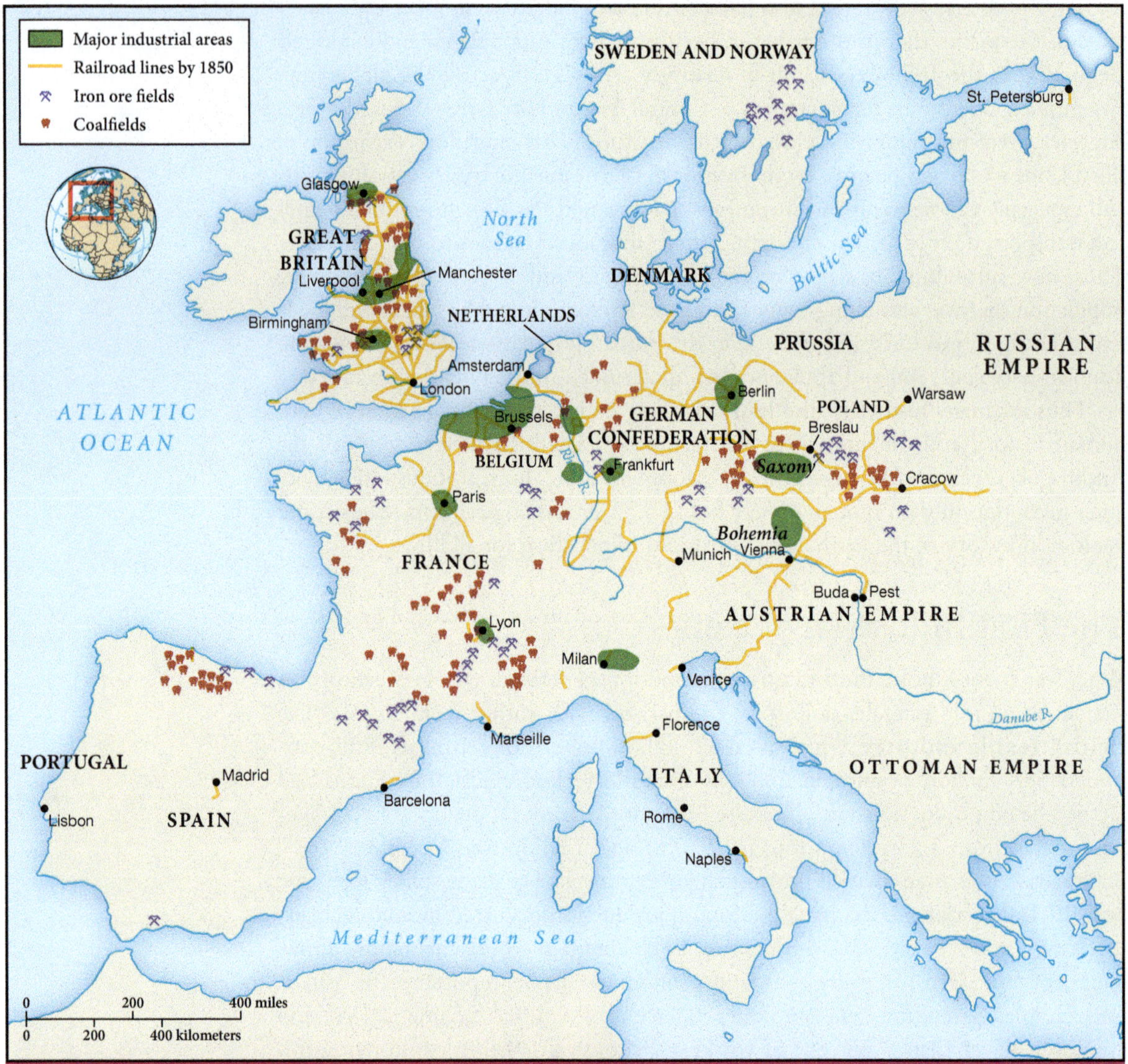

MAPPING HISTORY

Map 17.1 The Early Phase of Europe's Industrial Revolution

From its beginning in Great Britain, industrialization had spread by 1850 across Western Europe to include parts of France, Germany, Belgium, Bohemia, and Italy.

READING THE MAP How would you describe the relationship between the major industrialized areas of Great Britain and deposits of coal and iron? How do railways impact your description? Do all the early major industrialized regions of Europe share a similar relationship with sources of raw materials?

INTERPRETING THE MAP Identify potential sites for further industrialization. Why did you choose these sites? Where might the building of further railway lines facilitate the growth of already established major industrial areas?

Railroads This 1830s image celebrates the opening of a railway line in Scotland linking the industrial center of Garnkirk (pictured in the background) with the major city of Glasgow about six miles away. The large crowd of spectators reflects the fascination of the public with this new technology. (Private Collection/Photo © Christie's Images/Bridgeman Images)

living, and greater participation in public life. The human gains and losses associated with the Industrial Revolution have been debated ever since. Amid the arguments, however, one thing is clear: not everyone was affected in the same way.

The British Aristocracy

Individual landowning aristocrats, long the dominant class in Britain, suffered little in material terms from the Industrial Revolution. In the mid-nineteenth century, a few thousand families still owned more than half of the cultivated land in Britain, most of it leased to tenant farmers, who in turn employed agricultural wage laborers to work it. A rapidly growing population and urbanization sustained demand for food products grown on that land. For most of the nineteenth century, landowners continued to dominate the British Parliament.

CORE IDEA

Identifying Change
In what ways did the Industrial Revolution transform British society?

As a class, however, the British aristocracy declined as a result of the Industrial Revolution, as did large landowners in every industrial society. As urban wealth became more important, landed aristocrats had to make way for the up-and-coming businessmen, manufacturers, and bankers, newly enriched by the Industrial Revolution. By the end of the century, landownership had largely ceased to be the basis of great wealth, and businessmen, rather than aristocrats, led the major political parties. Even so, the titled nobility of dukes, earls, viscounts, and barons retained great social prestige and considerable personal wealth. Many among them found an outlet for their energies and opportunities for status and enrichment in the vast domains of the British Empire, where they went as colonial administrators or settlers. Famously described as a "system of outdoor relief for the aristocracy," the empire provided a cushion for a declining class.

The Middle Classes

Describing Class What characterized the British middle class of the industrial era?

Those who benefited most conspicuously from industrialization were members of that amorphous group known as the middle class. At its upper levels, this middle class contained extremely wealthy factory and mine owners, bankers, and merchants. Such rising businessmen readily assimilated into aristocratic life, buying country houses, obtaining seats in Parliament, sending their sons to Oxford or Cambridge University, and gratefully accepting titles of nobility from Queen Victoria.

Far more numerous were the smaller businessmen, doctors, lawyers, engineers, teachers, journalists, scientists, and other professionals required in any industrial society. Such people set the tone for a distinctly **middle-class society** with its own values and outlooks. Politically they were liberals, favoring constitutional government, private property, free trade, and social reform within limits. Their agitation resulted in the Reform Bill of 1832, which broadened the right to vote to many men of the middle class, but not to middle-class women. Ideas of thrift and hard work, a rigid morality, "respectability," and cleanliness characterized middle-class culture. According to Samuel Smiles's famous book *Self-Help*, an enterprising spirit was what distinguished the prosperous middle class from Britain's poor. The misery of the poorer classes was "voluntary and self-imposed—the results of idleness, thriftlessness, intemperance, and misconduct."[13]

Women in such middle-class families were increasingly cast as homemakers, wives, and mothers, charged with creating an emotional haven for their men and a refuge from a heartless and cutthroat capitalist world. They were also expected to be the moral centers of family life, the educators of "respectability," and the managers of household consumption as "shopping"—a new concept in eighteenth-century Britain—became a central activity for the middle classes. An **ideology of domesticity** defined homemaking, child rearing, charitable endeavors, and "refined" activities such as embroidery and music as the proper sphere for women, while paid employment and the public sphere of life outside the home beckoned to men.

Male elites in many civilizations had long established their status by detaching women from productive labor. The new wealth of the Industrial Revolution now allowed larger numbers of families to aspire to that kind of status. With her husband as "provider," such a woman was now a "lady." "She must not work for profit," wrote the Englishwoman Margaretta Greg in 1853, "or engage in any occupation that money can command."[14] Employing even one servant became a proud marker of such middle-class status. But the withdrawal of middle-class women from the labor force turned out to be only a temporary phenomenon. By the late nineteenth century, some middle-class women began to enter the teaching, clerical, and nursing professions, and in the second half of the twentieth century, many more flooded into the labor force. By contrast, the withdrawal of children from productive labor into schools has proved a more enduring phenomenon as industrial economies increasingly required a more educated workforce.

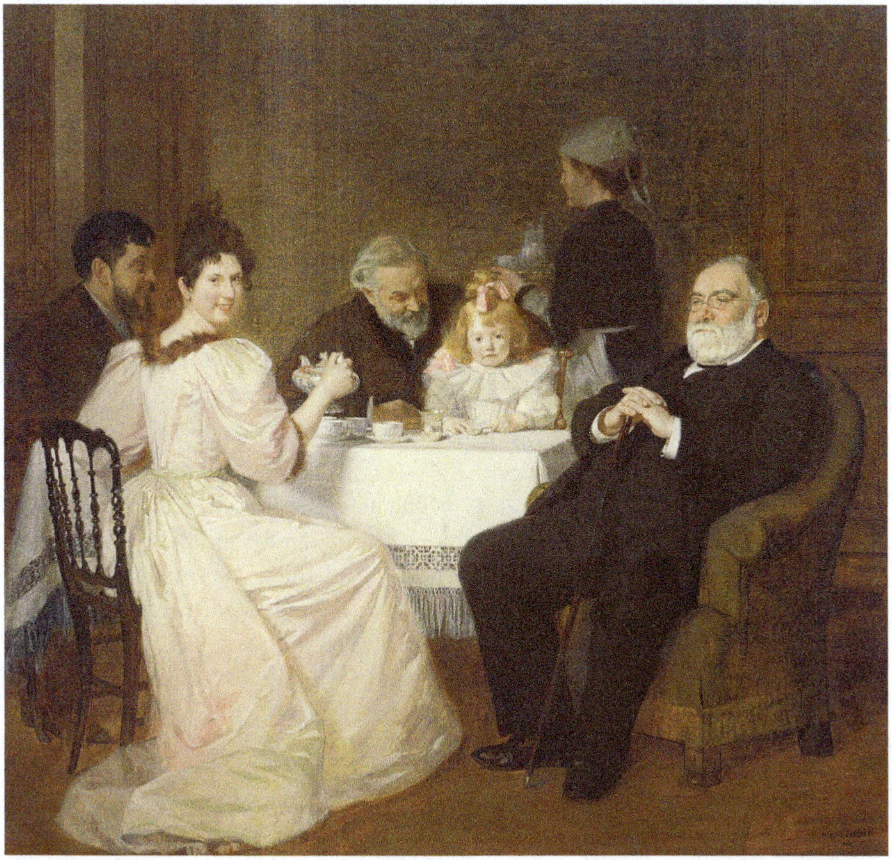

The Industrial Middle Class This late nineteenth-century painting shows a prosperous French middle-class family, attended by a servant. (Bridgeman Images)

As Britain's industrial economy matured, it also gave rise to a sizable **lower middle class**, which included people employed in the growing service sector as clerks, salespeople, bank tellers, hotel staff, secretaries, telephone operators, police officers, and the like. By the end of the nineteenth century, this growing segment of the middle class represented about 20 percent of Britain's population and provided new employment opportunities for women as well as men. In just twenty years (1881–1901), the number of female secretaries in Britain rose from 7,000 to 90,000. Almost all were single and expected to return to the home after marriage. For both men and women, such employment represented a claim on membership in the larger middle class and a means of distinguishing themselves clearly from a working class tainted by manual labor. The mounting ability of these middle classes to consume all manner of material goods—and their appetite for doing so—were among the factors that sustained the continuing growth of the industrializing process.

The Laboring Classes

The overwhelming majority of Britain's nineteenth-century population—some 70 percent or more—were neither aristocrats nor members of the middle classes. They were manual workers in the mines, ports, factories, construction sites, workshops, and farms of an industrializing Britain. Although their conditions varied considerably and changed over time, it was the **laboring classes** who suffered most and benefited least from the epic transformations of the Industrial Revolution. Their efforts to accommodate, resist, protest, and change those conditions contributed much to the texture of the first industrial society.

The lives of the laboring classes were shaped primarily by the rapid urbanization of the industrial era. Liverpool's population alone grew from 77,000 to 400,000 in the first half of the nineteenth century. By 1851, a majority of Britain's population lived in towns and cities, an enormous change from the overwhelmingly rural life of almost all previous civilizations.

DEATH'S DISPENSARY.
OPEN TO THE POOR, GRATIS, BY PERMISSION OF THE PARISH.

The Urban Poor of Industrial Britain This 1866 political cartoon shows an impoverished urban family forced to draw its drinking water from a polluted public well, while a figure of Death operates the pump.

These cities were vastly overcrowded and smoky, with wholly insufficient sanitation, periodic epidemics, few public services or open spaces, and inadequate and often-polluted water supplies. This was the environment in which most urban workers lived in the first half of the nineteenth century. By 1850, the average life expectancy in England was only 39.5 years, less than it had been some three centuries earlier. Nor was there much personal contact between the rich and the poor of industrial cities. Benjamin Disraeli's novel *Sybil*, published in 1845, described these two ends of the social spectrum as "two nations between whom there is no intercourse and no sympathy; who are ignorant of each other's habits, thoughts and feelings, as if they were dwellers in different zones or inhabitants of different planets."[15]

The industrial factories to which growing numbers of desperate people looked for employment offered a work environment far different from the artisan's shop or the tenant's farm. Long hours, low wages, and child labor were nothing new for the poor, but the routine and monotony of work, dictated by the factory whistle and the needs of machines, imposed novel and highly unwelcome conditions of labor. Also objectionable were the direct and constant supervision and the rules and fines aimed at enforcing work discipline. In addition, the ups and downs of a capitalist economy made industrial work insecure as well as onerous.

In the early decades of the nineteenth century, Britain's industrialists favored girls and young unmarried women as employees in the textile mills, for they were often willing to accept lower wages, while male owners believed them to be both docile and more suitable for repetitive tasks such as tending machines. A gendered hierarchy of labor emerged in these factories, with men in supervisory and more skilled positions, while women occupied the less skilled and "lighter" jobs that offered little opportunity for advancement. Nor were women welcome in the unions that eventually offered men some ability to shape the conditions under which they labored.

Thus, unlike their middle-class counterparts, many girls and young women of the laboring classes engaged in industrial work or found jobs as domestic servants for upper- and middle-class families to supplement meager family incomes. But after marriage, they too usually left outside paid employment because a man who could not support his wife was widely considered a failure. Within the home, however, many working-class women continued to earn money by taking in boarders, doing laundry, or sewing clothes in addition to the domestic and child-rearing responsibilities long assigned to women.

Social Protest

For workers of the laboring classes, industrial life "was a stony desert, which they had to make habitable by their own efforts."[16] Such efforts took many forms. By 1815, about 1 million workers, mostly artisans, had created a variety of "friendly societies." With dues contributed by members, these working-class self-help groups provided insurance against sickness, a decent funeral, and an opportunity for social life in an otherwise bleak environment. Other skilled artisans who had been displaced by machine-produced goods and forbidden to organize in legal unions sometimes wrecked the offending machinery and burned the mills that had taken their jobs. (See Zooming In: The English Luddites and Machine Breaking, page 748.) The class consciousness of working people was such that one police informer reported that "most every creature of the lower order both in town and country are on their side."[17] Others acted within the political arena by joining movements aimed at obtaining the vote for working-class men, a goal that was gradually achieved in the second half of the nineteenth century. When trade unions were legalized in 1824, growing numbers of factory workers joined these associations in their efforts to achieve better wages and working conditions. Initially their strikes, attempts at nationwide organization, and threat of violence made them fearful indeed to the upper classes. One British newspaper in 1834 described unions as "the most dangerous institutions that were ever permitted to take root, under shelter of law, in any country,"[18] although they later became rather more "respectable" organizations.

ZOOMING IN

The English Luddites and Machine Breaking

> If you do Not Cause those Dressing Machines to be Remov'd Within the Bounds of Seven Days . . . your factory and all that it Contains Will and Shall Surely Be Set on fire . . . it is Not our Desire to Do you the Least Injury, But We are fully Determin'd to Destroy Both Dressing Machines and Steam Looms.[19]

Luddites smashing a loom.

photo: Chronicle/Alamy

Between 1811 and 1813, this kind of warning was sent to hundreds of English workshops in the woolen and cotton industry, where more efficient machines, some of them steam-powered, threatened the jobs and livelihoods of workers. Over and over, that threat was carried out as well-organized bands of skilled artisans destroyed the offending machines, burned buildings, and on occasion attacked employers. These were the Luddites, taking their name from a mythical Robin Hood–like figure, Ned Ludd. A song called "General Ludd's Triumph" expressed their sentiments: "These Engines of mischief were sentenced to die / By unanimous vote of the Trade / And Ludd who can all opposition defy / Was the Grand executioner made."

So widespread and serious was this Luddite uprising that the British government sent 12,000 troops to suppress it, more than it was then devoting to the struggle against Napoleon in continental Europe. And a new law, rushed through Parliament as an "emergency measure" in 1812, made those who destroyed mechanized looms subject to the death penalty. Some sixty to seventy alleged Luddites were in fact hanged, and sometimes beheaded as well, for machine breaking.

In the governing circles of England, Luddism was widely regarded as blind protest, an outrageous, unthinking, and futile resistance to progress. It has remained in more recent times a term of insult applied to those who resist or reject technological innovation. And yet, a closer look suggests that the Luddites deserve some sympathy as an understandable response to a painful transformation of social life when few alternatives for expressing grievances were available.

At the time of the Luddite uprising, England was involved in an increasingly unpopular war with Napoleon's France,

Socialist ideas of various kinds gradually spread within the working class, challenging the assumptions of a capitalist society. Robert Owen (1771–1858), a wealthy British cotton textile manufacturer, urged the creation of small industrial communities where workers and their families would be well treated. He established one such community, with a ten-hour workday, spacious housing, decent wages, and education for children, at his mill in New Lanark in Scotland.

Of more lasting significance was the socialism of **Karl Marx** (1818–1883). German by birth, Marx spent much of his life in England, where he witnessed the brutal conditions of Britain's Industrial Revolution and wrote voluminously about history and economics. His probing analysis led him to conclude that industrial capitalism was an inherently unstable system, doomed to collapse in a revolutionary upheaval that would give birth to a classless socialist society, thus ending forever the and mutual blockades substantially reduced trade and hurt the textile industry. The country was also in the early phase of an Industrial Revolution in which mechanized production was replacing skilled artisan labor. All of this, plus some bad weather and poor harvests, combined to generate real economic hardship, unemployment, and hunger. Bread riots and various protests against high prices proliferated.

Furthermore, English elites were embracing new laissez-faire, or free market, economic principles, which eroded customary protections for the poor and working classes. Over the previous several decades, many laws that had regulated wages and apprenticeships and prohibited certain laborsaving machines had been repealed, despite repeated workers' appeals to Parliament to maintain some minimal protections for their older way of life. A further act of Parliament in 1799 had forbidden trade unions and collective bargaining. In these circumstances, some form of direct action is hardly surprising.

At one level, the Luddite machine-breaking movement represented "collective bargaining by riot," a way of pressuring employers when legal negotiations with them had been outlawed. And the issues involved more than laborsaving machines. Luddites also argued for price reductions, minimum wages, and prohibitions on the flooding of their industry by unapprenticed workers. They wanted to return to a time when "full fashioned work at the old fashioned price is established by custom and law," according to one of their songs. More generally, Luddites sought to preserve elements of an older way of life in which industry existed to provide a livelihood for workers, in which men could take pride in their craft, in which government and employers felt some paternalistic responsibility to the lower classes, and in which journeymen workers felt some bonds of attachment to a larger social and moral order. All of this was rapidly eroding in the new era of capitalist industrialization. In these ways, the Luddite movement looked backward to idealized memories of an earlier time.

And yet in other ways, the rebels anticipated the future with their demands for a minimum wage and an end to child labor, their concern about inferior-quality products produced by machines, and their desire to organize trade unions. At the height of the Luddite movement, some among them began to move beyond local industrial action toward a "general insurrection" that might bring real political change to the entire country. In one letter from a Luddite in 1812, the writer expressed "hope for assistance from the French emperor [Napoleon] in shaking off the yoke of the rottenest, wickedest, and most tyranious government that ever existed." He continued, "Then we will be governed by a just republic."

After 1813, the organized Luddite movement faded away. But it serves as a cautionary reminder that what is hailed as progress claims victims as well as beneficiaries.

QUESTIONS

To what extent did the concerns of the Luddites come to pass as the Industrial Revolution unfolded? How does your understanding of the Luddites affect your posture toward technological change in our time?

ancient conflict between rich and poor. (See Working with Evidence, Source 17.1, Socialism According to Marx and Engels, page 769.)

In Marx's writings, the combined impact of Europe's industrial, political, and scientific revolutions found expression. Industrialization created both the social conditions against which Marx protested so bitterly and the enormous wealth he felt would make socialism possible. The French Revolution, still a living memory in Marx's youth, provided evidence that grand upheavals, giving rise to new societies, had in fact taken place and could do so again. Moreover, Marx regarded himself as a scientist, discovering the laws of social development in much the same fashion as Newton discovered the laws of motion. His was therefore a "scientific socialism," embedded in these laws of historical change; revolution was a certainty and the socialist future was inevitable.

Understanding Change
How did Karl Marx's ideas about the Industrial Revolution affect the industrializing world in the nineteenth century?

It was a grand, compelling, prophetic, utopian vision of human freedom and community—and it inspired socialist movements of workers and intellectuals amid the grim harshness of Europe's industrialization in the second half of the nineteenth century. Socialists established political parties in most European states and linked them together in international organizations as well. These parties recruited members, contested elections as they gained the right to vote, agitated for reforms, and in some cases plotted revolution.

In the later decades of the nineteenth century, such ideas echoed among more radical trade unionists and some middle-class intellectuals in Britain, and even more so in a rapidly industrializing Germany and elsewhere. By then, however, the British working-class movement was not overtly revolutionary. When a working-class political party, the **Labour Party**, was established in the 1890s, it advocated a reformist program and a peaceful democratic transition to socialism, largely rejecting the class struggle and revolutionary emphasis of classical Marxism. Generally known as "social democracy," this approach to socialism was especially prominent in Germany during the late nineteenth century and spread more widely in the twentieth century, when it came into conflict with the more violent and revolutionary movements calling themselves "communist."

Improving material conditions during the second half of the nineteenth century helped move the working-class movement in Britain, Germany, and elsewhere away from a revolutionary posture. Marx had expected industrial capitalist societies to polarize into a small wealthy class and a huge and increasingly impoverished proletariat. However, standing between "the captains of industry" and the workers was a sizable middle and lower middle class, constituting perhaps 30 percent of the population, most of whom were not wealthy but were immensely proud that they were not manual laborers. Marx had not foreseen the development of this intermediate social group, nor had he imagined that workers could better their standard of living within a capitalist framework. But they did. Wages rose under pressure from unions; cheap imported food improved working-class diets; infant mortality rates fell; and shops and chain stores catering to working-class families multiplied. As English male workers gradually obtained the right to vote, politicians had an incentive to legislate in their favor, by abolishing child labor, regulating factory conditions, and even, in 1911, inaugurating a system of relief for the

Socialist Art Dating from 1901, this iconic painting entitled "The Fourth Estate" (the working classes) by the Italian artist Giuseppe Pellizza da Volpedo depicts striking workers peacefully marching toward a better future. It has become a symbol and rallying point for many socialists who find inspiration in the sense of determination, unity, and humanity conveyed by the workers in the image. (Museo del Novecento, Milan, Italy/Photo © A. Dagli Orti/De Agostini Picture Library/Bridgeman Images)

unemployed. Sanitary reform considerably cleaned up the "filth and stink" of early nineteenth-century cities, and urban parks made a modest appearance. Contrary to Marx's expectations, capitalist societies demonstrated some capacity for reform.

Further eroding working-class radicalism was a growing sense of nationalism, which bound workers to their middle-class employers, offsetting to some extent the economic and social antagonism between them. When World War I broke out, the "workers of the world," far from uniting against their bourgeois enemies as socialist leaders had urged, instead set off to slaughter one another in enormous numbers on the battlefields of Europe. National loyalty had trumped class loyalty.

Nonetheless, as the twentieth century dawned, industrial Britain was hardly a stable or contented society. Immense inequalities still separated the classes. Some 40 percent of the working class continued to live in conditions then described as "poverty." A mounting wave of strikes from 1910 to 1913 testified to the intensity of class conflict. The Labour Party was becoming a major force in Parliament. Some socialists and some feminists were becoming radicalized. "Wisps of violence hung in the English air," wrote Eric Hobsbawm, "symptoms of a crisis in economy and society, which the [country's] self-confident opulence . . . could not quite conceal."[20] The world's first industrial society remained dissatisfied and conflicted.

It was also a society in economic decline relative to industrial newcomers such as Germany and the United States. Britain paid a price for its early lead, for its businessmen became committed to machinery that became obsolete as the century progressed. Latecomers invested in more modern equipment and in various ways had surpassed the British by the early twentieth century.

Europeans in Motion

Europe's Industrial Revolution prompted a massive migratory process that uprooted many millions, setting them in motion both internally and around the globe. Within Europe itself, by the mid-nineteenth century half or more of the region's people had relocated from the countryside to the cities. More significant for world history was the exodus between 1815 and 1939 of fully 20 percent of Europe's population, some 50 to 55 million people, who left home for the Americas, Australia, New Zealand, South Africa, and elsewhere (see Map 17.2). They were pushed by poverty, a rapidly growing population, and the displacement of peasant farming and artisan manufacturing. And they were pulled abroad by the enormous demand for labor overseas, the ready availability of land in some places, and the relatively cheap transportation of railroads and steamships. But not all found a satisfactory life in their new homes, and perhaps 7 million returned to Europe.[21]

This huge process had a transformative global impact, temporarily increasing Europe's share of the world's population and scattering Europeans around the world. In 1800, less than 1 percent of the total world population consisted of overseas Europeans and their descendants; by 1930, they represented 11 percent.[22] In some regions, the impact was profound. Australia and New Zealand became settler colonies, outposts of European civilization in the South Pacific that overwhelmed

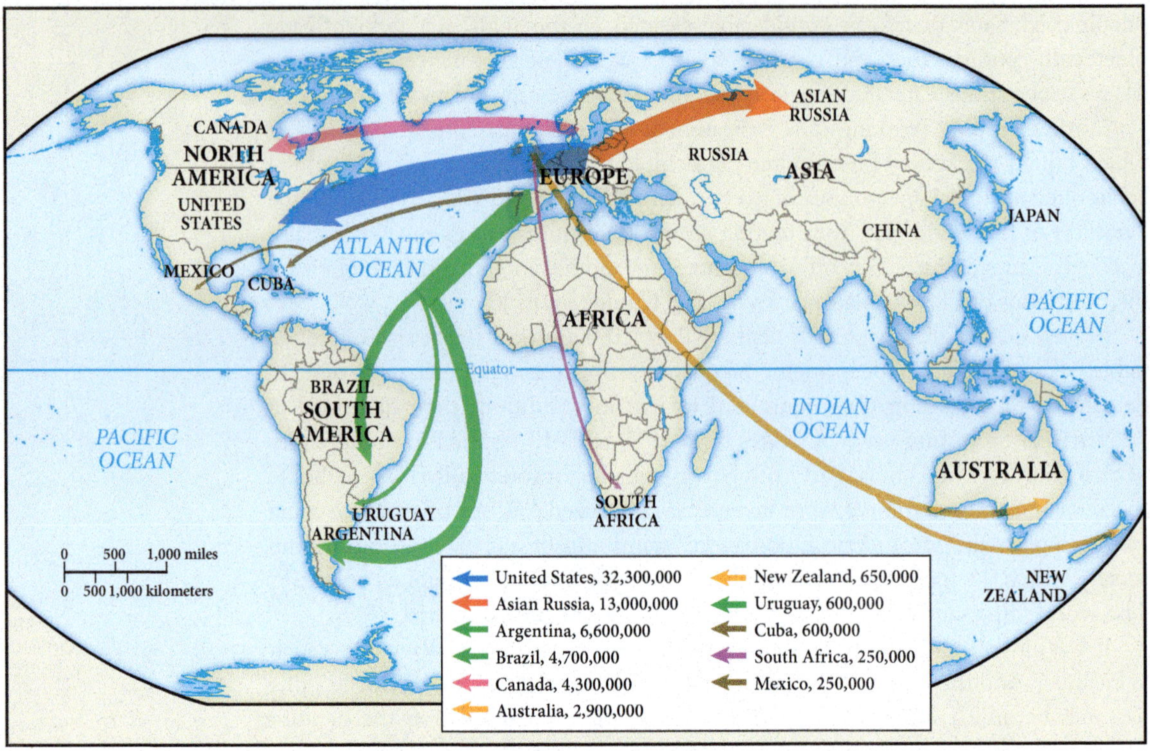

Map 17.2 European Migration in the Industrial Age
The Industrial Revolution not only transformed European society but also scattered millions of Europeans to the far corners of the world.

their native populations through conquest, acquisition of their lands, and disease. Smaller numbers of Europeans found their way to South Africa, Kenya, Rhodesia, Algeria, and elsewhere, where they injected a sharp racial divide into those colonized territories.

But it was the Americas that felt the brunt of this huge movement of people. Latin America received about 20 percent of the European migratory stream, mostly from Italy, Spain, and Portugal, with Argentina and Brazil accounting for some 80 percent of those immigrants. Considered "white," they enhanced the social weight of the European element in those countries and thus enjoyed economic advantages over the multiracial, Indian, and African populations.

In several ways the immigrant experience in the United States was distinctive. It was far larger and more diverse than elsewhere, with some 32 million newcomers arriving from all over Europe between 1820 and 1930. Furthermore, the United States offered affordable land to many and industrial jobs to many more, neither of which were widely available in Latin America. And the United States was unique in turning the immigrant experience into a national myth—that of the melting pot. Despite this ideology of assimilation, the earlier immigrants, mostly Protestants from Britain and Germany, were anything but welcoming to Catholics and Jews from Southern and

Eastern Europe who arrived later. The newcomers were seen as distinctly inferior, even "un-American," and blamed for crime, labor unrest, and socialist ideas. Nonetheless, this surge of immigration contributed much to the westward expansion of the United States, to the establishment of a European-derived culture in a vast area of North America, and to the displacement of the native peoples of the region.

In the vast domains of the Russian Empire, a parallel process of European migration likewise unfolded. After the freeing of the serfs in 1861, some 13 million Russians and Ukrainians migrated to Siberia, where they overwhelmed the native population of the region, while millions more settled in Central Asia. The availability of land, the prospect of greater freedom from tsarist restrictions and from the exploitation of aristocratic landowners, and the construction of the trans-Siberian railroad—all of this facilitated the continued Europeanization of Siberia. As in the United States, the Russian government encouraged and aided this process, hoping to forestall Chinese pressures in the region and relieve growing population pressures in the more densely settled western lands of the empire.

Variations on a Theme: Industrialization in the United States and Russia

Not for long was the Industrial Revolution confined to Britain. It soon spread to continental Western Europe, and by the end of the nineteenth century it was well under way in the United States, Russia, and Japan. The globalization of industrialization had begun. Everywhere it took hold, industrialization bore a range of broadly similar outcomes. New technologies and sources of energy generated vast increases in production and spawned an unprecedented urbanization as well. Class structures changed as aristocrats, artisans, and peasants declined as classes, while the middle classes and a factory working class grew in numbers and social prominence. Middle-class women generally withdrew from paid labor altogether, and their working-class counterparts sought to do so after marriage. Working women usually received lower wages than their male counterparts, had difficulty joining unions, and were accused of taking jobs from men. Working-class frustration and anger gave rise to trade unions and socialist movements, injecting a new element of social conflict into industrial societies.

Nevertheless, different histories, cultures, and societies ensured that the Industrial Revolution unfolded variously. Differences in the pace and timing of industrialization, the size and shape of major industries, the role of the state, the political expression of social conflict, and many other factors have made this process rich in comparative possibilities. French industrialization, for example, occurred more slowly and perhaps less disruptively than did that of Britain. Germany focused initially on heavy industry—iron, steel, and coal—rather than on the textile industry with which Britain had begun. Moreover, German industrialization was far more highly concentrated in huge companies called cartels, and it generated a rather more militant and Marxist-oriented labor movement than in Britain.

Nowhere were the variations in the industrializing process more apparent than in those two vast countries that lay on the periphery of Europe. To the west across the Atlantic Ocean was the United States, a young, vigorous, democratic, expanding country, populated largely by people of European and African descent. To the east was Russia, with its Eastern Orthodox Christianity, an autocratic tsar, a huge population of serfs, and an empire stretching across northern Asia. By the early twentieth century, industrialization had turned the United States into a major global power and had spawned in Russia an enormous revolutionary upheaval that made that country the first outpost of global communism.

The United States: Industrialization without Socialism

American industrialization began in the textile factories of New England during the 1820s but grew explosively in the half century following the conclusion of the Civil War in 1865 (see Map 17.3). The country's huge size, the ready availability of natural resources, its expanding domestic market, and its relative political stability

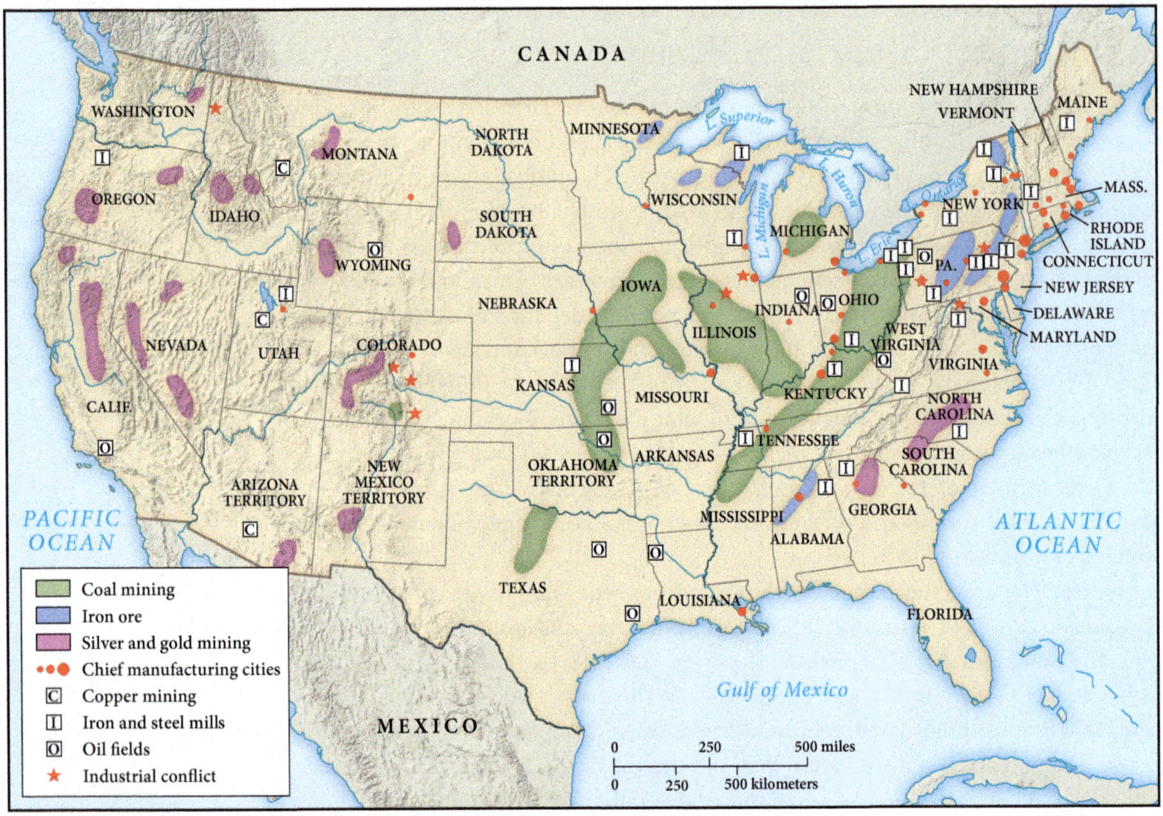

Map 17.3 The Industrial United States in 1900

By the early twentieth century, manufacturing industries were largely in the Northeast and Midwest, whereas mining operations were more widely scattered across the country.

combined to make the United States the world's leading industrial power by 1914. At that time, it produced 36 percent of the world's manufactured goods, compared to 16 percent for Germany, 14 percent for Great Britain, and 6 percent for France. Furthermore, U.S. industrialization was closely linked to that of Europe. About one-third of the capital investment that financed its remarkable growth came from British, French, and German capitalists.

As in other later industrializing countries, the U.S. government played an important role, though less directly than in Germany or Japan. Tax breaks, huge grants of public land to the railroad companies, laws enabling the easy formation of corporations, and the absence of much overt regulation of industry all fostered the rise of very large business enterprises. The U.S. Steel Corporation, for example, by 1901 had an annual budget three times the size of the federal government's budget. In this respect, the United States followed the pattern of Germany but differed from that of France and Britain, where family businesses still predominated.

CORE IDEA

■ **Making Comparisons**

How did industrialization differ in the United States and Russia?

The United States also pioneered techniques of mass production, using interchangeable parts, the assembly line, and "scientific management" to produce for a mass market. The nation's advertising agencies, Sears Roebuck's and Montgomery Ward's mail-order catalogs, and urban department stores generated a middle-class "culture of consumption." When the industrialist Henry Ford in the early twentieth century began producing the Model T at a price that many ordinary people could afford, he famously declared: "I am going to democratize the automobile." More so than in Europe, with its aristocratic traditions, self-made American industrialists of fabulous wealth such as Henry Ford, Andrew Carnegie, and John D. Rockefeller became cultural heroes, widely admired as models of what anyone could achieve with daring and hard work in a land of endless opportunity.

Nevertheless, well before the first Model T rolled off the assembly line, serious social divisions of a kind common to European industrial societies mounted. Preindustrial America had boasted of a relative social equality, quite unlike that of Europe, but by the end of the nineteenth century a widening gap separated the classes. In Carnegie's Homestead steel plant near Pittsburgh, employees worked every day except Christmas and the Fourth of July, often for twelve hours a day. In Manhattan, where millions of European immigrants disembarked, many lived in five- or six-story buildings with four families and two toilets on each floor. In every large city, such conditions prevailed close by the mansions of elite neighborhoods. To some, the contrast was a betrayal of American ideals, while others saw it as a natural outcome of competition and "the survival of the fittest."

As elsewhere, such conditions generated much labor protest, the formation of unions, strikes, and sometimes violence. In 1877, when the eastern railroads announced a 10 percent wage cut for their workers, strikers disrupted rail service across the eastern half of the country, smashed equipment, and rioted. Both state militias and federal troops were called out to put down the movement. Class consciousness and class conflict were intense in the industrial America of the late nineteenth and early twentieth centuries.

■ Explaining Difference
Why did Marxist socialism fail to flourish in the United States?

Unlike in many European countries, however, no major political party emerged in the United States to represent the interests of the working class. Nor did the ideas of socialism, especially those of Marxism, appeal to American workers nearly as much as they did to European laborers. At its high point, the Socialist Party of America garnered just 6 percent of the vote for its presidential candidate in the 1912 election, whereas socialists at the time held more seats in Germany's Parliament than any other party. Even in the depths of the Great Depression of the 1930s, no major socialist movement emerged to champion American workers. How might we explain the relative weakness of **socialism in the United States**?

One answer lies in the relative conservatism of major American union organizations, especially the American Federation of Labor. Its focus on skilled workers excluded the more radical unskilled laborers, and its refusal to align with any party limited its influence in the political arena. Furthermore, massive immigration from Europe, beginning in the 1840s, created a very diverse industrial labor force on top of the country's sharp racial divide. This diversity contrasted sharply with the more homogeneous populations of many European countries. Catholics and Protestants; whites and blacks; English, Irish, Germans, Slavs, Jews, and Italians—such differences undermined the class solidarity of American workers, making it far more difficult to sustain class-oriented political parties and a socialist labor movement. Moreover, the country's remarkable economic growth generated on average a higher standard of living for American workers than their European counterparts experienced. Land was cheaper, and homeownership was more available. Workers with property generally found socialism less attractive than those without. By 1910, a particularly large group of white-collar workers in sales, services, and offices outnumbered factory laborers. Their middle-class aspirations further diluted impulses toward radicalism.

But political challenges to the abuses of capitalist industrialization did arise. In the 1890s, among small farmers in the U.S. South, West, and Midwest, "populists" railed against banks, industrialists, monopolies, the existing money system, and both major political parties, all of which they thought were dominated by the corporate interests of the eastern elites. More successful, especially in the early twentieth century, were the **Progressives**, who pushed for specific reforms, such as wages-and-hours legislation, better sanitation standards, antitrust laws, and greater governmental intervention in the economy. Socialism, however, came to be defined as fundamentally "un-American" in a country that so valued individualism and so feared "big government." It was a distinctive feature of the American response to industrialization.

Russia: Industrialization and Revolution

As a setting for the Industrial Revolution, it would be hard to imagine two more different environments than the United States and Russia. If the United States was the Western world's most exuberant democracy during the nineteenth century, Russia remained the sole outpost of absolute monarchy, in which the state exercised far greater control over individuals and society than anywhere in the Western world.

At the beginning of the twentieth century, Russia still had no national parliament, no legal political parties, and no nationwide elections. The tsar, answerable to God alone, ruled unchecked. Furthermore, Russian society was dominated by a titled nobility of various ranks. Its upper levels included great landowners, who furnished the state with military officers and leading government officials. Until 1861, most Russians were peasant serfs, bound to the estates of their masters, subject to sale, greatly exploited, and largely at the mercy of their owners. Even after emancipation, a vast cultural gulf separated these two classes. Many nobles were highly westernized, some speaking French better than Russian, whereas their serfs were steeped in a backwoods Orthodox Christianity that incorporated pre-Christian spirits, spells, curses, and magic.

A further difference between Russia and the United States lay in the source of social and economic change. In the United States, such change bubbled up from society as free farmers, workers, and businessmen sought new opportunities and operated in a political system that gave them varying degrees of expression. In autocratic Russia, change was far more often initiated by the state, in its continuing efforts to catch up with its more powerful and innovative European competitors. This kind of "transformation from above" found expression in the freeing of the serfs in 1861 by an order from the tsar. Russia's industrial development, which began in the 1860s, was also heavily directed from the top by the state, far more so than was the case in Western Europe or the United States.

Russian Serfs This 1872 photograph shows a wealthy Russian landowner and his wife being pulled in a cart by serfs, who had been legally freed just eleven years earlier but continued to serve their master. They are attending a high-society wedding of another local estate owner. (© SZ Photo/Scherl/Bridgeman Images)

By the 1890s, Russia's Industrial Revolution was launched and growing rapidly. It focused particularly on railroads and heavy industry and was fueled by a substantial amount of foreign investment. By 1900, Russia ranked fourth in the world in steel production and had major industries in coal, textiles, and oil. Its industrial enterprises, still modest in comparison to those of Europe, were concentrated in a few major cities—Moscow, St. Petersburg, and Kiev, for example—and took place in factories far larger than in most of Western Europe.

Explaining Revolution
What factors set the stage for the Russian Revolution in the early twentieth century?

All of this contributed to the explosive social outcomes of Russian industrialization. A growing middle class of businessmen and professionals increasingly took shape. As modern and educated people, many in the middle class objected strongly to the deep conservatism of tsarist Russia and sought a greater role in political life, but they were also dependent on the state for contracts and jobs and for suppressing the growing radicalism of the workers, which they greatly feared. Although factory workers constituted only about 5 percent of Russia's total population, they quickly developed a radical class consciousness, based on harsh conditions and the absence of any legal outlet for their grievances. As in Western Europe, millions flocked to the new centers of industrial development. By 1897, over 70 percent of the population in Moscow and St. Petersburg were recent migrants from the rural areas. Their conditions of life resembled those of industrial migrants in New York or Berlin. One observer wrote: "People live in impossible conditions: filth, stench, suffocating heat. They lie down together barely a few feet apart; there is no division between the sexes and adults sleep with children."[23] Until 1897, a thirteen-hour working day was common, while ruthless discipline and overt disrespect from supervisors created resentment. In the absence of legal unions or political parties, these grievances often erupted in the form of large-scale strikes.

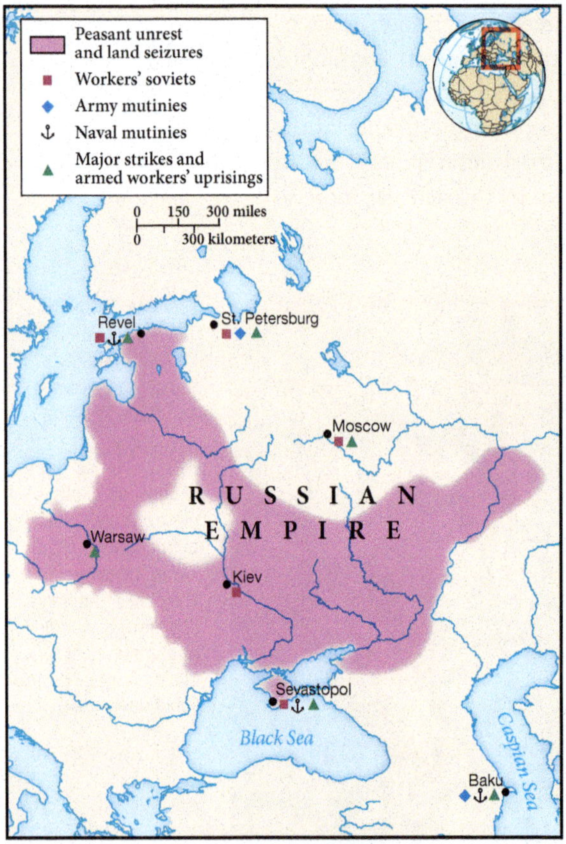

Map 17.4 Industrialization and Revolution in Russia, 1905
Only in Russia did industrialization lead to violent revolutionary upheavals, both in 1905 and more successfully in 1917.

In these conditions, a small but growing number of educated Russians found in Marxist socialism a way of understanding the changes they witnessed daily as well as hope for the future in a revolutionary upheaval of workers. In 1898, they created an illegal Russian Social Democratic Labor Party and quickly became involved in workers' education, union organizing, and, eventually, revolutionary action. By the early twentieth century, the strains of rapid change and the state's continued intransigence had reached the bursting point, and in 1905, following its defeat in a naval war with Japan, Russia erupted in spontaneous insurrection (see Map 17.4). Workers in Moscow and St. Petersburg went on strike and created their own representative councils, called soviets. Peasant uprisings, student demonstrations, revolts of non-Russian nationalities, and mutinies in the military all contributed to the upheaval. Recently formed political parties, representing intellectuals of various persuasions, came out into the open.

The **Russian Revolution of 1905**, though brutally suppressed, forced the tsar's regime to make more substantial reforms than it had ever contemplated. It granted a constitution, legalized both trade unions and political parties, and permitted the election of a national assembly, called the Duma. Censorship was eased, and plans were under way for universal primary education. Industrial development likewise continued at a rapid rate, so that by 1914 Russia stood fifth in the world in terms of overall output. But in the first half of that year, some 1,250,000 workers, representing about 40 percent of the entire industrial workforce, went out on strike.

Thus the tsar's limited political reforms, which had been granted with great reluctance and were often reversed in practice, failed to tame working-class radicalism or to bring social stability to Russia. In Russian political life, the people generally, and even the middle class, had only a very limited voice. Representatives of even the privileged classes had become so alienated by the government's intransigence that many felt revolution was inevitable. Various revolutionary groups, many of them socialist, published pamphlets and newspapers, organized trade unions, and spread their messages among workers and peasants. Particularly in the cities, these revolutionary parties had an impact. They provided a language through which workers could express their grievances; they created links among workers from different factories; and they furnished leaders who were able to act when the revolutionary moment arrived.

World War I provided that moment. The enormous hardships of that war, coupled with the immense social tensions of industrialization within a still autocratic political system, sparked the Russian Revolution of 1917 (see Chapter 20). That massive upheaval quickly brought to power the most radical of the socialist groups operating in the country—the Bolsheviks, led by the charismatic Vladimir Ilyich Ulyanov, better known as Lenin. Only in Russia was industrialization associated with violent social revolution. This was the most distinctive feature of Russia's modern historical development. And only in Russia was a socialist political party, inspired by the teachings of Karl Marx, able to seize power, thus launching the modern world's first socialist society, with enormous implications for the twentieth century.

CORE IDEA

■ Identifying Patterns

What was common to industrialization everywhere, and in what ways did it vary from place to place?

The Industrial Revolution and Latin America in the Nineteenth Century

Beyond the world of Europe and North America, only Japan underwent a major industrial transformation during the nineteenth century, part of that country's overall response to the threat of European aggression. (See "The Japanese Difference: The Rise of a New East Asian Power" in Chapter 19.) Elsewhere—in colonial India, Egypt, the Ottoman Empire, China, and Latin America—very modest

SNAPSHOT The Industrial Revolution and the Global Divide

During the nineteenth century, the Industrial Revolution generated an enormous and unprecedented economic division in the world, as measured by the share of manufacturing output. What patterns can you see in this table?

SHARE OF TOTAL WORLD MANUFACTURING OUTPUT (percentage)

	1750	1800	1860	1880	1900
EUROPE AS A WHOLE	23.2	28.1	53.2	61.3	62.0
United Kingdom	1.9	4.3	19.9	22.9	18.5
France	4.0	4.2	7.9	7.8	6.8
Germany	2.9	3.5	4.9	8.5	13.2
Russia	5.0	5.6	7.0	7.6	8.8
UNITED STATES	0.1	0.8	7.2	14.7	23.6
JAPAN	3.8	3.5	2.6	2.4	2.4
THE REST OF THE WORLD	73.0	67.7	36.6	20.9	11.0
China	32.8	33.3	19.7	12.5	6.2
South Asia (India/Pakistan)	24.5	19.7	8.6	2.8	1.7

Source: Data from Paul Kennedy, *The Rise and Fall of the Great Powers* (New York: Random House, 1987), 149.

experiments in modern industry were undertaken, but nowhere did they drive the kind of major social transformation that had taken place in Europe, North America, and Japan. However, even in societies that did not experience their own Industrial Revolution, the profound impact of European and North American industrialization was hard to avoid. Such was the case in Latin America during the nineteenth century. (See Snapshot: The Industrial Revolution and the Global Divide.)

After Independence in Latin America

The struggle for independence in Latin America had lasted far longer and proved far more destructive than in North America. Decimated populations, diminished herds of livestock, flooded or closed silver mines, abandoned farms, shrinking international trade and investment capital, and empty national treasuries—these were the conditions that greeted Latin Americans upon independence. Furthermore, the four major administrative units (viceroyalties) of Spanish America ultimately dissolved into eighteen separate countries, and regional revolts wracked Brazil in the early decades of its independent life. A number of international wars in the post-independence century likewise shook these new nations. Peru and Bolivia briefly united and then broke apart in a bitter conflict (1836–1839); Mexico lost huge territories to the United States (1846–1848); and an alliance of Argentina, Brazil, and Uruguay went to war with Paraguay (1864–1870) in a conflict that devastated Paraguay's small population.

Within these new countries, political life was turbulent and unstable. Conservatives favored centralized authority and sought to maintain the social status quo of the colonial era in alliance with the Catholic Church, which at independence owned perhaps half of all productive land. Their often bitter opponents were liberals, who attacked the Church in the name of Enlightenment values, sought at least modest social reforms, and preferred federalism. In many countries, conflicts between these factions, often violent, enabled military strongmen known as ***caudillos*** (kaw-DEE-yos) to achieve power as defenders of order and property, although they too succeeded one another with great frequency. One of them, Antonio López de Santa Anna of Mexico, was president of his country at least nine separate times between 1833 and 1855. Constitutions too replaced one another with bewildering speed. Bolivia had ten constitutions during the nineteenth century, while Ecuador and Peru each had eight.

Social life did not change fundamentally in the aftermath of independence. As in Europe and North America, women remained disenfranchised and wholly outside of formal political life. Slavery was abolished in most of Latin America by mid-century, although it persisted in both Brazil and Cuba until the late 1880s. Most of the legal distinctions among various racial categories also disappeared, and all free people were considered, at least officially, equal citizens. Nevertheless, productive economic resources such as businesses, ranches, and plantations remained overwhelmingly in the hands of creole white men, who were culturally oriented toward Europe. The military provided an avenue of mobility for a few skilled and ambitious mestizo men, some of whom subsequently became caudillos. Other multiracial men and women found a place in a small middle class as teachers, shopkeepers, or artisans. The vast majority—blacks, Indians, and many multiracial people of both sexes—remained impoverished, working small subsistence farms or laboring in the mines or on the *haciendas* (ah-see-EHN-duhz) (plantations) of the well-to-do. Only rarely did the poor and dispossessed actively rebel against their social betters. One such case was the Caste War of Yucatán (1847–1901), a prolonged struggle of the Maya people of Mexico aimed at cleansing their land of European and mestizo intruders.

Facing the World Economy

During the second half of the nineteenth century, a measure of political consolidation took hold in Latin America, and countries such as Mexico, Peru, and Argentina entered periods of greater stability. At the same time, Latin America as a whole became more closely integrated into a world economy driven by the industrialization of Western Europe and North America. The new technology of the steamship cut the sailing time between Britain and Argentina almost in half, while the underwater telegraph instantly brought the latest news and fashions of Europe to Latin America.

The most significant economic outcome of this increasing integration was a rapid growth of Latin American exports to the industrializing countries, which now needed the food products, raw materials, and markets of these new nations. Latin American landowners, businessmen, and governments proved eager to supply

CORE IDEA

■ Analyzing Connections
How was Latin America linked to the global economy of the nineteenth century, and what was the impact of those links?

those needs, and in the sixty years or so after 1850, a **Latin American export boom** increased the value of goods sold abroad by a factor of ten.

Mexico continued to produce large amounts of silver, providing more than half the world's new supply until 1860. Now added to the list of raw materials flowing out of Latin America were copper from Chile, a metal that the growing electrical industry required; tin from Bolivia, which met the mounting demand for tin cans; wild rubber from the Amazon rain forest, in great demand for bicycle and automobile tires; and nitrates from Chile and guano (bird droppings) from Peru, both of which were used for fertilizer. Bananas from Central America, beef from Argentina, cacao from Ecuador, coffee from Brazil and Guatemala, and sugar from Cuba also found eager markets in industrializing countries. In return for these primary products, Latin Americans imported the textiles, machinery, tools, weapons, and luxury goods of Europe and the United States (see Map 17.5).

Accompanying this burgeoning commerce was large-scale investment of foreign capital in Latin America, most of it from Great Britain but also from France, Germany, Italy, and the United States. By 1910, U.S. business interests controlled 40 percent of Mexican property and produced half of its oil. Much of this capital was used to build railroads, largely to funnel Latin American exports to the coast, where they were shipped to overseas markets. Mexico had only 390 miles of railroad in 1876; it had 15,000 miles in 1910. By 1915, Argentina, with 22,000 miles of railroad, had more track per person than the United States had.

Becoming like Europe?

To the economic elites of Latin America, intent on making their countries resemble Europe or the United States, all of this was progress. Economies were growing, producing more than ever before. The population was also burgeoning; it increased from about 30 million in 1850 to more than 77 million in 1912 as public health measures (such as campaigns to eliminate mosquitoes that carried yellow fever) brought down death rates.

Urbanization also proceeded rapidly. By the early twentieth century, wrote one scholar, "Latin American cities lost their colonial cobblestones, white-plastered walls, and red-tiled roofs. They became modern metropolises, comparable to urban giants anywhere. Streetcars swayed, telephones jangled, and silent movies flickered from Montevideo and Santiago to Mexico City and Havana."[24] Buenos Aires, Argentina's metropolitan center, boasted 750,000 people in 1900 and billed itself as the "Paris of South America." There the educated elite discussed European literature, philosophy, and fashion, usually in French.

■ **Making Comparisons**
Did Latin America follow or diverge from the historical path of Europe during the nineteenth century?

To become more like Europe, Latin America sought to attract more Europeans. Because civilization, progress, and modernity apparently derived from Europe, many Latin American countries actively sought to increase their "white"

Map 17.5 Latin America and the World, 1825–1935

During the nineteenth and early twentieth centuries, Latin American countries interacted with the industrializing world via investment, trade, immigration, and military intervention from the United States.

populations by deliberately recruiting impoverished Europeans with the promise, mostly unfulfilled, of a new and prosperous life in the New World. Argentina received the largest wave of European immigrants (some 2.5 million between 1870 and 1915), mostly from Spain and Italy.

Only a quite modest segment of Latin American society saw any great benefits from the export boom and all that followed from it. Upper-class landowners certainly gained as exports flourished and their property values soared. Middle-class urban dwellers—merchants, office workers, lawyers, and other professionals—also grew in numbers and prosperity as their skills proved valuable in a modernizing society. As a percentage of the total population, however, these were small elites. In Mexico in the mid-1890s, for example, the landowning upper class made up no more than 1 percent and the middle classes perhaps 8 percent of the population. All other people were lower class, and most of them were impoverished.[25]

A new but quite small segment of this vast lower class emerged among urban workers who labored in the railroads, ports, mines, and a few factories. They initially organized themselves in a variety of mutual aid societies, but by the end of the nineteenth century they were creating unions and engaging in strikes. To authoritarian governments interested in stability and progress, such activity was highly provocative and threatening, and they acted harshly to crush or repress unions and strikes. In 1907 more than 1,000 men, women, and children were slaughtered by police in the Chilean city of Iquique when nitrate miners protested their wages and working conditions.

The vast majority of the lower class lived in rural areas, where they suffered the most and benefited the least from the export boom. Government attacks on communal landholding and peasant indebtedness to wealthy landowners combined to push many farmers off their land or into remote and poor areas where they could barely make a living. Many wound up as dependent laborers or peons on the haciendas of the wealthy, where their wages were often too meager to support a family. Thus women and children, who had earlier remained at home to tend the family plot, were required to join their menfolk as field laborers.

Although local protests and violence were frequent, only in Mexico did these vast inequalities erupt into a nationwide revolution. There, in the early twentieth century, middle-class reformers joined with workers and peasants to overthrow the long dictatorship of Porfirio Díaz (r. 1876–1911). What followed was a decade of bloody conflict (1910–1920) that cost Mexico some 1 million lives, or roughly 10 percent of the population. Huge peasant armies under charismatic leaders such as Pancho Villa and Emiliano Zapata helped oust Díaz. Intent on seizing land and redistributing it to the peasants, they then went on to attack many of Mexico's large haciendas. But unlike the leaders of the later Russian and Chinese revolutions, whose most radical elements seized state power, Villa and Zapata proved unable to do so on any long-term basis, in part because they were hobbled by factionalism and focused on local or regional issues. Despite this limitation and its own internal conflicts, the **Mexican Revolution** transformed the country. When the dust settled, Mexico had a new constitution (1917) that proclaimed universal male suffrage; provided for the redistribution of land; stripped the Catholic Church of any role in public education and forbade it to own land; announced unheard-of rights for workers, such as a minimum wage and an eight-hour workday; and placed restrictions on foreign ownership of property. Much of Mexico's history in the twentieth century involved working out the implications of these nationalist and reformist changes. The revolution's direct influence, however, was largely limited to Mexico itself and a few places in Central America and the Andes; the upheaval did not have the wider international impact of the Russian and Chinese revolutions.

The Mexican Revolution Women were active participants in the Mexican Revolution. They prepared food, nursed the wounded, washed clothes, and at times served as soldiers on the battlefield, as illustrated in this cover image from a French magazine in 1913. (Apic/Getty Images)

Perhaps the most significant outcome of the export boom lay in what did *not* happen, for nowhere in Latin America did it jump-start a thorough Industrial Revolution. The reasons are many. A social structure that relegated some 90 percent of its population to an impoverished lower class generated only a very small market for manufactured goods. Moreover, economically powerful groups such as landowners and cattlemen benefited greatly from exporting agricultural products and had little incentive to invest in manufacturing. Domestic manufacturing enterprises could only have competed with cheaper and higher-quality foreign goods if they had been protected for a time by high tariffs. But Latin American political leaders had thoroughly embraced the popular European doctrine of prosperity through free trade, and many governments depended on taxing imports to fill their treasuries.

Instead of their own Industrial Revolution, Latin Americans developed a form of economic growth that was largely financed by capital from abroad and dependent on European and North American prosperity and decisions. Brazil experienced this kind of dependence when its booming rubber industry suddenly collapsed in 1910–1911, after seeds from the wild rubber tree had been illegally exported to Britain and were used to start competing and cheaper rubber plantations in Malaysia.

Later critics saw this **dependent development** as a new form of colonialism, expressed in the power exercised by foreign investors. The influence of the U.S.-owned United Fruit Company in Central America was a case in point. Allied with large landowners and compliant politicians, the company pressured the governments of these "banana republics" to maintain conditions favorable to U.S. business. This indirect or behind-the-scenes imperialism was supplemented by repeated U.S. military intervention in support of American corporate interests in Cuba, Haiti, the Dominican Republic, Nicaragua, and Mexico. The United States also controlled the Panama Canal and acquired Puerto Rico as a territory in the aftermath of the Spanish-American War (see Map 17.5, page 763).

Thus, despite Latin America's domination by people of European descent and its close ties to the industrializing countries of the Atlantic world, that region's historical trajectory in the nineteenth century diverged considerably from that of Europe and North America.

CONCLUSIONS AND REFLECTIONS

Reflecting on the Industrial Revolution

Only twice in world history has there been a revolutionary transformation of human life on a planetary scale. The first was the Agricultural Revolution, which began some 12,000 years ago, emerged separately in many places, and over thousands of years gradually encompassed the entire world. The ongoing Industrial Revolution, which is the second major transformation of human life, took shape very differently. It began little more than two centuries ago in a single place (Great Britain) and has already become global. Its significance has been an enduring issue of controversy and debate.

In the European heartland of the early Industrial Revolution, its social and economic transformations attracted the most attention. Technological innovations such as the steam engine enabled the production of goods to soar, though as always that unprecedented wealth was very unevenly distributed. Many Europeans viewed their technological mastery as a sure sign of their cultural and racial superiority as they came to use "machines as the measure of men."[26] Equally novel was the large-scale movement of Europeans to the cities or to altogether new homes in the Americas, Australia, South Africa, and elsewhere. With this shift, the landowning aristocracy lost ground to the emerging middle classes and wealthy industrialists, even as rural peasants declined in numbers relative to the growing urban working classes. These new forms of inequality generated sharp social conflict that led to the rise of trade unions and Marxist or socialist movements. Clearly, the Industrial Revolution did not generate social harmony.

Very quickly, industrialization had a global impact beyond Great Britain and Western Europe. Already in the nineteenth century, the United States and Japan initiated substantial industrialization programs of their own, each of them distinctive. So too did Russia, where industrialization led to a vast revolutionary upheaval and the beginnings of world communism. Latin American countries experienced a great expansion in their exports of raw materials and received much European investment, though without generating an Industrial Revolution of their own. Much of Asia and Africa came under European colonial rule as the Industrial Revolution provided Europeans with both the motives and means to exercise power on a global scale.

By the early twenty-first century, public concern about industrialization focused largely on its dire threat to the natural environment. Even as many governments and individuals continued to pursue the dream of greater economic growth through industrialization, profound questions about the sustainability of modern industrial life had prompted the emergence of a global environmental movement. By 2020, widespread discussion about a "climate crisis," "tipping points," and the possible "collapse of civilization" had pushed environmental issues higher on the political agenda. (See "The Environment in the Anthropocene Era" in Chapter 23.)

But such widespread fear about environmental consequences was conspicuous by its absence in the early years of the Industrial Revolution. Scattered European or American scientists, writers, and government officials during the nineteenth century did highlight the negative impact of industrial life—its pollution of air and water, its encroachment on the wilderness, and more. For the most part, however, industrialization was seen as "progress" and its unfortunate byproducts were a price well worth paying. Furthermore, those problems were perceived as local, rather than national or global. Earth systems seemed larger and more stable then, with little sense that human activity could seriously disrupt them. Thus when protests erupted in the early industrial era, they were about social rather than environmental issues.

During the nineteenth century, the Industrial Revolution was widely viewed as hopeful. Karl Marx understood it as ensuring the end of poverty and class conflict, even if he despised the capitalist system in which it was embedded. Even today, many still view industrialization in that positive light, for clearly it has enabled billions of people to live longer, healthier, and more materially abundant lives. But alongside that sensibility, the last fifty years or so has witnessed the emergence of a very different perspective on the industrial era, characterized more by fear than by hope. Navigating that tension will surely be the central task of humankind during the balance of this century.

Revisiting Chapter 17

Revisiting Specifics

steam engine, 736
British textile industry, 741
middle-class society, 744
ideology of domesticity, 744
lower middle class, 745
laboring classes, 746
Karl Marx, 748
Labour Party, 750

socialism in the United States, 756
Progressives, 756
Russian Revolution of 1905, 759
caudillos, 761
Latin American export boom, 762
Mexican Revolution, 764
dependent development, 766

Revisiting Core Ideas

1. **Establishing Context** What is the significance of the Industrial Revolution in the larger framework of world history?
2. **Identifying Change** In what ways did the Industrial Revolution transform British society?
3. **Making Comparisons** How did industrialization differ in the United States and Russia?
4. **Identifying Patterns** What was common to industrialization everywhere, and in what ways did it differ from place to place?
5. **Analyzing Connections** How was Latin America linked to the global economy of the nineteenth century, and what was the impact of those links?

A Wider View

1. What did humankind gain from the Industrial Revolution, and what did it lose?
2. In what ways might the Industrial Revolution be understood as a global rather than simply a European phenomenon?
3. The Industrial Revolution transformed social as well as economic life. What evidence might support this statement?
4. How do you think the Industrial Revolution will be viewed 50, 100, or 200 years into the future?
5. **Looking Back** How did the Industrial Revolution interact with the Scientific Revolution and the French Revolution to generate Europe's modern transformation?

To learn more about the topics in this chapter, see **For Further Study** at the end of this book.

WORKING WITH EVIDENCE

The Socialist Vision and Its Enemies

Among the ideologies and social movements that grew out of Europe's Industrial Revolution, none was more important than socialism. When it emerged in the nineteenth century, "socialism" referred to public or state ownership and control of the means of production and distribution (land, railroads, and factories, for example). Socialists rejected the inequalities created by the competitive and cutthroat capitalism of an industrializing Europe. Instead they envisioned a society where the benefits of the new industrial economy were far more equally shared. By the end of the nineteenth century, socialism had become a major element of the political and intellectual life of Europe's industrializing countries, and it enjoyed a modest presence in the United States and Japan and among a handful of intellectuals elsewhere. But the rise of socialism galvanized a ferocious opposition. These enemies of socialism feared that it would destroy economies, tear at the social fabric of nations, and undermine deeply rooted cultural values. The documents that follow illustrate some of the ways that socialism was expressed and contested as it emerged and took root in Europe.

SOURCE 17.1 Socialism According to Marx and Engels

Almost everywhere, modern socialism has been linked to the life and work of Karl Marx (1818–1883). This German-born intellectual lived during the harshest phase of European industrialization, before the benefits of this new and highly productive system were widely shared. But in this brutal process, Marx discerned the inevitable approach of a new socialist world. In his writings, he praised the productive capacity of the Industrial Revolution while providing devastating criticism of the social inequalities, the economic instability, and the blatant exploitation that accompanied this process. In short, Marx distinguished sharply between the technological achievements of industrialization and the capitalist socioeconomic system in which it occurred.

Source 17.1 presents excerpts from the most famous of Marx's writings, *The Communist Manifesto*, first published in 1848. In this effort and throughout much of his life, Marx was assisted by another German thinker, Friedrich Engels (1820–1895), the son of a successful textile manufacturer. Engels became radicalized as he witnessed the devastating social results of capitalist industrialization. Their *Manifesto* begins with a summary description of the historical process. Much of the document then analyzes what the authors call the "bourgeoisie" or the "bourgeois epoch," terms that refer to the age of industrial capitalism.

- How do Marx and Engels understand the motor of change in human history? What are their criticisms of the existing social system? What do they see as its major achievements?
- Why do they believe that the capitalist system is doomed? On what basis do Marx and Engels argue that only a revolution, "the forcible overthrow of all existing social conditions," will enable the creation of a socialist society? What kind of society do they envisage after the collapse of capitalism?
- Which of Marx and Engels's descriptions and predictions ring true even now? In what respects was their analysis disproved by later developments?

KARL MARX AND FRIEDRICH ENGELS | *The Communist Manifesto* | 1848

The history of all hitherto existing society is the history of class struggles. . . . Our epoch, the epoch of the bourgeoisie, possesses, however, this distinct feature: it has simplified class antagonisms. Society as a whole is more and more splitting up into two great hostile camps, into two great classes directly facing each other—bourgeoisie and proletariat.

Modern industry has established the world market, for which the discovery of America paved the way. This market has given an immense development to commerce, to navigation, to communication by land. . . .

[T]he bourgeoisie has at last, since the establishment of Modern Industry and of the world market, conquered for itself, in the modern representative state, exclusive political sway. The executive of the modern state is but a committee for managing the common affairs of the whole bourgeoisie. . . .

The bourgeoisie, wherever it has got the upper hand, has put an end to all feudal, patriarchal, idyllic relations. It has . . . left no other nexus between people than naked self-interest, than callous "cash payment." . . . It has resolved personal worth into exchange value, and in place of the numberless indefeasible chartered freedoms, has set up that single, unconscionable freedom—Free Trade. In one word, for exploitation, veiled by religious and political illusions, it has substituted naked, shameless, direct, brutal exploitation.

The bourgeoisie has stripped of its halo every occupation hitherto honored and looked up to with reverent awe. It has converted the physician, the lawyer, the priest, the poet, the man of science, into its paid wage laborers.

The bourgeoisie has torn away from the family its sentimental veil, and has reduced the family relation into a mere money relation. . . .

It has been the first to show what man's activity can bring about. It has accomplished wonders far surpassing Egyptian pyramids, Roman aqueducts, and Gothic cathedrals. . . .

The need of a constantly expanding market for its products chases the bourgeoisie over the entire surface of the globe. It must nestle everywhere, settle everywhere, establish connections everywhere. . . .

All old-established national industries have been destroyed or are daily being destroyed. They are dislodged by new industries . . . , that [use] raw material drawn from the remotest zones; industries whose products are consumed, not only at home, but in every quarter of the globe. In place of the old wants, satisfied by the production of the country, we find new wants, requiring for their satisfaction the products of distant lands and climes. In place of the old local and national seclusion and self-sufficiency, we have intercourse in every direction, universal interdependence of nations. . . .

The bourgeoisie . . . has created enormous cities, has greatly increased the urban population as compared with the rural, and has thus rescued a considerable part of the population from the idiocy of rural life. Just as it has made the country dependent on the towns, so it has made barbarian and semibarbarian countries dependent on the civilized ones, nations of peasants on nations of bourgeois, the East on the West. . . .

The bourgeoisie, during its rule of scarce one hundred years, has created more massive and more colossal productive forces than have all preceding generations together. Subjection of nature's forces to man, machinery, application of chemistry to industry and agriculture, steam navigation, railways, electric telegraphs, clearing of whole continents for cultivation, canalization of rivers, whole populations conjured out of the ground. . . .

It is enough to mention the commercial crises that, by their periodical return, put the existence of the entire bourgeois society on its trial, each time more threateningly. . . . In these crises, there breaks out an epidemic that, in all earlier epochs, would have seemed an absurdity—the epidemic of overproduction. . . .

But not only has the bourgeoisie forged the weapons that bring death to itself; it has also called into existence the men who are to wield those weapons—the modern working class—the proletarians. . . .

These laborers, who must sell themselves piecemeal, are a commodity, like every other article of commerce, and are consequently exposed to all the vicissitudes of competition, to all the fluctuations of the market.

Owing to the extensive use of machinery, and to the division of labor, the work of the proletarians has lost all individual character, and, consequently, all charm for the workman. He becomes an appendage of the machine, and it is only the most simple, most monotonous, and most easily acquired knack, that is required of him. . . .

Masses of laborers, crowded into the factory . . . they are daily and hourly enslaved by the machine, by the overlooker, and, above all, by the individual bourgeois manufacturer himself. . . .

The lower strata of the middle class—the small tradespeople, shopkeepers, and retired tradesmen generally, the handicraftsmen and peasants—all these sink gradually into the proletariat. . . . Thus, the proletariat is recruited from all classes of the population. . . .

What the bourgeoisie therefore produces, above all, are its own grave-diggers. Its fall and the victory of the proletariat are equally inevitable. . . .

[T]he first step in the revolution by the working class is to raise the proletariat to the position of ruling class, to win the battle of democracy. The proletariat will use its political supremacy to wrest, by degree, all capital from the bourgeoisie, to centralize all instruments of production in the hands of the state. . . . When, in the course of development, class distinctions have disappeared, and all production has been concentrated in the hands of a vast association of the whole nation, the public power will lose its political character. . . . In place of the old bourgeois society, with its classes and class antagonisms, we shall have an association in which the free development of each is the condition for the free development of all. . . .

The Communists disdain to conceal their views and aims. They openly declare that their ends can be attained only by the forcible overthrow of all existing social conditions. Let the ruling classes tremble at a communist revolution. The proletarians have nothing to lose but their chains. They have a world to win.

Source: John E. Toews, ed., *The Communist Manifesto by Karl Marx and Frederick Engels with Related Documents*, 2nd ed. (Boston: Bedford/St. Martin's, 2018), 64–95.

SOURCE 17.2 Socialism without Revolution

Karl Marx and Friedrich Engels provided the set of ideas that informed much of the European socialist movement during the second half of the nineteenth century. Organized in various national parties and joined together in international organizations as well, socialists usually referred to themselves as social democrats, for they were seeking to extend the principles of democracy from the political arena (voting rights, for example) into the realm of the economy and society. By the 1890s, however, some of them had begun to question at least part of Marx's teachings, especially the need for violent revolution. The chief spokesperson for this group of socialists, known as "revisionists," was Eduard Bernstein (1850–1932), a prominent member of the German Social Democratic Party. His ideas provoked a storm of controversy within European socialist circles. Source 17.2 is drawn from the preface of Bernstein's 1899 book, *Evolutionary Socialism*.

- In what ways and for what reasons was Bernstein critical of Marx and Engels's analysis of capitalism?
- What strategy does Bernstein recommend for the German Social Democratic Party?
- What does he mean by saying that "the movement means everything for me and . . . 'the final aim of socialism' is nothing"?
- Why would some of Marx's followers have considered Bernstein a virtual traitor to the socialist cause?

EDUARD BERNSTEIN | *Evolutionary Socialism* | 1899

It has been maintained in a certain quarter that the practical deductions from my treatises would be the abandonment of the conquest of political power by the proletariat organized politically and economically. That [idea] . . . I altogether deny.

I set myself against the notion that we have to expect shortly a collapse of the bourgeois economy. . . .

The adherents of this theory of a catastrophe, base it especially on the conclusions of the *Communist Manifesto*. This is a mistake. . . .

Social conditions have not developed to such an acute opposition of things and classes as is depicted in the *Manifesto*. It is not only useless, it is the greatest folly to attempt to conceal this from ourselves. The number of members of the possessing classes is today not smaller but larger. The enormous increase of social wealth is not accompanied by a decreasing number of large capitalists but by an increasing number of capitalists of all degrees. The middle classes change their character but they do not disappear from the social scale.

The concentration in productive industry is not being accomplished even today in all its departments with equal thoroughness and at an equal rate. . . .

In all advanced countries we see the privileges of the capitalist bourgeoisie yielding step by step to democratic organizations. Under the influence of this, and driven by the movement of the working classes which is daily becoming stronger, a social reaction has set in against the exploiting tendencies of capital. . . . Factory legislation, the democratizing of local government, and the extension of its area of work, the freeing of trade unions and systems of cooperative trading from legal restrictions, the consideration of standard conditions of labor in the work undertaken by public authorities—all these characterize this phase of the evolution.

But the more the political organizations of modern nations are democratized, the more the needs and opportunities of great political catastrophes are diminished. . . .

[Engels] points out in conformity with this opinion that the next task of the party should be "to work for an uninterrupted increase of its votes" or to carry on a slow *propaganda of parliamentary activity*. . . .

Shall we be told that he [Engels] abandoned the conquest of political power by the working classes . . . ?

[F]or a long time yet the task of social democracy is, instead of speculating on a great economic crash, "to organize the working classes politically and develop them as a democracy and to fight for all reforms in the State which are adapted to raise the working classes and transform the State in the direction of democracy." . . .

[T]he movement means everything for me and that what is *usually* called "the final aim of socialism" is nothing. . . .

The conquest of political power by the working classes, the expropriation of capitalists, are not ends themselves but only means for the accomplishment of certain aims and endeavors. . . . But the conquest of political power necessitates the possession of political *rights*; German social democracy [must] devise the best ways for the extension of the political and economic rights of the German working classes.

Source: Eduard Bernstein, *Evolutionary Socialism*, translated by Edith C. Harvey (New York: Schocken Books, 1961), xxiv–xxx.

SOURCE 17.3 Socialist Perspectives in Art: The Present and the Future

Socialists expressed in art both their understanding of existing capitalist society and a vision of what a socialist future might look like. Source 17.3A represents the former and Source 17.3B the latter.

- How does Source 17.3A express Marx's understanding of "bourgeois society"?
- Which of Marx's predictions about the socialist future is evoked in Source 17.3B? How does the artist deal with tension between nation and class?

SOURCE 17.3A

INDUSTRIAL WORKERS OF THE WORLD | *A Pyramid of Capitalist Society* | 1911

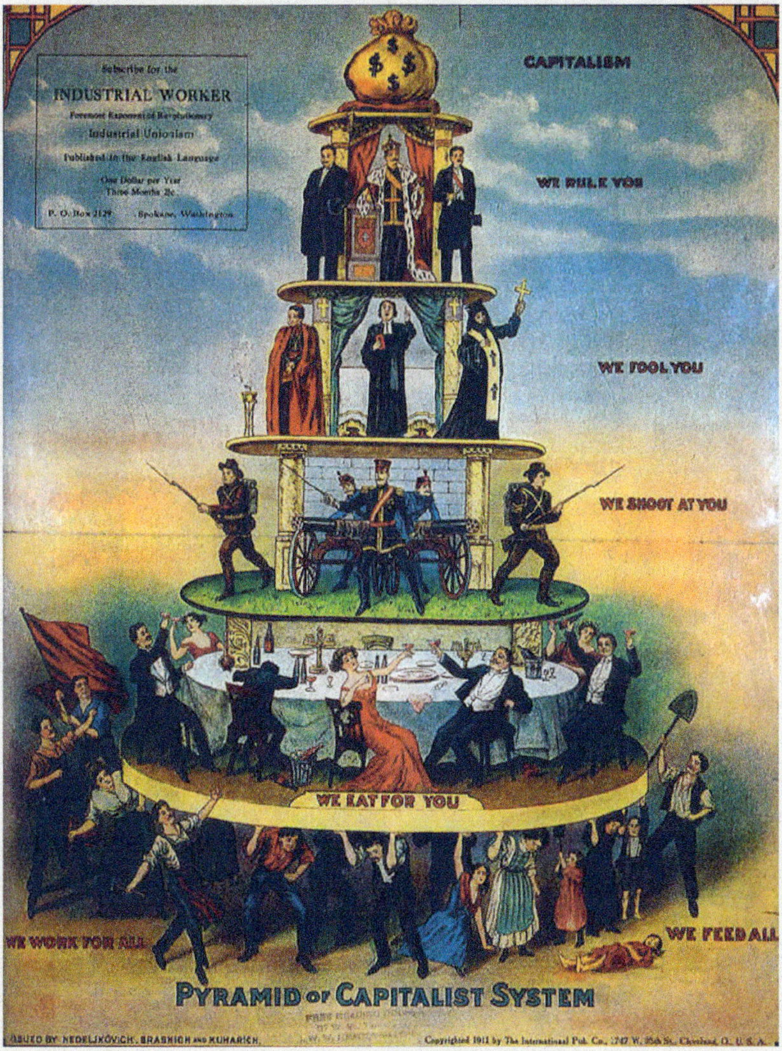

IAM/akg-images

SOURCE 17.3B

Poster Advertising International Trade Union Congress | **1896**

SOURCE 17.4 Socialism in Song

While socialist intellectuals like Marx and Bernstein developed a particular understanding of history and of capitalism, ordinary workers, many animated by socialist ideals, gave voice to their experience and aspirations in song. The hymn of the socialist movement was *The Internationale,* composed in 1871 by Eugène Pottier, a French working-class activist, poet, and songwriter. Source 17.4 offers an English translation made in 1900 by Charles Kerr, an American publisher of radical books. The song gave expression to both the oppression and the hopes of ordinary people as they worked for a socialist future.

- What evidence of class consciousness is apparent in the song? What particular grievances are expressed in it?
- How does *The Internationale* portray the struggle and the future?
- What evidence of Marxist thinking can you find in its lyrics?

EUGÈNE POTTIER | *The Internationale* | 1871

Arise, ye prisoners of starvation!
Arise, ye wretched of the earth!
For justice thunders condemnation,
A better world's in birth!
No more tradition's chains shall bind us,
Arise ye slaves, no more in thrall!
The earth shall rise on new foundations,
We have been nought, we shall be all. (Chorus)

Chorus
'Tis the final conflict,
Let each stand in his place.
The international working class
Shall be the human race.

We want no condescending saviors
To rule us from a judgment hall;
We workers ask not for their favors;
Let us consult for all.
To make the thief disgorge his booty
To free the spirit from its cell,
We must ourselves decide our duty,
We must decide, and do it well. (Chorus)

The law oppresses us and tricks us,
Wage slav'ry drains the workers' blood;
The rich are free from obligations,
The laws the poor delude.
Too long we've languished in subjection,
Equality has other laws;
"No rights," says she, "without their duties,
No claims on equals without cause." (Chorus)

Behold them seated in their glory
The kings of mine and rail and soil!
What have you read in all their story,
But how they plundered toil?
Fruits of the workers' toil are buried
In the strong coffers of a few;
In working for their restitution
The men will only ask their due. (Chorus)

Toilers from shops and fields united,
The union we of all who work;
The earth belongs to us, the workers,
No room here for the shirk.
How many on our flesh have fattened;
But if the noisome birds of prey
Shall vanish from the sky some morning,
The blessed sunlight still will stay. (Chorus)

Source: Charles H. Kerr (compiler and translator), *Socialist Songs with Music* (Chicago: Charles H. Kerr, 1901), No. 2.

■ ■ ■

SOURCE 17.5 British Poster Depicting the Socialist Threat

The growth of socialist movements was immensely threatening to many elements of the established order, and across Europe opponents organized to counter "the socialist menace." In Britain the Conservative Party provided a focus for those who feared that socialism would undermine the nation's economy and social fabric, including many industrialists, capitalists, members of the middle class, and social conservatives. Source 17.5 is a Conservative Party poster from 1909 that depicts a demonic socialist figure throttling (strangling) Britannia, a female allegorical figure representing Great Britain. Usually depicted as a powerful warrior sporting an ancient Greek helmet, a shield, and a trident (representing Britain's naval power), Britannia appeared on the back of British coinage and on many public buildings. In this image, she is overwhelmed by the socialist demon's frenzied attack. The image catches the moment when she drops her trident, having already lost her shield bearing the British Union Jack flag. Around her waist is a belt labeled "prosperity."

- What roles do Britannia and the demon play in this image?
- What messages about socialism and its impact on Great Britain does the artist who created this image wish to convey? What specific elements of the image reinforce these messages?
- How might Bernstein in Source 17.2 react to this image? How might the artists who created Sources 17.3A and 17.3B react to it? What specific criticisms might they offer?

■ ■ ■

CONSERVATIVE PARTY | *Socialism Throttling the Country* | **1909**

Pictorial Press Ltd/Alamy

SOURCE 17.6 Outlawing Socialism in Germany

Many opponents of socialism sought to use the authority and institutions of government to advance their goals. Nowhere was this more evident than in Germany, where the powerful Chancellor Otto von Bismarck (1815–1898), who was implacably opposed to socialism, used a conservative majority in the legislature to pass the Anti-Socialist Law of 1878. The act outlawed all socialist organizations (known as "societies") that aimed to overthrow the existing political and social order and included specific passages aimed at limiting a wide variety of activities. Before it lapsed in 1890, about 1,500 people were sentenced to prison time under the law. For socialists this period of repression became a source of solidarity and shared identity—a "heroic period" in the socialist struggle.

- What specific activities are banned by the law? What do you think that Bismarck hoped to accomplish by banning these specific activities?
- What did Bismarck mean by "the harmony among all classes"? Why was it so important to him?
- In what ways do Sources 17.5 and 17.6 convey similar messages about the threat of socialism? What differences can you identify?

Law against the Publicly Dangerous Endeavors of Social Democracy | 1878

1. Societies which aim at the overthrow of the existing political or social order through social-democratic, socialistic, or communistic endeavors are to be prohibited. This applies also to societies in which social-democratic, socialistic, or communistic endeavors aiming at the overthrow of the existing political or social order are manifested in a manner dangerous to the public peace, and, particularly to the harmony among the classes of the population. Associations of every kind are the same as societies. . . .

9. Meetings in which social-democratic, socialistic, or communistic endeavors which aim at the overthrow of the existing political or social order are manifested are to be dissolved. . . . Public festivities and processions shall be treated the same as meetings. . . .

11. Publications in which social-democratic, socialistic, or communistic endeavors aimed at the overthrow of the existing political or social order are manifested in a manner calculated to endanger the public peace, and particularly the harmony among all classes of the population, are to be prohibited. In the case of periodical publications, the prohibition may extend to further issues as soon as a single issue has been prohibited on the basis of this law. . . .

16. The collection of contributions for the furtherance of social democratic, socialistic, or communistic endeavors aiming at the overthrow of the existing political and social order, as well as a public appeal for such contributions, are to be prohibited by the police. The prohibition is to be announced publicly. . . .

17. Whoever participates as a member in a prohibited society, or carries on an activity in its interest, is to be punished by a fine of not more than five hundred marks or with imprisonment not exceeding three months. . . . Imprisonment of not less than one month and not more than one year is to be inflicted on those who participate in a society or assembly as chairmen, leaders, monitors, agents, speakers, or treasurers, or on those who issue invitations to attend the meeting.

18. Whoever provides a prohibited society or meeting with a place of assembly is to be punished with imprisonment of from one month to one year.

19. Whoever distributes, continues, or reprints a prohibited publication or a provisionally confiscated publication is to be punished with a fine not exceeding one thousand marks or with imprisonment not exceeding six months. . . .

23. . . . [I]nnkeepers, barkeepers, persons carrying on a retail business in brandy or liquors, book publishers, booksellers, librarians in lending libraries and proprietors of reading rooms, may, in addition to imprisonment, be forbidden to continue their business.

Source: Vernon L. Lidtke, *The Outlawed Party: Social Democracy in Germany, 1878–1890*, Appendix C (Princeton, NJ: Princeton University Press, 1966), 339, 341–44.

■ ■ ■

DOING HISTORY

1. **Defining the Socialist Vision** How might you describe the socialist critique of capitalist society and its expectation of the future?
2. **Considering the Appeal of Socialism** To what people might the socialist vision be most appealing? And to whom might it seem threatening?
3. **Analyzing Opposition to the "Socialist Menace"** In what ways did opponents of socialism seek to limit its influence on European society? What did opponents most fear about socialism?
4. **Connecting Socialist Thinking with the Atlantic Revolutions** To what extent did socialist thinking reflect the concerns of the Atlantic revolutions explored in Chapter 16? In what ways did it diverge from those earlier revolutionary movements?
5. **Identifying Differences** What different understandings of socialism and socialist movements can you identify in these sources?

HISTORIANS' VOICES

The Legacy of Karl Marx in the Twenty-First Century

Approaching 150 years after the death of Marx, scholars and activists alike continue to debate his relevance in the twenty-first century. Voice 17.1 comes from British educator and author Allan Todd and explores the relationship between recent events and the receptivity to Marxist ideas. In Voice 17.2, Terry Eagleton, a British professor of literature, argues for the continued usefulness of Marxist thinking in contemporary life and society.

- What events or circumstances does Allan Todd believe have shaped postures toward Marx and Marxism in recent decades?
- Why does Terry Eagleton in Voice 17.2 believe that Marx remains relevant in the twenty-first century?
- **Integrating Primary and Secondary Sources** What evidence from the primary sources might these authors use to support their arguments?

VOICE 17.1

Allan Todd on Marx and Current History | 2016

The opening words of Marx and Engels' *The Communist Manifesto*, first published in 1848, are: "A spectre is haunting Europe, the spectre of communism." Given the visible collapse of most states claiming to be communist, this "spectre" would appear to have been laid to rest. Certainly the failure of attempts in the Soviet Union and Eastern Europe to construct socialism led to a "retreat from Marxism" in the first decades after the collapse of these regimes.

Yet Marx's analysis had claimed that capitalist globalization was bound to lead to periodic and serious economic crises. . . . And indeed the financial crash of 2008 and the global economic crisis of 2011 . . . along with the ecological crises associated with the unrestricted drive for profit suggest that . . . Marx's theories might still have some relevance for the 21st century.

Thus historians such as E. Hobsbawm have argued that the events of 1989–91 and afterwards do not necessarily mark the end of Marxism or communism. They have pointed out that Marxist theory and communist practice arose from conditions of poverty, the destruction of war, and strong desires for liberty, fairness, and equality.

Other commentators have observed that Marxism . . . was in large part an extension of the French Revolution's ideals of "liberty, equality, and fraternity." . . . Movements calling for the full implementation of these ideals continue to emerge around the globe in the 21st century. Thus it may be rather too early for historians to proclaim the death and funeral of communism [Marxism].

Source: Allan Todd, *The Soviet Union and Post-Soviet Russia* (Cambridge: Cambridge University Press, 2016), 294–96.

VOICE 17.2

Terry Eagleton on the Continuing Relevance of Marx | 2011

Very few thinkers . . . have changed the course of actual history as decisively as [Marx]. . . . He transformed our understanding of human history. . . .

Marx was the first to identify the historical object known as capitalism—to show how it arose, by what laws it worked and how it might be brought to an end. . . . Marx unmasked our everyday life to reveal an imperceptible entity known as the capitalist mode of production. . . .

About Marxism as a moral and cultural critique. . . . Alienation, the "commodification" of social life, a culture of greed, aggression, mindless hedonism . . . , the steady hemorrhage of meaning and value from human existence—it is hard to find an intelligent discussion of these questions that is not indebted to the Marxist tradition.

Marxism is a critique of capitalism. . . . It is also the only such critique that has transformed large sectors of the globe. . . . As long as capitalism is in business, Marxism must be as well.

Marx himself predicted a decline of the working class and the steep rise of white collar work. . . . He also foresaw so-called globalization. He is accused of being outdated by champions of a capitalism that is rapidly reverting to Victorian levels of inequality. . . . In our own time, as Marx predicted, inequalities of wealth have dramatically deepened.

Capitalism has brought about great material advances. But though this way of organizing our affairs has had a long time to demonstrate that it is capable of satisfying human demands all around, it seems no closer to doing so than ever.

Source: Terry Eagleton, *Why Marx Was Right* (New Haven, CT: Yale University Press, 2011), x, xi, 2, 3, 8, 10.

TopFoto

CHAPTER 18

Colonial Encounters in Asia, Africa, and Oceania

1750–1950

CONNECTING PAST AND PRESENT

"It is . . . clear that the crimes and abominations from 1904 to 1908 were what we today describe as genocide."[1] So concluded a high German official in 2019 about a mass slaughter of Africans in what was then the German colony of Southwest Africa. At that time, early in the twentieth century, the German military commander in the colony, seeking to suppress a rebellion by the Herero people, had declared that "every Herero, with or without a gun, with or without cattle, will be shot. I will no longer accept [spare] women and children."[2] Some 80 percent of the Herero people perished in that suppression. Since the colony's independence in 1990 as the African state of Namibia, its government has pressed Germany for an apology and compensation. The German government has been the largest donor of development assistance to Namibia and has returned a number of bones and skulls of people killed during the rebellion. But as of 2020, contentious negotiations about a formal state apology and financial reparations remained unresolved. In such ways the colonial past has continued to echo in both Germany and Namibia more than a century later.

For many millions of Africans, Asians, and Pacific islanders, colonial rule by Western Europeans, Russians, or Americans was the major new element in their historical experience during the long nineteenth century (1750–1900) and up to the mid-twentieth century. Of course, no single colonial experience characterized this vast region. Much depended on the

« **The Imperial Durbar of 1903** To mark the coronation of British monarch Edward VII and his installation as the emperor of India, colonial authorities in India mounted an elaborate assembly, or durbar. The durbar was intended to showcase the splendor of the British Empire, and its pageantry included sporting events; a state ball; a huge display of Indian arts, crafts, and jewels; and an enormous parade in which a long line of British officials and Indian princes passed by on bejeweled elephants.

cultures and prior history of various colonized people, and the policies of the colonial powers sometimes differed sharply and changed over time. Men and women experienced the colonial era differently, as did traditional elites, Western-educated groups, artisans, peasant farmers, and migrant laborers. Furthermore, the varied actions and reactions of such people, despite their oppression and exploitation, shaped the colonial experience, perhaps as much as the policies, practices, and intentions of their temporary European rulers. All of them—colonizers and colonized alike—were caught up in the flood of change that accompanied this new burst of European imperialism.

SEEKING THE MAIN POINT

How was colonial rule experienced by the societies that it encompassed? And in what ways did colonized people respond to it?

Industry and Empire

Behind much of Europe's nineteenth-century expansion lay the massive fact of its Industrial Revolution, a process that gave rise to new economic needs, many of which found solutions abroad. The enormous productivity of industrial technology and Europe's growing affluence now created the need for extensive raw materials and agricultural products: wheat, meat, bananas, rubber, cocoa, palm oil, cotton, copper, and much more. This demand radically changed patterns of economic and social life in their places of origin.

CORE IDEA

■ Analyzing Cause and Effect

In what ways did the Industrial Revolution shape the character of nineteenth-century European imperialism?

Furthermore, Europe needed to sell its own products abroad, since its factories churned out more goods than its own people could afford to buy. By 1840, for example, Britain was exporting 60 percent of its cotton-cloth production, annually sending 200 million yards to Europe, 300 million yards to Latin America, and 145 million yards to India. Part of European and American fascination with China during the nineteenth and twentieth centuries lay in the enormous market potential represented by its huge population. Much the same could be said for capital, for European investors often found it more profitable to invest their money abroad than at home. Between 1910 and 1913, Britain was sending about half of its savings overseas as foreign investment. Large-scale overseas investment continued even after the collapse of European territorial empires in the mid-twentieth century, underpinning what some have termed the "economic imperialism" of the second half of the twentieth century (see Then and Now: Imperialism, page 784).

Wealthy Europeans also saw social benefits to foreign markets because they kept Europe's factories humming and its workers employed. The English imperialist Cecil Rhodes confided his fears to a friend in the late nineteenth century:

> Yesterday I attended a meeting of the unemployed in London and having listened to the wild speeches which were nothing more than a scream for bread, I returned home convinced more than ever of the importance of imperialism. . . . In order to save the 40 million inhabitants of the United Kingdom from a murderous civil war, the colonial politicians must open up new areas to absorb the excess population and create new markets for the products of the mines and factories.[3]

Landmarks for Chapter 18

1775 | 1800 | 1825 | 1850 | 1875 | 1900 | 1925 | 1950

EUROPE AND UNITED STATES

1750–1900 Europe's Industrial Revolution

1820s Quinine isolated and mass-produced

1846–1848 Mexican–United States War

1850–1900 Scientific racism and social Darwinism prominent

1862 Development of Gatling gun, a hand-driven machine gun

1875–1900 Intensification of European rivalries over African territories

1898 Spanish-American War

AFRICA

1830s France invades Algeria

1869 Opening of Suez Canal

1875–1900 European conquest of Africa

1890s–1908 King Leopold's reign of terror in the Congo

1896 Ethiopia defeats Italy at Battle of Adowa

1899–1902 Boer War

1904–1905 Maji Maji rebellion in German East Africa

ASIA/PACIFIC

1757–1858 East India Company governs India

1788 Initial European settlement of Australia

1830s–1870 Cultivation system in Netherlands East Indies

1857–1858 Indian Rebellion against rule of British East India Company

1858–1947 British government rules India

1858–1893 French conquest of Indochina

1898 United States acquires Hawaii and Philippines

1910 Japanese annexation of Korea

Imperialism

Imperialism thrived in the nineteenth century. The British famously boasted that the sun never set on their global empire. All across Asia, Africa, and Pacific Oceana, Western European powers created territorial empires that brought large lands and many peoples under their formal control. Likewise during this time, Russians expanded into Central Asia, as did Americans across their continent, and Japan into parts of East Asia. Almost everywhere, it was a bloody process. But for the colonizing nations and many of their citizens, imperialism was seen as something to celebrate. It confirmed their sense of racial or cultural superiority even as it persuaded many that they were bringing civilization and progress to inferior or less fortunate peoples.

By the late 1970s, however, almost all of this imperialism was gone. Nationalist movements had dissolved empires, bringing many dozens of "new nations" into existence, fifty-four of them in Africa alone. The collapse of the Soviet Union in 1991 brought an end to much of the Russian Empire, creating another fifteen newly independent countries. Only the continental empire of the United States remained intact, though few of its citizens, with the exception of Native Americans, Hawaiians, and Puerto Ricans, thought of their country as an imperial state. Even more startling was the sharp turnaround in thinking about empires. Imperialism had become illegitimate and morally reprehensible, a term of insult rather than praise, a matter of shame rather than pride. This amazing transformation of values registered globally in 1960, when the United Nations acknowledged "the passionate yearning for freedom in all dependent peoples" and declared that colonial rule represented a "denial of fundamental human rights."

So, with the disintegration of territorial empires, had the age of imperialism come to an end? Or had it merely changed its form?

For many observers, the international behavior of the United States and the Soviet Union during the Cold War (1950–1991) was usefully described in terms of empire. The case for a continuing American empire was rooted in multiple factors: its dominant economic power and the global penetration of its multinational corporations; its enormous military capacity, widespread network of military bases, and frequent military interventions such as those in Central America, Korea, Vietnam, Afghanistan, and Iraq; its leadership of many alliances such as the North Atlantic Treaty Organization; its promotion of democracy and capitalist market economies through aid programs like the Peace Corps; and the international spread of its culture (rock and roll, McDonald's, blue jeans, movies).

Something similar generated the notion of a Soviet empire during the Cold War. Certainly the Soviet Union's domination of Eastern Europe; its use of economic and military aid to draw developing countries into its orbit; its military interventions in Hungary, Czechoslovakia, Cuba, and Afghanistan; and its promotion of a communist culture of social equality and anticolonialism parallel the contours of the American empire. Ironically, both the United States and the Soviet Union created new kinds of empires while opposing the older European-style territorial empires.

A third country recently charged with imperial ambitions is China. Begun in 2013, its multi-trillion-dollar global infrastructure project, known as the Belt and Road Initiative, envisaged an array of roads, railways, port facilities, and energy pipelines stretching all across the Eastern Hemisphere and parts of Latin America as well. Funded in large part with Chinese capital and involving agreements with some 125 countries, it gave China a global economic footprint. In the eyes of some, it was an "empire-building strategy." Certainly some developing countries that eagerly took Chinese loans came to fear indebtedness and a dependence on China that limited their own sovereignty.

Thus a new vocabulary of "imperialism" has emerged to describe the different ways in which empire has found expression beyond political and territorial aims. "Economic imperialism," sometimes called "neocolonialism," suggests the ability of rich countries to gain advantage over poorer ones without the need to exercise direct political control or use military force. The notion of "cultural imperialism" refers to the domination of foreign cultural patterns over those of one's own country or people. The most prominent target of cultural imperialism has been "Americanization" as critics have deplored the growing influence of American movies, foods, fashion, political practices, manufactured goods, and much more. "Linguistic imperialism" points

U.S. imperialism has been a frequent subject of political cartoons, such as this one entitled "Yummy!" from 2010. Wilfred Hildonen via CartoonStock, www.cartoonstock.com/cartoonview.asp?catref=whin209

to the widespread adoption or imposition of particular languages (English, Spanish, French, Russian, Chinese) to the detriment of less widely spoken languages. "Religious imperialism" highlights the decline of local religions as world religions such as Buddhism, Christianity, or Islam have gained converts.

Almost all of these uses of "imperialism" in recent decades have been highly critical. They reflect the recent change in values about empire even as they have enlarged the meaning of "imperialism." In contemporary usage, imperialism no longer requires political control or military force, as it did in the nineteenth century. Rather, the term suggests that almost any exercise of unequal power qualifies as "imperialism" and is therefore morally questionable. Is this new understanding useful because it points to the essence of imperialism—inequality, domination, and exploitation? Or does it confuse our understanding of imperialism by lumping together quite different things without making necessary distinctions?

Despite the recent widespread condemnation of imperialism, a kind of "imperial nostalgia" has also surfaced. Turkey's nationalist President Erdogan has linked his country closely to the Ottoman Empire, which is widely celebrated in films and TV programs, while seeking to carve out for Turkey an Ottoman-like centrality in the Middle East. In a similar fashion, Russia's President Putin declared the collapse of the Soviet Union the "greatest geopolitical tragedy" of the twentieth century, while many have seen his policies in former Soviet states as an attempt to revive an earlier Russian/Soviet empire. And in Western Europe, a recent poll found that some 30 percent of the British and 50 percent of the Dutch were more proud than ashamed of their imperial past.[4] Some British historians, notably Niall Ferguson, have recently written quite favorably about the British Empire, arguing that colonial rule was better for its subjects than their earlier governments. "It's hard to make the case . . . ," Ferguson declared, "that somehow the world would have been better off if the Europeans had stayed home."[5]

So the question remains: did the imperialism of the nineteenth century persist in the twentieth, or did it fundamentally change?

QUESTIONS

What different kinds of imperialism have arisen over the past two centuries? To what extent does it still persist?

Colonial Rivalries This image shows Africa as a sleeping giant, while various European countries stake their rival claims to parts of the continent. It was published in 1911 in *Puck*, a British magazine of humor and satire. (Library of Congress, Prints and Photographs Division, LC-DIG-ppmsca-27783)

Thus imperialism promised to solve the class conflicts of an industrializing society while avoiding revolution or the serious redistribution of wealth.

But what made imperialism so broadly popular in Europe, especially in the last quarter of the nineteenth century, was the growth of mass nationalism. By 1871, the unification of Italy and Germany intensified Europe's already competitive international relations. Much of this rivalry spilled over into the struggle for overseas colonies or economic concessions, which became symbols of "Great Power" status for a nation. Their acquisition was a matter of urgency, even if they possessed little immediate economic value. After 1875, it seemed to matter, even to ordinary people, whether some remote corner of Africa or some obscure Pacific island was in British, French, or German hands. Imperialism, in short, appealed on economic and social grounds to the wealthy or ambitious, seemed politically and strategically necessary in the game of international power politics, and was emotionally satisfying to almost everyone. It was a potent mix!

Industrialization also provided new means for achieving those goals. Steam-driven ships moving through the new Suez Canal, completed in 1869, allowed Europeans to reach distant Asian, African, and Pacific ports more quickly and predictably and to penetrate interior rivers as well. The underwater telegraph made possible almost instant communication with far-flung outposts of empire. The discovery of quinine to prevent malaria greatly reduced European death rates in the tropics. Breech-loading rifles and machine guns vastly widened the military gap between Europeans and everyone else.

The nineteenth century also marked a change in the way Europeans perceived themselves and others. In earlier centuries, Europeans had defined others largely in religious terms. "They" were heathen; "we" were Christian. With the advent of the industrial age, however, Europeans developed a secular arrogance that fused with or in some cases replaced their notions of religious superiority. They had, after all, unlocked the secrets of nature, created a society of unprecedented wealth, and used both to produce unsurpassed military power. These became the criteria by which Europeans judged both themselves and the rest of the world.

Analyzing Change What contributed to changing European views of Asians and Africans during the nineteenth century?

By such standards, it is not surprising that their opinions of other cultures dropped sharply. The Chinese, who had been highly praised in the eighteenth century, were reduced in the nineteenth century to the image of "John Chinaman"—weak, cunning, obstinately conservative, and, in large numbers, a distinct threat labeled a "yellow peril." African societies, which even in the slave-trade era had been regarded as nations and their leaders as kings, were demoted in nineteenth-century European eyes to the status of tribes led by chiefs as a means of emphasizing their "primitive" qualities.

Peoples of Pacific Oceania and elsewhere could be regarded as "big children," who lived "closer to nature" than their civilized counterparts and correspondingly distant from the high culture with which Europeans congratulated themselves. Upon visiting Tahiti in 1768, the French explorer Bougainville concluded: "I thought I was walking in the Garden of Eden."[6] Such views could be mobilized to criticize the artificiality and materialism of modern European life, but they could also serve to justify the conquest of people who were, apparently, doing little to improve what nature had granted them. Writing in 1854, a European settler in Australia declared: "The question comes to this; which has the better right—the savage, born in a country, which he runs over but can scarcely be said to occupy . . . or

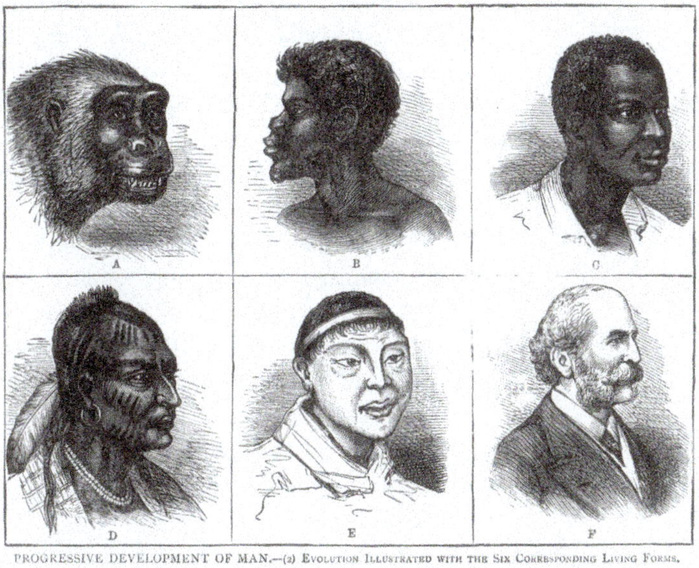
A
B
C
D
E
F
PROGRESSIVE DEVELOPMENT OF MAN.—(2) Evolution Illustrated with the Six Corresponding Living Forms.

European Racial Images This nineteenth-century chart, depicting the "Progressive Development of Man" from apes to modern Europeans, reflected the racial categories that were so prominent at the time. It also highlights the influence of Darwin's evolutionary ideas as they were applied to varieties of human beings. (Granger NYC—All rights reserved)

the civilized man, who comes to introduce into this . . . unproductive country, the industry which supports life?"[7]

Increasingly, Europeans viewed the culture and achievements of Asian and African peoples through the prism of a new kind of **scientific racism**. Although physical differences had often been a basis of fear or dislike, in the nineteenth century Europeans increasingly used the prestige and apparatus of science to support their racial preferences and prejudices. Phrenologists, craniologists, and sometimes physicians used allegedly scientific methods and numerous instruments to classify the size and shape of human skulls and concluded, not surprisingly, that those of whites were larger and therefore more advanced. Nineteenth-century biologists, who classified the varieties of plants and animals, applied these notions of rank to varieties of human beings as well. The result was a hierarchy of races, with the whites on top and the less developed "child races" beneath them. Race, in this view, determined human intelligence, moral development, and destiny. "Race is everything," declared the British anatomist Robert Knox in 1850. "Civilization depends on it."[8] Furthermore, as the germ theory of disease took hold in nineteenth-century Europe, it was accompanied by fears that contact with "inferiors" threatened the health and even the biological future of more advanced or "superior" peoples.

These ideas influenced how Europeans viewed their own global expansion. Almost everyone saw it as inevitable, a natural outgrowth of a superior civilization. For many, though, this viewpoint was tempered with a genuine, if condescending, sense of responsibility to the "weaker races" that Europe was fated to dominate. "Superior races have a right, because they have a duty . . . to civilize the inferior races," declared the French politician Jules Ferry in 1883.[9] That **civilizing mission** included bringing Christianity to the heathen, good government to disordered lands, work discipline and production for the market to "lazy natives," a measure of education to the ignorant and illiterate, clothing to the naked, and health care to the sick, all while suppressing "native customs" that ran counter to Western ways of living. In European thinking, this was "progress" and "civilization."

A harsher side to the ideology of imperialism found expression in **social Darwinism**. Its adherents applied Charles Darwin's evolutionary concept of "the survival of the fittest" to human society. This outlook suggested that European dominance inevitably led to the displacement or destruction of backward peoples or "unfit" races. Such views made imperialism, war, and aggression seem both natural and progressive, for weeding out "weaker" peoples of the world would allow the "stronger" to flourish. These were some of the ideas with which industrializing and increasingly powerful Europeans confronted the peoples of Asia and Africa in the nineteenth century.

A Second Wave of European Conquests

The imperialism of the long nineteenth century (1750–1900) continued the process of European colonial conquests that had begun with the takeover of the

Americas during the sixteenth and seventeenth centuries. Now it was focused in Asia, Africa, and Oceania rather than in the Western Hemisphere. And it featured a number of new players—Germany, Italy, Belgium, the United States, and Japan—who were not at all involved in the earlier phase, while the Spanish and Portuguese now had only minor roles. In general, Europeans preferred informal control, which operated through economic penetration and occasional military intervention but without a wholesale colonial takeover. Such a course was cheaper and less likely to provoke wars. But where rivalry with other European states made it impossible or where local governments were unable or unwilling to cooperate, Europeans proved more than willing to undertake the expense and risk of conquest and outright colonial rule.

Once established in a region, they frequently took advantage of moments of weakness in local societies to strengthen their control. "Each global drought was the green light for an imperialist landrush," wrote one scholar when examining the climatic instability that caused monsoon rains across Asia and parts of Africa to repeatedly fail in the second half of the nineteenth century.[10] Nowhere was this more evident than in Africa, where a drought in the southern part of the continent in 1877 coincided with British success in reining in Zulu independence, and famine in Ethiopia starting in the late 1880s coincided with Italian efforts to subdue the Horn of Africa.

The construction of these new European empires in the Afro-Asian world, like empires everywhere, involved military force or the threat of it. Increasingly in the nineteenth century, Europeans possessed overwhelming advantages in firepower, derived from the recently invented repeating rifles and machine guns. Nonetheless, Europeans had to fight, often long and hard, to create their new empires, as countless wars of conquest attest. In the end, though, they prevailed almost everywhere. Thus gathering and hunting bands in Australia, agricultural village societies or chiefdoms on Pacific islands and in parts of Africa, pastoralists of the Sahara and Central Asia, residents of states large and small, and virtually everyone in the large and complex civilizations of India and Southeast Asia—all of them alike lost the political sovereignty and freedom of action they had previously exercised.

CORE IDEA

■ Comparing Differences
In what different ways was colonial rule established in the various regions of Africa and Asia?

The passage to colonial status occurred in various ways. For the peoples of India and Indonesia, colonial conquest grew out of interaction with European trading firms that were authorized to conduct military operations and exercise political and administrative control over large areas. The British East India Company, rather than the British government directly, played the leading role in the colonial takeover of South Asia. The fragmentation of the Mughal Empire and the absence of any overall sense of cultural or political unity both invited and facilitated European penetration. A similar situation of many small and rival states assisted the Dutch acquisition of Indonesia. However, neither the British nor the Dutch had a clear-cut plan for conquest. Rather, in India it evolved slowly as local authorities and European traders made and unmade a variety of alliances with local states over roughly a century (1750–1850). In Indonesia, a few areas held out until the early twentieth century (see Map 18.1).

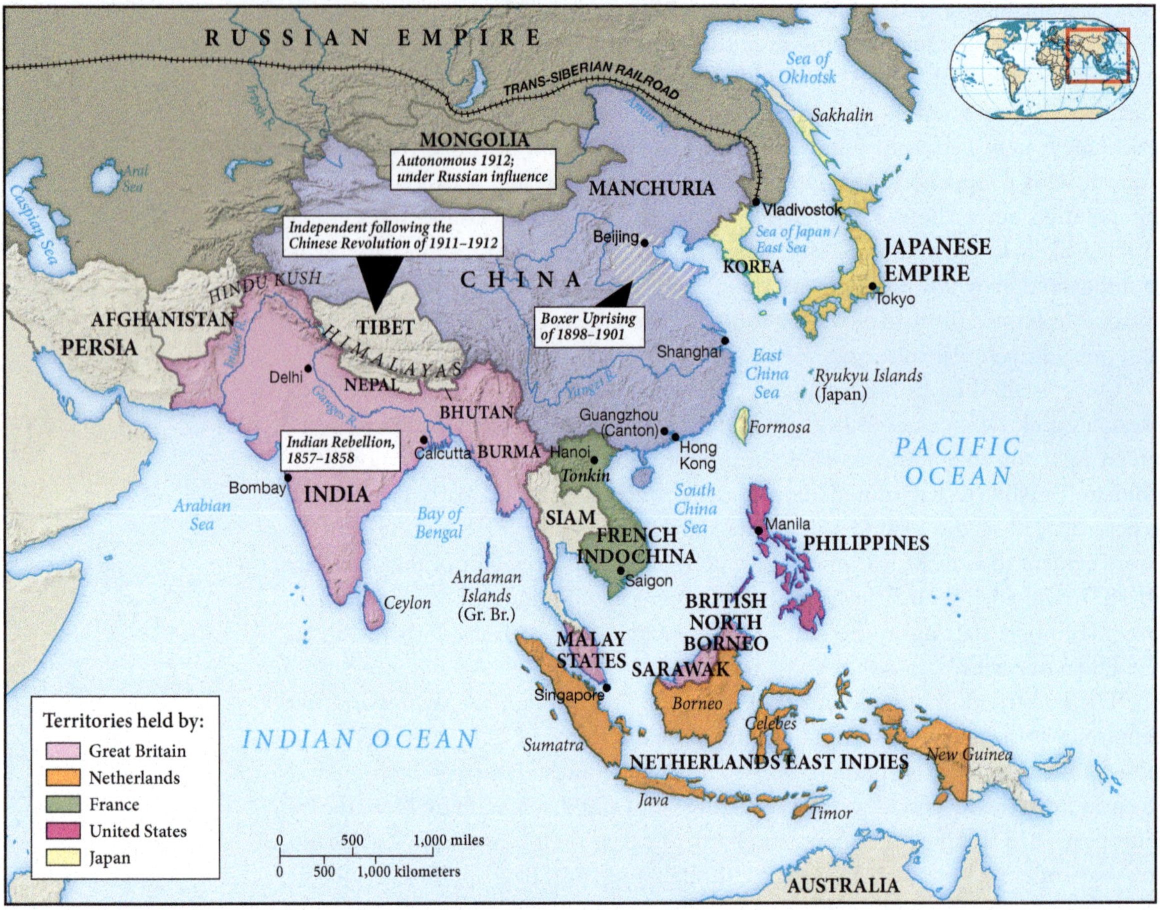

Map 18.1 Colonial Asia in the Early Twentieth Century

By the early twentieth century, several of the great population centers of Asia had come under the colonial control of Britain, the Netherlands, France, the United States, or Japan.

For most of Africa, mainland Southeast Asia, and the Pacific islands, colonial conquest came later, in the second half of the nineteenth century, and rather more abruptly and deliberately than in India or Indonesia. The "**scramble for Africa**," for example, pitted half a dozen European powers against one another as they partitioned the entire continent among themselves in only about twenty-five years (1875–1900). (See Working with Evidence: Colonial Conquest, page 817, for various perspectives on the "scramble.") European leaders themselves were surprised by the intensity of their rivalries and the speed with which they acquired huge territories, about which they knew very little.

That process involved endless but peaceful negotiations among the competing Great Powers about "who got what" and extensive and bloody military action, sometimes lasting decades, to make their control effective on the ground.

Among the most difficult to subdue were those decentralized societies without any formal state structure. In such cases, Europeans confronted no central authority with which they could negotiate or that they might decisively defeat. It was a matter of village-by-village conquest against extended resistance. As late as 1925, one British official commented on the process as it operated in central Nigeria: "I shall of course go on walloping them until they surrender. It's a rather piteous sight watching a village being knocked to pieces and I wish there was some other way, but unfortunately there isn't."[11] Another very difficult situation for the British lay in South Africa, where they were initially defeated by a Zulu army in 1879 at the Battle of Isandlwana. And twenty years later, in what became known as the Boer War (1899–1902), the Boers, white descendants of the earlier Dutch settlers in South Africa, fought bitterly for three years before succumbing to British forces (see Map 18.2). The colonial conquest of Africa was intensely resisted.

Europeans and Americans had been drawn into the world of Pacific Oceania during the eighteenth century through exploration and scientific curiosity, by the missionary impulse for conversion, and by their economic interests in sperm whale oil, coconut oil, guano, mineral nitrates and phosphates, sandalwood, and other products. Primarily in the second half of the nineteenth century, these entanglements morphed into competitive annexations as Britain, France, the Netherlands, Germany, and the United States, now joined by Australia, claimed control of all the islands of Oceania (see Map 18.1). Chile too, in search of valuable guano and nitrates, entered the fray and gained a number of coastal islands as well as Rapa Nui (Easter Island), the easternmost island of Polynesia.

The colonization of the South Pacific territories of Australia and New Zealand, both of which were taken over by the British during the nineteenth century, was more similar to the earlier colonization of North America than to contemporary patterns of Asian and African conquest. In both places, conquest was accompanied by large-scale European settlement and diseases that reduced native numbers by 75 percent or more by 1900. Like Canada and the United States, these became **settler colonies**, "neo-European" societies in the Pacific. Aboriginal Australians constituted only about 2.4 percent of their country's population in the early twenty-first century, and the indigenous Maori were a minority of about 15 percent in New Zealand. In other previously isolated regions as well—Polynesia, Amazonia, Siberia—disease took a terrible toll on peoples who lacked immunities to European pathogens. For example, the population of Hawaii declined from around 142,000 in 1823 to only 39,000 in 1896. Unlike these remote areas, most African and Asian regions shared with Europe a broadly similar disease environment and so were less susceptible to the pathogens of the conquerors.

Elsewhere other variations on the theme of imperial conquest unfolded. The westward expansion of the United States, for example, overwhelmed Native American populations and involved the country in an imperialist war with Mexico.

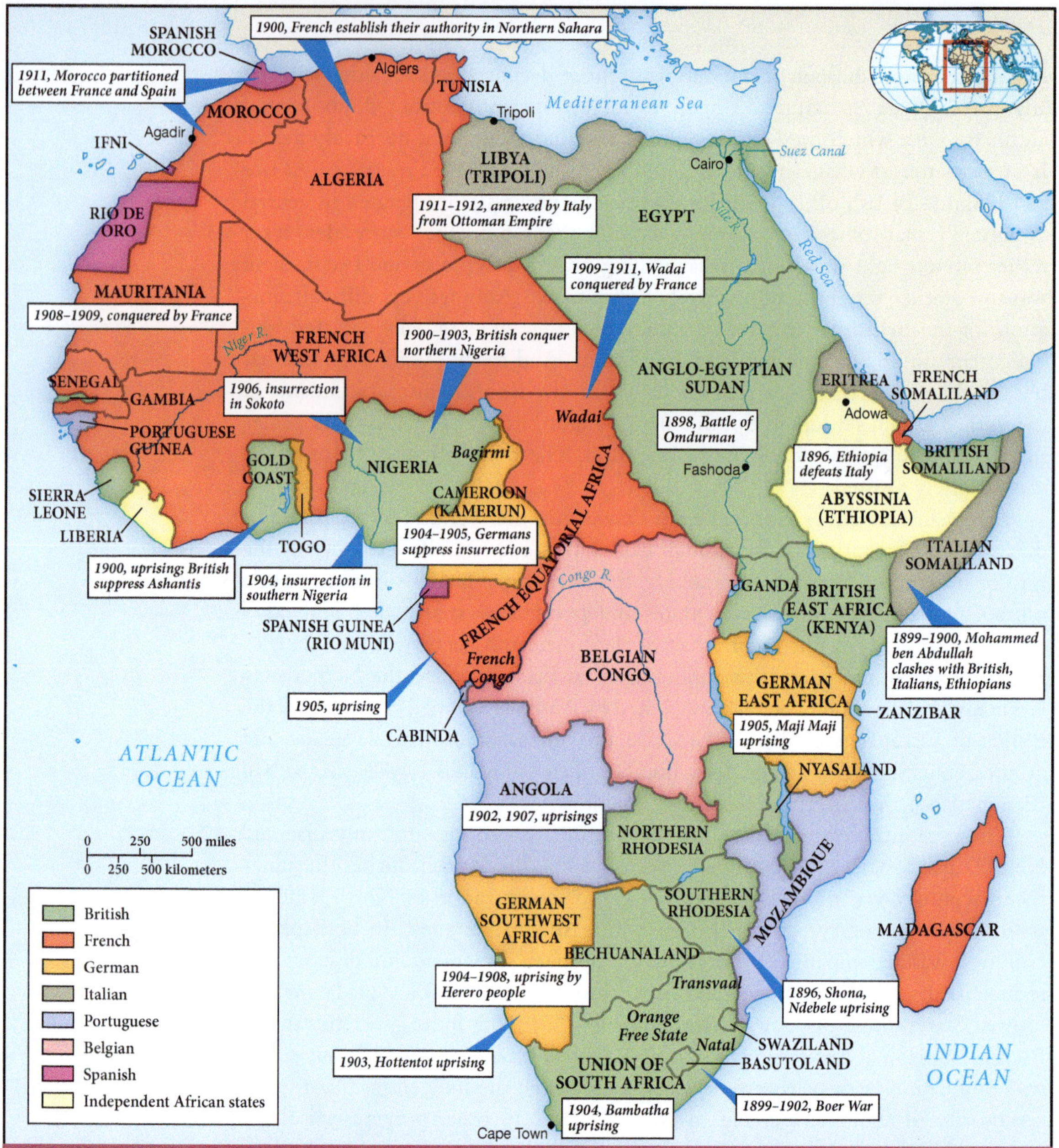

MAPPING HISTORY

Map 18.2 Conquest and Resistance in Colonial Africa

By the early twentieth century, the map of Africa reflected the outcome of the scramble for Africa, a conquest that was heavily resisted in many places.

READING THE MAP "France's colonial possessions were concentrated in north and west Africa, with Britain's colonies focused in eastern and southern Africa." To what extent is this statement accurate? What problems can you identify with this generalization?

INTERPRETING THE MAP Which European colonial powers experienced uprisings and insurrections more frequently than others? What regions of Africa experienced the most uprisings and insurrections? Can you make any generalizations concerning uprisings and insurrections based on these observations?

Seeking territory for white settlement, the United States practiced a policy of removing, sometimes almost exterminating, indigenous peoples. On the "reservations" to which they were confined and in boarding schools to which many of their children were removed, reformers sought to "civilize" the remaining Native Americans, eradicating tribal life and culture, under the slogan "Kill the Indian and Save the Man."

Japan's takeover of Taiwan and Korea bore marked similarities to European actions, as that East Asian nation joined the imperialist club. Russian penetration of Central Asia brought additional millions under European control as the Russian Empire continued its earlier territorial expansion. Filipinos acquired new colonial rulers when the United States took over from Spain following the Spanish-American War of 1898. Seeking greater freedom than was possible at home, some 13,000 formerly enslaved people from the United States migrated to West Africa, where they became, ironically, a colonizing elite in the land they named Liberia.

Ethiopia and Siam (Thailand) were notable for avoiding the colonization to which their neighbors succumbed. Those countries' military and diplomatic skills, their willingness to make modest concessions to the Europeans, and the rivalries of the imperialists all contributed to these exceptions to the rule of colonial takeover in East Africa and Southeast Asia. Ethiopia, in fact, considerably expanded its own empire, even as it defeated Italy at the Battle of Adowa in 1896.

These broad patterns of colonial conquest contained thousands of separate encounters as the target societies of Western empire builders were confronted with decisions about how to respond to encroaching European power in the context of their local circumstances. Many initially sought to enlist Europeans in their own internal struggles for power or in their rivalries with neighboring states or peoples. As pressures mounted and European demands escalated, some tried to play off imperial powers against one another, while others resorted to military action. Many societies were sharply divided between those who wanted to fight and those who believed that resistance was futile. After extended resistance against French aggression, the nineteenth-century Vietnamese emperor Tu Duc argued with those who wanted the struggle to go on: "Do you really wish to confront such a power with a pack of [our] cowardly soldiers? . . . With what you presently have, do you really expect to dissolve the enemy's rifles into air or chase his battleships into hell?"[12] Still others negotiated, attempting to preserve as much independence and power as possible. The rulers of the East African kingdom of Buganda, for example, saw opportunity in the British presence and negotiated an arrangement that substantially enlarged their state and personally benefited the kingdom's elite class.

Under European Rule

In many places and for many people, incorporation into European colonial empires was a traumatic experience. Especially for small-scale societies, the loss of life, homes, cattle, crops, and land was devastating. In 1902, a British soldier in East

Africa described what happened in a single village: "Every soul was either shot or bayoneted. . . . We burned all the huts and razed the banana plantations to the ground."[13]

For the Vietnamese elite, schooled for centuries in Chinese-style Confucian thinking, conquest meant that the natural harmonies of life had been badly disrupted, that "water flowed uphill." Nguyen Khuyen (1835–1909), a senior Vietnamese official, retired to his ancestral village to farm and write poetry after the French conquest, expressing his anguish at the passing of the world he had known. Many others also withdrew into private life, feigning illness when asked to serve in public office under the French.

Cooperation and Rebellion

Although violence was a prominent feature of colonial life both during conquest and after, various groups and many individuals willingly cooperated with colonial authorities to their own advantage. Many men found employment, status, and security in European-led armed forces. The shortage and expense of European administrators and the difficulties of communicating across cultural boundaries made it necessary for colonial rulers to rely heavily on a range of local intermediaries. Thus Indian princes, Muslim emirs, and African rulers, often from elite or governing families, found it possible to retain much of their earlier status and many of their privileges while gaining considerable wealth by exercising authority, legally and otherwise, at the local level. For example, in French West Africa, an area eight times the size of France and with a population of about 15 million in the late 1930s, the colonial state consisted of just 385 French administrators and more than 50,000 African "chiefs." Thus colonial rule rested on and reinforced the most conservative segments of colonized societies.

■ Analyzing Decisions
Why might subject peoples choose to cooperate with or to actively resist the colonial regime?

Both colonial governments and private missionary organizations had an interest in promoting a measure of European education. From this process arose a small Western-educated class, whose members served the colonial state, European businesses, and Christian missions as teachers, clerks, translators, and lower-level administrators. A few received higher education abroad and returned home as lawyers, doctors, engineers, or journalists. As colonial governments and business enterprises became more sophisticated, Europeans increasingly depended on the Western-educated class at the expense of the more traditional elites.

If colonial rule enlisted the willing cooperation of some, it provoked the bitter opposition of many others. Thus periodic rebellions, both large and small, erupted in colonial regimes everywhere. The most famous among them was the **Indian Rebellion of 1857–1858**, triggered by a mutiny among disaffected Indian troops in Meerut, near Delhi. Behind this incident were many groups of people with a whole series of grievances generated by the British colonial presence: troops whose religious beliefs and practices were transgressed, local rulers who had lost power, landlords deprived of their estates or their rent, peasants overtaxed and exploited by urban moneylenders and landlords alike, unemployed weavers displaced by machine-manufactured textiles, and religious leaders outraged by missionary preaching. Soon parts of India were aflame. Some rebel leaders presented their cause as an effort to revive an almost-vanished Mughal Empire. Although it was crushed in 1858, the rebellion greatly widened the racial divide in colonial India. It also convinced the British government to assume direct control over India, ending the era of British East India Company rule in the subcontinent. Fear of provoking another rebellion also made the British more conservative and cautious about deliberately trying to change Indian society.

Colonial Empires with a Difference

CORE IDEA

Identifying Distinctive Features What was distinctive about European colonial empires of the nineteenth century?

At one level, European colonial empires were but the latest in a very long line of imperial creations, all of which had enlisted cooperation and experienced resistance from their subject peoples, but the nineteenth-century European version of empire was distinctive in several remarkable ways. One was the prominence of race in distinguishing rulers as "superior" to the ruled, as the high tide of scientific racism in Europe coincided with the acquisition of Asian and African colonies. In East Africa, for example, white men expected to be addressed as *bwana* (Swahili for "master"), whereas Europeans regularly called African men "boy." Particularly affected by European racism were those whose Western education and aspirations most clearly threatened the racial divide. For example, a proposal in 1883 to allow Indian judges to hear cases involving whites provoked outrage and massive demonstrations among European inhabitants of India.

In those colonies that had a large European settler population, the expression of racial distinctions was much more pronounced than in places that had few permanently settled whites. The most extreme case was South Africa, where a large European population and the widespread use of African labor in mines and industries brought blacks and whites into closer and more prolonged contact than elsewhere. Racial fears among whites resulted in extraordinary efforts to establish race as a legal, not just a customary, feature of South African society. This racial system provided for separate "homelands," educational systems, residential areas, public facilities, and much more. In what was eventually known as apartheid, South African whites attempted the impossible task of creating an industrializing economy based on cheap African labor while limiting African social and political integration in every conceivable fashion.

A further distinctive feature of nineteenth-century European empires lay in the extent to which colonial states were able to penetrate the societies they governed. Centralized tax-collecting bureaucracies, new means of communication and transportation, imposed changes in landholding patterns, integration of colonial economies into a global network of exchange, public health and sanitation measures, and the activities of missionaries—all of this touched the daily lives of many people far more deeply than in earlier empires. Not only were Europeans foreign rulers, but they also bore the seeds of a very different way of life that had grown out of their own modern transformation.

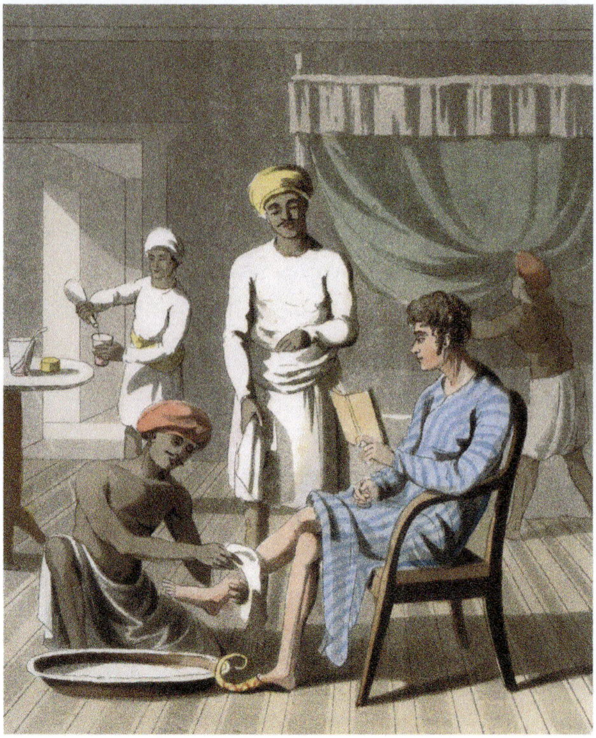

European Master and Indian Servants This image, dating to 1812, shows a young European gentleman attended by multiple servants in colonial India. It illustrates the exalted status available to quite ordinary Europeans in a colonial setting as well as the sharp racial divide separating Europeans and Indians. (Historia/Shutterstock)

Nineteenth-century European colonizers were extraordinary as well in their penchant for counting and classifying their subject people. With the assistance of anthropologists and missionaries, colonial governments collected a vast amount of information, sought to organize it "scientifically," and used it to manage the unfamiliar, complex, varied, and fluctuating societies that they governed. In India, the British found in classical texts and Brahmin ideology an idealized description of the caste system, based on the notion of four ranked and unchanging varnas. It was a vast simplification of the immense complexity and variety of caste as it actually operated. Thus the British invented or appropriated a Brahmin version of "traditional India" that they favored and sought to preserve, while scorning as "non-Indian" the new elite who had been educated in European schools and were enthusiastic about Western ways of life. This view of India reflected the great influence of Brahmins on British thinking and clearly served the interests of this Indian upper class.

Likewise, within African colonies Europeans identified, and sometimes invented, distinct tribes, each with its own clearly defined territory, language, customs, and chief. The notion of a "tribal Africa" expressed the Western view that African societies were primitive or backward, representing an earlier stage of human development. It was also a convenient idea, for it reduced the enormous complexity and fluidity of African societies to a more manageable state and thus made colonial administration easier.

Gender too entered into the efforts of Europeans to define both themselves and their newly acquired subject peoples. European colonizers—mostly male—took pride in their "active masculinity" while defining the "conquered races" as soft, passive, and feminine. Indian Bengali men, wrote a British official in 1892, "are disqualified for political enfranchisement by the possession of essentially feminine characteristics."[14] By linking the inferiority of women with that of people of color, imperialists joined gender ideology and race prejudice in support of colonial rule. But the intersection of race, gender, and empire was complex and varied. European men in the colonies often viewed their own women as the bearers and emblems of civilization, "upholding the moral dignity of the white community" amid the darkness of inferior peoples.[15] As such, European women had to be above reproach in sexual matters, protected against the alleged lust of native men by their separation from local societies. Furthermore, certain colonized people, such as the Sikhs and Gurkhas in India, the Kamba in Kenya, and the Hausa in Nigeria, were gendered as masculine or "martial races" and targeted for recruitment into British military or police forces.

Finally, the colonial policies of Europeans contradicted their own core values and their practices at home to an unusual degree. While nineteenth-century Britain and France were becoming more democratic, their colonies were essentially dictatorships, where few colonial subjects participated as citizens. Empire, of course, was wholly at odds with European notions of national independence, and ranked racial classifications went against the grain of both Christian and Enlightenment ideas of human equality. Furthermore, many Europeans were distinctly reluctant to encourage within their colonies the kind of modernization—urban growth, industrialization, individual values, religious skepticism—that was sweeping their own societies. They feared that this kind of social change, often vilified as "detribalization," would encourage unrest and challenge colonial rule. As a model for social development, they much preferred "traditional" rural society, with its established authorities and social hierarchies, though shorn of abuses such as slavery and *sati* (widow burning). Such contradictions between what Europeans embraced at home and what they practiced in the colonies became increasingly apparent to many Asians and Africans and played a major role in undermining the foundations of colonial rule in the twentieth century.

Ways of Working: Comparing Colonial Economies

Colonial rule affected the lives of its subject people in many ways, but the most pronounced change was in their ways of working. The colonial state—with its power to tax, to seize land for European enterprises, to compel labor, and to build railroads, ports, and roads—played an important role in these transformations. Even more powerful was the growing integration of colonized societies into a world economy that increasingly demanded their gold, diamonds, copper, tin, rubber, coffee, cotton, sugar, cocoa, and many other products. But the economic transformations born of these twin pressures were far from uniform. Various groups—migrant workers and cash-crop farmers, plantation laborers and domestic servants, urban elites and day laborers, men and women—experienced the colonial era differently as their daily working lives underwent profound changes.

To various degrees, old ways of working were eroded almost everywhere in the colonial world. Subsistence farming, in which peasant families produced largely for their own needs, diminished as growing numbers directed at least some of their energies to working for wages or selling what they produced for a cash income. That money was both necessary to pay taxes and school fees and useful for buying the various products—such as textiles, bicycles, and kerosene—that the industrial economies of Europe sent their way. As in Europe, artisans suffered greatly when cheaper machine-manufactured merchandise displaced their own handmade goods.

CORE IDEA

Comparing Changes

In what different ways did the colonial experience reshape the economic lives of Asian and African societies?

A flood of inexpensive textiles from Britain's new factories ruined the livelihood of tens of thousands of India's handloom weavers. Iron smelting largely disappeared in Africa, and occupations such as blacksmithing and tanning lost ground. Furthermore, Asian and African merchants, who had earlier handled the trade between their countries and the wider world, were squeezed out by well-financed European commercial firms.

Economies of Coercion: Forced Labor and the Power of the State

Many of the new ways of working that emerged during the colonial era derived directly from the demands of the colonial state. The most obvious was required and unpaid labor on public projects, such as building railroads, constructing government buildings, and transporting goods. In French Africa, all "natives" were legally obligated to do "statute labor" for ten to twelve days a year, a practice that lasted through 1946. It was much resented. A resident of British West Africa, interviewed in 1996, bitterly recalled this feature of colonial life: "They [British officials] were rude, and they made us work for them a lot. They came to the village and just rounded us up and made us go off and clear the road or carry loads on our heads."[16]

■ Assessing Cause and Effect
How did the policies of colonial states change the economic lives of their subjects?

The most infamous cruelties of forced labor occurred during the early twentieth century in the **Congo Free State**, then governed personally by King Leopold II of Belgium. Private companies in the Congo, operating under the authority of the state, forced villagers to collect rubber, which was much in demand for bicycle and automobile tires, with a reign of terror and abuse beginning in the 1890s that cost millions of lives. One refugee from these horrors described the process:

> We were always in the forest to find the rubber vines, to go without food, and our women had to give up cultivating the fields and gardens. Then we starved. . . . We begged the white man to leave us alone, saying we could get no more rubber, but the white men and their soldiers said "Go. You are only beasts yourselves. . . ." When we failed and our rubber was short, the soldiers came to our towns and killed us. Many were shot, some had their ears cut off; others were tied up with ropes round their necks and taken away.[17]

Eventually such outrages were widely publicized in Europe, where they created a scandal, forcing the Belgian government to take control of the Congo in 1908 and ending Leopold's reign of terror.

A variation on the theme of forced labor took shape in the so-called **cultivation system** of the Netherlands East Indies (Indonesia) during the nineteenth century. Peasants were required to cultivate 20 percent or more of their land in cash crops such as sugar or coffee to meet their tax obligation to the state. Sold to government contractors at fixed and low prices, those crops, when resold on the world market, proved highly profitable for Dutch traders as well as for the Dutch state and its citizens. According to one scholar, the cultivation system "performed a miracle for the

Dutch economy," enabling it to avoid taxing its own people and providing capital for its Industrial Revolution.[18] It also enriched and strengthened the position of those "traditional authorities" who enforced the system, often by using lashings and various tortures, on behalf of the Dutch. For the peasants of Java, however, it meant a double burden of obligations to the colonial state as well as to local lords. Many became indebted to moneylenders when they could not meet those obligations. Those demands, coupled with the loss of land and labor now excluded from food production, contributed to a wave of famines during the mid-nineteenth century in which hundreds of thousands perished.

On occasion, the forced cultivation of cash crops was successfully resisted. In German East Africa, for example, colonial authorities in the late nineteenth century imposed the cultivation of cotton, which seriously interfered with production of local food crops. Here is how one man remembered the experience:

> Every village was allotted days on which to cultivate. . . . After arriving you all suffered very greatly. Your back and your buttocks were whipped and there was no rising up once you stooped to dig. . . . And yet he [the German] wanted us to pay him tax. Were we not human beings?[19]

Colonial Violence in the Congo Horrific photos of mutilated children had an important impact on public opinion about imperial rule in the Congo Free State. They came to symbolize widespread abuses, including murders, rapes, starvation, and the burning of villages, associated with efforts to obtain supplies of wild rubber for use in industrialized societies. (Universal History Archive/Getty Images)

Such conditions prompted a massive rebellion in 1904–1905, known as Maji Maji, and persuaded the Germans to end the forced growing of cotton. Thus the actions of colonized peoples could alter or frustrate the plans of the colonizers.

Economies of Cash-Crop Agriculture: The Pull of the Market

Many Asian and African peoples had produced quite willingly for an international market long before they were enclosed within colonial societies. They offered for trade items such as peanuts and palm oil in West Africa, cotton in Egypt, spices in Indonesia, and pepper and textiles in India. In some places, colonial rule created conditions that facilitated and increased **cash-crop production** to the advantage of local farmers. British authorities in Burma, for example, acted to encourage rice production among small farmers by ending an earlier prohibition on rice exports, providing irrigation and transportation facilities, and enacting land tenure laws that facilitated private ownership of small farms. Under these conditions, the population of the Irrawaddy Delta boomed, migrants from Upper Burma and India poured into the region, and rice exports soared. Local small farmers benefited considerably because they were now able to own their own land, build substantial houses, and buy imported goods. For several decades in the late nineteenth century, standards of living improved sharply, and huge increases in rice production fed millions of people in other parts of Asia and elsewhere. It was a very different situation from that of peasants forced to grow crops that seriously interfered with their food production.

Analyzing Change How did cash-crop agriculture transform the lives of colonized peoples?

But that kind of colonial development, practiced also in the Mekong River delta of French-ruled Vietnam, had important environmental consequences. It involved the destruction of mangrove forests and swamplands along with the fish and shellfish that supplemented local diets. New dikes and irrigation channels inhibited the depositing of silt from upstream and thus depleted soils in the deltas of these major river systems. And, unknown to anyone at the time, this kind of agriculture generates large amounts of methane gas, a major contributor to global warming.

Profitable cash-crop farming also developed in the southern Gold Coast (present-day Ghana), a British territory in West Africa. Unlike in Burma, it was African farmers themselves who took the initiative to develop export agriculture. Planting cacao trees in huge quantities, they became the world's leading supplier of cocoa, used to make chocolate, by 1911. Cacao was an attractive crop because, unlike cotton, it was compatible with the continued production of foods and did not require as much labor. In the early twentieth century, it brought a new prosperity to many local farmers. But that success brought new problems in its wake. A shortage of labor fostered the employment of former enslaved people as dependent and exploited workers and also generated tensions between the sexes when some men married women for their labor but refused to support them adequately. Moreover, the labor shortage brought a huge influx of migrants from the drier interior parts of West Africa, generating ethnic and class tensions. Another problem was that many colonies came to specialize in one or two cash crops, creating an unhealthy dependence when world market prices dropped. Thus African and Asian farmers were increasingly subject to the uncertain rhythms of the international marketplace as well as to those of weather and climate.

Economies of Wage Labor: Migration for Work

Yet another new way of working in colonial societies involved wage labor in some European enterprise. Driven by the need for money, by the loss of land adequate to support their families, or sometimes by the orders of colonial authorities, millions of colonial subjects across Asia, Africa, and Oceania sought employment in European-owned plantations, mines, construction projects, and homes. Often this required migration to distant work sites, many of them overseas. In this process, colonized migrants were joined by millions of Chinese, Japanese, and others who lived in more independent states. Together they generated vast streams of migration that paralleled and at least equaled in numbers the huge movement of Europeans during the nineteenth and early twentieth centuries. For Europeans, Asians, and Africans alike, the globalizing world of the colonial era was one of people in motion. (See the Snapshot on long-distance migration.)

The African segment of this migratory stream moved in several directions. For much of the nineteenth century, the Atlantic slave trade continued, funneling well over 3 million additional people to the Americas, mostly to Brazil. As the slave trade diminished and colonial rule took shape in Africa, internal migration mounted within or among particular colonies. More than in Asia, Africans migrated to farms or plantations controlled by Europeans because they had lost their own land. In the settler colonies of Africa—Algeria, Kenya, Southern Rhodesia (Zimbabwe), and South Africa, for example—permanent European communities, with the help of colonial governments, obtained huge tracts of land, much of which had previously been home to Africans. A 1913 law in South Africa legally defined 88 percent of the land as belonging to whites, who were then about 20 percent of the population. Much of highland Kenya, an enormously rich agricultural region that was home to the Gikuyu and Kamba peoples, was taken over by some 4,000 white farmers. In such places, some Africans stayed on as "squatters," working for the new landowners as the price of remaining on what had been their own land. Others were displaced to "native reserves," limited areas that could not support their growing populations. In South Africa, such reserved areas became greatly overcrowded: soil fertility declined, hillsides were cleared, forests shrank, and erosion scarred the land. This kind of ecological degradation forced ever more Africans into wage labor in European enterprises.

SNAPSHOT Long-Distance Migration in an Age of Empire, 1846–1940

The age of empire was also an age of global migration. Beyond the three major patterns of long-distance migration shown here, shorter migrations within particular regions or colonies set millions more into motion.

Origins	Destination	Numbers
Europe	Americas	55–58 million
India, southern China	Southeast Asia, Indian Ocean rim, South Pacific	48–52 million
Northeast Asia, Russia	Manchuria, Siberia, Central Asia, Japan	46–51 million

Source: Data from Adam McKeown, "Global Migration, 1846–1940," *Journal of World History* 15, no. 2 (2004): 156.

The gold and diamond mines of South Africa likewise set in motion a huge pattern of labor migration that encompassed all of Africa south of the Belgian Congo. With skilled and highly paid work reserved for white miners, Africans worked largely as unskilled laborers at a fraction of the wages paid to whites. Furthermore, they were recruited on short-term contracts, lived in all-male prison-like barracks that were often surrounded by barbed wire, and were forced to return home periodically to prevent them from establishing a permanent family life near the mines.

Asians too were in motion and in large numbers. Some 29 million Indians and 19 million Chinese migrated variously to Southeast Asia, the South Pacific, East and South Africa, the Caribbean, or the lands around the Indian Ocean basin. All across Southeast Asia in the later nineteenth and early twentieth centuries, huge plantations sprouted that were financed from Europe and that grew sugarcane, rubber, tea, tobacco, sisal (used for making rope), and more. Impoverished workers by the hundreds of thousands came from great distances (India and China) to these plantations, where they were subject to strict control, often housed in barracks, and paid poorly, with women receiving 50 to 75 percent of a man's wage. Disease was common, and death rates were at least double that of the colony as a whole. In 1927 in southern Vietnam alone, one in twenty plantation workers died. British colonial authorities facilitated the migration of millions of Indians to work sites elsewhere in the British Empire—Trinidad, Jamaica, Fiji, Malaysia, Ceylon, South Africa, Kenya, Uganda, among others. Some worked as indentured laborers, receiving free passage and enough money to survive in return for five to seven years of heavy labor. Others operated as independent merchants. Particularly in the Caribbean region, Indian migration rose as the end of slavery created a need for additional labor. Since the vast majority of these Asian migrants were male, gender ratios were altered on the islands and in their countries of origin, where women faced increased workloads.

Economic Change in the Colonial World These workers at a Malayan tin-mining facility in the early twentieth century were just a few of the millions drawn from as far away as China and India to labor in the mines and on the plantations of Southeast Asia. (© Look and Learn/Bridgeman Images)

Mines were another source of wage labor for many Asians. In the British-ruled Malay States (Malaysia), tin mining accelerated greatly in the late nineteenth century, and by 1895 that colony produced some 55 percent of the world's tin. Operated initially by Chinese and later by European entrepreneurs, Malaysian tin mines drew many millions of impoverished Chinese workers on strictly controlled three-year contracts. Appalling living conditions, disease, and accidents generated extraordinarily high death rates.

Assessing Choice What kinds of wage labor were available in the colonies, and why might people choose this work? How did doing so affect their lives?

Beyond Southeast Asia, Chinese migrants moved north to Manchuria in substantial numbers, encouraged by a Chinese government eager to prevent Russian encroachment in the area. The gold rushes of Australia and California also attracted hundreds of thousands of Chinese, who often found themselves subject to sharp discrimination from local people, including recently arrived European migrants. For example, Dennis Kearney, who led a California anti-immigrant labor organization with the slogan "The Chinese must go," was himself an Irish-born immigrant. Canada, Australia, New Zealand, and the United States all enacted measures to restrict or end Chinese immigration in the late nineteenth century.

A further destination of African and Asian migrants lay in the rapidly swelling cities of the colonial world—Lagos, Nairobi, Cairo, Calcutta, Rangoon, Batavia, Singapore, Saigon. Racially segregated, often unsanitary, and greatly overcrowded, these cities nonetheless were seen as meccas of opportunity for people all across the social spectrum. Traditional elites, absentee landlords, and wealthy Chinese businessmen occupied the top rungs of Southeast Asian cities. Western-educated people everywhere found opportunities as teachers, doctors, and professional specialists, but more often as clerks in European business offices and government bureaucracies. Skilled workers on the railways or in the ports represented a working-class elite, while a few labored in the factories that processed agricultural goods or manufactured basic products such as beer, cigarettes, cement, and furniture. Far more numerous were the construction workers, rickshaw drivers, food sellers, domestic servants, prostitutes, and others who made up the urban poor of colonial cities. In 1955, a British report on life in Nairobi, the capital of Kenya, found that low wages, combined with the high cost of housing and food, "makes family life impossible for the majority."[20] After a half century of colonial rule, it was quite an admission.

Women and the Colonial Economy: Examples from Africa

If economic life in European empires varied greatly from place to place, even within the same colony, it also offered a different combination of opportunities and hardships to women than it did to men, as the experience of colonial Africa shows.[21] In precolonial Africa, women were almost everywhere active farmers, with responsibility for planting, weeding, and harvesting in addition to food preparation and child care. Men cleared the land, built houses, herded the cattle, and in some cases assisted with field work. Within this division of labor, women were expected to feed their own families and were usually allocated their own fields for that purpose. Many were also involved in local trading activity. Though clearly subordinate to men, African women nevertheless had a measure of economic autonomy.

Analyzing Change
In what ways did colonial economies affect the lives of African women?

As the demands of the colonial economy grew, women's lives increasingly diverged from those of men. In colonies where cash-crop agriculture was dominant, men often withdrew from subsistence production in favor of more lucrative export crops. Among the Ewe people of southern Ghana, for example, men almost completely dominated the highly profitable cacao farming, whereas women assumed nearly total responsibility for domestic food production. Thus when men focused on cash-crop agriculture, the subsistence workload of women increased. One study from Cameroon estimated that women's working hours increased from forty-six per week in precolonial times to more than seventy by 1934.

Further increasing women's workload and differentiating their lives from those of men was labor migration. As growing numbers of men sought employment in the cities, on settler farms, or in the mines, their wives were left to manage the domestic economy almost alone. In many cases, women also had to supply food to men in the cities to compensate for very low urban wages. They often took over such traditionally male tasks as breaking the ground for planting, milking the cows, and supervising the herds, in addition to their normal responsibilities. In South Africa, where the demands of the European economy were particularly heavy, some 40 to 50 percent of able-bodied adult men were absent from the rural areas, and women headed 60 percent of households. In Botswana, which supplied much male labor to South Africa, married couples by the 1930s rarely lived together for more than two months at a time. Increasingly, men and women lived in different worlds, with one focused on the cities and working for wages and the other on village life and subsistence agriculture.

Women coped with these difficult circumstances in a number of ways. Many sought closer relations with their families of birth rather than with their absent husbands' families, as would otherwise have been expected. Among the Luo of Kenya, women introduced laborsaving crops, adopted new farm implements, and earned some money as traders. In the cities, they established a variety of self-help associations, including those for prostitutes and for brewers of beer.

The colonial economy sometimes provided a measure of opportunity for enterprising women, particularly in small-scale trade and marketing. In some parts of West Africa, women came to dominate this sector of the economy by selling foodstuffs, cloth, and inexpensive imported goods, while men or foreign firms controlled the more profitable wholesale and import-export trade. Such opportunities sometimes gave women considerable economic autonomy. By the 1930s, for example, Nupe women in northern Nigeria had gained sufficient wealth as itinerant traders that they were contributing more to the family income than their husbands and frequently lent money to them. Among some Igbo groups in southern Nigeria, men were responsible for growing the prestigious yams, but women's crops—especially cassava—came to have a cash value during the colonial era, and women were entitled to keep the profits from selling them. "What is man? I have my own money" was a popular saying that expressed the growing economic independence of such women.[22]

At the other end of the social scale, women of impoverished rural families, by necessity, often became virtually independent heads of household in the absence of their husbands. Others took advantage of new opportunities in mission schools, towns, and mines to flee the restrictions of rural patriarchy. Such challenges to patriarchal values elicited various responses from men, including increased accusations of witchcraft against women. Among the Shona in Southern Rhodesia, and no doubt elsewhere, senior African men repeatedly petitioned the colonial authorities for laws and regulations that would criminalize adultery and restrict women's ability to leave their rural villages. The control of women's sexuality and mobility was a common interest of European and African men.

Women and Peanut Production in Gambia In this photograph from the British colony of Gambia in West Africa, women are threshing peanuts, separating the nuts from the plants on which they grow. Throughout the colonial era, peanuts were the colony's major export crop, and women were heavily involved in their production. (Popperfoto/Getty Images)

Assessing Colonial Development

Beyond the many and varied changes that transformed the working lives of millions in the colonial world lies the difficult and highly controversial question of the overall economic impact of colonial rule on Asian and African societies. Defenders, both then and now, praise it for jump-starting modern economic growth, but numerous critics cite a record of exploitation and highlight the limitations and unevenness of that growth.

Amid the continuing debates, three things seem reasonably clear. First, colonial rule served, for better or worse, to further the integration of Asian and African economies into a global network of exchange, now centered in Europe. Within the colonial world far more land and labor were devoted to production for the global market at the end of the colonial era than at its beginning. Many colonized groups and individuals benefited from their new access to global markets—Burmese rice farmers and West African cocoa farmers, for example. Others were devastated. In India, large-scale wheat exports to Britain continued unchecked—or even increased—despite a major drought and famine that claimed between 6 and 10 million lives in the late 1870s. A colonial government committed to free market principles and white superiority declined to interfere with those exports or to provide much by way of relief. One senior official declared it "a mistake to spend so much money to save a lot of black fellows."[23]

■ Assessing Change
Did colonial rule bring economic "progress" in its wake?

Second, Europeans could hardly avoid conveying to the colonies some elements of their own modernizing process. It was in their interests to do so, and many felt duty bound to "improve" the societies they briefly governed. Modern administrative and bureaucratic structures facilitated colonial control; transportation and communication infrastructure (railroads, ports, telegraphs, postal services) moved products to the world market; schools trained the army of intermediaries on which colonial rule depended; and modest health care provisions fulfilled some of the "civilizing mission" to which many Europeans felt committed. These elements of modernization made an appearance, however inadequately, during the colonial era.

Third, nowhere in the colonial world did a major breakthrough to modern industrial society occur. When India became independent after two centuries of colonial rule by the world's first industrial society, it was still one of the poorest of the world's developing countries. The British may not have created Indian poverty, but neither did they overcome it to any substantial degree. Scholars continue to debate the reasons for that failure: was it the result of deliberate British policies, or was it due to the conditions of Indian society? The nationalist movements that surged across Asia and Africa in the twentieth century had their own answer. To their many millions of participants, colonial rule, whatever its earlier promise, had become an economic dead end, whereas independence represented a grand opening to new and more hopeful possibilities. Taking off from a famous teaching of Jesus, Kwame Nkrumah, the first prime minister of an independent Ghana, declared, "Seek ye first the political kingdom, and all these other things [schools, factories, hospitals, for example] will be added unto you."

Believing and Belonging: Identity and Cultural Change

Beyond profound economic transformations, the experience of colonial rule—its racism, its exposure to European culture, its social and economic upheavals—also generated new patterns of identity within Asian, African, and Oceanic societies. Millions of people underwent substantial and quite rapid changes in what they believed and in how they defined the communities to which they belonged. Those new ways of believing and belonging echoed long after European rule had ended.

Education

For an important minority, it was the acquisition of Western education, obtained through missionary or government schools, that generated a new identity. To previously illiterate people, the knowledge of reading and writing of any kind often suggested an almost magical power. Within the colonial setting, it could mean an escape from some of the most onerous obligations of living under European control, such as forced labor. More positively, it meant access to better-paying positions in government bureaucracies, mission organizations, or business firms and to the exciting imported goods that their salaries could buy. Moreover, education often provided social mobility and elite status within colonized peoples' own communities and an opportunity to achieve, or at least approach, equality with whites in racially defined societies. An African man from colonial Kenya described an encounter he had as a boy in 1938 with a relative who was a teacher in a mission school:

> Aged about 25, he seems to me like a young god with his smart clothes and shoes, his watch, and a beautiful bicycle. I worshipped in particular his bicycle that day and decided that I must somehow get myself one. As he talked with us, it seemed to me that the secret of his riches came from his education, his knowledge of reading and writing, and that it was essential for me to obtain this power.[24]

CORE IDEA

Analyzing Change
How were new cultural identities forged during the colonial era?

Many such people ardently embraced European culture, dressing in European clothes, speaking French or English, building European-style houses, getting married in long white dresses, and otherwise emulating European ways. Some of the early Western-educated Bengalis from northeastern India boasted about dreaming in English and deliberately ate beef, to the consternation of their elders. In a well-known poem titled "A Prayer for Peace," Léopold Senghor, a highly educated West African writer and political leader, enumerated the many crimes of colonialism and yet confessed, "I have a great weakness for France." Asian and African colonial societies now had a new cultural divide: between the small numbers who had mastered to varying degrees the ways of their rulers and the vast majority who had not. Literate Christians in the East African kingdom of Buganda referred with contempt to their "pagan" neighbors as "those who do not read."

Many among the Western-educated elite saw themselves as a modernizing vanguard, leading the regeneration of their societies in association with colonial authorities. For them, at least initially, the colonial enterprise was full of promise for a better future. The Vietnamese teacher and nationalist Nguyen Thai Hoc, while awaiting execution in 1930 by the French for his revolutionary activities, wrote about his earlier hopes: "At the beginning, I had thought to cooperate with the French in Indochina in order to serve my compatriots, my country, and my people, particularly in the areas of cultural and economic development."[25]

Assessing Impact
What impact did Western education have on colonized societies?

In nineteenth-century India, Western-educated men organized a variety of reform societies that drew inspiration from the classic texts of Hinduism while seeking a renewed Indian culture that was free of idolatry, caste restrictions, and other "errors" that had entered Indian life over the centuries. Much of this reform effort centered on improving the status of women. Thus reformers campaigned against *sati*, the ban on remarriage of widows, female infanticide, and child marriages, while advocating women's education and property rights. For a time, some of these Indian reformers saw themselves working in tandem with British colonial authorities. One of them, Keshub Chunder Sen, addressed his fellow Indians in 1877: "You are bound to be loyal to the British government that came to your rescue, as God's ambassador, when your country was sunk in ignorance and superstition. . . . India in her present fallen condition seems destined to sit at the feet of England for many long years, to learn western art and science."[26]

The Educated Elite Throughout the Afro-Asian world of the nineteenth century, the European presence generated a small group of people who enthusiastically embraced the culture and lifestyle of Europe. Here King Chulalongkorn of Siam poses with the crown prince and other young students, all of them impeccably garbed in European clothing. (Hulton Deutsch/Getty Images)

Those who held such hopes for the modernization of their societies within a colonial framework would be bitterly disappointed. Europeans generally declined to treat their Asian and African subjects—even those with a Western education—as equal partners in the enterprise of renewal. The frequent denigration of Asian and African cultures as primitive, backward, or uncivilized certainly rankled, particularly among the well educated. "My people of Africa," wrote the West African intellectual James Aggrey in the 1920s, "we were created in the image of God, but men have made us think that we are chickens, and we still think we are; but we are eagles. Stretch forth your wings and fly."[27] In the long run, the educated classes in colonial societies everywhere found European rule far more of an obstacle to their countries' development than a means of achieving it. Turning decisively against a now-despised foreign imperialism, they led the many struggles for independence that came to fruition in the second half of the twentieth century.

Religion

Religion too provided the basis for new or transformed identities during the colonial era. Most dramatic were those places where widespread conversion to Christianity took place, such as Pacific Oceania and especially non-Muslim Africa. Some 10,000 missionaries had descended on Africa by 1910; by the 1960s, about 50 million Africans, roughly half of the non-Muslim population, claimed a Christian identity. The attractions of the new faith were many. As in the Americas centuries earlier, military defeat shook confidence in the old gods and local practices, fostering openness to new sources of supernatural power that could operate in the wider world now impinging on Oceanic and African societies. Furthermore, Christianity was widely associated with modern education, and, especially in Africa, mission schools were its primary providers. The young, the poor, and many women—all of them oppressed groups in many African societies—found new opportunities and greater freedom in some association with missions. Moreover, the spread of the Christian message was less the work of European missionaries than of those many thousands of African teachers, catechists, and pastors who brought the new faith to remote villages as well as the local communities that begged for a teacher and supplied the labor and materials to build a small church or school. In Oceania, local authorities, such as those in Fiji, Tonga, and Hawaii, sought to strengthen their position by associating with Christian missionaries, widely regarded as linked to the growing influence of European or American power in the region. In many of these small island societies, mission Christianity with its schools, clinics, political counsel, and new social conventions provided a measure of social cohesion for peoples devastated by disease and other disruptions that accompanied Western incursions.

■ Assessing Religious Appeal
What were the attractions of Christianity in colonial Africa? What kinds of conflicts did it generate?

But missionary teaching and practice also generated conflict and opposition, particularly when they touched on gender roles. A wide range of issues focusing on the lives of women proved challenging for missionaries and spawned opposition from converts or potential converts. Female nudity offended Western notions of modesty. Polygyny contradicted Christian monogamy, though such prescriptions sat uneasily beside the biblical testimony that Old Testament figures such as Abraham, Jacob, David, and Solomon all had multiple wives. And the question of what male converts should do with their additional wives was always difficult. To many missionaries, bride wealth made marriage seem "a mere mercantile transaction." Marriages between Christians and non-Christians remained problematic. Sexual activity outside of monogamous marriage often resulted in disciplinary action or expulsion from the church. Missionaries' efforts to enforce Western gender norms were in part responsible for considerable turnover in the ranks of African church members.

Among the more explosive issues that agitated nascent Christian communities in colonial Kenya was that of **female circumcision**, the excision of a pubescent girl's clitoris and adjacent genital tissue as a part of initiation rites marking her coming-of-age. To the Gikuyu people, among whom it was widely practiced, it was a prerequisite for adult status and marriage. To missionaries, it was physically damaging to girls and brought "unnecessary attention . . . to the non-spiritual aspects of sex."[28] When missionaries in 1929 sought to enforce a ban on the practice among their African converts, outrage ensued. Thousands abandoned mission schools and churches, but they did not abandon Christianity or modern education. Rather, they created a series of independent schools and churches in which they could practice their new faith and pursue their educational goals without missionary intrusion. Some recalled that the New Testament itself had declared that "circumcision is nothing and uncircumcision is nothing." Accordingly, wrote one angry convert to a local missionary, "Has God spoken to you this time and informed you that those who circumcise will not enter in to God's place? It is better for a European like you to leave off speaking about such things because you can make the Gospel to be evil spoken of."[29]

As elsewhere, Christianity in Africa soon adapted to local cultural patterns. This **Africanization of Christianity** took many forms. Within mission-based churches, many converts continued using protective charms and medicines and consulting local medicine men, all of which caused their missionary mentors to speak frequently of "backsliding." Other converts continued to believe in their old gods and spirits but now deemed them evil and sought their destruction. Furthermore, thousands of separatist movements established a wide array of independent churches that were thoroughly Christian but under African rather than missionary control and that in many cases incorporated African cultural practices and modes of worship. It was a twentieth-century "African Reformation."

The Missionary Factor Among the major change agents of the colonial era were the thousands of Christian missionaries who brought not only a new religion but also elements of European medicine, education, gender roles, and culture. Here is an assembly at a mission school for girls in New Guinea in the early twentieth century. (Library of Congress, Prints & Photographs Division, Reproduction number LC-USZ62-46884 [b&w film copy neg. of half stereo])

In India, where Christianity made only very modest inroads, leading intellectuals and reformers began to define their region's endlessly varied beliefs, practices, sects, rituals, and philosophies as a more distinct, unified, and separate religion, now known as **Hinduism**. It was in part an effort to provide for India a religion wholly equivalent to Christianity, "an accessible tradition and a feeling of historical worth when faced with the humiliation of colonial rule."[30] To Swami **Vivekananda** (1863–1902), one of nineteenth-century India's most influential religious figures, as well as others active in reform movements, a revived Hinduism, shorn of its distortions, offered a means of uplifting the country's village communities, which were the heart of Indian civilization. It also served to distinguish a "spiritual East" from a "materialistic West." (See Zooming In: Vivekananda, a Hindu Monk in America, page 812.)

Explaining Religious Change
How and why did Hinduism emerge as a distinct religious tradition during the colonial era in India?

This new notion of Hinduism provided a cultural foundation for emerging ideas of India as a nation, but it also contributed to a clearer sense of Muslims as a distinct community in India. Before the British takeover, little sense of commonality united the many diverse communities who practiced Islam—urban and rural dwellers; nomads and farmers; artisans, merchants, and state officials. But the British had created one set of inheritance laws for all Muslims and another set for all Hindus; in their census taking, they counted the numbers of people within these now sharply distinguished groups; and they allotted seats in local councils according to these artificial categories. As some anti-British patriots began to cast India in Hindu terms, the idea of Muslims as a separate community that was perhaps threatened by the much larger number of Hindus began to make sense to some who practiced Islam. In the early twentieth century, a young Hindu Bengali schoolboy noticed that "our Muslim school-fellows were beginning to air the fact of their being Muslims rather more consciously than before and with a touch of assertiveness."[31] Here were the beginnings of what became in the twentieth century a profound religious and political division within the South Asian peninsula.

"Race" and "Tribe"

In Africa as well, intellectuals and ordinary people alike forged new ways of belonging as they confronted the upheavals of colonial life. Central to these new identities were notions of race and ethnicity. By the end of the nineteenth century, a number of African thinkers, familiar with Western culture, began to define the idea of an "**African identity**." Previously, few if any people on the continent had regarded themselves as Africans. Rather, they were members of particular local communities, usually defined by language; some were also Muslims; and still others inhabited some state or empire. Now, however, influenced by the common experience of colonial oppression and by a highly derogatory European racism, well-educated Africans began to think in broader terms, similar to those of Indian reformers who were developing the notion of Hinduism. It was an effort to revive the cultural self-confidence of their people by articulating a larger, common, and respected "African tradition," equivalent to that of Western culture.

This effort took various shapes. One line of argument held that African culture and history in fact possessed the very characteristics that Europeans exalted. Knowing that Europeans valued large empires and complex political systems, African intellectuals pointed with pride to the ancient kingdoms of Axum/Ethiopia, Mali,

ZOOMING IN

Vivekananda, a Hindu Monk in America

The modern colonial era is associated with the "westernization" of the peoples of Asia, Africa, and the Middle East. Less frequently noticed has been traffic in the other direction, as Eastern, and especially Indian, religious culture penetrated Europe and the Americas. At his cabin on Walden Pond in the mid-1840s, Henry David Thoreau remarked, "In the morning I bathe my intellect in the stupendous . . . philosophy of the Bhagavad Gita . . . in comparison with which our modern world and its literature seem puny and trivial."[32]

A more seminal moment in the coming of Indian spirituality to the United States occurred in Chicago during September 1893. The occasion was the World's Parliament of Religions, an interfaith gathering that drew representatives from many of the world's religious traditions. The man who made the most vivid impression at the conference was a handsome thirty-year-old Hindu monk known as Swami Vivekananda. Appearing in an orange robe and a yellow turban and speaking fluent and eloquent English, he had only recently arrived from India, where he had received an excellent European education as well as a deep immersion in Hindu philosophy and practice.

Swami Vivekananda.

In his initial speech to the parliament on its opening day, Vivekananda declared, "I am proud to belong to a religion which has taught the world both tolerance and universal acceptance. . . . We accept all religions as true." He concluded with a plea that the parliament might mark the end of sectarianism, fanaticism, and persecution "between persons wending their way to the same goal."

In further speeches at the parliament and in subsequent travels around the country, Vivekananda expressed the

photo: akg-images

Songhay, and others. C. A. Diop, a French-educated scholar from Senegal, insisted that Egyptian civilization was in fact the work of black Africans. Reversing European assumptions, Diop argued that Western civilization owed much to Egyptian influence and was therefore derived from Africa. Black people, in short, had a history of achievement fully comparable to that of Europe and therefore deserved just as much respect and admiration.

■ Defining Cultural Change
In what ways were "race" and "tribe" new identities in colonial Africa?

An alternative approach to defining an African identity lay in praising the differences between African and European cultures. The most influential proponent of such views was **Edward Blyden** (1832–1912), a West African born in the West Indies and educated in the United States who later became a prominent scholar and political official in Liberia. Blyden accepted the assumption that the world's various races were different but argued that each had its own distinctive contribution to make to world civilization. The uniqueness of African culture, Blyden wrote, lay in its communal, cooperative, and egalitarian societies, which contrasted sharply with Europe's highly individualistic, competitive, and class-ridden societies; in its major themes of his modernized Hindu outlook: that all human beings possess a divine nature; that awakening to that nature can be pursued through a variety of paths; and that spiritual practice and realization are far more important than dogma or doctrine. He argued that the disciplines of the mind and body that derived from Hindu tradition represented a psychological, experimental, and almost scientific approach to spiritual development and certainly did not require "conversion" to an alien faith. On occasion, he was sharply critical of Christian missionaries for their emphasis on conversion. "The people of India have more than religion enough," he declared. "What they want is bread." He described England as "the most prosperous Christian nation in the world with her foot on the neck of 250 million Asiatics."

Vivekananda emerged from the parliament a sensation and a celebrity, widely acclaimed but also widely criticized. His critique of Christian missionaries offended many. More conservative Christians objected to his assertion of the equality of all religious traditions. "We believe that Christianity is to supplant all other religions," declared the leading organizer of the parliament.

Vivekananda's time in the United States represented India speaking back to the West. After a century of European missionary activity and colonial rule in his country, he was declaring that India could offer spiritual support to a Western world mired in materialism and militarism. He proclaimed, "The whole of the Western world is a volcano which may burst tomorrow. . . . Now is the time to work so that India's spiritual ideas may penetrate deep into the West."[33]

In exposing Americans to Indian spirituality, Vivekananda's followers did not seek converts, but invited participants to apply Hindu principles and practices within their own religious traditions. They spoke about Jesus with great respect and displayed his image along with that of the Buddha and various Hindu sacred figures. In the early twentieth century, these ideas attracted a modest following among Americans who were disillusioned with the superficiality of modern life as well as with the rigidity of Christian doctrine and the many divisions and conflicts among Christian churches. In the 1960s and later, interest in Eastern religion exploded in the West as hundreds of Indian teachers arrived, many of them bearing the same universal message that Vivekananda had presented in Chicago. The growing numbers of Americans who claim to be "spiritual but not religious" are following in the path of that orange-robed monk.

QUESTION

What accounts for the appeal of Vivekananda's message, and what accounts for opposition to it?

harmonious relationship with nature as opposed to Europe's efforts to dominate and exploit the natural order; and particularly in its profound religious sensibility, which Europeans had lost in centuries of attention to material gain. Like Vivekananda in India, Blyden argued that Africa had a global mission "to be the spiritual conservatory of the world."[34]

In the twentieth century, such ideas resonated with a broader public. Hundreds of thousands of Africans took part in World War I, during which they encountered other Africans as well as Europeans. Some were able to travel widely. Contact with American black leaders, such as Booker T. Washington, W. E. B. Du Bois, and Marcus Garvey, as well as various West Indian intellectuals further stimulated among a few a sense of belonging to an even larger pan-African world. Such notions underlay the growing nationalist movements that contested colonial rule as the twentieth century unfolded.

For the vast majority, however, the most important new sense of belonging that evolved from the colonial experience was not the notion of "Africa"; rather, it was the **idea of "tribe"** or, in the language of contemporary scholars, that of ethnic identity. African peoples, of course, had long recognized differences among themselves based on language, kinship, clan, village, or state, but these were seldom clearly defined. Boundaries fluctuated and were hazy; local communities often incorporated a variety of culturally different peoples. The idea of an Africa sharply divided into separate and distinct "tribes" was in fact a European notion that facilitated colonial administration and reflected Europeans' belief in African primitiveness. By requiring people to identify their "tribe" on applications for jobs, schools, and identity cards, colonial governments spread the idea of tribe widely within their colonies.

But new ethnic identities were not simply imposed by Europeans, for Africans themselves increasingly found ethnic or tribal labels useful. This was especially true in rapidly growing urban areas. Surrounded by a bewildering variety of people and in a setting where competition for jobs, housing, and education was very intense, migrants to the city found it helpful to categorize themselves and others in larger ethnic terms. Thus, in many colonial cities, people who spoke similar languages, shared a common culture, or came from the same general part of the country began to think of themselves as a single people—a new tribe. They organized a rich variety of ethnic or tribal associations to provide mutual assistance while in the cities and to send money back home to build schools or clinics. Migrant workers, far from home and concerned about protecting their rights to land and to their wives and families, found a sense of security in being part of a recognized tribe, with its chiefs, courts, and established authority.

The Igbo people of southeastern Nigeria represent a case in point. Prior to the twentieth century, they were organized in a series of independently governed village groups. Although they spoke related languages, they had no unifying political system and no myth of common ancestry. Occupying a region of unusually dense population, many of these people eagerly seized on Western education and moved in large numbers to the cities and towns of colonial Nigeria. There they gradually discovered what they had in common and how they differed from the other peoples of Nigeria. By the 1940s, they were organizing on a national level and calling on Igbos everywhere to "sink all differences" to achieve "tribal unity, cooperation, and progress of all the Igbos." Fifty years earlier, however, no one had regarded himself or herself as an Igbo. One historian summed up the process of creating African ethnic identities: "Europeans believed Africans belonged to tribes; Africans built tribes to belong to."[35]

CONCLUSIONS AND REFLECTIONS

Who Makes History?

Winners may write history, at least temporarily, but they do not make history, at least not alone. Dominant groups everywhere—imperial rulers, upper classes, and men generally—have found their actions constrained and their choices limited by the sheer presence of subordinated people and the ability of those people to act. So it was in the colonial encounters of the long nineteenth century.

European colonial rulers clearly held the upper hand in those encounters. Their military power—repeating rifles and machine guns, for example—made conquest possible almost everywhere, enabled them to compel the labor and taxes of conquered people, and allowed them to create new states with new boundaries. Their industrializing economies drove imperial expansion and shaped the lives of millions as their demand for colonial foodstuffs, raw materials, investment opportunities, and export markets took hold around the world. In the colonies these processes transformed the working lives of colonial subjects as farmers increasingly produced for the world market and laborers migrated to distant sites for jobs in the mines and on the farms or plantations of Europeans. Colonial rulers also imported elements of their culture to the colonies—their languages, their Christian religion, their ideas about gender and sexuality, their racial prejudices, their educational systems, their medical practices, and more.

But colonized peoples were certainly not passive in these encounters, nor were European policies and intentions always realized in practice. Colonial conquest, though ultimately successful, was no cakewalk, as extended military resistance impeded European takeovers in many parts of Asia and Africa. Even after colonial rule was established, frequent rebellions, such as the massive Indian Rebellion of 1857–1858, punctuated the imposed peace of empire. Furthermore, some state authorities actively negotiated with European powers; through such means, Ethiopia and the Kingdom of Siam (Thailand) were able to maintain their precarious independence. Elsewhere, rulers in Buganda and Botswana in Africa and many Indian princes carved out a degree of autonomy for their states. Many individuals joined the administrative service or military forces of their colonial rulers, which permitted established elites to maintain their privileged positions and others to elevate their social position.

In economic life, West African farmers grew cocoa and Burmese farmers grew rice for export to their own economic benefit. But Europeans who sought to make their home countries self-sufficient in cotton by requiring colonized Africans to grow it were generally frustrated as African farmers effectively resisted that onerous and unprofitable work. African women took advantage of opportunities to grow cash crops, engage in small-scale trading, and brew beer in urban areas. In regions such as southern Africa, the absence of men who had left home as migratory workers required women to assume traditionally male roles as heads of households.

Particularly in sub-Saharan Africa, many became Christians, adapting that religion to their own cultures in a massive movement of independent churches. Throughout the colonial world, young people eagerly sought Western education but later, as leaders of nationalist movements, turned it against the colonizers. Colonized peoples also shaped or reshaped their social and cultural identities, as Africans forged new ethnic groupings and Indian intellectuals and reformers generated a modern form of Hinduism. In these and many other ways, colonized people actively shaped the history of the colonial era, even in highly oppressive conditions.

"Men make their own history," Karl Marx famously wrote, "but they do not make it as they please nor under conditions of their own choosing." In the colonial experience of the nineteenth and early twentieth centuries, both the colonizers and the colonized "made history," but neither were able to do so precisely as they pleased.

Revisiting Chapter 18

Revisiting Specifics

Revisiting Core Ideas

1. **Analyzing Cause and Effect** In what ways did the Industrial Revolution shape the character of nineteenth-century European imperialism?
2. **Comparing Differences** In what different ways was colonial rule established in the various regions of Africa and Asia?
3. **Identifying Distinctive Features** What was distinctive about European colonial empires of the nineteenth century?
4. **Comparing Changes** In what different ways did the colonial experience reshape the economic lives of Asian and African societies?
5. **Analyzing Change** How were new cultural identities forged during the colonial era?

A Wider View

1. In what ways did colonial rule rest on violence and coercion, and in what ways did it elicit voluntary cooperation or generate benefits for some people?
2. In what respects were colonized people more than victims of colonial conquest and rule? To what extent could they act in their own interests within the colonial situation?
3. Was colonial rule a transforming, even a revolutionary, experience, or did it freeze or preserve existing social and economic patterns? What evidence can you find to support both sides of this argument?
4. **Looking Back** How would you compare the colonial experience of Asian and African peoples during the long nineteenth century to the earlier colonial experience in the Americas?

To learn more about the topics in this chapter, see **For Further Study** at the end of this book.

WORKING WITH EVIDENCE

Colonial Conquest: The Scramble for Africa

The centerpiece of Europe's global expansion during the nineteenth century occurred in the so-called scramble for Africa, during which a half dozen or so European countries divided up almost the entire continent into colonial territories (see Map 18.2, page 792). The "scramble" took place very quickly (between roughly 1875 and 1900), surprising even the European leaders who initiated it, as well as the many African societies that suddenly found themselves confronting highly aggressive and well-armed foreign forces. Remarkably, the entire partition of Africa took place without any direct military conflict between the competing imperial countries. But in establishing their control on the ground, Europeans faced widespread African resistance, making the scramble an extremely bloody process of military conquest. The sources that follow illustrate some of the distinctive features of the scramble for Africa as well as the differing ways in which it was perceived and represented.

SOURCE 18.1 Competition and Conquest ▶

As the scramble for Africa got under way in earnest in the 1880s and 1890s, it became a highly competitive process. French designs on Africa, for example, focused on obtaining an uninterrupted east-west link from the Red Sea to the Atlantic Ocean. But the British, entrenched in Egypt and in control of the Suez Canal, were determined that no major European power should be allowed to control the headwaters of the Nile on which Egypt depended. Those conflicting goals came to a head in 1898, when British forces moving south from Egypt met a French expedition moving northeast from the Atlantic coast of what is now Gabon. That encounter took place along the Nile River at Fashoda in present-day South Sudan, threatening war between France and Great Britain. In the end, negotiations persuaded the French to withdraw.

Source 18.1, the cover of a French publication, shows the commander of the French expedition, Jean-Baptiste Marchand, who gained heroic stature by leading his troops on an epic journey across much of Africa that lasted more than eighteen months.

- How did the artist portray Marchand? How might a British artist have portrayed him?
- What does this source suggest about the role of violence in the scramble for Africa?
- Notice the large number of African troops among Marchand's forces. What does that suggest about the process of colonial conquest? Why might Africans have agreed to fight on behalf of a European colonial power?
- How do you understand the fallen soldier lying between Marchand's legs?

CHARLES TICHON | *Commandant Marchand across Africa* | 1900

SOURCE 18.2 "Pacification" in East Africa

In European eyes, conquest was frequently termed "pacification," with the goal of ending all active resistance to colonial authorities. For African communities, it often meant devastating violence. Source 18.2 provides a vivid example of what the scramble for Africa meant at the level of a single village. It comes from the diary of a young British soldier who took part in the takeover of what is now Kenya.

- What posture did this soldier take toward this military action?
- How might this experience be described from the viewpoint of one of the surviving young women?
- How does the violence depicted in this account differ from that shown in Source 18.1?

RICHARD MEINERTZHAGEN | *A Small Slaughter* | 1902

I have performed a most unpleasant duty today. I made a night march to the village at the edge of the forest where the white settler had been so brutally murdered the day before yesterday. Though the war drums were sounding throughout the night, we reached the village without incident and surrounded it. By the light of the fires, we could see savages dancing in the village, and our guides assured me that they were dancing around the mutilated body of the white man.

I gave orders that every living thing except children should be killed without mercy. I hated the work and was anxious to get through with it. So soon as we could see to shoot we closed in. Several of the men tried to break out but were immediately shot. I then assaulted the place before any defense could be prepared. Every soul was either shot or bayoneted, and I am happy to say that there were no children in the village. They, together with the younger women, had already been removed by the villagers to the forest. We burned all the huts and razed the banana plantations to the ground.

Source: R. Meinertzhagen, *Kenya Diary* (London: Oliver and Boyd, 1957), 51–52.

SOURCE 18.3 From Cape to Cairo

Nowhere did the vaulting ambition of European colonial powers in Africa emerge more clearly than in the British vision of a north-south corridor of British territories along the eastern side of the continent stretching from South Africa to Egypt, or in the popular phrase of the time, "from the Cape to Cairo." A part of this vision was an unbroken railroad line running the entire length of the African continent. That grand idea was popularized by Cecil Rhodes, a British-born businessman and politician who made a fortune in South African diamonds and became an enthusiastic advocate of British imperialism. Source 18.3, an 1892 cartoon published in the popular British magazine of satire and humor named *Punch*, shows Rhodes bestriding the continent with one foot in Egypt and the other in South Africa.

- Is this famous image criticizing or celebrating Rhodes's Cape-to-Cairo dream? Explain your reasoning.
- What does this source suggest about the purpose of the Cape-to-Cairo scheme and the means to achieve it?
- How did the artist portray the African continent? What does the absence of African people suggest?

The Rhodes Colossus | 1892

THE RHODES COLOSSUS
STRIDING FROM CAPE TOWN TO CAIRO.

SOURCE 18.4 Ethiopia and the Scramble for Africa

The East African state of Ethiopia played an intriguing role during the scramble, for alone in all of Africa, it successfully resisted incorporation into a European empire. But Ethiopia also participated in the scramble, almost doubling the size of the country at the expense of neighboring peoples. Source 18.4A presents a letter written in 1891 from the Ethiopian emperor Menelik II to the great powers of Europe announcing his outlook and intentions as the scramble for Africa picked up speed. This warning, however, did not prevent the Italians from claiming a protectorate over Ethiopia, an action that led to war. Source 18.4B records Menelik's call to arms in 1895 as that war unfolded. The famous Battle of Adowa, which followed in 1896, marked a decisive victory for Ethiopia over the Italians. Ethiopia had preserved its independence, becoming a symbol of African resistance and bravery. The people forcibly incorporated into a growing Ethiopian empire, no doubt, saw things differently.

- How would you summarize Menelik's goals as expressed in Source 18.4A?
- How does Menelik try to distinguish his kingdom from others in Africa? In what ways does he try to appeal to European sensibilities?
- On what basis does Menelik appeal to his people to mobilize against the Italians in Source 18.4B?

SOURCE 18.4A
MENELIK II | *Letter to the European Great Powers* | 1891

Being desirous to make known to our friends the Powers (Sovereigns) of Europe the boundaries of Ethiopia, we have addressed also to you (your Majesty) the present letter.

These are the boundaries of Ethiopia: [Then follows a detailed description of Ethiopia's boundaries.]

While tracing today the actual boundaries of my Empire, I shall endeavour, if God gives me life and strength, to re-establish the ancient frontiers (tributaries) of Ethiopia up to Khartoum, and as far as Lake Nyanza with all the Gallas.

Ethiopia has been for fourteen centuries a Christian island in a sea of pagans. If powers at a distance come forward to partition Africa between them, I do not intend to be an indifferent spectator.

As the Almighty has protected Ethiopia up to this day, I have confidence He will continue to protect her, and increase her borders in the future. I am certain He will not suffer her to be divided among other Powers.

Formerly the boundary of Ethiopia was the sea. Having lacked strength sufficient, and having received no help from Christian Powers, our frontier on the sea coast fell into the power of the Muslim-man [Muslims].

At present we do not intend to regain our sea frontier by force, but we trust that the Christian Powers, guided by our Saviour, will restore to us our sea-coast line, at any rate, certain points on the coast.

Source: Mohamed Osman Omar, *The Scramble in the Horn of Africa* (New Delhi: Somali Publications, 2001), 143.

SOURCE 18.4B

MENELIK II | *Mobilization Proclamation* | 1895

Enemies have now come upon us to ruin our country and to change our religion. Our enemies have begun the affair by advancing and digging into our country like moles. With the help of God, I will not deliver my country to them. Today, you who are strong, give me your strength, and you who are weak, help me by prayer. Men of my country, up to now I believe I have never wronged you and you have never caused me sorrow. If you refuse to follow me, beware. You will hate me, for I shall not fail to punish you. I swear in the name of Mary that I shall never accept any plea of pardon. . . . Meet me at Were Illu [the place of assembly for Menelik's forces], and may you be there by the middle of [October]. So says Menelik, elect of God, king of kings.

Source: Quoted in Rick Duncan, *Man, Know Thyself* (Bloomington, IN: XLibris, 2013), 1:330.

SOURCE 18.5 Empire Building in North Africa

In North Africa, the primary European rivalries for territory involved Great Britain, which occupied Egypt in 1881; France, which came to control Tunisia, Algeria, and Morocco; and Italy, which seized Libya in 1912. Source 18.5 portrays two of these rivals—Britain, on the right, and France, on the left—toasting one another while standing on piles of skeletons. This image appeared in the Cairo *Punch*, a British-owned magazine in Egypt published in Arabic, probably around 1910.

This image refers specifically to two incidents. On the British side, the cartoon evokes a 1906 quarrel between British soldiers hunting pigeons and local villagers of Denshway that resulted in the death of one of the soldiers. In response, outraged British authorities hanged several people and flogged dozens of others. The following year in Morocco, French civilians building a small railway near the harbor of Casablanca dug up parts of a Muslim cemetery, "churning up piles of bones." When attacks against European laborers followed, killing eight, the French bombarded the Arab quarter of the city, with many casualties—European and Arab alike—in the fighting that ensued. Both incidents stimulated nationalist feelings in these two North African countries.

- What references to the incidents described here can you find in Source 18.5?
- The British and French generally saw themselves as rivals in the scramble for Africa. How are they portrayed here?
- What posture toward colonial rule does this image reflect? While the artist remains unknown, do you think it more likely to have been an Egyptian or a European?

British and French in North Africa | **ca. 1910**

SOURCE 18.6 An African American Voice on the Scramble for Africa

Writing in 1915, shortly after the outbreak of World War I, the African American scholar and activist W. E. B. Du Bois reflected on the scramble for Africa, arguing that it was a leading cause of the war.

- How does Du Bois characterize the process of the scramble?
- With which of the earlier sources does the tone of his essay most clearly resonate?
- What connection does Du Bois see between the partition of Africa and World War I?

W. E. B. DU BOIS | *The African Roots of War* | 1915

Africa is a prime cause of this terrible overturning of civilization [World War I]. . . .

The Berlin Conference to apportion the rising riches of Africa among the white peoples met on the fifteenth day of November, 1884 . . . and before the Berlin Conference had finished its deliberations, [Germany] had annexed . . . an area over half as large again as the whole German Empire in Europe. Only in its dramatic suddenness was this undisguised robbery of the land of seven million natives different from the methods by which Great Britain and France got four million square miles each, Portugal three quarters of a million, and Italy and Spain got smaller but substantial areas.

The methods by which this continent has been stolen have been contemptible and dishonest beyond expression. Lying treaties, rivers of rum, murder, assassination, mutilation, rape, and torture have marked the progress of Englishman, German, Frenchman, and Belgian on the dark continent. . . .

The present world war is, then, the result of jealousies engendered by the recent rise of armed [nations] . . . whose aim is the exploitation of the wealth of the world mainly outside the European circle of nations . . . , and particularly in Africa. . . .

[I]n the minds of yellow, brown, and black men the brutal truth is clearing: a white man is privileged to go to any land where advantage beckons and behave as he pleases; the black or colored man is being more and more confined to those parts of the world where life for climatic, historical, economic, and political reasons is most difficult to live and most easily dominated by Europe for Europe's gain.

Source: W. E. B. Du Bois, "The African Roots of War," *Atlantic Monthly* (May 1915), 707–8, 712.

DOING HISTORY

1. **Distinguishing Viewpoints** From what different perspectives do these sources represent the scramble for Africa? What criticisms and justifications of the scramble can you read in them?
2. **Portraying Africans and Europeans** In what different ways are Europeans and Africans portrayed in these sources?
3. **Considering Motives** Scholars have sometimes argued that the scramble for Africa was driven less by concrete economic interests than by emotional, even romantic, notions of national grandeur and personal adventure. In what ways do these sources support or challenge this interpretation?
4. **Considering Moral Visions** How do these sources deal with issues of morality or visions of right and wrong?

HISTORIANS' VOICES

The Invasion of Africa

Two major issues have informed historians' inquiry about the scramble for Africa—the motives of the Europeans and the responses of Africans. Voice 18.1 deals with the first of these issues. It comes from British historian Thomas Pakenham's award-winning history of the scramble. In Voice 18.2 the West African scholar A. Adu Boahen, a pioneer in the field of African history, addresses the second problem.

- What range of European motivations underlay the scramble for Africa according to Voice 18.1?
- How does Boahen in Voice 18.2 classify African responses to the European intrusion, and why does he believe Africans were unable to maintain their independence?
- **Integrating Primary and Secondary Sources** How might Pakenham (Voice 18.1) use Sources 18.1 and 18.3 to substantiate his argument? In which of his three categories of African response to the scramble might Boahen place Menelik in Source 18.4?

VOICE 18.1

Thomas Pakenham on European Motivations | 1992

Why this undignified rush by the leaders of Europe to build empires in Africa? . . . [T]hey all conceived the crusade in terms of romantic nationalism. To imperialism—a kind of race nationalism—they brought a missionary zeal. Not only would they save Africa from itself. Africa would be the saving of their own countries.

At first, European governments were reluctant to intervene. But to most people in their electorates, there seemed a real chance of missing something. . . . There were dreams of El Dorado, of diamond mines and goldfields crisscrossing the Sahara. There might be new markets out there in this African Garden of Eden and tropical groves where golden fruit could be plucked by willing brown hands. . . .

[O]verseas empire would sooth the *amour proper* [self-esteem] of the French army, humiliated by its collapse in the Franco-Prussian war. And it would no less bolster the pride of the political *parvenus* [newcomers] of Europe [recently united Germany and Italy] . . . and what about a place in the sun for emigrants? . . .

In Britain . . . there was growing resentment toward the intruders. . . . Britain had pioneered the exploration and evangelization of Central Africa and she felt a proprietary right to most of the continent. . . . As the only great maritime empire, she needed to prevent her rivals obstructing the steamer routes to the East, via Suez and the Cape.

Source: Thomas Pakenham, *The Scramble for Africa* (New York: Avon Books, 1992), xxi–xxiii.

VOICE 18.2

A. Adu Boahen on African Strategies | 1987

Africans devised three main strategies [for responding to the scramble]. . . . [First] some African rulers readily submitted to the European invaders . . . either because they became aware of the futility and cost of confronting the imperialists or . . . because they themselves urgently needed European protection.

The second main strategy adopted . . . was that of alliance. . . . These African rulers sought to achieve the very sovereignty of their state, and what they saw themselves doing was not collaborating but rather allying with the incoming invaders to achieve this national end.

The third strategy . . . was confrontation . . . and an overwhelming majority of the Africans adopted the military option. . . . Most of these African armies were nonprofessional and not properly trained. . . . African armies were, in many cases, numerically inferior to European armies. . . . Most of the armies of the European imperialists consisted of African soldiers. . . . Above all, technologically and logistically, African armies were at a great disadvantage.

[And] no African state was strong enough economically to have sustained any protracted warfare. . . . Most African rulers failed to form . . . alliances [among themselves]. Not only did this weaken them militarily, but it also enabled European imperialists to play one African power against the other. . . . It was above all . . . because the Europeans had the maxim gun and the Africans did not that an overwhelming number of African states lost their independence.

Source: A. Adu Boahen, *African Perspectives on Colonialism* (Baltimore, MD: Johns Hopkins University Press, 1987), 39–57.

Bridgeman Images

CHAPTER

19

Empires in Collision

Europe, the Middle East, and East Asia

1800–1900

CONNECTING PAST AND PRESENT

"Several centuries ago, China was strong. . . . In over 100 years after the 1840 Opium War, China suffered immensely from aggression, wars and chaos."[1] Speaking in early 2017, Chinese president Xi Jinping thus reminded his listeners of Britain's nineteenth-century violent intrusion into China's history bearing shiploads of highly addictive opium. This conflict marked the beginning of what the Chinese still describe as a "century of humiliation." In official Chinese thinking, it was only the victory of the Chinese Communist Party that enabled China to finally escape from that shameful past. Memories of the Opium War remain a central element of China's "patriotic education" for the young, serving as a warning against uncritical admiration of the West and providing a rejoinder to any Western criticism of China. Approximately 180 years after that clash between the Chinese and British empires, the Opium War retains an emotional resonance for many Chinese and offers a politically useful tool for the country's government.

China was among the countries that confronted an aggressive and industrializing West while maintaining its formal independence, unlike the colonized areas discussed in Chapter 18. So too did Japan, the Ottoman Empire, Persia (now Iran), Ethiopia, and Siam (now Thailand). Latin America also belongs in this category (see "The Industrial Revolution and Latin America in the Nineteenth Century" in Chapter 17). These states avoided outright incorporation into Western colonial empires, retaining some ability to resist

« **Carving Up the Pie of China** In this French cartoon from the late 1890s, the Great Powers of the day (from left to right: Great Britain's Queen Victoria, Germany's Kaiser Wilhelm, Russia's Tsar Nicholas II, a female figure representing France, and the Meiji emperor of Japan) participate in dividing China, while a Chinese figure behind them tries helplessly to stop the partition of his country.

aggression and to reform or transform their own societies. But they shared with their colonized counterparts the need to deal with four dimensions of the European moment in world history. First, they faced the immense military might and political ambitions of the major imperial powers. Second, they became enmeshed in networks of trade, investment, and sometimes migration that arose from an industrializing and capitalist Europe to generate a new world economy. Third, they were touched by various aspects of traditional European culture, as some among them learned the French, English, or German language; converted to Christianity; or studied European literature and philosophy. Fourth, they too engaged with the culture of modernity—its scientific rationalism; its technological achievements; its belief in a better future; and its ideas of nationalism, socialism, feminism, and individualism. In those epic encounters, they sometimes resisted, at other times accommodated, and almost always adapted what came from the West. They were active participants in the global drama of nineteenth-century world history, not simply its passive victims or beneficiaries.

At the same time, these societies were dealing with their own internal issues. Population growth and peasant rebellion wracked China; internal social and economic changes eroded the stability of Japanese public life; the great empires of the Islamic world shrank or disappeared; rivalry among competing elites troubled Latin American societies. China, the Ottoman Empire, and Japan provide a range of experiences, responses, and outcomes and many opportunities for comparison, as they navigated this era of colliding empires.

SEEKING THE MAIN POINT

What differences can you identify in how China, the Ottoman Empire, and Japan experienced Western imperialism and responded to it? How might you account for those differences?

Reversal of Fortune: China's Century of Crisis

In 1793, just a decade after King George III of Britain lost his North American colonies, he received yet another rebuff, this time from China. In a famous letter to the British monarch, the Chinese emperor Qianlong (chyan-loong) sharply rejected British requests for a less restricted trading relationship with his country. "Our Celestial Empire possesses all things in prolific abundance," he declared. "There was therefore no need to import the manufactures of outside barbarians." Qianlong's snub simply continued the pattern of the previous several centuries, during which Chinese authorities had strictly controlled and limited the activities of European missionaries and merchants. But by 1912, little more than a century later, China's long-established imperial state had collapsed, and the country had been transformed from a central presence in the global economy to a weak and dependent participant in a European-dominated world system in which Great Britain was the major economic and political player. It was a stunning reversal of fortune for a country that in Chinese eyes was the civilized center of the entire world—in their terms, the Celestial Empire or the Middle Kingdom.

Landmarks for Chapter 19

1775 | 1800 | 1825 | 1850 | 1875 | 1900 | 1925

CHINA

1793 China rejects British request for open trade

1840–1842 First Opium War

1850–1864 Taiping Uprising

1856–1858 Second Opium War

1898–1901 Boxer Uprising

1911–1912 Chinese revolution; end of Qing dynasty

OTTOMAN EMPIRE

1789–1807 Reforms of Sultan Selim III

1839–1876 Tanzimat reforms

1870 Teacher training college for women opened

1876–1909 Reign of Sultan Abd al-Hamid II

1908 Military coup by Young Turks

JAPAN

1830s Famine, peasant uprisings, urban protests

1853 Commodore Perry's arrival in Japan

1868 Meiji Restoration

1880s Small feminist movement emerges

1889 Japanese constitution proclaimed

1894–1895 Japan defeats China

1904–1905 Japan defeats Russia

The Crisis Within

In some ways, China was the victim of its own earlier success. Its robust economy and American food crops had enabled substantial population growth, from about 100 million people in 1685 to some 430 million in 1853. Unlike in Europe, though, where a similar population spurt took place, no Industrial Revolution accompanied this vast increase in the number of people, nor was agricultural production able to keep up. Neither did China's internal expansion to the west and south generate anything like the wealth and resources that derived from Europe's overseas empires. The result was growing pressure on the land, smaller farms for China's huge peasant population, and, in all too many cases, unemployment, impoverishment, misery, and starvation.

CORE IDEA

■ Defining Challenges
How did China's internal and external challenges intersect during the nineteenth century?

Furthermore, China's governing institutions did not keep pace with the growing population. Thus the state was increasingly unable to effectively perform its many functions, such as tax collection, flood control, social welfare, and public security. Gradually the central state lost power to provincial officials and local gentry. Among such officials, corruption was endemic, and harsh treatment of peasants was common. According to an official report issued in 1852, "Day and night soldiers are sent out to harass taxpayers. Sometimes corporal punishments are imposed upon tax delinquents; some of them are so badly beaten to exact the last penny that blood and flesh fly in all directions."[2] Finally, European military pressure and economic penetration during the first half of the nineteenth century disrupted internal trade routes, created substantial unemployment, and raised peasant taxes.

This combination of circumstances, traditionally associated with a declining dynasty, gave rise to growing numbers of bandit gangs roaming the countryside and, even more dangerous, to outright peasant rebellion. Beginning in the late eighteenth century, such rebellions drew on a variety of peasant grievances and found leadership in charismatic figures proclaiming a millenarian religious message. Increasingly they also expressed opposition to the Qing dynasty because of its foreign Manchu origins. "We wait only for the northern region to be returned to a Han emperor," declared one rebel group in the early nineteenth century.[3]

China's internal crisis culminated in the **Taiping Uprising**, which set much of the country aflame between 1850 and 1864. This was a different kind of peasant upheaval. Its leaders largely rejected Confucianism, Daoism, and Buddhism alike, finding their primary ideology in a unique form of Christianity. Its leading figure, Hong Xiuquan (hong show-chwaan) (1814–1864), proclaimed himself the younger brother of Jesus, sent to cleanse the world of demons and to establish a "heavenly kingdom of great peace." Nor were these leaders content to restore an idealized Chinese society; instead they insisted on genuinely revolutionary change. They called for the abolition of private property, a radical redistribution of land, the end of prostitution and opium smoking, and the organization of society into sexually segregated military camps of men and women. Hong fiercely denounced the Qing dynasty as foreigners who had "poisoned China" and "defiled the emperor's throne." His cousin, Hong Rengan, developed plans for transforming China into an industrial nation, complete with railroads, health insurance for all, newspapers, and widespread public education.

Among the most revolutionary dimensions of the Taiping Uprising was its posture toward women and gender roles. This outlook reflected its origins among the minority Hakka people of southern China, where women were notably less restricted than Confucian orthodoxy prescribed. During the uprising, Hakka women, whose feet had never been bound, fought as soldiers in their own regiments, and in liberated regions, Taiping officials ordered that the feet of other women be unbound. The Taiping land reform program promised women and men equal shares of land. Women were now permitted to sit for civil service examinations and were appointed to supervisory positions, though usually ones in which they exercised authority over other women rather than men. Mutual attraction rather than family interests was promoted as a basis for marriage.

Taiping Uprising Western powers generally supported the Qing dynasty during the Taiping Uprising and even provided it with some military support. This image shows a group of the Taiping rebels and a British soldier they have captured. (Peter Newark Military Pictures/Bridgeman Images)

None of these reforms were consistently implemented during the short period of Taiping power, and the movement's leadership demonstrated considerable ambivalence about equality for women. Hong himself reflected a much more traditional understanding of elite women's role when he assembled a large personal harem and declared: "The duty of the palace women is to attend to the needs of their husbands; and it is arranged by Heaven that they are not to learn of the affairs outside."[4] Nonetheless, the Taiping posture toward women represented a sharp challenge to long-established gender roles and contributed to the hostility that the movement generated among many other Chinese, including women.

With a rapidly swelling number of followers, Taiping forces swept out of southern China and established their capital in Nanjing in 1853. For a time, the days of the Qing dynasty appeared to be over. But divisions and indecisiveness within the Taiping leadership, along with their inability to link up with several other rebel groups also operating separately in China, provided an opening for Qing dynasty loyalists to rally and by 1864 to crush this most unusual of peasant rebellions. Western military support for pro-Qing forces likewise contributed to their victory. It was not, however, the imperial military forces of the central government that defeated the rebels. Instead provincial military leaders, fearing the radicalism of the Taiping program, mobilized their own armies, which in the end crushed the rebel forces.

Analyzing Causation

What accounts for the massive peasant rebellions of nineteenth-century China?

Thus the Qing dynasty was saved, but it was also weakened as the provincial gentry consolidated their power at the expense of the central state. The intense conservatism of both imperial authorities and their gentry supporters postponed any resolution of China's peasant problem, delayed any real change for China's women, and deferred vigorous efforts at modernization until the communists came to power in the mid-twentieth century. More immediately, the devastation and destruction occasioned by this massive civil war seriously disrupted and weakened China's economy. Estimates of the number of lives lost range from 20 to 30 million. In human terms, it was the most costly conflict in the world during the nineteenth century, and it took China more than a decade to recover from its devastation. China's internal crisis in general and the Taiping Uprising in particular also provided a highly unfavorable setting for the country's encounter with a Europe newly invigorated by the Industrial Revolution.

Western Pressures

Nowhere was the shifting balance of global power in the nineteenth century more evident than in China's changing relationship with Europe, a transformation that registered most dramatically in the famous **Opium Wars**. Derived from Arab traders in the eighth century or earlier, opium had long been used on a small scale as a drinkable medicine; it was regarded as a magical cure for dysentery and described by one poet as "fit for Buddha."[5] It did not become a serious problem until the late eighteenth century, when the British began to use opium, grown and processed in India, to cover their persistent trade imbalance with China. By the 1830s, British, American, and other Western merchants had found an enormous, growing, and very profitable market for this highly addictive drug. From 1,000 chests (each weighing roughly 150 pounds) in 1773, China's opium imports exploded to more than 23,000 chests in 1832. (See Snapshot, page 835.)

Addiction to Opium Throughout the nineteenth century, opium imports created a massive addiction problem in China, as this photograph of an opium den from around 1900 suggests. Not until the early twentieth century did the British prove willing to curtail the opium trade from their Indian colony. (Hulton Deutsch/Getty Images)

By then, Chinese authorities recognized a mounting problem on many levels. Because opium importation was illegal, it had to be smuggled into China, thus flouting Chinese law. Bribed to turn a blind eye to the illegal trade, many officials were corrupted. Furthermore, a massive outflow of silver to pay for the opium reversed China's centuries-long ability to attract much of the world's silver supply, and this imbalance caused serious economic problems. Finally, China found itself with many millions of addicts—men and women, court officials, students preparing for exams, soldiers going into combat, and common laborers seeking

SNAPSHOT Chinese/British Trade at Canton, 1835–1836

What do these figures suggest about the role of opium in British trade with China? Calculate opium exports as a percentage of British exports to China, Britain's trade deficit without opium, and its trade surplus with opium. What did this pattern mean for China?

	Item	Value (in Spanish dollars)
British Exports to Canton	Opium	17,904,248
	Cotton	8,357,394
	All other items (sandalwood, lead, iron, tin, cotton yarn and piece goods, tin plates, watches, clocks)	6,164,981
	Total	32,426,623
British Imports from Canton	Tea (black and green)	13,412,243
	Raw silk	3,764,115
	Vermilion	705,000
	All other goods (sugar products, camphor, silver, gold, copper, musk)	5,971,541
	Total	23,852,899

Source: Data from Hsin-Pao Chang, ed., *Commissioner Lin and the Opium War* (New York: W. W. Norton, 1970), 226–27.

to overcome the pain and drudgery of their work. Following an extended debate at court in 1836 on whether to legalize the drug or crack down on its use, the emperor decided on suppression. An upright official, **Commissioner Lin Zexu** (lin zuh-SHOO), led the campaign against opium use as a kind of "drug czar." (See Zooming In: Lin Zexu, page 836.) The British, offended by the seizure of their property in opium and emboldened by their new military power, sent a large naval expedition to China, determined to end the restrictive conditions under which they had long traded with that country. In the process, they would teach the Chinese a lesson about the virtues of free trade and the "proper" way to conduct relations among countries. Thus began the first Opium War (1840–1842), in which Britain's industrialized military might proved decisive. The Treaty of Nanjing, which ended the war in 1842, largely on British terms, imposed numerous restrictions on Chinese sovereignty and opened five ports to European traders. Its provisions reflected the changed balance of global power that had emerged with Britain's Industrial Revolution. To the Chinese, that agreement represented the first of the "**unequal treaties**" that seriously eroded China's independence by the end of the century.

But it was not the last of those treaties. Britain's victory in a second Opium War (1856–1858) was accompanied by the brutal vandalizing of the emperor's exquisite Summer Palace outside Beijing and resulted in further humiliations. Still more ports were opened to foreign traders. Now those foreigners were allowed to

Assessing Change
How did Western pressures stimulate change in China during the nineteenth century?

ZOOMING IN

Lin Zexu: Confronting the Opium Trade

Commissioner Lin Zexu ordering the destruction of opium.

When the Chinese emperor decided in 1838 on firm measures to suppress the opium trade, he selected Lin Zexu to enforce that policy.[6] Born in 1785, Lin was the son of a rather poor but scholarly father who had never achieved an official position. Lin, however, excelled academically, passing the highest-level examinations in 1811 after two failed attempts and then rising rapidly in the ranks of China's bureaucracy. In the process, he gained a reputation as a strict and honest official; he was immune to bribery, genuinely concerned with the welfare of the peasantry, and unafraid to confront the corruption and decadence of rich and poor alike.

And so in December of 1838, after some nineteen personal audiences with the emperor, Lin found himself in Canton, the center of the opium trade and the only Chinese city legally open to foreign merchants. He was facing the greatest challenge of his professional life. Undertaken with the best of intentions, his actions were unable to prevent a war with Britain that propelled the country into a century of humiliating subservience to an industrializing Europe and forced growing numbers of Chinese to question their vaunted civilization.

In established Confucian fashion, Lin undertook his enormous task with a combination of moral appeals, reasoned argument, political pressure, and coercion, while hoping to avoid outright armed conflict. It was an approach that focused on both the demand and supply sides of the problem. In dealing with Chinese opium users, Lin emphasized the health hazards of the drug and demanded that people turn in their supplies of opium and the pipes used to smoke it. By mid-1839, he had confiscated some 50,000 pounds of the drug, together with over 70,000 pipes, and arrested some 1,700 dealers. Hundreds of local students were summoned to an assembly where they were invited to identify opium distributors and to suggest ways of dealing with the problem. Opium-using officials

photo: Pictures from History/TopFoto

travel freely and buy land in China, to preach Christianity under the protection of Chinese authorities, and to patrol some of China's rivers. Furthermore, the Chinese were forbidden to use the character for "barbarians" to refer to the British in official documents. Following later military defeats at the hands of the French (1885) and Japanese (1895), China lost control of Vietnam, Korea, and Taiwan. By the end of the century, the Western nations plus Japan and Russia had all carved out spheres of influence within China, granting themselves special privileges to establish military bases, extract raw materials, and build railroads. Many Chinese believed that their country was being "carved up like a melon" (see Map 19.1 and the chapter-opening image).

Coupled with its internal crisis, China's encounter with European imperialism had reduced the proud Middle Kingdom to dependency on the Western powers as it became part of a European-based "**informal empire**," an area dominated by Western powers but retaining its own government and a measure of independence.

became the target of investigations, and five-person teams were established to enforce the ban on opium smoking on one another.

Lin applied a similar mix of methods to the foreign suppliers of opium. A moralistic appeal to Queen Victoria argued that the articles the English imported from China—silk, tea, and rhubarb—were all beneficial. "By what right," he asked, "do [the barbarians] use this poisonous drug to injure Chinese people?" He pointedly reminded Europeans that new regulations, applying to Chinese and foreigners alike, fixed the penalty for dealing in opium at "decapitation or strangling." Then he demanded that foreign traders hand over their opium, and without compensation. When the merchants hesitated, Lin tightened the screws, ordering all Chinese employed by foreigners to leave their jobs and blockading the Europeans in their factories. After six weeks of negotiations, the Europeans capitulated, turning over some 3 million pounds of raw opium to Lin Zexu.

Disposing of the drug was an enormous task. Workers, stripped and searched daily to prevent looting, dug three huge trenches into which they placed the opium mixed with water, salt, and lime and then flushed the concoction into the sea. (See the image in this feature, which shows the commissioner overseeing this process.) Lin also offered a sacrifice to the Sea Spirit, apologizing for introducing this poison into its domain and "advising the Spirit to tell the creatures of the water to move away for a time." He informed the emperor that throngs of local people flocked to witness the destruction of the opium. And foreigners too came to observe the spectacle. Lin reported, "[The foreigners] do not dare to show any disrespect, and indeed I should judge from their attitudes that they have the decency to feel heartily ashamed."

Had Lin been correct in his appraisal, history would have taken a very different turn. But neither Lin nor his superiors anticipated the response that these actions provoked from the British government. They were also largely unaware that European industrial and military advances had decisively shifted the balance of power between China and the West. Arriving in 1840, a British military expedition quickly demonstrated its superiority and initiated the devastating Opium War that marked Lin's policies in Canton as a failure.

As a punishment for his unsatisfactory performance, the emperor sent Lin to a remote post in western China. Although his career rebounded somewhat after 1845, he died in 1850 while on the way to an appointment aimed at suppressing the Taiping rebellion. While his reputation suffered in the nineteenth century, it recovered in the twentieth as an intensely nationalist China recalled his principled stand against Western imperialism.

QUESTIONS

How might Lin Zexu have handled his task differently or more successfully? Or had he been given an impossible mission?

China was no longer the center of civilization to which barbarians paid homage and tribute, but just one weak and dependent nation among many others. The Qing dynasty remained in power, but in a weakened condition, which served European interests well and Chinese interests poorly. Restrictions imposed by the unequal treaties clearly inhibited China's industrialization, as foreign goods and foreign investment flooded the country largely unrestricted. Chinese businessmen mostly served foreign firms, rather than developing as an independent capitalist class capable of leading China's own Industrial Revolution.

The Failure of Conservative Modernization

Chinese authorities were not passive in the face of their country's mounting internal and external crises. Known as "**self-strengthening**," their policies during the 1860s and 1870s sought to reinvigorate a traditional China while borrowing

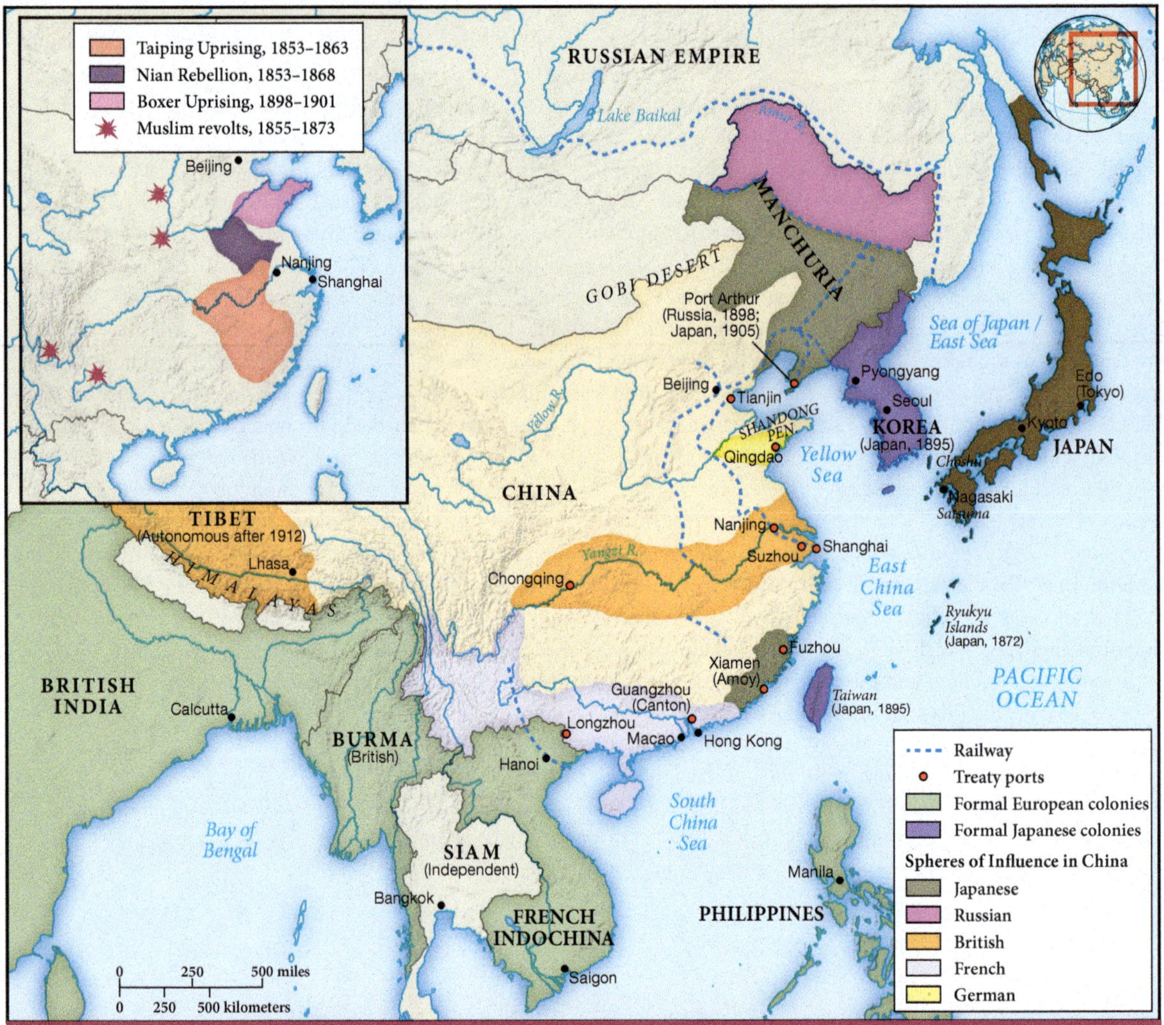

MAPPING HISTORY

Map 19.1 China and the World in the Nineteenth Century

As China was reeling from massive internal upheavals during the nineteenth century, it also faced external assaults from Russia, Japan, and various European powers. By the end of the century, large parts of China were divided into spheres of influence, each affiliated with one of the major industrial powers of the day.

READING THE MAP Which imperial powers created spheres of influence in China that were adjacent to territories that they already controlled? In which regions of China do the spheres of influence of major powers come into contact? Where would you predict that conflicts between major outside powers might occur in China?

INTERPRETING THE MAP How might you compare the success of Japanese and European colonialism in Asia?

cautiously from the West. An overhauled examination system, designed to recruit qualified candidates for official positions, sought the "good men" who could cope with the massive reconstruction that China faced in the wake of the Taiping rebellion. Support for landlords and the repair of dikes and irrigation helped restore rural social and economic order. A few industrial factories producing textiles and steel were established, coal mines were expanded, and a telegraph system was initiated. One Chinese general in 1863 confessed his humiliation that "Chinese weapons are far inferior to those of foreign countries."[7] A number of modern arsenals, shipyards, and foreign-language schools sought to remedy this deficiency.

CORE IDEA

■ Assessing Strategies
What strategies did China adopt to confront its various problems? Why were they so unsuccessful?

Self-strengthening as an overall program for China's modernization was inhibited by the fears of conservative leaders that urban, industrial, or commercial development would erode the power and privileges of the landlord class. Furthermore, the new industries remained largely dependent on foreigners for machinery, materials, and expertise. And they served to strengthen local authorities, who largely controlled those industries, rather than the central Chinese state.

The general failure of "self-strengthening" became apparent at the end of the century, when China suffered a humiliating military defeat by Japan (1894–1895). This failure was only confirmed when an antiforeign movement known as the **Boxer Uprising** (1898–1901) erupted in northern China. Led by militia organizations calling themselves the Society of Righteous and Harmonious Fists, the "Boxers" killed numerous Europeans and Chinese Christians and laid siege to the foreign embassies in Beijing. When Western powers and Japan occupied Beijing to crush the rebellion and imposed a huge payment on China as a punishment, it was clear that China remained a dependent country, substantially under foreign control.

No wonder, then, that growing numbers of educated Chinese, including many in official elite positions, became highly disillusioned with the Qing dynasty, which was both foreign and ineffective in protecting China. By the late 1890s, such people were organizing a variety of clubs, study groups, and newspapers to examine China's desperate situation and to explore alternative paths. The names of these organizations reflect their outlook—the National Rejuvenation Study Society, Society to Protect the Nation, and Understand the National Shame Society. They admired not only Western science and technology but also Western political practices that limited the authority of the ruler and permitted wider circles of people to take part in public life. They believed that only a truly unified nation in which rulers and ruled were closely related could save China from dismemberment at the hands of foreign imperialists. Despite the small number of women who took part in these discussions, traditional gender roles became yet another focus of opposition. No one expressed that issue more forcefully than Qiu Jin (1875–1907), the rebellious daughter of a gentry family who started a women's journal, arguing that liberated women were essential for a strong Chinese nation, and became involved in revolutionary politics. (For more on Qiu Jin, see Working with Evidence, Source 19.3, page 861.) Thus was born the immensely powerful force of Chinese nationalism, directed alike against Western imperialists, the foreign Qing dynasty, and aspects of China's traditional culture.

The Qing dynasty response to these new pressures proved inadequate. A flurry of progressive imperial edicts in 1898, known as the Hundred Days of Reform, was soon squelched by conservative forces. More extensive reform in the early twentieth century, including the end of the old examination system and the promise of a national parliament, was a classic case of too little too late. (See Working with Evidence: China: On the Brink of Change, page 859.) In 1912 the last Chinese emperor abdicated as the ancient imperial order that had governed China for two millennia collapsed, with only a modest nudge from organized revolutionaries. This **Chinese revolution of 1911–1912** marked the end of a long era in China's long history and the beginning of an immense struggle over the country's future.

The Ottoman Empire and the West in the Nineteenth Century

Like China, the Islamic world represented a highly successful civilization that felt little need to learn from the "infidels" or "barbarians" of the West until it collided with an expanding and aggressive Europe in the nineteenth century. Unlike China, though, Islamic civilization had been a near neighbor to Europe for 1,000 years. Its most prominent state, the Ottoman Empire, had long governed substantial parts of southeastern Europe and had posed a clear military and religious threat to Europe in the sixteenth and seventeenth centuries. But if its encounter with the West was less abrupt than that of China, it was no less consequential. Neither the Ottoman Empire nor China fell under direct colonial rule, but both were much diminished as the changing balance of global power took hold; both launched efforts at "defensive modernization" aimed at strengthening their states and preserving their independence; and in both societies, some people held tightly to old identities and values, even as others embraced new loyalties associated with nationalism and modernity.

"The Sick Man of Europe"

In 1750, the Ottoman Empire was still the central political fixture of a widespread Islamic world. From its Turkish heartland in Anatolia, it ruled over much of the Arab world, from which Islam had come. It protected pilgrims on their way to Mecca, governed Egypt and coastal North Africa, and incorporated millions of Christians in the Balkans. Its ruler, the sultan, claimed the role of caliph, successor to the Prophet Muhammad, and was widely viewed as the leader, defender, and primary representative of the Islamic world. But by the middle, and certainly by the end, of the nineteenth century, the Ottoman Empire was no longer able to deal with Europe from a position of equality, let alone superiority. Among the Great Powers of the West, it was now known as **"the sick man of Europe."** Within the Muslim world, the Ottoman Empire, once viewed as "the strong sword of Islam," was unable to prevent region after region—India, Indonesia, West Africa, Central Asia—from falling under the control of Christian powers.

The Ottoman Empire's own domains shrank considerably at the hands of Russian, British, Austrian, and French aggression (see Map 19.2). In 1798, Napoleon's invasion of Egypt, which had long been a province of the Ottoman Empire, was a particularly stunning blow. A contemporary observer, Abd al-Rahman al-Jabarti, described the French entry into Cairo:

> The French entered the city like a torrent rushing through the alleys and streets without anything to stop them, like demons of the Devil's army. . . . And the French trod in the Mosque of al-Azhar with their shoes, carrying swords and rifles. . . . They plundered whatever they found in the mosque. . . . They treated the books and Quranic volumes as trash. . . . Furthermore, they soiled the mosque, blowing their spit in it, pissing and defecating in it. They guzzled wine and smashed bottles in the central court.[8]

When the French left, a virtually independent Egypt pursued a modernizing and empire-building program of its own during the early and mid-nineteenth century and on one occasion came close to toppling the Ottoman Empire itself.

Beyond territorial losses to stronger European powers, other parts of the empire, such as Greece, Serbia, Bulgaria, and Romania, achieved independence based on their

CORE IDEA

■ Making Comparisons

In what ways were the histories of China and the Ottoman Empire similar during the nineteenth century? And how did they differ?

Map 19.2 The Contraction of the Ottoman Empire

Foreign aggression and nationalist movements substantially diminished the Ottoman Empire during the nineteenth century, but they also stimulated a variety of efforts to revive and reform Ottoman society.

own surging nationalism and support from the British or the Russians. The continued independence of the core region of the Ottoman Empire owed much to the inability of Europe's Great Powers to agree on how to divide it up among themselves.

Assessing Decline In what respects did the Ottoman Empire decline during the nineteenth century?

Behind the contraction of the Ottoman Empire lay other problems. As in China, the central Ottoman state had weakened, particularly in its ability to raise necessary revenue, as provincial authorities and local warlords gained greater power. Moreover, the Janissaries, once the effective and innovative elite infantry units of Ottoman military forces, lost their military edge, becoming a highly conservative force within the empire. The technological and military gap with the West was clearly growing.

Economically, the earlier centrality of the Ottoman and Arab lands in Afro-Eurasian commerce diminished as Europeans achieved direct oceanic access to the treasures of Asia. Competition from cheap European manufactured goods hit Ottoman artisans hard and led to urban riots protesting foreign imports. Furthermore, a series of agreements, known as capitulations, between European countries and the Ottoman Empire granted Westerners various exemptions from Ottoman law and taxation. Like the unequal treaties with China, these agreements facilitated European penetration of the Ottoman economy and became widely resented. Such measures eroded Ottoman sovereignty and reflected the changing position of that empire relative to Europe. So too did the growing indebtedness of the Ottoman Empire, which came to rely on foreign loans to finance its efforts at economic development. By 1881, its inability to pay the interest on those debts led to foreign control of much of its revenue-generating system, while a similar situation in Egypt led to its outright occupation by the British. Like China, the Ottoman Empire had fallen into a position of considerable dependency on Europe.

Reform and Its Opponents

Analyzing Responses In what different ways did the Ottoman state respond to its various problems?

The leadership of the Ottoman Empire recognized many of its problems and during the nineteenth century mounted increasingly ambitious programs of "defensive modernization" that were earlier, more sustained, and far more vigorous than the timid and halfhearted measures of self-strengthening in China. One reason perhaps lay in the absence of any internal upheaval, such as the Taiping Uprising in China, which threatened the very existence of the ruling dynasty. Nationalist revolts on the empire's periphery, rather than Chinese-style peasant rebellion at the center, represented the primary internal crisis of nineteenth-century Ottoman history. Nor did the Middle East in general experience the explosive population growth that contributed so much to China's nineteenth-century crisis. Furthermore, the long-established Ottoman leadership was Turkic and Muslim, culturally similar to its core population, whereas China's Qing dynasty rulers were widely regarded as foreigners from Manchuria.

Ottoman reforms began in the late eighteenth century when Sultan Selim III (r. 1789–1807) sought to reorganize and update the army, drawing on European advisers and techniques. Even these modest innovations stirred the hostility of

Ottoman Modernization Bustling major cities provided environments where Ottoman modernizers hoped to transform their society and economy. With ships anchored in Constantinople's harbor and the smokestacks of industry to the right, this 1890s colorized image of the Ottoman capital illustrates the outcomes of these modernization efforts. (Universal History Archive/Getty Images)

powerful factions among both the *ulama* (religious scholars) and the elite military corps of Janissaries, who saw them in conflict with both Islam and their own institutional interests. Opposition to his measures was so strong that Selim was overthrown in 1807 and then murdered. Subsequent sultans, however, crushed the Janissaries and brought the ulama more thoroughly under state control than elsewhere in the Islamic world.

Then, in the several decades after 1839, more far-reaching reformist measures, known as **Tanzimat** (tahn-zee-MAHT) (reorganization), took shape as the Ottoman leadership sought to provide the economic, social, and legal underpinnings for a strong and newly recentralized state. Factories producing cloth, paper, and armaments; modern mining operations; reclamation and resettlement of agricultural land; telegraphs, steamships, railroads, and a modern postal service; Western-style law codes and courts; new elementary and secondary schools—all of these new departures began a long process of modernization and westernization in the Ottoman Empire.

Even more revolutionary, at least in principle, were changes in the legal status of the empire's diverse communities, which now gave non-Muslims equal rights under the law. An imperial proclamation of 1856 declared:

> Every distinction or designation tending to make any class whatever of the subjects of my Empire inferior to another class, on account of their religion, language or race shall be forever effaced. . . . No subject of my Empire shall be hindered in the exercise of the religion that he professes. . . . All the subjects

> of my Empire, without distinction of nationality, shall be admissible to public employment.[9]

This declaration represented a dramatic change that challenged the fundamentally Islamic character of the state. Mixed tribunals with representatives from various religious groups were established to hear cases involving non-Muslims. More Christians were appointed to high office. A mounting tide of secular legislation and secular schools, drawing heavily on European models, now competed with traditional Islamic institutions.

Although Tanzimat-era reforms did not directly address gender issues, they did stimulate modest educational openings for women, mostly in Istanbul, with a training program for midwives in 1842, a girls' secondary school in 1858, and a teacher training college for women in 1870. Furthermore, the reform-minded class that emerged from the Tanzimat era generally favored greater opportunities for women as a means of strengthening the state, and a number of upper- and middle-class women were involved in these discussions. During the 1870s and 1880s, the prominent female poet Sair Nigar Hanim held weekly "salons" in which reformist intellectuals of both sexes participated.

■ Defining Identity
In what different ways did various groups define the Ottoman Empire during the nineteenth century?

The reform process raised profound and highly contested questions. What was the Ottoman Empire, and who were its people? Were they Ottoman subjects of a dynastic state, Turkish citizens of a national state, or Muslim believers in a religiously defined state? For decades, the answers oscillated, as few people wanted to choose decisively among these alternative identities.

To those who supported the reforms, the Ottoman Empire was an inclusive state, all of whose people were loyal to the dynasty that ruled it. This was the outlook of a new class spawned by the reform process itself—lower-level officials, military officers, writers, poets, and journalists, many of whom had a modern Western-style education. Dubbed the **Young Ottomans**, they were active during the middle decades of the nineteenth century, as they sought major changes in the Ottoman political system itself. They favored a more European-style parliamentary and constitutional regime that could curtail the absolute power of the sultan. Only such a political system, they felt, could mobilize the energies of the country to overcome backwardness and preserve the state against European aggression. Known as Islamic modernism, such ideas found expression in many parts of the Muslim world in the second half of the century. Muslim societies, the Young Ottomans argued, needed to embrace Western technical and scientific knowledge, while rejecting its materialism. Islam in their view could accommodate a full modernity without sacrificing its essential religious character. After all, the Islamic world had earlier hosted impressive scientific achievements and had incorporated elements of Greek philosophical thinking.

In 1876, the Young Ottomans experienced a short-lived victory when **Sultan Abd al-Hamid II** (r. 1876–1909) accepted a constitution and an elected parliament, but not for long. Under the pressure of war with Russia, the sultan soon suspended the reforms and reverted to an older style of despotic rule for the next

The First Ottoman Constitution This Ottoman-era postcard celebrates the short-lived constitutional period of 1876–1878 and the brief political victory of the Young Ottoman reformers. The country is represented by an unveiled woman being released from her chains, while an angel carries a banner inscribed with the slogan of the French Revolution: liberty, equality, fraternity. ("The Ottoman Constitution, December 1895." Color postcard, artist unknown/Visual Connection Archive)

thirty years, even renewing the claim that he was the caliph, the successor to the Prophet and the protector of Muslims everywhere.

Opposition to this revived despotism soon surfaced among both military and civilian elites known as the **Young Turks**. Largely abandoning any reference to Islam, they advocated a militantly secular public life, were committed to thorough modernization along European lines, and increasingly thought about the Ottoman Empire as a Turkish national state. "There is only one civilization, and that is European civilization," declared Abdullah Cevdet, a prominent figure in the Young Turk movement. "Therefore we must borrow western civilization with both its rose and its thorn."[10]

A military coup in 1908 finally allowed the Young Turks to exercise real power. They pushed for a radical secularization of schools, courts, and law codes; permitted elections and competing parties; established a single Law of Family Rights for all regardless of religion; and encouraged Turkish as the official language of the empire. They also opened modern schools for women, including access to Istanbul University; allowed women to wear Western clothing; restricted polygamy; and permitted women to obtain divorces in some situations. Women established a number of publications and organizations, some of them linked to British suffrage groups. In the western cities of the empire, some women abandoned their veils.

But the nationalist Turkish conception of Ottoman identity antagonized non-Turkic peoples and helped stimulate Arab and other nationalisms in response. For some, a secular nationality was becoming the most important public loyalty, with Islam relegated to private life. Nationalist sentiments contributed to the complete disintegration of the Ottoman Empire following World War I, but the secularizing and westernizing principles of the Young Turks informed the policies of the Turkish republic that replaced it.

Outcomes: Comparing China and the Ottoman Empire

By the beginning of the twentieth century, both China and the Ottoman Empire, recently centers of proud and vibrant civilizations, had experienced the consequences of a rapidly shifting balance of global power. Now they were "semi-colonies" within the "informal empires" of Europe, although they retained sufficient independence for their governments to launch catch-up efforts of defensive modernization, the Ottomans earlier and the Chinese later. But neither was able to create the industrial economies or strong states required to fend off European intrusion and restore their former status in the world. Despite their diminished power, however, both China and the Ottoman Empire gave rise to new nationalist conceptions of society that were initially small and limited in appeal but of great significance for the future.

In the early twentieth century, that future witnessed the end of both the Chinese and Ottoman empires. In China, the collapse of the imperial system in 1912 was followed by a vast revolutionary upheaval that by 1949 led to a communist regime within largely the same territorial space as the old empire. By contrast, the collapse of the Ottoman Empire following World War I led to the creation of the new but much smaller nation-state of Turkey in the Anatolian heartland of the old empire, which lost its vast Arab and European provinces.

China's twentieth-century revolutionaries rejected traditional Confucian culture far more thoroughly than the secularizing leaders of modern Turkey rejected Islam. Almost everywhere in the Islamic world, including Turkey, traditional religion retained its hold on the private loyalties of most people and later in the twentieth century became a basis for social renewal in many places. Islamic civilization, unlike its Chinese counterpart, had many independent centers and was never so closely associated with a single state. Furthermore, it was embedded in a deeply religious tradition that was personally meaningful to millions of adherents, in contrast to the more elitist and secular outlook of Confucianism. Many Chinese, however, retained traditional Confucian values such as filial piety, and Confucianism has made something of a comeback in China over the past several decades. Nonetheless, Islam retained a hold on its civilization in the twentieth century rather more firmly than Confucianism did in China.

The Japanese Difference: The Rise of a New East Asian Power

Like China and the Ottoman Empire, the island country of Japan confronted the aggressive power of the West during the nineteenth century. This threat took shape as U.S. commodore Matthew Perry's "black ships" steamed into Tokyo Bay in 1853 and forcefully demanded that this reclusive nation open up to more "normal" relations with the world. However, the outcome of that encounter differed sharply from the others. In the second half of the nineteenth century, Japan undertook a radical transformation of its society—a "revolution from above," according to some historians—that turned it into a powerful, modern, united, industrialized nation. It was an achievement that neither China nor the Ottoman Empire was able to duplicate. Far from succumbing to Western domination, Japan joined the club of imperialist countries by creating its own East Asian empire at the expense of China and Korea. In building a society that was both modern and distinctly Japanese, Japan demonstrated that modernity was not a uniquely European phenomenon. This "Japanese miracle," as some have called it, was both promising and ominous for the rest of Asia.

The Tokugawa Background

For 250 years prior to Perry's arrival, Japan had been governed by a shogun (a military ruler) from the Tokugawa family who acted in the name of a revered but powerless emperor who lived in Kyoto, 300 miles away from the seat of power in Edo (Tokyo). The chief task of this Tokugawa shogunate was to prevent the return of civil war among some 260 rival feudal lords, known as daimyo, each of whom had a cadre of armed retainers, the famed samurai warriors of Japanese tradition.

Based on their own military power and political skills, successive shoguns gave Japan more than two centuries of internal peace (1600–1850). To control the restive daimyo, they required these local authorities to create second homes in Edo, the country's capital, where they had to live during alternate years. When they left for their rural residences, families stayed behind, almost as hostages. Nonetheless, the daimyo, especially the more powerful ones, retained substantial autonomy in their own domains and behaved in some ways like independent states, with separate military forces, law codes, tax systems, and currencies. With no national army, no uniform currency, and little central authority at the local level, **Tokugawa Japan** was "pacified . . . but not really unified."[11] To further stabilize the country, the Tokugawa regime issued highly detailed rules governing the occupation, residence, dress, hairstyles, and behavior of the four hierarchically ranked status groups into which Japanese society was divided—samurai at the top, then peasants, artisans, and, at the bottom, merchants.

During these 250 years of peace, much was changing within Japan in ways that belied the control and orderliness of Tokugawa regulations. For one thing, the samurai, in the absence of wars to fight, evolved into a salaried bureaucratic or administrative class amounting to 5 to 6 percent of the total population, but they remained fiercely devoted to their daimyo lords and to their warrior code of loyalty, honor, and self-sacrifice.

■ **Identifying Change**
In what ways was Japan changing during the Tokugawa era?

More generally, centuries of peace contributed to a remarkable burst of economic growth, commercialization, and urban development. Entrepreneurial peasants, using fertilizers and other agricultural innovations, grew more rice than ever before and engaged in a variety of rural manufacturing enterprises as well. By 1750, Japan had become perhaps the world's most urbanized country, with about 10 percent of its population living in sizable towns or cities. Edo, with perhaps a million residents, was among the world's largest cities. Well-functioning networks of exchange linked urban and rural areas, marking Japan as an emerging market economy. The influence of Confucianism encouraged education and generated a remarkably literate population, with about 40 percent of men and 15 percent of women able to read and write. Although no one was aware of it at the time, these changes during the Tokugawa era provided a solid foundation for Japan's remarkable industrial growth in the late nineteenth century.

Such changes also undermined the shogunate's efforts to freeze Japanese society in the interests of stability. Some samurai found the lowly but profitable path of commerce too much to resist. "No more shall we have to live by the sword," declared one of them in 1616 while renouncing his samurai status. "I have seen that great profit can be made honorably. I shall brew *sake* and soy sauce, and we shall prosper."[12] Many merchants, though hailing from the lowest-ranking status group, prospered in the new commercial environment and supported a vibrant urban culture, while not a few daimyo found it necessary, if humiliating, to seek loans from these social inferiors. Thus merchants had money, but little status, whereas samurai enjoyed high status but were often indebted to inferior merchants. Both resented their positions.

Despite prohibitions to the contrary, many peasants moved to the cities, becoming artisans or merchants and imitating the ways of their social betters. A decree of 1788 noted that peasants "have become accustomed to luxury and forgetful of their status." They wore inappropriate clothing, used umbrellas rather than straw hats in the rain, and even left the villages for the city. "Henceforth," declared the shogun, "all luxuries should be avoided by the peasants. They are to live simply and devote themselves to farming."[13] This decree, like many others before it, was widely ignored.

More than social change undermined the Tokugawa regime. Corruption was widespread, to the disgust of many. The shogunate's failure to deal successfully with a severe famine in the 1830s eroded confidence in its effectiveness. At the same time, a mounting wave of local peasant uprisings and urban riots expressed the many grievances of the poor. The most striking of these outbursts left the city of Osaka in flames in 1837. Its leader, Oshio Heihachiro, no doubt spoke for many ordinary people when he wrote:

> We must first punish the officials who torment the people so cruelly; then we must execute the haughty and rich Osaka merchants. Then we must distribute the gold, silver, and copper stored in their cellars, and bands of rice hidden in their storehouses.[14]

From the 1830s on, one historian concluded, "there was a growing feeling that the *shogunate* was losing control."[15]

American Intrusion and the Meiji Restoration

It was foreign intervention that brought matters to a head. Since the expulsion of European missionaries and the harsh suppression of Christianity in the early seventeenth century, Japan had deliberately limited its contact with the West to a single port, where only the Dutch were allowed to trade. (See "Asians and Asian Commerce" in Chapter 14.) By the early nineteenth century, however, various European countries and the United States were knocking at the door. All were turned away, and even shipwrecked sailors or whalers were expelled, jailed, or executed. As it happened, it was the United States that forced the issue, sending Commodore Perry in 1853 to demand humane treatment for castaways, the right of American vessels to refuel and buy provisions, and the opening of ports for trade. Authorized to use force if necessary, Perry presented his reluctant hosts with, among other gifts, a white flag for surrender should hostilities follow.

In the end, the Japanese avoided war. Aware of what had happened to China as a result of resisting European demands, Japan agreed to a series of unequal treaties with various Western powers. That humiliating capitulation to the demands of the "foreign devils" further eroded support for the shogunate, triggered a brief civil

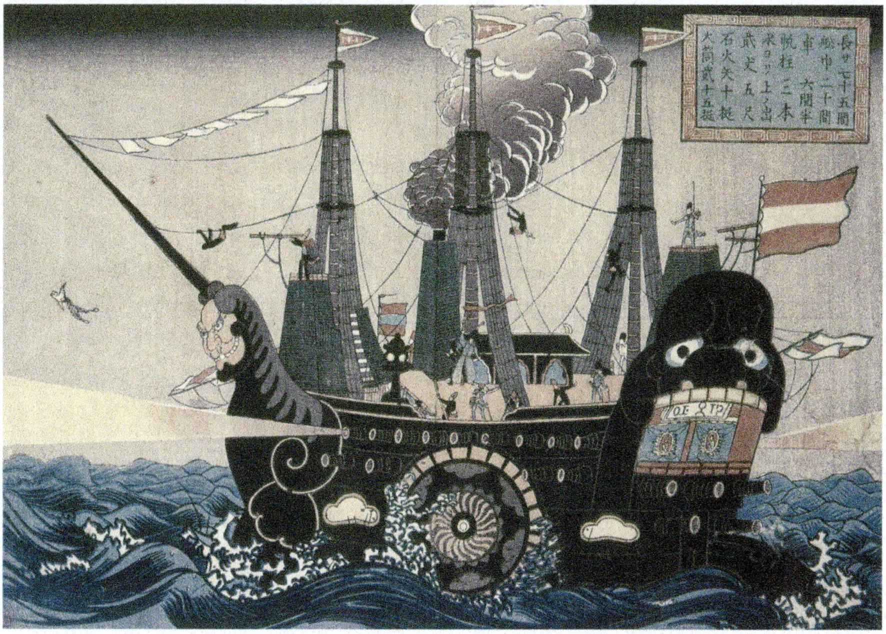

The Black Ships of the United States The initial occasion for serious Japanese reflection on the West occurred in 1853–1854, in the context of American commodore Matthew Perry's efforts to "open" Japan to regular commercial relationships with the United States. His nine coal-fired steamships, belching black smoke and carrying a crew of some 1,800 men and more than 100 mounted cannons, became known in Japan as the "black ships." Created around 1854, this image represents perhaps the best known of many such Japanese depictions of the American warships. (Granger, NYC—All rights reserved)

war, and by 1868 led to a political takeover by a group of young samurai from southern Japan. This decisive turning point in Japan's history was known as the **Meiji Restoration**, for the country's new rulers claimed that they were restoring to power the young emperor, then a fifteen-year-old boy whose throne name was Meiji (MAY-jee), or Enlightened Rule. Despite his youth, he was regarded as the most recent link in a chain of descent that traced the origins of the imperial family back to the sun goddess Amaterasu. Having eliminated the shogunate, the patriotic young men who led the takeover soon made their goals clear—to save Japan from foreign domination not by futile resistance, but by a thorough transformation of Japanese society drawing on all that the modern West had to offer. "Knowledge shall be sought throughout the world," they declared, "so as to strengthen the foundations of imperial rule."

Japan now had a government committed to a decisive break with the past, and it had acquired that government without massive violence or destruction. By contrast, the defeat of the Taiping Uprising had deprived China of any such opportunity for a fresh start, while saddling it with enormous devastation and massive loss of life. Furthermore, Japan was of less interest to Western powers than either China, with its huge potential market and reputation for riches, or the Ottoman Empire, with its strategic location at the crossroads of Asia, Africa, and Europe. The American Civil War and its aftermath likewise deflected U.S. ambitions in the Pacific for a time, further reducing the Western pressure on Japan.

Modernization Japanese-Style

These circumstances gave Japan some breathing space, and its new rulers moved quickly to take advantage of that unique window of opportunity. Thus they launched a cascading wave of dramatic changes that rolled over the country in the last three decades of the nineteenth century. Like the more modest reforms of China and the Ottoman Empire, Japanese modernizing efforts were defensive, based on fears that Japanese independence was in grave danger. Those reforms, however, were revolutionary in their cumulative effect, transforming Japan far more thoroughly than even the most radical of the Ottoman efforts, let alone the limited "self-strengthening" policies of the Chinese.

CORE IDEA

■ Assessing Change and Continuity

In what respects was Japan's nineteenth-century transformation revolutionary? And in what ways did it retain earlier Japanese traditions?

The first task was genuine national unity, which required an attack on the power and privileges of both the daimyo and the samurai. In a major break with the past, the new regime soon ended the semi-independent domains of the daimyo, replacing them with governors appointed by and responsible to the national government. The central state, not the local authorities, now collected the nation's taxes and raised a national army based on conscription from all social classes.

Thus the samurai relinquished their ancient role as the country's warrior class and with it their cherished right to carry swords. The old Confucian-based social order with its special privileges for various classes was largely dismantled, and almost all Japanese became legally equal as commoners and as subjects of the emperor. Limitations on travel and trade likewise fell as a nationwide economy came to parallel the centralized state. Although there was some opposition to these measures, including a brief rebellion of resentful samurai in 1877, it was on the whole a remarkably peaceful process in which a segment of the old ruling class abolished its own privileges. Many, but not all, of these displaced elites found a soft landing in the army, bureaucracy, or business enterprises of the new regime, thus easing a painful transition.

Accompanying these social and political changes was a widespread and eager fascination with almost everything Western. Knowledge about the West—its science and technology; its various political and constitutional arrangements; its legal and educational systems; its dances, clothing, and hairstyles—was enthusiastically sought out by official missions to Europe and the United States, by hundreds of students sent to study abroad, and by many ordinary Japanese at home. Western writers were translated into Japanese. "Civilization and Enlightenment" was the slogan of the time, and both were to be found in the West. The most prominent popularizer of Western knowledge, Fukuzawa Yukichi, summed up the chief lesson of his studies in the mid-1870s—Japan was backward and needed to learn from the West: "If we compare the knowledge of the Japanese and Westerners, in letters, in technique, in commerce, or in industry, from the largest to the smallest matter, there is not one thing in which we excel. . . . In Japan's present condition there is nothing in which we may take pride vis-à-vis the West."[16]

After this initial wave of uncritical enthusiasm for everything Western receded, Japan proceeded to borrow more selectively and to combine foreign and Japanese elements in distinctive ways. For example, drawing heavily on German models, the constitution of 1889 introduced a framework for political representation, including an elected parliament, that many in Japan had been pushing for, but that constitution was presented as a gift from a sacred emperor descended from the sun goddess. The parliament could advise, but ultimate power, and particularly control of the military, lay theoretically with the emperor and in practice with an oligarchy of prominent reformers acting in his name. Likewise, a modern educational system, which achieved universal primary schooling by the early twentieth century, was laced with Confucian-based moral instruction and exhortations of loyalty to the emperor. Christianity made little headway in Meiji Japan, but Shinto, an ancient religious tradition featuring ancestors and nature spirits, was elevated to the status of an official state cult. Japan's experience many centuries before of borrowing massively but selectively from Chinese culture perhaps served it better in these new circumstances than either the Chinese disdain for foreign cultures or the reluctance of many Muslims to see much of value in the infidel West.

Like their counterparts in China and the Ottoman Empire, some reformers in Japan—male and female alike—argued that the oppression of women was an obstacle to the country's modernization and that family reform was essential to gaining the respect of the West. Fukuzawa Yukichi, who was widely read, urged an

Japan's Political Modernization This woodblock print shows a meeting of the House of Peers, one of the new institutions created during the Meiji Restoration that was modeled on European institutions. The peers were chosen primarily from Japan's hereditary nobility. Note the Western dress worn by the peerage at this meeting. (Pictures from History/Bridgeman Images)

end to concubinage and prostitution, advocated more education for girls, and called for gender equality in matters of marriage, divorce, and property rights. But most male reformers understood women largely in the context of family life, seeing them as "good wife, wise mother." By the 1880s, however, a small feminist movement arose, demanding—and modeling—a more public role for women. Some even sought the right to vote at a time when only a small fraction of men could do so. A leading feminist, Kishida Toshiko, not yet twenty years old, astonished the country in 1882 when she undertook a two-month speaking tour during which she addressed huge audiences. Only "equality and equal rights," she argued, would allow Japan "to build a new society." Japan must rid itself of the ancient habit of "respecting men and despising women."

While the new Japanese government included girls in its plans for universal education, it was with a gender-specific curriculum and in schools segregated by sex. Any thought of women playing a role in public life was harshly suppressed. A Peace Preservation Law of 1887, in effect until 1922, forbade women from joining political parties and even from attending meetings where political matters were discussed. The Civil Code of 1898 accorded absolute authority to the male head of the family, while grouping all wives with "cripples and disabled persons" as those who "cannot undertake any legal action." To the authorities of Meiji

Japan, a serious transformation of gender roles was more of a threat than an opportunity.

At the core of Japan's effort at defensive modernization lay its state-guided industrialization program. More than in Europe or the United States, the government itself established a number of enterprises, later selling many of them to private investors. It also acted to create a modern infrastructure by building railroads, creating a postal service, and establishing a national currency and banking system. From the 1880s on, the Japanese government developed a distinctive form of "labor-intensive industrialization" that relied more heavily on the country's abundant workforce and less on the replacement of labor by machinery and capital than in Western Europe or North America.[17]

By the early twentieth century, Japan's industrialization, organized around a number of large firms called *zaibatsu*, was thriving in major urban areas. The country became a major exporter of textiles, in part to pay for imports of raw materials, such as cotton, that were necessary because Japan had limited natural resources. Soon the country was able to produce its own munitions and industrial goods as well. Its major cities enjoyed mass-circulation newspapers, movie theaters, and electric lights. All of this was accomplished through its own resources and without the massive foreign debt that so afflicted Egypt and the Ottoman Empire. No other country outside of Europe and North America had been able to launch its own Industrial Revolution in the nineteenth century. It was a distinctive feature of Japan's modern transformation.

Less distinctive, however, were the social results of that process. Taxed heavily to pay for Japan's ambitious modernization program, many peasant families slid into poverty. Their sometimes violent protests peaked in 1883–1884 as the Japanese countryside witnessed infanticide, the sale of daughters, and starvation.

While state authorities rigidly excluded women from political life and denied them adult legal status, they badly needed female labor in the country's textile industry, which was central to Japan's economic growth. Accordingly, the majority of Japan's textile workers were young women from poor families in the countryside. Recruiters toured rural villages, contracting with parents for their daughters' labor in return for a payment that the girls had to repay from their wages. That pay was low and their working conditions were terrible. Most lived in factory-provided dormitories and worked twelve or more hours per day. While some committed suicide or ran away and many left after earning enough to pay off their contracts, others organized strikes and joined the anarchist or socialist movements that were emerging among a few intellectuals. One such woman, Kanno Sugako, was hanged in 1911 for participating in a plot to assassinate the emperor. Efforts to create unions and organize strikes, both illegal in Japan at the time, were met with harsh repression even as corporate and state authorities sought to depict the company as a family unit to which workers should give their loyalty, all under the beneficent gaze of the divine emperor.

Japanese Women Workers Young women were prominent in Japan's emerging textile industry. The women in this photograph from a silk factory around 1900 are spinning silk threads from raw cocoons. (Pictures from History/Bridgeman Images)

Japan and the World

Japan's modern transformation soon registered internationally. By the early twentieth century, its economic growth, openness to trade, and embrace of "civilization and enlightenment" from the West persuaded the Western powers to revise the unequal treaties in Japan's favor. This had long been a primary goal of the Meiji regime, and the Anglo-Japanese Treaty of 1902 now acknowledged Japan as an equal player among the Great Powers of the world.

Not only did Japan escape from its semi-colonial entanglements with the West, but it also launched its own empire-building enterprise, even as European powers and the United States were carving up much of Asia, Africa, and Pacific Oceania into colonies or spheres of influence. It was what industrializing Great Powers did in the late nineteenth century, and Japan followed suit, in part to compensate for the relative poverty of its natural resource base. A successful war against China (1894–1895) established Japan as a formidable military competitor in East Asia, replacing China as the dominant power in the region. Ten years later in the **Russo-Japanese War** (1904–1905), which was fought over rival imperial ambitions in Korea and Manchuria, Japan became the first Asian state to defeat a major European power. Through those victories, Japan also gained colonial control of Taiwan and Korea and a territorial foothold in Manchuria. And in the aftermath of World War I, Japan acquired a growing influence in China's Shandong Peninsula and control over a number of Micronesian islands under the auspices of the League of Nations.

CORE IDEA

Analyzing Change
How did Japan's relationship to the larger world change during its modernization process?

Japan's entry onto the broader global stage was felt in many places (see Map 19.3). It added yet one more imperialist power to those already burdening a beleaguered China. Defeat at the hands of Japanese upstarts shocked Russia and

Map 19.3 The Rise of Japan
As Japan modernized after the Meiji Restoration, it launched an empire-building program that provided a foundation for further expansion in the 1930s and during World War II.

triggered the 1905 revolution in that country. To Europeans and Americans, Japan was now an economic, political, and military competitor in Asia.

In the world of subject peoples, the rise of Japan and its defeat of Russia generated widespread admiration among those who saw Japan as a model for their own modern development and perhaps as an ally in the struggle against imperialism. Some Poles, Finns, and Jews viewed the Russian defeat in 1905 as an opening for their own liberation from the Russian Empire and were grateful to Japan for the opportunity. Despite Japan's aggression against their country, many Chinese reformers and nationalists found in the Japanese experience valuable lessons for themselves. Thousands flocked to Japan to study its achievements. Newspapers throughout the Islamic world celebrated Japan's victory over Russia as an "awakening of the East" that might herald Muslims' own liberation. Some Turkish women gave their children Japanese names. Indonesian Muslims from Aceh wrote to the Meiji emperor asking for help in their struggle against the Dutch, and Muslim poets wrote odes in his honor. The Egyptian nationalist Mustafa Kamil spoke for many when he declared: "We are amazed by Japan because it is the first Eastern government to utilize Western civilization to resist the shield of European imperialism in Asia."[18]

Those who directly experienced Japanese imperialism in Taiwan or Korea no doubt had a less positive view, for its colonial policies matched or exceeded the brutality of European practices. In the twentieth century, China and much of Southeast Asia suffered bitterly under Japanese imperial aggression. Nonetheless, both the idea of Japan as a liberator of Asia from the European yoke and the reality of Japan as an oppressive imperial power in its own right derived from the country's remarkable modern transformation and its distinctive response to the provocation of Western intrusion.

CONCLUSIONS AND REFLECTIONS

Success and Failure in History

In our endless efforts to understand the past, all of us make judgments about success and failure. In 1900, Europeans often congratulated themselves on their successes during the previous century. They had created unprecedented wealth through their industrial technology; their sciences had penetrated the secrets of nature; their empires spanned the globe; and they had bested both the ancient civilization of China and the previously fearsome Ottoman Empire.

By contrast, thoughtful Chinese in 1900 had much to lament as they pondered their country's failures. They had endured a terribly disruptive civil war that killed many millions; they had suffered numerous military defeats at the hands of Europeans and Japanese, forcing the Chinese into humiliating concessions to these foreigners. Their once powerful state had proved unable to cope with these catastrophes.

Like the Chinese, Ottoman observers around 1900 might well have contemplated the failures of the past century. Their empire had shrunk dramatically, was economically dependent on Europe, and had been unable to create a strong state or economy despite implementing a far more robust reform program than China. In the early twentieth century, both of these old imperial systems collapsed.

But many Japanese, on the eve of the twentieth century, had good reason to celebrate their country's successes. They had created an efficient state and an industrialized economy, which had forestalled European aggression and made Japan one of the Great Powers of the world with the beginnings of an empire of its own.

So had Europe and Japan "succeeded" in the nineteenth century, while China, the Ottoman Empire, and the many colonized peoples of the world had "failed"? The historical record is complex, and we might want to be very careful about how we apply these notions to the past.

If the measure of success is national wealth and power, then Europeans and Japanese had reason to boast about their nineteenth-century achievements, while China and the Ottoman Empire had cause for disappointment. But success for whom? Not everyone shared equally in national prosperity. British artisans who lost their livelihood to industrial machines and Japanese women textile workers who suffered through the early stages of industrialization might be forgiven for not appreciating the "success" of their country's transformation, even if their middle-class counterparts and subsequent generations benefited. Furthermore, European and Japanese success as measured by their empires meant defeat, humiliation, and untold suffering for millions of their colonial subjects.

Success is frequently associated with good judgment and wise choices, yet actors in the historical drama are never completely free in making their decisions, and none, of course, have historians' benefit of hindsight. Did the leaders of China and the Ottoman Empire fail to push industrial development more strongly, or were they not in a position to do so? Were Japanese leaders wiser and more astute than their counterparts elsewhere, or did their knowledge of China's earlier experience and their unique national history simply provide them with circumstances more conducive to modern development?

Finally, national wealth and power are surely not the only criteria for success. Modern science and technology have certainly made human life healthier, longer, and more comfortable for millions. Surely a great success! But they have also eroded the face-to-face relationships of village life, undermined the comforts of religious belief, and generated massive environmental changes—global warming in particular—that pose severe threats to modern societies.

Questions about success and failure have no clear-cut answers, but they usefully highlight the ambiguity and uncertainty of historical judgments and foster humility in the face of immense complexity.

Revisiting Chapter 19

Revisiting Specifics

Taiping Uprising, 832
Opium Wars, 834
Commissioner Lin Zexu, 835
unequal treaties, 835
informal empires, 836
self-strengthening, 837
Boxer Uprising, 839
Chinese revolution of 1911–1912, 840
"the sick man of Europe," 840
Tanzimat, 843
Young Ottomans, 844
Sultan Abd al-Hamid II, 844
Young Turks, 845
Tokugawa Japan, 847
Meiji Restoration, 850
Russo-Japanese War, 854

Revisiting Core Ideas

1. **Defining Challenges** How did China's internal and external challenges intersect during the nineteenth century?
2. **Assessing Strategies** What strategies did China adopt to confront its various problems? Why were they so unsuccessful?
3. **Making Comparisons** In what ways were the histories of China and the Ottoman Empire similar during the nineteenth century? And how did they differ?
4. **Assessing Change and Continuity** In what respects was Japan's nineteenth-century transformation revolutionary? And in what ways did it retain earlier Japanese traditions?
5. **Analyzing Change** How did Japan's relationship to the larger world change during its modernization process?

A Wider View

1. "The response of each society to European imperialism grew out of its larger historical development and its particular internal problems." What evidence might support this statement?
2. Were deliberate government policies or historical circumstances more important in shaping the history of China, the Ottoman Empire, and Japan during the nineteenth century?
3. What kinds of debates, controversies, and conflicts were generated by European intrusion within each of the societies examined in this chapter?
4. **Looking Back** How did the experiences of China, the Ottoman Empire, Japan, and Latin America, all of which retained their independence despite much European pressure, differ from those of Africa, India, Southeast Asia, and Pacific Oceania, which fell under formal colonial rule?

To learn more about the topics in this chapter, see **For Further Study** at the end of the book.

WORKING WITH EVIDENCE

China: On the Brink of Change

By the end of the nineteenth century, growing numbers of thoughtful Chinese recognized that their country was in crisis. A decisive military defeat in a war with Japan (1894–1895) represented a further humiliation to a country already reduced to being a semi-colonial dependent of various European powers. And the Boxer rebellion (1898–1901) disclosed a virulent antiforeign and anti-Christian outlook even among rural people. This upheaval demonstrated—once again—the ability of China's vast peasant population to make its presence felt in the political life of the country, as it had in the Taiping Uprising of the 1850s and 1860s (see "The Crisis Within" earlier in this chapter). Its outcome—foreign occupation of Beijing and large reparation payments from China's government—revealed China's continuing weakness relative to European powers and Japan.

In this context, many educated Chinese began to consider various alternatives to the status quo. Some sought reform of various kinds, aimed at preserving the Qing dynasty regime. And several such projects were initiated: ending the traditional civil service examination system, modernizing the military, having consultations about a constitution, and creating elected provincial assemblies. Other voices were more revolutionary, seeking to replace dynastic China with a new society and political system altogether. The climax of this process occurred in 1912 with the collapse of the Qing dynasty and the end of several millennia of imperial rule. The sources that follow provide a glimpse of the various possibilities that awaited China on the brink of dramatic transformation.

SOURCE 19.1 Toward a Constitutional Monarchy

Among the leading advocates of reform in the aftermath of China's defeat by Japan was Kang Youwei (1858–1927), a brilliant Confucian scholar and political thinker. Understanding Confucius as a reformer, he argued that the emperor could be an active agent for China's transformation while operating in a parliamentary and constitutional setting. With its emphasis on human goodness, self-improvement, and the moral example of superiors, Confucianism could provide a framework for real change even as it protected China from "moral degeneration" and an indiscriminate embrace of Western culture. In an appeal to the emperor in early 1898, Kang Youwei spelled out his understanding of what China needed.

- In what ways does Kang Youwei express a Confucian outlook, and in what respects does he show an awareness of a larger world?
- What obstacles to reform does Kang Youwei identify?
- Why does he advocate the Russia of Peter the Great and Meiji Japan as models for China rather than Western Europe and the United States?

KANG YOUWEI | *An Appeal to Emperor Guangxu* | 1898

A survey of all states in the world will show that those states that undertook reforms became stronger while those states which clung to the past perished. . . . If Your Majesty, with your discerning brilliance, observes the trends in other countries, you will see that if we can change, we can preserve ourselves; but if we cannot change, we shall perish. . . .

It is a principle of things that the new is strong but the old is weak. . . . [T]here are no institutions that should remain unchanged for a hundred years. Moreover our present institutions are but unworthy vestiges of the Han, Tang, Yuan, and Ming dynasties. . . . [T]hey are the products of fancy writing and corrupt dealing of the petty officials rather than the original ideas of the ancestors. To say that they are ancestral institutions is an insult to the ancestors. Furthermore institutions are for the purpose of preserving one's territories. Now that the ancestral territory cannot be preserved, what good is it to maintain the ancestral institutions? . . .

Nowadays the court has been undertaking some reforms, but the action of the emperor is obstructed by the ministers, and the recommendations of the able scholars are attacked by old-fashioned bureaucrats. If the charge is not "using barbarian ways to change China," then it is "upsetting ancestral institutions." . . . I beg Your Majesty to make up your mind and to decide on the national policy.

After studying ancient and modern institutions, Chinese and foreign, I have found that . . . ancient times were different from today. I hope that Your Majesty will daily read Mencius [a famous Confucian writer] and follow his example of loving the people . . . but it should be remembered that the [present] age of universal unification is different from that of sovereign nations. . . . As to the republican governments of the United States and France and the constitutional governments of Britain and Germany, these countries are far away and their customs are different from ours. . . . Consequently I beg Your Majesty to adopt the purpose of Peter the Great of Russia as our purpose and to take the Meiji Reform of Japan as the model of our reform. The time and place of Japan's reforms are not remote and her religion and customs are somewhat similar to ours. Her success is manifest; her example can be followed.

Source: Wm. Theodore de Bary and Richard Lufrano, eds., *Sources of Chinese Tradition: From 1600 through the Twentieth Century* (New York: Columbia University Press, 2000), 269–70.

SOURCE 19.2 Resistance to Change

A growing reform movement also triggered conservative opposition, rooted in particular understandings of China's Confucian tradition. These brief excerpts from more traditionally oriented Chinese scholars illustrate that opposition.

- What specific values or principles are evoked in these excerpts?
- How might Kang Youwei respond to them?

Conservative Reactions after the Sino-Japanese War | **late 19th–early 20th centuries**

From Zeng Lian: "The state (dynasty) belongs to the ancestors; the emperor merely maintains the dynasty for them. He cannot change the permanent laws laid down by the ancestors."

From Chu Chengbo: ". . . [O]ur trouble is not that we lack good institutions, but that we lack upright minds. If we seek to reform institutions, we must first reform men's minds. Unless all men of ability assist each other, good laws become mere paper documents; unless those who supervise them are fair and enlightened, the venal will end up occupying the places of the worthy. . . ."

From Ye Dehui: "An examination of the causes of success and failure in government reveals that in general the upholding of Confucianism leads to good government and the adoption of foreignism leads to disorder. . . . Confucianism represents the supreme expression of justice in the principles of Heaven and the hearts of men."

Source: Wm. Theodore de Bary and Richard Lufrano, eds., *Sources of Chinese Tradition: From 1600 through the Twentieth Century* (New York: Columbia University Press, 2000), 274–75, 279–80.

SOURCE 19.3 Gender, Reform, and Revolution

Among those seeking to change China, the question of women's roles in society frequently arose. The most well-known advocate for women was Qiu Jin (1875–1907). Born into a well-to-do family with liberal inclinations and married to a much older man at age eighteen, she was distinctly unsatisfied in such a conventional life and developed a growing feminist awareness, sometimes dressing in men's clothes and Western styles. In 1903, Qiu Jin left her husband and children to pursue an education in Japan, selling her jewelry to finance the trip. Returning to China in 1906, she started a women's magazine, the *Chinese Women's Journal*, which was a strong advocate for women's independence and education. Soon Qiu Jin became active in revolutionary circles. For her role in an abortive plot to overthrow the Qing dynasty, she was arrested, tortured, and beheaded in 1907 at the age of thirty-two. The selection that follows comes from her most famous appeal for the rights of women.

- How does Qiu Jin describe the difficulties that faced Chinese women?
- How does she account for these sad conditions?
- What does she advocate as a remedy for the problems she identifies? Does she seem to have a political agenda?
- To what extent do you think she was writing from personal experience?

QIU JIN | *Address to Two Hundred Million Fellow Countrywomen* | 1904

Alas, the most unfairly treated things on this earth are the two hundred million who are born as Chinese women. We consider ourselves lucky to be born to a kind father. If we are unlucky, our father will be an ill-tempered and unreasonable person who . . . will resent us and say things like "she's eventually going to someone else's family" and give us cold and contemptuous looks. When we grow a few years older, without bothering to ask us our thoughts, they will bind our tender, white and natural feet with a strip of cloth. . . . In the end, the flesh is mangled and the bones broken, all so that relatives, friends and neighbors can say, "the girl from so and so's family has tiny feet."

When the time comes (for the parents) to select a husband . . . , the daughter's parents will go along with any proposal as long as his family is rich and powerful. . . . On the wedding day, one will sit in the brightly decorated bridal sedan chair barely able to breathe. When we arrive at the new home, if the husband is . . . no good, her family will blame it "on our wrong conduct in a previous life," or simply "bad luck." If we dare complain, or otherwise try to counsel our husbands, then a scolding and beating will befall us. Others who hear of the abuse will say: "She is a woman of no virtue. She does not act as a wife should!" Can you believe such words? . . . Further inequities will follow if the husband dies. The wife will have to wear a mourning dress for three years and will not be allowed to remarry. Yet, if the wife dies, the husband only needs to wear a blue (mourning) braid. Some men find even that unbecoming and do not bother to wear it at all. Even when the wife has only been dead for three days, he can go out and cavort and indulge himself. . . . In the beginning, Heaven created all people with no differences between men and women. . . . Why are things so unjust? Everyday these men say, "We ought to be equal and treat people kindly." Then why do they treat women so unfairly and unequally as if they were African slaves?

A woman has to learn not to depend on others, but to rely on herself instead. . . . Why can't we reject footbinding? Are they afraid of women being educated, knowledgeable, and perhaps surpassing them? Men do not allow us to study. We must not simply go along with their decision without even challenging them. . . .

However, from now on I hope we can leave the past behind us and focus on our future. . . . If you have a decent husband who wants to establish a school, do not stop him. If you have a fine son who wishes to study abroad, do not stop him. . . . If you have a son, send him to school. Do the same for your daughter and never bind her feet. If you have a young girl, the best choice would be for her to attend school, but even if she is unable to attend schools, you should teach her to read and write at home. If you come from a family of officials that has money, you should persuade your husband to establish schools and factories and do good deeds that will help common people. If your family is poor, you should work hard to help your husband. . . . These are my hopes. All of you are aware that we are about to lose our country. Men can scarcely protect themselves. How can we rely on them? We must revitalize ourselves. Otherwise all will be too late when the country is lost. Everybody! Everybody! Please keep my hopes alive!

Source: David G. Atwill and Lurong Y. Atwill, *Sources in Chinese History* (Upper Saddle River, NJ: Prentice Hall, 2010), 140–41.

SOURCE 19.4 Cutting the Queue

Another sign of changing times in late nineteenth-century China was the growing frequency with which more radical Chinese men began to cut or hide their *queue*, the long braided tail of hair that descended from their largely shaved heads. That hairstyle had been forcibly imposed by Manchu rulers of the Qing dynasty and had been periodically resisted since the seventeenth century. From the mid-1890s on, cutting the queue became a symbol of opposition to the Qing dynasty, of a favorable attitude toward modernization, and of a commitment to substantial political change in China. Source 19.4 provides an illustration from 1911 of this radical political action.

- How do you imagine the responses to this event of the various figures visible in the image? Notice especially the man in the lower left with his hands upraised and the man in Western dress in the lower right.
- How does the public setting for this event shape your understanding of its significance? Keep in mind also that earlier in its history, the Qing dynasty had applied the death penalty for those cutting their queue.

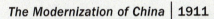

The Modernization of China | **1911**

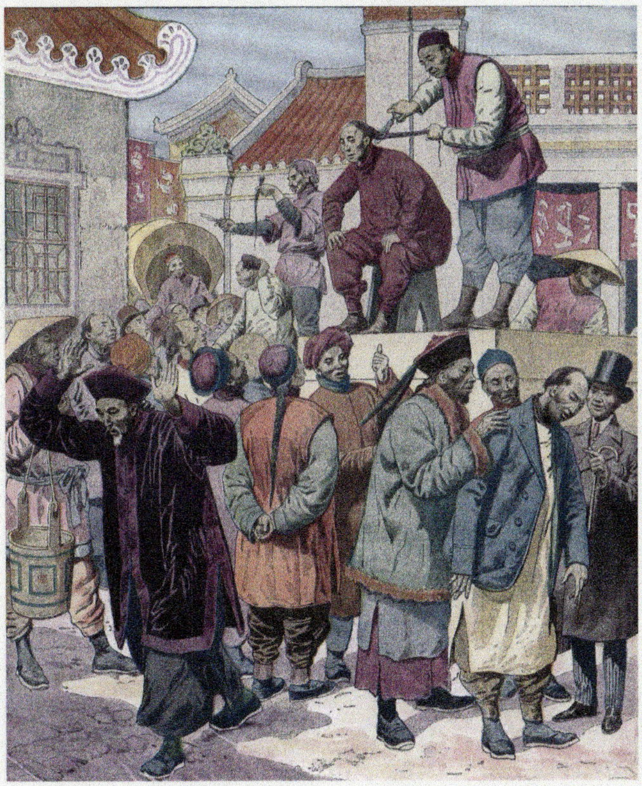

Historia/Shutterstock

SOURCE 19.5 Toward Revolution

While some advocates for change pressed for various reforms within the framework of Qing dynasty China, others felt that the millennia-old monarchy itself had to be overthrown if China was to modernize and prosper as a nation. Among them was Wang Jingwei, a political figure who had studied in Japan and later joined the revolutionary movement. When the Chinese government in 1908 announced plans for developing a quite conservative constitution, Wang Jingwei wrote a ferocious rebuttal, excerpted in Source 19.5. At the time, he was in prison awaiting execution for his revolutionary activities.

- Why does Wang Jingwei believe that an effective constitutional government can be achieved only after a revolution?
- What kind of revolution does he prescribe?
- How might Kang Youwei respond to this revolutionary manifesto?

WANG JINGWEI | ***We Want a Republic, Not a Constitutional Monarchy*** | **April 25, 1910**

The constitutionalists say that . . . the establishment of a constitutional monarchy will lead to the establishment of a good government. But we revolutionaries emphatically do not share this optimism. . . . [U]nless the monarchal power is destroyed, there is no way of eliminating the existing state system and replacing it with something new.

For several thousand years China has practiced nothing but autocracy. . . . The state power is vested with the monarch, and officials on all levels, central or local, are merely his servants or slaves, whom he can order to whatever he pleases. Suddenly enchanted with the good name of constitution, this autocratic China decided to promote one.

It is our belief that only under a constitutional government established in the wake of a revolution can the principles of nationalism and democracy be carried out. . . .

Speaking of [China's] relations with the outside world, we cannot but feel frightened and alarmed; she is so weak that her chance of survival, for all practical purposes, has become very slim indeed. Knowing her impending peril, how can any Chinese enjoy peace of mind . . . ?

[W]ith a constitutional government scheduled to be established, everyone believes that all of China's problems, foreign and domestic, will be automatically resolved. Like a man who has taken hallucinatory drugs, we are fascinated with appearance at the expense of reality.

Neither will the situation improve nor can she be rejuvenated unless there is a basic change in political structure. The time for making this change is very late, but by no means too late.

Source: Wang Ching-wei, "We Want a Republic, Not a Constitutional Monarchy," in *China in Transition: 1517–1911*, ed. Dun J. Li (New York: Van Nostrand Reinhold, 1969), 319–24.

SOURCE 19.6 The Chinese Revolution of 1911

In late 1911 and early 1912, more than 2,000 years of Chinese imperial history came to an inglorious end amid the confused maneuverings of various revolutionary groups, Qing dynasty loyalists, and constitutional reformers. The young boy-emperor Puyi abdicated the imperial throne, and power passed to a prominent military leader, Yuan Shikai. Revolutionary ideas had penetrated the ranks of both officers and soldiers in China's modernizing "New Army," which had been in the making since 1901. Source 19.6, from a French newspaper of 1911, provides a visual account of the evolution of the Chinese military, with figures on the left representing older and now outdated Qing dynasty units, and those on the right depicting the modernized forces of the New Army that were so instrumental in the revolution of 1911. As it happened, those dramatic events were but the prelude for a far deeper and more violent revolutionary transformation of China in the half century that followed. At the time, however, they marked a momentous turning point for an ancient civilization poised at the edge of a tumultuous upheaval.

- What distinguishes these two groups of military men from one another?
- What does the image imply about their attitudes toward one another?
- How might the authors of the other sources respond to the 1911 revolution?

About the Insurrectional Movement in China | **1911**

DOING HISTORY

1. **Defining Obstacles to Change** What hindrances to China's effective transformation are stated or implied in these sources?
2. **Assessing Outcomes** What do these sources contribute to an understanding of the eventual collapse of the Qing dynasty?
3. **Assessing Goals** "China as a culture and a political system must be destroyed in order to preserve China as a nation." To what extent would the creators of these sources have agreed or disagreed with this statement?
4. **Identifying Differences** Imagine a conversation among the authors of the written sources in this collection. What points of agreement might they find? What conflicts would likely arise among them?

The Sino-Japanese War of 1894–1895

The war between China and Japan during 1894–1895, fought largely over control of Korea, signaled a radical reversal in the historical relationship of these two East Asian countries. It also marked major turning points in the internal development of both countries. Voice 19.1, from two Chinese historians, David Atwill and Yurong Atwill, describes the significance of that war for China, while historian James Huffman does the same for Japan in Voice 19.2.

- In what ways was the Sino-Japanese War devastating for China?
- What impact did the Sino-Japanese War have on Japan?
- **Integrating Primary and Secondary Sources** What evidence from the primary sources might support the Atwills' conclusion that the Sino-Japanese War "marks the beginning of the end for the Qing dynasty"?

VOICE 19.1

David Atwill and Yurong Atwill on the Significance of the War for China | 2010

[N]o military loss affected the Qing court and the Chinese populace quite as much as their defeat at the hands of the Japanese. . . . For centuries China had sat at the center of a vast tributary network, with neighboring countries acknowledging China's dominant military, political and commercial importance. . . . Contemporary observers all assumed Japan would be defeated quickly. It was a horrible shock to China when Japan not only routed Chinese troops dispatched to Korea, but with devastating precision devastated China's navy. These defeats dealt a savage blow to China's national pride. . . .

If the war eroded China's confidence, the peace was excruciating. With the Treaty of Shimonoseki, Japan proved itself fully as capable as its European counterparts at extracting concessions, indemnities, and territories. The Chinese public, who had been sheltered from the Qing's lack of military modernization, were whipped into a frenzy over the defeats and were further enraged at [China's] submissive acceptance of Japan's peace terms. While the Qing dynasty survived for another fifteen years, it would never recover psychologically from the humiliation it received at the hands of the Japanese. This truly marks the beginning of the end for the Qing dynasty.

Source: David G. Atwill and Yurong Y. Atwill, *Sources in Chinese History* (Upper Saddle River, NJ: Prentice Hall, 2010), 89–90.

VOICE 19.2

James L. Huffman on the Significance of the War for Japan | 2010

More important than the victory . . . was the explosion of patriotic fervor the war ignited at home. "The excitement generated among the Japanese people was beyond imagination," the commentator Ubukata Toshiro recalled. . . . By war's end, Japan had become a different place; proud of defeating Asia's giant, confident in its military might, thirsty for more territory.

The postwar years saw a rush of support for this vision of strength, even as Japan's cities became both modern and massive. . . . In part, that reflected a rise in industry—and city jobs—as the Sino-Japanese War indemnity poured more than 300 million yen into the economy. . . . When Japan provided roughly half of the international force that put down China's Boxer Rebellion in 1900, and then shared handsomely in the indemnity, the pride that had marked the Sino-Japanese War was reignited.

Source: James L. Huffman, *Japan in World History* (Oxford: Oxford University Press, 2010), 86, 88.

PART 6

The Long Twentieth Century

1900–present

THE BIG PICTURE

The Long Twentieth Century: A New Period in World History?

The years since 1900, or perhaps a little earlier, appear to many historians as a new and distinct phase of the human journey, in large part because the pace of change has so sharply accelerated during this relatively brief time. The world wars during the first half of the twentieth century were far more destructive than earlier conflicts, and the development of nuclear weapons has provided humankind a completely unprecedented capacity for destruction. Both fascism and communism challenged established

PHOTOS: left, © Look and Learn/Bridgeman Images; center, SIMON MAINA/AFP/Getty Images; right, Image created by Reto Stockli, Nazmi El Saleous, and Marit Jentoft-Nilsen, NASA GSFC

Western values as they presented new political ideologies to the world. The architecture of global politics changed several times—from a world dominated by European imperial powers, to one structured around the rivalry of two superpowers among some 200 independent states, and by the end of the twentieth century to a global system with one military superpower and a widening array of other centers of economic, military, and political influence.

Beneath the surface of these dramatic events, more significant and enduring processes likewise accelerated at an unprecedented rate. Industrialization quickly became a genuinely global phenomenon, accompanied by a massive increase in energy consumption and overall wealth, a soaring population, and rapid urbanization. Furthermore, long-distance migration mixed the world's peoples in novel ways, generating new social patterns and cultural identities. Feminists mounted an unprecedented attack on patriarchal attitudes and practices, while religious fundamentalists renewed their faith, often in opposition to established political and religious authorities.

But the most fundamental of these processes involved an extraordinary and mounting human impact on the environment. The well-known world historian David Christian has written that "the big story of the twentieth century is how one species began to dominate the energy and resources of the biosphere as a whole."[1] By the late twentieth century, that dominance had taken humankind well into what many scientists have been calling the Anthropocene era, the age of man, in which human activity is leaving an enduring and global mark on the geological, atmospheric, and biological history of the planet itself. All of this has been part of an astonishing and sometimes disorienting rate of change in human life.

A further distinctive feature of the human story during the past 100 years or so is an increasingly thick connectedness or entanglement that we commonly refer to as "globalization." It found expression in the worldwide empires of major European powers, in a great increase of international trade and investment, in the flow of ideas and cultural patterns around the world, in the large-scale movements of people, and in the global spread of diseases. War, economic crises, communism, fundamentalism, feminism, and the warming of the planet all operated on a global scale. The speed with which this globalizing world took shape and the density of the connections it forged—these too arguably mark the past century or more as a new era in world history.

But if speed and change mark the past century or so, there were also elements of continuity with the more distant past. Interaction among distinct societies, civilizations, and regions has a very long history. "Contact with strangers possessing new and unfamiliar skills," wrote world historian William McNeill, has long been "the principal factor promoting historically significant social change."[2] In that sense, modern globalization has an ancient pedigree. Furthermore, the collapse of empires during the past century resonates with the dissolution of many earlier empires. Technological innovation too has been a feature of human societies since the beginning, and human activity has left its mark on the planet since our gathering and hunting ancestors decimated a number of large animal species. Billions of people continue to operate in the tradition of long-established religions. Not everything has been new since 1900.

And even if world historians emphasize global networks and connections, what was local, regional, and particular continued to matter. Communism may have been a global phenomenon, but its Russian, Chinese, and Cuban variants were hardly identical. Feminism in the Global North certainly differed from that of the Global South. Economic globalization elicited both a warm embrace among corporate and technological elites and bitter rejection from those whose livelihoods and values were threatened by global linkages. Family, village, city, and nation remain deeply meaningful communities even in an interconnected world. Not everything has been global in this most recent era of world history.

In recounting this history, the four chapters of Part 6 do emphasize what was new, what was rapidly changing, and what was global, but with an eye on what persisted from the past and what was unique to particular places. Chapters 20 and 21 highlight the major events or "milestones" of this era. Thus Chapter 20 focuses on the first half of the twentieth century: the world wars, the Great Depression, the rise of fascist and authoritarian movements and states, and the beginnings of communism in Russia and China, all of this cast in a global context. Chapter 21 then carries this narrative of events from roughly 1950 to 2021. It examines the postwar recovery of Europe, the Soviet Union, and Japan; the emergence of a distinctive Chinese communism; the cold war; the end of European empires in Asia and Africa; the emergence of dozens of new states on the global stage; the demise of communism; and international tensions in the three decades since the end of the cold war.

With these "milestones" of the past century in mind, Chapters 22 and 23 turn to the larger and perhaps even more consequential processes occurring beneath the surface of major public events. Chapter 22 treats the enormous acceleration of technological innovation as a decisive driver of a deeply interconnected world economy and of pervasive social change. Chapter 23 then turns the spotlight on the explosive growth of human numbers, on the movement of many people to the cities and to new lives abroad, and on the cultural transformations that accompanied modern life during the past century. The chapter — and the book — conclude by examining the enormous and continuing impact of human activity on the entire biosphere, which represents by far the most significant long-term process of this new era and the most critical challenge of the next century.

The accelerating changes of this globalizing century have elicited a wide range of responses. Some individuals and communities welcomed changes that brought them unheard-of levels of material comfort and opportunities for an enriched personal life. Others resisted, denied, or sought to endure and adapt to changes that produced loss, disappointment, impoverishment, and sometimes horror beyond imagination. Reflecting on the flux and flow of this tumultuous era allows all of us—historians and students of history alike—to assess these recent transformations of the human condition, to locate ourselves in this torrent of change, and to ponder what lies ahead.

FIRST REFLECTIONS

1. **Questioning Chronology** How might you support the idea that the time spanning the twentieth century to today is a distinct period of world history? How might you criticize this idea? What alternative possibilities occur to you?
2. **Assessing Markers of Change** Do you think that events (World War I, the Russian Revolution, the end of European empires) or processes (population growth, globalization, technological innovation, climate change) provide the best indicators of new phases of world history?
3. **Comparing Significance** Do you think that population growth, globalization, technological innovation, or climate change has had the greatest impact on the course of world history over the past century? What criteria did you use to make this assessment?
4. **Thinking Like a World Historian** What events and processes in the twentieth century do you think will appear as most significant to historians living a hundred years from now? What will likely garner less attention? Why?

Landmarks in World History (ca. 1900–present)

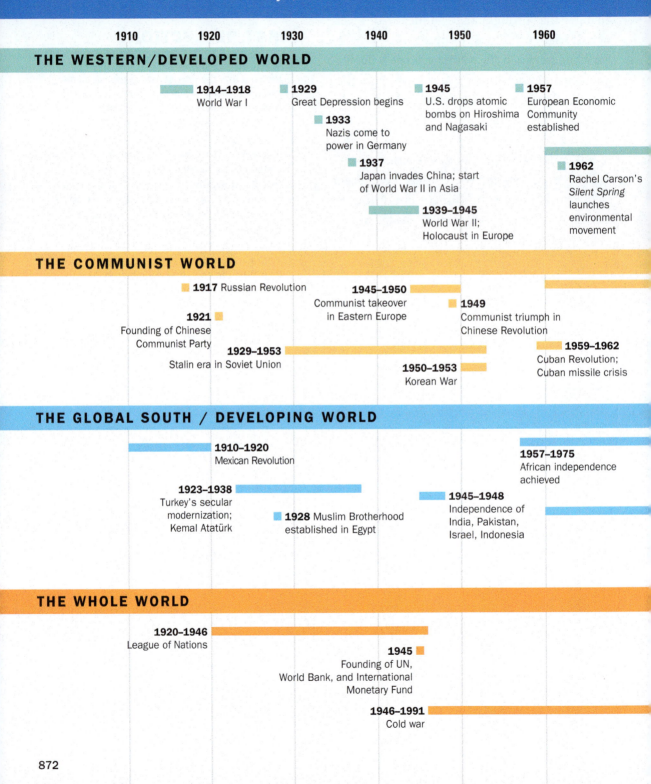

1910 | 1920 | 1930 | 1940 | 1950 | 1960

THE WESTERN/DEVELOPED WORLD

1914–1918 World War I

1929 Great Depression begins

1933 Nazis come to power in Germany

1937 Japan invades China; start of World War II in Asia

1939–1945 World War II; Holocaust in Europe

1945 U.S. drops atomic bombs on Hiroshima and Nagasaki

1957 European Economic Community established

1962 Rachel Carson's *Silent Spring* launches environmental movement

THE COMMUNIST WORLD

1917 Russian Revolution

1921 Founding of Chinese Communist Party

1929–1953 Stalin era in Soviet Union

1945–1950 Communist takeover in Eastern Europe

1949 Communist triumph in Chinese Revolution

1950–1953 Korean War

1959–1962 Cuban Revolution; Cuban missile crisis

THE GLOBAL SOUTH / DEVELOPING WORLD

1910–1920 Mexican Revolution

1923–1938 Turkey's secular modernization; Kemal Atatürk

1928 Muslim Brotherhood established in Egypt

1945–1948 Independence of India, Pakistan, Israel, Indonesia

1957–1975 African independence achieved

THE WHOLE WORLD

1920–1946 League of Nations

1945 Founding of UN, World Bank, and International Monetary Fund

1946–1991 Cold war

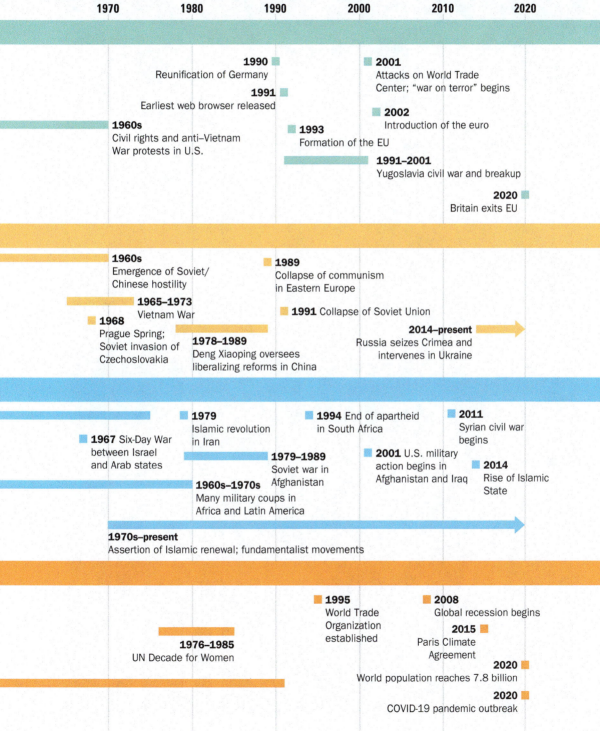

1970 | 1980 | 1990 | 2000 | 2010 | 2020

1990 Reunification of Germany

1991 Earliest web browser released

1960s Civil rights and anti–Vietnam War protests in U.S.

1993 Formation of the EU

2001 Attacks on World Trade Center; "war on terror" begins

2002 Introduction of the euro

1991–2001 Yugoslavia civil war and breakup

2020 Britain exits EU

1960s Emergence of Soviet/Chinese hostility

1965–1973 Vietnam War

1968 Prague Spring; Soviet invasion of Czechoslovakia

1978–1989 Deng Xiaoping oversees liberalizing reforms in China

1989 Collapse of communism in Eastern Europe

1991 Collapse of Soviet Union

2014–present Russia seizes Crimea and intervenes in Ukraine

1967 Six-Day War between Israel and Arab states

1979 Islamic revolution in Iran

1979–1989 Soviet war in Afghanistan

1960s–1970s Many military coups in Africa and Latin America

1994 End of apartheid in South Africa

2001 U.S. military action begins in Afghanistan and Iraq

2011 Syrian civil war begins

2014 Rise of Islamic State

1970s–present Assertion of Islamic renewal; fundamentalist movements

1976–1985 UN Decade for Women

1995 World Trade Organization established

2008 Global recession begins

2015 Paris Climate Agreement

2020 World population reaches 7.8 billion

2020 COVID-19 pandemic outbreak

PhotoQuest/Getty Images

CHAPTER

20 War and Revolution

1900–1950

CONNECTING PAST AND PRESENT

"The First World War was described at the time as the war to end all wars. It did nothing of the sort."[1] So said UN secretary general Ban Ki-moon at an event in 2014 marking one hundred years since the outbreak of that global conflict. And in 2017, the one-hundredth anniversary of the Russian Revolution, Russian president Vladimir Putin offered a commentary on that event. "Could we not have evolved by way of gradual and consistent forward movement," he asked, "rather than at the cost of destroying our statehood and the ruthless fracturing of millions of human lives?"[2] Both men reflected a widespread and intense sense of disappointment, even futility, about events that had earlier been greeted with great expectations.

However they are evaluated, these two immense upheavals—World War I and the Russian Revolution—initiated a chain of events that shaped much of world history during the past century. They were followed by the economic meltdown of the Great Depression, by the rise of Nazi Germany and the horror of the Holocaust, and by an even bloodier and more destructive World War II, a struggle that encompassed much of the world. Among the major outcomes of that war was the Chinese Revolution, which brought a modern Communist Party to power in that ancient land. Within the colonial world of Africa, Asia, and the Middle East, these events set in motion processes of change that would

« **Global War** This propaganda poster created during World War II and entitled "Together" depicts soldiers from various parts of Britain's far-flung empire marching in unity. While it celebrates an alleged spirit of cooperation between Europeans and their colonial subjects during this global conflict, the war contributed in many ways to the breakup of these empires described in Chapter 21.

SEEKING THE MAIN POINT

In what ways were war, depression, and revolution motors of global change during the first half of the twentieth century?

shortly put an end to Europe's global empires. It was, to put it mildly, an eventful half century, and many of its developments had their origins in the First World War and the Russian Revolution.

The First World War: A European Crisis with a Global Impact, 1914–1918

Since 1500, Europe had assumed an increasingly prominent position on the global stage, reflected in its military capacity, its colonial empires, and its Scientific and Industrial Revolutions (see Map 20.1). That unique situation provided the foundation for Europeans' pride, self-confidence, and sense of superiority. In 1900, few could have imagined that this "proud tower" of European dominance would lie shattered less than a half century later. The starting point in that unraveling was the First World War.

Origins: The Beginnings of the Great War

Europe's modern transformation and its global ascendancy were certainly not accompanied by a growing unity or stability among its own peoples—in fact, quite the opposite. The historical rivalries of its competing nation-states further sharpened as both Italy and Germany joined their fragmented territories into two major new powers around 1870. A powerful and rapidly industrializing Germany, seeking its "place in the sun," was a particularly disruptive new element in European political life, especially for the more established powers, such as Britain, France, and Russia. Since the defeat of Napoleon in 1815, a fragile and fluctuating balance of power had generally maintained the peace among Europe's major countries. By the early twentieth century, that balance of power was expressed in two rival alliances, the Triple Alliance of Germany, Italy, and the Austro-Hungarian Empire and the Triple Entente of Russia, France, and Britain. Those commitments, undertaken in the interests of national security, transformed a relatively minor incident in the Balkans (southeastern Europe) into a conflagration that consumed almost all of Europe.

That incident occurred on June 28, 1914, when a Serbian nationalist assassinated the heir to the Austro-Hungarian throne, Archduke Franz Ferdinand. To the rulers of Austria-Hungary, the surging nationalism of Serbian Slavs was a mortal threat to the cohesion of their fragile multinational empire, which included other Slavic peoples as well. Thus they determined to crush it. But behind Austria-Hungary lay its far more powerful ally, Germany; and behind tiny Serbia lay Russia, with its self-proclaimed mission of protecting other Slavic peoples. Allied to Russia were the French and the British. Thus a system of alliances intended to keep the

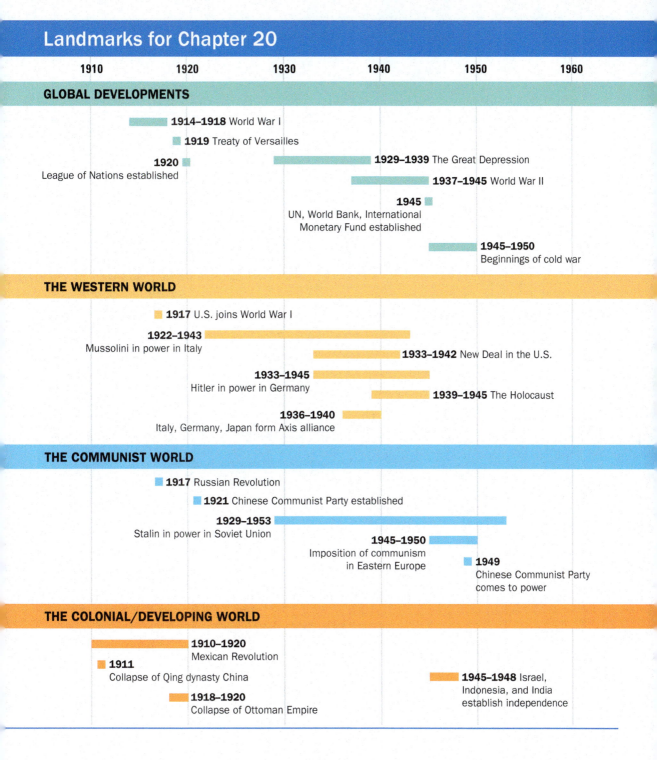

Landmarks for Chapter 20

1910 | 1920 | 1930 | 1940 | 1950 | 1960

GLOBAL DEVELOPMENTS

- **1914–1918** World War I
- **1919** Treaty of Versailles
- **1920** League of Nations established
- **1929–1939** The Great Depression
- **1937–1945** World War II
- **1945** UN, World Bank, International Monetary Fund established
- **1945–1950** Beginnings of cold war

THE WESTERN WORLD

- **1917** U.S. joins World War I
- **1922–1943** Mussolini in power in Italy
- **1933–1942** New Deal in the U.S.
- **1933–1945** Hitler in power in Germany
- **1939–1945** The Holocaust
- **1936–1940** Italy, Germany, Japan form Axis alliance

THE COMMUNIST WORLD

- **1917** Russian Revolution
- **1921** Chinese Communist Party established
- **1929–1953** Stalin in power in Soviet Union
- **1945–1950** Imposition of communism in Eastern Europe
- **1949** Chinese Communist Party comes to power

THE COLONIAL/DEVELOPING WORLD

- **1910–1920** Mexican Revolution
- **1911** Collapse of Qing dynasty China
- **1945–1948** Israel, Indonesia, and India establish independence
- **1918–1920** Collapse of Ottoman Empire

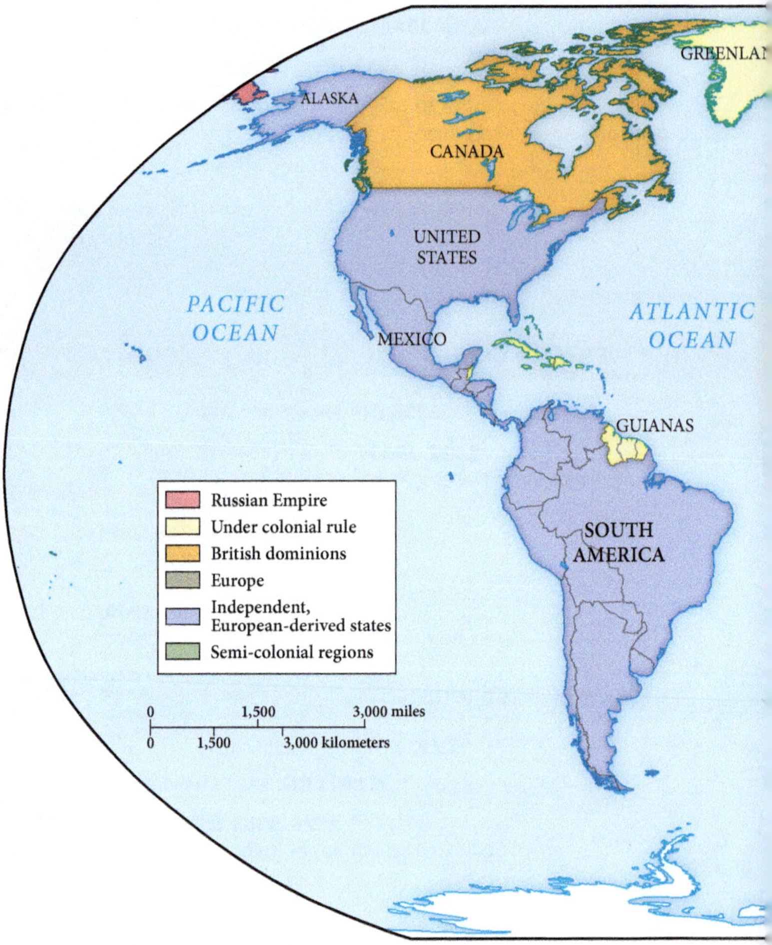

Map 20.1 The World in 1914

A map of the world in 1914 shows an unprecedented situation in which one people—Europeans or those of European descent—exercised enormous control and influence over virtually the entire planet.

peace created obligations that drew these Great Powers of Europe into a general war by early August 1914 (see Map 20.2).

■ Identifying Continuities
What elements of Europe's earlier history shaped the course of the First World War?

The outbreak of **World War I** was something of an accident, in that none of the major states planned or predicted the archduke's assassination or deliberately sought a prolonged conflict, but the system of rigid alliances made Europe vulnerable to that kind of accident. Moreover, behind those alliances lay other factors that contributed to the eruption of war and shaped its character. One of them was a mounting popular nationalism (see "Nations and Nationalism" in Chapter 16).

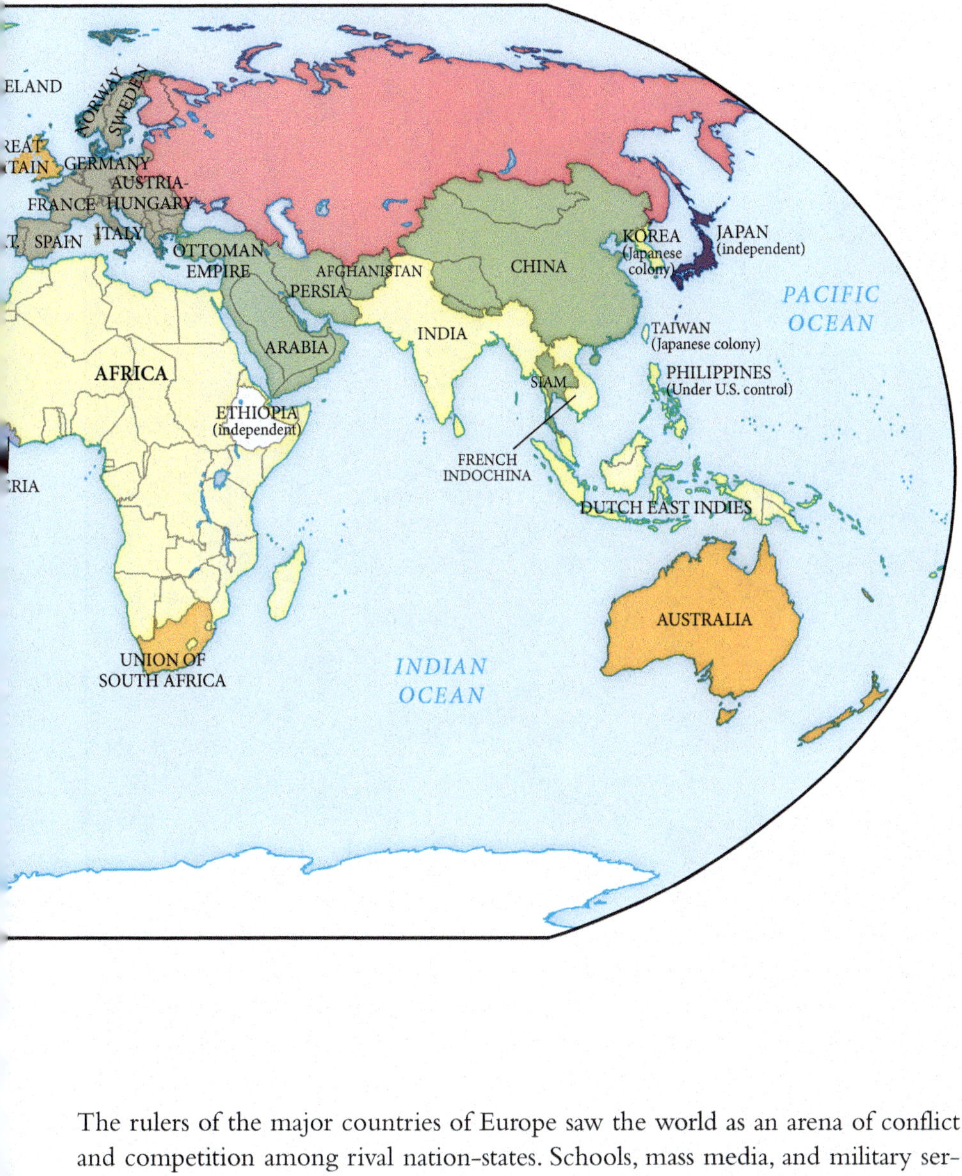

The rulers of the major countries of Europe saw the world as an arena of conflict and competition among rival nation-states. Schools, mass media, and military service had convinced millions of ordinary Europeans that their national identities were profoundly and personally meaningful. The public pressure of these competing nationalisms allowed statesmen little room for compromise and ensured widespread popular support, at least initially, for the decision to go to war. Many men rushed to recruiting offices, fearing that the war might end before they could enlist, and celebratory parades sent them off to the front. For conservative governments,

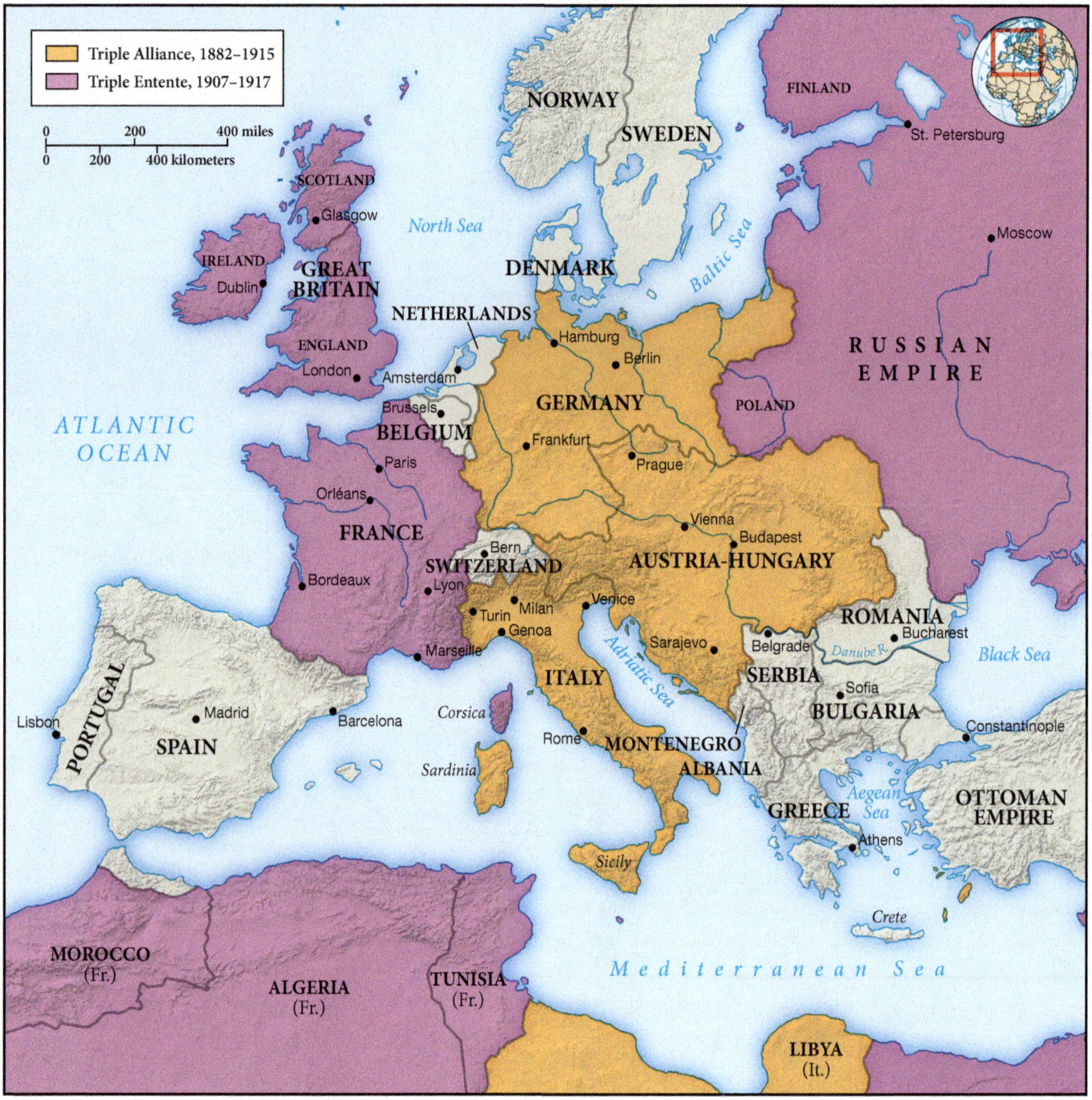

Map 20.2 Europe on the Eve of World War I
Despite many elements of common culture, Europe in 1914 was a powder keg, with its major states armed to the teeth and divided into two rival alliances. In the early stages of the war, Italy changed sides to join the French, British, and Russians.

the prospect of war was a welcome occasion for national unity in the face of the mounting class- and gender-based conflicts in European societies.

Also contributing to the war was an industrialized militarism. Europe's armed rivalries had long ensured that military men enjoyed great social prestige, and most heads of state wore uniforms in public. All of the Great Powers had substantial standing armies and, except for Britain, relied on conscription (compulsory military service) to staff them. Furthermore, each of the major states had developed elaborate "war plans" that spelled out in great detail the movement of men and materials that should occur immediately upon the outbreak of war. Such plans created a hair-trigger mentality because each country had an incentive to strike first so that its particular strategy could be implemented on schedule and without interruption or surprise. The rapid industrialization of warfare generated an array of novel weapons, including submarines, tanks, airplanes, poison gas, machine guns, and barbed wire. This new military technology contributed to the staggering casualties of the war, including some 10 million deaths, the vast majority male; perhaps twice that number were wounded, crippled, or disfigured. For countless women, as a result, there would be no husbands or children.

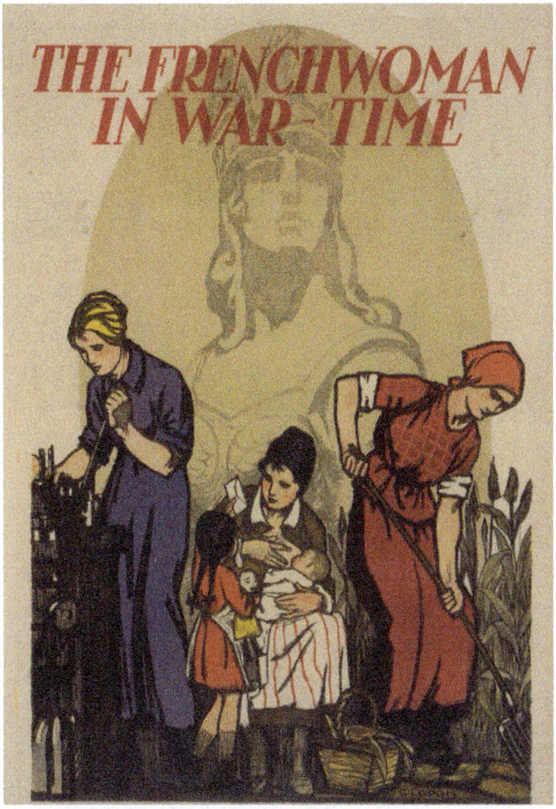

Women and the Great War World War I temporarily brought a halt to the women's suffrage movement as well as to women's activities on behalf of international peace. Most women on both sides actively supported their countries' war efforts, as suggested by this French wartime poster, showing women contributing to the war effort in industrial, agricultural, and domestic settings. (Library of Congress, Prints & Photographs Division, Reproduction number LC-USZC2-4067 [color film copy slide])

Europe's imperial reach around the world likewise shaped the scope and conduct of the war. It funneled colonial troops and laborers by the hundreds of thousands into the war effort, with men from Africa, India, China, Southeast Asia, Australia, New Zealand, and Canada taking part in the conflict. British and French forces seized German colonies in Africa and the South Pacific. Japan, allied with Britain, took various German possessions in China and the Pacific and demanded territorial and economic concessions from China itself. The Ottoman Empire, which entered the conflict on the side of Germany, became the site of intense military actions and witnessed an Arab revolt against Ottoman Turkish control. Finally, the United States, after initially seeking to avoid involvement in European quarrels, joined the war in 1917 when German submarines threatened American shipping. Thus the war, though centered in Europe, had global dimensions and certainly merited its title as a "world war."

Outcomes: Legacies of the Great War

CORE IDEA

Identifying Change
In what ways did World War I mark new departures in the history of the twentieth century?

The Great War shattered almost every expectation. Most Europeans believed in the late summer of 1914 that "the boys will be home by Christmas," but instead the war ground relentlessly on for more than four years before ending in a German defeat in November 1918. Moreover, it had become a **total war**, requiring the mobilization of each country's entire population. Thus the authority of governments expanded greatly. As the German state, for example, assumed further control over the economy, its policies became known as "war socialism," thus continuing a long-term strengthening of state power across much of Europe. Vast propaganda campaigns sought to arouse citizens by depicting a cruel and inhuman enemy who killed innocent children and violated women. Labor unions agreed to suspend strikes and accept sacrifices for the common good, while women, replacing the men who had left the factories for the battlefront, temporarily abandoned the struggle for the vote.

No less surprising were the longer-term outcomes of the war. In the European cockpit of that conflict, unprecedented casualties, particularly among elite and well-educated groups, and physical destruction, especially in France, led to a widespread disillusionment among intellectuals with their own civilization. For many, the war seemed to mock the Enlightenment values of progress, tolerance, and rationality, and some began to doubt that the West was superior or that its vaunted science and technology were unquestionably good things. In the most famous novel to emerge from the war, the German veteran Erich Remarque's *All Quiet on the Western Front*, one soldier expressed what many no doubt felt: "It must all be lies and of no account when the culture of a thousand years could not prevent this stream of blood being poured out."

The aftermath of war also brought substantial social and cultural changes to ordinary Europeans and Americans. Women were urged to leave the factory work they had taken up during the war and return to their homes, where they would not compete against returning veterans for "men's jobs." Nonetheless, the war had loosened the hold of tradition in various ways. Enormous casualties promoted social mobility, allowing the less exalted to move into positions previously dominated by the upper classes. As the war ended, suffrage movements revived and women received the right to vote in a number of countries—Britain, the United States, Germany, the Soviet Union, Hungary, and Poland—in part perhaps because of the sacrifices they had made during the conflict. Young middle-class women, sometimes known as "flappers," began to flout convention by appearing at nightclubs, smoking, dancing, drinking hard liquor, cutting their hair short, wearing revealing clothing, and generally expressing a more open sexuality. Technological innovations, mass production, and pent-up demand after the austerities of wartime fostered a new consumerism, particularly in the United States, encouraging those who could to acquire cars, washing machines, vacuum cleaners, electric irons, gas ovens, and other newly available products. Radio and the movies now became vehicles of popular culture, transmitting American jazz to Europe and turning Hollywood stars into international celebrities.

The war also transformed international political life. From the collapse of the German, Russian, and Austro-Hungarian empires emerged a new map of Central Europe with an independent Poland, Czechoslovakia, Yugoslavia, and other nations (see Map 20.3). Such new states were based on the principle of "national self-determination," a concept championed by U.S. president Woodrow Wilson, but

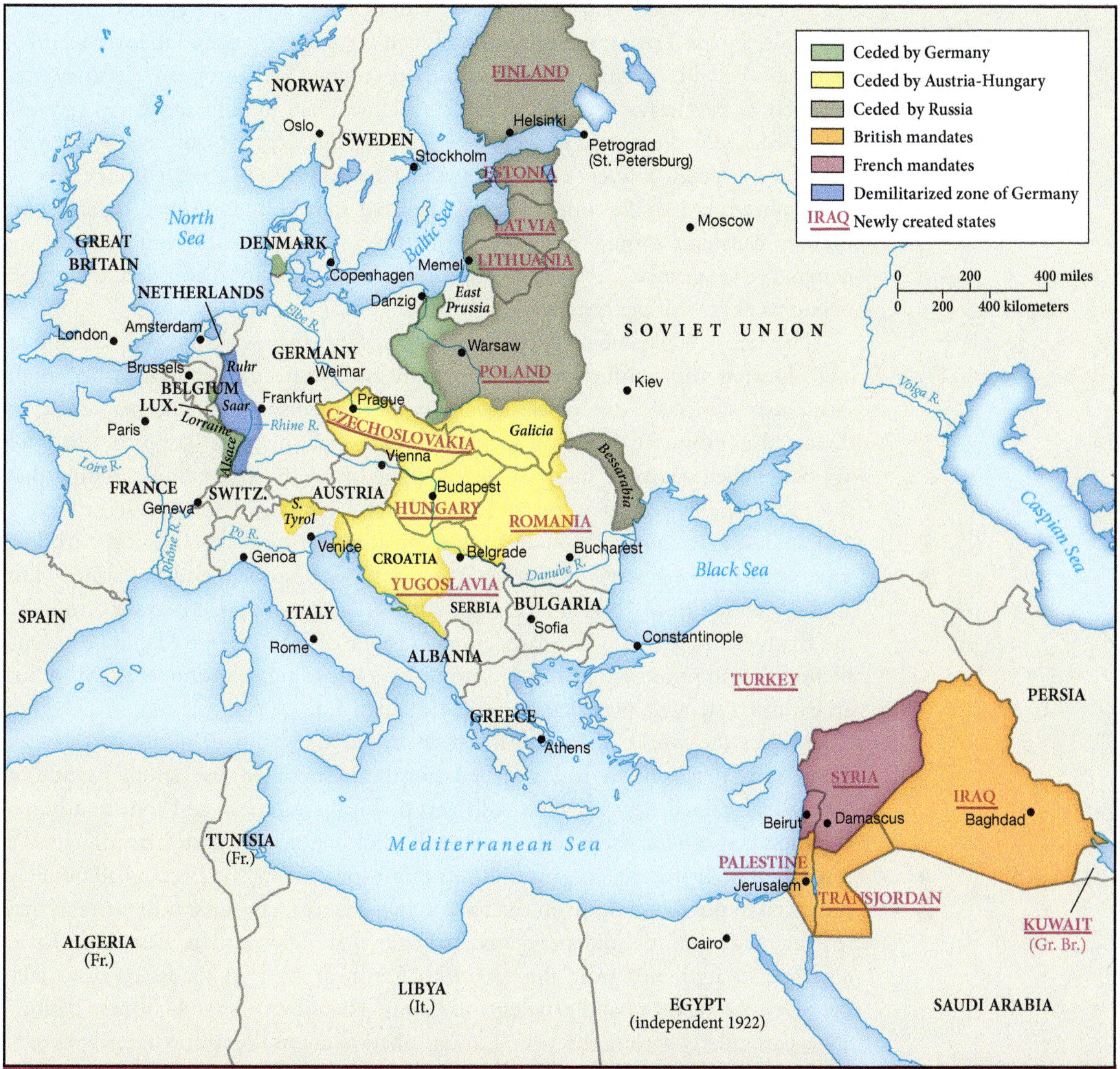

MAPPING HISTORY

Map 20.3 Europe and the Middle East after World War I

The Great War brought into existence a number of new states that were carved out of the old German, Austro-Hungarian, Russian, and Ottoman empires. Some were independent, while others were administered by Britain or France as mandates of the League of Nations.

READING THE MAP In which regions were new countries created in the aftermath of World War I? Which of the new states were independent, and which were administered by Britain and France as mandates of the League of Nations?

INTERPRETING THE MAP "The peace settlement at the end of World War I brought an end to empires in the Europe and the Middle East." To what extent does the map support this assertion?

each of them also contained dissatisfied ethnic minorities who claimed the same principle. By the **Treaty of Versailles**, which formally concluded the war in 1919, Germany lost its colonial empire and 15 percent of its European territory, was required to pay heavy reparations to the winners, had its military forces severely restricted, and was required to accept sole responsibility for the outbreak of the war. All of this created immense resentment in Germany. One of the country's many demobilized and disillusioned soldiers declared in 1922: "It cannot be that two million Germans should have fallen in vain. . . . No, we do not pardon, we demand—vengeance."[3] His name was Adolf Hitler, and within two decades he had begun to exact that vengeance.

The Great War generated profound changes in the world beyond Europe as well. During the conflict, Ottoman authorities, suspecting that some of their Armenian subjects were collaborating with the Russian enemy, massacred or deported an estimated 1 million Armenians. Although the term "genocide" had not yet been invented, some historians have applied it to those atrocities, arguing that they established a precedent on which the Nazis later built. The war also brought a final end to a declining Ottoman Empire, creating the modern map of the Middle East, with the new states of Turkey, Syria, Iraq, Transjordan, and Palestine. Thus Arabs emerged from Turkish rule, but many of them were governed for a time by the British or French, as "mandates" of the League of Nations (see Map 20.3). Conflicting British promises to both Arabs and Jews regarding Palestine set the stage for an enduring struggle over that ancient and holy land.

And in the world of European colonies, the war echoed loudly. Millions of Asian and African men had watched Europeans butcher one another without mercy, had gained new military skills and political awareness, and returned home with less respect for their rulers and with expectations for better treatment as a reward for their service. To gain Indian support for the war, the British had publicly promised to put that colony on the road to self-government, an announcement that set the stage for the independence struggle that followed. In East Asia, Japan emerged strengthened from the war, with European support for its claim to take over German territory and privileges in China. That news enraged Chinese nationalists, particularly among the young, and pushed many of them into a more revolutionary posture, as it seemed to signify the continuation of an arrogant imperialist attitude among Europeans toward the Chinese people.

Furthermore, the First World War brought the United States to center stage as a global power. Its manpower had contributed much to the defeat of Germany, and its financial resources turned the United States from a debtor nation into Europe's creditor. When the American president Woodrow Wilson arrived in Paris for the peace conference in 1919, he was greeted with an almost religious enthusiasm. His famous Fourteen Points seemed to herald a new kind of international life, one based on moral principles rather than secret deals and imperialist machinations. Particularly appealing to many was his idea for the League of Nations, a new international peacekeeping organization committed to the principle of "collective security" and intended to avoid any repetition of the horrors that had just ended. Wilson's idealistic vision largely failed, however. Germany was treated more harshly than he had wished. National self-determination in the multiethnic states of Europe and elsewhere was very difficult, and Wilson's rhetoric inspired hopes in the colonies that could not be immediately fulfilled. In his own country, the U.S. Senate refused to join the League, which was established in 1920, fearing that Americans would be forced to bow to "the will of other nations." That refusal seriously weakened the League of Nations as a vehicle for Wilson's new international order.

The Russian Revolution and Soviet Communism

Among the most significant outcomes of World War I was the beginning of world communism, which played such an enormous role in the history of the twentieth century. Modern communism found its political and philosophical roots in nineteenth-century European socialism, inspired by the teachings of Karl Marx. Most European socialists had come to believe that they could achieve their goals peacefully and through the democratic process, but not so in Russia, where democracy barely existed. Many Russian socialists therefore advocated uncompromising revolution as the only possible route to a socialist future. That revolution occurred during World War I in 1917. (For the background to the Russian Revolution, see "Russia: Industrialization and Revolution" in Chapter 17.)

CORE IDEA

Assessing Cause and Effect
What factors contributed to the Russian Revolution and the victory of the Bolsheviks?

The catalyst for the **Russian Revolution** was World War I, which was going very badly for the Russians. Under this pressure the accumulated tensions of Russian society exploded. Workers—men and women alike, along with the wives of soldiers—took to the streets to express their outrage at the incompetence and privileges of the elites. Activists organized demonstrations, published newspapers, and plotted revolution. By early 1917, Tsar Nicholas II had lost almost all support and was forced to abdicate the throne, thus ending the Romanov dynasty, which had ruled Russia for more than three centuries. What followed was a Provisional Government, led by major political figures from various parties. But the Russian Revolution had only begun.

The tsar's abdication opened the door for a massive social upheaval. Ordinary soldiers, seeking an end to a terrible war and despising their upper-class officers, deserted in substantial numbers. In major industrial centers such as St. Petersburg and Moscow, new trade unions arose to defend workers' interests, and some workers seized control of their factories. Grassroots organizations of workers and soldiers, known as soviets, emerged to speak for ordinary people. Peasants, many of whom had been serfs only a generation or two earlier, seized landlords' estates, burned their manor houses, and redistributed the land among themselves. Non-Russian nationalists in Ukraine, Poland, Muslim Central Asia, and the Baltic region demanded greater autonomy or even independence.

This was social revolution, and it provided an environment in which a small socialist party called the Bolsheviks was able to seize power by the end of 1917 under the

The Russian Civil War through Bolshevik Eyes This Bolshevik poster from 1921, titled "Electrification and Counterrevolution," presents a communist view of the civil war that followed the Russian Revolution. It shows a worker bringing electricity and more generally the light of modernity and progress to a backward country, while depicting his opponents, which include a priest, a general, and a businessman, as seeking to extinguish that light. (The New York Public Library/Art Resource, NY)

leadership of its determined and charismatic leader, Vladimir Ilyich Ulyanov, more commonly known as **Lenin**. In the desperate circumstances of 1917, his party's message—an end to the war, land for the peasants, workers' control of factories, self-determination for non-Russian nationalities—resonated with an increasingly rebellious public mood, particularly in the major cities.

A three-year civil war followed in which the Bolsheviks, now officially calling their party "communist," battled an assortment of enemies—tsarist officials, landlords, disaffected socialists, and regional nationalist forces, as well as troops from the United States, Britain, France, and Japan, all of which were eager to crush the fledgling communist regime. Remarkably, the Bolsheviks held on and by 1921 had staggered to victory over their divided and uncoordinated opponents. They renamed their country the Union of Soviet Socialist Republics (USSR or Soviet Union) and set about its transformation. For the next twenty-five years, the Soviet Union remained a communist island in a capitalist sea.

■ **Describing Ideology**
What were the major features of Soviet communism during the Stalin era?

Once they had consolidated power and resolved their leadership struggles, Russian communists soon began the task of constructing a socialist society under the control of Joseph **Stalin** (1878–1953), who emerged as the principal Soviet leader by the late 1920s. To Stalin and communists generally, building socialism meant first of all the modernization and industrialization of a backward Russian society. They sought, however, a distinctly socialist modernity with an emphasis on social equality and the promotion of cultural values of selflessness and collectivism.

Those imperatives generated a political system thoroughly dominated by the Communist Party. Top-ranking party members enjoyed various privileges but were expected to be exemplars of socialism in the making by being disciplined, selfless, and utterly loyal to their country's Marxist ideology. The party itself penetrated society in ways that Western scholars called "totalitarian," for other parties were forbidden, the state controlled almost the entire economy, and political authorities ensured that the arts, education, and the media conformed to approved ways of thinking. Mass organizations for women, workers, students, and various professional groups operated under party control, with none of the independence that characterized civil society in the West.

In the rural areas, building socialism meant the end of private ownership of land and the **collectivization of agriculture**. Between 1928 and 1933, peasants were forced, often against great resistance, into large-scale collective farms, which were supposedly more productive and better able to utilize modern agricultural machinery than the small family farms that had emerged from the revolution. Stalin singled out the richer peasants, known as *kulaks* (koo-LAHKS), for exclusion from the new collective farms. Some were killed, and many others were deported to remote areas of the country. With little support or experience in the countryside, the urban activists who enforced collectivization were viewed as intrusive outsiders in Russian peasant villages. A terrible famine ensued, with some 5 million deaths from starvation or malnutrition.

Mobilizing Women for Communism As the Soviet Union mobilized for rapid economic development in the 1930s, women entered the workforce in great numbers. Here two young women are mastering the skills of driving a tractor on one of the large collective farms that replaced the country's private agriculture. (Sovfoto/Getty Images)

In the cities, the task was rapid industrialization. The Soviet approach to industrial development, so different from that of the capitalist West, involved state ownership of property, centralized planning embodied in successive five-year plans, priority to heavy industry, massive mobilization of the nation's human and material resources, and intrusive Communist Party control of the entire process. For a time, it worked. During the 1930s, while the capitalist world floundered amid the massive unemployment of the Great Depression, the Soviet Union largely eliminated unemployment and constructed the foundations of an industrial society that proved itself in the victory over Nazi Germany in World War II. In addition, the USSR achieved massive improvements in literacy rates and educational opportunities, allowing far greater social mobility for millions of people than ever before. As in the West, industrialization fostered rapid urbanization, exploitation of the countryside to provide resources for modern industry in the cities, and the growth of a privileged bureaucratic and technological elite intent on pursuing their own careers and passing on their new status to their children.

Despite its totalitarian tendencies, the communist society of the Soviet Union was laced with conflict. Under Stalin's leadership, those conflicts erupted in a search for enemies that terribly disfigured Soviet life. An elastic concept of "enemy" came to include not only surviving remnants from the prerevolutionary elites but also, and more surprisingly, high-ranking members and longtime supporters of the Communist Party, who allegedly had been corrupted by bourgeois ideas, as evidenced by their opposition to some of Stalin's harsh policies. Refracted through the lens of Marxist thinking, these people became "class enemies" who had betrayed the revolution and were engaged in a vast conspiracy, often linked to foreign imperialists, to subvert the socialist enterprise and restore capitalism.

That process culminated in Stalin's Terror, or the Great Purges, of the late 1930s, which enveloped tens of thousands of prominent communists, including virtually all of Lenin's top associates, and millions of more ordinary people. Based on suspicious associations in the past, denunciations by colleagues, connections to foreign countries, or simply bad luck, such people were arrested, usually in the dead of night, and then tried and sentenced either to death or to long years in harsh and remote labor camps known as the gulag. A series of show trials publicized the menace that these "enemies of the people" allegedly posed to the country and its revolution. Close to 1 million people were executed between 1936 and 1941. An additional 4 or 5 million were sent to the gulag, where they were forced to work in horrendous conditions and died in appalling numbers. Such was the outcome of the world's first experiment with communism.

Capitalism Unraveling: The Great Depression

While the Soviet Union was constructing the world's first communist society, the capitalist world languished in the **Great Depression**, which began with an abrupt stock market crash in October 1929 and then lasted for a decade. If World War I represented the political collapse of Europe, this economic catastrophe suggested that Western capitalism was likewise failing, as Marx had predicted. All across the Euro-American heartland of the industrialized capitalist world, this vaunted economic system seemed to unravel. For the rich, it meant contracting stock prices that wiped out paper fortunes almost overnight. Banks closed, and many people lost their life savings. Investment dried up, world trade dropped by 62 percent within a few years, and businesses contracted or closed. Unemployment soared everywhere, and in both Germany and the United States it reached 30 percent or more by 1932. Vacant factories, soup kitchens, bread lines, shantytowns, and beggars came to symbolize the human reality of this economic disaster.

CORE IDEA

■ **Identifying Global Connections**

In what respects was the Great Depression a global phenomenon?

This economic breakdown began in the United States, which had experienced a booming economy during the 1920s. By the end of that decade, its farms and factories were producing more goods than could be sold, either at home or abroad. Meanwhile, a speculative stock market frenzy had driven up stock prices to an unsustainable level. When that bubble burst in late 1929, its ripple effects quickly encompassed the industrialized economies of Europe, which were intimately connected to the United States through ties of trade, debt, and investment.

Much as Europe's worldwide empires had globalized the Great War, so too its economic linkages globalized the Great Depression. Countries or colonies tied to exporting one or two products were especially hard-hit. Colonial Southeast Asia, the world's major rubber-producing region, saw the demand for its primary export drop dramatically as automobile sales in Europe and the United States were cut in half. In Britain's West African colony of the Gold Coast (present-day Ghana), farmers who had staked their economic lives on producing cocoa for the world market were badly hurt by the collapse of commodity prices. Latin American countries saw the value of their exports cut by half, generating widespread unemployment and social tensions. In response to these problems, governments sought to steer their economies away from exports toward producing for the internal market, a policy known as import substitution. In Mexico, the Depression opened the way to reviving the principles of the Mexican Revolution under the leadership of Lázaro Cárdenas (1934–1940), who pushed land reform, favored Mexican workers against foreign interests, and nationalized an oil industry dominated by American capital.

The Great Depression also sharply challenged the governments of industrialized capitalist countries. The apparent failure of a market economy to self-correct led many people to look twice at the Soviet Union. There, the dispossession of the propertied classes and a state-controlled economy had generated an impressive

Contrasts of the Great Depression This 1937 *Life* magazine image by famed photographer Margaret Bourke-White shows black victims of a flood in Louisville, Kentucky, standing in a breadline during the Depression while behind them rises a billboard depicting a happy and prosperous white family. (Margaret Bourke-White/Time & Life Pictures/Getty Images)

economic growth with almost no unemployment in the 1930s, even as the capitalist world was reeling. No Western country opted for the dictatorial and draconian socialism of the Soviet Union, but in Britain, France, and Scandinavia, the Depression energized a "democratic socialism" that sought greater regulation of the economy and a more equal distribution of wealth through peaceful means and electoral politics. The Great Depression, like the world wars, strengthened the power of the state.

The United States illustrated this trend as President Franklin Roosevelt's New Deal (1933–1942) took shape, permanently altering the relationship among government, the private economy, and individual citizens. The New Deal involved immediate programs of public spending (for dams, highways, bridges, and parks); longer-term reforms, such as the Social Security system, the minimum wage, and various relief and welfare programs; support for labor unions; and subsidies for farmers. A mounting number of government agencies marked a new degree of federal regulation and supervision of the economy.

Ultimately, the New Deal's programs were unable to bring the Great Depression to an end. Not until the massive government spending required by World War II kicked in did economic disaster abate in the United States. The most successful efforts to cope with the Depression came from unlikely places—Nazi Germany and an increasingly militaristic Japan.

Democracy Denied: The Authoritarian Alternative

Despite the victory of the democratic powers in World War I—Britain, France, and the United States—their democratic political ideals and their cultural values celebrating individual freedom came under sharp attack in the aftermath of that bloody conflict. One challenge derived from communism, which was initiated in the Russian Revolution of 1917. In the 1920s and 1930s, however, the more immediate challenge to the victors in the Great War came from highly authoritarian, intensely nationalistic, territorially aggressive, and ferociously anticommunist regimes, particularly those that took shape in Italy, Germany, and Japan. (See Working with Evidence: Ideologies of the Axis Powers, page 913.) The common political goals of these three countries drew them together by 1936–1937 in an alliance directed against the Soviet Union and international communism. In 1940, they solidified their relationship in a formal military alliance, creating the so-called Axis powers. Within this alliance, Germany and Japan clearly stand out, though in quite different ways, in terms of their impact on the larger patterns of world history, for it was their efforts to "establish and maintain a new order of things," as the Axis Pact put it, that generated the Second World War both in East Asia and in Europe.

European Fascism

Between 1919 and 1945, a new political ideology, known as **fascism**, found expression across parts of Europe. While communists celebrated class conflict as the driving force of history, for fascists it was the conflict of nations. Fascism was intensely nationalistic, seeking to revitalize and purify the nation and to mobilize its people for some grand task. Its spokesmen praised violence against enemies as a renewing force in society, celebrated action rather than reflection, and placed their faith in a charismatic leader. Fascists also bitterly condemned individualism, liberalism, feminism, parliamentary democracy, and communism, all of which, they argued, divided and weakened the nation. In their determination to overthrow existing regimes, they were revolutionary; in their embrace of traditional values and their opposition to much of modern life, however, they were conservative or reactionary.

Such ideas appealed to aggrieved people all across the social spectrum. In the devastation that followed the First World War, the numbers of such people grew substantially. Some among the middle and upper classes felt the rise of socialism and communism as a dire threat; small-scale merchants, artisans, and farmers feared the loss of their independence to either big business or socialist revolution; demobilized soldiers had few prospects and nursed many resentments; and intellectuals were appalled by the materialism and artificiality of modern life. Such people had lost faith in the capacity of liberal democracy and capitalism to create a good society and to protect their interests. Some among them proved a receptive audience for the message of fascism. Fascist or other highly authoritarian movements appeared in many European countries, such as Spain, Romania, and Hungary, and some in Latin America, but it was in Italy and Germany that such movements achieved prolonged power in major states, with devastating consequences for Europe and the world.

Comparing Ideas
In what ways did fascism challenge the ideas and practices of European liberalism and democracy?

The fascist alternative took shape first in Italy. That nation had become a unified state only in 1870 and had not yet developed a thoroughly industrialized economy or a solidly democratic culture. The First World War gave rise to resentful veterans, many of them unemployed, and to patriots who believed that Italy had not gained the territory it deserved from the Treaty of Versailles. During the serious economic downturn after World War I, trade unions, peasant movements, and various communist and socialist parties threatened the established social order with a wave of strikes and land seizures.

Into this setting stepped a charismatic orator and a former journalist with a socialist background, Benito **Mussolini** (1883–1945). With the help of a private army of disillusioned veterans and jobless men known as the Black Shirts, Mussolini swept to power in 1922 amid considerable violence, promising an alternative to communism, order in the streets, an end to bickering party-based politics, and the maintenance of the traditional social order. That Mussolini's government allegedly made the trains run on time became evidence that these promises might be fulfilled.

In Mussolini's thinking, fascism was resolutely anticommunist, "the complete opposite . . . of Marxist socialism," and equally antidemocratic. "Fascism combats the whole complex system of democratic ideology, and repudiates it," he wrote. At the core of Mussolini's fascism was his conception of the state. "Fascism conceives of the State as an absolute, in comparison with which all individuals and groups are relative, only to be conceived of in their relation to the State." The state was a conscious entity with "a will and a personality" that represented the "spirit of the nation." Its expansion in war and empire building was "an essential manifestation of vitality."

Mussolini's government suspended democracy and imprisoned, deported, or sometimes executed opponents. Italy's fascist regime also disbanded independent labor unions and peasant groups as well as all opposing political parties. In economic life, a "corporate state" took shape, at least in theory, in which workers, employers, and various professional groups were organized into "corporations" that were supposed to settle their disagreements and determine economic policy under the supervision of the state.

Culturally, fascists invoked various aspects of traditional Italian life. Though personally an atheist, Mussolini embraced the Catholic culture of Italy in a series of agreements with the Church, known as the Lateran Accords of 1929, that made the Vatican a sovereign state and Catholicism Italy's national religion. In fascist propaganda, women were portrayed in highly traditional domestic terms, particularly as mothers creating new citizens for the fascist state, with no hint of equality or liberation. Nationalists were delighted when Italy invaded Ethiopia in 1935, avenging the embarrassing defeat that Italians suffered at the hands of Ethiopians in 1896. In the eyes of Mussolini and fascist believers, all of this was the beginning of a "new Roman Empire" that would revitalize Italian society and give it a global mission. (See Working with Evidence, Source 20.1, page 913.)

Hitler and the Nazis

Far more important in the long run was the German expression of European fascism, which took shape as the **Nazi Party** under the leadership of Adolf **Hitler** (1889–1945). In many respects, it was similar to its Italian counterpart. Both espoused an extreme nationalism, openly advocated the use of violence as a political tool, generated a single-party dictatorship, were led by charismatic figures, despised parliamentary democracy, hated communism, and viewed war as a positive and ennobling experience.[4] The circumstances that gave rise to the Nazi movement were likewise broadly similar to those of Italian fascism, although the Nazis did not achieve national power until 1933. Germany too was a new European nation, lacking a long-term democratic tradition. As in Italy, resentment about the Treaty of Versailles was widespread, especially among unemployed veterans. Fear of socialism or communism was prevalent among middle- and upper-class groups. But it was the Great Depression that provided the essential context for the victory of German fascism. The German economy largely ground to a halt in the early 1930s amid massive unemployment among workers and the middle class alike. Everyone demanded decisive action from the state.

Analyzing Nazism
What was distinctive about the German expression of fascism? How were Nazis able to gain widespread popular support?

This was the context in which Adolf Hitler's National Socialist, or Nazi, Party gained growing public support. Its message expressed an intense German nationalism cast in terms of racial superiority, bitter hatred for Jews as an alien presence, passionate opposition to communism, a determination to rescue Germany from the humiliating requirements of the Treaty of Versailles, and a willingness to decisively tackle the country's economic problems. All of this resonated widely, enabling the Nazis to win 37 percent of the vote in the election of 1932. The following year, Hitler was legally installed as the chancellor of the German government. Thus a weak democratic regime that never gained broad support gave way to the Third Reich.

Nationalism and Nazi Ideology A critical element of Nazi fascist ideology was the promotion of fierce nationalism cast in terms of racial superiority. In this image, Adolf Hitler salutes a mass gathering of the Hitler Youth, an organization whose purpose in part was to instill national fervor in Germany's children and adolescents. (Corbis/Getty Images.)

Once in power, Hitler moved quickly to consolidate Nazi control of Germany. All other political parties were outlawed; independent labor unions were ended; thousands of opponents were arrested; and the press and radio came under state control. Far more thoroughly than Mussolini in Italy, Hitler and the Nazis established their control over German society.

By the late 1930s, Hitler apparently had the support of a considerable majority of the population, in large measure because his policies successfully brought Germany out of the Depression. The government invested heavily in projects such as superhighways, bridges, canals, and public buildings and, after 1935, in rebuilding and rearming the country's diminished military forces. These policies drove down the number of unemployed Germans from 6.2 million in 1932 to fewer than 500,000 in 1937. Two years later Germany had a labor shortage. Erna Kranz, a teenager in the 1930s, later remembered the early years of Nazi rule as "a glimmer of hope . . . not just for the unemployed but for everybody because we all knew that we were downtrodden. . . . It was a good time . . . there was order and discipline."[5] Millions agreed with her.

Other factors as well contributed to Nazi popularity. Like Italian fascists, Hitler appealed to rural and traditional values that many Germans feared losing as their country modernized. In Hitler's thinking and in Nazi propaganda, Jews became the symbol of the urban, capitalist, and foreign influences that were undermining traditional German culture. Thus the Nazis reflected and reinforced a broader and long-established current of anti-Semitism that had deep roots in much of Europe. In his book *Mein Kampf* (My Struggle), Hitler outlined his case against the Jews and his call for the racial purification of Germany in vitriolic terms. (See Working with Evidence, Source 20.2, page 915.)

Far more than in Italy or elsewhere, this insistence on a racial revolution was a central feature of the Nazi program. Upon coming to power, Hitler implemented

The Ideal Nazi Family This painting by Wolfgang Willrich, a prominent Nazi artist, portrays the highly romanticized Nazi image of an ideal Aryan family. They have four children; most are dressed in plain peasant-style clothing; the mother wears her hair in a bun and does not use makeup; they live in a rural agricultural setting; the boy is wearing a Hitler Youth uniform; and all of them are blonde, with athletic bodies and ruddy complexions. (bpk Bildagentur/Art Resource, NY)

policies that increasingly restricted Jewish life. Soon Jews were excluded from universities, professional organizations, and civil employment. In 1935, the Nuremberg Laws ended German citizenship for Jews and forbade marriage or sexual relations between Jews and Germans. On the night of November 9, 1938, known as Kristallnacht ("Night of Crystal" or "Night of Broken Glass"), persecution gave way to terror, when Nazis smashed and looted Jewish shops. Such actions made clear the Nazis' determination to rid Germany of its Jewish population, thus putting into effect the most radical element of Hitler's program. Still, it was not yet apparent that this "racial revolution" would mean the mass killing of Europe's Jews. That horrendous development emerged only in the context of World War II.

Beyond race, gender too figured prominently in Nazi thought and policies. While Soviet communists sought to enroll women in the country's industrialization effort, Nazis wanted to limit women largely to the home, removing them from the paid workforce. To Hitler, the state was the natural domain of men, while the home was the realm of women. "Woman in the workplace is an oppressed and tormented being," declared a Nazi publication. Concerned about declining birthrates, Italy and Germany alike promoted a cult of motherhood, glorifying and rewarding women who produced children for the state. Accordingly, fascist regimes in both countries generally opposed abortion, contraception, family planning, and sex education, all of which were associated with feminist thinking. Yet such an outlook did not necessarily coincide with conservative or puritanical sexual attitudes. In Germany, a state-sponsored system of brothels was initiated in the mid-1930s, for it was assumed that virile men would be promiscuous and that soldiers required a sexual outlet if they were to contribute to the nation's military strength.

Also sustaining Nazi rule were massive torchlight ceremonies celebrating the superiority of the German race and its folk culture. In these settings, Hitler was the mystical leader, the Führer, a mesmerizing orator who would lead Germany to national greatness and individual Germans to personal fulfillment.

If World War I and the Great Depression brought about the political and economic collapse of Europe, the Nazi phenomenon represented a rejection of some of the values—rationalism, tolerance, democracy, human equality—that for many people had defined the core of Western civilization since the Enlightenment.

On the other hand, Nazis claimed the legacy of modern science, particularly in their concern to classify and rank various human groups. Thus they drew heavily on the "scientific racism" of the late nineteenth century and its expression in phrenology, which linked the size and shape of the skull to human behavior and personality (see "Industry and Empire" in Chapter 18). Moreover, in their effort to purify German society, the Nazis reflected the Enlightenment confidence in the perfectibility of humankind and in the social engineering necessary to achieve it.

By 1940, the European political landscape had altered dramatically from what it had been just a few decades earlier. At the beginning of the twentieth century, major European countries had embraced largely capitalist economies and to varying degrees increasingly democratic political systems with multiple parties and elected parliaments. But by the time World War II broke out, Europe's largest country, the Soviet Union, had altogether rejected capitalism in favor of a state-controlled economy and a political system dominated by a single communist political party. The fascist states of Germany and Italy likewise dismantled multiparty democracies, replacing them with highly authoritarian dictatorships. While these dictatorships retained major private ownership of property, the state played a large role in economic affairs. Communist and fascist states alike rejected the individualistic liberalism of the remaining democracies, celebrating the collective identities of "class" in the case of the Soviet Union and of nation or race in Italy and Germany. (See Snapshot, page 896.)

Japanese Authoritarianism

In various ways, the modern history of Japan paralleled that of Italy and Germany. All three were newcomers to Great Power status, with Japan joining the club of industrializing and empire-building states only in the late nineteenth century as its sole Asian member (see "The Japanese Difference" in Chapter 19). Like Italy and Germany, Japan had a rather limited experience with democratic politics, for its elected parliament was constrained by a very small electorate (only 1.5 million men in 1917) and by the exalted position of a semi-divine emperor and his small coterie of elite advisers. During the 1930s, Japan too moved toward authoritarian government and a denial of democracy at home, even as it launched an aggressive program of territorial expansion in East Asia. But in sharp contrast to Italy and Germany, Japan's participation in World War I was minimal, and its economy grew considerably as other industrialized countries were consumed by the European conflict. At the peace conference ending that war, Japan was seated as an equal participant, allied with the winning side of democratic countries such as Britain, France, and the United States.

During the 1920s, Japan seemed to be moving toward more democratic politics and Western cultural values. Universal male suffrage was achieved in 1925, and a two-party system began to emerge. Supporters of these developments, mostly urban and well-to-do, generally embraced the dignity of the individual, free expression of

SNAPSHOT Comparing German Fascism and Soviet Communism

COMMONALITIES BETWEEN GERMAN FASCISM AND SOVIET COMMUNISM

- Intense opposition to liberal democratic ideology and practice in the West
- A party-dominated state seeking to penetrate and control society and individuals
- Elimination of competing political parties
- A transformational and utopian ideology seeking personal and social regeneration
- Leadership by a single highly celebrated individual with enormous personal power
- Contraction of private or civic life; expansion of collective or public life
- Mobilization of mass support for the regime
- Extensive use of violence against perceived enemies

DIFFERENCES

Theme	German Fascism	Soviet Communism
Ideology	• Focus on race and nation • Superiority of German peoples • Desire to purify Germany of "alien" Jewish presence • Desire to avenge humiliation of the Versailles treaty • Territorial expansion for increased living space	• Focus on class conflict, leading to revolution and socialism • Russia as initial breakthrough to international communism • Industrialization needed to provide foundation for socialism
Theory of state	• The state as an absolute value • Individuals and groups defined by their relationship to the state	• State to "wither away" in time (in practice, the state grew large, powerful, and intrusive)
Economic system	• Retained major elements of capitalism: private property, profit motive, market exchange • State intervened to regulate, control, and direct	• Eliminated capitalism and private property • Agriculture collectivized and industry owned by the state • Expressed in "five-year plans" for entire economy
Posture toward women	• Deeply antifeminist; sought to limit women to home as their "natural domain" • Opposed abortion and contraception	• Liberation of women; legal equality in marriage; mobilized women for production as workers
Modern life	• Ambivalent about modernity • Romanticized Aryan racial purity and traditional German peasant communities • Embraced science, technology, and industry	• Thoroughly modernist • No romanticism about the past; peasant Russia viewed as in need of modernization • Valued all things industrial and urban
Religion	• Monitored and controlled churches; no frontal attack on Christianity • Severe persecution of Jehovah's Witnesses and Jews	• Major effort to eliminate religion and promote atheism

ideas, and greater gender equality. Education expanded; an urban consumer society developed; middle-class women entered new professions; and young women known as *moga* (modern girls) sported short hair and short skirts, while dancing with *mobo* (modern boys) at jazz clubs and cabarets. To such people, the Japanese were becoming global citizens and their country was becoming "a province of the world" as they participated increasingly in a cosmopolitan and international culture.

In this environment, the accumulated tensions of Japan's modernizing and industrializing processes found expression. "Rice riots" in 1918 brought more than a million people into the streets of urban Japan to protest the rising price of that essential staple. Union membership tripled in the 1920s as some factory workers began to think in terms of entitlements and workers' rights rather than the benevolence of their employers. In rural areas, tenant unions multiplied, and disputes with landowners increased amid demands for a reduction in rents. A mounting women's movement advocated a variety of feminist issues, including suffrage and the end of legalized prostitution. "All the sleeping women are now awake and moving," declared Yosano Akiko, a well-known poet, feminist, and social critic in 1911. A number of "proletarian (working class) parties"—the Labor-Farmer Party, the Socialist People's Party, and a small Japan Communist Party—promised in various ways to promote radical social change.

■ **Explaining Political Change**
What explains the rise and the limits of right-wing politics in Japan?

For many people in established elite circles—bureaucrats, landowners, industrialists, military officials—all of this was both appalling and alarming, suggesting echoes of the Russian Revolution of 1917. As in Germany, however, it was the impact of the Great Depression that paved the way for harsher and more authoritarian action. That worldwide economic catastrophe hit Japan hard. Shrinking world demand for silk impoverished millions of rural dwellers who raised silkworms. Japan's exports fell by half between 1929 and 1931, leaving a million or more urban workers unemployed. Many young workers returned to their rural villages only to find food scarce, families forced to sell their daughters to urban brothels, and neighbors unable to offer the customary money for the funerals of their friends. In these desperate circumstances, many began to doubt the ability of parliamentary democracy and capitalism to address Japan's "national emergency." Such conditions energized a growing movement in Japanese political life known as Radical Nationalism or the **Revolutionary Right**. Expressed in dozens of small groups, it was especially appealing to younger army officers. The movement's many separate organizations shared an extreme nationalism, hostility to parliamentary democracy, a commitment to elite leadership focused around an exalted emperor, and dedication to foreign expansion. The manifesto of one of those organizations, the Cherry Blossom Society, expressed these sentiments clearly in 1930:

> As we observe recent social trends, top leaders engage in immoral conduct, political parties are corrupt, capitalists and aristocrats have no understanding of the masses, farming villages are devastated, unemployment and depression are serious. . . . The rulers neglect the long term interests of the nation, strive

to win only the pleasure of foreign powers and possess no enthusiasm for external expansion. . . . The people are with us in craving the appearance of a vigorous and clean government that is truly based upon the masses, and is genuinely centered around the Emperor.[6]

CORE IDEA

■ Making Comparisons
What did Italian fascism, German Nazism, and Japanese authoritarianism have in common? How did they differ?

In sharp contrast to developments in Italy and Germany, however, no right-wing or fascist party gained wide popular support in Japan, and no such party was able to seize power. Nor did Japan produce any charismatic leader on the order of Mussolini or Hitler. People arrested for political offenses were neither criminalized nor exterminated, as in Germany, but instead were subjected to a process of "resocialization" that brought the vast majority of them to renounce their "errors" and return to the "Japanese way." Japan's established institutions of government were sufficiently strong, and traditional notions of the nation as a family headed by the emperor were sufficiently intact, to prevent the development of a widespread fascist movement able to take control of the country.

In the 1930s, though, Japanese public life clearly changed in ways that reflected the growth of right-wing nationalist thinking. The military in particular came to exercise a more dominant role in Japanese political life, reflecting the long-standing Japanese respect for the samurai warrior class. Censorship limited the possibilities of free expression, and a single news agency was granted the right to distribute all national and most international news to the country's newspapers and radio stations. Established authorities also adopted many of the ideological themes of the Revolutionary Right. In 1937, the Ministry of Education issued a new textbook, *Cardinal Principles of the National Entity of Japan*, for use in all Japanese schools (see Working with Evidence, Source 20.4, page 917). That document proclaimed the Japanese to be "intrinsically quite different from the so-called citizens of Occidental [Western] countries." Those nations were "conglomerations of separate individuals" with "no deep foundation between ruler and citizen to unite them." In Japan, by contrast, an emperor of divine origin related to his subjects as a father to his children. It was a natural, not a contractual, relationship, expressed most fully in the "sacrifice of the life of a subject for the Emperor."

The Growth of Japanese Militarism This poster celebrating the Japanese navy was created by the National Defense Women's Association in 1938. It reflects the increasing role of the military in Japanese national life and seeks to encourage female support for it. (Pictures from History/Bridgeman Images)

The state's success in quickly bringing the country out of the Depression likewise fostered popular support. As in Nazi Germany, state-financed credit, large-scale spending on armaments, and public works projects enabled Japan to emerge from the Depression more rapidly and more fully than major Western countries. "By the end of 1937," noted one Japanese laborer, "everybody in the country was working."[7] By the mid-1930s, the government increasingly assumed a supervisory or managerial role in economic affairs. Private property, however, was retained, and the huge industrial enterprises called *zaibatsu* continued to dominate the economic landscape.

Although Japan during the 1930s shared some common features with fascist Italy and Nazi Germany, it remained, at least internally, a less repressive and more pluralistic society than either of those European states. Japanese intellectuals and writers had to contend with government censorship, but they retained some influence in the country. Generals and admirals exercised great political authority as the role of an elected parliament declined, but they did not govern alone. Political prisoners were few and were not subjected to execution or deportation as in European fascist states. Japanese conceptions of their racial purity and uniqueness were directed largely against foreigners rather than an internal minority. Nevertheless, like Germany and Italy, Japan developed extensive imperial ambitions. Those projects of conquest and empire building collided with the interests of established imperial powers such as the United States and Britain, launching a second, and even more terrible, global war.

A Second World War, 1937–1945

World War II, even more than the Great War, was a genuinely global conflict with independent origins in both Asia and Europe. Dissatisfied states in both continents sought to fundamentally alter the international arrangements that had emerged from World War I. Many Japanese, like their counterparts in Italy and Germany, felt stymied by Britain and the United States as they sought empires that they regarded as essential for their national greatness and economic well-being.

The Road to War in Asia

World War II began in Asia before it occurred in Europe. In the late 1920s and the 1930s, Japanese imperial ambitions mounted as the military became more powerful in Japan's political life and as an earlier cultural cosmopolitanism gave way to more nationalist sentiments. An initial problem was the rise of Chinese nationalism, which seemed to threaten Japan's sphere of influence in Manchuria, acquired by Japan after the Russo-Japanese War of 1904–1905. Acting independently of civilian authorities in Tokyo, units of the Japanese military seized control of Manchuria in 1931 and established a puppet state called Manchukuo. This action was condemned by China, the United States, and the League of Nations alike, but there was no effective military response to the Japanese aggression. The condemnation, however,

CORE IDEA

■ Making Comparisons

How did the origins, course, and outcomes of World War II differ from those of World War I?

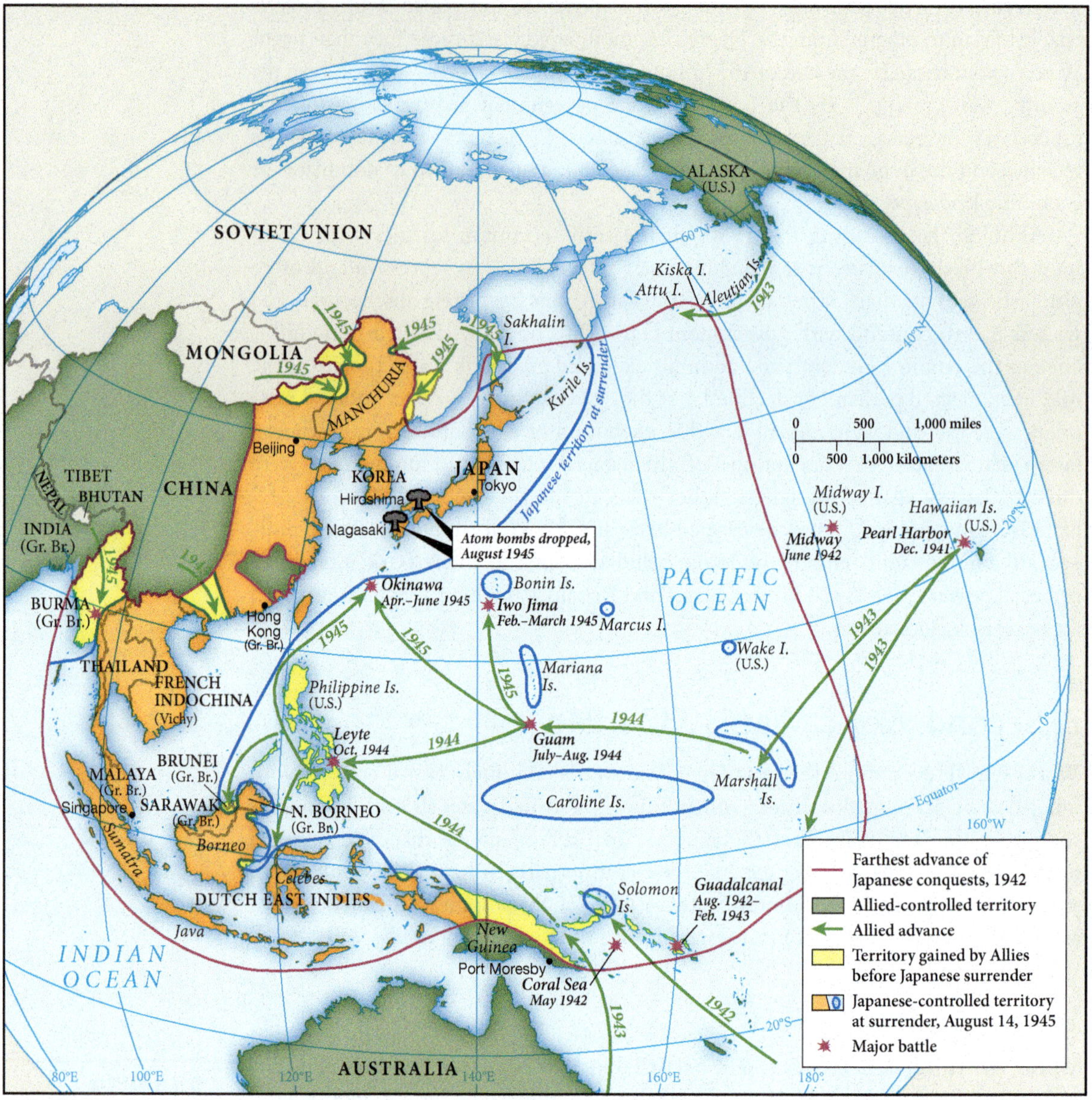

Map 20.4 World War II in Asia and the Pacific
Japanese aggression temporarily dislodged the British, French, Dutch, and Americans from their colonial possessions in Asia, while inflicting vast devastation on China. Much of the American counterattack involved "island hopping" across the Pacific until the dropping of the atomic bombs on Hiroshima and Nagasaki finally prompted the Japanese surrender in August 1945.

prompted Japan to withdraw from the League of Nations and in 1936 to align more closely with Germany and Italy. By that time, relations with an increasingly nationalist China had deteriorated further, leading to a full-scale attack on heartland China in 1937 and escalating a bitter conflict that would last another eight years. **World War II in Asia** had begun (see Map 20.4).

As Japan's war against China unfolded, the view of the world held by Japanese authorities and many ordinary people hardened. Increasingly, they felt isolated, surrounded, and threatened. Anti-Japanese immigration policies in the United States convinced some Japanese that racism prevented the West from acknowledging Japan as an equal power. Furthermore, Japan was quite dependent on foreign and especially American sources of strategic goods—oil, for example—even as the United States was becoming increasingly hostile to Japanese ambitions in Asia. Moreover, Western imperialist powers—the British, French, and Dutch—controlled resource-rich colonies in Southeast Asia. Finally, the Soviet Union, proclaiming an alien communist ideology, loomed large in northern Asia. To growing numbers of Japanese, their national survival was at stake.

Thus in 1940–1941, Japan extended its military operations to the French, British, Dutch, and American colonies of Southeast Asia—Malaya, Burma, Indonesia, Indochina, and the Philippines—in an effort to acquire those resources that would free it from dependence on the West. In carving out this Pacific empire, the Japanese presented themselves as liberators and modernizers, creating an "Asia for Asians" and freeing their continent from European and American dominance. Experience soon showed that Japan's concern was far more for Asia's resources than for its liberation and that Japanese rule exceeded in brutality even that of the Europeans.

A decisive step in the development of World War II in Asia lay in the Japanese attack on the United States at Pearl Harbor in Hawaii in December 1941. Japanese authorities undertook that attack with reluctance and only after negotiations to end American hostility to Japan's empire-building enterprise proved fruitless and an American oil embargo was imposed on Japan in July 1941. In the face of this hostility, Japan's leaders felt that the alternatives for their country boiled down to either an acceptance of American terms, which they feared would reduce Japan to a second- or third-rank power, or a war with an uncertain outcome. Given those choices, the decision for war was made more with foreboding than with enthusiasm. A leading Japanese admiral made the case for war in this way in late 1941: "The government has decided that if there were no war the fate of the nation is sealed. Even if there is a war, the country may be ruined. Nevertheless a nation that does not fight in this plight has lost its spirit and is doomed."[8]

As a consequence of the attack on Pearl Harbor, the United States entered the war in the Pacific, beginning a long and bloody struggle that ended only with the use of atomic bombs against Hiroshima and Nagasaki in 1945. Since Japan was allied with Germany and Italy, the Pearl Harbor action also joined the Asian theater of the war with the ongoing conflict in Europe into a single global struggle that pitted Germany, Italy, and Japan (the Axis powers) against the United States, Britain, and the Soviet Union (the Allies).

The Road to War in Europe

If Japan was the dissatisfied power in Asia, Nazi Germany occupied that role in Europe. As a consequence of their defeat in World War I and the harsh terms of the

■ **Making Comparisons**
How did the origins of World War II in Europe differ from that of Asia?

Treaty of Versailles, many Germans harbored deep resentments about their country's position in the international arena. Taking advantage of those resentments, the Nazis pledged to rectify the treaty's perceived injustices. Thus, to most historians, the origins of **World War II in Europe** lie squarely in German aggression, although with many twists and turns and encouraged by the initial unwillingness of Britain, France, or the Soviet Union to confront that aggression forcefully. If World War I was accidental and unintended, World War II was deliberate and planned—perhaps even desired—by the German leadership and by Hitler in particular.

Slowly at first and then more aggressively, Hitler rearmed the country for war as he also pursued territorial expansion, annexing Austria and the German-speaking parts of Czechoslovakia. At a famous conference in Munich in 1938, the British and the French gave these actions their reluctant blessing, hoping that this "appeasement" of Hitler could satisfy his demands and avoid all-out war. But it did not. On September 1, 1939, Germany unleashed a devastating attack on Poland, triggering the Second World War in Europe, as Britain and France declared war on Germany. Quickly defeating France, the Germans launched a destructive air war against Britain and in 1941 turned their war machine loose on the Soviet Union. By then, most of Europe was under Nazi control (see Map 20.5).

The Second World War was quite different from the first. It was not welcomed with the kind of mass enthusiasm across Europe that had accompanied the opening of World War I in 1914. The bitter experience of the Great War suggested to most people that only suffering lay ahead. The conduct of the two wars likewise differed. The first war had quickly bogged down in trench warfare that emphasized defense, whereas in the second war the German tactic of *blitzkrieg* (lightning war) coordinated the rapid movement of infantry, tanks, and airpower over very large areas.

Such military tactics were initially successful and allowed German forces, aided by their Italian allies, to sweep over Europe, the western Soviet Union, and North Africa. The tide began to turn in 1942 when the Soviet Union absorbed the German onslaught and then began to counterattack, slowly and painfully moving westward toward the German heartland. The United States, with its enormous material and human resources, joined the struggle against Germany in 1942 and led the invasion of northern France in 1944, opening a long-awaited second front in the struggle against Hitler's Germany. Years of bitter fighting ensued before these two huge military movements ensured German defeat in May 1945.

Consequences: The Outcomes of a Second Global Conflict

The Second World War was the most destructive conflict in world history, with total deaths estimated at around 60 million, some six times that of World War I. More than half of those casualties were civilians. Partly responsible for this horrendous toll were the new technologies of warfare—heavy bombers, jet fighters, missiles, and atomic weapons. Equally significant, though, was the almost complete blurring of the traditional line between civilian and military targets, as entire cities

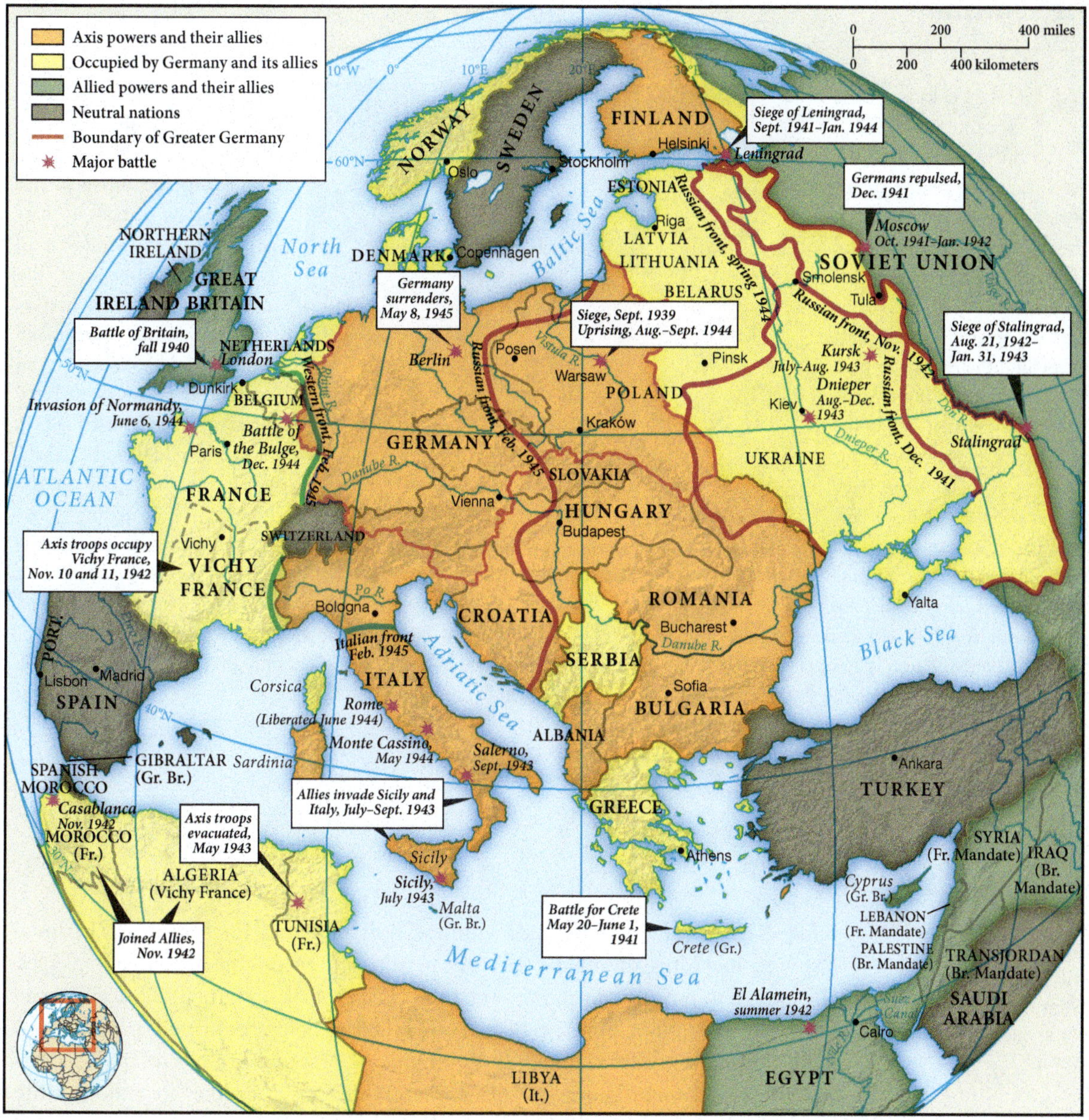

Map 20.5 World War II in Europe and Africa
For a brief moment during World War II, Nazi Germany came close to bringing all of Europe and North Africa under its rule. Then in late 1942, the Allies began a series of counterattacks that led to German surrender in May 1945.

and whole populations came to be defined as the enemy. Nowhere was that blurring more complete than in the Soviet Union, which accounted for more than 40 percent of the total deaths in the war—probably around 25 million, with an equal number made homeless and thousands of towns, villages, and industrial enterprises destroyed. In China as well, perhaps 15 million deaths and uncounted

ZOOMING IN

Hiroshima

"If the radiance of a thousand suns were to burst at once into the sky, that would be the splendor of the Mighty One."[9] This passage from the Bhagavad Gita, an ancient Hindu sacred text, occurred to J. Robert Oppenheimer, a leading scientist behind the American push to create a nuclear bomb, as he watched the first successful test of a nuclear weapon in the desert south of Santa Fe, New Mexico, on the evening of July 16, 1945. Years later, he recalled that another verse from the same sacred text had also entered his mind: "I am become Death, the shatterer of worlds." And so the atomic age was born amid Oppenheimer's thoughts of divine splendor and divine destruction.

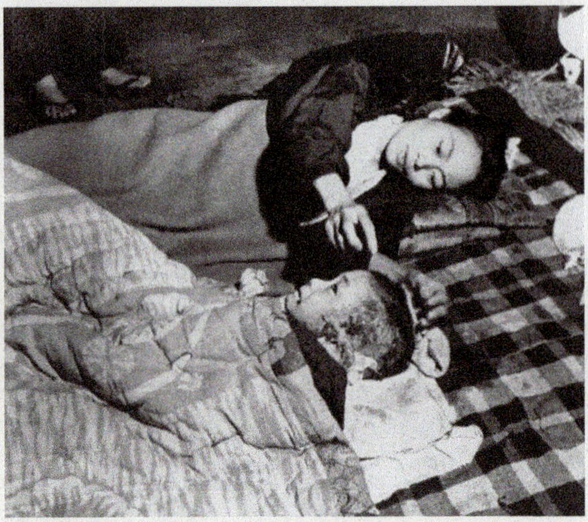

A mother and child, victims of Hiroshima, on the floor of a makeshift hospital, two months after the attack.

Several weeks later, the whole world became aware of this new era when American forces destroyed the Japanese cities of Hiroshima and Nagasaki with nuclear bombs. The U.S. government decided to use this powerful new weapon partially to hasten the end of World War II, but also to strengthen the United States' position in relation to the Soviet Union in the postwar world. Whether the bomb was necessary to force Japan to surrender is a question of some historical debate. What is not in dispute was the horrific destruction and human suffering wrought by the two bombs. The centers of both cities were flattened, and as many as 80,000 inhabitants of Hiroshima and 40,000 of Nagasaki perished almost instantly from the force and intense heat of the explosions.

photo: AP Images

■ Identifying Outcomes
What were the major consequences of World War II?

refugees grew out of prolonged Chinese resistance and the shattering Japanese response, including the killing of every person and every animal in many villages. Within a few months, during the infamous Rape of Nanjing in 1937–1938, some 200,000 to 300,000 Chinese civilians were killed and often mutilated, and countless women were sexually assaulted. Indiscriminate German bombing of British cities and the Allied firebombing of Japanese and German cities likewise reflected the new morality of total war, as did the dropping of atomic bombs on Hiroshima and Nagasaki, which in a single instant vaporized tens of thousands of people. This was total war with a scale, intensity, and indiscriminate brutality that exceeded even the horrors of World War I. (See Zooming In: Hiroshima.)

A further dimension of total war lay in governments' efforts to mobilize their economies, their people, and their propaganda machines even more extensively than before. Colonial resources were harnessed once again. The British in particular made extensive use of colonial troops and laborers from India and Africa. Japan compelled several hundred thousand women from Korea, China, and elsewhere to

The harrowing accounts of survivors offer some sense of the suffering that followed. Iwao Nakamura, a schoolboy in Hiroshima who lived through the attack, recalled "old people pleading for water, tiny children seeking help, students unconsciously calling for their parents." He remembered that "there was a mother prostrate on the ground, moaning with pain but with one arm still tightly embracing her dead baby."[10] But for many of these survivors, the suffering had only begun. It is estimated that by 1950 as many as 200,000 additional victims had succumbed to their injuries, especially burns and the terrible effects of radiation. Cancer and genetic deformations caused by exposure to radiation continue to affect survivors and their descendants today.

Human suffering on a massive scale was a defining feature of total war during the first half of the twentieth century. In this sense, the atomic bomb was just the latest development in an arms race that drew on advances in manufacturing, technology, and science to create ever more horrific weapons of mass destruction. But no other weapon from that period was as revolutionary as the atomic bomb, which made use of recent discoveries in theoretical physics to harness the fundamental forces of the universe for war. The subsequent development of those weapons has cast an enormous shadow on the world ever since.

That shadow lay in a capacity for destruction previously associated only with an apocalypse of divine origin. Now human beings have acquired that capacity. A single bomb in a single instant can obliterate any major city in the world, and the detonation of even a small fraction of the weapons in existence today would reduce much of the world to radioactive rubble and social chaos. The destructive power of nuclear weapons has led responsible scientists to contemplate the possible extinction of our species—by our own hands. It is hardly surprising that the ongoing threat of nuclear war has led many survivors of the Hiroshima and Nagasaki bombings to push for a world free of nuclear weapons by highlighting the human suffering that they cause. In a speech to a United Nations Special Session on Disarmament in 1982, Senji Yamaguchi, a survivor of the Nagasaki bombing, pleaded for those present to look at his burnt face and hands, before calling for "no more Hiroshimas, no more Nagasakis, no more war, no more [survivors of nuclear attacks]."[11]

QUESTION

How might you define both the short- and long-term outcomes of the Hiroshima bombing?

serve the sexual needs of Japanese troops as so-called comfort women, who often accommodated twenty to thirty men a day.

As in World War I, though on a much larger scale, the needs of the war drew huge numbers of women into both industry and the military. In the United States, "Rosie the Riveter" represented those women who now took on heavy industrial jobs, which previously had been reserved for men. In the Soviet Union, women constituted more than half of the industrial workforce by 1945 and almost completely dominated agricultural production. Soviet women also participated actively in combat, with some 100,000 of them winning military honors. A much smaller percentage of German and Japanese women were mobilized for factory work, but a Greater Japan Women's Society enrolled some 19 million members, who did volunteer work and promised to lay aside their gold jewelry and abandon extravagant weddings. As always, war heightened the prestige of masculinity, and given the immense sacrifices that men had made, few women were inclined to directly challenge the practices of patriarchy immediately following the war.

Among the most haunting outcomes of the war was the **Holocaust**. The outbreak of war closed off certain possibilities, such as forced emigration, for implementing the Nazi dream of ridding Germany of its Jewish population. It also brought millions of additional Jews in Poland and the Soviet Union under German control and triggered among Hitler's enthusiastic subordinates various schemes for a "final solution" to the Jewish question. From this emerged the death camps that included Auschwitz, Treblinka, and Sobibór. Altogether, some 6 million Jews perished in a technologically sophisticated form of mass murder that set a new standard for human depravity. Millions more whom the Nazis deemed inferior, undesirable, or dangerous—Russians, Poles, and other Slavs; Gypsies, or the Roma; mentally or physically handicapped people; homosexuals; communists; and Jehovah's Witnesses—likewise perished in Germany's efforts at racial purification.

Although the Holocaust was concentrated in Germany, its significance in twentieth-century world history has been huge. It has haunted postwar Germany in particular and the Western world in general. How could such a thing have occurred in a Europe bearing the legacy of both Christianity and the Enlightenment? More specifically, it sent many of Europe's remaining Jews fleeing to Israel and gave urgency to the establishment of a modern Jewish nation in the ancient Jewish homeland. That action outraged many Arabs, some of whom were displaced by the arrival of the Jews, and has fostered an enduring conflict in the Middle East. Furthermore, the Holocaust defined a new category of crimes against humanity—genocide, the attempted elimination of entire peoples.

On an even larger scale than World War I, this second global conflict rearranged the architecture of world politics. As the war ended, Europe was impoverished, its industrial infrastructure shattered, many of its great cities in ruins, and millions of its people homeless or displaced. Within a few years, this much-weakened Europe was effectively divided, with its western half operating willingly under an American security umbrella and the eastern half subject to Soviet control, but less willingly. It was clear that Europe's dominance in world affairs was finished. Not only had the war weakened both the will and the ability of European powers to hold on to their colonies, but it had also emboldened nationalist and anticolonial movements everywhere (see "Toward Independence in Asia and Africa" in Chapter 21). Japanese victories in Southeast Asia had certainly damaged European prestige. Furthermore, tens of thousands of Africans had fought for the British or the French, had seen white people die, had enjoyed the company of white women, and had returned home with very different ideas about white superiority and the permanence of colonial rule. Colonial subjects everywhere were very much aware that U.S. president Franklin Roosevelt and British prime minister Winston Churchill had solemnly declared in 1941 that "we respect the right of all peoples to choose the form of government under which they will live." Increasingly, Asian and African leaders demanded that such principles should apply to them as well.

■ Interpreting History

Is it more useful to consider World Wars I and II as separate and distinct conflicts or as a single briefly interrupted phenomenon?

The horrors of two world wars within a single generation prompted a renewed interest in international efforts to maintain the peace in a world of competing and sovereign states. The chief outcome was the United Nations (UN), established in 1945 as a successor to the moribund League of Nations. As a political body dependent on agreement among its most powerful members, the UN proved more effective as a forum for international opinion than as a means of resolving the major conflicts of the postwar world, particularly the Soviet/American hostility during the cold war decades. Further evidence for a growing internationalism lay in the creation in late 1945 of the World Bank and International Monetary Fund, whose purpose was to regulate the global economy, prevent another depression, and stimulate economic growth, especially in the poorer nations. What these initiatives shared was the dominant presence of the United States, as the half century following the end of World War II witnessed its emergence as a global superpower. This was among the major outcomes of the Second World War and a chief reason for the remarkable recovery of a badly damaged and discredited Western civilization.

Communist Consolidation and Expansion: The Chinese Revolution

Yet another outcome of World War II lay in the consolidation and extension of the communist world. The Soviet victory over the Nazis, though bought at an unimaginable cost in blood and treasure, gave immense credibility to that communist regime and to its leader, Joseph Stalin. Whatever atrocities he had committed, many in the Soviet Union credited Stalin with leading the country's heroic struggle against Nazi aggression. Furthermore, Stalin also presided over a major expansion of communist control in Eastern Europe, much of which was occupied by Soviet forces as the war ended. He insisted that Soviet security required "friendly" governments in the region to permanently end the threat of invasion from the West. Stalin also feared that large-scale American aid for Europe's economic recovery, which began in 1948, sought to incorporate Eastern Europe into a Western and capitalist economic network. Thus he acted to install fully communist governments, loyal to himself, in Poland, East Germany, Czechoslovakia, Hungary, Romania, and Bulgaria. Backed by the pressure and presence of the Soviet army, **communism in Eastern Europe** was largely imposed from the outside rather than growing out of a domestic revolution, as had happened in Russia itself. The situation in Yugoslavia differed sharply from the rest of Eastern Europe. There a genuinely popular communist movement had played a leading role in the struggle against Nazi occupation and came to power on its own with little Soviet help. Its leader, Josef Broz, known as Tito, openly defied Soviet efforts to control Yugoslav communism, claiming that "our goal is that everyone should be master in his own house."

In Asia too communism took root after World War II. Following Japan's defeat, its Korean colony was partitioned, with the northern half coming under Soviet and therefore communist control. In Vietnam, a much more locally based communist movement, active since the mid-1920s under the leadership of **Ho Chi Minh** (1890–1969), embodied both a socialist vision and Vietnamese nationalism as it battled Japanese, French, and later American invaders and established communist control first in the northern half of the country and after 1975 throughout the whole country. The victory of the Vietnamese communists spilled over into neighboring Laos and Cambodia, where communist parties took power in the mid-1970s.

Far and away the most striking expansion of communism occurred in China, where that country's Communist Party triumphantly seized power in 1949. As in Russia, that victory came on the heels of war and domestic upheaval. But the **Chinese Revolution of 1949**, which was a struggle of decades rather than a single year, was far different from its earlier Russian counterpart. The Chinese imperial system had collapsed in 1911, under the pressure of foreign imperialism, its own inadequacies, and mounting internal opposition (see "The Failure of Conservative Modernization" in Chapter 19). Unlike in Russia, where intellectuals had been discussing socialism for half a century or more before the revolution, the ideas of Karl Marx were barely known in China in the early twentieth century. Not until 1921 was a small Chinese Communist Party (CCP) founded, aimed initially at organizing the country's minuscule urban working class.

CORE IDEA

■ Explaining Success
How might you explain the success of the Chinese Communist Party in coming to power by 1949?

Over the next twenty-eight years, that small party, with an initial membership of only sixty people, grew enormously, transformed its strategy, found a charismatic leader in **Mao Zedong** (1893–1976), engaged in an epic struggle with its opponents, fought the Japanese heroically, and in 1949 emerged victorious as the rulers of the world's most populous country. That victory was all the more surprising because the CCP faced a far more formidable foe than the weak Provisional Government over which the Bolsheviks had triumphed in Russia. That opponent was the **Guomindang** (GWOH-mihn-dahng) (Nationalist Party), which governed China after 1928. Led by a military officer, Chiang Kai-shek, that party promoted a measure of modern development (railroads, light industry, banking, airline services) in the decade that followed. However, the impact of these achievements was limited largely to the cities, leaving the rural areas, where most people lived, still impoverished. The Guomindang's base of support was also narrow, deriving from urban elites, rural landlords, and Western powers.

Whereas the Bolsheviks had found their primary audience among workers in Russia's major cities, Chinese communists, in a striking adaptation of European Marxism, increasingly looked to the country's peasant villages for support. But Chinese peasants did not rise up spontaneously against their landlords, as Russian peasants had. Instead, years of guerrilla warfare, experiments with land reform in areas under communist control, and the creation of a communist military force to protect liberated areas slowly gained for the CCP a growing measure of respect and support among China's peasants, particularly during the 1930s. In the process, Mao Zedong, the son of a prosperous Chinese peasant family and a professional revolutionary since the early 1920s, emerged as the party's leader. A central event in Mao's rise to prominence was the Long March of 1934–1935, when beleaguered communist forces in southern China made a harrowing but successful retreat to a new base area in the northwest of the country, an epic journey of some 5,600 miles that soon acquired mythical dimensions in communist lore.

Mao Zedong and the Long March An early member of China's then-minuscule Communist Party, Mao rose to a position of dominant leadership during the Long March of 1934–1935, when beleaguered communists from southeastern China trekked to a new base area in the north. This photograph shows Mao on his horse during that epic journey. (© Collection J. A. Fox/Magnum Photos)

To recruit women for the revolution, communists drew on a theoretical commitment to their liberation and in the areas under their control established a Marriage Law that outlawed arranged or "purchased" marriages, made divorce easier, and gave women the right to vote and own property. Women's associations enrolled hundreds of thousands of women and promoted literacy, fostered discussions of women's issues, and encouraged handicraft production such as making clothing, blankets, and shoes, so essential for the revolutionary forces. But resistance to such radical measures from more traditional rural villagers, especially the male peasants and soldiers on whom the communists depended, persuaded the party leaders to modify these measures. Women were not permitted to seek divorce from men on active military duty. Women's land deeds were often given to male family heads and were regarded as family property. Female party members found themselves limited to work with women or children.

It was Japan's brutal invasion of China that gave the CCP a decisive opening, for that attack destroyed Guomindang control over much of the country and forced it to retreat to the interior, where it became even more dependent on conservative landlords. The CCP, by contrast, grew from just 40,000 members in 1937 to more than 1.2 million in 1945, while the communist-led People's Liberation Army mushroomed to 900,000 men, supported by an additional 2 million militia troops. Much of this growing support derived from the vigor with which the CCP waged war against the Japanese invaders. Using guerrilla warfare techniques learned in the struggle against the Guomindang, communist forces established themselves behind enemy lines and, despite periodic setbacks, offered a measure of security to many Chinese faced with Japanese atrocities. The Guomindang, by contrast, sometimes seemed to be more interested in eliminating the communists than in actively fighting the Japanese. Furthermore, in the areas it controlled, the CCP reduced rents, taxes, and interest payments for peasants; taught literacy to adults; and mobilized women for the struggle. As the war drew to a close, more radical action followed. Teams of activists encouraged poor peasants to "speak bitterness" in public meetings, to "struggle" with landlords, and to "settle accounts" with them.

Thus the CCP frontally addressed both of China's major problems—foreign imperialism and peasant exploitation. It expressed Chinese nationalism as well as a demand for radical social change. It gained a reputation for honesty that contrasted sharply with the massive corruption of Guomindang officials. It put down deep roots among the peasantry in a way that the Bolsheviks never did. And whereas the Bolsheviks gained support by urging Russian withdrawal from the highly unpopular First World War, the CCP won support by aggressively pursuing the struggle against Japanese invaders during World War II. In 1949, four years after the war's end, the Chinese communists swept to victory over the Guomindang, many of whose followers fled to Taiwan. Mao Zedong announced triumphantly that "the Chinese people have stood up."

CONCLUSIONS AND REFLECTIONS

Historical Intersections and Their Implications

Major historical events, such as the world wars, the Russian and Chinese revolutions, and the Great Depression, did not turn on a dime. Rather they emerged at intersections or crossroads where multiple paths converged, where many factors played a role, and where the aspirations of various individuals and groups encountered one another.

World War I, for example, was shaped by the unstable balance of power among the major countries of Europe, by the growth of mass nationalism, by the highly destructive weaponry born of the Scientific and Industrial Revolutions, and by the rivalry of Europe's global empires. The Russian Revolution occurred when the immediate pressures of World War I were coupled with the long-term inequalities of Russian society and the more recent development of an aggrieved group of industrial workers. The legacy of World War I—debt, protectionism, and reparations demanded of Germany—also aggravated the long-term instabilities of capitalism to generate the Great Depression, which spread across the world along the economic linkages of globalization. Among the factors that facilitated the rise of the Nazis were the resentments following World War I, the economic tragedy of the Great Depression, and fear of Soviet communism.

And what about the role of particular people as they intersected with major events of the twentieth century? How much did the personal qualities of Lenin in Russia, Hitler in Germany, or Mao in China contribute to the movements they led?

Ordinary people as well—hungry Russian women, impoverished Chinese peasants, millions of soldiers—also decided how to act amid these vast upheavals. Historians continue to debate the relationship between larger historical processes and the actions of individuals.

An awareness of this immense complexity has had implications for how historians respond to several commonplace notions about the past. One of them is the idea that history has "lessons" that can be applied in the present. About this, many historians are skeptical. The historical record, after all, is sufficiently rich and multifaceted to allow people to draw quite different lessons from it. The world wars of the twentieth century represent a case in point, as writer Adam Gopnik has pointed out:

> The First World War teaches that territorial compromise is better than full-scale war, that an "honor-bound" allegiance of the great powers to small nations is a recipe for mass killing, and that it is crazy to let the blind mechanism of armies and alliances trump common sense. The Second [World War] teaches that searching for an accommodation with tyranny by selling out small nations only encourages the tyrant, that refusing to fight now leads to a worse fight later on. . . . The First teaches us never to rush into a fight, the Second never to back down from a bully.[12]

History offers a rich reservoir of past experiences to ponder, but their lessons are not always clear or consistent to those seeking to learn from them.

A second notion to which historians bring considerable skepticism is that "history repeats itself." While historians often notice repetitive patterns in the past—wars, revolutions, and empires, for example—they usually focus more sharply on the complexity and distinctiveness of particular events such as World War I or the Chinese Revolution. They are also acutely aware of the surprising nature of historical events. Few people in 1914 anticipated the duration and carnage of World War I. The Holocaust was literally unimaginable when Hitler took power in 1933 or even at the outbreak of the Second World War in 1939. So while all of us quite naturally look to the past as we try to imagine the future, for many scholars history repeats itself most certainly in its unexpectedness.

Revisiting Chapter 20

Revisiting Specifics

World War I, 878
total war, 881
Treaty of Versailles, 884
Russian Revolution, 885
Lenin, 886
Stalin, 886
collectivization of agriculture, 887
Great Depression, 888
fascism, 890
Mussolini, 891
Nazi Party, 892
Hitler, 892
Revolutionary Right (Japan), 897
World War II in Asia, 900

World War II in Europe, 902
Holocaust, 906
communism in Eastern Europe, 907
Ho Chi Minh, 907
Chinese Revolution of 1949, 908
Mao Zedong, 908
Guomindang, 908

Revisiting Core Ideas

1. **Identifying Change** In what ways did World War I mark new departures in the history of the twentieth century?
2. **Assessing Cause and Effect** What factors contributed to the Russian Revolution and the victory of the Bolsheviks?
3. **Identifying Global Connections** In what respects was the Great Depression a global phenomenon?
4. **Making Comparisons** What did Italian fascism, German Nazism, and Japanese authoritarianism have in common? How did they differ?
5. **Making Comparisons** How did the origins, course, and outcomes of World War II differ from those of World War I?
6. **Explaining Success** How might you explain the success of the Chinese Communist Party in coming to power by 1949?

A Wider View

1. The disasters that befell Europe in the first half of the twentieth century derived from fundamental flaws in its civilization. Do you agree? Why or why not?
2. To what extent did the two world wars settle the issues that caused them? What legacies for the future did they leave?
3. In what ways did Europe's internal conflicts between 1914 and 1945 have global implications?
4. In what ways did communism have an impact on world history in the first half of the twentieth century?
5. **Looking Back** In what ways were the major phenomena of the first half of the twentieth century—world wars, communist revolutions, the Great Depression, fascism, the Holocaust, the emergence of the United States as a global power—rooted in earlier times?

To learn more about the topics in this chapter, see **For Further Study** at the end of this book.

Ideologies of the Axis Powers

Even more than the Great War of 1914–1918, the Second World War was a conflict of ideas and ideologies as well as a struggle of nations and armies. The ideas of the losing side in that war, repellant as they were to their enemies and probably to many people today, had for a time attracted considerable support. Described variously as fascist, authoritarian, right-wing, or radically nationalist, the ideologies of the Axis powers—Italy, Germany, and Japan—differed in tone and emphasis. But they shared a repudiation of mainstream Western liberalism and democracy, an intense hatred of Marxist communism, and a desire for imperial expansion. The sources that follow provide a sample of this thinking as it took shape in those three countries.

SOURCE 20.1 Italian Fascism: Creating a New Roman Empire ▶

Empire was central in the thinking of Italy's Benito Mussolini and his understanding of fascism. "For Fascism," he wrote, "the growth of Empire, that is to say the expansion of the nation, is an essential manifestation of vitality, and its opposite a sign of decadence."[13] And for Mussolini, the model for empire was decidedly Roman. Following the conquest of Ethiopia in 1936, he triumphantly celebrated "the reappearance of empire on the fated hills of Rome." "Italy finally has its own empire," he proclaimed. "An empire of civilization and of humanity for all the populations of Ethiopia. This is in the tradition of Rome. . . ."[14] One year later, marking the first anniversary of that victory, the image in Source 20.1 was on the cover of school exercise books. Mussolini appears in the foreground in military uniform including a combat helmet, while in the background looms a famous national monument commemorating the unification of Italy in 1871. Located near the heart of ancient Rome, this monument used classical architectural and sculptural styles to evoke the revival of Italy's glorious past. The golden winged figure, busy inscribing the date of the empire's foundation on a tablet, is Victoria, the Roman goddess of victory, widely revered in Roman armies and worshipped by returning generals. The caption reads: "In the first year of the foundation of the Empire, the Italian people renew the victorious Duce [Mussolini] with fervent testimonies of gratitude and devotion."

- Why might the artist have chosen to present Mussolini in the context of the ancient Roman Empire?
- Why might Mussolini want to link his recent conquest of Ethiopia with the nineteenth-century reunification of Italy?
- What does the arrangement of the image suggest about how Mussolini wanted to be viewed? What attitudes or postures does this portrayal of Mussolini project?

School Exercise Book Celebrating Italy's Victory over Ethiopia | 1937

SOURCE 20.2 Hitler on Nazism

The ideology of German Nazism found its classic expression in Adolf Hitler's *Mein Kampf* (My Struggle), written while he was briefly imprisoned in 1923 and published a few years later. Armed with these ideas, Hitler assumed the leadership of Germany in 1933.

- What larger patterns in European thinking do Hitler's ideas reflect, and what elements of European thought does he reject? Consider in particular his use of social Darwinism, then an idea with wide popularity in Europe.
- How does Hitler distinguish between Aryans and Jews? How does he understand the role of race in human affairs?
- What kind of political system does Hitler advocate?

ADOLF HITLER | *Mein Kampf (My Struggle)* | 1925–1926

There are truths that are so obvious that they are not seen, or at least not recognized, by ordinary people. . . . In the struggle for daily bread the weak and sickly, as well as the less resolute, succumb, while in the struggle of the males for the female only the healthiest is granted the right or opportunity to propagate. . . . However little Nature wishes that the weaker mate with the stronger, even less does she desire the blending of a higher race with a lower. . . . All great cultures of the past collapsed only because the originally creative race died off from the poisoning of their blood. . . .

Those who want to live, must also fight, and those who will not fight in this world of eternal struggle do not deserve to live. . . . All that we see before us today of human culture, all the achievements of art, science, and technology, is almost exclusively the creative product of the Aryan race. . . . [H]e alone was the founder of all higher forms of humanity, and thus represents the very prototype of all that we understand by the word "human." He is the Prometheus of mankind from whose bright forehead the divine spark of genius has always sprung. . . .

Everything in this world that is not of good race is chaff. All occurrences in world history, for better and for worse, are simply the expression of the racial instinct for self-preservation. . . .

The Jew represents the most formidable opponent of the Aryan. . . . Because the Jew . . . has never possessed a culture of his own, the foundations of his intellectual work have always been provided by others. . . . If the Jews were alone in this world, not only would they suffocate in filth and offal, but they would also seek, in their hate-filled struggles, to cheat and to destroy each another. . . . [T]he Jew is led by nothing more than the naked egoism of the individual. . . .

The black-haired Jewish youth, satanic joy in his face, lurks in wait for the unsuspecting girl whom he defiles with his blood, thus stealing her from her people. He uses every means to taint the racial foundations of the people he has set out to subjugate. . . . And thus he tries to systematically lower the racial level [of a people] by the continuous poisoning of individuals. . . . He has found, in the organized masses of Marxism, the weapon that allows him . . . to subjugate and to "govern" the peoples with a dictatorial and brutal fist. . . .

If we mentally review all the reasons for the German collapse [defeat in World War I], the ultimate and most decisive remains the failure to recognize the racial problem and especially the Jewish menace. . . . The lost purity of the blood is enough to destroy the inner happiness [of a people] forever . . . the consequences of which can never be eliminated from body and from spirit. . . . All really significant symptoms of decay from the prewar period can be traced back to racial causes. . . .

. . . [T]he state is a means to an end. Its purpose lies in the preservation and advancement of a society of physically and spiritually homogenous beings. . . .

States that do not serve this purpose are misbegotten, indeed they are monstrosities. . . .

The highest purpose of the folkish state is therefore concern for the preservation of those original cultural-bestowing racial elements that create the beauty and dignity of higher humanity. We, as Aryans, conceive of the state simply as the living organism of a nation that not only ensures the preservation of the nation, but through the development of its spiritual and intellectual abilities leads it to the highest freedom. . . .

This world is surely moving toward a great revolution. And the only question is whether it will rebound to the salvation of Aryan mankind or to the profit of the eternal Jew. . . .

. . . [T]he folkish state must accordingly free the political leadership . . . entirely from the parliamentarian principle of majority or mass rule, and instead absolutely guarantee the right of the personality. . . . The best state constitution and state form is the one with the instinctual certainty to raise the best minds of the national community to leading prominence and influence. . . . There will be no majority decisions, only responsible individuals, and the word "counsel" will be restored to its original meaning. Every man will have advisers by his side to be sure, but the decision will be made by one man. . . .

With respect to the feasibility of these ideas, I beg you not to forget that the parliamentary principle of democratic majority rule has not always governed mankind, but rather is to be found only in the briefest periods of history, which are invariably eras of decay of peoples and states.

Source: Adolf Hitler, *Mein Kampf. Zwei Bände in einem Band,* translated by Sarah Panzer (München: Zentralverlag der NSDAP, 1943), 311, 312–13, 316, 317, 324, 329, 330, 331, 357, 359, 360, 433, 434, 475, 500, 501, 502.

■ ■ ■

SOURCE 20.3 Nazi Anti-Semitism ▶

Hatred of Jews was central to Nazi ideology. This image, which served as the cover of a Nazi publication titled *Der Ewige Jude* (The Eternal Jew), summed up many of the themes in Nazi anti-Semitism.

- How does this image illustrate Hitler's understanding of Jews as expressed in Source 20.2?
- Notice particular aspects of the image: the coins in the man's right hand, the whip in his left hand, the map of Russia with a hammer and sickle. What does each of these suggest about the Nazi case against the Jews?
- Notice also the general appearance and dress of the figure. What does this contribute to the image of Jews that Nazis are trying to convey?

H. SCHLUTER | *Der Ewige Jude (The Eternal Jew)* | 1937

akg-images

■ ■ ■

SOURCE 20.4 The Japanese Way

In the Japanese language, the word *kokutai* is an evocative term that refers to the national essence or the fundamental character of the Japanese nation and people. Drawing both on long-established understandings and on recently developed nationalist ideas, the Ministry of Education in 1937 published a small volume, widely distributed in schools and homes throughout the country, titled *Kokutai No Hongi* (Cardinal Principles of the National Entity of Japan). That text, excerpted in Source 20.4, defined the uniqueness of Japan and articulated the philosophical foundation of its authoritarian regime. When the Americans occupied a defeated and devastated Japan in 1945, they forbade the further distribution of the book.

- According to *Cardinal Principles*, what is *kokutai*? How does the document define the national essence of Japan? How do its authors compare Japan to the West?
- What was the ideal role of the individual in Japanese society?
- Why do you think the American occupation authorities banned the document?

Cardinal Principles of the National Entity of Japan | 1937

[T]he foreign ideologies imported into our country are in the main ideologies of the [European] Enlightenment. . . . The views of the world and of life that form the basis of these ideologies . . . lay the highest value on, and assert the liberty and equality of, individuals. . . .

We subjects [of the Japanese emperor] are intrinsically quite different from the so-called citizens of the Occidental [Western] countries. . . .

Our country is established with the Emperor. . . . For this reason, to serve the Emperor and to receive the Emperor's great august Will as one's own is the rationale of making our historical "life" live in the present. . . .

Loyalty means to reverence the Emperor as [our] pivot and to follow him implicitly. . . . Hence, offering our lives for the sake of the Emperor does not mean so-called self-sacrifice, but the casting aside of our little selves to live under his august grace and the enhancing of the genuine life of the people of a State. . . . An individual is an existence belonging to the State and her history, which forms the basis of his origin, and is fundamentally one body with it. . . .

We must sweep aside the corruption of the spirit and the clouding of knowledge that arises from setting up one's "self" and from being taken up with one's "self" and return to a pure and clear state of mind that belongs intrinsically to us as subjects, and thereby fathom the great principle loyalty. . . .

Indeed, loyalty is our fundamental Way as subject, and is the basis of our national morality. Through loyalty are we become Japanese subjects; in loyalty do we obtain life and herein do we find the source of all morality.

Source: J. O. Gauntlett, trans., and R. K. Hall, ed., *Kokutai No Hongi* (*Cardinal Principles of the National Entity of Japan*) (Cambridge, MA: Harvard University Press, 1949), 52, 80–83.

SOURCE 20.5 Japanese Imperialism

Empire was a major theme in Japanese ideology of the 1930s and 1940s. It began to be put into practice in the early 1930s, when Japanese forces seized parts of northeastern China, calling it Manchukuo. Source 20.5 presents a Japanese propaganda poster, created in 1933, showing anti-Japanese Manchurians in hell (on the left), while pro-Japanese supporters (on the right) enjoy a blissful paradise.

- What contrasts can you identify between the two panels? How does the imagery in both panels enhance the message of the poster? What kinds of figures dominate each panel of the image, and what are they doing?
- To whom might this image be directed?
- How does this portrayal of Japanese empire building compare with that of Italian imperialism in Source 20.1?

Japanese Propaganda Poster of Manchuria under Japanese Occupation | 1933

ullstein bild/Getty Images

DOING HISTORY

1. **Making Comparisons** What broad similarities and differences in outlook can you identify among these sources? What aspects of the Japanese *Cardinal Principles* text might Hitler have viewed with sympathy, and what parts of it might he have found distasteful or offensive?
2. **Criticizing the West** In what ways did Mussolini, Hitler, and the authors of *Cardinal Principles* find fault with mainstream Western societies and their political and social values?
3. **Considering Ideas and Action** To what extent did the ideas articulated in these sources find expression in particular actions or policies of political authorities?
4. **Placing Sources in Context** To what extent were the ideas in these sources new and revolutionary? In what respects did they draw on long-standing traditions? In what ways did they embrace modern life, and what aspects of it did they reject? Have these ideas been completely discredited, or do they retain some resonance in contemporary political discourse?

HISTORIANS' VOICES

Anti-Semitism

Because hatred and fear of Jews were central to Nazi ideology, the history of anti-Semitism and its relationship to the Holocaust have loomed large in historians' efforts to understand the Nazi phenomenon. Voice 20.1, by historian Beth A. Griech-Polelle, shows how Nazi anti-Semitism drew on ideas built up over centuries to create a sense of Jews as radically "other" and threatening. Voice 20.2, derived from a book by the prominent historian Christopher Browning, takes a shorter-term perspective by exploring why Nazi policies were at least tacitly supported by millions of Germans upon whom the fate of the Jews "weighed lightly or not at all."

- In what ways did anti-Semitism define Jews as radically "other"?
- Why does Browning believe that many millions of "ordinary" Germans at least tacitly accepted Nazi anti-Semitic policies?
- What elements of the Nazi program were most widely criticized by "ordinary" Germans and why?
- **Integrating Primary and Secondary Sources** How might these two historians use Sources 20.2 and 20.3 to support their arguments?

VOICE 20.1

Beth A. Griech-Polelle on Anti-Semitism Creating "Otherness" | 2017

In this "Us" vs "Them" world, insiders are told that their very existence is threatened by an enemy who seeks to define, pollute, and destroy the coherence of "us." The threatening imagery of "the Jew" . . . was built up over the course of centuries. Destructive legends, myths, and stereotypes all contributed to a type of acceptable language about Jews that enabled Hitler to play on well-established tropes. Images of the "diabolical, cunning" Jew could be used to instill fear and anxiety and could serve as an explanation as to why an average German person felt stymied in their personal and professional development. They were told repeatedly that the enemy, the Jew, was standing in their way of creating a peaceful harmonious society. . . . In order for the German people to live, Jews had to die. . . .

The "other" is portrayed in language that suggests Jews are dirty, foreign, corrupt, corrupting, and never to be trusted. They are depicted as being in league with the devil, perpetrating every evil known to mankind. . . . Germans had to attack Jews in a kind of preemptive strike. . . . The Germans were only acting in self-defense to protect themselves from an imagined future annihilation. . . .

The image of "the Jew" was now a figure standing outside of history, an eternal enemy of "us."

Source: Beth A. Griech-Polelle, *Anti-Semitism and the Holocaust* (London: Bloomsbury Academic, 2017), 1–2.

VOICE 20.2

Christopher Browning on Why Many Ordinary Germans Tacitly Supported Nazi Anti-Semitic Policies | 2004

Hitler's coming to power would not only "unleash" the Nazis and their right-wing allies . . . to harm the Jews, but would do so with the tacit support of millions of Germans for whom the fate of the Jews weighed lightly or not at all . . . and increasingly with the support of millions of Germans eager to catch the political tide. . . . Germany ceased to be a pluralistic society, and there were no significant "countervailing" forces outside the alliance of Nazis and conservative nationalists on which the regime rested.

. . . It is most unlikely that the conservatives on their own would have proceeded beyond the initial discriminatory measures of 1933–34 that drove the Jews out of the civil and military services, the professions, and cultural life . . . [but] with strikingly few exceptions they had no remorse or regret for the fate of the Jews.

What can be said of the German people at large in the 1930s? . . . The majority of "ordinary" Germans . . .

accepted the legal measures of the regime . . . yet this majority was critical of the hooliganistic violence of activists. . . . Many Germans who were indifferent or even hostile toward Jews were not indifferent to the public flouting of deeply ingrained values concerning the preservation of order, propriety, and property. But anti-Semitic measures carried out in an orderly and legal manner were widely accepted. . . . This was a major accomplishment for the regime, but it still did not offer the prospect that most ordinary Germans would approve of, much less participate in, the mass murder of European Jewry.

Source: Christopher R. Browning, *The Origins of the Final Solution: The Evolution of Nazi Jewish Policy, September 1939–March 1942* (Lincoln: University of Nebraska Press, 2004), 8–10.

INDEPENDENCE
DAY MARCH 6TH 1957
McB

CHAPTER 21

A Changing Global Landscape

1950–present

CONNECTING PAST AND PRESENT

"What good is independence in the age of neocolonialism? Europe still plays the flute and our government dances. We owe billions to the World Bank and the International Monetary Fund. Western nonprofits arrive at a steady speed to improve our education and health care systems. Chinese interests have descended on our resources, taking away the livelihoods of many."[1] This was the view of Imbolo Mbue, a Cameroonian novelist writing in early 2020. She was describing the situation in her Central African country sixty years after its independence from colonial rule in 1960.

A rather different view of the six decades since independence comes from Omar Victor Diop, a photographer from Senegal in West Africa, also writing in 2020: "I have faith in our ability to forgive ourselves for not being where we thought we'd be, 60 years after 1960; building a nation and a functioning republic takes time. I have faith in our ability to see that we've done great things, staying together in peace being the greatest among them. . . . I will have the honor to witness the greatness of my hopeful, elegant and future-loving people."[2]

These contrasting assessments of the post-independence era in Africa highlight the significance of the end of European empires in Asia, Africa, and elsewhere, which marked a dramatic change in the political landscape of the world in the second half of the twentieth century. So too did the continuing struggles of dozens

« **African Independence Achieved** This poster depicts an Independence Day celebration in the new West African nation of Ghana in 1957. Its exuberance reflects the sense of great achievement that came with the defeat of colonial rule and the immense hopes for the future that independence raised.

of "new nations" to create stable, unified, and prosperous societies. But this epic transformation intersected with other profound changes during these years. A devastated Europe rebuilt its modern economy and moved toward greater union. Communism expanded its reach into Eastern Europe, China, Southeast Asia, and Cuba. A cold war between the United States and the Soviet Union, both of them armed with nuclear weapons of unprecedented destructive power, structured much of international life until the communist experiment largely collapsed at the end of the twentieth century. By the early twenty-first century, China had become a powerful and prominent player in the global arena, challenging the dominance of the United States, while the Middle East emerged as a major exporter of oil and a center of conflict and instability.

These are among the major developments in world history during the past seven decades. Each of them had roots in the past, and each had a profound impact on many millions of people. Together they transformed human life across the planet.

SEEKING THE MAIN POINT

In what ways has the structure of global political life changed in the decades since the end of World War II?

Recovering from the War

The tragedies that afflicted Europe in the first half of the twentieth century—fratricidal war, economic collapse, the Holocaust—were wholly self-inflicted, and yet that civilization had not permanently collapsed. In the twentieth century's second half, Europeans rebuilt their industrial economies and revived their democratic political systems. Three factors help to explain this astonishing recovery. One is the apparent resiliency of an industrial society, once it has been established. The knowledge, skills, and habits of mind that enabled industrial societies to operate effectively remained intact, even if the physical infrastructure had been substantially destroyed. Thus even the most terribly damaged countries—Germany, the Soviet Union, and Japan—had largely recovered by 1960, amid a worldwide economic boom during the 1950s.

CORE IDEA

Explaining Postwar Recovery
What enabled Europe, the Soviet Union, and Japan to recover from the devastation of war?

A second factor lay in the ability of the major Western European countries to integrate their recovering economies, putting aside some of their prickly nationalism in return for enduring peace and common prosperity. That process took shape during the 1950s, giving rise to the **European Economic Community** (EEC), established in 1957, whose members reduced their tariffs and developed common trade policies. Over the next half century, the EEC expanded its membership to include almost all of Europe, including many former communist states. In 1993, the EEC was renamed the European Union (see Map 21.1), and in 2002 twelve of its members, later increased to nineteen, adopted a common currency, the euro. All of this sustained Europe's remarkable economic recovery and expressed a larger European identity.

A third element of European recovery lay in the United States, which emerged after 1945 as the dominant center of Western civilization and a global superpower. An early indication of the United States' intention to exercise global leadership took

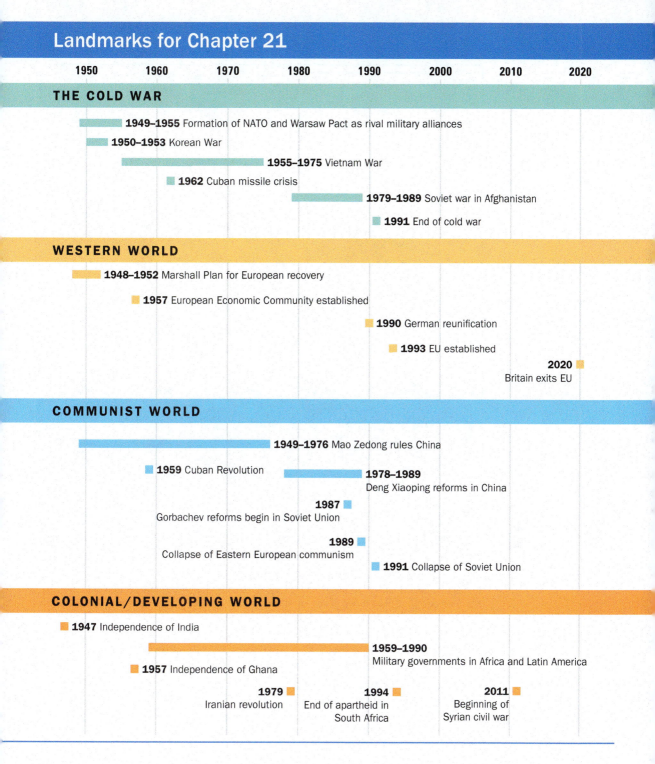

Landmarks for Chapter 21

1950 | 1960 | 1970 | 1980 | 1990 | 2000 | 2010 | 2020

THE COLD WAR

- **1949–1955** Formation of NATO and Warsaw Pact as rival military alliances
- **1950–1953** Korean War
- **1955–1975** Vietnam War
- **1962** Cuban missile crisis
- **1979–1989** Soviet war in Afghanistan
- **1991** End of cold war

WESTERN WORLD

- **1948–1952** Marshall Plan for European recovery
- **1957** European Economic Community established
- **1990** German reunification
- **1993** EU established
- **2020** Britain exits EU

COMMUNIST WORLD

- **1949–1976** Mao Zedong rules China
- **1959** Cuban Revolution
- **1978–1989** Deng Xiaoping reforms in China
- **1987** Gorbachev reforms begin in Soviet Union
- **1989** Collapse of Eastern European communism
- **1991** Collapse of Soviet Union

COLONIAL/DEVELOPING WORLD

- **1947** Independence of India
- **1959–1990** Military governments in Africa and Latin America
- **1957** Independence of Ghana
- **1979** Iranian revolution
- **1994** End of apartheid in South Africa
- **2011** Beginning of Syrian civil war

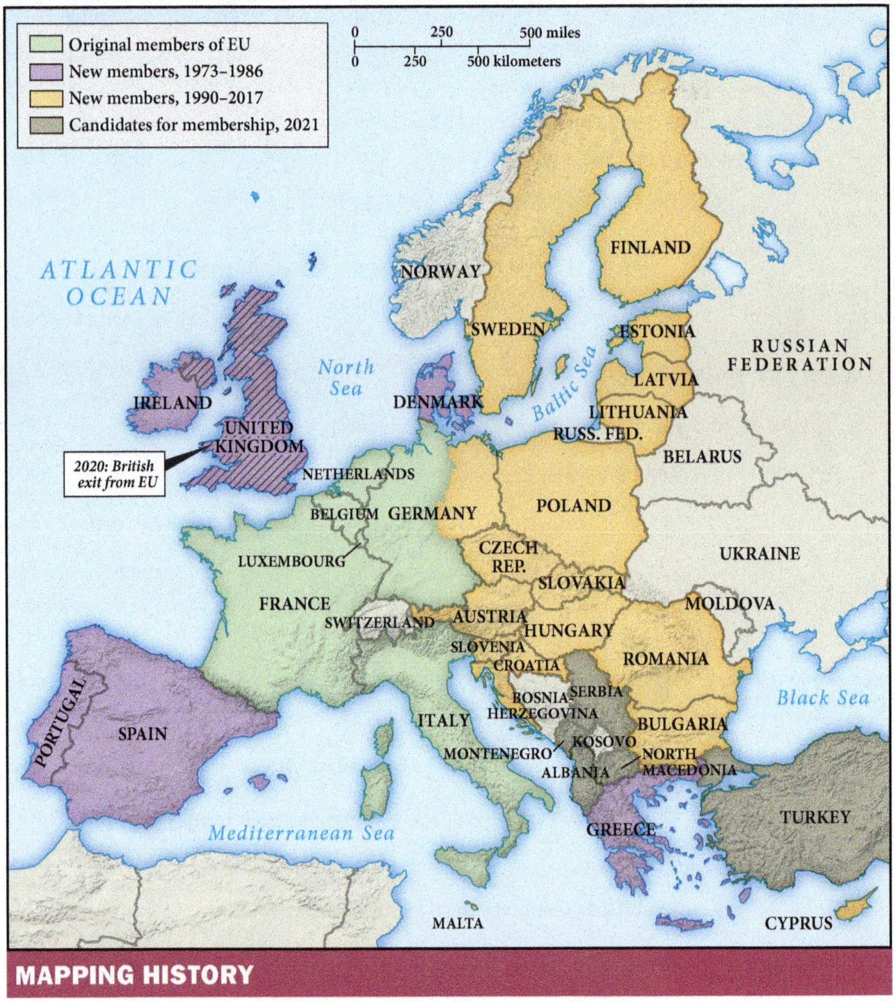

Map 21.1 The Growth of European Integration

During the second half of the twentieth century, Europeans gradually put aside their bitter rivalries and entered into various forms of economic cooperation with one another, although these efforts fell short of complete political union. This map illustrates the growth of what is now called the European Union (EU).

READING THE MAP Where did the European Union start, and into which regions did it expand? How would you describe the growth of the European Union through time?

INTERPRETING THE MAP Why might Russia have found the recent growth of the European Union threatening to its interests?

shape in its effort to rebuild and reshape shattered European economies. Known as the **Marshall Plan**, that effort funneled into Europe some $12 billion (roughly $121 billion in 2017 dollars), together with numerous advisers and technicians. It was motivated by some combination of genuine humanitarian concern, a desire to prevent a new depression by creating overseas customers for American industrial goods, and an interest in undermining the growing appeal of European communist parties. This economic recovery plan, along with access to American markets, was successful beyond all expectations. Between 1948 and the early 1970s, Western European economies grew rapidly, generating a widespread prosperity and improving living standards. Beyond economic assistance, the American commitment to Europe soon came to include political and military security against the distant possibility of renewed German aggression and the more immediate communist threat from the Soviet Union. Thus was born the military and political alliance known as the North Atlantic Treaty Organization (NATO) in 1949. It committed the United States and its nuclear arsenal to the defense of Europe against the Soviet Union, and it firmly anchored West Germany within the Western alliance. It also allowed Western Europe to avoid heavy military expenditures.

A parallel process in Japan, which was under American occupation between 1945 and 1952, likewise revived that country's devastated but already industrialized economy. In the two decades following the occupation, Japan's economy grew remarkably, and the nation became an economic giant on the world stage. The democratic constitution imposed on Japan by American occupation authorities required that "land, sea, and air forces, as well as other war potential, will never be maintained." This meant that Japan, even more so than Europe, depended on the United States for its military security.

Recovery in the Soviet Union, so terribly damaged by the war, occurred under very different conditions from that of Japan and Western Europe. The last years of Stalin's rule (1945–1953) were extraordinarily harsh, with no tolerance for dissent of any kind. One result was a huge and growing convict labor force of 3 to 4 million people who provided a major source of cheap labor for the recovery effort. Furthermore, that program was a wholly state-planned effort that favored heavy industry, agricultural production, and military expenditure at the expense of basic consumer goods, such as shoes and clothing. But Stalin's regime did gain some popular support by substantially lowering the price of bread and other essentials. Finally, the Soviet Union benefited greatly from its seizure of industrial complexes, agricultural goods, raw materials, gold, and European art from Germany, Poland, and elsewhere. Viewed as looting or plunder in the West, this appropriation in Soviet eyes was seen as the "spoils of war" and was justified by the massive damage, both human and material, that the Nazi invasion had caused in the USSR. By the mid-1950s, economic recovery was well under way.

Communism Chinese-Style

While Europe, Japan, and the Soviet Union were emerging from the chaos of World War II, China was likewise recovering from decades of civil war and from its devastating struggle against Japanese imperialism. And it was doing so under the direction of the Chinese Communist Party and its leader **Mao Zedong**. In a longer-term perspective, China's revolution represented the real beginning of that country's emergence from a century of imperialist humiliation and semi-colonial rule, the development of a distinctive Chinese approach to modern development, and its return to a position of prominence on the global stage.

CORE IDEA

■ **Making Comparisons**

What was distinctive about the Chinese experience of communism compared to that of the Soviet Union?

As a communist country, China began its task of "building socialism" in a very different international environment than its Soviet counterpart had experienced. In 1917 Russian Bolsheviks faced a hostile capitalist world alone, while Chinese communists, coming to power over thirty years later, had an established Soviet Union as a friendly northern neighbor and ally. Furthermore, Chinese revolutionaries had actually governed parts of their huge country for decades, gaining experience that the new Soviet rulers had altogether lacked, since they had come to power so quickly. And the Chinese communists were firmly rooted in the rural areas and among the country's vast peasant population, while their Russian counterparts had found their support mainly in the cities.

If these comparisons generally favored China in its efforts to "build socialism," in economic terms that country faced even more daunting prospects than did the Soviet Union. Its population was far greater, its industrial base far smaller, and the availability of new agricultural land far more limited than in the Soviet Union. China's literacy and modern education, as well as its transportation network, were likewise much less developed. Even more than the Soviets, Chinese communists had to build a modern society from the ground up.

The Great Leap Forward This Chinese poster from 1960 celebrates both the agricultural and industrial efforts of the Great Leap Forward. The caption reads: "Start the movement to increase production and practice thrift, with foodstuffs and steel at the center, with great force!" The great famine that accompanied this "great leap" belied the optimistic outlook of the poster. (Stefan R. Landsberger Collections/International Institute of Social History, Amsterdam/www.chineseposters.net)

Building a Modern Society

Initially China sought to follow the Soviet model of socialist modernization, though with important variations. In sharp contrast to the Soviet experience, the collectivization of agriculture in China during the 1950s was a generally peaceful process, owing much to the close relationship between the Chinese Communist Party and the peasantry that had been established during three decades of struggle. China, however, pushed collectivization even further than the Soviet Union did, particularly in huge "people's communes" in the late 1950s. It was an effort to mobilize China's enormous population for rapid development and at the same time to move toward a more fully communist society with an even greater degree of social equality and collective living. (See Working with Evidence, Source 21.2, page 962.)

China's industrialization program was also modeled on the earlier Soviet experience, with an emphasis on large-scale heavy industries, urban-based factories, centralized planning by state and party authorities, and the mobilization of women for the task of development. As in the Soviet Union, impressive economic growth followed, as did substantial migration to the cities and the emergence of a bureaucratic elite of planners, managers, scientists, and engineers (see Snapshot). And both countries favored urban over rural areas and privileged an educated, technically trained elite over workers and peasants. Stalin and his successors largely accepted these inequalities, while Mao certainly did not. Rather, he launched recurrent efforts to combat these

SNAPSHOT China under Mao, 1949–1976

The following table reveals some of the achievements, limitations, and tragedies of China's communist experience during the era of Mao Zedong.

Steel production	from 1.3 million to 23 million tons
Coal production	from 66 million to 448 million tons
Electric power generation	from 7 million to 133 billion kilowatt-hours
Fertilizer production	from 0.2 million to 28 million tons
Cement production	from 3 million to 49 million tons
Industrial workers	from 3 million to 50 million
Scientists and technicians	from 50,000 to 5 million
"Barefoot doctors" posted to countryside	1 million
Annual growth rate of industrial output	11 percent
Annual growth rate of agricultural output	2.3 percent
Total population	from 542 million to 1 billion
Average population growth rate per year	2 percent
Per capita consumption of rural dwellers	from 62 to 124 yuan annually
Per capita consumption of urban dwellers	from 148 to 324 yuan annually
Overall life expectancy	from 35 to 65 years
Counterrevolutionaries killed (1949–1952)	between 1 million and 3 million
People labeled "rightists" in 1957	550,000
Deaths from famine during Great Leap Forward	30 million to 45 million
Deaths during Cultural Revolution	500,000
Officials sent down to rural labor camps during Cultural Revolution	3 million or more
Urban youth sent down to countryside	17 million (1967–1976)

Source: Such figures are often highly controversial. See Maurice Meisner, *Mao's China and After* (New York: Free Press, 1999), 413–25; Roderick MacFarquhar, ed., *The Politics of China* (Cambridge: Cambridge University Press, 1997), 243–45.

perhaps inevitable tendencies of any industrializing process and to revive and preserve the revolutionary spirit that had animated the Communist Party during its long struggle for power.

By the mid-1950s, Mao and some of his followers had become persuaded that the Soviet model of industrialization was leading China away from socialism and toward new forms of inequality, toward individualistic and careerist values, and toward an urban bias that favored the cities at the expense of the countryside. The **Great Leap Forward** of 1958–1960 marked Mao's first response to these distortions of Chinese socialism. It promoted small-scale industrialization in the rural areas rather than focusing wholly on large enterprises in the cities; it tried to foster widespread and practical technological education for all rather than relying on a small elite of highly trained technical experts; and it envisaged an immediate transition to full communism in the "people's communes" rather than waiting for industrial development to provide the material basis for that transition. The Great Leap, however, generated a national catastrophe and an unprecedented human tragedy that temporarily discredited Mao's radicalism. Administrative chaos, disruption of marketing networks, and bad weather combined to produce a massive famine, the worst in human history according to some scholars, that killed some 30 million people or more between 1959 and 1962, dwarfing the earlier Soviet famine.

Nonetheless, in the mid-1960s, Mao launched yet another campaign—the Great Proletarian **Cultural Revolution**—to combat the capitalist tendencies that he believed had penetrated even the highest ranks of the Communist Party itself. The Cultural Revolution also involved new efforts to bring health care and education to the countryside and to reinvigorate earlier attempts at rural industrialization under local rather than central control. In these ways, Mao struggled, though without great success, to overcome the inequalities associated with China's modern development and to create a model of socialist modernity quite distinct from that of the Soviet Union.

Eliminating Enemies

China under Mao, like the Soviet Union under Stalin, found itself caught up in a gigantic search for enemies beginning in the 1950s. In the Soviet Union, that process occurred under the clear control of state authorities. In China, however, it became much more public, escaping the control of the leadership, particularly during the most intense phase of the Cultural Revolution (1966–1969). Convinced that many within the Communist Party had been seduced by capitalist values of self-seeking and materialism, Mao called for rebellion against the Communist Party itself. Millions of young people responded, and, organized as Red Guards, they set out to rid China of those who were "taking the capitalist road." Following gigantic and ecstatic rallies in Beijing, they fanned out across the country and attacked local party and government officials, teachers, intellectuals, factory managers, and others they defined as enemies. Many were "sent down" to the countryside for hard physical labor and to "learn from the peasants." Others were humiliated, beaten, and sometimes killed. (See Working with Evidence, Source 21.6, page 967.) Rival revolutionary groups soon began fighting with one another, violence erupted throughout the country, and civil war threatened China. Mao was forced to call in the military to restore order and Communist Party control. Both Stalin's Terror and the Chinese Cultural Revolution badly discredited the very idea of socialism and contributed to the ultimate collapse of the communist experiment at the end of the century.

East versus West: A Global Divide and a Cold War

CORE IDEA

■ Making Comparisons

In what different ways was the cold war expressed and experienced?

Not only did communist regimes bring revolutionary changes to the societies they governed, but their very existence launched a global conflict that restructured international life and touched the lives of almost everyone, particularly in the twentieth century's second half. That rift had begun soon after the Russian Revolution when the new communist government became the source of fear and loathing to many in the Western capitalist world. The common threat of Nazi Germany temporarily made unlikely allies of the Soviet Union, Britain, and the United States, but a few years after World War II ended, that division erupted again in what became known as the **cold war**. Underlying that conflict were the geopolitical and ideological realities of the postwar world. The Soviet Union and the United States were now the world's major political and military powers, replacing the shattered and diminished states of Western Europe, but they represented sharply opposed views of history, society, politics, and international relations. In retrospect, conflict seemed almost inevitable, as both sides felt they were riding the tides of historical progress.

Military Conflict and the Cold War

The initial arena of the cold war was Eastern Europe, where Soviet insistence on security and control clashed with American and British desires for open and democratic societies with ties to the capitalist world economy. What resulted were rival military alliances. The **North Atlantic Treaty Organization (NATO)**, created in 1949, brought the United States and various West European countries together to defend themselves against the threat of Soviet aggression. Then in 1955 the **Warsaw Pact** joined the Soviet Union and East European communist countries in an alliance intended to provide a counterweight to NATO and to prevent Western influence in the communist bloc. These alliances created a largely voluntary American sphere of influence in Western Europe and an imposed Soviet sphere in Eastern Europe. The heavily fortified border between Eastern and Western Europe came to be known as the Iron Curtain. Thus Europe was bitterly divided. But although tensions flared across this dividing line, particularly in Berlin, no shooting war occurred between the two sides (see Map 21.2).

By contrast, the extension of communism into Asia—China, Korea, and Vietnam—globalized the cold war and occasioned its most destructive and

Map 21.2 The Global Cold War
The cold war witnessed a sharp division between the communist world and the Western democratic world. It also divided the continent of Europe; the countries of China, Korea, Vietnam, and Germany; and the city of Berlin. In many places, it also sparked crises that brought the nuclear-armed superpowers of the United States and the USSR to the brink of war, although in every case they managed to avoid direct military conflict between themselves. Many countries in Africa and Asia claimed membership in a Non-Aligned Movement that sought to avoid entanglements in cold war conflicts.

prolonged "hot wars." A North Korean invasion of South Korea in 1950 led to both Chinese and American involvement in a bitter three-year conflict (1950–1953), which ended in an essential standoff that left the Korean peninsula still divided in the early twenty-first century. Likewise in Vietnam, military efforts by South Vietnamese communists and the already communist North Vietnamese government to unify their country prompted massive American intervention in the 1960s. To American authorities, a communist victory would open the door to

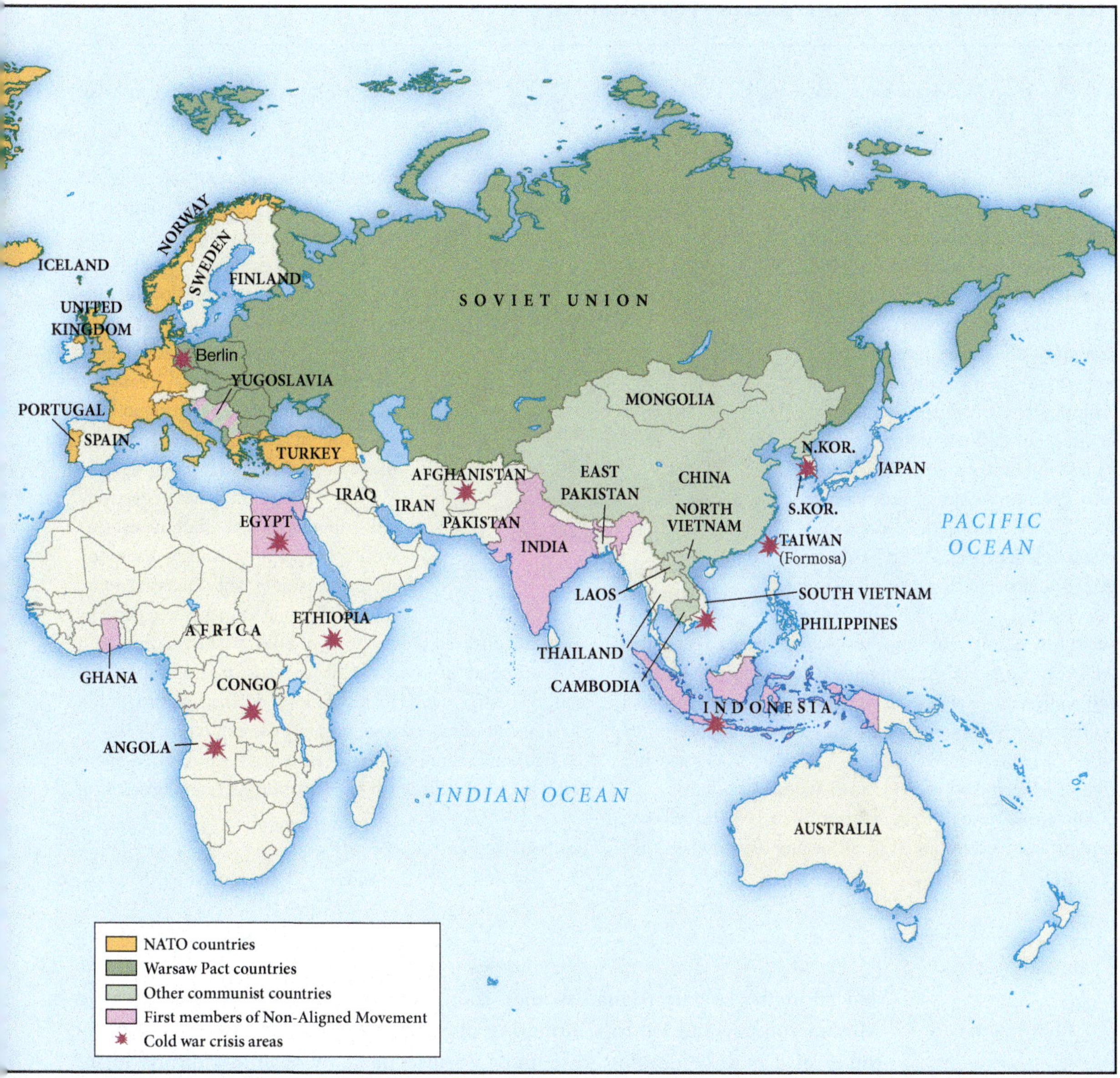

further communist expansion in Asia and beyond. Armed and supported by the Soviets and Chinese and willing to endure enormous losses, the Vietnamese communists bested the Americans, who were hobbled by growing protest at home. The Vietnamese united their country under communist control by 1975.

A third major military conflict of the cold war era occurred in Afghanistan, where a Marxist party had taken power in 1978. Soviet leaders were delighted at this extension of communism on their southern border, but radical land reforms

ZOOMING IN

Fidel Castro and the Cuban Revolution

"You Americans must realize what Cuba means to us old Bolsheviks," declared a high-ranking Soviet official, Anastas Mikoyan, in 1960. "We have been waiting all our lives for a country to go communist without the Red Army. It has happened in Cuba, and it makes us feel like boys again."[3] The triumph of the Cuban revolutionaries must have been exhilarating for communists everywhere because it occurred in such an unlikely place. Located just ninety miles from Florida, Cuba had been a virtual protectorate of the United States in the decades following its independence from Spain in 1902. Moreover, U.S. companies had long exerted considerable influence over the weak and corrupt Cuban government and dominated key sectors of the economy, including sugar, the island's most important export. Nonetheless, Fidel Castro, son of a wealthy sugar plantation owner, led a successful popular insurrection that transformed Cuba into a Marxist socialist state just off the southern coast of the United States.

Fidel Castro fighting in the mountains of Cuba in 1957.

The armed revolt began disastrously. In 1953, the Cuban army defeated Castro and 123 of his supporters when they attacked two army barracks in what was their first major military operation. Castro himself was captured, sentenced to jail, and then released into exile. However, fortunes shifted in 1956, when Castro slipped back into Cuba and succeeded in bringing together many opponents of the current regime in an armed nationalist insurgency dedicated to radical economic and social reform. Upon seizing power in 1959, Castro and his government acted decisively to implement their revolutionary agenda. Within a year, they had effectively redistributed 15 percent of the nation's wealth by granting land to the poor, increasing wages, and lowering rents. In the following year, the new government nationalized the property of both wealthy Cubans and U.S. corporations. Many Cubans, particularly among the elite, fled into exile. "The revolution," declared Castro, "is the dictatorship of the exploited against the exploiters."[4]

Economic and political pressure from the United States followed, culminating in the Bay of Pigs, a failed invasion of

and efforts to liberate Afghan women soon alienated much of this conservative Muslim country and led to a mounting opposition movement. Fearing the overthrow of a new communist state and its replacement by Islamic radicals, Soviet forces intervened militarily and were soon bogged down in a war they could not win. For a full decade (1979–1989), that war was a "bleeding wound," sustained in part by U.S. aid to Afghan guerrillas. Under widespread international pressure, Soviet forces finally withdrew in 1989, and the Afghan communist regime soon collapsed. In Vietnam and Afghanistan, both superpowers painfully experienced the limits of their power.

The most haunting battle of the cold war era was one that never happened. The setting was Cuba, where a communist regime under the leadership of Fidel Castro had emerged by the early 1960s. (See Zooming In: Fidel Castro and the Cuban the island in 1961 by Cuban exiles with covert support from the U.S. government. American hostility pushed the revolutionary nationalist Castro closer to the Soviet Union, and gradually he began to think of himself and his revolution as Marxist. In response to Cuban pleas for support against American aggression, the Soviet premier Khrushchev deployed nuclear missiles on the island, sparking the Cuban missile crisis. While the compromise reached between the two superpowers resulted in the withdrawal of the missiles, it did include assurances from the United States that it would not attack Cuba.

In the decades that followed, Cuba sought to export its brand of revolution beyond its borders, especially in Latin America and Africa. Che Guevara, an Argentine who had fought in the Cuban Revolution, declared, "Our revolution is endangering all American possessions in Latin America. We are telling these countries to make their own revolution."[5] Cuba supported revolutionary movements in many regions; however, none succeeded in creating a lasting Cuban-style regime.

The legacy of the Cuban Revolution has been mixed. The new government devoted considerable resources to improving health and education on the island. By the mid-1980s, Cuba possessed both the highest literacy rate and the lowest infant mortality rate in Latin America. Over the same period, life expectancy increased from fifty-eight to seventy-three years, putting Cuba on a par with the United States. Living standards for most improved as well. Indeed, Cuba became a model for development in other Latin American countries.

However, earlier promises to establish a truly democratic system never materialized. Castro declared in 1959 that elections were unneeded because "this democracy . . . has found its expression, directly, in the intimate union and identification of the government with the people."[6] The state placed limits on free expression and arrested opponents or forced them into exile. Cuba has also failed to achieve the economic development originally envisioned at the time of the revolution. Sugar remains its chief export crop, and by the 1980s Cuba had become almost as economically dependent on the Soviet Union as it had been upon the United States. Desperate consequences followed when the Cuban economy shrank by a third following the collapse of the Soviet Union.

Like communist experiments in the Soviet Union and China, Cuba experienced real improvements in living standards, especially for the poor, but these gains were accompanied by sharp restraints on personal freedoms and mixed results in the economy. Such have been the ambivalent outcomes of many revolutionary upheavals.

QUESTIONS

Compare the Cuban Revolution to those in Russia and China. What are the similarities and differences? How might you assess the successes and failures of the Cuban Revolution?

Revolution.) Intense American hostility to this nearby outpost of communism prompted the Soviet leader Nikita Khrushchev (KROOSH-chef), who had risen to power after Stalin's death in 1953, to secretly deploy nuclear-tipped Soviet missiles to Cuba, believing that this would deter further U.S. action against Castro. When the missiles were discovered in October 1962, the world held its breath for thirteen days as American forces blockaded the island and prepared for an invasion. A nuclear exchange between the superpowers seemed imminent, but that catastrophe was averted by a compromise between Khrushchev and U.S. president John F. Kennedy. Under its terms, the Soviets removed their missiles from Cuba in return for an American promise not to invade the island. That promise was kept and a communist regime persisted in Cuba, though much changed, well into the twenty-first century.

Nuclear Standoff and Third-World Rivalry

The **Cuban missile crisis** gave concrete expression to the most novel and dangerous dimension of the cold war—the arms race in nuclear weapons. An initial American monopoly on those weapons prompted the Soviet Union to redouble its efforts to acquire them, and in 1949 it succeeded. Over the next forty years, the world moved from a mere handful of nuclear weapons to a global arsenal of close to 60,000 warheads. Delivery systems included submarines, bomber aircraft, and missiles that could rapidly propel numerous warheads across whole continents and oceans with accuracies measured in hundreds of feet. During those decades, the entire world lived in the shadow of weapons whose destructive power is scarcely within the bounds of human imagination.

Awareness of this power is surely the primary reason that no shooting war of any kind occurred between the two superpowers, for leaders on both sides knew beyond any doubt that a nuclear war would produce only losers and utter catastrophe. Already in 1949, Stalin had observed that "atomic weapons can hardly be used without spelling the end of the world."[7] Particularly after the frightening Cuban missile crisis of 1962, both sides carefully avoided further nuclear provocation, even while continuing to build up their respective arsenals. Moreover, because they feared that a conventional war would escalate to the nuclear level, they implicitly agreed to sidestep any direct military confrontation at all.

The Hydrogen Bomb During the 1950s and early 1960s, tests in the atmosphere of ever larger and more sophisticated hydrogen bombs made images of enormous fireballs and mushroom-shaped clouds the universal symbol of these weapons, which were immensely more powerful than the atomic bombs dropped on Japan. The American test pictured here took place in 1957. (Photo courtesy of National Nuclear Security Administration/Nevada Site Office)

Still, opportunities for conflict abounded as the U.S.-Soviet rivalry spanned the globe. Using military and economic aid, educational opportunities, political pressure, and covert action, both sides courted countries emerging from colonial rule. The Soviet Union aided anticolonial and revolutionary movements in many places, including South Africa, Mozambique, Vietnam, and Cuba. Cold war fears of communist penetration prompted U.S. intervention, sometimes openly and often secretly, in Iran, the Philippines, Guatemala, El Salvador, Chile, the Congo, and elsewhere. In the process the United States frequently supported anticommunist but corrupt and authoritarian regimes. However, neither superpower was able to completely dominate its supposed allies, many of whom resisted the role of pawns in superpower rivalries. Some countries, such as India, took a posture of nonalignment in the cold war, while others tried to play off the superpowers against each other. Indonesia received large amounts of Soviet and Eastern European aid, but that did not prevent it from destroying the Indonesian Communist Party in 1965, killing half a million suspected communists in the process. When the Americans refused to assist Egypt in building the Aswan Dam in the mid-1950s, that country developed a close relationship with the Soviet Union. Later, in 1972, Egypt expelled 21,000 Soviet advisers, following disagreements over the extent of Soviet military aid, and again aligned more clearly with the United States.

The Cold War and the Superpowers

World War II and the cold war provided the context for the emergence of the United States as a global superpower. Much of that effort was driven by the perceived demands of the cold war, during which the United States spearheaded the Western effort to contain a worldwide communist movement that seemed to be advancing. By 1970, one writer observed, "the United States had more than 1,000,000 soldiers in 30 countries, was a member of four regional defense alliances and an active participant in a fifth, had mutual defense treaties with 42 nations, was a member of 53 international organizations, and was furnishing military or economic aid to nearly 100 nations across the face of the globe."[8] Sustaining this immense international effort was a flourishing U.S. economy and an increasingly middle-class society. The United States was the only major industrial country to escape the physical devastation of war on its own soil. As World War II ended with Europe, the Soviet Union, and Japan in ruins, the United States was clearly the world's most productive economy.

On the communist side, the cold war was accompanied by considerable turmoil within and among the various communist states. In the Soviet Union, the superpower of the communist world, the mid-1950s witnessed devastating revelations of Stalin's many crimes, shocking the communist faithful everywhere. And in Hungary (1956–1957), Czechoslovakia (1968), and Poland (early 1980s), various reform movements registered sharp protest against highly repressive and Soviet-dominated communist governments.

■ Identifying Divisions
What divisions surfaced within the communist world during the cold war years?

Soviet Invasion, Prague In the 1950s and 1960s, the Soviet Union sent troops into supposedly allied countries in Eastern Europe to crush nascent reform movements. In this image from 1968, protesters in Prague, Czechoslovakia, swarm around and on top of Russian military equipment in a doomed effort to oppose a Russian crackdown. (AP Photo/Libor Hajsky/CTK)

Many in the West had initially viewed world communism as a monolithic force whose disciplined members meekly followed Soviet dictates in cold war solidarity against the West. And Marxists everywhere contended that revolutionary socialism would erode national loyalties as the "workers of the world" united in common opposition to global capitalism. Nonetheless, the communist world experienced far more bitter and divisive conflict than did the Western alliance, which was composed of supposedly warlike, greedy, and highly competitive nations.

In Eastern Europe, Yugoslav leaders early on had rejected Soviet domination of their internal affairs and charted their own independent road to socialism. Fearing that reform might lead to contagious defections from the communist bloc, Soviet forces actually invaded their supposed allies in Hungary and Czechoslovakia to crush such movements, and they threatened to do so in Poland. Such actions gave credibility to Western perceptions of the cold war as a struggle between tyranny and freedom and badly tarnished the image of Soviet communism as a reasonable alternative to capitalism.

Even more startling, the two communist giants, the Soviet Union and China, found themselves sharply opposed, owing to territorial disputes, ideological differences, and rivalry for communist leadership. In 1960, the Soviet Union backed away from an earlier promise to provide China with the prototype of an atomic bomb and abruptly withdrew all Soviet advisers and technicians who had been assisting Chinese development. By the late 1960s, China on its own had developed a modest nuclear capability, and the two countries were at the brink of war, with the Soviet Union hinting at a possible nuclear strike on Chinese military targets. Beyond this central conflict, communist China in fact went to war against communist Vietnam in 1979, even as Vietnam invaded communist Cambodia. Nationalism, in short, proved more powerful than communist solidarity, even in the face of cold war hostilities with the capitalist West.

Despite its many internal conflicts, world communism remained a powerful global presence during the 1970s, achieving its greatest territorial reach. China was emerging from the chaos of the Cultural Revolution, while the Soviet Union had matched U.S. military might. Despite American hostility, Cuba remained a communist outpost in the Western Hemisphere, with impressive achievements in education and health care for its people and a commitment to supporting revolutionary movements in Africa and Latin America. Communism triumphed in Vietnam, dealing a major setback to the United States. A number of African countries also affirmed their commitment to Marxism. Few people anywhere expected that within two decades most of the twentieth century's experiment with communism would be gone.

Toward Freedom: Struggles for Independence

From an American or Soviet perspective, cold war struggles dominated international life from the 1940s through the early 1990s. But viewed from the world of Asia and Africa, a rather different global struggle was unfolding. Its central focus was colonial rule, subordination, poverty, and racism. Variously called the struggle for independence or **decolonization**, that process marked a dramatic change in the world's political architecture, as nation-states triumphed over the empires that had structured much of the world's political life in the nineteenth and early twentieth centuries. It mobilized millions of people, thrusting them into political activity and sometimes into violence and warfare. Decolonization signaled the declining legitimacy of both empire and race as a credible basis for political or social life. It promised not only national freedom but also personal dignity, opportunity, and prosperity.

In 1900, European colonial empires in Africa, Asia, the Caribbean region, and Pacific Oceania appeared as enduring features of the world's political landscape. Well before the end of the twentieth century, they were gone. The first major breakthroughs occurred in Asia and the Middle East in the late 1940s, when the Philippines, India, Pakistan, Burma, Indonesia, Syria, Iraq, Jordan, and Israel achieved independence. The decades from the mid-1950s through the mid-1970s were an age of African independence as colony after colony, more than fifty in total, emerged into what was then seen as the bright light of freedom. During the 1970s, many of the island societies of Pacific Oceania—Samoa, Fiji, Tonga, the Solomon Islands, Kiribati—joined the ranks of independent states, almost entirely peacefully and without much struggle as the various colonial powers willingly abandoned their right to rule. Hawaiians, however, sought incorporation as a state within the United States, rather than independence. Finally, a number of Caribbean societies—the Bahamas, Barbados, Belize, Jamaica, Trinidad and Tobago—achieved independence during the 1960s and 1970s, informed by a growing awareness of a distinctive Caribbean culture. Cuba, although formally independent since 1902, dramatically declared its rejection of American control in its revolutionary upheaval in 1959. By 1983 the Caribbean region hosted sixteen separate independent states.

The End of Empire in World History

At one level, this vast process was but the latest case of imperial dissolution, a fate that had overtaken earlier empires, including those of the Assyrians, Romans, Arabs, and Mongols. But never before had the end of empire been so associated with the mobilization of the masses around a nationalist ideology. More comparable perhaps was that earlier decolonization in which the European colonies in the Americas had thrown off British, French, Spanish, or Portuguese rule during the late eighteenth and early nineteenth centuries (see "Comparing Atlantic Revolutions" in Chapter 16). Like their earlier counterparts, the new nations of the mid-to-late twentieth century claimed an international status equivalent to that of their former rulers. In the Americas, however, many of the colonized people were themselves of European origin, sharing much of their culture with their colonial rulers. In that respect, the freedom struggles of the twentieth century were very different, for they not only asserted political independence but also affirmed the vitality of their cultures, which had been submerged and denigrated during the colonial era.

The twentieth century witnessed the demise of many empires. The Austrian and Ottoman empires collapsed following World War I, giving rise to a number of new states in Europe and the Middle East. The Russian Empire also unraveled, although it was soon reassembled under the auspices of the Soviet Union. World War II ended the German and Japanese empires. African and Asian movements for independence shared with these other end-of-empire stories the ideal of national self-determination. This novel idea—that humankind was naturally divided into distinct peoples or nations, each of which deserved an independent state of its own—was loudly proclaimed by the winning side of both world wars. It gained a global acceptance, particularly in the colonial world, during the twentieth century and rendered empire illegitimate in the eyes of growing numbers of people.

Empires without territory, such as the powerful influence that the United States exercised in Latin America, likewise came under attack from highly nationalist governments. An intrusive U.S. presence was certainly one factor stimulating the Mexican Revolution, which began in 1910. One of the outcomes of that upheaval was the nationalization in 1937 of Mexico's oil industry, much of which was owned by American and British investors. Similar actions accompanied Cuba's revolution of 1959–1960 and also occurred in other places throughout Latin America and elsewhere. National self-determination and freedom from Soviet control likewise lay behind the Eastern European revolutions of 1989. The disintegration of the Soviet Union itself in 1991 brought to an inglorious end one of the last major territorial empires of the twentieth century and the birth of fifteen new national states.

China's Central Asian empire, however, remained intact despite considerable resistance in Tibet and elsewhere. Although the winning of political independence for Europe's African and Asian colonies was perhaps the most spectacular challenge to empire in the twentieth century, that process was part of a larger pattern in modern world history (see Map 21.3).

Toward Independence in Asia and Africa

As the twentieth century closed, the end of European empires seemed in retrospect almost inevitable, for colonial rule had lost any credibility as a form of political order. What could be more natural than for people to seek to rule themselves? Yet at the beginning of the century, few observers were predicting the collapse of these empires, and the idea that "the only legitimate government is national self-government" was not nearly as widespread as it subsequently became. How might historians explain the rapid collapse of European colonial empires and the emergence of a transformed international landscape with dozens of new nation-states?

One approach focuses attention on fundamental contradictions in the entire colonial enterprise. The rhetoric of Christianity, Enlightenment thought, and material progress sat awkwardly with the realities of colonial racism, exploitation, and poverty. The increasingly democratic values of European states ran counter to the essential dictatorship of colonial rule. The ideal of national self-determination was profoundly at odds with the possession of colonies that were denied any opportunity to express their own national character. The enormously powerful force of nationalism, having earlier driven the process of European empire building, now played a major role in its disintegration. From this perspective, colonial rule dug its own grave because its practice ran counter to established European values of democracy and national self-determination.

CORE IDEA

■ Accounting for Change

What factors contributed to the end of European colonial empires in Africa and Asia?

But why did this "fatal flaw" of European colonial rule lead to independence in the post–World War II decades rather than earlier or later? Here, historians have found useful the notion of "conjuncture": the coming together of several separate developments at a particular time. At the international level, the world wars had weakened Europe while discrediting any sense of European moral superiority. Both the United States and the Soviet Union, the new global superpowers, generally opposed the older European colonial empires, even as they created empire-like international relationships of their own. Meanwhile, the United Nations provided a prestigious platform from which to conduct anticolonial agitation. Within the colonies, the dependence of European rulers on the cooperation of local elites, and increasingly on Western-educated men, rendered those empires vulnerable to the withdrawal of that support. All of this contributed to the global illegitimacy of empire, a novel and stunning transformation of social values that was enormously encouraging to anticolonial movements everywhere.

At the same time, social and economic processes within the colonies themselves generated the human raw material for anticolonial movements. By the early twentieth

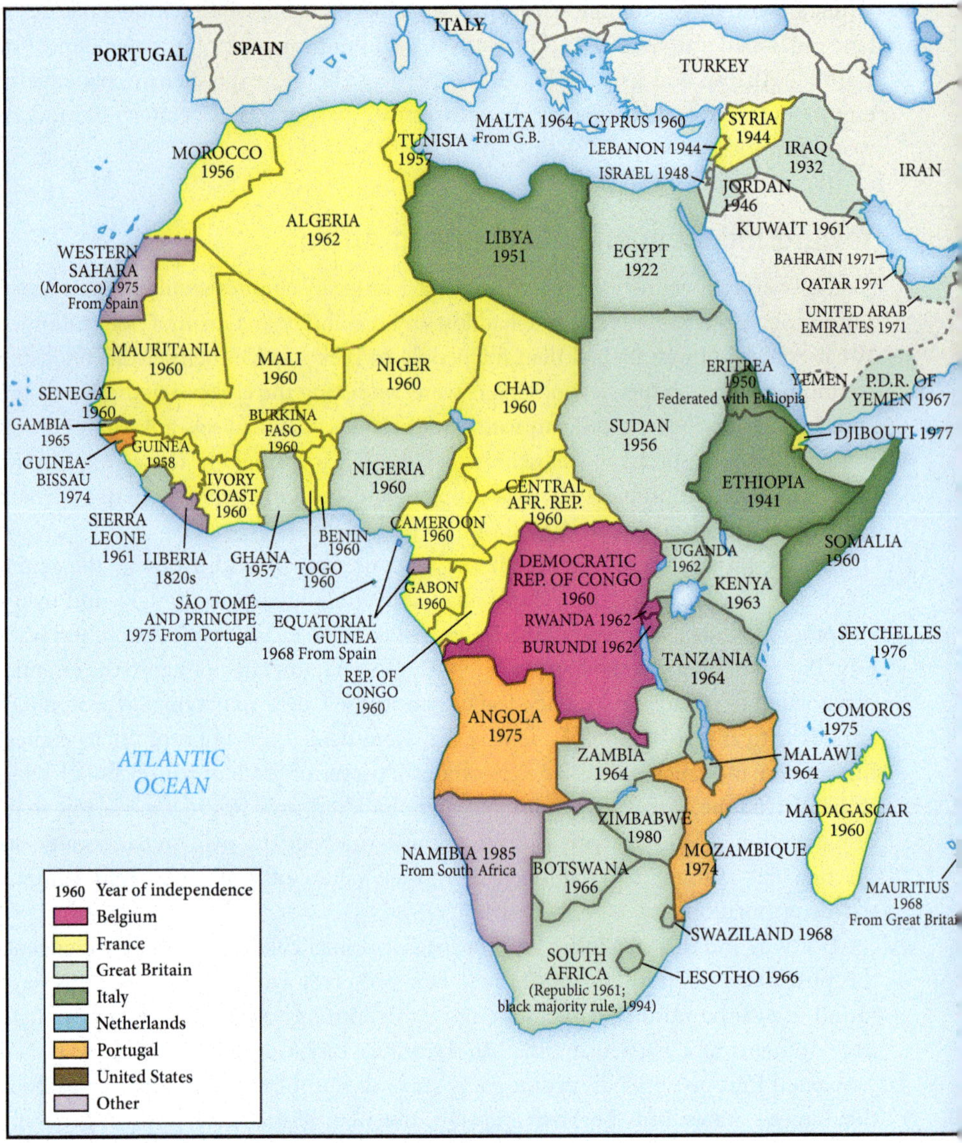

Map 21.3 The End of Empire in Africa and Asia
In the second half of the twentieth century, under pressure from nationalist movements, Europe's Asian and African empires dissolved into dozens of new independent states, dramatically altering the structure of international life.

century in Asia and the mid-twentieth century in Africa, a second or third generation of Western-educated elites, largely male, had arisen throughout the colonial world. These young men were thoroughly familiar with European culture; they were deeply aware of the gap between its values and its practices; they no longer viewed colonial rule as a vehicle for their peoples' progress as their fathers had; and they increasingly

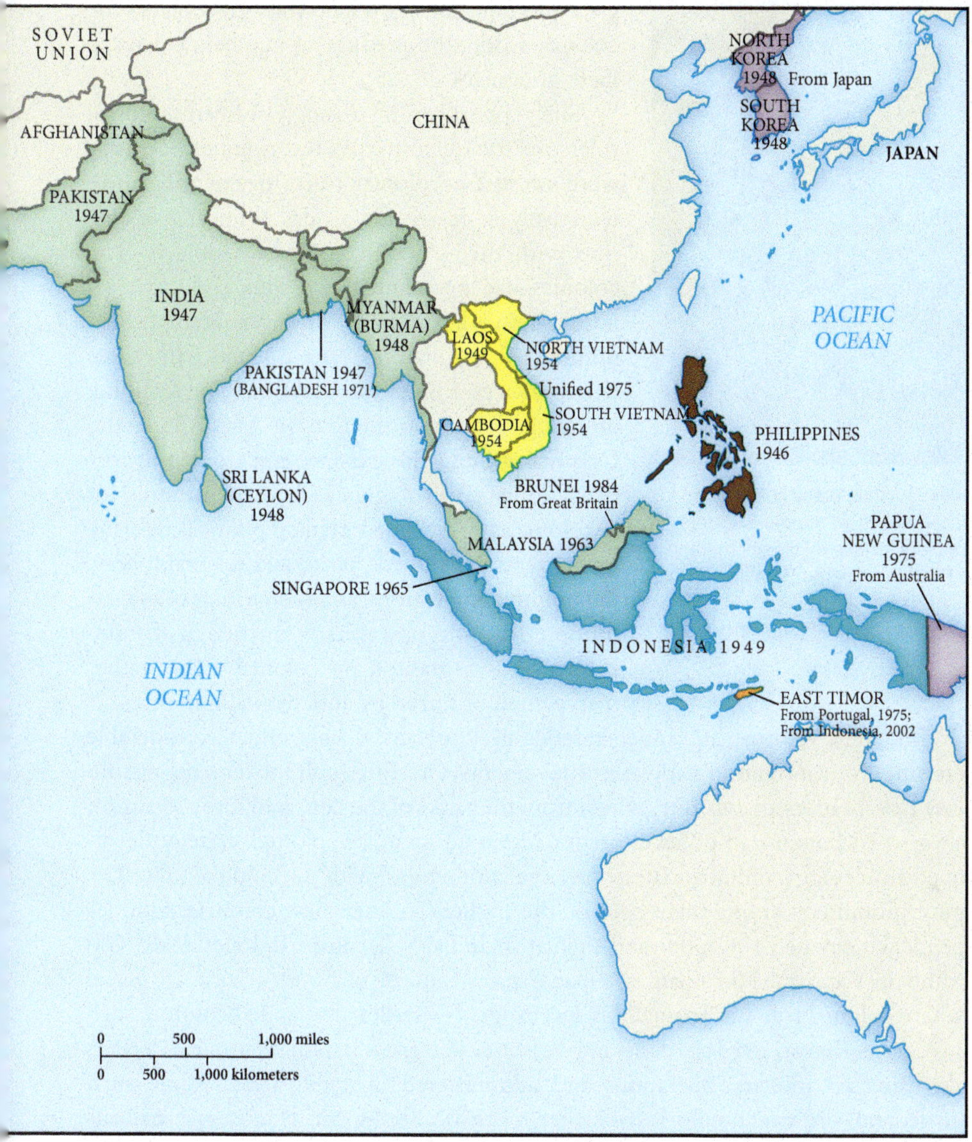

insisted on immediate independence. Moreover, growing numbers of ordinary people—women and men alike—were receptive to this message. Veterans of the world wars; young people with some education but few jobs commensurate with their expectations; a small class of urban workers who were increasingly aware of their exploitation; small-scale female traders resentful of European privileges; rural dwellers who had lost land or suffered from forced labor; impoverished and insecure newcomers to the cities—all of these groups had reason to believe that independence held

Military Struggles for Independence While many colonies won their independence through peaceful political pressure, others found it necessary to adopt a military strategy. This photograph from 1975 shows a nationalist Rhodesian fighter training for the long-running guerrilla war against British rule. In 1980, South Rhodesia finally won its independence, becoming modern Zimbabwe. (AFP Contributor/Getty Images)

great promise. And as populations grew across the colonial world, the pressure of numbers enhanced these grievances.

Such pressures increasingly placed colonial rulers on the defensive. As the twentieth century wore on, these colonial rulers began to plan—tentatively at first—for a new political relationship with their Asian and African subjects. The colonies had been integrated into a global economic network, and local elites were largely committed to maintaining those links. In these circumstances, Europeans could imagine retaining profitable economic interests in Asia, Africa, and Oceania without the expense and trouble of formal colonial governments. Deliberate planning for decolonization included gradual political reforms; investments in railroads, ports, and telegraph lines; the holding of elections; and the writing of constitutions. To some observers, it seemed as if independence was granted by colonial rulers rather than gained or seized by anticolonial initiatives.

But these reforms, and independence itself, occurred only under considerable pressure from mounting nationalist movements. Creating such movements was no easy task. Leaders, drawn everywhere from the ranks of the educated few and almost always male, organized political parties, recruited members, plotted strategy, developed an ideology, and negotiated with one another and with the colonial state. The most prominent among them became the "fathers" of their new countries as independence dawned—Gandhi and Nehru in India, Sukarno in Indonesia, Ho Chi Minh in Vietnam, Nkrumah in Ghana, and Mandela in South Africa. In places where colonial rule was particularly intransigent—settler-dominated colonies such as Algeria, Kenya, and Rhodesia and Portuguese territories, for example—leaders also directed military operations and administered liberated areas. While such movements drew on memories of earlier, more localized forms of resistance, nationalist leaders did not seek to restore a vanished past. Rather, they looked forward to joining the world of independent nation-states, to membership in the United Nations, and to the wealth and power that modern technology promised.

A further common task of the nationalist leadership involved recruiting a mass following, and to varying degrees, they did. Millions of ordinary men and women joined Gandhi's nonviolent campaigns in India; tens of thousands of freedom fighters waged guerrilla warfare in Algeria, Kenya, Mozambique, and Zimbabwe; in West Africa workers went on strike and market women joined political parties, as did students, farmers, and the unemployed.

But struggles for independence were rarely if ever cohesive movements of uniformly oppressed people. More often, they were fragile alliances representing different classes, ethnic groups, religions, or regions. Beneath the common goal of independence, they struggled with one another over questions of leadership, power, strategy, ideology, and the distribution of material benefits, even as they fought and negotiated with their colonial rulers. Sometimes the relationship between nationalist leaders and their followers was fraught with tension. One such Indonesian leader, educated in Holland, spoke of his difficulty in relating to the common people: "Why am I vexed by the things that fill their lives, and to which they are so attached? Why are the things that contain beauty for them . . . only senseless and displeasing for me? We intellectuals here are much closer to Europe or America than we are to the primitive Islamic culture of Java and Sumatra."[9] In colonial Nigeria, the independence movement took shape as three major political parties, each of them identified primarily with a particular ethnic group, Igbo, Yoruba, or Hausa. Thus the very notion of "national self-government" posed obvious but often contentious questions: What group of people constituted the "nation" that deserved to rule itself? And who should speak for it?

■ Assessing Nationalist Movements
What divisions or conflicts accompanied struggles for independence in Asia and Africa?

India's independence movement, which found expression in the **Indian National Congress** or Congress Party, provides a compelling example of these divisions and controversies. Its primary leader, **Mohandas Gandhi**, rejected modern industrialization as a goal for his country, while his own chief lieutenant, Jawaharlal Nehru, thoroughly embraced science, technology, and industry as essential to India's future. Nor did everyone accept Gandhi's nonviolent philosophy or his inclusive definition of India as embracing all religions, regions, and castes. Some believed that Gandhi's efforts to improve the position of women or untouchables were a distraction from the chief task of gaining independence. Whether to participate in British-sponsored legislative bodies prior to complete independence also became a divisive issue. Furthermore, a number of smaller parties advocated on behalf of particular regions or castes.

By far the most serious threat to a unified movement derived from the growing divide between the country's Hindu and Muslim populations. As a distinct minority within India, some Muslims feared that their voice could be swamped by numerically dominant Hindus, despite Gandhi's inclusive sensibility. Some Hindu politicians confirmed those fears when they cast the nationalist struggle in Hindu religious terms, hailing their country, for example, as a goddess, Bande Mataram (Mother India). This approach, as well as Hindu efforts to protect cows from slaughter, antagonized Muslims. Their growing skepticism about the possibility of a single Indian state found expression in the **Muslim League**, whose leader, Muhammad Ali Jinnah (JIN-uh), argued that those parts of India that had a Muslim majority should have a separate political status. They called it Pakistan, the land of the pure. In this view, India was not a single nation, as Gandhi had long argued. Jinnah put his case succinctly: "The Muslims and Hindus belong to two different religious philosophies, social customs, and literatures. They neither intermarry nor interdine [eat] together and, indeed, they belong to two different civilizations."[10] With great reluctance and amid mounting violence, Gandhi and the Congress Party finally agreed to partition as the British declared their intention to leave India after World War II.

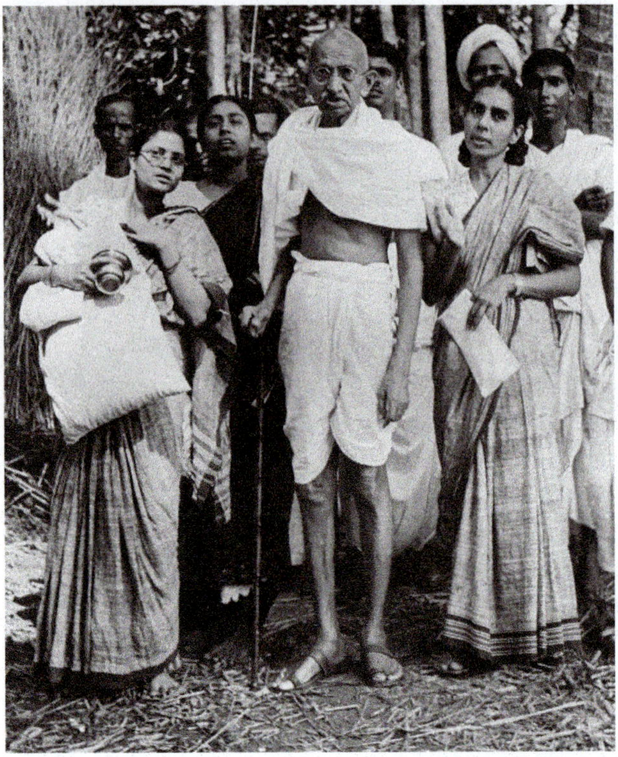

Mahatma Gandhi on the Salt March The most widely recognized and admired figure in the global struggle against colonial rule was Mohandas Gandhi, often known as Mahatma, or "Great Soul." He is shown here with his granddaughter Ava (left) and his personal physician Dr. Sushila Nayar (right). (Bettmann/Getty Images)

Thus colonial India became independent in 1947 as two countries—a Muslim Pakistan, itself divided into two wings 1,000 miles apart, and a mostly Hindu India governed by a secular state. Dividing colonial India in this fashion was horrendously painful. A million people or more died in the communal violence that accompanied partition, and some 12 million refugees moved from one country to the other to join their religious compatriots. Gandhi himself, desperately trying to stem the mounting tide of violence, refused to attend the independence celebrations. Only a year after independence, he was assassinated by a Hindu extremist. The great triumph of independence, secured from the powerful British Empire, was overshadowed by the great tragedy of violent partition.

Beyond their internal divisions, nationalist movements seeking independence differed sharply from one another. In some places, that struggle, once begun, produced independence within a few years, four in the case of the Belgian Congo. Elsewhere it was measured in decades. Nationalism had surfaced in Vietnam in the early 1900s, but the country achieved full political independence only in the mid-1970s, having fought French colonial rulers, Japanese invaders during World War II, and U.S. military forces in the 1960s and 1970s, as well as Chinese forces during a brief war in 1979. And the struggle in South Africa was distinctive in many ways. It was not waged against a distant colonial power, but against a white settler minority representing about 20 percent of the population that had already been granted independence from Great Britain in 1910. It took place in a mature industrialized and urbanized nation and in the face of the world's most rigid and racially repressive regime, known as apartheid. These factors help to explain why South Africa gained its "independence" from colonial oppression only in 1994.

Tactics too varied considerably. In many places, such as West Africa, nationalists relied on peaceful political pressure—demonstrations, strikes, mass mobilization, and negotiations—to achieve independence. Elsewhere armed struggle was required. Eight years of bitter guerrilla warfare preceded Algerian independence from France in 1962.

While all nationalist movements sought political independence for modern states, their ideologies and outlooks also differed. Many in India and the Islamic world viewed their new nations through the prism of religion, while elsewhere more secular outlooks prevailed. In Indonesia an early nationalist organization, the Islamic Union, appealed on the basis of religion, while later groups espoused Marxism. Indonesia's primary nationalist leader, Sukarno, sought to embrace and reconcile these various outlooks. "What is Sukarno?" he asked. "A nationalist? An Islamist? A Marxist? . . . Sukarno is a mixture of all these isms."[11] Nationalist movements led by communist parties, such as those in Vietnam and China, sought major social transformations as well as freedom from foreign rule, while those in most of Africa focused on ending racial discrimination and achieving political independence with little concern about emerging patterns of domestic class inequality.

However it was achieved, the collapse of colonial rule and the emergence of these new nations onto the world stage as independent and assertive actors have been distinguishing features of world history in this most recent century.

After Freedom

Having achieved the long-sought status of independent nation-states, how would those states be governed? And how would they undertake the tasks of nation building and modern development? Those were the questions that confronted both the former colonies and those already independent, such as China, Thailand, Ethiopia, Iran, Turkey, and Central and South America. Together they formed the bloc of nations known variously as the third world, the developing countries, or the Global South.

All across the developing world, efforts to create a new political order had to contend with a set of common conditions. Populations were exploding, and expectations for independence ran very high, often exceeding the available resources. Many developing countries were culturally very diverse, with little loyalty to a central state. Nonetheless, public employment mushroomed as the state assumed greater responsibility for economic development. In conditions of widespread poverty and weak private economies, groups and individuals sought to capture the state, or parts of it, both for the salaries and status it offered and for the opportunities for private enrichment that public office provided.

This was the formidable setting in which developing countries had to hammer out new political systems. The range of that effort was immense: Communist Party control in China, Vietnam, and Cuba; multiparty democracy in India and South Africa; one-party democracy in Mexico, Tanzania, and Senegal; military regimes for a time in much of Latin America, Africa, and the Middle East; personal dictatorships in Iraq, Uganda, and the Philippines. In many places, one kind of political system followed another in kaleidoscopic succession.

■ Assessing Democracy
To what extent did Western-style democracy take root in the newly independent states?

As colonial rule drew to a close, European authorities in many places attempted to transplant democratic institutions to colonies they had long governed with such a heavy and authoritarian hand. They established legislatures, permitted elections, allowed political parties to operate, and in general anticipated the development of constitutional, parliamentary, multiparty democracies similar to their own.

It was in India that such a political system established its deepest roots. There Western-style democracy, including regular elections, multiple parties, civil liberties, and peaceful changes in government, has been practiced almost continuously since independence. Elsewhere in the colonial world, democracy proved a far more fragile transplant. Among the new states of Africa, for example, few retained their democratic institutions beyond the initial post-independence decade. Many of the apparently popular political parties that had led the struggle for independence lost mass support and were swept away by military coups, one-party systems, or "big man" dictatorships. Across much of Africa, economic disappointments, class resentments, and ethnic conflicts provided the context for numerous military takeovers. By the early 1980s, the military had intervened in at least thirty of Africa's forty-six independent states and actively governed more than half of them. Army officers swept aside the old political parties and constitutions and vowed to begin anew, while promising to return power to civilians and restore democracy at some point in the future. A similar wave of military interventions swept over Latin America during the 1960s and 1970s, leaving Brazil, Argentina, Peru, Chile, Uruguay, Bolivia, the Dominican Republic, and other countries governed at times by their military officers. However, the circumstances in Latin America were quite different from those in Africa. While military rule was something new and unexpected in Africa, Latin American armed forces had long intervened in political life. The region had also largely escaped the bitter ethnic conflicts that afflicted so many African states, though its class antagonisms were more clearly defined and expressed. Furthermore, Latin American societies in general were far more modernized and urbanized than those of Africa. And while newly independent African states remained linked to their former European rulers, long-independent Latin American states lived in the shadow of a dominant United States.

The late twentieth century, however, witnessed a remarkable political reversal, a **globalization of democracy** that brought popular movements, multiparty elections, and new constitutions to many countries all around the world. This included the end of military and autocratic rule in Spain, Portugal, and Greece as well as the stunning rise of democratic movements, parties, and institutions amid the collapse of communism in the Soviet Union and Eastern Europe. But the most extensive expression of this global reemergence of democracy lay in the developing countries. By 2000, almost all Latin American countries had abandoned their military-controlled regimes and returned to some form of democratic governance. So too did most African states previously ruled by soldiers, dictators, or single parties. In Asia, authoritarian regimes, some long established, gave way to more pluralistic and participatory political systems in South Korea, Taiwan, Thailand, the Philippines, Iraq, and Indonesia. And in 2011, in what came to be called the Arab Spring, mass movements in various Arab countries—Tunisia, Egypt, Libya, Syria, Bahrain, Yemen—challenged the hold of entrenched, corrupt, and autocratic rulers, while proclaiming their commitment to democracy, human dignity, and honest government.

By the final quarter of the twentieth century, democracy was increasingly viewed as a universal political principle to which all could aspire rather than an alien and imposed system deriving from the West. It was therefore more available as a vehicle for social protest in the rest of the world. Meanwhile, established authoritarian governments had often failed abysmally to promote economic growth or to curb pervasive corruption. Many no doubt agreed with the West African critic George Ayittey when he labeled various African governments as "vampire states" led by "gangsters, thugs and crooks . . . who use the state to enrich themselves."[12] Growing numbers of people were outraged. The growth of civil society with its numerous voluntary groups provided a social foundation, independent of the state, for demanding change. Disaffected students, professionals, urban workers, religious organizations, women's groups, and more joined in a variety of grassroots movements, some of them mobilized through social media, to insist on democratic change as a means to a better life.

But the consolidation of democratic practice was an uncertain and highly variable process. Some elected leaders, such as Hugo Chávez in Venezuela, Vladimir Putin in Russia, and Recep Erdogan in Turkey, turned authoritarian once in office. Even where parliaments existed, they were often quite circumscribed in their powers. Outright electoral fraud tainted democratic institutions in many places, while established elites and oligarchies found it possible to exercise considerable influence even in formal democracies. Chinese authorities brutally crushed a democratic movement in 1989. The Algerian military sponsored elections in 1992 and then abruptly canceled them when an Islamic party seemed poised to win. And the political future of the Arab Spring remained highly uncertain, as a military strongman became a civilian politician and returned to power in Egypt in 2014 and Syria degenerated into brutal civil war. In Hungary and Poland, right-wing populist movements had moved their countries' political systems in an authoritarian direction by 2020. While no longer exclusively Western, democracy remained a fragile experiment in many parts of the world.

The End of the Communist Era

As the emergence of dozens of "new nations" from colonial rule reshaped the international political landscape during the second half of the twentieth century, so too did the demise of world communism during the last quarter of that century. It effectively ended the cold war, diminished the threat of a nuclear holocaust, and marked the birth of another twenty or so new nation-states.

Surprisingly enough, the communist era came to an end far more peacefully than it had begun. That ending might be viewed as a drama in three acts. Act One began in China during the late 1970s, following the death of its towering revolutionary leader Mao Zedong in 1976. Over the next several decades, the CCP gradually abandoned almost everything that had been associated with Maoist communism, even as the party retained its political control of the country. Act Two took place in Eastern Europe in the "miracle year" of 1989, when popular movements toppled despised communist governments one after another all across the region. The climactic act in this "end of communism" drama occurred in 1991 in the Soviet Union, where the entire "play" had opened seventy-four years earlier. There the reformist leader Mikhail Gorbachev (GORE-beh-CHOF) had come to power in 1985 intending to revive and save Soviet socialism from its accumulated dysfunctions. Those efforts, however, only exacerbated the country's many difficulties and led to the political disintegration of the Soviet Union on Christmas Day 1991. The curtain had fallen on the communist era.

Behind these separate stories lay two general failures of the communist experiment, measured both by communists' own standards and by those of the larger world. The first was economic. Despite their early successes, communist economies by the late 1970s showed no signs of catching up to the more advanced capitalist countries. The highly regimented Soviet economy in particular was largely stagnant; its citizens were forced to stand in long lines for consumer goods and complained endlessly about their poor quality and declining availability. This was enormously embarrassing, for it had been the proud boast of communist leaders everywhere that they had found a better route to modern prosperity than their capitalist rivals. Furthermore, these unflattering comparisons were increasingly well known, thanks to the global information revolution. A lagging economy had political and national security implications as well, for economic growth, even more than military capacity, was increasingly the measure of state power and widely expected among the general population as consumerism took hold around the world. The second failure was moral. The horrors of Stalin's Terror and the gulag, of Mao's Cultural Revolution, of something approaching genocide in communist Cambodia—all of this wore away at communist claims to moral superiority over capitalism. Moreover, this erosion occurred as global political culture more widely embraced democracy and human rights as the universal legacy of humankind, rather than the exclusive possession of the capitalist West. In both economic and moral terms, the communist path to the modern world was increasingly seen as a road to nowhere.

Communist leaders were not ignorant of these problems, and particularly in China and the Soviet Union, they moved aggressively to address them. But their approach to doing so varied greatly, as did the outcomes of those efforts. Thus, much as the Russian and Chinese revolutions differed and their approaches to building socialism diverged, so too did these communist giants chart distinct paths during the final years of the communist experiment.

Beyond Mao in China

In China the reform process took shape under the leadership of **Deng Xiaoping** (dung shee-yao-ping), who emerged as China's "paramount leader" in 1978, following the death of Mao Zedong. Particularly dramatic were Deng's dismantling of the country's system of collectivized farming and a return to something close to small-scale private agriculture. Impoverished Chinese peasants eagerly embraced these new opportunities and pushed them even further than the government had intended. Industrial reform proceeded more gradually. Managers of state enterprises were given greater authority and encouraged to act like private owners, making many of their own decisions and seeking profits. China opened itself to the world economy and welcomed foreign investment in "special enterprise zones" along the coast, where foreign capitalists received tax breaks and other inducements. Local governments and private entrepreneurs joined forces in thousands of flourishing "township and village enterprises" that produced food, clothing, building materials, and much more.

CORE IDEA

■ Making Comparisons

In what different ways was the erosion of communism experienced in China and the Soviet Union?

The outcome of these reforms was stunning economic growth and a new prosperity for millions. Better diets, lower mortality rates, declining poverty, massive urban construction, and surging exports—all of this accompanied China's state-directed rejoining of the world economy and contributed to a much-improved material life for millions of its citizens. China was the rising economic giant of the twenty-first century. That economic success provided the foundation for China's emergence as one of the Great Powers of the new century, able to challenge American dominance in eastern Asia and the Pacific.

After Communism in China Although the Communist Party still governed China in the early twenty-first century, communist values of selflessness, community, and simplicity had been substantially replaced for many by Western-style consumerism. This New Year's Good Luck poster from 1993 illustrates the new interest in material wealth in the form of American dollars and the return of older Chinese cultural patterns represented by the traditional gods of wealth, happiness, and longevity. The caption reads: "The gods of wealth enter the home from everywhere." (Zhejiang People's Art Publishing House/Stefan R. Landsberger Collections/International Institute of Social History, Amsterdam/www.chineseposters.net)

On the other hand, the country's burgeoning economy also generated massive corruption among Chinese officials, sharp inequalities between the coast and the interior, a huge problem of urban overcrowding, terrible pollution in major cities, and periodic inflation as the state loosened its controls over the economy. Urban vices such as street crime, prostitution, gambling, drug addiction, and a criminal underworld, which had been largely eliminated after 1949, surfaced again in China's booming cities. Nonetheless, something remarkable had occurred in China: a largely capitalist economy had been restored, and by none other than the Communist Party itself. Mao's worst fears had been realized, as China "took the capitalist road."

Although the party was willing to abandon many communist economic policies, it was adamantly unwilling to relinquish its political monopoly or to promote democracy at the national level. "Talk about democracy in the abstract," Deng Xiaoping declared, "will inevitably lead to the unchecked spread of ultra-democracy and anarchism, to the complete disruption of political stability, and to the total failure of our modernization program. . . . China will once again be plunged into chaos, division, retrogression, and darkness."[13] Such attitudes associated democracy with the chaos and uncontrolled mass action of the Cultural Revolution. Thus, when a democracy movement spearheaded by university and secondary school students surfaced in the late 1980s, Deng ordered the brutal crushing of its brazen demonstration in Beijing's Tiananmen Square before the television cameras of the world.

The Collapse of the Soviet Union

A parallel reform process unfolded quite differently in the USSR under the leadership of **Mikhail Gorbachev**, beginning in the mid-1980s. Like Deng Xiaoping in China, Gorbachev was committed to aggressively tackling the country's many problems—economic stagnation, a flourishing black market, public apathy, and cynicism about the party. His economic program, launched in 1987 and known as *perestroika* (per-uh-STROI-kuh) (restructuring), paralleled aspects of the Chinese approach by freeing state enterprises from the heavy hand of government regulation, permitting small-scale private businesses called cooperatives, offering opportunities for private farming, and cautiously welcoming foreign investment in joint enterprises.

Explaining Change What factors help to explain the collapse of the Soviet Union?

But in cultural and political affairs, Gorbachev moved far beyond Chinese reforms. His policy of *glasnost* (GLAHS-nohst) (openness) now permitted an unprecedented range of cultural and intellectual freedoms. In the late 1980s, glasnost hit the Soviet Union like a bomb. Newspapers and TV exposed social pathologies—crime, prostitution, child abuse, suicide, elite corruption, and homelessness—that previously had been presented solely as the product of capitalism. "Like an excited boy reads a note from his girl," wrote one poet, "that's how we read the papers today."[14] Plays, poems, films, and novels that had long been buried "in the drawer" were now released to a public that virtually devoured them. Films broke the ban on nudity and explicit sex. Soviet history was also reexamined as revelations of Stalin's crimes poured out of the media. The Bible and the Quran became more widely available, atheistic propaganda largely ceased, and thousands of churches and mosques were returned to believers and opened for worship. And beyond glasnost lay democratization and a new parliament with real powers, chosen in competitive elections. When those elections occurred in 1989, dozens of leading communists were rejected at the polls. In foreign affairs, Gorbachev moved to end the cold war by making unilateral cuts in Soviet military forces, engaging in arms control negotiations with the United States, and refusing to intervene as communist governments in Eastern Europe were overthrown.

But almost nothing worked out as Gorbachev had anticipated. Far from strengthening socialism and reviving a stagnant Soviet Union, the reforms led to its further weakening and collapse. In a dramatic contrast with China's booming economy, the Soviet Union spun into a sharp decline as its planned economy was dismantled before a functioning market-based system could emerge. Inflation mounted; consumer

Breaching the Berlin Wall In November 1989, anticommunist protesters broke through the Berlin Wall dividing the eastern and western sections of the city, even as East Berlin citizens joyfully entered their city's western zone. That event has become an iconic symbol of the collapse of communism in Eastern Europe and heralded the reunification of Germany and the end of the cold war, which had divided Europe since the late 1940s. (Tom Stoddart/Reportage via Getty Images)

goods were in short supply, and ration coupons reappeared; many feared the loss of their jobs. Unlike Chinese peasants, few Soviet farmers were willing to risk the jump into private farming, and few foreign investors found the Soviet Union a tempting place to do business.

Furthermore, the new freedoms provoked demands that went far beyond what Gorbachev had intended. A democracy movement of unofficial groups and parties now sprang to life, many of them seeking a full multiparty democracy and a market-based economy. They were joined by independent labor unions, which actually went on strike, something unheard of in the "workers' state." Most corrosively, a multitude of nationalist movements used the new freedoms to insist on greater autonomy, or even independence, from the Soviet Union. In the face of these mounting demands, Gorbachev resolutely refused to use force to crush the protesters, another sharp contrast with the Chinese experience.

Events in Eastern Europe intersected with those in the Soviet Union. Gorbachev's reforms had lit a fuse in these Soviet satellites, where communism had been imposed and maintained from outside. If the USSR could practice glasnost and hold competitive elections, why not Eastern Europe as well? This was the background for the "miracle year" of 1989. Massive demonstrations, last-minute efforts at reforms, the breaching of the Berlin Wall, the surfacing of new political groups—all of this and more overwhelmed the highly unpopular communist regimes of Poland, Hungary, East Germany, Bulgaria, Czechoslovakia, and Romania, which were quickly swept away. This success then emboldened nationalists and democrats in the Soviet Union. If communism had been overthrown in Eastern Europe, perhaps it could be overthrown in the USSR as well. Soviet conservatives and patriots, however, were outraged. To them, Gorbachev had stood idly by while the political gains of World War II, for which the Soviet Union had paid in rivers of blood, vanished before their eyes. It was nothing less than treason.

A brief and unsuccessful attempt to restore the old order through a military coup in August 1991 triggered the end of the Soviet Union and its communist regime. From the wreckage there emerged fifteen new and independent states, following the internal political divisions of the USSR. Arguably the Soviet Union had collapsed less because of its multiple problems and more from the unexpected consequences of Gorbachev's efforts to address them.

The Soviet collapse represented a unique phenomenon in the world of the late twentieth century. Simultaneously, the world's largest state and its last territorial empire vanished; the world's first Communist Party disintegrated; a powerful command economy broke down; an official socialist ideology was repudiated; and a forty-five-year global struggle between the East and the West ended, at least temporarily. In Europe, Germany was reunited, and a number of former communist states joined NATO and the European Union, ending the division of the continent. At least for the moment, capitalism and democracy seemed to triumph over socialism and authoritarian governments. In many places, the end of communism allowed simmering ethnic tensions to explode into open conflict. Beyond the disintegration of the Soviet Union, both Yugoslavia and Czechoslovakia fragmented. Chechens in Russia, Abkhazians in Georgia, Russians in the Baltic states and Ukraine, Tibetans and Uighurs in China—all of these minorities found themselves in opposition to the states in which they lived.

After Communism

As the twenty-first century dawned, the communist world had shrunk considerably from its high point just three decades earlier. In the Soviet Union and Eastern Europe, communism had disappeared entirely as the governing authority and dominant ideology. In the immediate aftermath of the Soviet collapse, Russia experienced a sharply contracting economy, widespread poverty and inequality, and declining life expectancy. Not until 2006 did its economy recover to the level of 1991. China had largely abandoned its communist economic policies as a market economy took shape, spurring remarkable economic growth. Like China, Vietnam and Laos remained officially communist, even while they pursued Chinese-style reforms, though more cautiously. Even Cuba, which was beset by economic crisis in the 1990s after massive Soviet subsidies ended, allowed small businesses, private food markets, and tourism to grow, while harshly suppressing opposition political groups. Cubans were increasingly engaged in private enterprise, able to buy and sell cars and houses, and enthusiastically embracing mobile phones and computers. In 2015 diplomatic relations with the United States were restored after more than a half century of hostility between the two countries. An impoverished and highly nationalistic North Korea, armed with nuclear weapons, remained the most unreformed and repressive of the remaining communist countries. But either as a primary source of international conflict or as a compelling path to modernity and social justice, communism was effectively dead. The brief communist era in world history had ended.

■ **Identifying Change** In what ways did international life change following the end of the communist era?

The end of the cold war and the thorough discrediting of communism, however, did not usher in any extended period of international tranquility as many had hoped, for the rivalries of the Great Powers had certainly not ended. As the bipolar world of the cold war faded away, the United States emerged as the world's sole superpower, but Russia and China alike continued to challenge American dominance in world affairs. Russian president Vladimir Putin deeply resented the loss of his country's international stature after the breakup of the Soviet Union and what he regarded as U.S. efforts to intrude upon Russia's legitimate interests. Issues such as the eastward expansion of NATO, Russia's intervention in Ukraine and its outright annexation of the Crimea, rival involvements in Syria's civil war, Russian meddling in American elections, and the withdrawal of the United States from several arms control agreements had brought the relationship of Russia and the United States by 2020 to something resembling cold war–era hostility, though without the sharp ideological antagonism of that earlier conflict.

The rising economic and military power of China generated many tensions with its neighbors as China sought to assert its interests and influence in East Asia and the South China Sea. Relations between China and the United States also deteriorated, when, following his election in 2016, President Donald Trump raised tariffs on Chinese imports and limited the sale of cutting-edge technology to Chinese companies in reaction to what his administration viewed as unfair trading practices.

Beyond the antagonisms among the major world powers, the Middle East emerged as a vortex of instability and conflict that echoed widely across the world. The struggles between the new Jewish state of Israel, granted independence in 1948, and the adjacent Palestinian Muslim territories generated periodic wars and upheavals that have persisted into the post–cold war era. Both near neighbors, such as Syria, Jordan, Turkey, and Egypt, as well as distant powers, such as the United States and Russia, have been drawn into the **Israeli-Palestinian conflict** on both sides. The **Iranian revolution** of 1979

The Middle East, ca. 2000

established a radically Islamist government in that ancient land, helped to trigger a long and bloody war with neighboring Iraq during the 1980s, posed a serious threat to Israel, and launched a continuing rivalry with Saudi Arabia for dominant influence in the region. A contentiously negotiated international agreement in 2015 brought to a halt Iran's alleged efforts to acquire nuclear weapons capability, but the unilateral withdrawal of the United States from the agreement in 2018 and the subsequent restarting of the Iran nuclear program put the agreement in doubt.

The most globally unsettling and novel aspect of post–cold war international life has been the proliferation of "terrorist" attacks undertaken by radical Islamist groups such as the Taliban, al-Qaeda, Boko Haram, and the Islamic State or by individuals inspired by their message. (See "Religion and Global Modernity" in Chapter 23.) The random character of these attacks, their unpredictability, and their targeting of civilians have generated immense fear and insecurity in many places. In terms of their international consequences, the most significant of these attacks was that launched against several U.S. targets, including the World Trade Center, in September of 2001, for that event prompted large-scale U.S. military intervention and prolonged wars in both Afghanistan and Iraq. In both places old regimes were replaced by new ones amid enormous and continuing conflict and carnage. But the United States has certainly not been the sole target of terrorist violence. Many European and Russian cities have experienced such attacks in the twenty-first century, and terrorism has claimed far more victims in the Islamic world itself, as Islamic radicals have sought to oust what they view as corrupt and un-Islamic governments. Thus terrorism and the so-called war on terrorism have become a global issue in the post–cold war era.

The Syrian Refugee Crisis Among the most wrenching aspects of the Syrian civil war were the millions of refugees that it generated, many of them fleeing to Turkey or Europe and winding up in refugee camps. This photograph shows an anguished woman arriving on the Greek island of Lesbos, having survived a hazardous crossing of the Aegean Sea from Turkey in late 2015. Five other migrants had died during that crossing. (DIMITAR DILKOFF/Getty Images)

A final source of international tension deriving from the Middle East has been the flood of refugees from war-torn and economically desperate societies in the region and adjacent African states, many of them headed for Europe. The **Syrian civil war**, beginning in 2011, had by itself generated over 12 million refugees by mid-2016, with about 1 million seeking asylum in Europe, almost 5 million relocated to Turkey and other neighboring countries, and another 6.5 million displaced within Syria. That conflict became thoroughly internationalized as Russia, the United States, and various Muslim governments and radical groups took sides.

It also sharpened the regional rivalry between Iran and Saudi Arabia, which contained both an ethnic Persian/Arab dimension and a religious Shia/Sunni element.

Beyond the Middle East, conflicts between India and Pakistan, between North Korea and its various neighbors, and between China and Taiwan continued to roil the waters of international life. That all of these countries except Taiwan possessed nuclear weapons compounded the potential dangers of these conflicts. Furthermore, the East-West struggles of the cold war era gave way to tension between the wealthy countries of the Global North and the developing countries of the Global South, led by such emerging powers as India, Indonesia, Brazil, Mexico, and South Africa. And any number of civil wars or ethnically based separatist movements took shape in Yugoslavia, Rwanda, Russia, Ukraine, Myanmar (Burma), Iraq, Somalia, Afghanistan, and Libya, among other places.

The pattern of global military spending in the postcommunist era reflected all of these continuing or emerging tensions in international life. After a brief drop during the 1990s, global military spending rose during the early twenty-first century to exceed cold war levels by 2010. The United States led this global pattern, with sharp spending increases after the attacks of 2001, as the "war on terror" took hold. Although the United States accounted for roughly 35 to 40 percent of this spending in the twenty-first century, China has steadily increased its military budget during this time and is now second only to the United States in expenditures for war. Clearly, no prolonged period of international stability and no lasting "peace dividend" accompanied the passing of the cold war into history.

CONCLUSIONS AND REFLECTIONS

Twentieth-Century Communism

Among the major shapers of twentieth-century world history was the phenomenon of global communism, beginning with its initial breakthrough in the Russian Revolution of 1917. Communist regimes everywhere sought a radical transformation of their societies as they set about "building socialism." Fear and hatred of communism were major factors in the ideology and appeal of fascist movements in Italy, Germany, and elsewhere. Communism likewise motivated American aid to a recovering Western Europe as well as the creation of NATO as an anticommunist alliance.

Communism and Western opposition to it gave rise to the cold war and the various military conflicts that it spawned, such as in Korea, Vietnam, Cuba, and Afghanistan. The decades-long rivalry between the communist Soviet Union and the democratic capitalist United States generated the arms race in nuclear weapons, which hung like a dark cloud over the entire world for over forty years.

Communism and cold war rivalries also intersected with the end of European empires. Both the Soviet Union and the United States opposed European-style colonial empires, thus encouraging independence movements in Asia and Africa. But both sides also sought allies among the "new nations" of Asia and Africa.

Resistance to these efforts gave rise to the idea of a "third world" consisting of countries seeking to avoid entanglement in Great Power rivalries, while focusing on their own economic development. China, itself a communist country after 1949, aspired to a major role in the third world even as it challenged the Soviet Union for leadership in the communist world. And for a time, a number of countries (Cuba, Vietnam, India, Ethiopia, Mozambique) adopted a Marxist or communist approach to governing their countries.

The collapse of communism, particularly in the Soviet Union and Eastern Europe, also had global geopolitical implications, largely ending the ideological cold war, though not the rivalry between Russia and the United States. It also gave birth to about two dozen new states and many ethnic conflicts. Of the remaining communist states, North Korea remains a flashpoint of global tension, while China has embraced many elements of a market economy even as it is still governed by a Communist Party.

Particularly during the cold war, efforts to study communism encountered many obstacles. In the United States, which lacks a major socialist tradition, sometimes saying anything positive about communism or even noting its appeal to millions of people has brought charges of whitewashing the crimes of the most brutal communist leaders. Within the communist world, even modest criticism of the government was usually regarded as counterrevolutionary and was largely forbidden and harshly punished. Certainly few observers were neutral in their assessment of the communist experiment.

Were the Russian and Chinese revolutions a blow for human freedom and a cry for justice on the part of oppressed people, or did they simply replace one tyranny with another? Did Stalin and Mao lead successful efforts to industrialize backward countries or a ferocious assault on their moral and social fabric? Did Chinese reforms of the late twentieth century represent a return to sensible policies of modernization, a continued denial of basic democratic rights, or an opening to capitalist inequalities, corruption, and acquisitiveness? Passionate debate continues on all of these questions.

Communism, like many human projects, has been an ambiguous enterprise. On the one hand, communism brought hope to millions by addressing the manifest injustices of the past; by providing new opportunities for women, workers, and peasants; by promoting rapid industrial development; and by ending Western domination. On the other hand, communism was responsible for mountains of crimes—millions killed and wrongly imprisoned; massive famines partly caused by radical policies; human rights violated on an enormous scale; lives uprooted and distorted by efforts to achieve the impossible.

Studying communism challenges our inclination to want definitive answers and clear moral judgments. Can we hold contradictory elements in some kind of tension? Can we affirm our own values while acknowledging the ambiguities of life, both past and present? Doing so is arguably among the essential tasks of growing up and achieving a measure of intellectual maturity. In that undertaking, history can be helpful.

Revisiting Chapter 21

Revisiting Specifics

European Economic Community, 924
Marshall Plan, 926
Mao Zedong, 927
Great Leap Forward, 930
Cultural Revolution, 930
cold war, 931
North Atlantic Treaty Organization (NATO), 931
Warsaw Pact, 931
Cuban missile crisis, 936
decolonization, 939
Indian National Congress, 945
Mohandas Gandhi, 945
Muslim League, 945
globalization of democracy, 948
Deng Xiaoping, 950
Mikhail Gorbachev, 952
Israeli-Palestinian conflict, 955
Iranian revolution, 955
Syrian civil war, 956

Revisiting Core Ideas

1. **Explaining Postwar Recovery** What enabled Europe, the Soviet Union, and Japan to recover from the devastation of war?
2. **Making Comparisons** What was distinctive about the Chinese experience of communism compared to that of the Soviet Union?
3. **Making Comparisons** In what different ways was the cold war expressed and experienced?
4. **Accounting for Change** What factors contributed to the end of European colonial empires in Africa and Asia?
5. **Making Comparisons** In what different ways was the erosion of communism experienced in China and the Soviet Union?

A Wider View

1. Two major international conflicts shaped the second half of the twentieth century: the cold war struggle between the communist and capitalist worlds and the anticolonial struggles of Afro-Asian peoples against the Western imperial powers. How might you compare these two conflicts, and how did they intersect with one another?
2. How would you compare the historical experiences of India and China since World War II?
3. In what ways did the struggle for independence shape the agenda of developing countries in the second half of the twentieth century?
4. "The end of communism was as revolutionary as its beginning." Do you agree with this statement? Explain your thinking.
5. **Looking Back** To what extent did the struggle for independence and the postcolonial experience of African and Asian peoples in the twentieth century parallel or diverge from the experience of the earlier "new nations" in the Americas in the eighteenth and nineteenth centuries?

To learn more about the topics in this chapter, see **For Further Study** at the end of this book.

WORKING WITH EVIDENCE

Mao's China

Within the communist world of the twentieth century, the experience of the Chinese people was distinctive, particularly during the decades when Mao Zedong led the country (1949–1976). The sources that follow provide a glimpse into those tumultuous decades, at times hopeful for some and at other times tragic for many.

SOURCE 21.1 Revolution in Long Bow Village

The Chinese Revolution occurred in thousands of separate villages as Communist Party activists called "cadres" encouraged peasants to "speak the bitterness" of their personal experience, to "struggle" with their landlords, and to "settle accounts" with them. Source 21.1 provides a brief account of one such struggle as it unfolded in Long Bow Village in northern China in 1948. It was written by the American farmer and activist William Hinton, who had worked in China with the U.S. government during World War II and later with the United Nations. He personally observed and took part in the events he describes.

- What grievances found expression as peasants challenged landlords and husbands in Long Bow Village?
- In what specific ways did these gatherings take shape?
- What change in consciousness had occurred in the course of these events? How might you imagine the conversations that occurred at the New Year's feast that evening or following the women's gathering?

WILLIAM HINTON | ***Confronting Landlords and Husbands*** | **1948**

There was no holding back. . . . So vicious had been Ching-ho's practices and so widespread his influence that more than half the families in the village had scores to settle with him. Old women who had never spoken in public before stood up to accuse him. Even Li Mao's wife—a woman so pitiable she hardly dared look anyone in the face—shook her fist before his nose and cried out, "Once I went to glean wheat on your lands but you cursed me . . . and beat me. Why did you seize the wheat I had gleaned?" Altogether over 180 opinions were raised. Ching-ho had no answer to any of them. He stood there with his head bowed. . . . When the committee of our [Peasant] Association met to figure up what he owed, it came to 400 bags of milled grain. . . .

That evening all the people went to Ching-ho's courtyard to help take over his property. We went in to register his grain and altogether found . . . only a quarter of what he owed us. Right then and there we decided to call another meeting. People said he must have a lot of silver dollars. . . .

We called him out of the house and asked him what he intended to do since the grain was not nearly enough. He said, "I have land and house."

"But all this is not enough," shouted the people. So then we began to beat him. Finally he said, "I have 40 silver dollars under the *k'ang*." We went in and dug it up. The money stirred up everyone. We beat him again. He told us where to find another hundred after that. But no-one believed that this was the end of his hoarding. We beat him again and several militiamen began to heat an iron bar in one of the fires. . . .

Altogether we got $500 from Ching-ho that night. . . . We were tired and hungry. . . . So we decided to eat all of the things that Ching-ho had prepared to pass the New Year.

All said, "In the past we never lived through a happy new year, because he always asked for his rent and interest then and cleaned our houses bare. This time we'll eat what we like."

[*The revolution in Long Bow also encouraged women to confront abusive husbands. When one of those women registered a complaint against her husband, the local Women's Association took action.*]

In front of this unprecedented gathering of determined women, a demand was made that Man-ts'ang explain his actions. Man-ts'ang, arrogant and unbowed, readily complied. He said that he beat his wife because she went to [political] meetings and "the only reason women go to meetings is to gain a free hand for flirtations and seduction."

This remark aroused a furious protest from the women assembled before him. Words soon led to deeds. They rushed at him from all sides, knocked him down, kicked him, tore his clothes, scratched his face, pulled his hair, and pummeled him until he could no longer breathe. . . .

"Stop. I'll never beat her again," gasped the panic stricken husband. . . . From that day onward, Man-ts'ang never dared beat his wife and from that day onward his wife became known to the whole village by her maiden name, Ch'eng Ai-lien, instead of simply by the title of Man-ts'ang's wife, as had been the custom since time began.

Source: William Hinton, *Fanshen* (New York: Random House, 1966), 137–38, 158.

SOURCE 21.2 A Vision of the New China

In the eyes of its leaders, the Chinese Communist Party's victory in 1949 by no means meant the end of the struggle with enemies. Former landowners and capitalists had to be confronted, as did those within the Communist Party who had become infected with "bourgeois values" such as materialism, careerism, and individualism and were suspected of opposition to some of Mao's radical policies. What the party called the "Four Olds"—old customs, cultures, habits, and ideas—had to be destroyed so that a wholly "new world" might take shape. Source 21.2, a poster from the Cultural Revolution era (1966–1976), effectively presented the major features of this imagined new society. Its caption urged everyone to "encourage late marriage, plan for birth, and work hard for the new age."

- How does this poster define the "new age" to which the Chinese Communist Party was beckoning its people?
- What kind of gender relationships does the poster favor?
- What elements of prerevolutionary Chinese life might be included in the "Four Olds," which had to be rooted out?
- The caption also speaks of "encouraging late marriage and planning for birth." What might such values contribute to creating the "new age"?

Poster: "Work Hard for a New Age" | **1970s**

工业学大庆
提倡晚婚 计划生育 为实现新时期的总任务而奋斗

DaTo Images/Bridgeman Images

SOURCE 21.3 Socialism in the Countryside

The centerpiece of Mao's plans for the vast Chinese countryside lay in the "people's communes." Established during the Great Leap Forward in the late 1950s, these were huge political and economic units intended to work the land more efficiently and collectively, to undertake large-scale projects such as building dams and irrigation systems, to create small-scale industries in rural areas, and to promote local self-reliance. They were also intended to move China more rapidly toward genuine communism by eliminating virtually every form of private property and emphasizing social equality and shared living. Commune members ate together in large dining halls, and children were cared for during the day in collective nurseries rather than by their own families. Source 21.3A contains Mao's vision of these communes, expressed at a party conference in 1958, while Source 21.3B shows a highly idealized image of one such commune in a poster created in 1958 under the title "The People's Communes Are Good."

The actual outcomes of the commune movement departed radically from its idealistic goals. Economic disruption occasioned by the creation of communes contributed a great deal to the enormous famines of the late 1950s and early 1960s, in which many millions perished. Furthermore, efforts to involve the peasants in iron and steel production through the creation of much-heralded "backyard furnaces," illustrated in Source 21.3B, proved a failure. Most of the metal produced in these primitive facilities was of poor quality and essentially unusable. Such efforts further impoverished the rural areas, as peasants were encouraged to contribute their pots, pans, and anything made of iron to the smelting furnaces.

- What do these sources suggest about the long-term goals of the Chinese Communist Party leadership?
- What aspects of Mao's description of communal life are illustrated in the poster? One of Mao's chief goals was to overcome the sharp division between industrial cities and the agricultural countryside. How is this effort expressed in these sources?

SOURCE 21.3A
MAO ZEDONG | *On Communes* | 1958

The characteristics of the people's communes are (1) big and (2) public. [They have] vast areas of land and abundant resources [as well as] a large population; [they can] combine industry, agriculture, commerce, education and military affairs as well as farming, forestry, animal husbandry, side-line production and fisheries—being "big" is terrific. [With] many people, there's lots of power. [We say] public because they contain more socialism . . . [and] they will gradually eradicate the vestiges of capitalism—for example the eradication of private plots and private livestock rearing and the running of public mess halls, nurseries, and tailoring groups so that all working women can be liberated. They will implement a wage system and agricultural factories [in which] every single man, woman, old person and youth receives his own wage, in contrast to the former [system of] distribution to the head of household. . . . This eradicates the patriarchal system and the system of bourgeois rights. Another advantage of [communes] being public is that labor efficiency can be raised. . . .

Source: Roderick MacFarquhar, Timothy Cheek, and Eugene Wu, eds., *The Secret Speeches of Chairman Mao* (Cambridge, MA: Council on East Asian Studies/Harvard University, 1989), 431.

SOURCE 21.3B

Poster: "The People's Communes Are Good" | **1958**

SOURCE 21.4 Women, Nature, and Industrialization

Among the core values of Maoist communism were human mastery over the natural order, rapid industrialization, and the liberation of women from ancient limitations and oppressions in order to mobilize them for the task of building socialism. Source 21.4, a 1970 poster, illustrates these values. Its caption reads: "Women hold up half of heaven, and, cutting through rivers and mountains, change to a new attitude."

- In what ways does this poster reflect Chinese communism's core values?
- How is the young woman in this image portrayed? What does the expression on her face convey? Notice her clothing and the shape of her forearms, as well as the general absence of a feminine figure. Why do you think she is portrayed in this largely sexless fashion? What does this suggest about the communist attitude toward sexuality?
- What does this image suggest about how the party sought to realize gender equality? What is the significance of the work the young woman is doing? What is the "new attitude" to which the caption refers?
- Notice the lights that illuminate a nighttime work scene. What does this suggest about attitudes toward work and production?

Poster: "Women Hold Up Half of Heaven" | **1970**

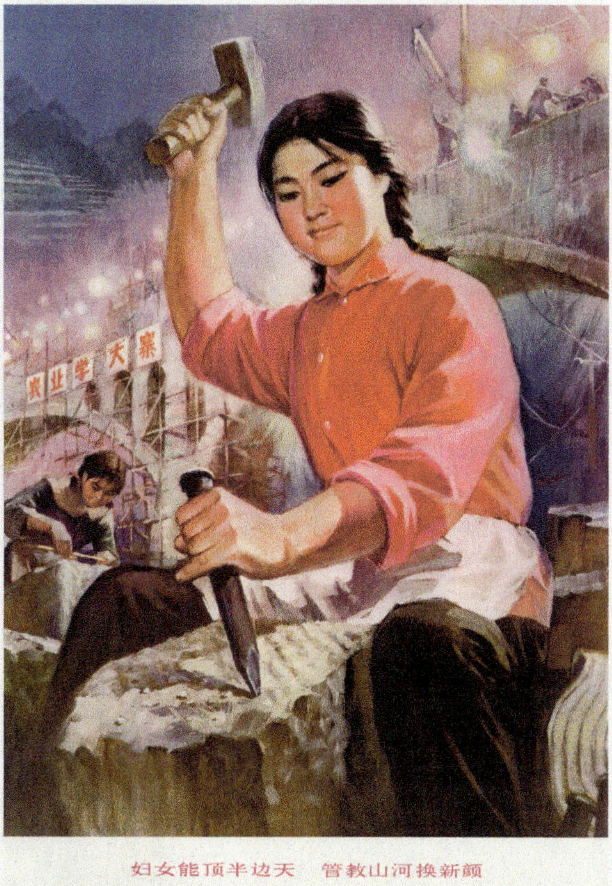

业学大寨
妇女能顶半边天　管教山河换新颜

Bridgeman Images

SOURCE 21.5 The Cult of Mao

A central feature of Chinese communism, especially during the Cultural Revolution of 1966–1976, was the growing veneration, even adoration, of Chairman Mao. Portraits, statues, busts, and Mao badges proliferated. Everyone was expected to read repeatedly the "Red Treasured Book," which offered a selection of quotations from Mao's writings, believed to facilitate solutions to almost all problems, both public and private. Many families erected "tablets of loyalty" to Mao, much like those previously devoted to ancestors. People made pilgrimages to "sacred shrines" associated with key events in his life.

During the Cultural Revolution, millions of young people, organized as Red Guards and committed to revolutionary action, flocked to Beijing, where enormous and ecstatic rallies allowed them to catch a glimpse of their beloved leader and to unite with him in the grand task of creating communism in China. Source 21.5, a poster created in 1968, depicts such a rally. Its caption reads: "The reddest, reddest, red sun in our heart, Chairman Mao, and us together." Following such events, these young people fanned out across the country to attack Mao's alleged enemies, those who were "taking the capitalist road." (See "Communism Chinese-Style" earlier in this chapter.)

- What relationship between Mao and his young followers does the poster suggest? Why might some scholars have seen a quasi-religious dimension to that relationship?
- How do you understand the significance of the "Red Treasured Book" of quotations from Mao that the young people are waving?
- How might you account for the unbridled enthusiasm expressed by the Red Guards? Can you think of other comparable cases of such mass enthusiasm?

***Poster: "Chairman Mao and Us Together"* | 1968**

SOURCE 21.6 Experiencing the Cultural Revolution

As the Cultural Revolution unfolded, teachers and other intellectuals became a particular target of the young revolutionary Red Guards, who publicly humiliated, tortured, or killed those they believed to be enemies of Mao and the revolution. Source 21.6 contains an account of such confrontations or "struggle meetings." It was written by Gao Yuan some twenty years after it occurred. Some of the victims of these confrontations committed suicide to escape the horror that befell them.

- What actions did the Red Guards take toward their teachers? What were the actions intended to accomplish?
- How might you imagine the motivations of those who participated in these sessions?

GAO YUAN | *Born Red* | 1987

The list of accusations grew longer by the day: hooligans and bad eggs, filthy rich peasants and son-of-a-bitch landlords, bloodsucking capitalists and neo-bourgeoisie . . . counterrevolutionaries . . . imperialist running dogs and spies. Students stood in the role of prosecutor, judge, and police. No defense was allowed. Any teacher who protested was certainly a liar.

The indignities escalated as well. Some students cut or shaved teachers' hair into curious patterns. The most popular was the yin-yang cut, which featured a full head of hair on one side and a clean shaven scalp on the other. Some said this style represented Chairman Mao's theory of the "unity of opposites." It made me think of the punishments of ancient China, which included shaving the head, tattooing the face, cutting off the nose or feet, castration, or dismemberment by five horse-drawn carts.

At struggle meetings, students would often force teachers into the "jet-plane" position. Two people would stand on either side of the accused, push him to his knees, pull back his head by the hair, and hold his arms out in back like airplane wings. We tried it on each other and found it caused great strain on the back and neck. . . .

A few students even argued that we should use a bit more force. After all, weren't many of these bad eggs Kuomintang [Guomindang] and American agents? . . .

A young teacher from a worker's family was charged with emphasizing academics over politics and a young woman of poor peasant origin was criticized for wearing high heels, proof that she had betrayed her class. Each apologized in a public meeting.

Source: Gao Yuan, *Born Red* (Stanford, CA: Stanford University Press, 1987), 53–55.

DOING HISTORY

1. **Analyzing Communist Intentions** Based on these sources, how would you describe the kind of society that the Chinese Communist Party sought to create in China during Mao's lifetime?
2. **Distinguishing Image and Reality** Based on these sources and the chapter narrative, to what extent do these sources accurately represent the successes of Maoist communism? What insights do they shed on its failures?
3. **Defining Audience and Appeal** To whom do you think these sources were directed? What appeal might they have had for the intended audience?
4. **Noticing Change** How could you use these sources to define the dramatic changes that transformed China since 1949? How might a traditional Chinese official from the nineteenth century respond to them?

HISTORIANS' VOICES

Assessing Mao

The towering significance of Mao Zedong in China's recent history has led to no end of effort to assess his role and legacy. By some mysterious mathematical reckoning, the Chinese Communist Party declared him 70 percent correct and 30 percent wrong. Historians too have weighed in on the question. Voice 21.1 by Maurice Meisner, a prominent historian of modern China, highlights Mao's role as a modernizing figure in China's history, while lamenting his limitations as a builder of democratic socialism. In Voice 21.2, the Dutch historian of China, Frank Dikotter, proclaims Mao's responsibility for perhaps the greatest famine in world history, which emerged from the Great Leap Forward.

- In what respects was Mao a successful modernizer and a failed builder of socialism according to Meisner?
- How does Dikotter explain the "great famine" of 1958–1962?
- **Integrating Primary and Secondary Sources** How might the primary sources in this feature be used to support or challenge the arguments of Meisner and Dikotter?

VOICE 21.1

Maurice Meisner on Mao, Modernization, and Socialism | 1999

Mao Zedong was far more successful as an economic modernizer than as a builder of socialism. . . . Between 1952 . . . and 1977, the output of Chinese industry increased at an average annual rate of 11.3 percent, as rapid a pace of industrialization as has ever been achieved by any country in a comparable period in modern world history. . . . [T]he Maoist era was the time of China's modern industrial revolution. . . . It is a record that compares favorably with comparable stages in the industrialization of Germany, Japan and Russia. . . . Maoist industrialization proceeded without benefit of foreign loans or investment. . . . The near doubling of average life expectancy over the quarter century of Mao's rule . . . offers dramatic statistical evidence for the material and social gains that the Communist revolution brought to the great majority of the Chinese people.

More questionable . . . is his lingering, if tarnished, image as the builder of a socialist society. . . . As industrial development proceeded, new bureaucratic and technological elites emerged. The rural areas were exploited for the benefit of the cities. . . . And industrial values of economic rationality and bureaucratic professionalism became the dominant social norms, subordinating the socialist goals [of equality, selflessness, service to the collective]. . . . The Maoist state machine became increasingly separated from the society it ruled . . . and the division between rulers and ruled became ever more pronounced. . . . Maoism . . . was not a doctrine that recognized popular democracy as both the necessary means to realize socialism and one of its essential ends as well.

Source: Maurice Meisner, *Mao's China and After* (New York: Free Press, 1999), 414–15, 417–19, 421–22.

VOICE 21.2

Frank Dikotter on Mao's Great Famine | 2011

Between 1958 and 1962 China descended into hell. Mao Zedong . . . threw his country into a frenzy with the Great Leap Forward, an attempt to catch up with and overtake Britain in less than 15 years. By unleashing China's greatest asset, a labor force that was counted in the hundreds of millions, Mao thought he could catapult his country past its competitors. . . . In pursuit of a utopian paradise, everything was collectivized as villagers were herded together in giant communes which heralded the advent of communism. People in the countryside were robbed of their work, their home, their land, their belongings, and their livelihood. Food, distributed by the spoonful in collective canteens according to merit, became a weapon to force people to follow the party's every dictate. Irrigation campaigns forced up to half the villagers to work for weeks on end on giant water conservancy projects, often far from home, without adequate food and rest. The experiment ended in the greatest catastrophe the country had ever known, destroying tens of millions of lives. . . . [A]t least 45 million people died unnecessarily between 1958 and 1962. . . .

[A] vision of promised abundance . . . also inflicted unprecedented damage on agriculture, trade, industry, and transportation. Pots, pans, and tools were thrown into backyard furnaces to increase the country's steel output, which was seen as one of the magic markers of progress. Livestock declined precipitously . . . despite extravagant schemes for giant piggeries that would bring meat to every table. . . . As everyone cut corners in the relentless pursuit of higher output, factories spewed out inferior goods. . . . Corruption seeped into the fabric of life, tainting everything from soy sauce to hydraulic dams.

Source: Frank Dikotter, *Mao's Great Famine* (London: Bloomsbury, 2011), xi–xiii.

SIMON MAINA/AFP/Getty Images

CHAPTER 22

Global Processes

Technology, Economy, and Society

1900–present

CONNECTING PAST AND PRESENT

Around 2012, Bella, an eighteen-year-old Indonesian girl seeking to escape a difficult family situation at home, applied for a job as a "sales promotion girl" on a distant island. There she found herself trapped as a sex worker in a night club, where she became indebted and was terribly abused. "They turned women into animals," reported Bella's mother. "[They] claimed they owed debts that they obviously could not repay. The women there were helpless."[1]

At roughly the same time, another Indonesian, a fisherman named Samysuddin, found his livelihood threatened as coral reefs degraded in the face of global warming and fish became scarce. "If the reefs continue to degrade," he declared, "then there won't be any fish here. There won't be anything left for us to do."[2]

Yet a third Indonesian whose life was shaped by the changing conditions of a globalized world was Arfian Faudi, a young engineer, who with only a vocational high school education built a successful high-tech firm, DTech Engineering. In an international design contest sponsored by General Electric, he and his younger brother twice won first place, winning a prize of $7,000 in 2013. "We created products that were basically non-existent in the market," he remarked. "As long as we got the opportunity, we were willing to learn."[3]

For all three of these Indonesians, life in the early twenty-first century was defined not so much by war, revolution, or liberation struggles, but by powerful though less visible processes such as migration and sex trafficking for Bella, climate change and impoverishment for Samysuddin,

« **Technological Globalization** In 2019 a Kenyan woman uses her cell phone following prayers marking the end of the Muslim holy month of Ramadan. This image illustrates the intersection of tradition and modernity for billions across the globe who have integrated contemporary technologies into the rhythms of their everyday lives.

and technological innovation and economic globalization for Arfian. And so it has been for billions of others during the past century. Therefore, the two final chapters of Part 6 turn the historical spotlight away from the dominant events of the past century, recounted in Chapters 20 and 21, to focus more explicitly on such immensely transformative processes, all of which have played out on a deeply interconnected global stage.

SEEKING THE MAIN POINT

In what ways was technology a major driver of economic and social change during the past century?

Science and Technology: The Acceleration of Innovation

Behind both the major events and the global processes of the past century lay the decisive power of those twin processes of scientific discovery and technological innovation. Breakthroughs in both domains initially occurred largely within the Western world, where the Scientific and Industrial Revolutions had first taken shape. The accumulated wealth and experience derived from these earlier processes enabled this region to maintain its momentum as the primary source of global innovation well into the twentieth century. By the end of the century, however, the science and technology enterprise had become global, with major expressions in Mexico, Brazil, China, Vietnam, India, Indonesia, and elsewhere.

Particularly after World War II, a potent combination of universities, governments, and large corporations relentlessly drove the process of scientific and technological development. University-based scientific research provided the foundational knowledge from which new conceptions of the universe and all manner of technical applications emerged. Governments enmeshed in wars and concerned about national security funded some basic scientific research and were particularly interested in military applications such as weaponry, medicine, communications, aircraft, rocketry, and computing. And large corporations, eager for profits and motivated to create or meet consumer demand, invested heavily in both basic science and new products. Thus advances in chemistry generated the plastics industry; developments in physics enabled aerospace technologies; and new understandings in biology gave rise to antibiotics, a polio vaccine, chemotherapy, and much more.

A Second Scientific Revolution

Like the Scientific Revolution of the sixteenth and seventeenth centuries, the scientific breakthroughs of the past century in astronomy, physics, biochemistry, and biology have given rise to profound changes in our understanding of the cosmos with important cultural implications. In the first place, this new picture of the universe is one of mind-bending dimensions. We are now aware of the enormous duration of the universe—13.8 billion years and counting. We now measure astronomical distance in light years, just one of which is about 5.879 trillion miles. Our Milky Way galaxy alone measures about 100,000 light years across. And the universe contains an estimated 100 to 200 billion galaxies, each of which contains

Landmarks for Chapter 22

1900 · 1920 · 1940 · 1960 · 1980 · 2000 · 2020

THE DEVELOPED INDUSTRIAL WORLD / GLOBAL NORTH

1882–1920 Electric grids developed in industrial countries

1908 Mass production of automobiles begins

1940s Earliest digital computers

1960 Birth control pill approved in U.S.

1960s Second-wave feminism begins

1991 Earliest web browser released

1999 Seattle protests against the WTO

2008 Housing bubble collapse in U.S.

2020 Britain exits EU

2017 U.S. withdraws from Trans-Pacific Partnership

THE DEVELOPING WORLD / GLOBAL SOUTH

1920–1940 Land reform in Mexico

1923–1938 Women's emancipation in Turkey

1970s Developing countries demand "new international economic order"

1978–2013 Rapid economic growth in China

1979 Islamic revolution in Iran

1980–2014 China's one-child family policy

2004 Morocco's Family Law Code advances women's rights

THE WHOLE WORLD

1929–1940 The Great Depression

1930s–1960s Green Revolution technologies developed and applied

1945–1970 Postwar economic boom

1975 United Nations: International Women's Year

2006 UN Convention on the Elimination of All Forms of Discrimination against Women ratified by 183 nations hundreds of millions or even billions of stars. Such numbers are merely educated guesses by scientists, but at this level they almost exceed our ability to feel them as meaningful. Our universe is incomprehensibly large.

Furthermore, the world we know through modern science is one of constant flux or change. The current "big bang" theory imagines a singular beginning of things, in an explosion of unimaginable power and temperature, perhaps only the most recent of many "big bangs" and many universes. In this understanding of the universe, everything changes, constantly. Even stars are born, generate in their fusion furnaces the elements known to students of chemistry, and eventually use up their fuel and die. For billions of years, the universe itself has been expanding very rapidly and, according to some, at accelerating rates. As one science writer put it: "The eternal heavens aren't. We are the first generation to live in a dynamic universe."[4] We have discovered, in short, that the cosmos has a history.

So too does the earth, which initially took shape some 4.5 billion years ago, along with its neighboring planets. One aspect of that history that emerged only in the 1960s and 1970s is "plate tectonics," which explains how the continents have migrated across the surface of the earth for at least 2.5 billion years, how mountain chains arose, and how earthquakes function. Climate has also changed, as ice ages with extensive glaciation have alternated with warmer periods. The most significant change on earth was the emergence of life from the chemical soup of the early planet about 3.5 billion years ago. And life also changed or evolved, particularly in the past 600 million years, when larger multi-celled plants and animals became abundant. New species arose, changed, and died out in periodic "extinction events." At the tail end of this enormous unfolding of cosmic and planetary evolution, just several hundred thousand years ago, human life emerged. In this new picture of the world, everything changes.

But if everything changes, it seems to do so in the direction of greater complexity, from simple hydrogen and helium atoms to the development of stars to life on earth embodied in cells. "Even the simplest cell is far more complex than any inanimate object," wrote a leading astrophysicist.[5] Each cell membrane encloses many millions of molecules that are constantly interacting with one another. And then cells began to coordinate and work together, sharing information, giving rise to trees, whales, and people. "The human brain," writes the American physicist Michio Kaku, "has 100 billion neurons [nerve cells], each neuron connected to 10,000 other neurons. Sitting on your shoulders is the most complicated object in the known universe."[6]

In addition to this picture of increasing complexity, recent science has disclosed the connectivity of things. Everything, it seems, is connected to everything else; nothing can be understood by itself. Matter and energy, Einstein declared, are two manifestations of the same thing. Atoms, molecules, cells, and organs are entangled in vast networks of relationships in our bodies. Plants, animals, and the environment are linked in ecologies of interaction. And humankind is intimately connected to both cosmic and planetary history.

This novel understanding of the world has invited a reconsideration of old questions in a new context with profound cultural implications. Does the world exhibit purpose, direction, coherence, or unity? What is the significance of human consciousness in the face of cosmic vastness? Has science undermined religion or enhanced our experience of wonder, awe, and mystery? About such cultural matters, there is endless debate. What is not controversial, however, is the enormous role that science has played in seeding the massive acceleration of technological innovation that has so decisively shaped the history of the past century.

Fossil Fuel Breakthroughs

Access to the stored energy of fossil fuels—coal, oil, and natural gas—has provided the foundation of the modern world economy, beginning with the Industrial Revolution in the nineteenth century. But it was the twentieth century that became the **age of fossil fuels** as their consumption skyrocketed (see Figure 22.1). Coal production increased by some 700 percent during that century, and in its second half oil overtook coal as the dominant source of energy. Natural gas became a growing element in the energy equation in the latter decades of the century. In 2019 fossil fuels provided about 84 percent of the energy that powered the world economy.

Technological innovations allowed humankind to turn the potential energy of fossil fuels into useful energy. One such innovation involved the generation of electricity, the basic principles of which were discovered in the early nineteenth century in Great Britain. The subsequent development of coal-, oil-, or gas-fired power stations, alternating current, transformers, and batteries permitted electricity to be generated on a commercial scale, moved across great distances, and stored.

This more widespread availability of electricity was the product of electric grids, which generated power and transmitted it widely to homes and businesses. The development of such grids began in the late nineteenth century in the already industrialized countries, but it spread rapidly in capitalist, communist, colonial, and developing countries alike. By 2016, some 87 percent of the world's population had access to electricity, though not always reliably. Europe, Russia, North America, and Japan achieved

CORE IDEA

■ Identifying Change
What was new about energy production in the twentieth century?

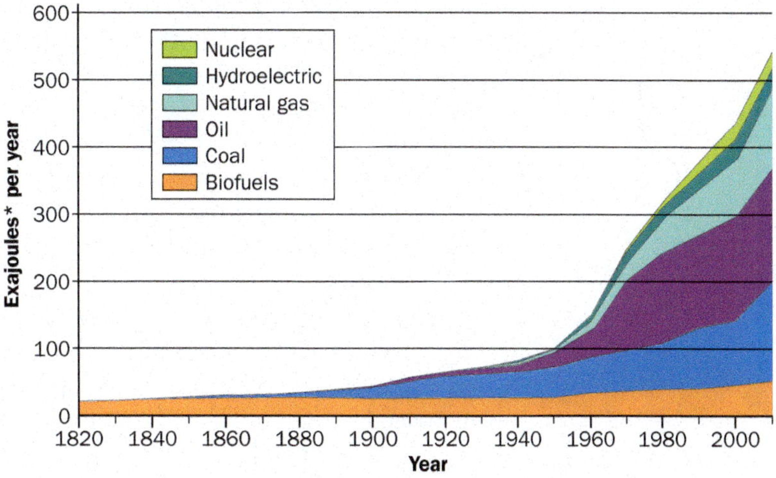

*An exajoule is a large-scale unit of energy.

Figure 22.1 Sources of World Energy Consumption, 1820–2010
It was access to fossil fuels that allowed world energy production to skyrocket during the twentieth century. (Data from Gail Tverberg, OurFiniteWorld.com, from https://ourfiniteworld.com/2012/03/12/world-energy-consumption-since-1820-in-charts)

100 percent electrification first, but China, North Africa, Latin America, and parts of India achieved or approached that figure in the early twenty-first century.[7] By any historical standard, global electrification represents a very rapid transition to new ways of living.

Electrification lit up the world, especially at night, and much more cheaply than oil or gas lighting, allowing students to study, people to play, and employees to work around the clock. Electric motors powered all manner of industrial machinery far more productively than steam engines, and they made possible a vast array of consumer goods. Electrification became a crucial component of all economic development planning.

CORE IDEA

Assessing Change
How did electricity and the internal combustion engine transform human life during the past century?

Another breakthrough in the generation of useful energy via fossil fuels was the gasoline- or oil-driven internal combustion engine, pioneered in the late nineteenth century in Western Europe and applied widely throughout the world in the twentieth century. That innovation created a huge new industry that became central to modern economic life; it led to a sharp decline in the use of horses; it enabled the far more rapid and efficient movement of goods and people, transforming the patterns of daily life for much of humankind; and it has been a potent source of the greenhouse gases that have driven climate change. Together, electricity and the internal combustion engine have enormously increased the energy available to humankind, even as access to that energy has favored the most highly industrialized economies (see Map 22.1).

Transportation Breakthroughs

Nowhere did this new availability of energy register more dramatically than in the technology of transportation, which built upon the revolutionary development of railroads and steamships in the nineteenth century. To those innovations, the twentieth century added cars, buses, and trucks; containerized shipping and supertankers; and airplanes and air freight. This was the technological infrastructure that has made possible the surging movement of goods and people in the globalized world of recent times. By the early twenty-first century, the planet was densely crisscrossed on land by roads, railways, and pipelines, on the seas by shipping routes, and in the air by flight patterns.

Among these transportation technologies, none achieved a greater social and cultural impact than the automobile. In 1900, there were only about 10,000 cars in the global inventory, all of them expensive luxury items for the rich and most of them driven by steam or electric power. But the growing availability of cheap gasoline established the internal combustion engine as the means of propulsion for cars for the next century. It was Henry Ford's Model T, initially built in 1908, that launched the democratization of the automobile and made the United States the first country to market cars for the masses, followed by European countries and Japan after World War II. By 2010, the world had over 1 billion cars, with developing countries contributing substantially to that number. China and India alone

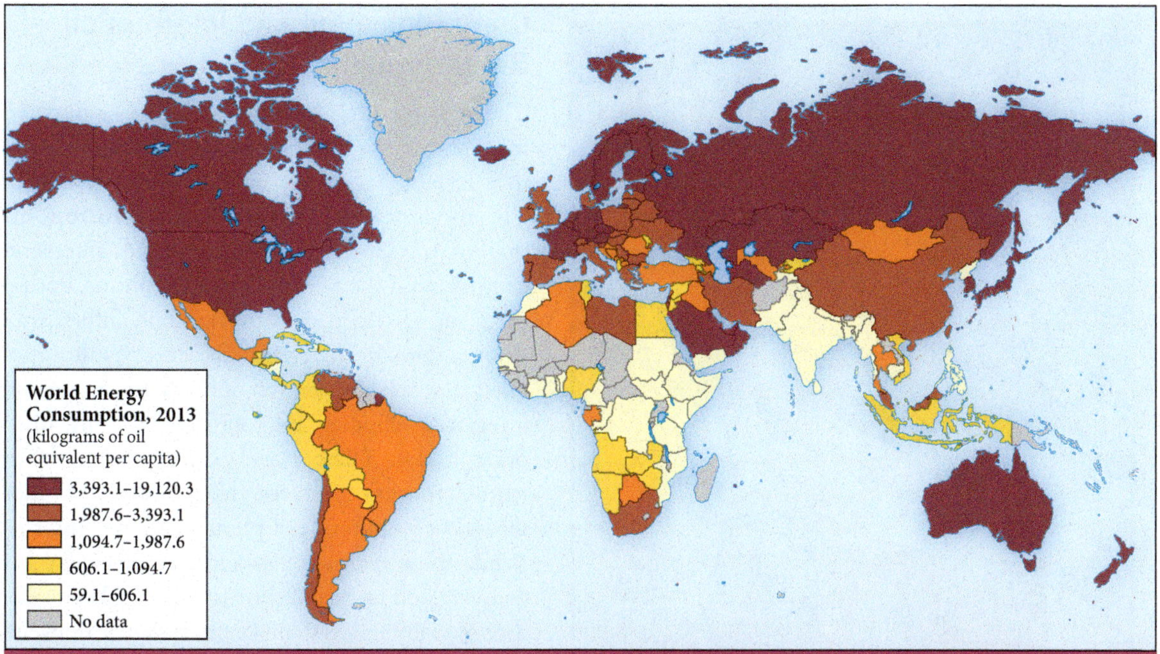

MAPPING HISTORY

Map 22.1 World Energy Consumption per Capita, 2013
While global energy production soared during the past century, access to that energy remained highly uneven in the early twenty-first century when measured on a per person basis. (Data from World Bank)

READING THE MAP Which continents used the least amount of energy per capita in 2013? Was energy consumption relatively uniform on these continents, or were there significant variations between countries in these lower-use regions?

MAKING CONNECTIONS Compare this map with Map 20.1: The World in 1914. What might you infer about the legacy of colonialism by comparing relative energy consumption in 2013 in former imperial countries and their colonies?

produced 28 percent of the world's cars in that year. The age of the automobile had become a global phenomenon.

Cars have shaped modern society and culture in many ways. Ownership of a car conveyed a sense of freedom, individuality, personal empowerment, and status. Like electrification, the car linked remote rural areas more firmly into national life. A farmwife in Georgia wrote to Henry Ford in 1918 about the Model T: "Your car lifted us out of the mud. It brought joy into our lives."[8] In urban areas, car ownership facilitated the growth of burgeoning suburbs. In doing so, it also created pervasive traffic jams and contributed much to air pollution, greenhouse gas emissions, and traffic fatalities. Like most technologies, the car conveyed both great benefits and heavy costs, but the world's love affair with the automobile has shown few signs of waning.

The Automobile In the early twentieth century, the automobile represented unparalleled freedom of movement. The early driver was a mounted knight, observed the British intellectual Kenneth Boulding, while pedestrians were mere peasants. This French poster dating from around 1920 catches something of the car's mystique by depicting an automobile hurtling across the landscape guided by the ancient Greek messenger god Mercury wearing his winged helmet and sandals. (Popperfoto/Getty Images)

Communication and Information Breakthroughs

The past century has also witnessed a flurry of innovations in communication and information that have transformed life for almost everyone. The modern **communication revolution**, like that of transportation, began in the nineteenth century with the telegraph and telephone, both of them using electricity to transmit information along a wire. In the twentieth century, innovation piled on innovation: vacuum tubes, transistors, integrated circuits, microprocessors, and fiber-optic cables. These novel technologies enabled radios, motion pictures, televisions, and most recently computers, cell phones, and the Internet. While these technologies and products were initially created in the West or Japan, they have taken root globally in less than a century, albeit unevenly. Radios have spread most widely, with over 75 percent of households in developing countries having access to a radio in 2012. TV coverage is more variable but surprisingly widespread. In much of Latin America, North Africa, the Middle East, and East Asia, 90 percent or more of households had a TV in the early twenty-first century. Internet access has soared globally since the introduction of web browsers in 1991, connecting about 59 percent of the world's population by 2020. The availability of cell phones has also spread very rapidly since the first mobile call in 1973 and the first smart phone in 1992. In much of Africa, for example, close to 80 percent of adults had access to a cell phone in 2017, allowing much of the continent to avoid installing more expensive land lines.

These communication technologies have reshaped human life across the planet and have spawned numerous debates about their consequences. Radio enabled even remote villagers to become aware of national and international events, even as it empowered authoritarian and democratic governments alike. Hitler's minister of propaganda, Joseph Goebbels, claimed in 1933 that "it would not have been possible for us [Nazis] to take power or to use it in the ways we have without the radio."[9] And Franklin Roosevelt used his radio "fireside chats" to reassure the American public during the Depression and World War II. But radio also challenged governments that sought to restrict their people's access to information. The availability of short-wave radio broadcasts from Europe and the United States eroded the capacity of the Soviet regime to monopolize the mass media and contributed to the collapse of Communist Party rule in the Soviet Union. Television and the movies have generated a particularly sharp debate. Supporters have praised their ability to inform, educate, and entertain, but critics fear that American or Western domination of the media might erode local or national cultures, regret the generally low cultural level of TV programming, lament the effects of TV violence on children, and argue about the portrayal of women, minorities, Muslims, and others.

■ Assessing Cause and Effect What impact has modern communication technology had on the world in the past century?

The impact of personal computers and their numerous uses (the Internet, e-mail, social media, cell phones) has been pervasive and contested ever since they began to be widely available, at least in the West, during the 1980s. They made possible virtually unlimited access to information, enabling people the world over to participate creatively in this technological revolution. Education in many parts of the world has been transformed as online courses, "smart" classrooms, and digital books have proliferated, while computer science has become a major new field of study. Computer applications have become central to almost every aspect of business and economic life, spawning entirely new industries and forms of commerce. In many African countries, mobile banking has allowed millions to access financial services, with over two-thirds of Kenyans using their cell phones for this purpose in 2018. Online commerce has grown rapidly in the twenty-first century. China has become the world's largest e-commerce country, with its Internet giant, the Alibaba Group, replacing Walmart as the world's leading retailer in 2014.

Computer applications have also transformed personal life as online dating has spread to urban areas all around the world. Internet pornography has also become pervasive, though it is legally banned in China, India, the Islamic world, and elsewhere. Facebook, launched in 2004, had connected some 2.6 billion active users, about a third of the world's population, to an array of "friends" by 2020. Recreation also has been transformed as computer-based gaming has spread globally, with China emerging as the largest video game market in the world.

But these information technologies have generated anxieties

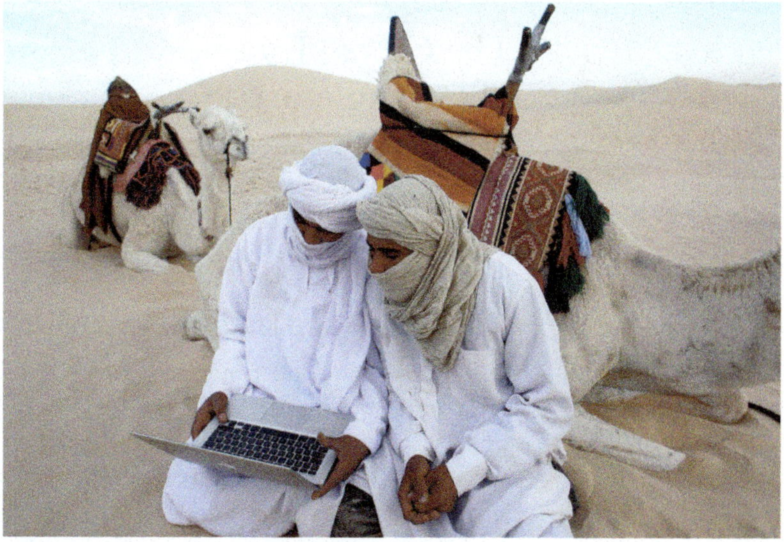

Computers and Camels The global penetration of computer technology is illustrated in this 2012 image of two Tunisian Bedouins consulting their laptop in the Sahara Desert. (akg-images/UIG/Godong)

and criticism. Individuals fear being bullied by peers, monitored and controlled by governments, and manipulated by corporations able to track their buying preferences. Debate has arisen as to whether the Internet facilitates or undermines personal relationships. Hacking of government records and corporate secrets has raised concerns about cyber-warfare, while the entire complex system remains vulnerable to outages, sabotage, and natural disaster. Democratic countries have increasingly worried about cyber interference in their elections.

Military Weapons Breakthroughs

A final example of accelerated innovation lies in technologies of destruction. The late nineteenth-century development of high-power explosives such as dynamite as well as machine guns found application in World War I, along with other new technologies such as submarines, tanks, poison gas, radio, and military aircraft. World War II refined and enhanced these technologies, while adding radar, computers, jet engines, battle tanks, fighter aircraft, aircraft carriers, and atomic bombs to the mix. The cold war generated ever more sophisticated nuclear weapons, from enormous hydrogen bombs to smaller tactical nuclear weapons. New means of delivering them with almost pinpoint accuracy also emerged, using ballistic missiles launched from airplanes, land-based silos, or submarines. At the height of the cold war and ever since, we have been able to imagine, realistically, a nuclear war that would result in instant death for tens of millions of people, the collapse of modern civilization, and perhaps the extinction of the human species. Military technologies, of course, have also had numerous civilian spin-offs, including radar, nuclear power plants, the Internet, space exploration, and communication satellites.

The Global Economy: The Acceleration of Entanglement

Accelerating technological innovation decisively shaped the world economy of the past century, enabling what we now refer to as **economic globalization**, particularly during the seven decades following World War II. A central element of that process has been the spread of industrialization among the peoples of the Global South.

Industrial Globalization: Development in the Global South

As decolonization, independence, and revolution rolled over much of Africa, Asia, and Latin America, economic development and industrialization became everywhere a central priority. It was an essential promise of all revolutions and independence struggles, and it was increasingly the standard by which people measured and granted legitimacy to their governments.

Achieving economic development, however, was no easy or automatic task for societies sharply divided by class, religion, ethnic group, and gender and facing explosive population growth. In many places, colonial rule had provided only the most slender foundations for modern development, as new nations often came to independence with low rates of literacy, few people with managerial experience, a weak private economy, and little industrial infrastructure. Furthermore, the entire effort occurred in a world split by rival superpowers and economically dominated by the powerful capitalist economies of the West.

Noticing Differences
How has global industrial development varied across the world during the past century?

Beyond these difficulties lay the vexing question of what strategies to pursue. Should state authorities take the lead, or was it wiser to rely on private enterprise and the market? Should industrial production be aimed at the domestic market in an "import substitution" approach, or was it more effective to specialize in particular products, such as cars, clothing, or electronics, for an export market?

For developing countries, it was an experimental process, and the outcomes varied considerably. (See Snapshot, page 986.) In general, East Asian countries that produced products primarily for export have had the strongest record of economic growth. South Korea, Taiwan, Singapore, and Hong Kong were dubbed **Asian Tigers** or newly industrialized countries. Following the death of Mao Zedong in 1976, China soon became a spectacular economic success story, boasting the most rapid economic growth in the world by the end of the twentieth century while replacing Japan as the world's second-largest economy and edging up on the United States. In the 1990s, Asia's other giant, India, opened itself more fully to the world market and launched rapid economic growth with a powerful high-tech sector and major steel, chemical, automotive, and pharmaceutical industries. Oil-producing countries reaped a bonanza when they were able to demand much higher prices for that essential commodity in the 1970s and after. By 2016, Mexico, Turkey, Malaysia, Thailand, Vietnam, India, and Indonesia numbered in the top twenty of the most competitive manufacturing countries, with China ranking number one. Limited principally to Europe, North America, and Japan in the nineteenth century, industrialization and modern economic growth had become a global phenomenon by the early twenty-first century. It was also an uneven process, as much of Africa and various other countries (such as Afghanistan, Myanmar, Bangladesh, and Haiti) lagged behind.

Economic Globalization: Deepening Connections

Accompanying the worldwide spread of modern development and industrial growth was a tightening network of global economic relationships that cut across the world's separate countries and regions, binding them together more closely, but also more contentiously, during the second half of the twentieth century. It signaled a renewal and a great acceleration of earlier trends that had linked the economies of the world.

The capitalist victors in World War II, led by the United States, were determined to avoid any return to the kind of economic contraction and nationalist excesses associated with World War I and the Great Depression. At a conference in Bretton Woods, New Hampshire, in 1944, they forged a set of agreements and institutions (the World Bank and the International Monetary Fund [IMF]) that laid the foundation for postwar globalization. This **Bretton Woods system** negotiated the rules for commercial

Containerized Shipping The growth of global trade has been facilitated by containerized shipping, a highly mechanized process of moving goods that requires far fewer workers and has substantially reduced transportation costs. This photograph illustrates that process as it occurred in the Chinese port of Qingdao in mid-2017. (STR/Getty Images)

and financial dealings among the major capitalist countries, while promoting relatively free trade, stable currency values linked to the U.S. dollar, and high levels of capital investment.

By the 1970s, leading figures in capitalist countries such as the United States and Great Britain, as well as in major international lending agencies such as the World Bank, increasingly viewed the entire world as a single market. This approach to the world economy, widely known as neoliberalism, favored the reduction of tariffs, the free global movement of capital, a mobile and temporary workforce, the privatization of many state-run enterprises, the curtailing of government efforts to regulate the economy, and both tax and spending cuts. In this view, the market, operating both globally and within nations, was the most effective means of generating the holy grail of economic growth. As communism collapsed by the end of the twentieth century, "capitalism was global and the globe was capitalist."[10]

CORE IDEA

Assessing Cause and Effect

In what ways have global economic linkages deepened during the past century, and with what impact?

Such policies, together with major changes in transportation and communication technology, accompanied a dramatic quickening of global economic transactions after World War II, expressed in the accelerating circulation of both goods and capital. World trade, for example, skyrocketed from a value of some $57 billion in 1947 to about $18.3 trillion in 2012. For those with enough money, it meant access to the goods of the world. It also meant employment. In the United States in 2008, exports supported some 10 million jobs and represented about 13 percent of the country's gross domestic product (GDP). Many developing countries, however, were far more dependent on exports, usually raw materials and agricultural products. Ghana, for example, relied on exports for 44 percent of its GDP in 2014, mostly gold, cocoa beans, and timber products. Cocoa alone supported some 700,000 farming families. Mounting trade entangled the peoples of the world to an unprecedented degree.

Economic entanglement was financial as well as commercial. "Foreign direct investment," whereby a firm in, say, the United States opens a factory in China or Mexico, exploded after 1960 as companies in rich countries sought to take advantage of cheap labor, tax breaks, and looser environmental regulations in developing countries. Money also surged around the planet as investors and financiers annually spent trillions of dollars purchasing foreign currencies or stocks that were likely to increase in value and often selling them quickly thereafter, with unsettling consequences. The personal funds of individuals likewise achieved a new mobility as international credit cards took hold almost everywhere.

Central to the acceleration of economic globalization have been huge global businesses known as **transnational corporations** (TNCs), which produce goods or deliver services simultaneously in many countries. Toyota, the world's largest automaker in 2016, sold cars around the world and had manufacturing facilities in some twenty-eight countries on five continents. Burgeoning in number since the 1960s, TNCs such as Royal Dutch Shell, Sony, and General Motors often were so enormous and had such economic clout that their assets and power dwarfed those of many countries. By 2000, fifty-one of the world's hundred largest economic units were in fact TNCs, not countries. In the permissive economic climate of recent decades, such firms have been able to move their facilities quickly from place to place in search of the lowest labor costs or the least restrictive environmental regulations. During one five-year period, for example, Nike closed twenty factories and opened thirty-five others, often thousands of miles apart.

Growth, Instability, and Inequality

The impact of these tightening economic linkages has prompted enormous debate and controversy. (See Controversies: Debating Globalization, page 984.) Amid the swirl of contending opinion, one thing seemed reasonably clear: economic globalization accompanied, and arguably helped generate, the most remarkable spurt of economic growth in world history. On a global level, total world output grew from a value of $7 trillion in 1950 to $73 trillion in 2009 and on a per capita basis from $2,652 to $10,728.[11] While world population quadrupled during the twentieth century, the output of the world economy grew by a factor of 14 and industrial output by a factor of 40. This represents an immense, rapid, and unprecedented creation of wealth with a demonstrable impact on human welfare. Everywhere people lived longer. Global average life expectancy has more than doubled since 1900, to 73.2 years in 2020. Everywhere, far fewer children died before the age of five: in 1960 the global average was 18.2 percent; in 2018, 3.8 percent. And everywhere more people were literate. Some 80 percent of adults could read and write at some level by 2000, while only 21 percent could do so in 1900. The UN Human Development Report in 1997 concluded that "in the past 50 years, poverty has fallen more than in the previous 500."

Far more problematic have been the instability of this emerging world economy and the distribution of the immense wealth it has generated. Amid overall economic growth, periodic crises and setbacks have shaped recent world history. Soaring oil prices in 1973–1974 resulted in several years of economic stagnation for many industrialized countries, great hardship for many developing countries, and an economic windfall for oil-producing countries. Inability to repay mounting debts triggered a major financial crisis in Latin America during the 1980s and resulted in a "lost decade" in terms of economic development. Another financial crisis in Asia during the late

CONTROVERSIES

Debating Globalization

By the early 1990s, "globalization" had become a buzzword among scholars, journalists, and ordinary people alike because it succinctly captured something of the deeply connected and entangled world of the late twentieth century. The economists, sociologists, and political scientists who first embraced the term presented "globalization" as novel and unprecedented: the world was becoming "a single place," and human history was entering a wholly new era of global connectedness and global consciousness.

World historians, however, were not so sure about the novelty of "globalization." They had, after all, long traced patterns of interaction, communication, and exchange among distant regions and civilizations: the Silk Road commercial networks across Eurasia; the movement of technologies and disease; the transcontinental spread of Buddhism, Christianity, and Islam; the making of an Atlantic world linking Europe, Africa, and the Americas; and the globe-spanning empires of Europe. Did all of this count as "globalization," pushing its origins deep into the past?

Yet another controversy involved the "drivers" of globalization. For some, they were impersonal forces—"the inexorable integration of markets, nation-states, and technologies"—according to leading journalist Thomas Friedman. In such a view, no one was in control, and the process, once begun, was inevitable and unstoppable. Others believed that powerful economic elites and political leaders, acting from a free market ideology, deliberately shaped policies (such as low tariffs) and institutions (the World Trade Organization, for example) that opened the door to corporate globalization.

The economic outcomes of recent globalization have also generated much debate. Did globalization increase or reduce inequality? Answers depend very much on what is being measured. If the measure is income, most economists think that inequality on a global level has substantially increased. One study concluded that the per capita income gap between the United States and various regions of the Global South roughly tripled since 1960.[12] The rich were getter richer much faster than the poor were gaining income.

But if the measure of economic outcomes involves "quality of life indicators," the picture changes considerably. Average global life expectancy, for example, more than doubled since 1900, reaching 73.2 years in 2020. Thus many countries in the Global South now approach the 79-year life span of U.S. citizens: China, 76 years; Brazil, 74; India, 69. Even poorer countries have dramatically increased their life expectancies, with sub-Saharan African rates improving from 40 years in 1960 to 59 years in 2014.[13] Clearly, despite growing inequality in income, inequality in longevity has lessened. So which is the more important measure of inequality: income measured in dollars or life expectancy measured in years?

Yet another controversy involves the impact of globalization on nation-states. Many elements of the globalized world have arguably diminished the ability of nation-states to act freely in their own interests—agreements favoring free trade and the power of huge transnational corporations, for example. The more enthusiastic advocates of globalization have imagined a future in which the nation-state has vanished, or at least greatly weakened, in the face of global flows of people, capital, goods, services, and ideas.

Others, however, view such opinions as exaggerated. It was, after all, the decisions of some states that created a free trade international system after World War II, even as other states, especially in the communist bloc, refused to take part in it. And what states create they can also change. China joined the World Trade Organization in 2001 after decades of declining to take part in the global marketplace;

1990s resulted in the collapse of many businesses, widespread unemployment, and political upheaval in Indonesia and Thailand. And in 2008 an inflated housing market—or "bubble"—in the United States collapsed, triggering millions of home foreclosures, growing unemployment, the tightening of credit, and declining consumer spending. Soon this crisis rippled around the world. In Sierra Leone, some 90 percent of the country's diamond-mine workers lost their jobs. Impoverished Central American and Caribbean families, dependent on money sent home by family members working the United Kingdom decided in 2016 to leave the European Union; the Trump administration in the United States announced American withdrawal from the Trans-Pacific Partnership agreement in early 2017. Even developing countries have some leverage. Both Mexico and Cuba have nationalized American industries in their countries in the twentieth century. And the oil-producing states of the Middle East upended the global markets in the late 1970s when they dramatically raised the price of oil. All of this testifies to the continuing power of state action to shape the world economy.

Cultural globalization too prompted debate and controversy. Has the world become more culturally homogeneous in the global age? Many feared that the answer was "yes" as "cultural imperialism" in the shape of westernization or Americanization swept the planet, displacing many established cultural patterns and ways of living. The prevalence of English and modern science; the popularity of McDonald's, blue jeans, Barbie dolls, and American films; shopping malls and Western-style consumerism across the world; cell phones and the Internet—all of this and much more suggested the emergence of a "global culture."

But perhaps globalization produces or reinforces cultural difference as well as commonality. The rise of Islamic fundamentalism represented strong resistance to the intrusion of Western secular culture. French efforts to prevent the importation of too many American films or TV programs and to prohibit the wearing of headscarves by Muslim women likewise reflected a desire to preserve major elements of French national culture in an age of globalization. A proliferation of ethnic nationalist movements articulated demands to ensure the integrity of particular and local cultures. Furthermore, a phenomenon known as "glocalization" refers to the process by which foreign products or practices are adapted to local cultural patterns. Yoga in the West often became a form of exercise or relaxation, losing much of its original spiritual significance, while McDonald's restaurants in India and China now include various rice-based menu offerings.

Globalization is commonly regarded as a still-unfolding process leading to an uncertain destination, often called "globality" or "entanglement on a global scale." Two prominent historians have recently contested this understanding, arguing that "globality" has long been a "done deal," a condition already achieved. The question then is not whether to participate in this globalized world, but rather "how to change in order to keep pace with, hold out against, or adapt to a world of continuous and inescapable interactivity."[14]

And yet, is it possible to imagine global connections unraveling? Is globalization really a "done deal"? Various events of the early twenty-first century have caused many to wonder: the global recession of 2008; the sharp economic contraction during the COVID-19 pandemic of 2020; the exit of Great Britain from the European Union; the election of Donald Trump promising that "Americanism not globalism will be our credo"; the reaction against immigration in the United States and Western Europe; and the rise of assertive nationalist movements in much of Europe, Turkey, Iran, China, India, and elsewhere. Does this mean that globalization is in retreat? The debate continues, as it does for almost everything related to globalization.

QUESTIONS TO CONSIDER

1. How might you describe in your own words the major debates and controversies that are associated with the concept of globalization? Can you think of other questions that arise from the use of this term?
2. How do you think the authors of this book have answered those questions in Chapter 22? Or have they avoided doing so?

abroad, suffered further as those remittances dropped sharply. Contracting economies contributed to debt crises in Greece, Italy, and Spain and threatened to unravel European economic integration. Whatever the overall benefits of globalization, economic stability and steady progress were not among them.

Nor did globalization resolve the problem of inequality. (See Snapshot, page 986.) Despite substantial gains in life expectancy, infant mortality, literacy, and the reduction of poverty, economic inequality on a global level has been stubbornly

SNAPSHOT Global Development and Inequality, 2011

This table shows thirteen commonly used indicators of "development" and their variations in 2011 across four major groups of countries defined by average level of per capita income. In which areas has the Global South most nearly caught up with the Global North?

Gross National Income per Capita with Sample Countries	Low Income: $995 or Less (Congo, Kenya, Ethiopia, Afghanistan, Myanmar)	Lower Middle Income: $996–$3,945 (India, China, Egypt, Algeria, Indonesia, Nigeria)	Upper Middle Income: $3,946–$12,195 (Mexico, Brazil, Turkey, Russia, Iran)	Upper Income: $12,196 or More (USA, Western Europe, Japan, South Korea, Australia)
Life expectancy: M/F in years	58/60	66/70	68/75	77/83
Deaths under age 5 per 1,000 live births	120	60	24	7
Deaths from infectious disease: %	36	14	11	7
Access to toilets: %	35	50	84	99
Years of education	7.9	10.3	13.8	14.5
Literacy rate: %	66	80	93	99
Population growth: % annual	2.27	1.27	.96	.39
Urban population: %	27	41	74	78
Cell phones per 100 people	22	47	92	106
Internet users per 100 people	2.3	13.7	29.9	68.3
Personal computers per 100 people	1.2	4.3	11.9	60.4
Cars per 1,000 people	5.8	20.3	125.2	435.1
Carbon dioxide emissions: metric tons per capita	1	3	5	13

Source: Data from "Map Supplement," *National Geographic* (Washington, DC: National Geographic Society, March 2011).

persistent and by some measures growing. In 1870 the average per capita income in the world's ten richest countries was six times that of the ten poorest countries. By 2002 that ratio was 42 to 1.[15] That gap has been evident, often tragically, in great disparities in incomes, medical care, availability of clean drinking water, educational and employment opportunities, access to the Internet, and dozens of other ways. It has shaped the life chances of practically everyone. Even among developing countries, great inequalities were apparent. The oil-rich economies of the Middle East had little in common with the banana-producing countries of Central America. The rapidly industrializing states of China, India, and South Korea had quite different economic agendas than impoverished African countries.

Economic globalization has contributed to inequalities not only among countries and regions, but also within individual nations, rich and poor alike. In the United States, for example, income inequality has sharply increased since the late 1970s. The American economy shed millions of manufacturing jobs, with some companies moving their operations to Asia or Latin America, where labor costs were lower. More important, however, was automation. The U.S. steel industry, for example, lost 75 percent of its workforce between 1962 and 2005, while producing roughly the same amount of steel. This left many American workers in the lurch, forcing them to work in the low-wage service sector, even as other Americans were growing prosperous in emerging high-tech industries. Globalization divided Mexico as well. The northern part of the country, with close business and manufacturing ties to the United States, grew much more prosperous than the south, which was a largely rural agricultural area and had a far more slowly growing economy. China's rapid economic growth likewise fostered mounting inequality between its rural households and those in its burgeoning cities, where income by 2000 was three times that of the countryside. Economic globalization may have brought people together as never before, but it has also divided them sharply.

Pushback: Resistance to Economic Globalization

Assessing Conflict
What criticisms of economic globalization have emerged, and from what sources did they derive?

Those who felt unfairly treated, left behind, or overwhelmed by a tsunami of change increasingly pushed back. One expression of this resistance derived from the Global South. As the East/West division of capitalism and communism faded, differences between the rich nations of the Global North and the developing countries of the Global South assumed greater prominence in world affairs. Highly contentious issues have included the rules for world trade, availability of and terms for foreign aid, representation in international economic organizations, the mounting problem of indebtedness, and environmental and labor standards. In the 1970s, for example, a large group of developing countries joined together to demand a "new international economic order" that was more favorable to the poor countries, though with little success. Developing countries have often contested protectionist restrictions on their agricultural exports imposed by the rich countries seeking to safeguard their own politically powerful farmers.

In the 1990s a growing popular movement, featuring a highly critical posture toward globalization, emerged as an international coalition of political activists, concerned scholars and students, trade unions, women's and religious organizations, environmental groups, and others, hailing from rich and poor countries alike. Though reflecting a variety of viewpoints, that opposition largely agreed that market-driven corporate globalization had lowered labor standards, fostered ecological degradation, prevented poor countries from protecting themselves against financial speculators, ignored local cultures, disregarded human rights, and enhanced global inequality, while favoring the interests of large corporations and rich countries.

This movement appeared dramatically on the world's radar screen in 1999 in Seattle at a meeting of the **World Trade Organization (WTO)**. An international

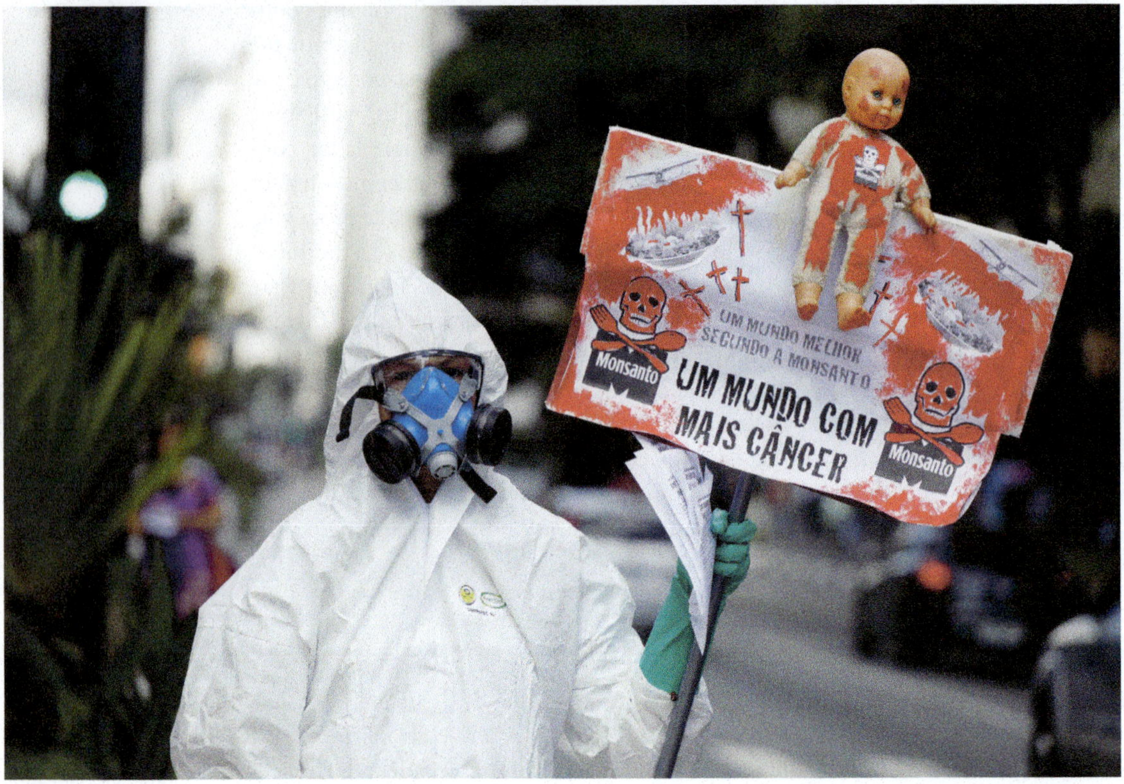

Anti-Globalization Protest A demonstrator in São Paulo, Brazil, in 2013, part of a worldwide protest against the biotech giant Monsanto, holds a sign reading: "A better world according to Monsanto is a world with more cancer." (Nelson Antoine/AP Images)

body now representing 164 nations and charged with negotiating the rules for global commerce and promoting free trade, the WTO had increasingly become a major target of globalization critics. "The central idea of the WTO," argued one such critic, "is that *free trade*—actually the values and interests of global corporations—should supersede all other values."[16] Tens of thousands of protesters from all over the world descended on Seattle in what became a violent, chaotic, and much-publicized protest. Such protests stimulated the creation in 2001 of the World Social Forum, an annual gathering of alternative globalization activists to coordinate strategy, exchange ideas, and share experiences, under the slogan "Another world is possible."

Local activists in various places likewise resisted the impact of globalization. In 1994 in southern Mexico, peasant resentment boiled over against the Mexican government and its privatizing of communally held land, which was related to the country's 1984 entry into the **North American Free Trade Agreement (NAFTA)**. The leader of this peasant upheaval referred to globalization as a "process to eliminate that multitude of people who are not useful to the powerful." Likewise in southern India, activist farmers during the late 1990s organized protests against the opening of

Kentucky Fried Chicken outlets as well as against the giant American chemical corporation Monsanto, uprooting and burning fields where Monsanto grew genetically modified cotton.

Opposition to globalization also emerged from more conservative circles, especially after the sharp economic downturn beginning in 2008. Britain's vote in 2016 to leave the European Union clearly represented a backlash against globalization, even as movements hostile to a more united Europe gained support in many countries. So too did the U.S. election of 2016, in which all of the candidates expressed reservations about international trade agreements as threatening American jobs. The most vociferous voice was that of the winner, Donald Trump, who withdrew the United States from the Trans-Pacific Partnership trade agreement and renegotiated NAFTA, replacing it with the United States–Mexico–Canada Agreement in 2020. Elsewhere as well—in Turkey, Russia, China, and India, for example—political leaders increasingly appealed to national pride and cultural purity. Observers wondered if this represented a rejection of earlier assumptions that international cooperation in reducing trade barriers fostered peace and prosperity for all concerned.

Producing and Consuming: The Shapes of Modern Societies

Technological innovation and economic globalization during the past century have dramatically reshaped human societies around the world. Further contributing to this reshaping of social structures have been the actions of state authorities through their laws, regulations, and policies. Broad global patterns such as the declining role of peasant farmers and the growing role of middle-class professionals found expression in many variations across the multiple divides of the modern world.

Life on the Land: The Decline of the Peasantry

A little over 20 percent of the world's population farmed full time in 2000, a dramatic drop from 66 percent in 1950 and around 80 percent in many preindustrial agricultural societies. One historian has described this development as "the death of the peasantry," which has allowed "an absurdly tiny percentage" of the population "to flood . . . the world with untold quantities of food."[17]

CORE IDEA

Identifying Change
What global social changes have accompanied economic globalization? How have those changes affected levels of social inequality?

A major factor in this decline was mechanization, as machinery such as tractors and combines made farmers more productive, earlier in North America and Australia and later elsewhere in the world. Furthermore, many farmers in the Global North and some regions of the Global South (India, Argentina, and Brazil) also embraced Green Revolution innovations, including chemical fertilizers and new types of seed, that were initially developed between the 1930s and the late 1960s. By the 1970s a corn farmer in the United States was between 100 and 1,000 times more productive than his nineteenth-century counterpart, but costs were also much higher as expenditures on machinery, fertilizer, and diesel fuel soared. Describing the impact of technology on his work, Ken Grimsdell, whose company raised crops in the Midlands of England, noted in 2015: "A tractor can be controlled by satellite, drones can fly over a crop, record pictures and send them back to the office. The technology has made for better farming."[18] It also made for fewer farmers.

Many of the most mechanized and efficient farms in the world remained dependent on seasonal labor at crucial moments in the agricultural year. The work of migrant laborers, often organized into teams that moved from place to place, was intense, repetitive, and sometimes dangerous, especially as the use of toxic pesticides increased with the Green Revolution. Migrant workers typically were outsiders in the communities where they worked and in the United States were often undocumented or possessed temporary work visas. Nevertheless, this difficult life attracted millions of Latin American and Caribbean migrants to the fields of the United States, as well as similar numbers of Eastern Europeans to the farms of Western Europe following the enlargement of the European Union in the early twenty-first century.

Ever cheaper transportation costs created an increasingly global market for food, forcing farmers, often on different continents, to compete with one another. Trade deals exposed small-scale farmers in the Global South to the mechanized and heavily subsidized farming industries of the Global North. In 1994, NAFTA allowed corn from the United States to flood the Mexican market, forcing 2 million small farmers in Mexico to abandon its cultivation. In 2006, Tirso Alvares Correa worried that no one would be left to work land that his family had tilled for generations. "Free trade has been a disaster for us. . . . Corn from abroad is taking a toll. . . . We can't sell our corn anymore."[19] Some displaced farmers found work on large estates geared toward raising crops like avocados for export. Many others immigrated to the United States, with some finding work on American farms.

While farmers as a percentage of the population declined dramatically in the second half of the twentieth century, nearly 27 percent of the world's population, about 2 billion people, still earned their living from the land in 2016, more than the total world population in 1850. Most remained small-scale or subsistence cultivators. In some regions, farming populations grew rapidly, paralleling the growth of population generally. Land reform movements in Mexico and elsewhere contributed to this trend by distributing small plots of land to farming families. Collectivization movements in the communist world also employed large numbers in agriculture as private ownership of land ended. Nonetheless, after millennia during which 80 percent or more of people toiled on the land, the past century has witnessed those who farm shrink to a distinct minority of humankind.

The Changing Lives of Industrial Workers

The opening decades of the twentieth century brought considerable changes to the lives of millions who labored in factories. American industry pioneered the moving production line and "scientific management" that broke down more complex activities into simple steps. While increasing productivity substantially, these changes fundamentally altered the pace and nature of factory work. More jobs became repetitive and boring. The moving assembly line removed nearly all control over the pace of work from those who performed it. Some employers, like the car manufacturer Henry Ford, offered better pay and somewhat shorter hours to his workers to entice them into his factories, while union movements and social reformers pressed for worker's rights, sometimes through strikes. Elements of these American innovations spread to factories in Europe, the Soviet Union, and to a lesser extent Japan by the 1930s.

In many heavily unionized industries, the two-day weekend became standard by the 1920s and along with higher wages created a growing culture of leisure and consumption, often called **consumerism**. "Industrial cities," wrote one scholar, "became places of leisure as well as labor."[20] Shopping at department stores and attending movies or sporting events emerged as popular pastimes among working-class families, who also increasingly purchased prepared foods rather than cooking. Fish and chips (French fries) became a particular favorite of the British working class, with over 30,000 shops across the country offering this new convenience food by the 1920s.

Plant closures during the Great Depression significantly disrupted the lives of factory workers, as did World War II through the rationing and physical destruction of wartime. But the shortage of wartime labor drew women into factories across the industrialized world in unprecedented numbers and also allowed them to fill positions traditionally reserved for men. After the war many women were forced to leave the factories altogether or at least abandon "male" jobs. In the 1950s and 1960s, stable and well-paid workforces often represented by strong unions typified the industrial sectors of Japan, the United States, and Western Europe. After decades of depression and wartime scarcity, industrial workers everywhere reacted to the good times by embracing consumerism. By 1970 nearly all urban households in Japan owned the "big three"—a television, washing machine, and refrigerator. Between 1945 and 1960 companies in the United States quadrupled their collective advertising expenditure, reflecting the buying power of the American worker. Europeans consumed more but also emphasized leisure, as one month of paid annual vacation became standard in many industries. In the communist world, large factory workforces enjoyed similar job security, even if their economies proved unable to produce the variety of consumer goods available to workers elsewhere.

Further changes awaited factory workers in the later twentieth century. Liberalization of global trade, automation and robots, relocation of factories to places with cheaper labor costs, and the rapid growth of manufacturing in the Global South—all of this led to the decline or "rusting out" of many well-established industrial centers in parts of Western Europe and the United States and the displacement of many less skilled workers. As the former Soviet Union and China opened up to global trade in the 1990s, many state-owned manufacturing enterprises collapsed or fell into decline, displacing many workers, even as a new factory working class formed in China's coastal regions, where foreign investors had created new industrial operations. Closure of factories around the world tore at the social fabric of communities and led many to seek better employment opportunities elsewhere. Speaking in 2015 about his two teenage daughters, Mark Semande, a former worker at the

Closed Factories and Displaced Industrial Workers As automation and outsourcing swept across the industrialized West, factories closed, employees lost their jobs, communities were disrupted, and protests ensued. Workers at a Goodyear tire plant in northern France responded to the company's plans to close the facility, eliminating some 1,000 jobs, by holding two managers hostage and setting fire to numerous tires in early 2014. (DENIS CHARLET/Getty Images)

closed Maytag appliance plant in Galesburg, Illinois, mused: "Maybe they could find jobs and live in the community but not if they want to do as well as [my wife and I]."[21] Nonetheless, in some heavily industrialized regions, new, more efficient automated manufacturing allowed factories to survive and compete in the global market, but with far fewer and more highly skilled workers.

Even as manufacturing declined in many of its traditional heartlands in the later twentieth century, it took root and thrived in new regions. Between 1980 and 2007 the global manufacturing workforce grew from 1.9 to 3.1 billion people, offering many new employment opportunities, especially in the developing world. Countries competed to attract manufacturers, luring them with weak labor laws, low wages, tax incentives, and special **export-processing zones (EPZs)** where international companies could operate with expedited building permits, exemptions from certain taxes and customs duties, and other benefits.

Many of the conditions for these workers remained much as they had been during the first Industrial Revolution. Women made up an important part of the global industrial workforce and typically earned less than men. At the turn of the twenty-first century, around 74 percent of the workers in the Philippine EPZs were women who earned on average 54 percent of what their male counterparts did. Also mirroring the first Industrial Revolution, workers frequently labored in dangerous conditions that resulted in tragedies like the collapse of the Rana Plaza garment factory in Bangladesh in April 2013, which killed 1,135 workers and injured a further 2,500. In some regions like South Africa during the apartheid era or China during the 1980s and 1990s, migrants from the countryside who worked in industrial zones commonly lacked official residency and work privileges, limiting their ability to oppose the demands of their employers and access services like education or health care. But as manufacturing became established in new regions, workers often voiced dissatisfaction and sought better pay and working conditions. In Brazil, South Africa, and South Korea, labor movements emerged within a generation of the auto industry establishing major production facilities.

The Service Sector and the Informal Economy

Beyond farm and factory, employment opportunities grew significantly in service industries, sales, and the knowledge economy, which included government, medicine, education, finance, communication, information technology, and media. Growth in these areas was driven in part by an emerging consumerism and increasing population and was encouraged by new communication and computation technologies, including the typewriter, telephone, and later the computer and the Internet. Some of these **service sector** enterprises employed highly educated, well-paid workers such as doctors, computer coders, and bankers, but many more were lower-skilled, lower-paid occupations such as cleaners, shopkeepers, taxi drivers, secretaries, and typists. Everywhere race and gender pay differentials existed, with jobs gendered female—manicurist, nurse, teacher—paying less than those gendered male—plumber, bank manager, engineer.

The last decades of the twentieth century witnessed a trend toward less stable employment in service industries and the knowledge economies of more developed regions as employers outsourced jobs to freelancers, independent contractors, contract workers, and temporary staffing agencies. Advances in telecommunications and the Internet allowed companies to relocate jobs in the service industry (call centers, data entry) and knowledge economy (computer coding, editing) to lower-wage countries. At the opening of the twenty-first century, zero-hour contracts, which required employees to be on call without any guarantee of work, grew more common in the retail sector, and new ride-sharing apps competed with taxi firms. In what has been described as the new "gig economy," jobs came with greater flexibility for workers but also less security, fewer fringe benefits, looser relationships with employers, and often longer workdays.

The **informal economy** (or "shadow" economy), which operated "off the books" and largely outside government regulation and taxation, grew rapidly as fewer employees worked in stable, permanent jobs. This growth occurred most notably in the Global South, where new immigrants to rapidly expanding cities often found employment as day laborers or small-scale traders and lived in crowded shantytowns, but it was also evident in the Global North. Greece's black market reached 20 to 25 percent of its total economy in 2017, and in the United States, an estimated $2 trillion of unreported income in 2012 suggested a substantial shadow economy. The expansion of such informal economies over the past several decades has led some scholars to conclude that the stable and well-defined workplaces in the mid-twentieth-century industrialized

North were an aberration rather than a new norm in the world of work.

Middle-Class Life in Nigeria One sign of an emerging middle class in the Global South was the proliferation of malls and huge retail outlets such as this Shoprite store, located in the new Delta Mall in Warri, Nigeria. Shoprite is Africa's largest food retailer, selling food, liquor, household goods, and small appliances. A recent customer commented: "A middle-class person can come into this mall and feel a sense of belonging."[22] (GLENNA GORDON/© The New York Times/Redux)

Global Middle Classes and Life at the Top

A prosperous middle class in the Global North was a defining feature of the twentieth century. By the 1950s factory workers, tradesmen, and increasing numbers of service, sales, clerical, and knowledge economy workers came to view themselves as "middle class," for they were earning stable wages that allowed them to live comfortably, own their homes, and secure access to health care, education, entertainment, and travel. In much of the Global South, "middle class" was defined differently—as those households earning significantly above the poverty line but less than the highest earners in their communities. In most developing countries, a large middle class of this kind only emerged at the opening of the twenty-first century. But by 2009, an estimated 1.8 billion people globally were "middle class."[23] The shifting of manufacturing and some service and knowledge economy employment to the Global South was an important driver in this remarkable growth.

However, at the opening of the twenty-first century, many in the global middle class felt that their position in society was insecure or under threat. In Europe, the United States, Japan, and other places in the industrial North, the middle class as a proportion of society has been stagnant or shrinking since the 1970s, and the living standards of many declined even as economic growth continued in these regions. As one Chicago steelworker whose plant shut down in the 1980s put it: "I'm working harder, making less money, got less of a future."[24] Less secure employment, the loss of manufacturing jobs, immigration, and the decline of labor unions have all taken their toll on the middle class, sparking populist political backlashes such as Britain's exit from the European Union in 2020 and the election of President Donald Trump in the United States in 2016. In the Global South as well, many in the middle class find their positions precarious. More than 60 percent of the middle class in Bolivia, Brazil, Chile, and Mexico work within the informal economy, often running their own very small businesses.

The last several decades also produced economic winners. Never before had the richest 1 percent controlled so much wealth as they did at the opening of the twenty-first century. In 2016 an OXFAM study concluded that the eight richest people in the world possessed roughly the same amount of wealth as the poorest 3.5 billion. The gap between the pay of top executives and employees at major firms has widened dramatically. One commentator in 2011 described it as "the winner-take-most economy," in which a small number of "superstar" performers enjoyed most of the newly generated wealth.[25]

The richest 1 percent looked very different in 2000 than a century earlier. More were self-made, with fewer having inherited their wealth. In the West and some other places, the globalization and deregulation of the financial industry from the 1980s on allowed some in the banking, private equity, and hedge fund industries to make fortunes even as a series of financial bubbles and collapses made finance more risky. At the same time, the remarkable growth of high-tech and especially Internet businesses made billionaires out of a lucky few. Following decolonization in the Global South, some 1 percenters made their fortunes by taking over the structures of the state, often profiting through embezzlement, kickbacks, and other forms of direct corruption. In Nigeria, for instance, billions in oil revenues were siphoned off into the personal accounts of officials. Similarly, following the collapse of the Soviet Union, well-connected individuals who frequently had held elite positions in the former regime purchased state assets on the cheap, becoming billionaires in the process.

The newly enriched rubbed shoulders with one another and with more traditional elites while living global lifestyles almost unimaginable to the rest. Owning multiple houses in desirable locations—London, Dubai, Hong Kong, New York—and moving between them on private jets or on luxury yachts established their place in the new elite, as did participation in exclusive gatherings like the annual Davos summit in Switzerland. More so than in the past, the superrich possessed a shared international outlook, educational background, and experiences that made them a self-conscious global class. "A person in Africa who runs a big African bank and went to Harvard Business School has more in common with me than he does with his neighbors, and I have more in common with him than I do with my neighbors," observed the private equity banker Glen Hutchins.[26] At the opening of the twenty-first century, humankind had never been so collectively wealthy. That wealth lifted billions out of poverty and created a growing global middle class, but it also accumulated in the hands of a privileged few, creating an unprecedentedly wealthy global plutocracy.

Getting Personal: Transformations of Private Life

The public face of social life, expressed in work, class, income, and wealth, has a more private counterpart, experienced in marriage, family, sexuality, and gender roles. These elements of personal life also changed dramatically amid the technological and economic transformations of the past century. Increasingly, individuals had to make choices about intimate matters that were previously regarded as determined by custom or law—who to marry, how many children to bear, when to begin sexual activity, and what it meant to be male or female. Amid much diversity and variation, many people the world over have experienced and celebrated those changes as liberation from ancient constraints and social oppression, while many others have felt them as an assault on the natural order of things and a threat to ways of living sanctioned by religion and tradition. These diverse reactions have driven matters long considered private or unspeakable into the public sphere of controversy, debate, and political action.

Modernity and Personal Life

Among the agents of change in personal life, none have been more fundamental than the multiple processes widely associated with modernity—science and technology, industrialization and urbanization, and globalization and migration. Consider, for example, their impact on family life, experienced earlier and most fully in the industrialized societies of Europe, North America, and Japan, but also more recently in the Global South.

CORE IDEA

Identifying Change
In what ways has personal or private life been transformed over the past century?

As industrial and urban life took hold across the world during the past two centuries, large business enterprises and the state took over functions that families had previously performed. Production moved from family farms and workshops to factories, offices, and large-scale agricultural enterprises, and opportunities for work outside the home beckoned to growing numbers of women as well as men. Education became the task of state-run schools rather than families, and the primary role of children became that of student rather than worker. Families increasingly functioned primarily to provide emotional and financial security in a turbulent and rapidly changing world. In this setting, modern families became smaller as children were increasingly seen as economic burdens and as both men and women married later. Furthermore, family life grew less stable as divorce became far more frequent and the stigma attached to it diminished. Modern life also witnessed an increasing variety of family patterns across the world: patriarchal families of several generations living together; small nuclear families of mother, father, and children; single-parent families, usually headed by women; unmarried couples living together, sometimes with children and often without; blended families as a result of second marriages; polygamous families; and gay and lesbian families.

These broad patterns of change in family life at the global level hide a great deal of diversity. While family size has dropped sharply in much of Asia and Latin America during the past century, it has remained quite high in sub-Saharan Africa, where women in the early twenty-first century produced on average 5 children during their reproductive years, compared to a global average of 2.5. Divorce rates too varied widely in the early twenty-first century, with 50 percent or more of marriages ending in divorce in the United States, France, Spain, Cuba, Hungary, and the Czech Republic, compared to much lower rates in Chile (3 percent), Brazil (21 percent), Egypt (17 percent), Iran (22 percent), and South Africa (17 percent). Since the mid-1990s, China has experienced a dramatic increase in divorce, prompting the Chinese government to intervene to address the issue. Most of the world's marriages during the past century have involved one man and one woman, though polygamy remains legal in much of Africa and the Islamic Middle East. And same-sex marriages have gained a measure of acceptance at least in some cultures in recent decades. While the past century has generally favored free choice or "love" marriages, many families in India and elsewhere still arrange marriages for their children.

Modern life has also deeply impacted sexuality. Technologies of contraception—condoms, IUDs, diaphragms, and above all "the pill"—have allowed many people to separate sexual life from reproduction. Especially since the 1960s, this change has contributed to the emergence of a highly sexualized public culture in many parts of the world, expressed in advertising and in an enormous pornography industry with a global reach. One investigator reported on a remote village in the West African country of Ghana: "The village has no electricity, but that doesn't stop a generator from being wheeled in, turning a mud hut into an impromptu porn cinema."[27] Sex tourism has also become big business, with major destinations in Thailand, Indonesia, the Philippines, Colombia, Brazil, and the Netherlands. Movies, TV, newspapers, and magazines openly display or discuss all manner of sexual topics that would have been largely forbidden in public discourse only a century ago: premarital sex, homosexuality, gay marriage, LGBTQ rights, sexually transmitted diseases, birth control, abortion, teen pregnancy, and much more. Sex education in schools has spread globally to varying degrees, while provoking sharp controversy in many places.

Sex, in short, has come out of the closet during the past century. Unsurprisingly, this has been associated with a considerable increase in premarital sex in many parts of the world, with the vast majority of Americans and Europeans participating in such activity by the late 1960s. A rapidly industrializing China has witnessed the frequency of premarital sex skyrocket since 1989, approaching levels in the United States.

But all of this has occurred in the face of much controversy and opposition. The hierarchies of the Catholic Church and many fundamentalist or evangelical Christian leaders have remained steadfastly opposed to the "sexual revolution" of the past century, even as many of their parishioners participate in it. Despite the sexual revolution, over 90 percent of Muslims in Indonesia, Jordan, Pakistan, Turkey, and Egypt found premarital sex unacceptable in the early twenty-first century, while fewer than 10 percent of the people in France, Germany, and Spain felt the same way.[28] Greater openness and assertiveness among gays and lesbians have triggered legal action against them, especially in Africa, where many countries have passed harsh antigay legislation, citing the AIDS crisis, a defense of traditional marriage, and the supposedly "un-African" character of homosexuality.

The State and Personal Life

■ Assessing State Policies
In what different ways did the policies of governments shape personal life during the past century?

States too have shaped personal life in the past century, as they grew more powerful and intrusive and as matters of marriage, family, gender, and sexuality became ever more entangled with politics. Nazi Germany, for example, prohibited birth control

China's One-Child Family China's vigorous efforts to limit its population growth represented a radical intrusion of state power into the private lives of its people. It was accompanied by a massive propaganda effort, illustrated by this urban billboard. (Barry Lewis/Alamy)

and rewarded large families during the 1930s in an effort to produce as many "good Germans" as possible. At the same time, they sterilized or executed those deemed "undesirable" and forbade marriage or sexual relations between Jews and Germans to prevent "contamination" of the Aryan race. For similar racial reasons, South Africa under the apartheid regime legally prohibited both sexual relationships and marriage between whites and nonwhites. In the aftermath of World War II, the Soviet Union sharply limited access to all contraception in an effort to rebuild a population devastated by war.

But as concerns about population growth mounted in the 1970s and beyond, some states moved to limit the numbers of their people. Acting under a state of emergency, the government of India sterilized some 11 million men and women between 1975 and 1977, using a combination of incentives and compulsion to gain consent. China pursued population control on an even larger scale through its **one-child family policy**, which lasted from 1980 until 2014. Under the pressure of financial incentives and penalties and intense pressure from local authorities, over 300 million women "agreed" to have IUD devices implanted, over 100 million were sterilized, and many were forced to undergo abortions.

Communist regimes intervened in personal life in other ways as well. Among the earliest and most revolutionary actions of the new communist government in the Soviet Union were efforts at liberating and mobilizing women. Almost immediately upon coming to power, communist authorities in the Soviet Union declared full legal and political equality for women; marriage became a civil procedure among freely consenting adults; divorce was legalized and made easier, as was abortion; illegitimacy was abolished; women no longer had to take their husbands' surnames; pregnancy leave for employed women was mandated; and women were actively mobilized as workers in the country's drive to industrialization. (See Zooming In: Anna Dubova, a Russian Woman, and the Soviet State, page 1000.) During the 1920s, a special party organization called the **Women's Department** (Zhenotdel) organized numerous conferences for women, trained women to run day-care centers and medical clinics, published newspapers and magazines aimed at a female audience, provided literacy and prenatal classes, and encouraged Muslim women to take off their veils.

Elsewhere as well, states acted in favor of women's rights and gender equality, most notably in Turkey, a thoroughly Muslim country, during the 1920s and 1930s. Turkey had emerged as an independent state, led by Kemal Atatürk, from the ashes of the Ottoman Empire following World War I. In Atatürk's view, the emancipation of women was a cornerstone of the new Turkey and a mark of the country's modernization. In a much-quoted speech, he declared: "If henceforward the women do not share in the social life of the nation . . . we shall remain irremediably backward, incapable of treating on equal terms with the civilizations of the West."[29] Thus polygamy was abolished; women were granted equal rights in divorce, inheritance, and child custody; and in 1934 Turkish women gained the right to vote and hold public office, a full decade before French women gained that right. Public beaches were opened to women, and Atatürk encouraged them to discard the veil or head covering, long associated with Muslim piety, in favor of Western styles of dress. As in the early Soviet Union, this was a state-directed feminism, responsive to Atatürk's modern views, rather than reflecting popular demands from women themselves.

But what the state granted to women, the state could also take away, as it did in Iran in the years following that country's Islamic revolution in 1979. The country's new Islamic government, headed by the Ayatollah Khomeini, moved to sharply tighten religiously inspired restrictions on women, while branding feminism and women's rights as a Western evil. By 1983, all women were required to wear loose-fitting clothing and the head covering known as hijab, a regulation enforced by roving groups of militants, or "revolutionary guards." Sexual segregation was imposed in schools, parks, beaches, and public transportation. The legal age of marriage for girls, set at eighteen under the prerevolutionary regime, was reduced to nine with parental consent. Married women could no longer file for divorce or attend school. Yet, despite such restrictions, many women supported the revolution and over the next several decades found far greater opportunities for employment and higher education than before. By the early twenty-first century, almost 60 percent of university students were women, women's right to vote remained intact, and some loosening of earlier restrictions on women had become apparent.

Feminism and Personal Life

A third source of change in personal life during the past century derived from social movements committed to liberation from ancient patterns of inequality and oppression. No expression of this global culture of liberation held a more profound potential for social change than feminism, for it represented a rethinking of the most fundamental and personal of all human relationships—that between women and men. Although feminism had begun in the West in the nineteenth century, it became global in the twentieth, as organized efforts to address the concerns of women took shape across the world.

ZOOMING IN

Anna Dubova, a Russian Woman, and the Soviet State

Born into a large peasant family near Smolensk in western Russia in 1916, Anna Dubova lived through the entire communist period in her country.[30] Her experience illustrates the impact of state policies on the life of one woman, as well as Anna's efforts to find her own way within a sometimes dangerous and often oppressive society.

Anna was one of fourteen children, of whom seven survived. Her family was dominated by a strict, hardworking, and highly religious father, who was choirmaster of the local church. Anna's father was suspicious of the communists when they came to power the year after Anna's birth, but her grandmother was more forthright. "The forces of the Antichrist have triumphed," she declared. Nonetheless, her father accepted an appointment in 1922 as chairman of the village soviet, the new communist organ of local government. During the 1920s, the village and Anna's family flourished under Lenin's New Economic Policy, which briefly permitted a considerable measure of private enterprise and profit making. Her father even opened a small shop in the village, where he sold goods purchased in the city.

A 1941 image of a woman factory worker in Moscow

By 1928, however, everything changed as the Soviet regime, now under Joseph Stalin's leadership, abruptly moved to collectivize agriculture and root out *kulaks*, supposedly wealthy peasants who were thought to bear the germ of a hated capitalism. Because of her father's shop, the family was labeled as kulak and their property was confiscated. "I remember so well how Mama sat and cried when they took away the cow," Anna recalled years later. The family forestalled their expected deportation to the far north of the Soviet Union only by promising Anna, then just thirteen, in marriage to the local Communist Party secretary. The marriage never took place, however, and the family was forced to leave. Later, Anna was permitted to join her older sister in Moscow, but approval for that much-coveted move

photo: Library of Congress, Prints and Photographs Division, LC-USW33-024241-C (P&P)

CORE IDEA

■ **Assessing Gender Roles**
What social, political, and cultural norms were challenged by women in the twentieth century?

Western feminism had lost momentum as an organized movement by the end of the 1920s, when many countries in Western Europe and North America had achieved women's suffrage. But it revived in the 1960s with a quite different agenda as women's participation in the paid workforce mounted rapidly. Millions of American women responded to Betty Friedan's book, *The Feminine Mystique* (1963), which disclosed the identity crisis of educated women, unfulfilled by marriage and motherhood. Some adherents of this **second-wave feminism** took up the equal rights agenda of their nineteenth-century predecessors, but with an emphasis now on employment and education rather than voting rights. A more radical expression of American feminism, widely known as "women's liberation," took broader aim at came at a very high price. Anna recalled, "I had to write out an official statement that I renounced my parents, that I no longer had any ties with them."

Thus Anna, a rural teenage girl, joined millions of other young women who flocked to the city to pursue the new opportunities that became available as the Soviet Union launched its industrialization drive, which required the labor of men and women alike. In Moscow, she gained a basic education, pursued a vocation in cake decorating, which she enjoyed, and did a brief stint as a mechanic and chauffeur, which she detested. All the while the shadow of her kulak label followed her. Had it been discovered, she could have lost her job and her permission to live in Moscow. And so she married a party activist from a poor peasant family, she explained years later, "just so I could cover up my background." Her husband drank heavily, leaving her with a daughter when he went off to war in 1941.

In the Soviet Union, the late 1930s witnessed the Terror when millions of alleged "enemies of the people" were arrested and hauled off to execution or labor camps. Anna recalled what it was like: "You'd come home and they'd say, Yesterday they took away Uncle Lesha. . . . You'd go to see a girlfriend, they'd say, We have an empty room now; they've exiled Andreitsev." Like most people not directly involved, Anna believed in the guilt of these people. And she feared that she herself might be mistakenly accused, for those with a kulak label were particular targets of the search for enemies.

Beyond her kulak background, Anna also felt compelled to hide a deep religious sensibility derived from her childhood. She remembered the disappearance of the village priest, the looting of the churches, and the destruction of icons. And so she never entered a church or prayed in front of others. But she wore a cross under her clothing. "I never stopped [believing]," she recalled. "But I concealed it. Deep down . . . I believed." Nor did she ever seek to join the Communist Party, though it may well have advanced her career prospects and standard of living.

In the decades following World War II and especially after Stalin's death in 1953, Anna's life seemed to stabilize. She entered into a thirty-year relationship with a man and found satisfying work in a construction design office, though the lack of higher education and party connections prevented her from moving into higher-paid jobs. Despite Anna's ability to forge a life for herself in an industrializing and repressive Soviet Union, she had come to value, perhaps nostalgically, the life of a peasant over that of an urban worker. "[As a peasant,] I would have lived on the fruits of my labor," she reflected. ". . . [Instead,] I've lived someone else's life."

QUESTIONS

In what ways did state policies shape Anna's life? What deliberate actions did she and her family take to make a life for themselves within the communist system?

patriarchy as a system of domination, similar to those of race and class. One manifesto from 1969 declared:

> We are exploited as sex objects, breeders, domestic servants, and cheap labor. We are considered inferior beings, whose only purpose is to enhance men's lives. . . . Because we live so intimately with our oppressors, we have been kept from seeing our personal suffering as a political condition.[31]

Thus liberation for women meant becoming aware of their own oppression, a process that took place in thousands of consciousness-raising groups across the United States. Women also brought into open discussion issues involving sexuality, insisting that free love, lesbianism, and celibacy should be accorded the same respect as heterosexual marriage.

Yet another strand of Western feminism emerged from women of color. For many of them, the concerns of white, usually middle-class, feminists were hardly relevant to their oppression. Black women had always worked outside the home and so felt little need to be liberated from the chains of homemaking. Whereas white women might find the family oppressive, African American women viewed it as a secure base from which to resist racism and poverty. Solidarity with black men, rather than separation from them, was essential in confronting racism.

As women mobilized across Asia, Africa, and Latin America, they faced very different situations than did white women in the United States and Europe. The predominant issues for **feminism in the Global South**—colonialism, racism, poverty, development, political oppression, and sometimes revolution—were not always directly related to gender. To many African feminists in the 1970s and later, the concerns of their American or European sisters were too individualistic, too focused on sexuality, and insufficiently concerned with issues of motherhood, marriage, and poverty to be of much use. Furthermore, they resented Western feminists' insistent interest in cultural matters such as female genital mutilation and polygamy, which sometimes echoed the concerns of colonial-era missionaries and administrators. Western feminism could easily be seen as a new form of cultural imperialism.

During the colonial era, much of women's political activity was aligned with the struggle for independence. Later, women's movements in the Global South took shape around a wide range of issues. In the East African country of Kenya, a major form of mobilization was the "women's group" movement. Some 27,000 small associations of women, an outgrowth of traditional self-help groups, enabled women to provide personal support for one another and took on community projects, such as building water cisterns, schools, and dispensaries. Some groups became revolving loan societies or bought land or businesses. One woman testified to the sense of empowerment she derived from membership in her group:

> I am a free woman. I bought this piece of land through my group. I can lie on it, work on it, keep goats or cows. What more do I want? My husband cannot sell it. It is mine.[32]

Elsewhere, other issues and approaches predominated. In the North African Islamic kingdom of Morocco, a more centrally directed and nationally focused feminist movement targeted the country's Family Law Code, which still defined women as minors. In 2004, a long campaign by Morocco's feminist movement, often with the help of supportive men and a liberal king, resulted in a new Family Law Code that recognized women as equals to their husbands and allowed them to initiate divorce and to claim child custody, all of which had previously been denied.

In Chile, a women's movement emerged as part of a national struggle against the military dictatorship of General Augusto Pinochet, who ruled the country from 1973 to 1990. Because they were largely regarded as "invisible" in the public sphere, women were able to organize extensively, despite the repression of the Pinochet regime. From this explosion of organizing activity emerged a women's movement that crossed class lines and party affiliations. Poor urban women by the tens of thousands organized soup kitchens, craft workshops, and shopping collectives, all aimed at the economic survival of their families. Smaller numbers of middle-class women brought more distinctly feminist perspectives to the movement and argued pointedly for "democracy in the country and in the home." This diverse women's movement was an important part of the larger national protest that returned Chile to democratic government in 1990.

Perhaps the most impressive achievement of feminism in the twentieth century was its ability to project the "woman question" as a global issue and to gain international recognition for the view that "women's rights are human rights." Like slavery and empire before it, patriarchy lost at least some of its legitimacy during this most recent century. Feminism registered as a global issue when the United Nations (UN), under pressure from women activists, declared 1975 as International Women's Year and the next ten years as the Decade for Women. By 2006, 183 nations, though not the United States, had ratified a UN Convention on the Elimination of All Forms of Discrimination against Women. Clearly, this international attention to women's issues set a global standard to which feminists operating in their own countries could aspire.

But feminism generated a global backlash among those who felt that its agenda undermined family life, the proper relationship of men and women, and civilization generally. To Phyllis Schlafly, a prominent American opponent of equal rights for women, feminism was a "disease" that brought in its wake "fear, sickness, pain, anger, hatred, danger, violence, and all manner of ugliness."[33] In the Islamic world, Western-style feminism, with its claims of gender equality and open sexuality, was highly offensive to many and fueled movements of religious revivalism that invited or compelled women to wear the veil and sometimes to lead highly restricted lives. The Vatican, some Catholic and Muslim countries, and at times the U.S. government took strong exception to aspects of global feminism, particularly its emphasis on reproductive rights, including access to abortion and birth control. Many African governments and many African men defined feminism of any kind as "un-African" and associated with a hated colonialism. Feminist support for gay and lesbian rights only solidified opposition to women's rights activists within socially conservative circles internationally. Thus feminism was global as the twenty-first century dawned, but it was very diverse and much contested.

CONCLUSIONS AND REFLECTIONS

On Contemporary History

Most of the history we study involves stories that have more or less clear endings, such as the Spanish conquest of the Aztec Empire, the Haitian Revolution, or the First World War. We also know something of their legacies, which often continue to resonate decades or even centuries after the event. But when dealing with more recent historical processes, our accounts of the past bump up directly against the present and extend into the future. In this situation, we know neither their ending point nor their legacies. This is contemporary history.

Scientific and technological innovation, for example, has accelerated sharply since World War II, with no end in sight, generating new conceptions of the universe, new sources of energy, new breakthroughs in medicine, and virtually endless applications in manufacturing, transportation, communication, and the military. These innovations continue to drive deepening economic entanglement all across the planet, reflected in the globalization of industrialization, in skyrocketing volumes of world trade and investment, and in the ever-growing activities of multinational corporations. In response to these processes, social life too has changed dramatically over the past century. Full-time farmers have declined sharply in numbers; many industrial workers have been displaced by technology or outsourcing; the already rich have increased their share of the world's wealth; sexual expression has become more open and varied; and feminism has generated many new possibilities for women. Each of these patterns seems likely to continue into the foreseeable future. Opposition to all of this likewise persists, based variously on environmental or social justice concerns, or fears that cherished cultural values are eroding.

In dealing with such contemporary matters, historians are often uneasy. That discomfort derives in part from the belief that only time can provide perspective. In writing about ongoing and unfinished processes, historians worry that they may lack enough distance to identify what is truly significant as opposed to what is of only passing interest. They may also lack sufficient detachment. Can historians write "objectively" or in some balanced fashion about matters in which they have been witnesses or even participants and about which they have strong personal opinions?

Yet another source of discomfort about contemporary history arises from questions about the future. Should historians speculate about "what's next"? Many people think that some understanding of the past gives historians a unique insight into the future. But historians themselves are often rather cautious about predictions because they are so aware that historical change can be unexpected and surprising. At the end of World War II, who could have anticipated the Internet, the collapse of the Soviet Union, or China's massive industrial growth?

Nevertheless, the study of contemporary history offers some contexts for the news of the day. Such contexts disclose where there is continuity with the past, as well as highlight where there is a departure from it. At its best, an understanding of contemporary history also provides a corrective to the self-serving uses of the past—and the outright lies—to which politicians are prone. Current issues also encourage historians to look at the past in different ways. It is surely no accident that as feminism and environmentalism have achieved global prominence, women's history and environmental history have flourished in recent decades.

Finally, for those seeking guidance for our personal lives and our societies, historical context is one of the few resources we have. So, like everyone before us, we stumble forward, using lessons from the past, as we feel our way into an always uncertain future.

Revisiting Chapter 22

Revisiting Specifics

age of fossil fuels, 975
communication revolution, 978
economic globalization, 980
Asian Tigers, 981
Bretton Woods system, 981
transnational corporations, 983
World Trade Organization (WTO), 987
North American Free Trade Agreement (NAFTA), 988
consumerism, 991
export-processing zones (EPZs), 992
service sector, 993
informal economy, 993
one-child family policy (China), 998
Women's Department (USSR), 998
second-wave feminism, 1000
feminism in the Global South, 1002

Revisiting Core Ideas

1. **Identifying Change** What was new about energy production in the twentieth century?
2. **Assessing Change** How did electricity and the internal combustion engine transform human life during the past century?
3. **Assessing Cause and Effect** In what ways have global economic linkages deepened during the past century, and with what impact?
4. **Identifying Change** What global social changes have accompanied economic globalization? How have those changes affected levels of social inequality?
5. **Identifying Change** In what ways has personal or private life been transformed over the past century?
6. **Assessing Gender Roles** What social, political, and cultural norms were challenged by women in the twentieth century?

A Wider View

1. In shaping the history of the past century, how might you assess the relative importance of the deliberate actions of human beings (such as social movements and government policies) and impersonal forces (such as technological innovation or economic change)?
2. How might you assess the costs and benefits of the processes discussed in this chapter?
3. How have the global developments examined in this chapter shaped your own life and community?
4. **Looking Back** How did the processes discussed in this chapter (energy revolution, technological change, globalization, and feminism) have an impact on the major events of the past century explored in Chapters 20 and 21 (war, revolution, fascism, communism, the cold war, and decolonization)?

To learn more about the topics in this chapter, see **For Further Study** at the end of the book.

WORKING WITH EVIDENCE

Global Feminism

With its focus on equal rights and opportunities for women, modern feminism has challenged the most ancient and perhaps deeply rooted of human inequalities—that of patriarchy or the dominance of men over women. Beginning in Western Europe and the United States during the nineteenth century, it was born in the context of democratic gains for men from which women were excluded. Like science, industrialism, socialism, and electoral democracy, feminism was a Western cultural innovation that acquired a global reach during the most recent century.

In doing so, feminism has found expression in many voices, giving rise to much controversy and many questions within feminist circles. How relevant has mainstream Western feminism been to women of color in the West and in the developing countries? To what extent do all women share common interests? In what ways do differences of class, race, nation, religion, sexual orientation, and economic condition generate quite distinct feminist agendas? How important is sexual freedom to the feminist cause? What tactics are most effective in realizing the varying goals of feminists? The documents that follow provide a sample of the divergent voices in which global feminism has been articulated during the past century.

SOURCE 22.1 Western Feminism in the Twenty-First Century ►

In the West, where modern feminism had begun, a new phase of that movement took shape during the 1960s and after. Moving well beyond the earlier focus on suffrage and property rights, second-wave feminists gave voice to a wide range of new issues: the value of housework, discrimination in the workplace, media portrayal of women, sexuality and the family, reproductive rights, lesbianism, violence against women, pornography, and prostitution.

At the opening of the twenty-first century, Western feminists continued to advance a broad agenda, as reflected in the two images that constitute Source 22.1. Source 22.1A depicts a 2012 "slutwalk" in London protesting against rape culture. This march was one of many around the world, the first of which occurred in Canada in 2011 when a policeman told a group of students that in order to avoid being raped "women should avoid dressing like sluts." Source 22.1B documents a 2017 protest in Toulouse, France, that advocated for women's rights in the workplace, another major goal of modern Western feminism. The banner in the foreground reads, "Precarious, underpaid, harassed. It's enough!"

- What strategies are these protesters employing to secure the changes that they advocate for?
- What do the issues raised by participants and the types of protest depicted in these images reveal about Western feminism in the first decades of the twenty-first century?

SOURCE 22.1A

A "Slutwalk" Protest in London | 2012

Patricia Phillips/Alamy

SOURCE 22.1B

A Demonstration for Women Workers' Rights in Toulouse, France | 2017

NurPhoto/Getty Images

SOURCE 22.2 Black American Feminism

Within North American feminism, a distinctive voice arose among women of color—especially blacks and Hispanics. Many among them resented the claims of white, middle-class feminists to speak for all women and objected to the exclusive prominence given to gender issues. Capitalism, race, class, and compulsory heterosexuality, they insisted, combined with patriarchy to generate an interlocking system of oppression that was unique to women of color. Such a perspective is reflected in the 1977 statement of the Combahee River Collective, a black feminist organization.

- What similarities and differences in perspective can you identify between this document and the images in Source 22.1?
- What issues divide black and white feminists in the United States?
- What difficulties have black American feminists experienced in gaining support for their movement?
- On what basis might this black feminist statement generate opposition and controversy?

COMBAHEE RIVER COLLECTIVE | *A Black Feminist Statement* | 1977

We are a collective of Black feminists who have been meeting together since 1974. . . . [W]e are actively committed to struggling against racial, sexual, heterosexual, and class oppression . . . based upon the fact that the major systems of oppression are interlocking. . . .

[W]e find our origins in the historical reality of Afro-American women's continuous life-and-death struggle for survival and liberation. . . . Black women have always embodied an adversary stance to white male rule. . . . Black feminist politics also have an obvious connection to movements for Black liberation, particularly those of the 1960s and 1970s. . . . It was our experience and disillusionment within these liberation movements, as well as experience on the periphery of the white male left, that led to the need to develop a politics that was anti-racist, unlike those of white women, and anti-sexist, unlike those of Black and white men. . . . [A]s we developed politically we [also] addressed ourselves to heterosexism and economic oppression under capitalism. . . .

Although we are feminists and Lesbians, we feel solidarity with progressive Black men and do not advocate the fractionalization that white women who are separatists demand. . . . We struggle together with Black men against racism, while we also struggle with Black men about sexism. . . . We are socialists because we believe that work must be organized for the collective benefit of those who do the work and create the products, and not for the profit of the bosses. . . . We need to articulate the real class situation of persons . . . for whom racial and sexual oppression are significant determinants in their working/economic lives. . . . No one before has ever examined the multilayered texture of Black women's lives. . . . "Smart-ugly" crystallized the way in which most of us had been forced to develop our intellects at great cost to our "social" lives. . . . We have a great deal of criticism and loathing for what men have been socialized to be in this society . . . [b]ut we do not have the misguided notion that it is their maleness, per se—i.e., their biological maleness—that makes them what they are.

The major source of difficulty in our political work is that we are . . . trying . . . to address a whole range of oppressions. . . . We do not have racial, sexual, heterosexual, or class privilege to rely upon. . . . The psychological toll of being a Black woman and the difficulties this presents in reaching political consciousness and doing political work can never be underestimated. . . . As an early group member once said, "We are all damaged people merely by virtue of being Black women." . . . The material conditions of most Black women would hardly lead them to upset both economic and sexual arrangements that seem to represent some stability in their lives. . . . Accusations that Black feminism divides the Black struggle are powerful deterrents to the growth of an autonomous Black women's movement.

The inclusiveness of our politics makes us concerned with any situation that impinges upon the lives of women, Third World and working people. . . . One issue that is of major concern to us and that we have begun to publicly address is racism in the white women's movement. . . . Eliminating racism in the white women's movement is by definition work for white women to do, but we will continue to speak to and demand accountability on this issue. . . .

Source: Zillah R. Eisenstein, ed., *Capitalist Patriarchy and the Case for Socialist Feminism* (New York: Monthly Review Press, 1979), 362–72.

■ ■ ■

SOURCE 22.3 Communist Feminism

Following the Russian Revolution of 1917, the communist Soviet Union was the site of a remarkable experiment in state-directed feminism. (See "The State and Personal Life" earlier in this chapter.) Early on women were granted full legal and political equality with men, divorce was legalized, and pregnancy leave was mandated for employed women. As part of a determined drive to industrialize the country, authorities also sought to liberate women from household responsibilities so that they could work outside the home. This poster from 1949 advertises the support available to Soviet women who chose to pursue careers in industry. The poster caption reads, "The broad development of a network of nursery schools, kindergartens, dining rooms and laundries will provide for the participation of women in socialist construction."

- How would you describe the woman in the center of the poster? What do you think that the artist wanted to convey about her?
- How are the specific services promised to women in the poster text depicted in the image? How might state provision of these services alter the daily life and family dynamics of working women?
- Compare this image of a female communist worker with the one depicted in Source 21.4, the Chinese poster "Women Hold Up Half of Heaven," on page 965. What similarities can you identify?
- How might the protesters in Source 22.1B react to this poster?

Soviet Poster Advertising Support for Women Workers | **1949**

Photo 12/Getty Images

■ ■ ■

SOURCE 22.4 Islamic Feminism

Beyond the Western world and the communist world, modern feminism has also found expression in the developing countries (see "Feminism and Personal Life" earlier in this chapter). Nowhere has this provoked greater controversy than in the Islamic world. For a few women, exposure to Western gender norms and liberal thought has occasioned the abandonment of Islam altogether. Far more common have been efforts to root gender equality in both personal and public life within the traditions of Islam. Such was the argument of Benazir Bhutto, several times the prime minister of Pakistan, in a speech delivered to a United Nations conference on women in 1995.

- What message does Bhutto feel her election and the election of other female Muslim heads of state provide to Muslim women everywhere?
- How does Bhutto account for the manifest inequality of women in so many Muslim societies?
- How might you compare Bhutto's case for feminism with those of Westerners and communists in the preceding documents?

BENAZIR BHUTTO | *Politics and the Muslim Woman* | 1995

I stand before you not only as a Prime Minister but as a woman and a mother proud of her cultural and religious heritage. . . . Muslim women have a special responsibility to help distinguish between Islamic teachings and social taboos spun by the traditions of a patriarchal society. . . .

[W]e must remember that Islam forbids injustice; injustice against people, against nations, against women. It shuns race, colour, and gender as a basis of distinction amongst fellow men. It enshrines piety as the sole criteria for judging humankind. It treats women as human beings in their own right, not as chattels. A woman can inherit, divorce, receive alimony and child custody. Women were intellectuals, poets, jurists and even took part in war. The Holy Book of the Muslims refers to the rule of a woman, the Queen of Sabah. The Holy Book alludes to her wisdom and to her country being a land of plenty. The Holy Prophet (peace be upon him) himself married a working woman. And the first convert to Islam was a woman, Bibi Khadija. Prophet Muhammad (peace be upon him) emphatically condemned and put an end to the practice of female infanticide in pre-Islamic Arabia. The Holy Quran reads:

When news is brought to one of them, of the birth
of a female (child),
his face darkens and he is filled with inward grief
what shame does he
hide himself from his people because of the bad
news he has had.
Shall he retain it on sufferance and contempt, or
bury it in the dust.
Ah! what an evil choice they decide on
(Surah Al-Nahl, Ayat 57, 58, 59)

Ladies and gentlemen! How true these words ring even today.

How many women are still "retained" in their families "on sufferance and contempt" growing up with emotional scars and burdens. How tragic it is that the pre-Islamic practice of female infanticide still haunts a world we regard as modern and civilized. Girl children are often abandoned or aborted. Statistics show that men now increasingly outnumber women in more than 15 Asian nations. . . . Boys are wanted because their worth is considered more than that of the girl. Boys are wanted to satisfy the ego: they carry on the father's name in this world. Yet too often we forget that for Muslims on the Day of Judgement, each person will be called not by their father's name but by the mother's name. . . . And it [the aborting or killing of female babies] continues, not because of religion in the case of Pakistan, but because of social prejudice. The rights Islam gave Muslim women have too often been denied.

Source: United Nations, Fourth World Conference on Women, September 4, 1995, http://www.un.org/esa/gopher-data/conf/fwcw/conf/gov/950904202603.txt, made available by the United Nations.

SOURCE 22.5 Mexican Zapatista Feminists

Mexican feminists, like those in much of Latin America, have operated in societies shaped by widespread poverty, sharp class inequalities, racial and ethnic conflict, and frequently authoritarian or corrupt governments. Thus feminists have often sought to address the ways in which multiple sources of oppression, not only gender relations, affect both women and men. Such was the case in the Zapatista rebellion that erupted in 1994 among the Maya people in the Chiapas region of southern Mexico. It was a protest against a long history of injustice and impoverishment for indigenous peoples. Women activists within this largely peasant movement had to confront the sexist attitudes of their male comrades as well as an oppressive Mexican government that marginalized its Maya citizens. Although they usually rejected the "feminist" label, these women articulated their demands in an Indigenous Women's Petition (Source 22.5A) and succeeded in embedding their concerns in a Women's Revolutionary Law (Source 22.5B).

- How would you describe the issues that these documents articulate? How do they reflect class, ethnic, and gender realities of Mexican life?
- Should these documents be regarded as feminist? Why or why not? Why might Zapatista women be reluctant to call themselves feminists?
- Which of these demands might provoke the strongest male resistance? Why?
- With which of the previous feminist sources might Zapatista women be most sympathetic?

SOURCE 22.5A
Indigenous Women's Petition | **March 1, 1994**

We, Indigenous campesino women, demand the immediate solution to our urgent needs, which the government has never resolved:

A: Childbirth clinics with gynecologists. . . .

B: That child care facilities be built in the communities.

C: We ask the government to send sufficient food for the children in all rural communities including: milk, cornflour, rice, corn, soy, oil, beans, cheese, eggs, sugar, soup, oats, etc.

D: That kitchens and dining halls be built for the children in the communities. . . .

E: We demand the construction of community corn dough mills and tortillerías based on the number of families in each community.

F: That they give us poultry, rabbit, sheep and pig

farm projects, and also that we be provided with technical assistance and veterinarians.

G: We ask for bakery projects, which include the provision of ovens and ingredients.

H: We want artisan workshops to be built, equipped with machinery and raw materials.

I: Markets in which to sell our crafts at fair prices.

J: That schools be built where women can get technical training.

K: That there be preschools and maternal schools in rural communities, where children can play and grow in a morally and physically healthy way.

L: That as women we have sufficient transportation for the products we produce in our various projects.

Source: *Zapatistas! Documents of the New Mexican Revolution (December 31, 1993–June 12, 1994)* (New York: Autonomedia, 1994), 243, accessed January 9, 2018, http://lanic.utexas.edu/project/Zapatistas/Zapatistas_book.pdf.

SOURCE 22.5B

The Women's Revolutionary Law | **January 1, 1994**

[T]aking into account the situation of the woman worker in Mexico, the revolution supports their just demands for equality and justice in the following Women's Revolutionary Law.

First: Women, regardless of their race, creed, color or political affiliation, have the right to participate in the revolutionary struggle in a way determined by their desire and capacity.

Second: Women have the right to work and receive a just salary.

Third: Women have the right to decide the number of children they will have and care for.

Fourth: Women have the right to participate in the affairs of the community and hold positions of authority if they are freely and democratically elected.

Fifth: Women and their children have the right to primary attention in matters of health and nutrition.

Sixth: Women have the right to an education.

Seventh: Women have the right to choose their partner, and are not to be forced into marriage.

Eighth: Women shall not be beaten or physically mistreated by their family members or by strangers. Rape and attempted rape will be severely punished.

Ninth: Women will be able to occupy positions of leadership in the organization and hold military ranks in the revolutionary armed forces.

Source: *Zapatistas! Documents of the New Mexican Revolution (December 31, 1993–June 12, 1994)* (New York: Autonomedia, 1994), 38–39, accessed January 9, 2018, http://lanic.utexas.edu/project/Zapatistas/Zapatistas_book.pdf.

DOING HISTORY

1. **Identifying Similarities** What common concerns animate these sources?
2. **Defining Differences** What variations or conflicting feminist perspectives can you identify in these sources? What accounts for those differences?
3. **Considering Change over Time** How do you think nineteenth-century Western feminists would have responded to each of these twentieth-century statements (see "Feminist Beginnings" in Chapter 16)?
4. **Evaluating Global Feminism** What aspects of global feminism were most revolutionary, liberating, or threatening to established authorities and ways of living? To what extent do you think the goals of these varying feminist efforts have been realized?

HISTORIANS' VOICES

Feminism: Tensions and Resistance

The globalization of the feminist movement after 1960 has transformed its scope and impact while also creating new tensions both within the movement and in the wider society. The two historians' voices that follow offer broad assessments of feminism. In Voice 22.1 Merry Wiesner-Hanks examines the movement's globalization after 1960 and the tensions that emerged among feminists. In Voice 22.2 Peter Stearns explores the different countercurrents that have resisted feminism since the 1960s.

- According to Voice 22.1, what roles did the United Nations play in the modern feminist movement?
- What motivations for opposing some goals of international feminism does Voice 22.2 identify?
- **Integrating Primary and Secondary Sources** How might Wiesner-Hanks and Stearns use the sources in this feature to support their overviews of the modern global feminist movement?

VOICE 22.1

Merry Wiesner-Hanks on International Feminism | 2011

By the 1960s, women in many parts of the world were dissatisfied with the pace at which they were achieving political and legal equality, and a second-wave women's movement began, often termed the "women's liberation movement." Women's groups pressured for an end to sex discrimination in hiring practices, pay rates, inheritance rights, and the granting of credit, they opened shelters for battered women, day care centers, and rape crisis centers, and pushed for university courses on women, and laws against sexual harassment. In Western countries they pushed for abortion rights, and in India they mobilized against dowries and dowry-related deaths. By the early 1970s, advocates of rights for homosexuals had also mobilized in many countries, sponsoring demonstrations, political action campaigns, and various types of self-help organizations. The United Nations declared 1975–1985 to be the International Decade for Women, and meetings discussing the status of women around the world were held under UN auspices in Mexico City (1975), Copenhagen (1980), Nairobi (1985), and Beijing (1995). These meetings were sometimes divisive, pointing out the great differences in women's concerns around the world, with sexual orientation and female genital cutting often the most explosive issues. The official Platform for Action of the Beijing Conference sought to avoid some of these divisions by calling for a general "empowerment of women," noting that this would mean different things in different areas of the world.

Source: Merry E. Wiesner-Hanks, *Gender in History: Global Perspectives*, 2nd ed. (Oxford: Wiley Blackwell, 2011), 157–58.

VOICE 22.2

Peter Stearns on Resistance to Global Feminism | 2015

Two related trends emerged. The first . . . was the resurgence of religious and other conservatism, often directed explicitly against changes in gender relations. . . . Islamic, Hindu and many Christian fundamentalists all urged more traditional gender hierarchy and the importance of female modesty. . . .

Equally interesting, if less important numerically, was the growing group of women's leaders who objected to international standards because they were too Western and too individualistic. These were people who wanted women to have an active voice in their lives and societies but who did not find the international formulas persuasive. An Indian women's magazine thus objected to global consumerism on the grounds that it tended to force women to waste time and effort on personal beauty in the hope of finding and keeping men. Far better, in terms of real women's interests, was the Indian custom of arranged marriages, which made the Western appearances game irrelevant. . . .

Finally . . . at the grass-roots level, many ordinary women sought to effect compromise, using new standards to a degree but combining them with older goals. Thus a grandmother in Kenya talks of the importance of education for women, so they can fend for themselves, and also accepts new levels of birth control. But beneath this interestingly cosmopolitan surface she hopes not for individual fulfillment for her granddaughters, but for a revived family cohesion in which different generations of women will take care of each other, regardless of what the men do. International influences have had some effect here, but more on the means by which goals were to be met than on the purposes themselves.

Source: Peter N. Stearns, *Gender in World History*, 3rd ed. (New York: Routledge, 2015), 194–95.

Image created by Reto Stockli, Nazmi El Saleous, and Marit Jentoft-Nilsen, NASA GSFC

CHAPTER 23

Global Processes

Demography, Culture, and the Environment

1900–present

CONNECTING PAST AND PRESENT

In the early twenty-first century, a forty-five-year-old vegetable grower named Omar Imma Assayar moved with his wife and ten children from their rural village of some 400 people in the West African country of Chad to the capital city of N'Djamena with a population of over a million. His decision to move was prompted by the death of all his cattle during a severe drought. Furthermore, while living in the village, he had to get up early and carry his produce by bicycle to the market in the city. "My life is easier now," he explained. "I live right next to the market. I have more time to be with my family, and I can get a better price for my vegetables as well. . . . My one big wish is for my children to go to school."[1]

Omar and his family have both witnessed and participated in some of the major drivers of world history during the past century. His ten children have contributed to the enormous increase in human numbers. In moving to the capital of Chad, Omar joined millions of others in Africa, Asia, and Latin America who are seeking a better life in the city. In his desire to educate his children, he has also taken part in the vast expansion of literacy that has swept the planet during the past century. Not far from his new home is Lake Chad, which has shrunk drastically in response to climate change and overuse, linking his country to global patterns of environmental degradation. The life of this single individual then is connected to the global processes that conclude

« **One World** This composite NASA photograph, showing both the earth and the moon, reveals none of the national, ethnic, religious, or linguistic boundaries that have long divided humankind. Such pictures have both reflected and helped create a new planetary consciousness among growing numbers of people.

SEEKING THE MAIN POINT

What has enabled the demographic, cultural, and environmental changes of the past century?

this account of the human journey during the twentieth century and beyond—massive population growth, widespread movement of people, changing patterns of cultural identity, and unprecedented human impact on the environment.

More People: Quadrupling Human Numbers

From about 1.65 billion people in 1900, world population soared to approximately 7.8 billion in 2020. In 120 years, the human species had more than quadrupled its numbers. It had taken humankind several hundred thousand years to reach 1 billion people in the early nineteenth century. That number then reached 2 billion in roughly 1930, 4 billion in 1975, 6 billion in 1999, and 7 billion by 2012. The speed and extent of this **population explosion** have no parallel in the human past or in the history of primate life on the planet.[2] Equally striking is the distribution of this massive growth, as some 90 percent of it occurred in the developing countries of Asia, Africa, the Middle East, and Latin America. (See Snapshot: World Population Growth, 1950–2100, page 1020.)

CORE IDEA

Explaining Population Growth

What accounts for the unprecedented growth in human numbers during the past century?

The explanation for this massive demographic change lies in lower death rates, while birth rates have remained high. In 1945 roughly 20 people died each year for every 1,000 people in the world's population. By 2014 that figure was 8.[3] Infant mortality dropped even more quickly, especially after the 1960s. New medical technologies such as antibiotics, as well as widespread public health programs, played a major role in this unprecedented change. Various mosquito control measures sharply reduced death from malaria and yellow fever, while extensive vaccination campaigns eradicated smallpox by 1977.

As populations grew, innovations in agriculture enabled food production globally to keep up with, and even exceed, growing human numbers. A new "**Green Revolution**" greatly increased agricultural output through the use of tractors and mechanical harvesters; the massive application of chemical fertilizers, pesticides, and herbicides; and the development of high-yielding varieties of wheat and rice. All of this sustained the enormous population growth in developing countries.

By the end of the twentieth century, the rate of global population growth had begun to slow, as birth rates dropped all around the world. This transition to fewer births had occurred first in the more industrialized countries, where birth control measures were widely available, women were educated and pursuing careers, and large families were economically burdensome. By 1975, births in Europe had fallen below the replacement rate. More recently, this pattern began to take hold in developing countries as well, associated with urbanization, with growing educational opportunities for girls, and with vigorous family-planning programs in many places. China's famous one-child family policy, introduced in 1980, was the most dramatic of these efforts. Nonetheless, the world's population has continued to rise and according to UN projections is expected to reach 9.7 billion in 2050 and 10.9 billion in 2100.

Landmarks for Chapter 23

1950 | 1960 | 1970 | 1980 | 1990 | 2000 | 2010 | 2020

THE WHOLE WORLD

- **1948** UN Universal Declaration of Human Rights
- **1975** Human population reaches 4 billion
- **1977** Smallpox eradicated
- **ca. 1981** Beginning of AIDS epidemic
- **2007** 50 percent of human population in towns/cities
- **2015** Paris Climate Agreement
- **2020** COVID-19 pandemic outbreak
- **2020** Human population reaches 7.8 billion

THE GLOBAL NORTH

- **1962** Rachel Carson's *Silent Spring* launches modern environmentalism
- **1986** Chernobyl nuclear disaster
- **1992** Collapse of Grand Banks cod fishery
- **2001** Terrorist attack on World Trade Center
- **2017** U.S. announces withdrawal from Paris Climate Agreement

THE GLOBAL SOUTH

- **1949** Apartheid in South Africa
- **ca. 1965** Beginning of widespread deforestation in Amazon basin
- **1979** Iranian revolution
- **ca. 1980** Beginning of massive Chinese migration to coastal cities
- **1988** Al-Qaeda established
- **ca. 1990** Growing prominence of Indian Bollywood films
- **2014** Rise of the Islamic State

SNAPSHOT **World Population Growth, 1950–2100 (projected)**

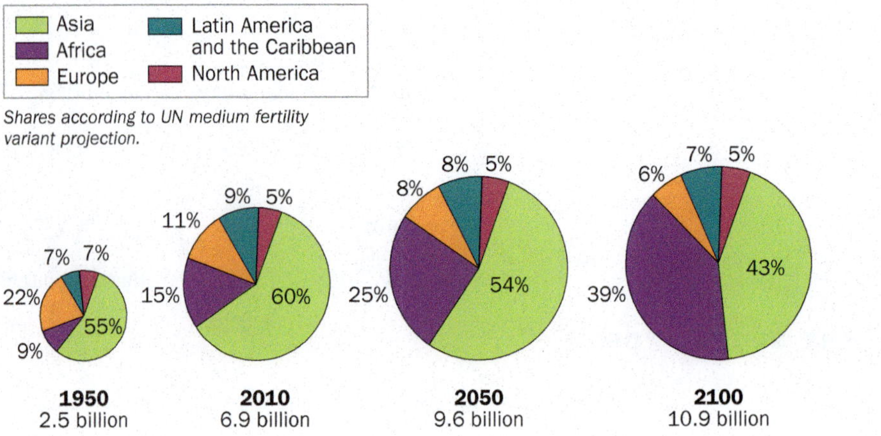

Source: The European Environment Agency.

People in Motion: Patterns of Migration

Growing numbers pushed more people to move. War, famine, climate change, poverty, industrialization, and urban growth drove migration, while new forms of transportation—steamships, trains, buses, cars, trucks, airplanes—facilitated this vast circulation of people.

To the Cities: Global Urbanization

In the early twenty-first century, humankind reached a remarkable, though largely unnoticed, milestone. For the first time more people around the world lived in towns and cities than in the countryside. Although urban populations had been slowly increasing for centuries, it was massive **global urbanization**, the explosive growth of cities after 1900, that made the world an "urban place."[4] City-dwellers made up 15 percent of the world's population in 1900 and about 25 percent in 1950 before doubling again to 50 percent by 2007.

CORE IDEA

■ Explaining Migration

What has caused such large-scale human movement to urban areas and other countries in the past century?

Mechanized farming and the Green Revolution had reduced the need for rural labor, even as population was growing rapidly, pushing many to migrate to cities. Opportunities for employment in manufacturing, commerce, government, and the service industry drew such people to urban centers, where life expectancies were rising because of improving infrastructure and health care. "These shifts in population," wrote historian Michael Hunt, "stripped villages of healthy young men and young, unmarried women. Their departure tore the social fabric of villages, leaving wives, young children, and the elderly behind."[5]

The timing of this movement to the cities varied. Europe and North America led the way, with about half their populations urbanized by 1950. Latin America, Africa, and Asia followed this general pattern in subsequent decades. And many of the urban centers to which people moved were large **megacities** with populations of over 10 million. In 1950, only New York and Tokyo had reached megacity status, but by 2020 the world counted thirty-seven such megacities on five continents. Joining Tokyo among the top five by population were Shanghai in China, Delhi in India, São Paolo in Brazil, and Mexico City in Mexico. From the 1970s on, the decline in manufacturing in some regions of the developed world prompted many industrial cities to reinvent themselves as hubs for education, health care, logistics, information technology, and other services. And as industrialization took hold in the Global South after 1950, cities grew at around twice the rate of already industrialized regions. In the 1980s, the Chinese government loosened residency restrictions that had kept much of the population in the countryside, unleashing an unprecedented wave of urban migrants, so that by 2018 nearly 60 percent of China's population lived in cities, dramatically up from 26 percent in 1990. Everywhere, cities attracted primarily young people from the countryside looking for better job prospects and educational, social, and cultural opportunities.

Even the most modern, well-managed cities had profound impacts on the environment, as large concentrations of people consumed huge amounts of food, energy, and water and in turn emitted enormous amounts of sewage, garbage, carbon dioxide, and toxic substances. Certainly, the poorly serviced slums and loosely regulated manufacturing enterprises of many cities across the planet created ecological disasters that destroyed the environment and damaged the health of residents, while elite neighborhoods boasted safe water, sewage systems, electricity, and fire and police services. On a per person basis, however, city living sometimes reduced electricity consumption and carbon emissions because public transportation, energy-efficient residences, and smaller families lessened the impact of humans on the environment.

Everywhere, wealth was concentrated in cities, but inequality was all the more apparent because the rich and poor often lived in close proximity, with luxury apartment buildings, office blocks, and

Slums and Skyscrapers The enormous disparities that have accompanied urbanization in Latin America and elsewhere are illustrated in this photograph from São Paulo, Brazil. (Florian Kopp/imageBROKER/AGE Fotostock)

malls overlooking slums and shantytowns. Improvements in public and private transport in the twentieth century allowed cities to spread out as never before. In the early twentieth century some cities, like Munich, Chicago, Sydney, and Cape Town, had large middle-class suburban communities composed of single-family houses, and after midcentury similar communities developed in cities across the globe where incomes and transportation networks allowed. In other cities, like Jakarta, Rio de Janeiro, Nairobi, and Lagos, rapid urban sprawl was driven primarily by recent arrivals who settled in slums on empty pieces of land with few public services, often at the edges of cities or in marginal spaces like steep hillsides or areas prone to flooding. In 2006, a visitor described the Kibera slum in Nairobi as "a squeezed square mile . . . home to nearly one million people. . . . Most of them live in one-room mud or wattle huts or in wooden or basic stone houses often windowless. . . . The Kenyan state provides the huge, illegal sprawl with nothing—no sanitation, no roads, no hospitals. It is a massive ditch of mud and filth, with a brown dribble of a stream running through it."[6] Clearly population growth and the rise of cities did not solve, and probably exacerbated in many places, the problem of urban poverty.

Moving Abroad: Long-Distance Migration

While most "people in motion" traveled to nearby cities, a growing number moved abroad. (See Map 23.1.) Older patterns of migration, from Europe to the Americas, for example, continued and even accelerated in the early twentieth century, but migration patterns changed as the century progressed. (For earlier patterns of migration, see "Europeans in Motion" in Chapter 17 and "Economies of Wage Labor: Migration for Work" in Chapter 18.) The number of migrants from Asia, Africa, and Latin America grew significantly, while Europe, earlier a leading source of long-distance emigrants, instead became an important destination for immigrants. From the 1920s on, the percentage of female migrants steadily grew, and in 2016 women constituted nearly half of all international migrants.

During the twentieth century states increasingly sought to control the flow of migrants across their borders, requiring travelers to possess passports and creating numerous administrative categories to describe migrants—asylum seekers, guest workers, refugees, tourists, students, climate refugees, illegals, and undocumented persons. Since World War II, these efforts to regulate borders have helped create enormous increases in refugees as desperate individuals find routes for flight shut off, leaving many millions living in refugee camps, often for generations.

Noticing Change
How did patterns of international migration change during the past century, and with what results?

The twentieth century also witnessed new patterns of human migration driven by war, revolution, the end of empire, and the emergence of new nation-states—many of which proved less tolerant of ethnic minorities than the empires that they replaced. The collapse of the Ottoman Empire following World War I prompted a large-scale exchange of populations as over a million Greek Orthodox Christians from Turkey relocated to Greece, while some 400,000 Turkish-speaking Muslims living in Greece moved in the other direction. Fleeing anti-Semitism, fascism, and the Holocaust, Jews immigrated to what is now Israel in large numbers, generating in the process a flow of Palestinian refugees to settlements in neighboring countries. Indian independence from Britain in 1947 resulted in the partition of the region along sectarian lines, forcing millions to migrate. In Rwanda, massacres by Hutus in July 1994 required over a million Tutsis to flee their homes, while the ultimate victory of the Tutsis sparked an even larger exodus of Hutus. Still other peoples moved as refugees fleeing violence or political oppression in places such as Vietnam, Cambodia, Sudan, Uganda, Cuba, Haiti, Venezuela, Iraq, Afghanistan, and Syria.

Perhaps the most significant pattern of global migration since the 1960s has featured a vast movement of people from the developing countries of Asia, Africa, and Latin America to the industrialized world of Europe and North America, with smaller flows to Australia and the oil-rich states of the Persian Gulf. Pakistanis, Indians, and West Indians have moved to Great Britain; Algerians and West Africans to France; Turks and Kurds to Germany; Filipinos, Koreans, Cubans, Mexicans, and Haitians to the United States; and Egyptians, Pakistanis, Bangladeshis, and smaller numbers of highly skilled Westerners to the Persian Gulf states.

Much of this movement has involved **labor migration**, as people have moved, often illegally and with few skills, to escape poverty in their own lands, drawn by a belief that employment opportunities and a better future await them in the developed countries. Often their journeys have been dangerous, as migrants have confronted long treks through burning deserts in the American Southwest or braved dangerous crossings of the Mediterranean Sea to Europe in rickety and overcrowded vessels. Many have depended on expensive and sometimes unreliable human smugglers. Smaller numbers of highly skilled and university-trained people, such as doctors and computer scientists, have come in search of professional opportunities less available in their own countries.

Everywhere migrants have struggled to find a place in their adopted communities. In some regions immigrant groups have for centuries assimilated into local societies without fully losing their distinct identities, a pattern that persisted into the twentieth century. Indians in East Africa, Chinese in Southeast Asia, and Japanese in Peru took advantage of their outsider status to become middlemen, forging links between existing groups in society as merchants, traders, or financiers. However, with the emergence or strengthening of national identities during the twentieth century, some of these minorities faced persecution. In Indonesia, huge numbers of ethnic Chinese who had lived in the region for generations were killed or driven from the country in 1965 by authorities suspicious that they held communist sympathies.

The most important countries of arrival for twentieth-century migrants—the United States, Canada, Australia, and, since the 1960s, Western Europe—all expected that immigrants would assimilate into their societies by adopting the language, political values, and cultural norms of the host society. Many migrants agreed, viewing assimilation as a pathway to better economic opportunities and social status even if it often took several generations for a migrant family to fully integrate into the host society. Despite this pressure toward assimilation, migrants also maintained aspects of

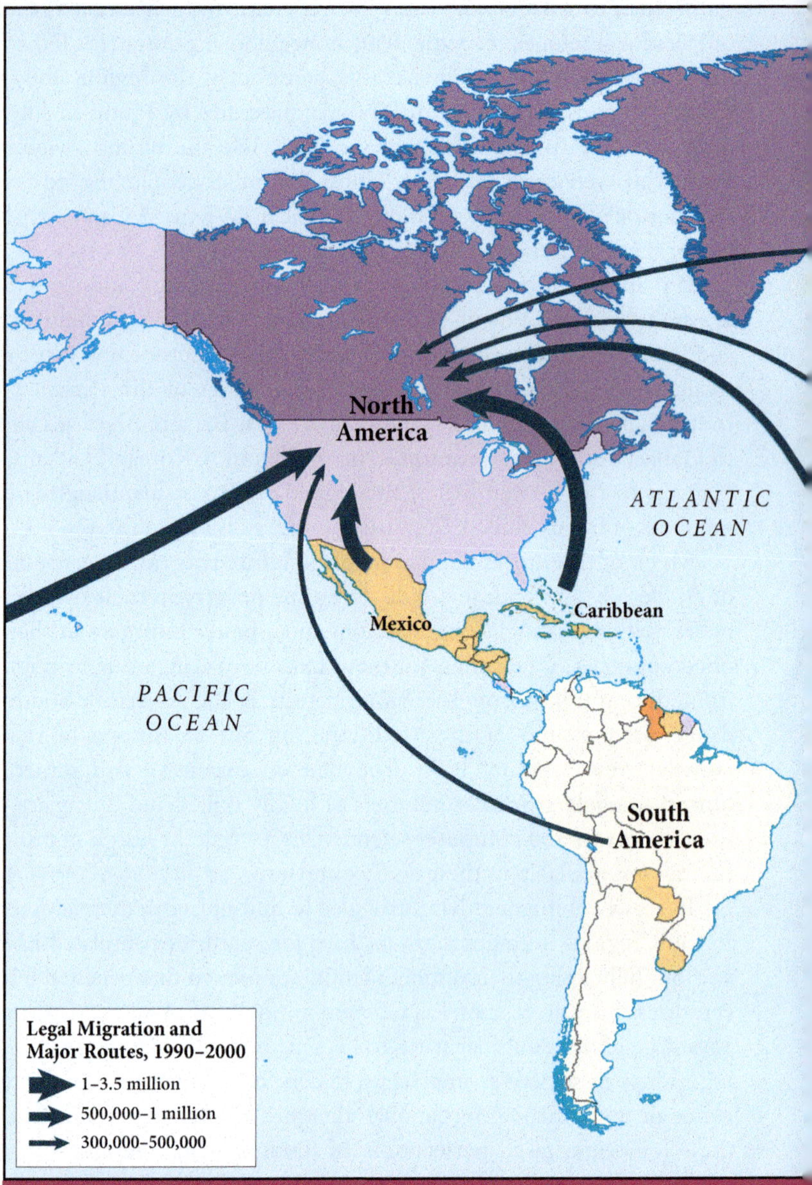

MAPPING HISTORY

Map 23.1 Global Migration Patterns, 1990–2005

The late twentieth and early twenty-first centuries witnessed a large-scale movement of people, primarily from the Global South to the Global North.

(Data from United Nations, World Bank, 2005; OEDC, 2001)

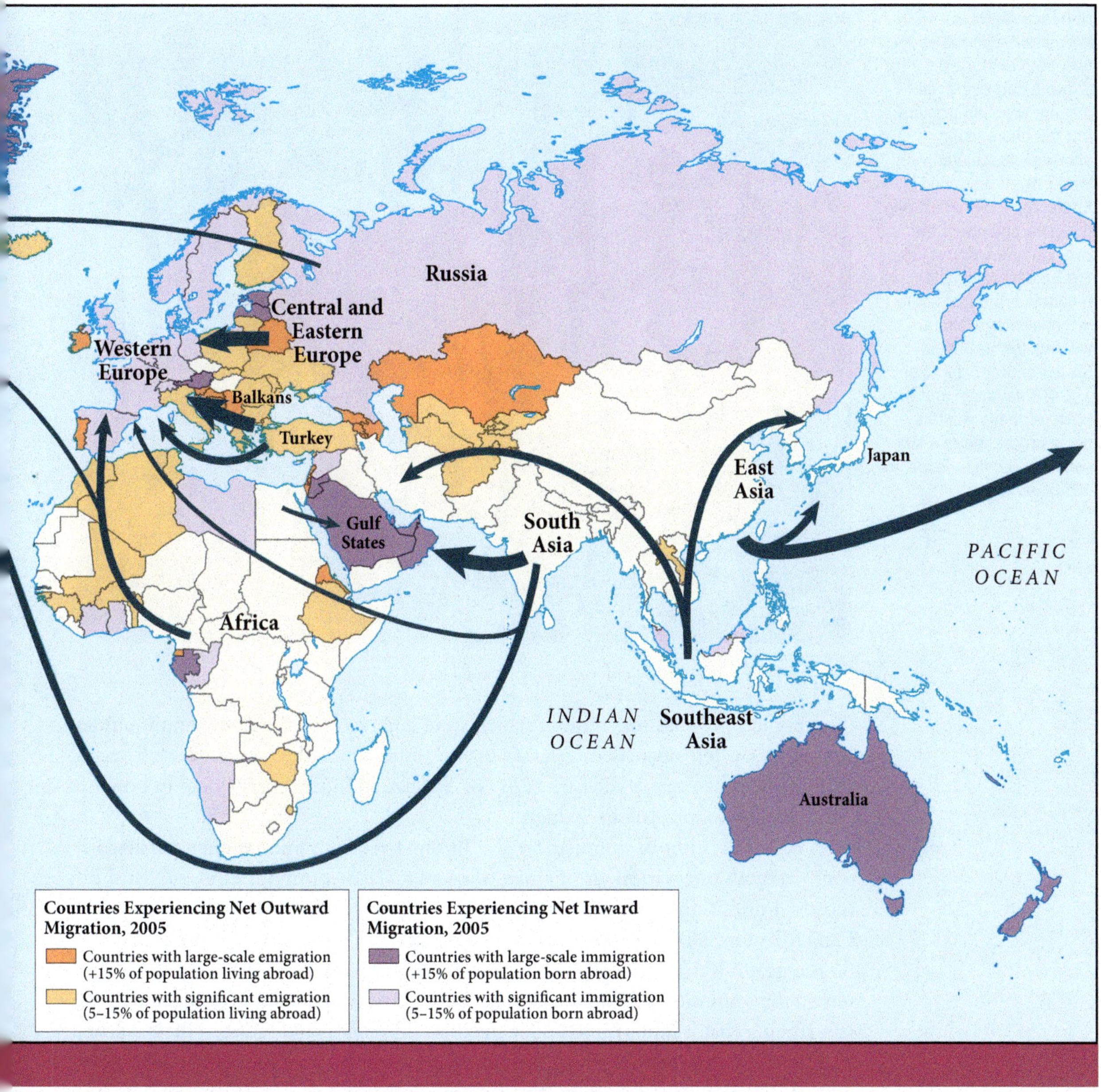

READING THE MAP Which regions produced the most emigrants in total numbers? Which regions produced the most outward migration measured as a percentage of the region's population? Do areas where the largest number of emigrants originated always correlate with regions with the highest percentage of outward migration?

MAKING CONNECTIONS Does this map offer any evidence to support the idea that migration patterns at the end of the twentieth century were still influenced by older links between Europe and its overseas empires?

Mexican Migrant Workers Since the early twentieth century, U.S. growers had employed migrant Mexican workers. But the acute labor shortage associated with World War II prompted a formal agreement between the governments of the two countries. Known as the Bracero (migrant labor) program, it brought some 4.5 million agricultural workers to the United States between 1942 and 1964. This image shows some of these workers being processed at a labor center in Hidalgo, Texas, in 1959. (AP Photo)

their homelands' cultures, some of which were embraced by their new communities. Immigrants often opened eateries featuring dishes from their countries of origin, such as a Mexican tamale food truck in Los Angeles, an Indian curry house in London, or a Chinese noodle café in Sydney.

The expectation of assimilation also brought tensions and conflict, particularly over cultural integration. In France, for instance, the immigration of Muslims, mostly from North Africa, has sparked controversy over women's clothing. A French law in 2004 forbade the practice of wearing headscarves in public schools on the grounds that it compromised the secularism of French education and represented the repression of women. But many Muslim women strongly objected to the law, arguing that it undermined their freedom of religion and violated their cultural traditions. As one woman put it, "France is supposed to be a free country. Nowadays women have the right to take their clothes off but not put them on."[7] In the United States, large-scale migration from Latin America in recent decades has led some to demand that English be designated the official language of the country. More recently, fears that immigrants openly hostile to Western values might bring terrorism to host societies have led to calls to limit or refuse admission to refugees from some Islamic countries. At the same time, other voices have advocated the benefits of multiculturalism for the globalized and knowledge-based societies and economies of the twenty-first century.

A final category of long-distance migrants has encompassed those engaged in short-term travel. International tourist arrivals grew from 25 million in 1950 to 988 million in 2011. Businesspeople in search of profits and students in search of education have crisscrossed the world in large numbers. These travelers have participated in "an unprecedented new era of transnational ties and mobility" that is only a few decades old.[8]

Microbes in Motion: Disease and Recent History

People in motion have carried not only their cultures but also their microbes. Everywhere growing populations, urban living, and unprecedented mobility have created more efficient pathways for deadly diseases to mutate and spread across the globe. Even before the emergence of commercial air travel, the early twentieth century witnessed one of the worst pandemics in human history when three waves of an **influenza pandemic** swept across the globe in 1918 and 1919, carried by soldiers, refugees, and other people dislocated by World War I. Infecting about one-third of the world's population, this pandemic killed at least 50 million people.

■ Identifying Differences
What differences can you notice among major pandemics of the past century?

Another new pathogen, human immunodeficiency virus (HIV), which causes acquired immune deficiency syndrome (AIDS), sparked a second global pandemic beginning in the 1980s. Unlike the influenza virus of 1918, **HIV/AIDS** spread primarily through sexual contact, contaminated blood products, or the sharing of needles by intravenous drug users. Nonetheless, the disease has spread rapidly across the globe. In 2018 nearly 38 million people lived with HIV, while some 32 million have died since the 1980s of AIDS or its complications. In sub-Saharan Africa, where the disease first emerged—and where nearly 70 percent of those currently infected reside—the disease was spread in part by long-distance truck drivers and the commercial sex workers they frequented on their travels. When the disease arrived in wealthier countries, drug companies responded by producing treatments, which have transformed this disease from a major killer into a serious but chronic and manageable disease for those with access to the latest medicines.

The twentieth century saw humankind mobilize its resources as never before to combat deadly pandemics. Modern communication meant that reports of new diseases spread faster than ever before. Concerned communities and their governments took action to try to keep diseases out or limit their spread by ordering measures like border checks and quarantines. Recognizing the potentially destabilizing economic, social, and political effects of pandemics, governments created both national and international institutions, like the World Health Organization in 1948, to help coordinate efforts to combat disease within national borders and beyond. In the early twenty-first century, new threats—severe acute respiratory syndrome (SARS), the Ebola virus, and the Zika virus, among others—prompted large-scale international efforts to identify, track, and stop their spread.

But despite these unprecedented advances in public health, starting in late 2019 much of the world was overwhelmed by COVID-19, a disease that for the first time

The COVID-19 Pandemic Many schools that initially closed in the face of the COVID-19 pandemic reopened after scrambling to institute measures that made their classrooms safer. This photograph taken in June of 2020 depicts students attending a high school in Cape Town, South Africa. They practice social distancing with their desks spaced widely apart and wear masks donated to their school by the Metropolitan Life Insurance Company. (Gallo Images/Getty Images)

became endemic in humans and that spread easily from person to person. First emerging in Wuhan, China, it spread across the globe in a matter of months as air travel quickly dispersed infected people to distant parts of the world. To avoid overwhelming health care systems and to buy time for the development of a vaccine or cure, governments in hard-hit places issued travel restrictions and shelter-at-home decrees that brought with them great economic costs. Deadly in a small but significant percentage of cases, the coronavirus provided a sobering reminder of the limits of human control over disease and the vulnerabilities to pandemics that come with our more highly entangled and urbanized world, our growing human population, and our ever-increasing intrusion into the shrinking domain of wild animals.

Cultural Identity in an Entangled World

Large and impersonal global processes (industrialization, migration, and urbanization, for example) have had a profound and personal impact at the level of individual identity—how people define the communities to which they belong, the religions with which they affiliate, and even the food they eat, the clothes they wear, and the music they enjoy. Certainly older patterns of cultural identity have been challenged as individuals have come up against people and cultures quite different from their own. Secular ideas and values were often at odds with traditional religious outlooks; feminist ideas confronted patriarchal assumptions; socialist or communist thinking undermined the legitimacy of deeply rooted social hierarchies. Among the identities in question during the past century, those of political and religious loyalty loomed large.

Race, Nation, and Ethnicity

Nineteenth-century Europe gave rise to an elaborate ideology of "race" as a fundamental distinction among human communities based on allegedly permanent biological characteristics. (See "Industry and Empire" in Chapter 18.) But it was in the twentieth century that such ideas achieved their greatest prominence, shaping individual behavior, institutional practices, and government policies alike. Three societies in particular stand out as openly racist regimes: Nazi Germany, the southern

United States from the 1890s to the 1950s, and apartheid-era South Africa. All of them officially sanctioned explicitly racist ideologies, prohibited marriage across racial lines, legislated extreme forms of social segregation, denied political rights to Jews or blacks, and deliberately kept them in poverty.

In many other places, race was a pervasive reality, though perhaps racist thinking was less officially endorsed. Racial distinctions and white supremacy were prominent in European thinking and central features within all of the European colonies in Africa and Asia, generating in turn a new racial awareness among many colonized people. Aime Cesaire, a poet from the French island of Martinique in the Caribbean region, coined the term "negritude," which he defined in 1939 as "the simple recognition of the fact that one is black."[9] Black, Indian, and multiracial people in Latin America and the United States clearly experienced discrimination and disadvantage in relationship to whites or Europeans, even in the absence of legal constraints.

CORE IDEA

Assessing Identity
In what ways have race, nation, and ethnicity found expression and played a role in world history during the past century?

During the second half of the twentieth century, race lost much of its public legitimacy as a social distinction, discredited in part by the horrors of the Nazi regime. As the American author Barbara Ehrenreich put it: "Hitler gave race a bad name." Furthermore, scholars thoroughly debunked the connection between biology and culture or behavior, which was so central to racial thinking. But perhaps most importantly, the sharp critique of white bigotry and discrimination that accompanied the surging independence movements across Asia and Africa made overt racism globally illegitimate. The 1948 UN Universal Declaration of Human Rights inscribed this rejection of racism as a new global moral standard.

Nonetheless, race remained a social reality in many places and continued to generate serious conflict. Even after the end of apartheid in South Africa, pervasive inequalities between whites and blacks in wealth, housing, jobs, and educational opportunities remained front and center in the life of the country. In the United States, the civil rights movement made important gains in the 1960s for black Americans in terms of voting rights, education, and employment. But what has come to be called **systemic racism** persisted, manifesting itself in deeply rooted cultural and social attitudes established over centuries. Combined with long-established wealth inequalities, these attitudes found expression in many institutional practices that hindered access to mortgages to buy homes and capital to start businesses. Systemic racism subjected black Americans to arbitrary arrest and police brutality, giving rise to the Black Lives Matter movement beginning in 2013.

In Europe as well, racial tensions grew as increasing numbers of Africans and Asians migrated to the continent after World War II. Immigrants often faced discrimination in employment and housing, and efforts by European countries to encourage cultural and social assimilation were a source of further tension. Calls for a greater reckoning with Europe's imperial and slave-trading past have also provided a focus for disagreement. Despite their loss of public legitimacy, entrenched racial attitudes have remained an enduring social reality in many parts of the world.

Even more pervasive than race as a form of individual identity and political loyalty has been nationalism, and the two have sometimes overlapped. Loyalty to national states and their presumed interests drove the world wars of the past century and undermined empires around the globe. But if nation-states and national loyalties largely triumphed during the past century, they also faced challenges. Pan-African and pan-Arab aspirations beckoned to those seeking a larger identity and loyalty, though they never achieved an effective political expression. The European Union did give concrete political meaning to a broader European identity in the aftermath of two disastrous wars, though by the early twenty-first century the Union appeared shaky in the face of rising nationalist sentiments and the British decision to withdraw. Globalization too challenged national loyalties as visions of a world without borders and destructive national rivalries appealed to many. The League of Nations and the United Nations gave expression to such visions. The growth of international economic linkages and an increasing global awareness of problems common to all of humankind generated for some a sense of global citizenship, a cosmopolitan feeling of being at home in the world as a whole. Pictures of the earth viewed from the moon or outer space—a beautiful but solitary planet in an immense cosmos—came to symbolize this one-world sensibility.

If globalization represented an external challenge to national loyalties and existing nation-states, a serious internal challenge took shape as ethnically based separatist movements. Most of the world's states, after all, contained several, and sometimes many, culturally distinct peoples. Such peoples readily adopted the rhetoric and logic of nationalism, arguing that they too deserved some separate political status, such as greater autonomy or full independence. Under the pressure of such movements, a number of states have in fact disintegrated. British India dissolved immediately upon independence into a Muslim Pakistan and largely Hindu India. In the 1990s, the multinational states of the Soviet Union, Czechoslovakia, and Yugoslavia dissolved into many separate ethnically based states. In northeastern Africa, Eritrea seceded from Ethiopia in 1993, and in 2011 South Sudan claimed independence from the Republic of Sudan, both of them following decades of civil war. Even where a separate state was not achieved, ethnic separatist movements have threatened the integrity of existing nation-states. Scotland has sought to exit from the United Kingdom, Quebec from Canada, Tibet from China, the Basques from Spain, Igbo-speaking peoples from Nigeria, and the Moro people from the Philippines. Many Russians living in eastern Ukraine would prefer annexation by Russia, and many Kurds living in Iraq, Iran, Syria, and Turkey aspire to an independent Kurdistan.

These various cultural identities—racial, national, ethnic, and global—have become politically and personally meaningful for much of the world's population even as they have mixed and mingled in many ways. German nationalism in the Nazi era found expression in racial terms. Some people found it possible to embrace both an ethnic heritage and loyalty to a larger nation with little contradiction, as many Irish, Italians, Hispanics, and African Americans have done in the United States. A sense of global citizenship, in the struggle against climate change, for example, remains compatible with loyalty to a particular country.

Ethnic Cleansing in Vukovar, Croatia The disintegration of the multiethnic state of Yugoslavia in southeastern Europe during the 1990s gave rise to numerous violent conflicts among its various ethnic groups. This photograph shows Croatians making their way through the rubble of the city of Vukovar, from which some 20,000 of them had been expelled by Serbian troops. The city was almost completely destroyed and largely "cleansed" of its non-Serb population. (Ron Haviv/VII/Redux)

Popular Culture on the Move

Related to these cultural and political identities have been the many elements of popular culture that have increasingly permeated social life during the past century. They too have been on the move around the world in a many-sided process widely known as **cultural globalization**, with the heaviest currents moving from the West to the rest of the world. Hollywood films; Western music (classical, jazz, rock and roll, and rap); American TV programming; American fast-food chains such as McDonald's and KFC—all of these have shaped patterns of taste globally. Furthermore, English has become a world language; Western sports such as soccer, cricket, basketball, and baseball have an international presence; and Western fashions—jeans, suits and ties, miniskirts, white wedding dresses—have become common in many places, sometimes losing their direct association with the West.

■ **Assessing Cultural Connections**
What elements of popular culture have moved globally during the past century?

All of this has been driven by the dominance of the West in world affairs over the past several centuries and the impulse of many to imitate the ways of the powerful. But the assimilation of Western cultural forms has also come to symbolize modernity, inclusion in an emerging global culture, and sometimes liberation or rebellion, especially among the young. Such a sensibility informed Kemal Atatürk's desire for "civilized, international dress" for Turkish men when he sought to impose Western-style clothing on them during the 1920s and 1930s. The outlook was similar for liberated young women in Japan who imitated the dress style of Western "flappers" during the same time. They were *moga* or "modern girls" whose country was becoming a "province of the world."

The global spread of Western culture has raised fears in many places about cultural homogenization or "cultural imperialism" threatening local or national cultures, values, and traditions. Like other forms of globalization, the cultural variant of this larger process has witnessed not only enthusiastic embrace but also pushback, much of which has targeted the outsized American influence in the world. Communist Party officials in the Soviet Union, for example, were suspicious of the growing popularity of American jazz and later rock and roll. Associating these musical forms with Western individualistic values of spontaneity, open sexuality, and opposition to authority, they tried periodically to suppress them, though without much success.

In the Islamic world, pushback against cultural "contamination" from the West has been particularly prominent, especially in religiously fundamentalist circles. The Ayatollah Khomeini, architect of Iran's Islamic revolution, strongly expressed this outlook:

> Just what is the social life we are talking about? Is it those hotbeds of immorality called theatres, cinemas, dancing, and music? Is it the promiscuous presence in the streets of lusting young men and women with arms, chests, and thighs bared? Is it the ludicrous wearing of a hat like the Europeans or the imitation of their habit of wine drinking . . . [or] the disrobed women to be seen on the thoroughfares and in swimming pools?[10]

Yoga in the United States The cultural dimension of globalization is illustrated in the spread of yoga, a mind-body practice from India that has become a part of global culture. This photo shows an outdoor yoga class held in New York's Time's Square to celebrate the summer solstice in 2017. (Brazil Photo Press/Alamy)

Efforts to protect national languages have also prompted resistance to cultural globalization. The French Academy, for example, has long been on the lookout for English terms that have crept into general usage while urging their replacement by French equivalents. Chinese authorities have sought to require foreign firms to use Chinese terms for their products, and in 2012 over 100 Chinese scholars urged the removal of English words from a prominent Chinese dictionary.

But the cultural flows of the past century have moved in many directions, not simply outward from the United States and Europe. In exchange for Big Macs, Americans and Europeans have received Chinese, Indian, Thai, Mexican, and Ethiopian cuisine. Yoga, originally a mind-body practice of Indian origin, has taken hold widely in the West and elsewhere, losing much of its earlier association with spiritual practice and becoming a form of exercise or relaxation. India's huge film industry, known as Bollywood, has had a major cultural impact in the Soviet Union, Western Europe, the United States, and Latin America. India-based Ayurvedic medicine and traditional Chinese medicine, including acupuncture, have become widely used "alternative" treatments in Europe and North America. Japanese and Chinese martial arts have attracted numerous participants in the West and have been featured in many highly popular films. Latin American telenovelas or "soap operas" have enthralled audiences around the world, and Korean popular culture, including TV dramas, movies, and music, has also spread far beyond Korean borders. Congolese music, sometimes blended with Latin American dance rhythms, has spread widely throughout Africa and by the 1980s attracted eager audiences in Europe as well. Jamaican-based reggae music has extended around the world, while its superstar Bob Marley became an international icon. In short, cultural traffic in the entangled world of the past century has moved in many directions.

Religion and Global Modernity

Among the various expressions of cultural identity during the past century, religion has provoked perhaps the deepest personal response among individuals and has provided a potent source of identity in social and political life. Some of these responses were highly critical of religion, while others affirmed and sought to renew or revitalize religious belief and practice.

On the critical side, many of the most "advanced" thinkers of the past several hundred years—Enlightenment writers in the eighteenth century, Karl Marx in the nineteenth, and many academics and secular-minded intellectuals in the twentieth—believed that religion was headed for extinction in the face of modernity, science, communism, or globalization. In some respects, that prediction seemed to come true during the twentieth century and beyond. Soviet authorities, viewing religion as a backward-looking bulwark of an exploiting feudal or capitalist class, closed many churches and seminaries, promoted atheism in public education, prohibited any display of religion in public or the media, and denied believers access to better jobs and official positions. In several modernizing Islamic countries, the role of religion in public life was sharply restricted. Kemal Atatürk in Turkey sought to relegate Islam to the personal and private realm, arguing that "Islam will be elevated, if it will cease to be a political instrument." (See Working with Evidence, Source 23.1, page 1053.)

Religion and Soviet Communism This postcard from the 1930s illustrates Soviet hostility to religion as it depicts a Soviet worker against the background of modern industrial life smashing the symbols of Muslim, Christian, and Jewish religion. (Bridgeman Images)

Even without such state action, religious belief and practice during the past century declined sharply in the major European countries such as Britain, France, Italy, and the Netherlands. A recent poll taken in 2019 found that 26 percent of Americans defined themselves as religiously unaffiliated, while only 31 percent claimed to attend religious services every week.[11] Moreover, the spread of a scientific culture around the world persuaded small minorities everywhere, often among the most highly educated, that the only realities worth considering were those that could be measured with the techniques of science. To such people, all else was superstition, born of ignorance.

Nevertheless, the far more prominent trends of the last century have involved the further spread of major world religions, their resurgence in new forms, their opposition to elements of a secular and global modernity, and their political role as a source of community identity and conflict. Contrary to earlier expectations, religion has played an unexpectedly powerful role in this most recent century.

Buddhism, Christianity, and Islam had long functioned as transregional cultures and continued to do so in the twentieth century. Buddhist ideas and practices such as meditation found a warm reception in the West, and Buddhism has been reviving in China since the 1970s. Christianity of various kinds spread widely in non-Muslim Africa and South Korea, less extensively in parts of India, and after 1975 was growing even in China. By 2019 Christianity was no longer a primarily European or North American religion, as some 67 percent of its adherents lived in Asia, Africa, Oceania, and Latin America. Islam too continued its centuries-long spread in Asia and Africa, while migrants from the Islamic world have planted their religion solidly in the West, constructing over 2,000 mosques in the United States by 2010. Sufi mystical practices have attracted the attention of many in the West who have grown disillusioned with conventional religion.

CORE IDEA

■ Making Comparisons

In what different ways have religious believers responded to the challenges of modern life?

Religious vitality in the twentieth century was expressed also in the vigorous response of those traditions to the modernizing and globalizing world. One such response has been widely called **religious fundamentalism**—a militant piety hostile to secularism and religious pluralism—that took shape to some extent in every major religious tradition. Many features of the modern world, after all, appeared threatening to established religion. The scientific and secular focus of global modernity challenged the core beliefs of religion, with its focus on an unseen realm of reality. Furthermore, the social upheavals connected with capitalism, industrialization, imperialism, and globalization thoroughly upset customary class, family, and gender relationships that had long been sanctified by religious tradition.

Making Comparisons
What do the various "fundamentalist" movements have in common? How have they differed?

To such threats deriving from a globalized modern culture, fundamentalism represented a religious response, characterized by one scholar as "embattled forms of spirituality . . . experienced as a cosmic war between the forces of good and evil."[12] The term "fundamentalism" came from the United States, where religious conservatives in the early twentieth century were outraged and threatened by many recent developments: the growth of secularism; critical and "scientific" approaches to the Bible; Darwin's concept of evolution; liberal versions of Christianity that emphasized ethical behavior rather than personal salvation; the triumph of communism in the Soviet Union, which adopted atheism as its official doctrine; and postwar labor strikes that carried echoes of the Russian Revolution to many conservatives.

Feeling that Christianity itself was at stake, they called for a return to the "fundamentals" of the faith, which included a belief in the literal truthfulness of the scriptures, in the virgin birth and physical resurrection of Jesus, and in miracles. After World War II, American Protestant fundamentalists came to oppose political liberalism and "big government," the sexual revolution of the 1960s, homosexuality and abortion rights, and secular humanism generally. From the 1970s on, they entered the political arena as the "religious right," determined to return America to a "godly path."

In the very different setting of independent India, another fundamentalist movement—known as **Hindutva** (Hindu nationalism)—took shape during the 1980s. Like American fundamentalism, it represented a politicization of religion within a democratic context. To its advocates, India was, and always had been, an essentially Hindu land, even though it had been overwhelmed in recent centuries by Muslim invaders, then by the Christian British, and most recently by the secular state of the post-independence decades. The leaders of modern India, they argued, and particularly its first prime minister, Jawaharlal Nehru, were "the self-proclaimed secularists who . . . seek to remake India in the Western image," while repudiating its basically Hindu religious character. The Hindutva movement took political shape in an increasingly popular party called the Bharatiya Janata Party (BJP), promoting a distinctly Hindu identity in education, culture, and religion. Muslims in particular were sometimes defined as outsiders, potentially more loyal to a Muslim Pakistan than to India. The BJP's sweeping victories in the 2014 and 2019 national elections offer evidence of substantial support for Hindu nationalism in twenty-first-century India.

Nowhere were fundamentalist religious responses to political, social, and cultural change more intense or varied than within the Muslim world. Conquest and colonial rule; awareness of the huge technological and economic gap between Islamic and European civilizations; the disappearance of the Ottoman Empire, long the chief Islamic state; elite enchantment with Western culture; the retreat of Islam for many to the realm of private life—all of this had sapped the cultural

ZOOMING IN

Barbie and Her Competitors in the Muslim World

"I think every Barbie doll is more harmful than an American missile," declared Iranian toy seller Masoumeh Rahimi in 2002. To Rahimi, Barbie's revealing clothing, her shapely appearance, and her close association with Ken, her longtime unmarried companion, were "foreign to Iran's culture."[13] Thus Rahimi warmly welcomed the arrival in 2002 of Sara and Dara, Iranian Muslim dolls meant to counteract the negative influence of Barbie, who had long dominated Iran's toy market. Created by the Iranian government, Sara and her brother, Dara, represented eight-year-old twins and were intended to replace Barbie and Ken, which the authorities had officially banned in the mid-1990s because they represented a "Trojan horse" for Western values. Sara came complete with a head-scarf to cover her hair in modest Muslim fashion and a full-length white chador enveloping her from head to toe. She and her brother were described as helping each other solve problems, while looking to their loving parents for guidance, hardly the message that Barbie and Ken conveyed.

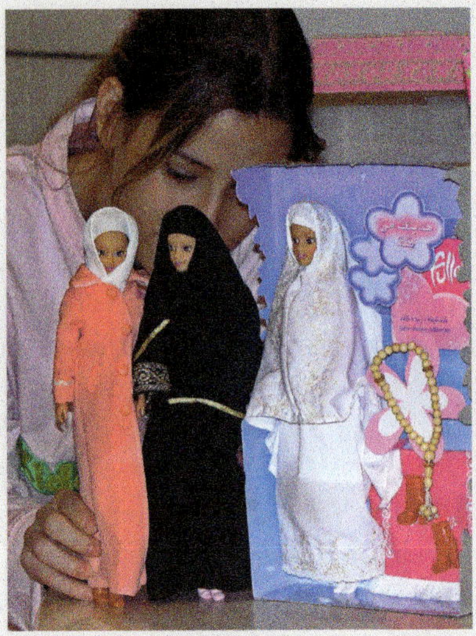

A Syrian girl examining Fulla dolls at a toy store in Damascus in 2005.

In 2003, a toy company based in Syria introduced Fulla, a doll depicting a young Muslim woman about the same age as Barbie, perhaps a grown-up version of Sara. Dressed modestly in a manner that reflected the norms of each national market, Fulla was described by her creator as representing "Muslim values." Unlike Barbie, with her boyfriend and a remarkable range of careers, including astronaut and president of the United States, Fulla was modeled on the ideal traditional Arab woman. She interacted with male family members rather than a boyfriend and was depicted only as a teacher or a doctor, both respected professions for women in the Islamic world. But she did share an eye for fashion with

photo: Khaled al-Hariri/Reuters/Newscom

self-confidence of many Muslims by the mid-twentieth century. Political independence for former colonies certainly represented a victory for Islamic societies, but it had given rise to major states—Egypt, Pakistan, Indonesia, Iraq, Algeria, and others—that pursued essentially Western and secular policies of nationalism, socialism, and economic development, often with only lip service to an Islamic identity.

Even worse, these policies were not very successful. Vastly overcrowded cities with few services, widespread unemployment, pervasive corruption, slow economic growth, a mounting gap between the rich and poor—all of this flew in the face of the great expectations that had accompanied the struggle against European domination. Despite formal independence, foreign intrusion still persisted. Israel, widely regarded as an outpost of the West, had been reestablished as a Jewish state in the very center of the Islamic world in 1948. In 1967, Israel inflicted a devastating defeat on Arab forces in the Six-Day War and seized various Arab territories, including the holy city of Jerusalem. Furthermore, broader signs of Western cultural

Barbie. Underneath her modest outer dress, Fulla wore stylish clothing, although it was less revealing than that of her American counterpart, and, like Barbie, she chose from an extensive wardrobe, sold separately of course. "This isn't just about putting the hijab [a headscarf covering a woman's hair and chest] on a Barbie doll," Fawaz Abidin, the Fulla brand manager, noted. "You have to create a character that parents and children want to relate to."[14]

Fulla proved far more popular than Sara among Muslim girls, becoming one of the best-selling dolls in the Islamic world. In part, the adoption by Fulla's creators of Western marketing techniques, similar to those that had been used to promote Barbie for decades, lay behind the doll's remarkable success. Fulla-themed magazines appeared on newsstands, and commercials advertising Fulla dolls and their accessories permeated children's television programming in the Muslim world. "When you take Fulla out of the house, don't forget her new spring abaya [a long, robe-like full-body covering]!" admonished one advertisement. Fulla's image was used to market an endless number of other licensed products, including branded stationery, backpacks, prayer rugs, bikes, and breakfast cereals, all in trademark "Fulla pink." In this respect, Fulla and Barbie shared a great deal.

Despite Fulla's success, Barbie has continued to enjoy a loyal following in the region, in part because of her exotic qualities. "All my friends have Fulla now, but I still like Barbie the best," one ten-year-old Saudi girl stated. "She has blonde hair and cool clothes. Every single girl in Saudi looks like Fulla. . . . What's so special about that?"

The widespread availability of Barbie in the Muslim world provides one small example of the power of global commerce in the world of the early twenty-first century. But Sara and Fulla illustrate resistance to the cultural values associated with this American product. Still, Sara, Fulla, and Barbie had something in common: nearly all were manufactured in East Asian factories. Indeed, the same factories frequently manufactured the rival dolls. This triangular relationship of the United States, the Muslim world, and East Asia symbolized the growing integration of world economies and cultures as well as their divergences and conflicts. These linked but contrasting patterns involve much more than dolls in the early twenty-first century, for they define major features of our entangled world.

QUESTIONS

What can Barbie, Sara, and Fulla tell us about the globalized world of the twenty-first century? What different values and sensibilities do they convey?

penetration persisted—secular schools, alcohol, Barbie dolls, European and American movies, miniskirts, and more. (See Zooming In: Barbie and Her Competitors in the Muslim World.)

To all of this, many Muslims objected strongly. An emerging fundamentalist movement argued that it was the departure from Islamic principles that had led the Islamic world into its sorry state, and only a return to the "straight path of Islam" would ensure a revival of Muslim societies. To politically militant Islamists, this meant the overthrow of those Muslim governments that had allowed these tragedies and their replacement by regimes that would purify Islamic practice while enforcing Islamic law and piety in public life. One of the leaders of an Egyptian Islamist group put the matter succinctly: "The first battlefield for jihad is the extermination of these infidel leaders and to replace them by a complete Islamic Order."[15]

Islamic fundamentalists won a significant victory in 1979 when the Iranian revolution chased out the country's long-reigning monarch, the shah of Iran. The leader of the revolution, the Ayatollah Khomeini, believed that the purpose of government was to apply the law of Allah as expressed in the *sharia*. The secular law codes under which the shah's government had operated were discarded in favor of those based solely on Islamic precedents. Some 200 universities and colleges closed for two years while textbooks, curricula, and faculty were "purified" of un-Islamic influences. Afterwards the history of Islam and Iran's revolution predominated in schools and the mass media. Sharp restriction of the lives of women represented a major element of this religious revolution. (See Historians' Voices: Perspectives on the Iranian Revolution, page 1063.)

Noticing Variations In what ways was Islamic radicalism expressed?

A further expression of **Islamic radicalism** lay in violent attacks, largely against civilian targets, undertaken by radical groups such as al-Qaeda, the Taliban, Boko Haram, and the Islamic State. The most widely known of these attacks occurred on September 11, 2001, when the World Trade Center in New York and other targets were attacked. Subsequent assaults targeted various European and Russian cities, but this kind of terrorist violence was directed far more often and with far greater casualties against targets in the Islamic world itself, including Iraq, Pakistan, Afghanistan, Saudi Arabia, India, Indonesia, Yemen, Somalia, and Nigeria.

Violence, however, was not the only response of Islamic fundamentalists or radicals. All over the Muslim world, from North Africa to Indonesia, Islamic renewal movements spawned organizations that operated legally to provide social services—schools, clinics, youth centers, legal-aid societies, financial institutions, publishing houses—that the state offered inadequately or not at all. Islamic activists took leadership roles in unions and professional organizations of teachers, journalists, engineers, doctors, and lawyers. Such people embraced modern science and technology but sought to embed these elements of modernity within a more distinctly Islamic culture. Some served in official government positions or entered political life and contested elections where it was possible to do so. The Algerian Islamic Salvation Front was poised to win elections in 1992, when a frightened military government intervened to cancel it, an action that plunged the country into a decade of bitter civil war. Egypt's Muslim Brotherhood did come to power peacefully in 2012, but it was removed by the military a year later amid widespread protests against its policies.

Confronting Islamic Radicalism The Nigerian Islamic radical group Boko Haram ("Western influence is a sacrilege") has waged a violent campaign of terror in support of a highly restrictive version of sharia law, killing thousands and displacing millions in northeastern Nigeria. In 2014 the group abducted over 200 schoolgirls, prompting this demonstration in Lagos to "bring back our girls." (Xinhua/Alamy)

Militant fundamentalism has certainly not been the only religious response to modernity and globalization within the Islamic world.

(See Working with Evidence: Contending for Islam, page 1053.) Considerable debate among Muslims has raised questions about the proper role of the state; the difference between the eternal law of God (sharia) and the human interpretations of it; the rights of women; the possibility of democracy; and many other issues. In 1996, Anwar Ibrahim, a major political and intellectual figure in Malaysia, insisted:

> Southeast Asian Muslims . . . would rather strive to improve the welfare of the women and children in their midst than spend their days elaborately defining the nature and institutions of the ideal Islamic state. They do not believe it makes one less of a Muslim to promote economic growth, to master the information revolution, and to demand justice for women.[16]

In 2004 and 2005 scholars from all major schools of Islamic thought called for Islamic unity, condemned terrorism, forbade Muslims from declaring one another as "apostate" or nonbelievers, and emphasized the commonalities shared by Muslims, Christians, and Jews.

Within other religious traditions as well, believers found various ways of responding to global modernity. A number of liberal and mainstream Christian groups spoke to the ethical issues arising from economic globalization and climate change. Many Christian organizations, for example, were active in agitating for debt relief for poor countries and the rights of immigrants. Adherents of "liberation theology," particularly in Latin America, sought a Christian basis for action in the areas of social justice, poverty, and human rights, while viewing Jesus as liberator as well as savior. In Asia, a growing movement known as socially engaged Buddhism addressed the needs of the poor through social reform, educational programs, health services, and peacemaking action during times of conflict and war. In short, religious responses to global modernity were articulated in many voices.

The Environment in the Anthropocene Era

The fossil fuel revolution and rapid technological innovation; industrialization and economic growth; urbanization and consumerism; population growth and migration; nationalism and global citizenship—all of these accelerating global processes of the past century connect with what is surely the most distinctive feature of that century: the human impact on the environment. As environmental historian J. R. McNeill put it: "This is the first time in human history that we have altered ecosystems with such intensity, on such a scale, and with such speed. . . . The human race, without intending anything of the sort, has undertaken a gigantic uncontrolled experiment on the earth."[17]

The Global Environment Transformed

By the early twenty-first century, that "experiment" had acquired a name: the **Anthropocene era** or the age of humankind. Many scientists and environmental historians now use this term to designate the contemporary era since the advent of

CORE IDEA

Assessing the Anthropocene
What evidence might support the notion that the earth has moved into the "age of humankind"?

the Industrial Revolution and more dramatically since 1950. It emphatically calls attention to the enduring impact of recent human activity on the planet. Species extinctions; mounting carbon dioxide emissions and climate change; the depletion of groundwater reserves; accumulating radioactive isotopes in the earth's surface; the enlargement of deserts; dead zones in the oceans; the prevalence of concrete and plastics—these and other environmental changes, all of them generated by human actions, will be apparent to archeologists many thousands of years in the future, should they be around to reflect on them. A prominent geologist recently declared: "We are the dominant geologic force shaping the planet. It's not so much river or ice or wind anymore. It's humans."[18]

As geologists reckon time, humankind has been living for the past 12,000 years in the **Holocene era**, a warmer and often wetter period that began following the end of the last Ice Age. During this Holocene era, environmental conditions were uniquely favorable for human thriving. It was, according to prominent earth scientist Johan Rockstrom, a "Garden of Eden" era, providing "a stable equilibrium of forests, savannahs, coral reefs, grasslands, fish, mammals, bacteria, air quality, ice cover, temperatures, fresh water availability, and productive soils."[19] These conditions enabled the development of agriculture, significant population growth, and the creation of complex civilizations. Human activity during the Holocene era certainly transformed the environment in many ways, as plants and animals were domesticated, as native vegetation and forests gave way to agricultural fields and grazing land, as soils were eroded or became salty, as cities grew, and in many other ways. However, these environmental impacts were limited, local, and sometimes temporary.

That began to change as industrialization and population growth took hold first in Europe, North America, and Japan during the nineteenth century, in the Soviet Union during the 1930s, and then after 1950 in many other parts of the world. Everywhere, the idea of economic growth or "development" as something possible and desirable took hold, in capitalist, communist, and developing countries alike. Thus, human impact on the environment has become pervasive, global, and permanent, eroding the "Garden of Eden" conditions of the Holocene era.

Among the chief indicators of the Anthropocene era were multiple transformations of the landscape.[20] The growing numbers of the poor and the growing consumption of the rich led to the doubling of cropland and pasturelands during the twentieth century. By 2015, some 40 percent of the world's land area was used to produce food for humans and their domesticated animals, whereas in 1750 that figure was only 4 percent. As grasslands and swampland contracted, so too did the world's forests. The most dramatic deforestation took place in tropical regions of Latin America, Africa, and Southeast Asia, making way for timbering and farming, even as some reforestation took hold in Europe, North America, and Japan. Furthermore, huge urban complexes have transformed the landscape in many places into wholly artificial environments of concrete, asphalt, steel, and glass. China alone lost some 6.7 million hectares of farmland, over 5 percent of its available agricultural land, to urban growth between 1996 and 2003.[21]

These human incursions reduced the habitat available to wild plants and animals, leading to the extinction of numerous species and declining biodiversity. Extinction is, of course, a natural phenomenon, but by the early twenty-first century the pace of species extinction had spiked far beyond the natural or "background rate" because of human interventions in the form of agriculture, lumbering, and urban growth. Tropical rain forest habitats, home to a far richer diversity of species than more temperate environments, were particularly susceptible to human intrusion.

This loss of biodiversity extended to the seas of the world as well. Fishing with industrial-style equipment has led to the collapse or near collapse of fisheries around the world. The 1992 breakdown of the Grand Banks cod fishery off the coast of Newfoundland persuaded the Canadian government to place a moratorium on further fishing in that area. By the early 1960s, most whale species were on the verge of extinction, though many have begun to recover as restrictions on whaling have been put in place. "For the first time since the demise of the dinosaurs 65 million years ago," wrote the director of the World Wildlife Federation, "we face a global mass extinction of wildlife."[22]

The global spread of modern industry, heavily dependent on fossil fuels, has generated dramatic changes in the air, water, soil, and atmosphere, with profound impacts on human life. China's spectacular economic growth since the 1980s, fueled largely by coal, has resulted in an equally spectacular pall of air pollution in its major cities. In 2004, the World Bank reported that twelve of the world's twenty most polluted cities were in China. Degradation of the world's rivers, seas, and oceans has also mounted, as pesticides, herbicides, chemical fertilizers, detergents, oil, sewage, industrial waste, and plastics have made their way from land to water. The Great Pacific Garbage Patch, an area of about 7 million square miles in the North Pacific, has trapped an enormous quantity of debris, mostly plastics, endangering oceanic food webs and proving deadly to creatures of the sea, which ingest or become entangled in this human garbage. Industrial pollution in the Soviet Union rendered about half of the country's rivers severely polluted by the late 1980s, while fully 20 percent of its population lived in regions defined as "ecological disasters." The release of chemicals known as chlorofluorocarbons thinned the ozone layer,

Urban Pollution in Beijing Deriving from auto exhausts, coal burning, and dust storms, the air pollution in China's capital city of Beijing has long been horrendous. In this photograph from early 2014, teenagers wear face masks to protect themselves from inhaling the noxious particles in the air. Many thousands of people across the globe die daily from the long-term effects of air pollution. (Rolex Dela Pena/EPA/Shutterstock)

which protects the earth from excessive ultraviolet radiation, before an international agreement put an end to the practice.

In other ways as well, human activity has left a lasting mark on the planet during the past century. Radioactive residue from the testing of nuclear weapons and from the storage of nuclear waste produced by power plants can remain detectable for tens or hundreds of thousands of years. Mining has also created a vast underground network of shafts and tunnels and above-ground scarring of open-pit mines and quarries. As the demand for water to serve growing populations, industries, and irrigation needs increased by 900 percent during the twentieth century, many of the planet's aquifers became substantially depleted. A number of large cities—Beijing, Mexico City, Bangkok, Tokyo, Houston, Jakarta, and Manila—have been measurably sinking over the past century due in part to groundwater depletion. All of these environmental changes deriving from human activity will be apparent to our descendants for a long time to come.

Changing the Climate

By the early twenty-first century, **climate change** had become the world's most pressing environmental issue. Since the Industrial Revolution took hold in Western Europe, higher concentrations of carbon dioxide and methane, generated by the burning of fossil fuels, as well as nitrous oxide derived largely from fertilizers, began to accumulate in the atmosphere, slowly at first and then much more rapidly after 1950. These so-called greenhouse gases act as a blanket around the world, limiting the escape of infrared energy from the earth's surface and so warming the planet. Carbon dioxide concentrations have increased by almost 50 percent since 1750, reaching around 412 parts per million (ppm) by the summer of 2020, a level well beyond the 350 ppm generally considered "safe" and greater than at any time during the over 200,000 years of human life on the planet. (See Figure 23.1 and Figure 23.2.) Average

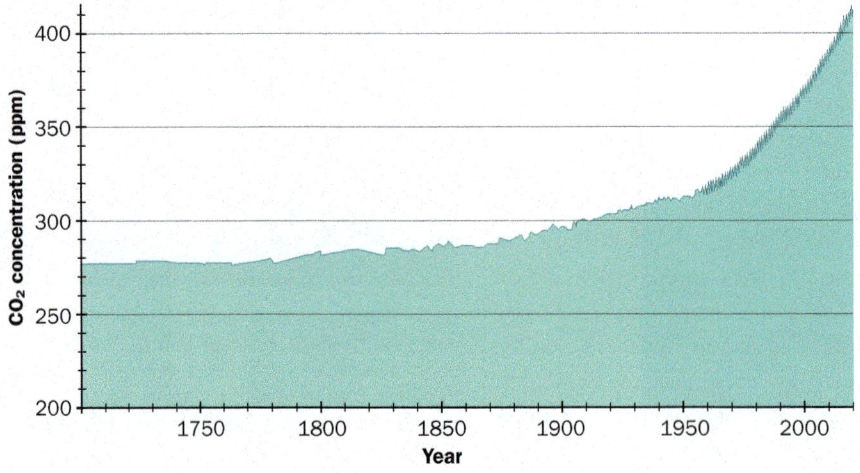

Figure 23.1 Carbon Dioxide Concentrations, 1750–2020
Rising concentrations of carbon dioxide in the atmosphere have been matched by a marked increase in global temperatures. (Data from Scripps Institution of Oceanography at the University of California San Diego)

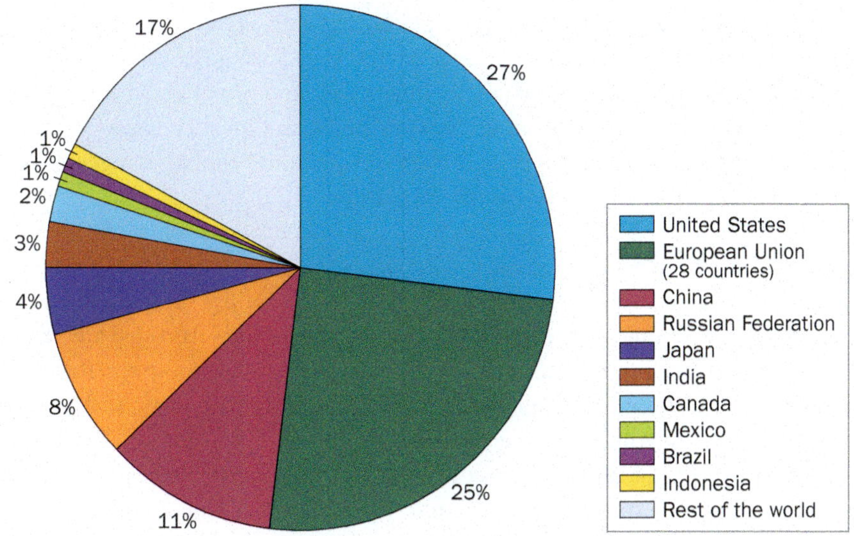

Figure 23.2
Distribution of Total World Carbon Dioxide Emissions, 1850–2011
The various regions or countries of the world have contributed very unevenly to carbon dioxide emissions over the past 160 years. By 2014, however, industrializing Asian economies had become major emitters, with China responsible for some 30 percent of global carbon dioxide discharges into the atmosphere in that year. (Data from World Resources Institute)

global temperature during this time increased by 1°C or more. While this temperature increase may seem numerically small, its consequences have already been substantial and are intensifying. Every year between 2001 and 2019 ranked in the top twenty hottest on record, and projections into the near future are alarming.

Scientists have associated this warming of the planet with all manner of environmental changes. One of them involves the accelerating melting of glaciers and polar ice caps. Arctic temperatures, unprecedented in the past 44,000 years, have been melting glaciers and sea ice at record levels. Coupled with expanded sea volumes as the oceans warm, this rapid melting has raised sea levels by roughly 8.5 inches since 1850. Particularly threatened have been a number of small island nations in Oceania—Tuvalu and Kiribati in particular. Coastal communities everywhere have become more vulnerable to storm surges. Low-lying regions of Bangladesh and the Philippines already flood almost every year and more catastrophically during particularly powerful storms, which seem to occur with increasing frequency and power as the planet warms. The first decade of the twenty-first century witnessed eight Category 5 hurricanes in the Atlantic Ocean, the most for any decade on record.

■ Assessing Cause and Effect
In what ways has global warming affected life on earth?

While global warming has exacerbated storms and rainfall in some regions, it has increased the prevalence and duration of droughts in others. Since the 1970s, droughts have been longer and more extreme in parts of Africa, the Middle East, southern Asia, and the western United States. In 2010 and 2011, extreme weather conditions characteristic of global warming—droughts, dust storms, fires, heavy rainfall—afflicted many grain-producing regions of the world, including Canada, Russia, China, Argentina, and Australia, causing a sharp spike in grain prices on the world market. The Middle East and North Africa, heavily dependent on grain imports, experienced sharply rising food prices, arguably aggravating social unrest and contributing to the political protests of the Arab Spring. In various parts of Africa, surging populations, record high temperatures, and prolonged drought have generated crop failures, devastation of livestock herds, and local conflicts over land and water. These pressures have turned many people into "climate refugees" who migrate to urban areas or northward toward Europe.

Climate change has also disrupted many aquatic ecosystems, as the world's oceans and lakes have become warmer and more acidic, absorbing some 25 percent of human-generated carbon dioxide. While this absorption has limited the extent of atmospheric warming to date, the resulting carbonic acid has damaged any number of marine organisms with calcium shells, such as oysters, clams, sea urchins, and plankton, and places entire aquatic food chains in jeopardy. The world's coral reefs have been especially vulnerable. Record-high oceanic temperatures in 2016 killed 67 percent of the coral in some areas of Australia's Great Barrier Reef. "The coral was cooked," declared one of the scientists studying this phenomenon.[23]

Nor have land-based communities of living organisms been spared the impact of global warming. Drier conditions, for example, have meant more forest fires. Those in the western United States have increased fourfold since 1970, and the fire season has been extended by more than two months. Both plants and animals adapted to a particular temperature range have been forced to migrate or die as temperatures have increased. In Ethiopia, this has meant that mosquitos bearing malaria have migrated higher up the country's mountains, bringing the disease to people who never knew it before. Warmer temperatures in western North America have enabled bark beetles, which cause great damage as they feed on the bark and wood of trees, to survive the less intense winters and move to new environments. They have killed over 150,000 square miles of trees in recent decades. Polar bears have become an iconic image of the impact of global warming, as the sea ice on which they depend vanishes.

Clearly climate change as a marker of the Anthropocene era is in its early stages, with more, much more, to follow if these emissions continue more or less unchecked. Projections to the year 2100, although subject to much dispute and controversy, paint a bleak picture: there will be carbon dioxide concentrations of 600 ppm and up; temperature increases of 1.8°C to 4°C; massive melting of glaciers and sea ice with sea level rise in the range of 2.5 to 6 feet; millions of homes and hundreds of cities at least partially under water; drought and falling food production in parts of Africa, leading to mass migrations; widespread species extinction of up to half of earth's higher life forms by one estimate; and frequent international conflicts over dwindling freshwater supplies. Under these conditions, serious observers have begun to speak about the possibility of a major collapse of modern civilization. Can humans restrain their activities enough to stop climate change when the world has never experienced anything like this in the past? (See Then and Now: Humanity and Nature, page 1046.) Environmental movements of the twenty-first century have certainly pushed for fundamental change in the face of current conditions and future possibilities.

Protecting the Planet: The Rise of Environmentalism

Long before climate change emerged as a global issue, a growing awareness of ecological damage and a desire to counteract it accompanied human entry into the Anthropocene era.[24] In the late eighteenth and early nineteenth centuries, Romantic English poets such as William Blake and William Wordsworth denounced the industrial era's "dark satanic mills," which threatened the "green and pleasant land" of an earlier England. In opposing the extension of railroads, the British writer John Ruskin declared in 1876 that "the frenzy of avarice is daily drowning our sailors, suffocating our miners, poisoning our children and blasting the cultivable surface of England into a treeless waste of ashes."[25] Another element in early environmentalism, especially prominent in the United States and Germany, derived from a concern with deforestation, drought, and desertification as pioneering settlers, lumbermen, miners, and the owners of colonial plantations inflicted terrible damage on the woodlands and pasturelands of the world. Articulated primarily by scientists often working in the colonial world, this approach sought to mobilize scientific expertise and state control to manage, contain, and tame modern assaults on the environment.

Protecting remaining wilderness areas was yet another piece of early environmentalism. The first international environmental conference, held in London in 1900, aimed at preserving African wildlife from voracious European hunters. In the United States it was the opening of the west to European settlers that threatened the natural order. "With no eye to the future," wrote naturalist John Muir in 1897, "these pious destroyers waged interminable forest wars . . . , spreading ruthless devastation ever wider and further. . . . Wilderness is a necessity . . . not only as fountains of timber and irrigating rivers, but as fountains of life."[26] This kind of sensibility found expression in the American national parks, the first of which, Yellowstone, was established in 1872.

CORE IDEA

Making Comparisons

In what different ways has environmentalism been expressed?

These early examples of environmental awareness were distinctly limited, largely a product of literary figures, scientists, and some government officials. None of them attracted a mass following or elicited a global response. But "**second-wave environmentalism**," beginning in the 1960s, certainly did. It began, arguably, with the publication in 1962 of Rachel Carson's *Silent Spring*, which exposed the chemical contamination of the environment with a particular emphasis on the use of pesticides. Ten years later, the Club of Rome, a global think tank, issued a report called *Limits to Growth*, which warned of resource exhaustion and the collapse of industrial society in the face of unrelenting economic and population growth. Soon a mounting wave of environmental books, articles, treatises, and conferences emerged in Europe and North America, pushing back in various ways against the postwar emphasis on "development,"

THEN AND NOW

Humanity and Nature

Homo sapiens, like all other living creatures, are a product of the natural world. The earth's environment has sustained our kind even as we have learned more and more how to harness and redirect its resources for our needs and desires. Natural challenges have repeatedly shaped our historical trajectory. Global warming at the end of the last Ice Age, for instance, enabled the emergence of agriculture, while tiny microbes carried by Europeans and Africans decimated Native American peoples in the sixteenth century.

Two ancient and persistent patterns have featured prominently in humankind's relationship with the natural world. First, humans have long been inspired by nature's impressive power and immense grandeur and understood themselves as deeply connected to it. Paleolithic cave art, Australian Dreamtime mythology, Chinese landscape paintings, and many religious traditions reflect this reverence for nature, often celebrating its ancient rhythms while inspiring practices that preserve elements of the natural world.

At the same time, humans have also long sought to use nature for their own benefit, often altering, degrading, or destroying the environment in the process. The arrival of the earliest human settlers in many places brought the rapid extinction of some species and the reshaping of environments to meet human needs through practices such as controlled burns, where humans intentionally set fires to parts of their environment to help favored species thrive. Then starting some 10,000 years ago, the spread of agriculture allowed humankind to harness ever more of nature's resources. But doing so often imposed great environmental costs, including deforestation, water pollution, and soil degradation.

For many centuries, the environmental impact of human activity remained limited and local. Very recently, however, humankind's relationship with nature has changed profoundly. Starting about two centuries ago but accelerating markedly over the past seventy years, we have increasingly entered a new era—the Anthropocene, or "age of humankind." For the first time in the history of our planet, a single species—us—has "acquired such control over the biosphere that it dominates change on the surface of the Earth."[27] This is what separates our relationship with the natural world now from all that has come before.

So what has caused this dramatic change in balance between humankind and nature in such a short time? Human numbers certainly played a role. Unprecedented in human history, our population expanded from 1 billion in the early nineteenth century to 7.8 billion in 2020. And energy use, associated with industrialization on a global scale, has increased even more quickly than the population, so that humankind today consumes twenty-five times more energy than it did in 1800, mostly thanks to the burning of fossil fuels.

Thus population and economic growth have granted humankind the means to drive change on an unprecedented scale. Humans now move more earth for construction, road building, and other projects than do all the natural processes of the planet, including erosion and glaciation. Greenhouse gas emissions far beyond anything in human history have melted glaciers and polar ice caps, raising sea levels by at least three inches since 1993. Species extinction rates are 1,000 times greater today than the average over the last few million years. As one leading scholar has recently put it, "we humans have become a planet-changing species."[28]

Already in the opening decades of the twentieth century, many predicted that the shifting balance between nature and humankind would continue and accelerate. The British science fiction author H. G. Wells envisioned futures in which humans became god-like masters of nature and thus their own fate. "The final goal . . . is a profound rearrangement of the entire living world," declared the communist Soviet intellectual Nikolai Kashchenko in 1929. "All living nature will live, thrive and die at none other than the will of humans and according to their designs."[29]

While some viewed this future as full of promise, other observers struck a more cautious tone. Was humankind really up to creating nature in its image? The German philosopher and intellectual Ludvig Klages expressed his doubts when he wrote that "in no conceivable case will human beings ever meet with success in their attempt to 'correct' nature."[30] And as the impact of human activity on the environment became more apparent over the course of the twentieth century, a growing number of scientists and environmentalists warned that mistreating and overwhelming nature might bring terrible repercussions. Already by 1948, the American conservationist and environmentalist Aldo Leopold gave expression to what later was dubbed a "deep ecology" outlook. "We abuse land," he wrote, "because we regard it as a commodity belonging to us. When we see land as a community to which we belong, we may begin to use it with love and respect."[31] In the 1960s, a growing environmentalist movement emerged that was dedicated to limiting humankind's imprint on the natural world and conserving the natural environment; notable successes included the improvement of air and water quality in many regions and the protection of some endangered species.

Electric lights have overturned night's limitations on humankind but also consume the earth's fuel. (Matthias Kulka/Getty Images)

But in the 2020s it remains an open question whether humankind will be able to slow, let alone stop, its unprecedented assault on the natural order, which is driven by powerful forces beyond the control of any single person or government: a rising human population, the universal desire for economic growth, the imperatives of capitalism, and the technological capacity to overcome limitations imposed by nature. The past offers us few lessons about the future, for our age has no parallel in our planet's 4.5-billion-year history. Never before has a single species gained a large element of control over change on earth. Can we recover a sense of ourselves as a part of the natural order rather than the masters of it? In short, can humanity restrain itself?

Or will nature restrain humankind? The COVID-19 pandemic provides a timely reminder of human vulnerability in the face of nature. In just a matter of months, the coronavirus jumped species through human contact with wild animals and then rode along modern transportation routes and became established almost everywhere. Another natural phenomenon, global warming, could prove an even greater constraint than disease. The burning of fossil fuels, which has been critical to humans' control over their environment, threatens to cause catastrophic climate changes that will bring into question the viability of our current way of life. The Anthropocene has arrived, but the duration and course of this "age of humankind" are unclear.

QUESTIONS

What separates humankind's relationship with the natural environment today from its relationship in the more distant past? Is the Anthropocene a permanent break from the past, or might the relationship between humankind and the natural environment return to older patterns in the future?

consumerism, and unending economic growth. That sensibility was aptly captured in the title of a best-selling book by British economist E. F. Schumacher in 1973, *Small Is Beautiful*.

But what most clearly distinguished second-wave environmentalism was widespread grassroots involvement and activism. By the late 1990s, millions of people in North America, Europe, Japan, Australia, and New Zealand had joined one of the rapidly proliferating environmental organizations, many of them local. The issues addressed in these burgeoning movements were many and various: pollution, resource depletion, toxic waste, protecting wildlife habitats, nuclear power and nuclear testing, limiting development, and increasingly at the top of the agenda in the twenty-first century, climate change. Beyond particular issues, proponents of "deep ecology" argued that human beings should no longer be considered central but understood as occupying a place of equivalence with other species. Those supporting an "environmental justice" outlook were more concerned with the impact of environmental devastation on the poor, minorities, and developing countries. This social justice perspective informed Pope Francis's 2015 environmental encyclical, which commanded global attention, as the world's most prominent Christian leader called for humankind to "care for our common home."

The tactics of these movements were as varied as the issues they addressed. Much attention was given to public education and to lobbying governments and corporations, often through professionally run organizations. In Germany, New Zealand, and Australia, environmentalists created Green parties, which contested elections and on occasion shared power. Teach-ins, demonstrations, street protests, and various local actions also played a role in the strategies of environmental activists.

In the communist world, environmentalism was constrained by highly authoritarian states that were committed to large-scale development. In the late 1980s, the Chinese government, for example, sharply repressed groups critical of the enormous Three Gorges Dam project across the Yangzi River. By the early twenty-first century, however, a grassroots environmental movement had taken root in China, expressed in hundreds of private groups and in state-sponsored organizations as well. Many of these sought to ground their activism in Buddhist or Daoist traditions that stressed the harmony of humankind and the natural order. In the Soviet Union during the 1970s and after, environmentalists were able to voice their concerns about the shrinking of the Aral Sea, pollution threats to Lake Baikal in Siberia, and poor air quality in many cities. After the nuclear disaster at Chernobyl in 1986, Gorbachev's policy of *glasnost* allowed greater freedom of expression as environmentalist concerns became part of a broader challenge to communism and Russian domination.

Quite quickly, during the 1970s and 1980s, environmentalism also took root in the Global South, where it frequently assumed a distinctive character compared to the more industrialized countries. There it was more locally based, with less connection to global issues or large national organizations than in the West; it involved more poor people in direct action rather than in political lobbying and corporate strategies; it was more concerned with issues of food security, health, and basic survival than with the rights of nature or wilderness protection; and it was more closely connected to movements for social justice. Thus, whereas Western environmentalists defended forests where few people lived, the Chikpo, or "tree-hugging," movement in India sought to protect the livelihood of farmers, artisans, and herders living in areas subject to extensive deforestation. A massive movement to prevent or limit the damming of India's Narmada River derived from the displacement of local people; similar anti-dam protests in the American Northwest were more concerned with protecting salmon runs.

Environmentalism in Action Many environmental activists have channeled their energies into direct action at the local level. In this photograph taken in 2020, two volunteers in kayaks—part of a flotilla of about 300 small craft—take part in a waste removal and cleanup campaign in Cairo, Egypt. The group that sponsored this event claims to have collected some thirty-seven tons of garbage from the Nile River over the past three years. (Khaled Desouki/Getty Images)

In the Global South, this "environmentalism of the poor" took shape in various ways, often in opposition to the gigantic development projects of national governments. Residents of the Brazilian Amazon basin, facing the loss of their livelihood to lumbering interests, ranchers, and government road-building projects, joined hands and directly confronted workers sent to cut down trees with their chainsaws. When the Thai government sought to create huge eucalyptus plantations, largely to supply Japanese-owned paper mills, Buddhist teachers, known as "ecology monks," mobilized peasants to put their case to public officials. In the Philippines, coalitions of numerous local groups mobilized large-scale grassroots movements against foreign-owned mining companies. Kenya's Green Belt Movement organized groups of village women to plant millions of trees to forestall the growth of deserts and protect the soil.

By the early twenty-first century, environmentalism had become a matter of global concern and had prompted action at many levels. A growing market for solar and wind power helped drive its cost sharply lower, moving it closer to being competitive with conventional forms of electric generation like coal. Governments acted to curtail pollution and to foster the use of renewable energy sources. Germany, for example, increased the proportion of its electricity from renewable sources from 6.3 percent in 2000 to 46 percent in 2019. China has enacted a large body of environmental laws and regulations and invested heavily in solar power. Brazil and Canada derive the bulk of their electricity from renewables, primarily hydropower. Some 6,000 national parks in over 100 countries served to protect wildlife and natural beauty.

Many businesses found it commercially useful and therefore profitable to brand themselves as "green." Reforestation programs were under way in China, Honduras, Kenya, and elsewhere. International agreements have come close to eliminating the introduction of ozone-depleting substances into the atmosphere. And after extensive negotiations, the **Paris Climate Agreement** of 2015 committed some 195 countries, 700 cities, and many companies to reduce greenhouse gas emissions sufficiently to avoid a 2°C increase in global temperatures. Furthermore, millions of individuals altered their ways of life, agreeing to recycle, to install solar panels, to buy fuel-efficient cars, to shop in local markets, and to forgo the use of plastic bags.

But resistance has also surfaced, partly because moving toward a clean energy economy would require lifestyle adjustment for citizens in the Global North and for elites everywhere. Powerful and entrenched interests in fossil fuel industries likewise generate resistance. Furthermore, large-scale international agreement on global warming has come up against sharp conflicts between the Global North and South. Both activists and governments in the developing countries have often felt that Northern initiatives to address atmospheric pollution and global warming would curtail their industrial development, leaving the North/South gap intact. A Malaysian official put the dispute succinctly: "The developed countries don't want to give up their extravagant lifestyles, but plan to curtail our development."[32]

Since signing the Paris Agreement in 2016, U.S. government policy toward climate change has shifted more dramatically between engagement and resistance than in any other major country in the world. In 2017 the new Trump administration began to partially dismantle existing climate change regulations and stunned the world by announcing U.S. withdrawal from the Paris Agreement. Then in 2021 the United States changed course under President Joe Biden by rejoining the agreement and beginning the process of reversing other actions taken by his predecessor. As one of the largest producers of greenhouse gases in the world, the path charted by the United States in coming years will have a critical impact on the success or failure of efforts to limit global warming. More than any other widespread movement, global environmentalism came to symbolize a focus on the common plight of humankind across the artificial boundaries of nation-states. It also marked a challenge to modernity itself, particularly its overriding commitment to endless growth and consumption. The ideas of sustainability and restraint, certainly not prominent in any list of modern values, entered global discourse and marked the beginnings of a new environmental ethic. This change in thinking, although limited, was perhaps the most significant achievement of global environmentalism.

CONCLUSIONS AND REFLECTIONS

World History and the Making of Meaning

Humans everywhere are meaning-making creatures. We find meaning in relationship with others, in causes and common efforts, in religious or spiritual experience, and in perceiving pattern or purpose both in the world generally and in our individual lives. In the absence of meaning, we do not flourish.

A large part of the historian's task involves identifying and describing the multiple meanings that individuals and societies in the past have ascribed to their world and to their behavior. Over the last century, for example, religiously committed people, pummeled by the multiple assaults of modern life, have sought meaning and a sense of belonging by returning to what they believed were earlier and more authentic forms of Hinduism, Christianity, or Islam. For many others, identification with a particular racial, national, or ethnic group has provided that sense of meaning, as in Nazi Germany. Still others have found significance in a sense of world citizenship or membership in larger international communities, such as a pan-African community, the European Union, or a global scientific association. Amid many signs of serious damage to the planet, environmentalists too have understood the world in ways that give meaning to what they see and what they value.

But historians are more than observers of past meanings. They also join the rest of humankind in creating meaning as they give definition to the human past. World historians, for example, have sometimes pointed to a broad trend toward greater social complexity and more connectivity among regions and peoples, especially in the twentieth century. They give some meaning to human tragedies such as wars and genocide by explaining their origins and development. In defining the past century as a new and distinctive age in world history, the "Anthropocene," historians assert that a special significance or meaning attaches to this period. In identifying particular patterns within the recent past—unprecedented population growth, widespread urbanization, international migration, recurring pandemics, cultural globalization, and global warming—historians seek to impose some shape and significance on the chaos of random events.

In doing so, they are insisting that history is more than "one damned thing after another," that it is possible to find a measure of coherence in the record of humankind. Some might argue that any such "shape" is an illusion, an artificial product of human self-serving. Certainly historians' formulations are endlessly contested and debated. But we are apparently impelled to seek pattern, structure, or meaning in the past. An infinite array of miscellaneous historical "facts" is neither satisfying nor useful.

The study of world history can also be helpful for each of us as we seek to make meaning in our own lives. As we witness the broad contours of the human journey and learn more about the wider world, we can more readily locate ourselves individually in the larger stream of that story. In short, world history provides context, which is so essential to the creation of meaning. If we base our understanding of the world only on what we personally experience in our own brief and limited lives, we render ourselves both impoverished and ineffective.

World history opens a marvelous window into the unfamiliar. It confronts us with the "ways of the world," the whole panorama of human achievement, tragedy, and sensibility. It allows us some modest entry into the lives of people far removed from us in time and place. And it offers us company for the journey of our own lives. Pondering the global past with a receptive heart and an open mind can assist us in enlarging and deepening our sense of self. In exposing us to the wider experience of "all under Heaven," as the Chinese put it, world history can aid us in constructing more meaningful lives. That is among the many gifts that the study of the global past offers to us all.

Revisiting Chapter 23

Revisiting Specifics

population explosion, 1018
Green Revolution, 1018
global urbanization, 1020
megacities, 1021
labor migration, 1023
influenza pandemic, 1027
HIV/AIDS, 1027
systemic racism, 1029
cultural globalization, 1031
religious fundamentalism, 1034
Hindutva, 1035
Islamic radicalism, 1038
Anthropocene era, 1039
Holocene era, 1040
climate change, 1042
second-wave environmentalism, 1045
Paris Climate Agreement, 1050

Revisiting Core Ideas

1. **Explaining Population Growth** What accounts for the unprecedented growth in human numbers during the past century?
2. **Explaining Migration** What has caused such large-scale human movement to urban areas and other countries in the past century?
3. **Assessing Identity** In what ways have race, nation, and ethnicity found expression and played a role in world history during the past century?
4. **Making Comparisons** In what different ways have religious believers responded to the challenges of modern life?
5. **Assessing the Anthropocene** What evidence might support the notion that the earth has moved into the "age of humankind"?
6. **Making Comparisons** In what different ways has environmentalism been expressed?

A Wider View

1. In what ways has population growth shaped the movement of people and the human impact on the environment?
2. How have cultural patterns evolved over the past century? What broader processes have contributed to those cultural changes?
3. To what extent do the changes described in these last two chapters justify considering the past century a new phase of world history?
4. How have the technological and economic changes explored in the previous chapter shaped the demographic, cultural, and environmental processes discussed in this chapter?
5. **Looking Back** How do the migration patterns explored in this chapter compare to those associated with the Industrial Revolution and imperialism that were examined in Chapters 17 and 18?

To learn more about the topics in this chapter, see **For Further Study** at the end of the book.

Contending for Islam

Over the past century, the growing intrusion of the West and of modern secular culture into the Islamic world has prompted acute and highly visible debate among Muslims. Which ideas and influences flowing from the West could Muslims safely utilize, and which should they decisively reject? Are women's rights and democracy compatible with Islam? To what extent should Islam find expression in public life as well as in private religious practice? The sources that follow show something of these controversies while illustrating sharp variations in the understanding of Islam.

SOURCE 23.1 A Secular State for an Islamic Society

Modern Turkey emerged from the ashes of the Ottoman Empire after World War I, adopting a distinctive path of modernization, westernization, and secularism under the leadership of Mustafa Kemal Atatürk (see "Religion and Global Modernity" earlier in the chapter). Such policies sought to remove Islam from any significant role in public life, restricting it to the realm of personal devotion. They included abolition of the caliphate, by which Ottoman rulers had claimed leadership of the entire Islamic world. In a speech delivered in 1927, Atatürk explained and justified these policies, which went against the grain of much Islamic thinking.

- On what grounds did Atatürk justify the abolition of the caliphate?
- What additional actions did he take to remove Islam from a public or political role in the new Turkish state?
- What can you infer about Atatürk's view of Islam?
- How did Atatürk's conception of a Turkish state differ from that of Ottoman authorities? In what ways did he build upon Ottoman reforms of the nineteenth century? (See "The Ottoman Empire and the West in the Nineteenth Century" in Chapter 19.)

MUSTAFA KEMAL ATATÜRK | *Speech to the General Congress of the Republican Party* | 1927

[Our Ottoman rulers] hoped to unite the entire Islamic world in one body, to lead it and to govern it. For this purpose, [they] assumed the title of Caliph [successor to the Prophet Muhammad]. . . . It is an unrealizable aim to attempt to unite in one tribe the various races existing on the earth, thereby abolishing all boundaries. . . .

If the Caliph and the Caliphate were to be invested with a dignity embracing the whole of Islam . . . , a crushing burden would be imposed on Turkey. . . . [Furthermore], will Persia or Afghanistan, which are [Muslim] states, recognize the authority of the Caliph in a single matter? No, and this is quite justifiable, because it would be in contradiction to the independence of the state, to the sovereignty of the people.

[The current constitution] laid down as the first duty of the Grand National Assembly that "the prescriptions of the Shari'a [Islamic law] should be put into force. . . ." [But] if a state, having among its subjects elements professing different religions and being compelled to act justly and impartially toward all of them . . . , it is obliged to respect freedom of opinion and conscience. . . . The Muslim religion includes freedom of religious opinion. . . . Will not every grown-up person in the new Turkish state be free to select his own religion? . . . When the first favorable opportunity arises, the nation must act to eliminate these superfluities [the enforcement of sharia] from our Constitution. . . .

Gentlemen, it was necessary to abolish the fez [a distinctive Turkish hat with no brim], which sat on our heads as a sign of ignorance, of fanaticism, of hatred to progress and civilization, and to adopt in its place the hat, the customary headdress of the whole civilized world, thus showing that no difference existed in the manner of thought between the Turkish nation and the whole family of civilized mankind. . . . [Thus] there took place the closing of the Tekkes [Sufi centers], of the convents, and of the mausoleums, as well as the abolition of all sects and all kinds of [religious] titles. . . .

Could a civilized nation tolerate a mass of people who let themselves be led by the nose by a herd of Sheikhs, Dedes, Seids, Tschelebis, Babas, and Emirs [various religious titles]? . . . Would not one therewith have committed the greatest, most irreparable error to the cause of progress and awakening?

Source: *A Speech Delivered by Ghazi Mustapha Kemal, October 1927* (Leipzig: K. F. Koehler, 1929), 377–79, 591–93, 595–98, 717, 721–22.

SOURCE 23.2 Toward an Islamic Society

Even as Kemal Atatürk was seeking to remove Islam from the public life of Turkey, a newly formed Muslim organization in Egypt was strongly advocating precisely the opposite course of action. Founded in 1928 by impoverished schoolteacher Hassan al-Banna (1906–1949), the Muslim Brotherhood argued in favor of "government that will act in conformity to the law and Islamic principles." As the earliest mass movement in the Islamic world advocating such ideas, the Brotherhood soon attracted a substantial following, including many poor urban residents recently arrived from the countryside. Long a major presence in Egyptian political life, the Brotherhood has frequently come into conflict with state authorities and briefly came to power in 2012. In 1936, it published a pamphlet, addressed to Egyptian and other Arab political leaders, that spelled out its views about the direction toward which a proper Islamic society should move.

- How does this document define the purposes of government?
- How does the Muslim Brotherhood understand the role of Islam in public life?
- To what extent was this document anti-Western in its orientation? What posture does it advocate toward capitalism and economic development?
- How might Kemal Atatürk respond to these views?

THE MUSLIM BROTHERHOOD | *Toward the Light* | 1936

After having studied the ideals which ought to inspire a renascent nation on the spiritual level, we wish to offer, in conclusion, some practical suggestions. . . .

I. In the political, judicial, and administrative fields:

1st. To prohibit political parties and to direct the forces of the nation toward the formation of a united front;

2nd. To reform the law . . . [to] be entirely in accordance with Islamic legal practice;

5th. To propagate an Islamic spirit within the civil administration . . .

6th. To supervise the personal conduct of officials . . .

9th. Government will act in conformity to the law and to Islamic principles; . . . The scheduling of government services ought to take account of the hours set aside for prayer. . . .

II. In the fields of social and everyday practical life:

2nd. To find a solution for the problems of women, a solution that will allow her to progress and which will protect her while conforming to Islamic principles.

3rd. To root out clandestine or public prostitution and to consider fornication as a reprehensible crime . . .

4th. To prohibit all games of chance (gaming, lotteries, races, golf)

5th. To stop the use of alcohol and intoxicants

7th. To develop an educational program for girls different than the one for boys

8th. Male students should not be mixed with female students

10th. To close dance halls; to forbid dancing;

11th. To censor theater productions and films;

12th. To supervise and approve music;

14th. To confiscate malicious articles and books as well as magazines displaying a grotesque character or spreading frivolity;

16th. To change the hours when public cafes are opened or closed

19th. To bring to trial those who break the laws of Islam, who do not fast, who do not pray, and who insult religion;

21st. Religious teaching should constitute the essential subject matter to be taught in all educational establishments and faculties;

24th. . . . Absolute priority to be given to Arabic over foreign languages;

25th. To study the history of Islam, the nation, and Muslim civilization;

27th. To combat foreign customs

29th. To safeguard public health . . . increasing the number of hospitals, doctors, and out-patient clinics;

30th. To call particular attention to the problems of village life (administration, hygiene, water supply, education, recreation, morality).

III. The economic field:

1st. Organization of the zakat tax [an obligatory payment to support the poor] according to Islamic precepts

2nd. To prevent the practice of usury [charging interest on loans]

3rd. To facilitate and to increase the number of economic enterprises and to employ the jobless . . . ,

4th. To protect workers against monopoly companies, to require these companies to obey the law, the public should share in all profits;

5th. Aid for low-ranking employees and enlargement of their pay, lowering the income of high-ranking employees; . . .

7th. To encourage agricultural and industrial works, to improve the situation of the peasants and industrial workers[.]

Source: Hassan al-Banna, "Towards the Light," in Robert Landen, *The Emergence of the Modern Middle East* (New York: Van Nostrand Reinhold, 1970), 261–64.

SOURCE 23.3 Two Images of Islamic Radicalism ►

By the late twentieth century, the most widely publicized face of Islam, at least in the West, derived from groups sympathetic to the views of the Muslim Brotherhood—Iran's revolutionary government, Saudi Arabia, and radical Islamist organizations such as al-Qaeda, the Islamic State, Boko Haram, and Hamas. These photographs illustrate two dimensions of Islamic radicalism. Its violent face is horrifically expressed in Source 23.3A, which shows a group of teenage Islamic State militants preparing to execute twenty-five Syrian prisoners in a Roman amphitheater in Palmyra in May 2015. That execution was carried out. On the other hand, Source 23.3B illustrates the kind of social services often provided by radical Islamist groups, such as the Palestinian militant organization Hamas, which governs the small territory of Gaza on the eastern coast of the Mediterranean Sea. The computer classroom pictured was part of a school established by Hamas, which was later destroyed in fighting between Hamas and Israeli forces.

- Why might the Islamic State choose children to perform executions? Why might they have chosen the ruins of a Roman amphitheater as the site for this event?
- What does the computer classroom suggest about the posture of Hamas to the modern world? Notice also the English textbook on the table.
- What do these contrasting images suggest about the appeal of Islamic radicalism?

SOURCE 23.3A

The Violent Face of Islamic Radicalism | 2015

Pictures from History/Newscom

SOURCE 23.3B

The Peaceful Face of Islamic Radicalism | 2015

Abed Rahim Khatib/Flash90/Redux

SOURCE 23.4 The Sufi Alternative

In sharp contrast to the Islamic secularists like Atatürk or Islamic radicals or fundamentalists such as the Muslim Brotherhood, the Sufis represent the more spiritual or mystical dimension of Islam. While most Sufis participate in conventional Islamic practices, they are generally more sharply focused on interior spiritual experience than on the precise prescriptions of the law. Thus they have resisted the legalistic prescriptions of Islamic radicals. And so Sufis have often been persecuted, their practices suppressed, and their places of worship attacked.

Others, however, view the Sufis as counteracting the appeal of Islamic radicals committed to violence. According to the prominent Iranian Sufi scholar Seyyed Nasr, "Sufism is the most powerful antidote to the religious radicalism called fundamentalism. . . . Its influence is immense; Sufism has kept alive the inner quality of ethics and spiritual virtues, rather than a rigid morality . . . and it provides access to knowledge of the divine reality."[33] This was the message that India's prime minister Narendra Modi delivered to the Sufi World Forum in Delhi in 2016. That it came from a prominent Hindu figure in India made the message all the more striking, given the historical tension between Muslims and Hindus.

- Why might Islamic fundamentalists such as those in the Muslim Brotherhood find Sufism "un-Islamic"?
- Why might a Hindu prime minister of India make a very public speech praising Sufism and Islam?
- What elements of Sufism do Prime Minister Modi and Seyyed Nasr believe can serve as an "antidote" to Islamic radicalism?

NARENDRA MODI | *Sufism and Islamic Radicalism* | 2016

At a time when the dark shadow of violence is becoming longer, you [Sufis] are the noor, or the light of hope. . . . And, you represent the rich diversity of the Islamic civilization that stands on the solid bedrock of a great religion. . . . It is a civilization that reached great heights by the 15th century in science, medicine, literature, art, architecture and commerce. . . . It set, once again, an enduring lesson of human history: it is through openness and enquiry, engagement and accommodation, and respect for diversity that humanity advances, nations progress and the world prospers. . . . And, this is the message of Sufism, one of the greatest contributions of Islam to this world.

From its origins in Egypt and West Asia, Sufism travelled to distant lands, holding aloft the banner of faith and the flag of human values, learning from spiritual thoughts of other civilisations, and attracting people with the life and message of its saints. . . . In the different settings of Saharan Africa or in Southeast Asia, in Turkey or in Central Asia, in Iran or India, Sufism reflected the universal human desire to go beyond the practice and precepts of religion for a deeper unity with the Almighty. . . .

For the Sufis, therefore, service to God meant service to humanity. . . . And, its humanism also upheld the place and status of women in society. Above all, Sufism is a celebration of diversity and pluralism. . . . Sufism is the voice of peace, co-existence, compassion and equality; a call to universal brotherhood.

Sufism became the face of Islam in India, even as it remained deeply rooted in the Holy Quran, and Hadiths. . . . Just as it once came to India, today Sufism from India has spread across the world.

Indeed, when terrorism and extremism have become the most destructive force of our times, the message of Sufism has global relevance. . . . Every year, we spend over 100 billion dollars on securing the world from terrorism, money that should have been spent on building lives of the poor. . . . [W]e must reject any link between terrorism and religion. Those who spread terror in the name of religion are anti-religious. . . . And, we must advance the message of Sufism that stands for the principles of Islam and the highest human values.

Source: NDTV, "Full Text of PM Narendra Modi's Speech at World Sufi Forum," March 17, 2016, http://www.ndtv.com/india-news/full-text-of-pm-narendra-modis-speech-at-world-sufi-forum-1288303.

■ ■ ■

SOURCE 23.5 Progressive Islam

All across the Islamic world, many Muslims argued that they could retain their distinctive religious sensibility while embracing democracy, women's rights, technological progress, freedom of thought, and religious pluralism. Such thinkers were following in the tradition of nineteenth-century Islamic modernism (see "Reform and Its Opponents" in Chapter 19), even as they recalled earlier centuries of Islamic intellectual and scientific achievement and religious tolerance. That viewpoint was expressed in a pamphlet composed in 2009 by a leading American Muslim scholar, translator, and teacher, Kabir Helminski. He was listed then as one of the 500 most influential Muslims in the world.

- Against what charges does Helminski seek to defend Islam? How does this document reflect the experience of 9/11?
- In what ways are his views critical of radical, or "fundamentalist," ideas and practices?
- How does this document articulate the major features of a more progressive or liberal Islam? What kinds of arguments does the author employ to make his case?
- To whom might these arguments appeal? How might Hassan al-Banna or Kemal Atatürk respond to these views?

KABIR HELMINSKI | *Islam and Human Values* | 2009

If the word "Islam" gives rise to fear or mistrust today, it is urgent that American Muslims clarify what we believe Islam stands for in order to dispel the idea that there is a fundamental conflict between the best values of Western civilization and the essential values of Islam. . . .

Islamic civilization, which developed out of the revelation of the Qur'an in the seventh century, affirms the truth of previous revelations, affirms religious pluralism, cultural diversity, and human rights, and recognizes the value of reason and individual conscience. . . .

[One issue] is the problem of violence. . . . Thousands of Muslim institutions and leaders, the great majority of the world's billion or more Muslims, have unequivocally condemned the hateful and violent ideologies that kill innocents and violate the dignity of all humanity. . . .

Islamic civilizations have a long history of encouraging religious tolerance and guaranteeing the rights of religious minorities. The Qur'an explicitly acknowledges that the diversity of religions is part of the Divine Plan and no religion has a monopoly on truth or virtue. . . .

Jerusalem, under almost continuous Islamic rule for nearly fourteen centuries, has been a place where Christians and Jews have lived side by side with Muslims, their holy sites and religious freedom preserved. Medieval Spain also created a high level of civilization as a multi-cultural society under Islamic rule for several centuries. The Ottoman Empire, the longest lived in history, for the more than six centuries of its existence encouraged ethnic and religious minorities to participate in and contribute to society. It was the Ottoman sultan who gave sanctuary to the Jews expelled from Catholic Spain. India was governed for centuries by Muslims, even while the majority of its people practiced Hinduism. . . .

[T]he acceptance of Islam must be an act of free will. Conversion by any kind of coercion was universally condemned by Islamic scholars. . . . There are many verses in the Qur'an that affirm the actuality and even the necessity of diversity in ways of life and religious belief.

In general, war is forbidden in Islam, except in cases of self-defense in response to explicit aggression. If there is a situation where injustice is being perpetrated or if the community is being invaded, then on a temporary basis permission is given to defend oneself.

[I]n recent decades . . . an intolerant ideology has been unleashed. A small minority of the world's one and a half billion Muslims has misconstrued the teachings of Islam to justify their misguided and immoral actions. It is most critical at this time for Muslims to condemn such extreme ideologies and their manifestations. It is equally important that non-Muslims understand that this ideology violates the fundamental moral principles of Islam and is repugnant to the vast majority of Muslims in the world. . . . So-called "suicide-bombers" did not appear until the mid-1990s. Such strategies have no precedent in Islamic history. The Qur'an says quite explicitly: *Do not kill yourselves* [4:29]. . . .

Islam and democracy are compatible and can coexist because Islam organizes humanity on the basis of the rule of law and human dignity. . . . The only principle of political governance expressed in the Qur'an is the principle of Consultation (Shura), which holds that communities will "*rule themselves by means of mutual consultation*" [Surah 42:38].

An American Muslim scholar, Abdul Aziz Sachedina, expresses it this way: "Islam does not encourage turning God into a political statement since humans cannot possess God. . . ."

[T]here is nothing in the Qur'an that essentially contradicts reason or science. . . . Repeatedly the Qur'an urges human beings to "reflect" and "use their intelligence."

Islam is not an alien religion. It does not claim a monopoly on virtue or truth. It follows in the way of previous spiritual traditions that recognized One Spirit operating within nature and human life. It continues on the Way of the great Prophets and Messengers of all sacred traditions.

Source: Selections from Kabir Helminski, *Islam and Human Values*, unpublished pamphlet, 2009.

SOURCE 23.6 Debating the Burqa

Among the contested issues in the Islamic world, none have been more prominent than those involving the lives—and the bodies—of women. The revolutionary Islamist government of Iran, for example, insisted on and enforced "good hijab" for women, which meant compulsory head covering and very conservative and modest attire. But the issue has surfaced in Europe as well. A prominent British Muslim woman, Saira Khan, called for banning the burqa, the head-to-toe covering worn by some Muslim women, in public places. "The veil is simply a tool of oppression," she declared. "The burkha is the ultimate visual symbol of female oppression."[34]

When the French government in 2011 began to enforce a law forbidding the concealment of the face in public, it was widely understood to be a prohibition of the burqa. To many French people, the burqa represented a security risk and violated the secularism of French life, while banning it prevented women from being forced by their families to wear it. But the new law prompted considerable protest in many places. One such protester outside Notre Dame Cathedral in Paris said: "We view this ban as an assault on our human rights."[35] Source 23.6 shows a group of Muslim women in Britain, clad in black burqas, protesting the law outside the French embassy in London.

- Based on the signs, how might you summarize the women's objections to the French ban on burqas?
- Why might this kind of dress for women be highly objectionable to many in France and elsewhere in Europe?
- How do you imagine that ordinary French people would respond to these signs?

Protests in London against French Ban of Face Concealment | **2011**

Peter Macdiarmid/Getty Images

DOING HISTORY

1. **Understanding the Issues** What issues might arise in a conversation among people holding the various perspectives represented here? Can you identify any areas of agreement? On which points would they probably never agree?
2. **Comparing Islamic Modernists** How do you think Kemal Atatürk would have responded to later Islamic modernists such as Kabir Helminski and perhaps Saira Khan?
3. **Comparing Islamic Radicals** How might the authors of the Muslim Brotherhood declaration of 1936 respond to the actions of Hamas and the women protesting the French ban on burqas?
4. **Explaining Variations** What accounts for the very different understandings of Islam that are reflected in these sources?

HISTORIANS' VOICES

Perspectives on the Iranian Revolution

The Iranian revolution of 1979 gave rise to a religiously inspired government that has sought to inscribe Islamist principles in the political, economic, and social fabric of a major Middle Eastern nation. In Voice 23.1, Francis Robinson, a prominent British historian of the Islamic world, describes the modern Islamic renewal movements that provide the larger context for the Iranian revolution. Then in Voice 23.2, John Esposito, a highly regarded American scholar of modern Islam, reflects on the specific conditions that gave rise to the Iranian revolution.

- How does Francis Robinson in Voice 23.1 explain the appeal of Islamist renewal movements since the 1970s?
- According to John Esposito in Voice 23.2, what conditions within Iran provided the raw material for revolution?
- **Integrating Primary and Secondary Sources** How might both of these authors use the primary sources to illustrate or support their arguments?

VOICE 23.1

Francis Robinson on Islamic Renewal Movements | 1996

A powerful movement of religious renewal has animated all parts of the Muslim world since the eighteenth century. . . .

Since the 1970s the desire to effect renewal has been more powerfully expressed in the Islamist movements. Often led by western-educated professionals and run by university students, these movements have aimed to fill the vacuum created by the failures of the state at the local level in cities and towns through much of the Islamic world. By providing schools, clinics, welfare, and psychological support, they have served the needs of urban communities disrupted by the penetration of the modern state and the international economy. They have also attracted the millions who have flocked to the cities in recent decades from the countryside. The rhetoric of these movements is profoundly opposed to western culture and western power. Their programmes, which start from the premise that the Quran and the holy law are sufficient for all human circumstances, aim to establish an Islamic system to match those of capitalism or socialism. They are to be implemented by seizing power in the modern nation state. This understanding of Islam as a system, an ideology is new in Islamic history. So too . . . is the complete merger between religion and political power.

Islamist movements . . . have brought Islam closer to the centre of political identity of Muslim peoples. In some places, such as Iran . . . , they have taken power.

Source: Francis Robinson, *The Cambridge Illustrated History of the Islamic World* (Cambridge: Cambridge University Press, 1996), 292, 293, 296.

VOICE 23.2

John Esposito on the Source of the Iranian Revolution | 1999

Iran [in 1979] captured the imagination of many throughout the Muslim world and the West. . . . A seemingly modern, enlightened and invincible shah was overthrown by a movement led by an ayatollah [a high-ranking religious scholar] in exile in France. Intellectuals, merchants, students, and journalists as well as clergy mobilized under the banner of Islam. Islam was . . . also a symbol of protest for all who opposed the shah. . . . Islamic symbols, rhetoric, and institutions provided the infrastructure for organization, protest, and mobilization of a coalition of forces calling for reform and in the end for revolution. . . .

Although the shah's modernization program did improve the lot of many, the benefits of modernization tended to favor disproportionately a minority of elites and urban centers. Economic, educational and military reforms were not accompanied by political liberalization. Traditional merchants and religious leaders . . . were alienated by the shah's religious and economic reforms. State control of religious affairs . . . and a tilt toward western markets and the corporate sector threatened their interests, authority, and power. Many modern educated academics, professionals, and journalists increasingly expressed concerns over the excessive dependence of Iran on the West. . . . Some . . . spoke of the dangers of "Westoxification," an excessive dependence on the West that threatened to rob Iranians of their independence and cultural identity. These were issues that resonated across many sectors of society.

Source: John Esposito, *The Oxford History of Islam* (Oxford: Oxford University Press, 1999), 661–62.

Notes

Prologue

1. See David Christian, *Maps of Time: An Introduction to Big History* (Berkeley: University of California Press, 2004).
2. Voltaire, *Treatise on Toleration*, chap. 22.
3. See David Christian, "World History in Context," *Journal of World History* 14, no. 4 (December 2003): 437–58.

Chapter 12

1. Columbus to Remove Christopher Columbus Statue at City Hall," *IdeaStream*, June 18, 2020, https://www.ideastream.org/news/columbus-to-remove-christopher-columbus-statue-at-city-hall.
2. Winona LaDuke, "We Are Still Here: The 500 Year Celebration," *Sojourners*, October 1991.
3. "The Truth about Columbus," http://www.truthaboutcolumbus.com/.
4. Brian Fagan, *Ancient North America* (London: Thames and Hudson, 2005), 503.
5. Quoted in Charles C. Mann, *1491: New Revelations of the Americas before Columbus* (New York: Alfred A. Knopf, 2005), 334.
6. Louise Levanthes, *When China Ruled the Seas* (New York: Simon and Schuster, 1994), 175.
7. Christine de Pisan, *The Book of the City of Ladies*, translated by Rosalind Brown-Grant (New York: Penguin Books, 1999), pt. 1, p. 1.
8. Frank Viviano, "China's Great Armada," *National Geographic*, July 2005, 34.
9. Quoted in John J. Saunders, ed., *The Muslim World on the Eve of Europe's Expansion* (Englewood Cliffs, NJ: Prentice Hall, 1966), 41–43.
10. Quoted in C. R. N. Routh, *They Saw It Happen in Europe: An Anthology of Eyewitnesses' Accounts of Events in European History, 1450–1600* (Oxford: Blackwell, 1965), 386.
11. Leo Africanus, *History and Description of Africa* (London: Hakluyt Society, 1896), 824–25.
12. Quoted in Craig A. Lockhard, *Southeast Asia in World History* (Oxford: Oxford University Press, 2009), 67.
13. Quoted in Patricia Risso, *Merchants and Faith* (Boulder, CO: Westview Press, 1995), 49.
14. Quoted in Stuart B. Schwartz, ed., *Victors and Vanquished* (Boston: Bedford/St. Martin's, 2000), 8.
15. Quoted in Michael E. Smith, *The Aztecs* (London: Blackwell, 2003), 108.
16. Smith, *The Aztecs*, 220.
17. Quoted in Miguel Leon-Portilla, *Aztec Thought and Culture*, translated from the Spanish by Jack Emory Davis (Norman: University of Oklahoma Press, 1963), 7.
18. For a summary of this practice among the Aztecs and Incas, see Karen Vieira Powers, *Women in the Crucible of Conquest* (Albuquerque: University of New Mexico Press, 2005), chap. 1.
19. Powers, *Women in the Crucible of Conquest*, 25.
20. Louise Burkhart, "Mexica Women on the Home Front," in *Indian Women of Early Mexico*, edited by Susan Schroeder et al. (Norman: University of Oklahoma Press, 1997), 25–54.
21. The "web" metaphor is derived from J. R. McNeill and William H. McNeill, *The Human Web* (New York: W. W. Norton, 2003).
22. Quoted in Jerry Brotton, *The Renaissance Bazaar: From the Silk Road to Michaelangelo* (Oxford: Oxford University Press, 2006), 51.
23. Quoted in Brotton, *Renaissance Bazaar*, 51.

Chapter 13

1. Thomas Escritt and Andrew Osborn, "Ukrainian Leader Says Putin Wants His Whole Country, Asks for NATO Help," Reuters, November 29, 2018, https://www.reuters.com/article/us-ukraine-crisis-russia/ukrainian-leader-says-putin-wants-his-whole-country-asks-for-nato-help-idUSKCN1NY1K5.
2. Claude Salhani, "One More Twist in Erdogan's Imperial Mindset," *Ahval*, January 17, 2020, https://ahvalnews.com/libya-turkey/one-more-twist-erdogans-imperial-mindset.
3. Quoted in Thomas E. Skidmore and Peter H. Smith, *Modern Latin America* (New York: Oxford University Press, 2001), 15.
4. George Raudzens, ed., *Technology, Disease, and Colonial Conquest* (Boston: Brill Academic, 2003), xiv.
5. Quoted in Noble David Cook, *Born to Die: Disease and the New World Conquest* (Cambridge: Cambridge University Press, 1998), 202.
6. Quoted in Cook, *Born to Die*, 206.
7. Quoted in Charles C. Mann, *1491: New Revelations of the Americas before Columbus* (New York: Alfred A. Knopf, 2005), 56.
8. Quoted in Geoffrey Parker, *Global Crisis* (New Haven, CT: Yale University Press, 2013), 464.
9. Quoted in Charles C. Mann, *1493: Uncovering the New World Columbus Created* (New York: Alfred A. Knopf, 2011), 165.
10. Felipe Fernandez-Armesto, "Empires in Their Global Context," in *The Atlantic in Global History*, edited by Jorge Canizares-Esguerra and Erik R. Seeman (Upper Saddle River, NJ: Prentice Hall, 2007), 105.
11. Quoted in Alejandro Lugo, *Fragmented Lives; Assembled Parts* (Austin: University of Texas Press, 2008), 53.
12. Quoted in Anthony Padgen, "Identity Formation in Spanish America," in *Colonial Identity in the Atlantic World, 1500–1800*, edited by Nicholas Canny and Anthony Padgen (Princeton, NJ: Princeton University Press, 1987), 56.
13. Quoted in James Lockhart and Stuart B. Schwartz, *Early Latin America* (Cambridge: Cambridge University Press, 1983), 206.
14. Mary Prince, *The History of Mary Prince* (1831; Project Gutenberg, 2006), http://www.gutenberg.org/ebooks/17851.
15. Quoted in Kevin Reilly et al., eds., *Racism: A Global Reader* (Armonk, NY: M. E. Sharpe, 2003), 136–37.
16. Benjamin Wadsworth, *The Well-Ordered Family* (1712), 39.

17. Willard Sutherland, *Taming the Wild Fields: Colonization and Empire on the Russian Steppe* (Ithaca, NY: Cornell University Press, 2004), 223–24.
18. Quoted in Michael Khodarkovsky, *Russia's Steppe Frontier* (Bloomington: Indiana University Press, 2002), 216.
19. Khodarkovsky, *Russia's Steppe Frontier*, 222.
20. Geoffrey Hosking, "The Freudian Frontier," *Times Literary Supplement*, March 10, 1995, 27.
21. Peter Perdue, *China Marches West: The Qing Conquest of Central Eurasia* (Cambridge, MA: Harvard University Press, 2005), 10–11.
22. Quoted in P. Lewis, *Pirs, Shrines, and Pakistani Islam* (Rawalpindi, Pakistan: Christian Study Centre, 1985), 84.
23. Quoted in Stanley Wolpert, *A New History of India* (New York: Oxford University Press, 1993), 160.
24. Quoted in Lewis Melville, *Lady Mary Wortley Montagu: Her Life and Letters* (Whitefish, MT: Kessinger, 2004), 88.
25. Jane I. Smith, "Islam and Christendom," in *The Oxford History of Islam*, edited by John Esposito (Oxford: Oxford University Press, 1999), 342.
26. Charles Thornton Forester and F. H. Blackburne Daniell, *The Life and Letters of Ogier Ghiselin de Busbecq* (London: C. Kegan Paul, 1881), 1:405–6.
27. Jean Bodin, "The Rise and Fall of Commonwealths," Chapter VII, Constitution Society, accessed February 21, 2012, http://www.constitution.org/bodin/bodin_4.htm.

Chapter 14

1. Vanessa Mbonu, "'Humbling,' 'Unforgettable,' Participants Reflect on Their Jamestown to Jamestown Experience as the Journey Comes to a Close," *NAACP*, August 27, 2019.
2. Quoted in M. N. Pearson, ed., *Spices in the Indian Ocean World* (Aldershot, UK: Valorium, 1996), xv.
3. Quoted in Paul Lunde, "The Coming of the Portuguese," *Saudi Aramco World*, July/August 2005, 56.
4. Quoted in Patricio N. Abinales and Donna J. Amoroso, *State and Society in the Philippines* (Lanham, MD: Rowman and Littlefield, 2005), 50.
5. Quoted in Craig A. Lockard, *Southeast Asia in World History* (Oxford: Oxford University Press, 2009), 85.
6. Anthony Reid, *Southeast Asia in the Age of Commerce, 1450–1680* (New Haven, CT: Yale University Press, 1993), 2:274, 290.
7. Anthony Reid, *Charting the Shape of Early Modern Southeast Asia* (Chiang Mai, Thailand: Silkworm Books, 1999), 227.
8. Quoted in Adam Clulow, "Like Lambs in Japan and Devils outside Their Land: Diplomacy, Violence, and Japanese Merchants in Southeast Asia," *Journal of World History* 24, no. 2 (2013): 343.
9. Kenneth Pomeranz and Steven Topik, *The World That Trade Created* (Armonk, NY: M. E. Sharpe, 2006), 28.
10. Quoted in Makrand Mehta, *Indian Merchants and Entrepreneurs in Historical Perspective* (Delhi: Academic Foundation, 1991), 54–58.
11. Andre Gunder Frank, *ReOrient: Global Economy in the Asian Age* (Berkeley: University of California Press, 1998), 131.
12. Quoted in Richard von Glahn, "Myth and Reality of China's Seventeenth Century Monetary Crisis," *Journal of Economic History* 56, no. 2 (1996): 132.
13. Quoted in Pomeranz and Topik, *The World That Trade Created*, 165.
14. Quoted in John Hemming, *The Conquest of the Inca* (New York: Harcourt, 1970), 372.
15. Dennis O. Flynn and Arturo Giraldez, "Born with a 'Silver Spoon,'" *Journal of World History* 6, no. 2 (1995): 210.
16. Quoted in Mark Elvin, *The Retreat of the Elephants* (New Haven, CT: Yale University Press, 2004), 37.
17. Quoted in Robert Marks, *The Origins of the Modern World* (Lanham, MD: Rowman and Littlefield, 2002), 81.
18. See John Richards, *The Endless Frontier* (Berkeley: University of California Press, 2003), pt. 4. Much of this section is drawn from this source.
19. Quoted in Elspeth M. Veale, *The English Fur Trade in the Later Middle Ages* (Oxford: Clarendon Press, 1966), 141.
20. Quoted in Herbert Milton Sylvester, *Indian Wars of New England* (Cleveland, 1910), 1:386.
21. Quoted in Timothy Brook, *Vermeer's Hat: The Seventeenth Century and the Dawn of the Global World* (London: Bloomsbury, 2008), 44.
22. Quoted in Richards, *Endless Frontier*, 499.
23. Richards, *Endless Frontier*, 504.
24. Quoted in Jeff Crane, *The Environment in American History* (New York: Routledge, 2015), 68.
25. Pamela McVay, *Envisioning Women in World History* (New York: McGraw-Hill, 2009), 86.
26. These figures derive from the Trans-Atlantic Slave Trade Database, accessed December 26, 2017, http://www.slavevoyages.org/assessment/estimates.
27. Quoted in Charles E. Curran, *Change in Official Catholic Moral Teaching* (Mahwah, NJ: Paulist Press, 2003), 67.
28. David Brion Davis, *Challenging the Boundaries of Slavery* (Cambridge, MA: Harvard University Press, 2003), 13.
29. Quoted in Bernard Lewis, *Race and Slavery in the Middle East* (New York: Oxford University Press, 1990), 52–53.
30. Audrey Smedley, *Race in North America* (Boulder, CO: Westview Press, 1993), 57.
31. Kevin Reilly et al., eds., *Racism: A Global Reader* (Armonk, NY: M. E. Sharpe, 2003), 131.
32. Quoted in Donald R. Wright, *The World and a Very Small Place in Africa* (Armonk, NY: M. E. Sharpe, 1997), 109–10.
33. John Thornton, *Africa and Africans in the Making of the Atlantic World* (Cambridge: Cambridge University Press, 1998), 72.
34. Thomas Phillips, "A Journal of a Voyage Made in the Hannibal of London in 1694," in *Documents Illustrative of the History of the Slave Trade to America*, edited by Elizabeth Donnan (Washington, DC: Carnegie Institute, 1930), 399–410.
35. Erik Gilbert and Jonathan T. Reynolds, *Africa in World History* (Upper Saddle River, NJ: Pearson Educational, 2004), 160.
36. This account is based largely on Thomas Bluett, *Some Memoirs of the Life of Job . . .* (London, 1734), http://docsouth.unc.edu/neh/bluett/bluett.html/; and James T. Campbell, *Middle Passages* (New York: Penguin Books, 2007), 1–14.
37. Francis Moore, *Travels into the Inland Parts of Africa* (London, 1755), 146–47.
38. Anne Bailey, *African Voices in the Atlantic Slave Trade* (Boston: Beacon Press, 2005), 153–54.

39. James Grehan, "Smoking and 'Early Modern' Sociability: The Great Tobacco Debate in the Ottoman Middle East (Seventeenth to Eighteenth Centuries)," *American Historical Review* 111, no. 5 (2006): 1352–77.
40. Quoted in Edwards Forbes Robinson, *Coffee Houses in England* (London: Kegan, Paul, Trench, Trübner & Co., 1893), 163.

Chapter 15

1. Lily Kuo, "Spread the Word: Africa's 'Reverse Missionaries' Are Bringing Christianity Back to the United Kingdom," *Quartz Africa*, October 11, 2017.
2. Quoted in Armin Siedlecki and Perry Brown, "Preachers and Printers," *Christian History*, Issue 118 (2016): 22.
3. Quoted in Glenn J. Ames, *Vasco da Gama: Renaissance Crusader* (New York: Pearson/Longman, 2005), 50.
4. Quoted in Marysa Navarro et al., *Women in Latin America and the Caribbean* (Bloomington: Indiana University Press, 1999), 37.
5. Quoted in James Rinehart, *Apocalyptic Faith and Political Violence* (New York: Palgrave Macmillan, 2006), 42.
6. Quoted in Nicolas Griffiths, *The Cross and the Serpent* (Norman: University of Oklahoma Press, 1996), 263.
7. Richard M. Eaton, "Islamic History as Global History," in *Islamic and European Expansion*, edited by Michael Adas (Philadelphia: Temple University Press, 1993), 25.
8. Patricia Buckley Ebrey, ed. and trans., *Chinese Civilization: A Sourcebook* (New York: Free Press, 1993), 257.
9. Quoted in Steven Shapin, *The Scientific Revolution* (Chicago: University of Chicago Press, 1996), 66.
10. Francis Bacon, *The Works of Francis Bacon*, edited by James Spedding, Robert Leslie Ellis, and Douglas Denon Heath (London: Longman, 1875), 114.
11. Girolamo Cardano, *The Book of My Life*, translated by Jean Stoner (London: J. M. Dent, 1931), 189.
12. Quoted in Kapil Raj, *Relocating Modern Science: Circulation and the Construction of Knowledge in South Asia and Europe, 1650–1900* (Basingstoke: Palgrave, 2007), 40.
13. Toby E. Huff, *The Rise of Early Modern Science* (Cambridge: Cambridge University Press, 2003), 339.
14. Quoted in Shapin, *Scientific Revolution*, 28.
15. Isaac Newton, *Sir Isaac Newton's Mathematical Principles of Natural Philosophy and His System of the World*, translated by Florian Cajori (Berkeley: University of California Press, 1966), 2:399.
16. Quoted in Shapin, *Scientific Revolution*, 33.
17. Quoted in Andrew Lossky, *The Seventeenth Century: Sources in Western Civilization* (New York: Free Press, 1967), 72.
18. For this observation, see Clifford R. Backman, *The Cultures of the West: A History* (Oxford: Oxford University Press, 2013), 473.
19. Pope John Paul II, "Faith Can Never Conflict with Reason," *L'Osservatore Romano*, November 4, 1992.
20. Quoted in Lossky, *Seventeenth Century*, 88.
21. H. S. Thayer, ed., *Newton's Philosophy of Nature: Selections from His Writings* (New York: Hafner Library of Classics, 1953), 42.
22. Immanuel Kant, "What Is Enlightenment?" translated by Peter Gay, in *Introduction to Contemporary Civilization in the West* (New York: Columbia University Press, 1954), 1071.
23. Voltaire, *Treatise on Tolerance* (1763), chap. 22, http://www.constitution.org/volt/tolerance.htm.
24. Quoted in Margaret C. Jacob, *The Enlightenment* (Boston: Bedford/St. Martin's, 2001), 103.
25. Quoted in Lynn Hunt et al., *The Making of the West: Peoples and Cultures* (Boston: Bedford/St. Martin's, 2012), 594.
26. Quoted in Hunt, *Making of the West*, 594.
27. Quoted in Karen Offen, *European Feminisms, 1700–1950* (Stanford, CA: Stanford University Press, 2000), 39.
28. Quoted in Alfred J. Andrea and James H. Overfield, *The Human Record: Sources of Global History* (Boston: Cengage, 2015), 2:141.
29. Mary Wollstonecraft, *A Vindication of the Rights of Men; with a Vindication of the Rights of Woman* (Cambridge: Cambridge University Press, 1995), 94 and 111.
30. Quoted in David R. Ringrose, *Expansion and Global Interaction, 1200–1700* (New York: Longman, 2001), 188.
31. Steven Weinberg, *To Explain the World: The Discovery of Modern Science* (New York: HarperCollins, 2015), xiii.
32. Weinberg, *To Explain the World*, xi.
33. Quoted in David Wooton, *The Invention of Science: A New History of the Scientific Revolution* (New York: Harper Perennial, 2016), 163.
34. John W. O'Malley et al., *The Jesuits* (Toronto: University of Toronto Press, 1999), 381.

PART 5

1. William H. McNeill, "*The Rise of the West* after 25 Years," *Journal of World History* 1, no. 1 (1990): 7.

Chapter 16

1. Robert Zaretsky, "The Old Regime and the Yellow Revolution," *Foreign Policy*, January 15, 2019, https://foreignpolicy.com/2019/01/15/the-yellow-revolution-france-macron/.
2. Quoted in Keith M. Baker, "A World Transformed," *Wilson Quarterly* (Summer 1989): 37.
3. Quoted in Thomas Benjamin et al., *The Atlantic World in the Age of Empire* (Boston: Houghton Mifflin, 2001), 205.
4. Quoted in Jack P. Greene, "The American Revolution," *American Historical Review* 105, no. 1 (2000): 96–97.
5. Quoted in Greene, "American Revolution," 102.
6. Quoted in Susan Dunn, *Sister Revolutions* (New York: Faber and Faber, 1999), 11, 12.
7. Quoted in Dunn, *Sister Revolutions*, 9.
8. Quoted in Lynn Hunt et al., *The Making of the West* (Boston: Bedford/St. Martin's, 2003), 625.
9. Quoted in Lynn Hunt, ed., *The French Revolution and Human Rights* (Boston: Bedford, 1996), 123.
10. Bonnie S. Anderson and Judith P. Zinsser, *A History of Their Own* (New York: Harper and Row, 1988), 283.
11. Hunt, *French Revolution*, 29.
12. From James Leith, "Music for Mass Persuasion during the Terror," copyright James A. Leith, Queen's University Kingston.
13. Franklin W. Knight, "The Haitian Revolution," *American Historical Review* 105, no. 1 (2000): 103.
14. Quoted in David P. Geggus, *Haitian Revolutionary Studies* (Bloomington: Indiana University Press, 2002), 27.

15. Peter Winn, *Americas: The Changing Face of Latin America and the Caribbean* (Berkeley: University of California Press, 2006), 83.
16. Quoted in Thomas E. Skidmore and Peter H. Smith, *Modern Latin America* (New York: Oxford University Press, 2001), 33.
17. Quoted in David Armitage and Sanjay Subrahmanyam, eds., *The Age of Revolutions in Global Context, c. 1760–1840* (New York: Palgrave Macmillan, 2010), xxiii.
18. James Walvin, "The Public Campaign in England against Slavery," in *The Abolition of the Atlantic Slave Trade*, edited by David Eltis and James Walvin (Madison: University of Wisconsin Press, 1981), 76.
19. Michael Craton, "Slave Revolts and the End of Slavery," in *The Atlantic Slave Trade*, edited by David Northrup (Boston: Houghton Mifflin, 2002), 200.
20. Joseph Dupuis, *Journal of a Residence in Ashantee* (London: Henry Colburn, 1824), 162–64.
21. Eric Foner, *Nothing but Freedom* (Baton Rouge: Louisiana State University Press, 1983).
22. Quoted in Daniel Moran and Arthur Waldron, eds., *The People in Arms: Military Myth and National Mobilization since the French Revolution* (Cambridge: Cambridge University Press, 2003), 14.
23. Barbara Winslow, "Feminist Movements: Gender and Sexual Equality," in *A Companion to Gender History*, edited by Teresa A. Meade and Merry E. Wiesner-Hanks (London: Blackwell, 2004), 186.
24. Quoted in Claire G. Moses, *French Feminism in the Nineteenth Century* (Albany: SUNY Press, 1984), 135.
25. Raden Adjeng Kartini, *Letters of a Javanese Princess* (New York: W. W. Norton, 1964). Unless otherwise noted, all quotes come from this source.
26. Quoted in Jooste Cote, "Raden Ajeng Kartini," in *Gender, Colonialism and Education*, edited by Joyce Goodman and Jayne Martin (London: Woburn Press, 2002), 204.

Chapter 17

1. http://news.xinhuanet.com/english/2017-06/05/c_136342098.htm.
2. https://citifmonline.com/2017/06/07/webster-university-holds-public-lecture-on-africa-china-relations/.
3. Edmund Burke III and Kenneth Pomeranz, eds., *The Environment and World History* (Berkeley: University of California Press, 2009), 41.
4. Gregory T. Cushman, *Guano and the Opening of the Pacific World* (Cambridge: Cambridge University Press, 2013), chaps. 1–3.
5. Ricardo Duchesne, *The Uniqueness of Western Civilization* (Leiden: Brill, 2011).
6. Eric Jones, *The European Miracle: Environments, Economics and Geopolitics in the History of Europe and Asia* (Cambridge: Cambridge University Press, 1981).
7. Kenneth Pomeranz, *The Great Divergence* (Princeton, NJ: Princeton University Press, 2000); Pier Vries, "Are Coal and Colonies Really Crucial?" *Journal of World History* 12 (2001): 411.
8. Peter Stearns, *The Industrial Revolution in World History*, 3rd ed. (Boulder, CO: Westview Press, 2007), 47.
9. Charles Dickens, *Barnaby Rudge. A Tale of the Riots of 'Eighty and Hard Times for These Times* (Boston: Chapman and Hall, 1858), 2:223.
10. Eric Hopkins, *Industrialization and Society* (London: Routledge, 2000), 2.
11. Joel Mokyr, *The Lever of Riches* (New York: Oxford University Press, 1990), 81.
12. Eric Hobsbawm, *Industry and Empire* (New York: New Press, 1999), 58. This section draws heavily on Hobsbawm's celebrated account of British industrialization.
13. Samuel Smiles, *Thrift* (London: John Murray, 1875), 39–40.
14. Quoted in Bonnie S. Anderson and Judith P. Zinsser, *A History of Their Own* (New York: Harper and Row, 1988), 2:131.
15. Benjamin Disraeli, *Sybil or the Two Nations* (New York: Routledge, 1845), 76.
16. Hobsbawm, *Industry and Empire*, 65.
17. Quoted in Peter Stearns and John H. Hinshaw, *Companion to the Industrial Revolution* (Santa Barbara, CA: ABC-CLIO, 1996), 150.
18. Quoted in Herbert Vere Evatt, *The Tolpuddle Martyrs* (Sydney: Sydney University Press, 2009), 49.
19. Much of this feature draws from E. P. Thompson, *The Making of the English Working Class* (New York: Vintage Books, 1966).
20. Hobsbawm, *Industry and Empire*, 171.
21. Dirk Hoeder, *Cultures in Contact* (Durham, NC: Duke University Press, 2002), 331–32.
22. Carl Guarneri, *America in the World* (Boston: McGraw-Hill, 2007), 180.
23. Quoted in Hoeder, *Cultures in Contact*, 318.
24. John Charles Chasteen, *Born in Blood and Fire* (New York: W. W. Norton, 2006), 181.
25. Peter Bakewell, *A History of Latin America* (Oxford: Blackwell, 1997), 425.
26. Michael Adas, *Machines as the Measure of Men* (Ithaca, NY: Cornell University Press, 1990).

Chapter 18

1. Reuters World News, "German Minister Calls Colonial-Era Killings in Namibia 'Genocide,'" September 2, 2019, https://www.reuters.com/article/us-germany-namibia/german-minister-calls-colonial-era-killings-in-namibia-genocide-idUSKCN1VN1DM.
2. Quoted in Marvin Perry, *Sources of the Western Tradition* (Boston: Wadsworth Cengage Learning, 2012), 2:256.
3. Quoted in Heinz Gollwitzer, *Europe in the Age of Imperialism* (London: Thames and Hudson, 1969), 136.
4. Robert Booth, "UK More Nostalgic for Empire than Other Ex-colonial Powers," *The Guardian*, March 11, 2020.
5. William Skidelsky, "Niall Ferguson: 'Westerners Don't Understand How Vulnerable Freedom Is,'" *The Guardian*, February 19, 2011, https://www.theguardian.com/books/2011/feb/20/niall-ferguson-interview-civilization.
6. Quoted in Steven Roger Fischer, *A History of the Pacific Islands* (New York: Palgrave Macmillan, 2013), 112.
7. Charles Griffith, *The Present State and Prospects of the Port Phillips District . . .* (Dublin: William Curry and Company, 1845), 169.
8. Robert Knox, *Races of Man* (Philadelphia: Lea and Blanchard, 1850), v.

9. Quoted in Ralph Austen, ed., *Modern Imperialism* (Lexington, MA: D. C. Heath, 1969), 70–73.
10. Mike Davis, *Late Victorian Holocausts: El Niño Famines and the Making of the Third World* (New York: Verso, 2001), 12.
11. Quoted in John Iliffe, *Africans: The History of a Continent* (Cambridge: Cambridge University Press, 1995), 191.
12. Quoted in Nicholas Tarling, "The Establishment of Colonial Regimes," in *The Cambridge History of Southeast Asia*, edited by Nicholas Tarling (Cambridge: Cambridge University Press, 1992), 2:76.
13. R. Meinertzhagen, *Kenya Diary* (London: Oliver and Boyd, 1957), 51–52.
14. Mrinalini Sinha, *Colonial Masculinity* (Manchester: Manchester University Press, 1995), 35; Jane Burbank and Frederick Cooper, *Empires in World History* (Princeton, NJ: Princeton University Press, 2010), 308–9.
15. Nupur Chaudhuri, "Clash of Cultures," in *A Companion to Gender History*, edited by Teresa A. Meade and Merry E. Wiesner-Hanks (London: Blackwell, 2004), 437.
16. Quoted in Donald R. Wright, *The World and a Very Small Place in Africa* (Armonk, NY: M. E. Sharpe, 2004), 170.
17. Quoted in Scott B. Cook, *Colonial Encounters in the Age of High Imperialism* (New York: HarperCollins, 1996), 53.
18. D. R. SarDesai, *Southeast Asia: Past and Present* (Boulder, CO: Westview Press, 1997), 95–98.
19. Quoted in G. C. K. Gwassa and John Iliffe, *Records of the Maji Maji Rising* (Nairobi: East African Publishing House, 1967), 1:4–5.
20. Quoted in Basil Davidson, *Modern Africa* (London: Longman, 1983), 79, 81.
21. This section draws heavily on Margaret Jean Hay and Sharon Stichter, eds., *African Women South of the Sahara* (London: Longman, 1984), especially chaps. 1–5.
22. Quoted in Robert A. Levine, "Sex Roles and Economic Change in Africa," in *Black Africa*, edited by John Middleton (London: Macmillan, 1970), 178.
23. Quoted in Davis, *Late Victorian Holocausts*, 37.
24. Josiah Kariuki, *Mau Mau Detainee* (London: Oxford University Press, 1963), 5.
25. Quoted in Harry Benda and John Larkin, *The World of Southeast Asia* (New York: Harper and Row, 1967), 182–85.
26. Quoted in William Theodore de Bary, *Sources of Indian Tradition* (New York: Columbia University Press, 1958), 619.
27. Quoted in Edward W. Smith, *Aggrey of Africa* (London: SCM Press, 1929).
28. Robert Strayer, *The Making of Mission Communities in East Africa* (London: Heinemann, 1978), 137.
29. Strayer, *The Making of Mission Communities,* 139.
30. C. A. Bayly, *The Birth of the Modern World* (Oxford: Blackwell, 2004), 343.
31. Nirad Chaudhuri, *Autobiography of an Unknown Indian* (London: John Farquharson, 1968), 229.
32. Unless otherwise noted, this essay and all the quotes derive from Philip Goldberg, *American Vedas* (New York: Harmony Books, 2010), 47–66; and Diana L. Eck, *A New Religious America* (New York: HarperCollins, 2001), 94–104.
33. Quoted in William Theodore de Bary, *Sources of Indian Tradition* (New York: Columbia University Press, 1958), 652.
34. Edward Blyden, *Christianity, Islam, and the Negro Race* (Edinburgh: Edinburgh University Press, 1967), 124.
35. John Iliffe, *A Modern History of Tanganyika* (Cambridge: Cambridge University Press, 1979), 324.

Chapter 19

1. Xi Jinping, "Xi Jinping: UN Climate Deal 'Must Not Be Derailed,'" *Climate Home News*, January 19, 2017, http://www.climatechangenews.com/2017/01/19/xi-jinping-un-climate-deal-must-not-be-derailed/.
2. Quoted in Dun J. Li, ed., *China in Transition, 1517–1911* (New York: Van Nostrand Reinhold, 1969), 112.
3. Quoted in Jonathan D. Spence, *The Search for Modern China* (New York: W. W. Norton, 1999), 169.
4. Quoted in Vincent Shih, *The Taiping Ideology: Its Sources, Interpretations, and Influences* (Seattle: University of Washington Press, 1967), 73.
5. Barbara Hodgson, *Opium: A Portrait of the Heavenly Demon* (San Francisco: Chronicle Books, 1999), 32.
6. This account of Lin Zexu draws from Spence, *Search for Modern China*; and Arthur Waley, *The Opium War through Chinese Eyes* (London: George Allen and Unwin, 1968).
7. Quoted in Teng Ssu and John K. Fairbanks, eds. and trans., *China's Response to the West* (New York: Atheneum, 1963), 69.
8. Quoted in Magali Morsy, *North Africa: 1800–1900* (London: Longman, 1984), 79.
9. Quoted in E. D. G. Prime, *Forty Years in the Turkish Empire; or, Memoirs of Rev. William Goodell* (New York: Carter and Brothers, 1875), 487.
10. Quoted in M. Sukru Hanioglu, *The Young Turks in Opposition* (New York: Oxford University Press, 1995), 17.
11. Marius B. Jansen, *The Making of Modern Japan* (Cambridge, MA: Harvard University Press, 2002), 33.
12. Quoted in Carol Gluck, "Themes in Japanese History," in *Asia in Western and World History*, edited by Ainslie T. Embree and Carol Gluck (Armonk, NY: M. E. Sharpe, 1997), 754.
13. Quoted in S. Hanley and K. Yamamura, *Economic and Demographic Change in Pre-Industrial Japan* (Princeton, NJ: Princeton University Press, 1977), 88–90.
14. Quoted in Harold Bolitho, "The Tempo Crisis," in *The Cambridge History of Japan*, vol. 5, *The Nineteenth Century*, edited by Marius B. Jansen (Cambridge: Cambridge University Press, 1989), 230.
15. Kenneth Henshall, *A History of Japan* (New York: Palgrave, 2004), 67.
16. Quoted in James L. McClain, *Japan: A Modern History* (New York: W. W. Norton, 2002), 177.
17. Kaoru Sugihara, "Global Industrialization: A Multipolar Perspective," in *The Cambridge World History* (Cambridge: Cambridge University Press, 2015), 7:117.
18. Quoted in Renée Worringer, *Ottomans Imagining Japan* (New York: Palgrave Macmillan2014), 59.

PART 6

1. David Christian et al., *Big History* (New York: McGraw-Hill, 2014), 283.
2. William McNeill, "*The Rise of the West* after 25 Years," *Journal of World History* 1, no. 1 (1990): 2.

Chapter 20

1. UN Secretary General, "Remarks to General Assembly . . . ," July 8, 2014, https://www.un.org/sg/en/content/sg/speeches/2014-07-08/remarks-general-assembly-commemoration-100th-anniversary-outbreak.
2. Andrew Osborn, "Putin, Wary of Political Tumult, Shuns Russian Revolution Centenary," Reuters, November 7, 2017, https://www.reuters.com/article/us-russia-revolution-anniversary/putin-wary-of-political-tumult-shuns-russian-revolution-centenary-idUSKBN1D71QA.
3. Quoted in John Keegan, *The First World War* (New York: Vintage Books, 1998), 3.
4. Stanley Payne, *History of Fascism, 1914–1945* (Madison: University of Wisconsin Press, 1995), 208.
5. Quoted in Claudia Koonz, *Mothers in the Fatherland* (New York: St. Martin's Press, 1987), 75.
6. Quoted in James L. McClain, *Japan: A Modern History* (New York: W. W. Norton, 2002), 414.
7. Quoted in Marius B. Jansen, *The Making of Modern Japan* (Cambridge, MA: Harvard University Press, 2000), 607.
8. Quoted in Jansen, *The Making of Modern Japan*, 639.
9. Quoted in Lincoln Barnett, "J. Robert Oppenheimer," *Life Magazine*, October 10, 1949, 133.
10. Quoted in Merry E. Wiesner-Hanks et al., *Discovering the Global Past*, 3rd ed. (Boston: Houghton Mifflin, 2007), 422.
11. Quoted in "A-Bomb Survivor, Anti-Nuclear Movement Leader Senji Yamacuchi Dies at 82," *Japanese Times*, July 6, 2013, https://www.japantimes.co.jp/news/2013/07/06/national/a-bomb-survivor-anti-nuclear-movement-leader-senji-yamaguchi-dies-at-82/.
12. Adam Gopnik, "The Big One: Historians Rethink the War to End All Wars," *New Yorker*, August 23, 2004, 78.
13. Benito Mussolini, *The Political and Social Doctrine of Fascism* (London: Hogarth Press, 1933), 25.
14. Quoted in Christopher Kelly, *The Roman Empire* (Oxford: Oxford University Press, 2006), 124.

Chapter 21

1. Quoted in "A Continent Remade: Reflections on 1960, the Year of Africa," *New York Times*, February 7, 2020, https://www.nytimes.com/interactive/2020/02/06/world/africa/africa-independence-year.html#mbue.
2. Quoted in "A Continent Remade: Reflections on 1960, the Year of Africa," *New York Times*, February 7, 2020, https://www.nytimes.com/interactive/2020/02/06/world/africa/africa-independence-year.html#diop.
3. Quoted in Dean Rusk, *As I Saw It* (New York: W.W. Norton, 1990), 245.
4. Quoted in Frank Mankiewicz and Kirby Jones, *With Fidel: A Portrait of Castro and Cuba* (New York: Ballantine Books, 1976), 83.
5. Quoted in Paul Mason, *Cuba* (New York: Marshall Cavendish, 2010), 14.
6. Quoted in Peter Roman, *People's Power: Cuba's Experience with Representative Government* (Lanham, MD: Rowman and Littlefield, 2003), 63.
7. Quoted in John L. Gaddis, *The Cold War: A New History* (New York: Penguin Press, 2005), 57.
8. Ronald Steel, *Pax Americana* (New York: Viking Press, 1970), 254.
9. Quoted in Craig A. Lockard, *Southeast Asia in World History* (Oxford: Oxford University Press, 2009), 138–39.
10. Quoted in Stanley Wolpert, *A New History of India* (Oxford: Oxford University Press, 1993), 331.
11. Quoted in J. D. Legge, *Sukarno: A Political Biography* (New York: Praeger, 1972), 341.
12. George B. N. Ayittey, "Why Africa Is Poor," 2002, http://ieas.unideb.hu/admin/file_6845.pdf.
13. Deng Xiaoping, "The Necessity of Upholding the Four Cardinal Principles in the Drive for the Four Modernizations," in *Major Documents of the People's Republic of China* (Beijing: Foreign Language Press, 1991), 54.
14. Quoted in Abraham Brumberg, *Chronicle of a Revolution* (New York: Pantheon Books, 1990), 225–26.

Chapter 22

1. Australian Embassy, Indonesia, "Human Trafficking (Remains) Rampant, Concealed in Various Guises," https://indonesia.embassy.gov.au/jakt/AR15-005.html#main.
2. Climate and Migration Coalition, "Moving Stories: Indonesia," September 26, 2013, http://climatemigration.org.uk/moving-stories-indonesia/.
3. Forbes Indonesia, "Solving the Impossible," June 2018, https://www.magzter.com/article/Business/Forbes-Indonesia/Solving-The-Impossible.
4. Paul R. Fleischman, *Wonder* (Amherst, MA: Small Batch Books, 2013), 333.
5. Alexei V. Filippenko, "Exploding Stars and the Accelerating Universe," *Bulletin of the American Academy of Arts and Sciences* (Winter 2016), https://www.amacad.org/news/exploding-stars-and-accelerating-universe.
6. Quoted in Nicole M. Gage and Bernard Baars, *Fundamentals of Cognitive Neuroscience* (London: Academic Press, 2018), 17.
7. International Energy Agency, "World Energy Outlook," 2015, http://www.worldenergyoutlook.org/resources/energydevelopment/energyaccessdatabase/; The World Bank, "World Development Indicators," http://databank.worldbank.org/data/reports.aspx?source=2&series=EG.ELC.ACCS.ZS&country=.
8. Quoted in Douglas Brinkley, *Wheels for the World* (New York: Viking, 2003), 118.
9. Quoted in Maja Adena et al., "Radio and the Rise of the Nazis in Pre-War Germany," *Quarterly Journal of Economics* 130, no. 4 (2015): 2.
10. Jeffrey Frieden, *Global Capitalism* (New York: W. W. Norton, 2006), 476.
11. "Gross World Product, 1950–2009," in *World on the Edge*, by Lester R. Brown (New York: W. W. Norton, 2011).

12. Jason Hickel, "Global Inequality May Be Much Worse Than We Think," *The Guardian*, April 8, 2016.
13. The World Bank, "Life Expectancy at Birth," http://data.worldbank.org/indicator/SP.DYN.LE00.IN.
14. Charles Bright and Michael Geyer, "Benchmarks of Globalization," in *A Companion to World History*, edited by Douglas Northrup (New York: Wiley-Blackwell, 2012), 290.
15. Branko Milanovic, "Global Income Inequality: What It Is and Why It Matters?" United Nations Department of Economic and Social Affairs, 2006, 9, www.un.org/esa/desa/papers/2006/wp26_2006.pdf.
16. Quoted in Frieden, *Global Capitalism*, 459.
17. Eric Hobsbawm, *The Age of Extremes: A History of the World, 1914–1991* (New York: Vintage, 1996), 289, 290, 292.
18. Quoted in John Vidal, "Hi-Tech Agriculture Is Freeing the Farmer from His Fields," *The Guardian*, October 20, 2015, https://www.theguardian.com/environment/2015/oct/20/hi-tech-agriculture-is-freeing-farmer-from-his-fields.
19. Quoted in Amy Clark, "Is NAFTA Good for Mexico's Farmers?" CBS Evening News, July 1, 2006, http://www.cbsnews.com/news/is-nafta-good-for-mexicos-farmers/.
20. Merry Wiesner-Hanks, *The Concise History of the World* (Cambridge: Cambridge University Press, 2015), 308.
21. Quoted in Binyamin Appelbaum, "Perils of Globalization When Factories Close and Towns Struggle," *New York Times*, May 17, 2015, https://www.nytimes.com/2015/05/18/business/a-decade-later-loss-of-maytag-factory-still-resonates.html?_r=0.
22. Norimitsu Onishi, "Nigeria Goes to the Mall," *New York Times*, January 5, 2016.
23. The Organisation for Economic Co-operation and Development (OECD) defined middle class as living in a household with a daily per capita income of between 10 and 100 U.S. dollars; Homi Kharas, *The Emerging Middle Class in Developing Countries*, Working Paper No. 285 (Paris: OECD, 2009), 6.
24. Studs Terkel, *The Great Divide: Second Thoughts on the American Dream* (New York: Pantheon, 1988), 175.
25. Chrystia Freeland, "The Rise of the New Global Elite," *Atlantic*, January/February 2011, https://www.theatlantic.com/magazine/archive/2011/01/the-rise-of-the-new-global-elite/308343/.
26. Quoted in Chrystia Freeland, *Plutocrats: The Rise of the New Global Super-Rich and the Fall of Everyone Else* (New York: Penguin, 2012), 59.
27. Tim Samuels, "Africa Goes Hardcore," *The Guardian*, August 30, 2009.
28. "Global Views on Premarital Sex 2013," Statista, https://www.statista.com/statistics/297288/global-views-on-premarital-sex/.
29. Quoted in Patrick B. Kinross, *Ataturk: A Biography of Mustafa Kemal* (New York: Morrow, 1965), 390.
30. Barbara Engel and Anastasia Posadskaya-Vanderbeck, eds., *A Revolution of Their Own* (Boulder, CO: Westview Press, 1998), 17–46.
31. Quoted in Sarah Shaver Hughes and Brady Hughes, *Women in World History* (Armonk, NY: M. E. Sharpe, 1997), 2:268.
32. Quoted in Wilhelmina Oduol and Wanjiku Mukabi Kabira, "The Mother of Warriors and Her Daughters: The Women's Movement in Kenya," in *Global Feminisms since 1945*, edited by Bonnie G. Smith (London: Routledge, 2000), 111.
33. Phyllis Schlafly, *The Power of the Christian Woman* (Cincinnati: Standard Publishers, 1981), 117.

Chapter 23

1. "Photojournal: Chad Urban Migrant's Story," *BBC News*, http://news.bbc.co.uk/2/shared/spl/hi/picture_gallery/06/africa_chad_urban_migrant0s_story/html/2.stm.
2. J. R. McNeill, "Energy, Population and Environmental Change since 1750," in *The Cambridge World History*, ed. J. R. McNeill and Kenneth Pomeranz (Cambridge: Cambridge University Press, 2015), vol. 7, part 1, pp. 63–67.
3. World Bank, "Death Rate, Crude," http://data.worldbank.org/indicator/SP.DYN.CDRT.IN.
4. David Clark, *Urban World/Global City* (London: Routledge, 1996), 1.
5. Michael H. Hunt, *The World Transformed: 1945 to the Present*, 2nd ed. (New York: Oxford University Press, 2016), 443.
6. Gareth McLean, "Where We're Headed," *The Guardian*, April 1, 2006.
7. Lizzy Davis, "The Young French Women Fighting to Defend the Full Face Veil," *The Guardian*, January 31, 2010.
8. Jose C. Moya and Adam McKeown, *World Migration in the Long Twentieth Century* (Washington, DC: American Historical Association, 2011), 39.
9. Quoted in John J. Simon, "Aime F. Cesaire: The Clarity of Struggle," *Monthly Review* 60 (2008): 2.
10. *Sayings of Ayatollah Khomeini* (New York: Bantam Books, 1980), 4.
11. Pew Research Center, "In U.S., Decline of Christianity Continues at Rapid Pace," 2019, https://www.pewforum.org/2019/10/17/in-u-s-decline-of-christianity-continues-at-rapid-pace/.
12. Karen Armstrong, *The Battle for God* (New York: Alfred A. Knopf, 2000), xi.
13. "Muslim Dolls Tackle 'Wanton' Barbie," *BBC News*, March 5, 2002, http://news.bbc.co.uk/2/hi/middle_east/1856558.stm.
14. Quoted in Katherine Zoepf, "Barbie Pushed Aside in Mideast Cultural Shift. Little Girls Obsessed with Fulla in Scarf," *International Herald Tribune*, September 22, 2005, 2. The passages concerning Fulla are largely drawn from this article.
15. Quoted in John Esposito, *Unholy War* (Oxford: Oxford University Press, 2002), 63.
16. Quoted in John Esposito and John Voll, *Makers of Contemporary Islam* (New York: Oxford University Press, 2001), 193.
17. J. R. McNeill, *Something New under the Sun* (New York: W. W. Norton, 2001), 3–4.
18. Ker Than, "The Atomic Age Ushered In the Anthropocene, Scientists Say," *Smithsonian.com*, January 7, 2016, http://www.smithsonianmag.com/science-nature/scientists-anthropocene-officially-thing-180957742/.
19. Johan Rockstrom et al., *Big World, Small Planet* (New Haven, CT: Yale University Press, 2015), 33.
20. This section draws heavily on the work of John McNeill, a leading environmental historian. See McNeill, "Energy, Population," 72–77; and McNeill, *Something New*.
21. George J. Gilboy and Eric Heginbotham, "The Latin Americanization of China," *Current History*, September 2004, 258.

22. Sophia DG, "Sixth Wildlife Mass Extinction May Happen in 2020, Experts Say," *Nature World News*, October 27, 2016, http://www.natureworldnews.com/articles/30805/20161027/year-2020-era-wildlife-mass-extinction.htm.
23. Hywel Griffith, "Great Barrier Reef Suffered Worst Bleaching on Record in 2016, Report Finds," *BBC News*, November 28, 2016, http://www.bbc.com/news/world-australia-38127320.
24. See Ramachandra Guha, *Environmentalism: A Global History* (New York: Longmans, 2000).
25. Quoted in Guha, *Environmentalism*, 14.
26. Quoted in Guha, *Environmentalism*, 50, 53.
27. David Christian, "The Anthropocene Epoch," in *The Oxford Illustrated History of the World*, ed. Felipe Fernández-Armesto (Oxford: Oxford University Press, 2019), 340.
28. Christian, "The Anthropocene Epoch," 340.
29. Quoted in Douglas Weiner, "The Predatory Tribute-Taking State: A Framework for Understanding Russian Environmental History," in *The Environment and World History*, ed. Edmund Burke III and Kenneth Pomeranz (Berkeley: University of California Press, 2009), 290.
30. Quoted in Edward Ross Dickinson, *The World in the Long Twentieth Century: An Interpretive History* (Berkeley: University of California Press, 2018), 328.
31. Aldo Leopold, *A Sand County Almanac* (Oxford: Oxford University Press, 1949), viii.
32. Quoted in Shiraz Sidhva, "Saving the Planet: Imperialism in a Green Garb," *UNESCO Courier*, April 2001, 41–43.
33. Quoted in Jane Lampman, "Sufism May Be Powerful Antidote to Islamic Extremism," *Christian Science Monitor*, December 5, 2007.
34. Saira Khan, "Why I, as a British Muslim Woman, Want the Burkha Banned from Our Streets," *Daily Mail*, June 24, 2009.
35. Peter Allen, "Burka Ban," *Daily Mail*, April 11, 2011.

Acknowledgments

Chapter 12

Excerpt beginning "Truly do we live on Earth?" from *Aztec Thought and Culture: A Study of the Ancient Nahuatl Mind*, by Miguel Leon Portilla. © 1963 University of Oklahoma Press. Republished with permission of University of Oklahoma Press. Permission conveyed through Copyright Clearance Center, Inc.

Source 12.5: Norman Housely, "Islam and Renaissance Europe, Pope Clement VI, Call for Crusade," from *Documents of the Later Crusades, 1274–1580,* 1st Edition by St. Martin's Press, Palgrave Macmillan. Copyright © 1996 by Springer Nature. Reproduced with permission of the Licensor through PLSclear.

Chapter 13

Source 13.4: Pedro De Cieza De León, *Incas of Pedro de Cieze de León.* © 1959 University of Oklahoma Press. Republished with permission of University of Oklahoma Press. Permission conveyed through Copyright Clearance Center, Inc.

Chapter 14

Source 14.2B: Donald Shively, "Sumptuary Regulation and Status in Early Tokugawa Japan," *Harvard Journal of Asiatic Studies*, 25 (1964–1965), 124–25, DOI:10.2307/2718340. Used with permission.

Chapter 15

Source 15.2: Ralph L. Roys et al., trans., *Book of Chilam Balam of Chumayel.* © 1967 University of Oklahoma Press. Republished with permission of University of Oklahoma Press. Permission conveyed through Copyright Clearance Center, Inc.

Chapter 17

Source 17.6: Vernon L. Lidtke, *The Outlawed Party: Social Democracy in Germany, 1878–1890,* Appendix C (Princeton, NJ: Princeton University Press, 1966), 339, 341–44. © 1966 Princeton University Press. Republished with permission of Princeton University Press. Permission conveyed through Copyright Clearance Center, Inc.

Chapter 19

Source 19.1: From Wm. Theodore de Bary and Richard J. Lufrano, eds., *Sources of Chinese Tradition.* Vol 2: *From 1600 through the Twentieth Century.* © 2000 Columbia University Press. Republished with permission of Columbia University Press. Permission conveyed through Copyright Clearance Center, Inc.

Source 19.2: From Wm. Theodore de Bary and Richard J. Lufrano, eds., *Sources of Chinese Tradition.* Vol 2: *From 1600 through the Twentieth Century.* © 2000 Columbia University Press. Republished with permission of Columbia University Press. Permission conveyed through Copyright Clearance Center, Inc.

Chapter 21

Source 21.1: From William Hinton, *Fanshen: A Documentary of Revolution in a Chinese Village.* Republished with permission of Monthly Review Press. Permission conveyed through Copyright Clearance Center, Inc.

Chapter 22

Source 22.2: From *Combahee River Collective, A Black Feminist Statement,* 1977, in Zillah R. Eisenstein, ed., *Capitalist Patriarchy and the Case for Socialist Feminism* (New York: Monthly Review Press, 1979). Used by permission of Zillah Eisenstein.

Chapter 23

Source 23.5: Selections from Kabir Helminski, "Islam and Human Values," unpublished pamphlet, 2009. Used by permission of the author.

For Further Study

Chapter 12

Alan Covey, *How the Incas Built Their Heartland* (2006). An interdisciplinary examination of the processes and strategies that allowed the Incas to create their empire.

Terence N. D'Altroy, *The Incas* (2002). A history of the Inca Empire that draws on recent archeological and historical research.

Edward L. Dreyer, *Zheng He: China and the Oceans in the Early Ming Dynasty* (2006). The most recent scholarly account of the Ming dynasty voyages.

Halil Inalcik and Donald Quataert, *An Economic and Social History of the Ottoman Empire, 1300–1914* (1994). A classic study of the Ottoman Empire.

Robin Kirkpatrick, *The European Renaissance, 1400–1600* (2002). A beautifully illustrated history of Renaissance culture as well as of the social and economic life of the period.

Charles C. Mann, *1491: New Revelations of the Americas before Columbus* (2005). A review of Western Hemisphere societies and academic debates about their pre-Columbian history.

J. R. McNeill and William H. McNeill, *The Human Web* (2003). A succinct account of the evolving webs or relationships among human societies in world history.

Michael Smith, *The Aztecs* (2003). A history of the Aztec Empire, with an emphasis on the lives of ordinary people.

Khan Academy, "An Introduction to the Ming Dynasty (1368–1644)," https://www.khanacademy.org/humanities/art-asia/imperial-china/ming-dynasty/a/an-introduction-to-the-ming-dynasty-13681644. A collection of brief essays, images, and videos about Ming dynasty China.

Joel Westerbrook, Executive Producer, "Inca: Secrets of the Ancestors," Time-Life, Lost Civilizations, 1995, https://www.youtube.com/watch?v=3GrcN24PqmE. A thoughtful video exploring this largest of pre-Columbian states.

Chapter 13

Jane Burbank and Frederick Cooper, *Empires in World History* (2010). Chapters 5 to 7 of this recent work describe and compare the empires of the early modern world.

Jorge Canizares-Esguerra and Erik R. Seeman, eds., *The Atlantic in Global History* (2007). A collection of essays that treats the Atlantic basin as a single interacting region.

Alfred W. Crosby, *The Columbian Voyages, the Columbian Exchange, and Their Historians* (1987). A classic account of changing understandings of Columbus and his global impact.

John Kicza, *Resilient Cultures: America's Native Peoples Confront European Colonization, 1500–1800* (2003). An account of European colonization in the Americas that casts the native peoples as active agents rather than passive victims.

Charles C. Mann, *1493: Uncovering the New World Columbus Created* (2011). A global account of the Columbian exchange that presents contemporary scholarship in a very accessible fashion.

Peter Perdue, *China Marches West: The Qing Conquest of Central Eurasia* (2005). Tells how China became an empire as it incorporated the non-Chinese people of Central Asia.

Willard Sutherland, *Taming the Wild Fields: Colonization and Empire on the Russian Steppe* (2004). An up-to-date account of Russian expansion in the steppes.

"Discover the Ottomans," http://www.theottomans.org. A series of essays and images that traces the history of the Ottoman Empire over six centuries.

"1492: An Ongoing Voyage," http://www.ibiblio.org/expo/1492.exhibit/Intro.html. An interactive website based on an exhibit from the Library of Congress that provides a rich context for exploring the meaning of Columbus and his voyages.

Chapter 14

Glenn J. Ames, *The Globe Encompassed: The Age of European Discovery, 1500–1700* (2007). An up-to-date survey of European expansion in the early modern era.

Andre Gunder Frank, *ReOrient: Global Economy in the Asian Age* (1998). An account of the early modern world economy that highlights the centrality of Asia.

Erik Gilbert and Jonathan Reynolds, *Trading Tastes: Commodity and Cultural Exchange to 1750* (2006). A world historical perspective on transcontinental commerce.

David Northrup, ed., *The Atlantic Slave Trade* (2002). A fine collection of essays about the origins, practice, impact, and abolition of Atlantic slavery.

John Richards, *The Endless Frontier* (2003). Explores the ecological consequences of early modern commerce.

John K. Thornton, *A Cultural History of the Atlantic World, 1250–1820* (2012). A recent account of the intersection of European, African, and Native American people.

"Voyages: The Trans-Atlantic Slave Trade Database," http://www.slavevoyages.org. An enormous and searchable collection of information, maps, charts, and graphs on the Atlantic slave system.

"Pepper: The Master Spice," *The Spice of Life*, British Broadcasting Corporation, 1983, https://www.youtube.com/watch?v=NuZujx-LMfg. A BBC film that presents the history of pepper, so central to the spice trade of the early modern era.

Chapter 15

William Burns, *The Scientific Revolution in Global Perspective* (2016). An up-to-date survey with a global perspective.

Natana J. Delong-Bas, *Wahhabi Islam: From Revival and Reform to Global Jihad* (2004). A careful study of the origins of Wahhabi Islam and its subsequent development.

Patricia Buckley Ebrey et al., *East Asia: A Cultural, Social, and Political History* (2005). A broad survey by major scholars in the field.

Geoffrey C. Gunn, *First Globalization: The Eurasian Exchange, 1500–1800* (2003). Explores the two-way exchange of ideas between Europe and Asia in the early modern era.

Diarmaid MacCulloch, *The Reformation: A History* (2005). A readable and wide-ranging survey of the European Reformation and Counter-Reformation.

Deva Sobel, *A More Perfect Heaven: How Copernicus Revolutionized the Cosmos* (2011). A fascinating account of a major breakthrough in the Scientific Revolution.

Mari Aguayo Tabor, "The Scientific Revolution in Europe," created for the Liberal Arts and Science Academy, Austin, Texas, 2014, https://www.youtube.com/watch?v=HhlX-17p4VEs. A brief and well-illustrated video with a focus on astronomy and anatomy in the early modern era.

"Sikhism, Religion of the Sikh People," Sikhs.org, 2011, https://www.sikhs.org/topics.htm. A highly informative website that covers the history, philosophy, and ways of life of the Sikh people.

Chapter 16

Benedict Anderson, *Imagined Communities: Reflections on the Origins and Spread of Nationalism* (1991). A now-classic though controversial examination of the process by which national identities were created.

Bonnie S. Anderson, *Joyous Greetings: The First International Women's Movement, 1830–1860* (2000). Describes the beginnings of transatlantic feminism.

David Armitage and Sanjay Subrahmanyam, eds., *The Age of Revolutions in Global Context, c. 1760–1840* (2010). A recent collection of scholarly essays that seeks to explore revolutions within a global framework.

Laurent Dubois and John Garrigus, *Slave Revolution in the Caribbean, 1789–1804* (2017). A brief and up-to-date summary of the Haitian Revolution, combined with a number of documents.

Eric Hobsbawm, *The Age of Revolution, 1789–1848* (1999). A highly respected survey by a well-known British historian.

Lynn Hunt, ed., *The French Revolution and Human Rights* (1996). A collection of documents, with a fine introduction by a prominent scholar.

Noland Walker (director), *Égalité for All: Toussaint Louverture and the Haitian Revolution,* 2009, http://www.youtube.com/watch?v=IOGVgQYX6SU. A thoughtful PBS documentary on the Haitian Revolution, focusing on its principal leader.

George Mason University and City University of New York, "Liberty, Equality, Fraternity: Exploring the French Revolution," http://chnm.gmu.edu/revolution/. A collection of essays, images, documents, songs, and maps illustrating the French Revolution.

Chapter 17

Robert C. Allen, *The Industrial Revolution: A Very Short Introduction* (2017). A concise, accessible, and up-to-date summary by a leading scholar in the field.

John Charles Chasteen, *Born in Blood and Fire* (2006). A lively and well-written account of Latin America's turbulent history since the sixteenth century.

Jack Goldstone, *Why Europe? The Rise of the West in World History, 1500–1850* (2009). An original synthesis of recent research provided by a leading world historian.

David S. Landes, *The Wealth and Poverty of Nations* (1998). An argument that culture largely shapes the possibilities for industrialization and economic growth.

Robert B. Marks, *The Origins of the Modern World* (2015). An effective summary of new thinking about the origins of European industrialization.

Peter Stearns, *The Industrial Revolution in World History* (2012). A global and comparative perspective on the Industrial Revolution.

BBC, "The Industrial Revolution," presented by Jeremy Black, 2013. https://www.youtube.com/watch?v=GYln_S2PVYA. This well-received documentary explores why the Industrial Revolution began in Britain and its global implications.

Chapter 18

A. Adu Boahen, *African Perspectives on Colonialism* (1987). An examination of the colonial experience by a prominent African scholar.

Adam Hochschild, *King Leopold's Ghost* (1999). A journalist's evocative account of the horrors of early colonial rule in the Congo.

Douglas Peers, *India under Colonial Rule* (2006). A concise and up-to-date exploration of colonial India.

Bonnie Smith, ed., *Imperialism* (2000). A fine collection of documents, pictures, and commentary on nineteenth- and twentieth-century empires.

Heather Streets-Salter and Trevor R. Getz, *Empires and Colonies in the Modern World: A Global Perspective* (2016). A highly readable survey of empires and colonies from the early modern period to the twenty-first century.

Margaret Strobel, *Gender, Sex, and Empire* (1994). A brief account of late twentieth-century historical thinking about colonial life and gender.

Saul David, "Slavery and the 'Scramble for Africa,'" BBC History, http://www.bbc.co.uk/history/british/abolition/scramble_for_africa_article_01.shtml. An examination of how abolitionism and the end of slavery in the nineteenth century shaped British interests in the colonization of Africa.

Chapter 19

Carter V. Finley, *The Turks in World History* (2004). A study placing the role of Turkish-speaking peoples in general and the Ottoman Empire in particular in a global context.

Marius B. Jansen, *The Making of Modern Japan* (2002). A well-regarded account of Japan since 1600 by a leading scholar.

Stephen R. Platt, *Autumn in the Heavenly Kingdom: China, the West, and the Epic Story of the Taiping Civil War* (2012). A dramatic account of the Taiping rebellion and the role of the West in it.

Jonathan D. Spence, *The Search for Modern China* (1999). Probably the best single-volume account of Chinese history from about 1600 through the twentieth century.

E. Patricia Tsurumi, *Factory Girls: Women in the Thread Mills of Meiji Japan* (1990). An examination of the lives of women in Japan's nineteenth-century textile factories.

Arthur Waley, *The Opium War through Chinese Eyes* (1968). An older classic that views the Opium War from various Chinese points of view.

"The Meiji Revolution," directed by Alex Gibney, The Annenberg CPB Project, 1992, https://www.youtube.com/watch?v=gURiHVTJX4A. A well-produced documentary on the rise of modern Japan, featuring major scholars in the field.

Shirvan Neftchi, "The Decline of the Ottoman Empire," The Caspian Report, https://www.youtube.com/watch?v=T-SUlb4rwls. A ten-minute video that offers an interpretation of the declining fortunes of the Ottoman Empire.

Chapter 20

Michael Burleigh, *The Third Reich: A New History* (2001). A fresh and thorough look at the Nazi era in Germany's history.

Sheila Fitzpatrick, *The Russian Revolution* (2008). The third edition of what has become a classic overview of the Russian Revolution.

John Keegan, *The Second World War* (2005). A comprehensive account by a well-known scholar.

Bernd Martin, *Japan and Germany in the Modern World* (1995). A comparative study of these two countries' modern history and the relationship between them.

Mark Mazower, *Dark Continent* (2000). A history of Europe in the twentieth century that views the era as a struggle among liberal democracy, fascism, and communism.

Michael S. Nieberg, *Fighting the Great War: A Global History* (2006). An exploration of the origins and conduct of World War I.

Dietman Rothermund, *The Global Impact of the Great Depression, 1929–1939* (1996). An examination of the origins of the Depression in America and Europe and its impact in Asia, Africa, and Latin America.

Adam Tooze, *The Deluge: The Great War and the Remaking of the Global Order 1916–1931* (2014). An exploration of the new global order that took shape in the tumultuous period from the closing years of World War I to the Great Depression.

Michael Duffy, ed., "First World War.com," 2009, http://www.firstworldwar.com. A website rich with articles, documents, photos, diaries, and more that illustrate the history of World War I.

Jewish Virtual Library, "The Holocaust," http://www.jewishvirtuallibrary.org/jsource/holo.html. A wealth of essays, maps, photographs, and timelines that explore the Holocaust and the context in which it arose.

Chapter 21

Archie Brown, *The Rise and Fall of Communism* (2009). A global overview of the communist phenomenon in the twentieth century by a respected scholar.

Timothy Cheek, *Mao Zedong and China's Revolutions* (2002). A collection of documents about the Chinese Revolution and a fine introduction to the life of Mao.

Frederick Cooper, *Africa since 1940* (2002). A readable overview of the coming of independence and efforts at development by a leading historian of Africa.

Ramachandra Guha, *India after Gandhi: The History of the World's Largest Democracy* (2007). A thoughtful account of India's first six decades of independence.

Michael H. Hunt, *The World Transformed: 1945 to the Present* (2015). An accessible survey of world history since World War II.

John Isbister, *Promises Not Kept* (2006). A well-regarded consideration of the obstacles to and struggles for development in the Global South.

Jan C. Jansen and Jurgen Osterhammel, *Decolonization: A Short History* (2017). An up-to-date survey of the end of empire in the twentieth century considered as a global process.

Odd Arne Westad, *The Cold War: A World History* (2017) A well-regarded history of the cold war from a global perspective.

"Soviet Archives Exhibit," http://www.ibiblio.org/expo/soviet.exhibit/entrance.html. A rich website from the Library of Congress, focusing on the operation of the Soviet system and relations with the United States.

"Teaching Decolonization Resource Collection," https://nationalhistorycenter.org/teaching-decolonization-resource-collection/. A rich and varied collection of primary and secondary sources organized by region and theme.

Chapter 22

Nayan Chanda, *Bound Together: How Traders, Preachers, Adventurers, and Warriors Shaped Globalization* (2007). An engaging, sometimes humorous, long-term view of the globalization process.

Sebastian Conrad, *What Is Global History?* (2016). A short introduction to the concepts of global history and globalization.

Lucy Delap, *Feminisms: A Global History* (2020). An accessible path-breaking study that offers a truly global history of feminism, organized into thematic chapters.

Chrystia Freeland, *Plutocrats: The Rise of the New Global Super-Rich and the Fall of Everyone Else* (2012). An insightful look at the lives and lifestyles of the 1 percent.

Jeffry A. Frieden, *Global Capitalism: Its Fall and Rise in the Twentieth Century* (2006). A thorough, thoughtful, and balanced history of economic globalization.

Michael H. Hunt, *The World Transformed: 1945 to the Present* (2015). A thoughtful global history of the second half of the twentieth century.

J. R. McNeill and Kenneth Pomeranz, eds., *The Cambridge World History*, vol. 6: *Production, Consumption and Connection 1750–Present* (2015). An extensive collection of essays by leading figures in their fields.

Jörn Barkemeyer and Jan Künzl, "Globalization," WissensWerte, 2011, https://www.youtube.com/watch?v=3oTLyPPrZE4. A brief eight-minute animated primer on the causes and consequences of globalization by two German filmmakers who produce video clips dealing with contemporary political themes.

"Women in Wartime," http://www.iwm.org.uk/history/women-in-wartime. A website of the British Imperial War Museum illustrating the impact of war on the lives of British women in the twentieth century.

Chapter 23

Karen Armstrong, *The Battle for God* (2000). A comparison of Christian, Jewish, and Islamic fundamentalism in historical perspective.

Wolfgang Behringer, *A Cultural History of Climate* (2010). Places contemporary issues of climate change in a broad world historical context.

Ian Law, *Racism and Ethnicity: Global Debates, Dilemmas, Directions* (2010). A broad historically grounded and global survey of the intersection of racial and ethnic identities.

J. R. McNeill, *Something New under the Sun: An Environmental History of the Twentieth-Century World* (2001). A much-acclaimed global account of the rapidly mounting human impact on the environment during the most recent century.

Rainer Munz and Albert Reiterer, *The Overcrowded World: Global Population and International Migration* (2009). Two German scholars place population growth, urbanization, and migration in a broad world historical context, but with an emphasis on the past century.

Jan Nederveen Pieterse, *Globalization and Culture: Global Mélange* (2015). Explores the cultural dimension of recent globalization within a longer historical context.

NASA, "Global Climate Change," https://climate.nasa.gov/. A NASA website full of articles, essays, images, and videos related to climate change.

"Overpopulation: The Human Explosion Explained," produced by Kurzgesagt, a Munich-based YouTube channel and design studio, https://www.youtube.com/watch?v=QsBT5EQt348. A thoughtful and informed animated film that describes and explains the recent and spectacular increase in human numbers.

Glossary

Abd al-Hamid II Ottoman sultan (r. 1876–1909) who accepted a reform constitution but then quickly suppressed it, ruling as a despotic monarch for the rest of his long reign. (Ch. 19)

abolitionist movement An international movement that condemned slavery as morally repugnant and contributed much to ending slavery in the Western world during the nineteenth century; the movement was especially prominent in Britain and the United States beginning in the late eighteenth century. (Ch. 16)

African diaspora The global spread of African peoples via the slave trade. (Ch. 14)

African identity A new way of thinking about belonging that emerged by the end of the nineteenth century among well-educated Africans; it was influenced by the common experience of colonial oppression and European racism and was an effort to revive the cultural self-confidence of their people. (Ch. 18)

Africanization of Christianity Process that occurred in non-Muslim Africa, where many who converted to Christianity sought to incorporate older traditions, values, and practices into their understanding of Christianity; often expressed in the creation of churches and schools that operated independently of the missionary and colonial establishment. (Ch. 18)

age of fossil fuels Twentieth-century shift in energy production with increased use of coal, oil, and natural gas, resulting in the widespread availability of electricity and the internal combustion engine; a major source of the greenhouse gases that drive climate change. (Ch. 22)

Akbar The most famous emperor of India's Mughal Empire (r. 1556–1605); his policies are noted for their efforts at religious tolerance and inclusion. (Ch. 13)

American Revolution Successful rebellion against British rule conducted by the European settlers in the thirteen colonies of British North America, starting in 1775; a conservative revolution whose success preserved property rights and class distinctions but established republican government in place of monarchy. (Ch. 16)

Anthropocene era A recently coined term denoting the "age of man," in general since the Industrial Revolution and more specifically since the mid-twentieth century. It refers to the unprecedented and enduring impact of human activity on the atmosphere, the geosphere, and the biosphere. (Ch. 23)

Asian Tigers Nickname for the East Asian countries of South Korea, Taiwan, Singapore, and Hong Kong, which experienced remarkable export-driven economic growth in the late twentieth century. (Ch. 22)

Aurangzeb Mughal emperor (r. 1658–1707) who reversed his predecessors' policies of religious tolerance and attempted to impose Islamic supremacy. (pron. ow-rang-ZEHB) (Ch. 13)

Aztec Empire Major state that developed in what is now Mexico in the fourteenth and fifteenth centuries; dominated by the semi-nomadic Mexica, who had migrated into the region from northern Mexico. (Ch. 12)

Benin West African kingdom (in what is now Nigeria) whose strong kings for a time sharply limited engagement with the slave trade. (Ch. 14)

Blyden, Edward (1832–1912) Prominent West African scholar and political leader who argued that each civilization, including that of Africa, has its own unique contribution to make to the world. (Ch. 18)

Boxer Uprising Antiforeign movement (1898–1901) led by Chinese militia organizations, in which large numbers of Europeans and Chinese Christians were killed. It resulted in military intervention by Western powers and the imposition of a huge payment as punishment. (Ch. 19)

Bretton Woods system Name for the agreements and institutions (including the World Bank and the International Monetary Fund) set up in 1944 to regulate commercial and financial dealings among the major capitalist countries. (Ch. 22)

British East India Company Private trading company chartered by the English around 1600, mainly focused on India; it was given a monopoly on Indian Ocean trade, including the right to make war and to rule conquered peoples. (Ch. 14)

British textile industry The site of the initial technological breakthroughs of the Industrial Revolution in eighteenth-century Britain, where multiple innovations transformed cotton textile production, resulting in an enormous increase in output. (Ch. 17)

cash-crop production Agricultural production of crops for sale in the market rather than for consumption by the farmers themselves; operated at the level of both individual farmers and large-scale plantations. (Ch. 18)

caudillos Military strongmen who seized control of a government in nineteenth-century Latin America, and were frequently replaced. (pron. kow-DEE-yos) (Ch. 17)

Chinese revolution of 1911–1912 The collapse of China's imperial order, officially at the hands of organized revolutionaries but for the most part under the weight of the troubles that had overwhelmed the imperial government for the previous century. (Ch. 19)

Chinese Revolution of 1949 An event that marks the coming to power of the Chinese Communist Party under the leadership of Mao Zedong, following a decades-long struggle against both domestic opponents and Japanese imperialism. (Ch. 20)

civilizing mission A European understanding of empire that emphasized Europeans' duty to "civilize inferior races" by bringing Christianity, good government, education, work discipline, and production for the market to colonized peoples, while suppressing "native customs," such as polygamy, that ran counter to Western ways of living. (Ch. 18)

climate change The warming of the planet, largely caused by higher concentrations of "greenhouse gases" generated by the burning of fossil fuels. It has become the most pressing environmental issue of the early twenty-first century. (Ch. 23)

cold war Geopolitical and ideological conflict between communist regimes and capitalist powers after World War II, spreading from Eastern Europe through Asia; characterized by the avoidance of direct military conflict between the USSR and the United States and an arms race in nuclear weapons. (Ch. 21)

collectivization of agriculture Communist policies that ended private ownership of land by incorporating peasants from small family farms into large-scale collective farms. Implemented forcibly in the Soviet Union (1928–1933), it led to a terrible famine and 5 million deaths; a similar process occurred much more peacefully in China during the 1950s. (Ch. 20)

Columbian exchange The enormous network of transatlantic communication, migration, trade, and the transfer of diseases, plants, and animals that began in the period of European exploration and colonization of the Americas. (Ch. 13)

communication revolution Modern transformation of communication technology, from the nineteenth-century telegraph to the present-day smart phone. (Ch. 22)

communism in Eastern Europe Expansion of post–World War II communism to Poland, East Germany, Czechoslovakia, Hungary, Romania, and Bulgaria, imposed with Soviet pressure rather than growing out of domestic revolution. (Ch. 20)

Condorcet The Marquis de Condorcet (1743–1794) was a French philosopher who argued that society was moving into an era of near-infinite improvability and could be perfected by human reason. (Ch. 15)

Congo Free State A private colony ruled personally by Leopold II, king of Belgium; it was the site of widespread forced labor and killing to ensure the collection of wild rubber; by 1908 these abuses led to reforms that transferred control to the Belgian government. (Ch. 18)

consumerism A culture of leisure and consumption that developed during the past century or so in tandem with global economic growth and an enlarged middle class; emerged first in the Western world and later elsewhere. (Ch. 22)

Copernicus, Nicolaus (1473–1543) Polish mathematician and astronomer who was the first to argue in 1543 for the existence of a sun-centered universe, helping to spark the Scientific Revolution. (Ch. 15)

Cortés, Hernán Spanish conquistador who led the expedition that conquered the Aztec Empire in modern Mexico. (Ch. 13)

Counter-Reformation An internal reform of the Catholic Church in the sixteenth century stimulated in part by the Protestant Reformation; at the Council of Trent (1545–1563), Catholic leaders clarified doctrine, corrected abuses and corruption, and put a new emphasis on education and accountability. (Ch. 15)

Cuban missile crisis Major standoff between the United States and the Soviet Union in 1962 over Soviet deployment of nuclear missiles in Cuba; the confrontation ended in compromise, with the USSR removing its missiles in exchange for the United States agreeing not to invade Cuba. (Ch. 21)

cultivation system System of forced labor used in the Netherlands East Indies in the nineteenth century; peasants were required to cultivate at least 20 percent of their land in cash crops, such as sugar or coffee, for sale at low and fixed prices to government contractors, who then earned enormous profits from resale of the crops. (Ch. 18)

cultural globalization The global spread of elements of popular culture such as film, language, and music from various places of origin, especially the spread of Western cultural forms to the rest of the world; has come to symbolize modernity, inclusion in global culture, and liberation or rebellion. It has prompted pushback from those who feel that established cultural traditions have been threatened. (Ch. 23)

Cultural Revolution China's Great Proletarian Cultural Revolution was a massive campaign launched by Mao Zedong in the mid-1960s to combat the capitalist tendencies that he believed reached into even the highest ranks of the Communist Party; the campaign threw China into chaos. (Ch. 21)

Dahomey West African kingdom in which the slave trade became a major state-controlled industry. (pron. deh-HOH-mee) (Ch. 14)

Declaration of the Rights of Man and Citizen Charter of political liberties, drawn up by the French National Assembly in 1789, that proclaimed the equal rights of all male citizens; the declaration gave expression to the essential outlook of the French Revolution and became the preamble to the French constitution completed in 1791. (Ch. 16)

decolonization Process in which many African and Asian states won their independence from Western colonial rule, in most cases by negotiated settlement and in some cases through violent military confrontations. (Ch. 21)

Deng Xiaoping (1904–1997) Leader of China from 1978 to 1997 whose reforms dismantled many of the distinctly communist elements of the Chinese economy. (pron. dung shee-yao-ping) (Ch. 21)

dependent development Term used to describe Latin America's economic growth in the nineteenth century, which was largely financed by foreign capital and dependent on European and North American prosperity and decisions; also viewed as a new form of colonialism. (Ch. 17)

devshirme A term that means "collection or gathering"; it refers to the Ottoman Empire's practice of removing young boys from their Christian subjects and training them for service in the civil administration or in the elite Janissary infantry corps. (pron. devv-shirr-MEH) (Ch. 13)

Dream of the Red Chamber, The Book written by Cao Xueqin that explores the life of an elite family with connections to the court; it was the most famous popular novel of mid-eighteenth-century China. (Ch. 15)

Dutch East India Company Private trading company chartered by the Netherlands around 1600, mainly focused on Indonesia; it was given a monopoly on Indian Ocean trade, including the right to make war and to rule conquered peoples. (Ch. 14)

economic globalization The deepening economic entanglement of the world's peoples, especially since 1950; accompanied by the spread of industrialization in the Global South and extraordinary economic growth following World War II; the process has also generated various forms of inequality and resistance as well as increasing living standards for many. (Ch. 22)

European Economic Community An alliance formed in 1957 by six Western European countries dedicated to developing common trade policies and reduced tariffs; it gradually developed into the larger European Union. (Ch. 21)

European Enlightenment European intellectual movement of the eighteenth century that applied the principles of the Scientific Revolution to human affairs and was noted for its commitment to open-mindedness and inquiry and the belief that knowledge could transform human society. (Ch. 15)

European Renaissance A "rebirth" of classical learning that is most often associated with the cultural blossoming of Italy in the period 1350–1500 and that included not just a rediscovery of Greek and Roman learning but also major developments in art, as well as growing secularism in society. It spread to Northern Europe after 1400. (Ch. 12)

export-processing zones (EPZs) Areas where international companies can operate with tax and other benefits, offered as an incentive to attract manufacturers. (Ch. 22)

fascism Political ideology that considered the conflict of nations to be the driving force of history; marked by intense nationalism and an appeal to post–World War I discontent. Fascists praised violence against enemies as a renewing force in society, celebrated action rather than reflection, and placed their faith in a charismatic leader. Fascists also bitterly condemned individualism, liberalism, feminism, parliamentary democracy, and communism. (Ch. 20)

female circumcision The excision of a pubescent girl's clitoris and adjacent genital tissue as part of initiation rites marking her coming-of-age; missionary efforts to end the practice sparked a widespread exodus from mission churches in colonial Kenya. (Ch. 18)

feminism in the Global South Mobilization of women across Asia, Africa, and Latin America; distinct from Western feminism because of its focus on issues such as colonialism, racism, and poverty, rather than those exclusively related to gender. (Ch. 22)

French Revolution Massive upheaval of French society (1789–1815) that overthrew the monarchy, ended the legal privileges of the nobility, and for a time outlawed the Catholic Church. The French Revolution proceeded in stages, becoming increasingly radical and violent until the period known as the Terror in 1793–1794, after which it became more conservative, especially under Napoleon Bonaparte (r. 1799–1815). (Ch. 16)

Fulbe West Africa's largest pastoral society, whose members gradually adopted Islam and took on a religious leadership role that led to the creation of a number of new states by the nineteenth century. (pron. fulb) (Ch. 12)

fur trade A global industry in which French, British, and Dutch traders exported fur from North America to Europe, using Native American labor and with great environmental cost to the Americas. A parallel commerce in furs operated under Russian control in Siberia. (Ch. 14)

Galileo (1564–1642) An Italian scientist who developed an improved telescope in 1609, with which he made many observations that undermined established understandings of the cosmos. (pron. gal-uh-LAY-oh) (Ch. 15)

Gandhi, Mohandas (1869–1948) Often known as "Mahatma" or "Great Soul," the political leader of the Indian drive for independence from Great Britain; rejected the goal of modern industrialization and advocated nonviolence. (Ch. 21)

General Crisis The near-record cold winters experienced in much of China, Europe, and North America in the mid-seventeenth century, sparked by the Little Ice Age; extreme weather conditions led to famines, uprisings, and wars. (Ch. 13)

globalization of democracy Late twentieth-century political shift that brought popular movements, multiparty elections, and new constitutions to countries around the world. (Ch. 21)

global urbanization The explosive growth of cities after 1900, caused by the reduced need for rural labor and more opportunities for employment in manufacturing, commerce, government, and the service industry. (Ch. 23)

Gorbachev, Mikhail (1931–) Leader of the Soviet Union from 1985 to 1991 whose efforts to reform the USSR led to its collapse. (pron. GORE-beh-CHOF) (Ch. 21)

Great Depression Worldwide economic contraction that began in 1929 with a stock market crash in the United States and continued in many areas until the outbreak of World War II. (Ch. 20)

Great Dying Term used to describe the devastating demographic impact of European-borne epidemic diseases on the Americas; in many cases, up to 90 percent of the pre-Columbian population died. (Ch. 13)

Great Jamaica Revolt Slave rebellion in the British West Indies (1831–1832) in which around 60,000 enslaved people attacked several hundred plantations; inspired by the Haitian Revolution, the discontent of the enslaved population and the brutality of the British response helped sway the British public to support the abolition of slavery. (Ch. 16)

Great Leap Forward Communist push for collectivization that created "people's communes" and aimed to mobilize China's population for rapid development. (Ch. 21)

Green Revolution Innovations in agriculture during the twentieth century, such as mechanical harvesters, chemical fertilizers, and the development of high-yielding crops, that enabled global food production to keep up with, and even exceed, growing human numbers. (Ch. 23)

Guomindang The Chinese Nationalist Party led by Chiang Kai-shek that governed from 1928 until its overthrow by the communists in 1949. (pron. GWOH-mihn-dahng) (Ch. 20)

Haitian Revolution The only fully successful slave rebellion in world history; the uprising in the French Caribbean colony of Saint Domingue (later renamed Haiti, which means "mountainous" or "rugged" in the native Taino language) was sparked by the French Revolution and led to the establishment of an independent state after a long and bloody war (1791–1804). Its first leader was Toussaint Louverture, a former enslaved person. (Ch. 16)

Hidalgo-Morelos rebellion Socially radical peasant rebellion in Mexico (1810) led by the priests Miguel Hidalgo and José Morelos. (Ch. 16)

Hinduism A religion based on the many beliefs, practices, sects, rituals, and philosophies in India; in the thinking of nineteenth-century Indian reformers, it was expressed as a distinctive tradition, an Indian religion wholly equivalent to Christianity. (Ch. 18)

Hindutva A Hindu nationalist movement that became politically important in India in the 1980s; advocated a distinct Hindu identity and decried government efforts to accommodate other faith communities, particularly Islamic. (Ch. 23)

Hitler, Adolf (1889–1945) Leader of the German Nazi Party and Germany's head of state from 1933 until his death. (Ch. 20)

HIV/AIDS A pathogen that spreads primarily through sexual contact, contaminated blood products, or the sharing of needles; after sparking a global pandemic in the 1980s, it spread rapidly across the globe and caused tens of millions of deaths. (Ch. 23)

Ho Chi Minh (1890–1969) Leader of the Vietnamese communist movement that established control first in the north and then the whole of Vietnam after 1975. (Ch. 20)

Holocaust Name commonly used for the Nazi genocide of Jews and other "undesirables" in German society. (Ch. 20)

Holocene era A warmer and often a wetter period that began approximately 12,000 years ago following the end of the last Ice Age. These environmental conditions were uniquely favorable for human thriving and enabled the development of agriculture, significant population growth, and the creation of complex civilizations. (Ch. 23)

idea of "tribe" A new sense of clearly defined ethnic identities that emerged in twentieth-century Africa, often initiated by Europeans intent on showing the primitive nature of their colonial subjects, but widely adopted by Africans themselves as a way of responding to the upheavals of modern life. (Ch. 18)

ideology of domesticity A set of ideas and values that defined the ideal role of middle-class women in nineteenth-century Europe, focusing their activity on homemaking, child rearing, charitable endeavors, and "refined" activities as the proper sphere for women. (Ch. 17)

Igbo People whose lands were east of the Niger River in what is now southern Nigeria in West Africa. They built a complex society that rejected kingship and centralized statehood, while relying on other institutions to provide social coherence. (pron. EE-boh) (Ch. 12)

Inca Empire The Western Hemisphere's largest imperial state in the fifteenth and early sixteenth centuries. Built by a relatively small community of Quechua-speaking people (the Incas), the empire stretched some 2,500 miles along the Andes Mountains, which run nearly the entire length of the west coast of South America, and contained perhaps 10 million subjects. (Ch. 12)

Indian National Congress The political party led by Mahatma Gandhi that succeeded in bringing about Indian independence from Britain in 1947. (Ch. 21)

Indian Ocean commercial network The massive, interconnected web of commerce in premodern times between the lands that bordered the Indian Ocean (including East Africa, India, and Southeast Asia); the network was transformed as Europeans entered it in the centuries following 1500. (Ch. 14)

Indian Rebellion of 1857–1858 Massive uprising of parts of India against British rule caused by the introduction to the colony's military forces of a new cartridge smeared with animal fat from pigs and cows, which caused strife among Muslims, who regarded pigs as unclean, and Hindus, who venerated cows. It came to express a variety of grievances against the colonial order. (Ch. 18)

influenza pandemic One of the worst pandemics in human history, caused by three waves of influenza that swept across the globe in 1918 and 1919, carried by demobilized soldiers, refugees, and other dislocated people returning home from World War I; at least 50 million people died in the pandemic. (Ch. 23)

informal economy Also known as the "shadow" economy; refers to unofficial, unregulated, and untaxed economic activity. (Ch. 22)

informal empires Term commonly used to describe areas that were dominated by Western powers in the nineteenth century but retained their own governments and a measure of independence (e.g., China). (Ch. 19)

Iranian revolution Establishment of a radically Islamist government in Iran in 1979; helped trigger a war with Iraq in the 1980s. (Ch. 21)

Iroquois Iroquois-speaking peoples in what is now New York State; around the fifteenth century they formed a loose alliance based on the Great Law of Peace, an agreement to settle disputes peacefully through a council of clan leaders. (Ch. 12)

Islamic radicalism Movements that promote strict adherence to the Quran and the sharia, often in opposition to key elements of Western culture. Particularly prominent since the 1970s, such movements often present themselves as returning to an earlier expression of Islam. Examples include the Iranian revolution, Taliban, al-Qaeda, and Islamic State. (Ch. 23)

Israeli-Palestinian conflict Struggle between the Jewish state of Israel and the adjacent Palestinian Muslim territories that has generated periodic wars and upheavals since 1948. (Ch. 21)

Jesuits in China Series of Jesuit missionaries from 1550 to 1800 who, inspired by the work of Matteo Ricci, sought to understand and become integrated into Chinese culture as part of their efforts to convert the Chinese elite, although with limited success. (Ch. 15)

kaozheng Literally, "research based on evidence"; Chinese intellectual movement whose practitioners were critical of conventional Confucian philosophy and instead emphasized the importance of evidence and analysis, applied especially to historical documents. (Ch. 15)

laboring classes The majority of Britain's nineteenth-century population, which included manual workers in the mines, ports, factories, construction sites, workshops, and farms of Britain's industrializing and urbanizing society; this class suffered the most and at least initially gained the least from the transformations of the Industrial Revolution. (Ch. 17)

labor migration The movement of people, often illegally, into another country to escape poverty or violence and to seek opportunities for work that are less available in their own countries. (Ch. 23)

Labour Party British working-class political party established in the 1890s and dedicated to reforms and a peaceful transition to socialism, in time providing a viable alternative to the revolutionary emphasis of Marxism. (Ch. 17)

Latin American export boom Large-scale increase in Latin American exports (mostly raw materials and foodstuffs) to industrializing countries in the second half of the nineteenth century, made possible by major improvements in shipping; the boom mostly benefited the upper and middle classes. (Ch. 17)

Latin American revolutions Series of risings in the Spanish and Portuguese colonies of Latin America (1808–1825) that established the independence of new states from European rule but that for the most part retained the privileges of the elites despite efforts at more radical social change by the lower classes. (Ch. 16)

Lenin (1870–1924) Born Vladimir Ilyich Ulyanov, leader of the Russian Bolshevik (later Communist) Party in 1917, when it seized power. (Ch. 20)

Lin Zexu, Commissioner Royal official charged with ending the opium trade in China; his concerted efforts to seize and destroy opium imports provoked the Opium Wars. (pron. lin zuh-SHOO) (Ch. 19)

Little Ice Age A period of unusually cool temperatures from the thirteenth to nineteenth centuries, most prominently in the Northern Hemisphere. (Ch. 13)

lower middle class Social stratum that developed in Britain in the nineteenth century and that consisted of people employed in the service sector as clerks, salespeople, secretaries, police officers, and the like; by 1900, this group comprised about 20 percent of Britain's population. (Ch. 17)

Luther, Martin (1483–1546) German priest who issued the Ninety-Five Theses and began the Protestant Reformation with his public criticism of the Catholic Church's theology and practice. (Ch. 15)

Manila The capital of the colonial Philippines, which by 1600 had become a flourishing and culturally diverse city; the site of violent clashes between the Spanish and Chinese residents. (Ch. 14)

Mao Zedong (1893–1976) Chairman of China's Communist Party and de facto ruler of China from 1949 until his death. (Chs. 20, 21)

maroon societies / Palmares Free communities of former enslaved people in remote regions of South America and the Caribbean; the largest such settlement was Palmares in Brazil, which housed 10,000 or more people for most of the seventeenth century. (Ch. 14)

Marshall Plan Huge U.S. government initiative to aid in the post–World War II recovery of Western Europe that was put into effect in 1948. (Ch. 21)

Marx, Karl (1818–1883) The most influential proponent of socialism, Marx was a German expatriate in England who predicted working-class revolution as the key to creating an ideal communist future. (Ch. 17)

maternal feminism Movement that claimed that women have value in society not because of an abstract notion of equality but because women have a distinctive and vital role as mothers; its exponents argued that women have the right to intervene in civil and political life because of their duty to watch over the future of their children. (Ch. 16)

megacities Very large urban centers with populations of over 10 million; by 2020, there were thirty-seven such cities on five continents. (Ch. 23)

Meiji Restoration The political takeover of Japan in 1868 by a group of young samurai from southern Japan. The samurai eliminated the shogun and claimed they were restoring to power the young emperor, Meiji. The new government was committed to saving Japan from foreign domination by drawing upon what the modern West had to offer to transform Japanese society. (pron. MAY-jee) (Ch. 19)

Melaka Muslim port city that came to prominence on the waterway between Sumatra and Malaya in the fifteenth century C.E.; it was the springboard for the spread of a syncretic form of Islam throughout the region. (Ch. 12)

mercantilism The economic theory that governments served their countries' economic interests best by encouraging exports and accumulating bullion (precious metals such as silver and gold); helped fuel European colonialism. (Ch. 13)

mestizo A term used to describe the multiracial population of Spanish colonial societies in the Americas. Recently, the word has been criticized for being associated with colonialism and racial stratification. (pron. mehs-TEE-zoh) (Ch. 13)

Mexican Revolution Long and bloody war (1910–1920) in which Mexican reformers from the middle class joined with workers and peasants to overthrow the dictator Porfirio Díaz and create a new, much more democratic political order. (Ch. 17)

middle-class society British social stratum developed in the nineteenth century, composed of small businessmen, doctors, lawyers, engineers, teachers, and other professionals required in an industrial society; politically liberal, they favored constitutional government, private property, free trade, and social reform within limits; had ideas of thrift, hard work, rigid morality, "respectability," and cleanliness. (Ch. 17)

Ming dynasty Chinese dynasty (1368–1644) that succeeded the Yuan dynasty of the Mongols; noted for its return to traditional Chinese ways and restoration of the land after the destructiveness of the Mongols. (Ch. 12)

Mirabai (1498–1547) One of India's most beloved bhakti poets, who transgressed the barriers of caste and tradition. (Ch. 15)

Mughal Empire A successful state founded by Muslim Turkic-speaking peoples who invaded India and provided a rare period of relative political unity (1526–1707); their rule was noted for efforts to create partnerships between Hindus and Muslims. (pron. MOO-guhl) (Chs. 12, 13)

mulattoes A derogatory term commonly used to describe people of mixed African and European blood. (Ch. 13)

Muslim League Political group formed in response to the Indian National Congress in India's struggle for independence from Britain; the League's leader, Muhammad Ali Jinnah, argued that regions of India with a Muslim majority should form a separate state called Pakistan. (Ch. 21)

Mussolini, Benito (1883–1945) Charismatic leader of the Italian Fascist Party who came to power in 1922 and ruled until his death. (Ch. 20)

Napoleon Bonaparte French head of state and general (r. 1799–1815); Napoleon preserved much of the French Revolution under a military dictatorship and was responsible for the spread of revolutionary ideals through his conquest of much of Europe. (Ch. 16)

nationalism The focusing of citizens' loyalty on the notion that they are part of a "nation" that merits an independent political life, with a unique culture, territory, and common experience; first became a prominent element of political culture in nineteenth-century Europe and the Americas. (Ch. 16)

Nazi Party German political party that established a fascist state dedicated to extreme nationalism, territorial expansion, and the purification of the German state. (Ch. 20)

Newton, Isaac (1642–1727) English scientist whose formulation of the laws of motion and mechanics is regarded as the culmination of the Scientific Revolution. (Ch. 15)

North American Free Trade Agreement (NAFTA) Free trade agreement between the United States, Mexico, and Canada, established in 1984. It was replaced in 2020 by a new agreement among the United States, Mexico, and Canada. (Ch. 22)

North Atlantic Treaty Organization (NATO) A military alliance, created in 1949, between the United States and various European countries; largely aimed at defending against the threat of Soviet aggression during the cold war. (Ch. 21)

one-child family policy (China) Chinese policy of population control that lasted from 1980 to 2014; used financial incentives and penalties to promote birth control, sterilization, and abortions in an effort to limit most families to a single child. (Ch. 22)

Opium Wars Two wars fought between Western powers and China (1840–1842 and 1856–1858) after China tried to restrict the importation of foreign goods, especially opium; China lost both wars and was forced to make major concessions. (Ch. 19)

Ottoman Empire Major Islamic state centered on Anatolia that came to include the Balkans, parts of the Middle East, and much of North Africa; lasted in one form or another from the fourteenth to the early twentieth century. (Chs. 12, 13)

Ottoman seizure of Constantinople The city of Constantinople, the capital and almost the only outpost left of the Byzantine Empire, fell to the army of the Ottoman sultan Mehmed II "the Conqueror" in 1453, an event that marked the end of Christian Byzantium. (Ch. 12)

Paris Climate Agreement An international agreement negotiated in 2015 among some 195 countries, 700 cities, and many companies to reduce greenhouse gas emissions sufficiently to avoid a 2°C increase in global temperatures. (Ch. 23)

Philippines (Spanish) An archipelago of Pacific islands colonized by Spain in a relatively bloodless process that extended for the century or so after 1565, a process accompanied by a major effort at evangelization; the Spanish named them the Philippine Islands in honor of King Philip II of Spain. (Ch. 14)

piece of eight The standard Spanish silver coin used by merchants in North America, Europe, India, Russia, West Africa, and China. (Ch. 14)

population explosion An extraordinarily rapid growth in human population during the twentieth and twenty-first centuries that quadrupled human numbers in little more than a century. Experienced primarily in the Global South. (Ch. 23)

Potosí City that developed high in the Andes (in present-day Bolivia) at the site of the world's largest silver mine and that became the largest city in the Americas, with a population of some 160,000 in the 1570s. (Ch. 14)

Progressives Followers of an American political movement (progressivism) in the period around 1900 that advocated reform measures such as wages-and-hours legislation to correct the ills of industrialization. (Ch. 17)

Protestant Reformation Massive schism within Christianity that had its formal beginning in 1517 with the German priest Martin Luther; the movement was radically innovative in its challenge to church authority and its endorsement of salvation by faith alone, and also came to express a variety of political, economic, and social tensions. (Ch. 15)

Qing expansion The growth of Qing dynasty China during the seventeenth and eighteenth centuries into a Central Asian empire that added a small but important minority of non-Chinese people to the empire's population and essentially created the borders of contemporary China. (Ch. 13)

religious fundamentalism Occurring within all the major world religions, fundamentalism is a self-proclaimed return to the alleged "fundamentals" of a religion and is marked by a militant piety, exclusivism, and a sense of threat from the modern secular world. (Ch. 23)

Revolutionary Right (Japan) Also known as Radical Nationalism, this was a movement in Japanese political life during the Great Depression that was marked by extreme nationalism, a commitment to elite leadership focused around the emperor, and dedication to foreign expansion. (Ch. 20)

Robespierre, Maximilien (1758–1794) Leader of the French Revolution during the Terror; his Committee of Public Safety executed tens of thousands of enemies of the revolution until he was arrested and guillotined. (pron. ROHBS-pee-air) (Ch. 16)

Russian Empire A Christian state centered on Moscow that emerged from centuries of Mongol rule in 1480; by 1800, it had expanded into northern Asia and westward into the Baltics and Eastern Europe. (Ch. 13)

Russian Revolution Massive revolutionary upheaval in 1917 that overthrew the Romanov dynasty in Russia and ended with the seizure of power by communists under the leadership of Lenin. (Ch. 20)

Russian Revolution of 1905 Spontaneous rebellion that erupted in Russia after the country's defeat at the hands of Japan in 1905; the revolution was suppressed, but it forced the government to make substantial reforms. (Ch. 17)

Russo-Japanese War (1904–1905) Fought over rival ambitions in Korea and Manchuria, this conflict ended in a Japanese victory, establishing Japan as a formidable military competitor in East Asia. The war marked the first time that an Asian country defeated a European power in battle, and it precipitated the Russian Revolution of 1905. (Ch. 19)

Safavid Empire Major Turkic empire established in Persia in the early sixteenth century and notable for its efforts to convert its people to Shia Islam. (pron. SAH-fah-vid) (Ch. 12)

scientific racism A new kind of racism that emerged in the nineteenth century that increasingly used the prestige and apparatus of science to support European racial prejudices and preferences. (Ch. 18)

Scientific Revolution The intellectual and cultural transformation that shaped a new conception of the material world between the mid-sixteenth and early eighteenth centuries in Europe; instead of relying on the authority of religion or tradition, its leading figures believed that knowledge was acquired through rational inquiry based on evidence, the product of human minds alone. (Ch. 15)

scramble for Africa The process by which European countries partitioned the continent of Africa among themselves in the period 1875–1900. (Ch. 18)

second-wave environmentalism A movement that began in the 1960s and triggered environmental movements in Europe and North America. It was characterized by widespread grassroots involvement focused on issues such as pollution, resource depletion, protection of wildlife habitats, and nuclear power. (Ch. 23)

second-wave feminism Women's rights movement that revived in the 1960s with a different agenda from earlier women's suffrage movements; second-wave feminists demanded equal rights for women in employment and education, women's right to control their own bodies, and the end of patriarchal domination. (Ch. 22)

self-strengthening China's program of internal reform in the 1860s and 1870s, based on vigorous application of traditional principles and limited borrowing from the West. (Ch. 19)

service sector Industries like government, medicine, education, finance, and communication that have grown due to increasing consumerism, population, and communication technologies. (Ch. 22)

settler colonies Imperial territories in which Europeans settled permanently in substantial numbers. Examples include British North America, Portuguese Brazil, Spanish Mexico and Peru, Australia, New Zealand, Algeria, South Africa. (Chs. 13, 18)

"the sick man of Europe" Western Europe's description of the Ottoman Empire in the nineteenth and early twentieth centuries, based on the empire's economic and military weakness and its apparent inability to prevent the shrinking of its territory. (Ch. 19)

signares The small number of African women who were able to exercise power and accumulate wealth through marriage to European traders. (Ch. 14)

Sikhism Religious tradition of northern India founded by Guru Nanak (1469–1539); combines elements of Hinduism and Islam and proclaims the brotherhood of all humans and the equality of men and women. (Ch. 15)

"silver drain" Term often used to describe the siphoning of money from Europe to pay for the luxury products of the East, a process exacerbated by the fact that Europe had few trade goods that were desirable in Eastern markets; eventually, the bulk of the world's silver supply made its way to China. (Ch. 14)

social Darwinism An outlook that suggested that European dominance inevitably led to the displacement or destruction of backward peoples or "unfit" races; this view made imperialism, war, and aggression seem both natural and progressive. (Ch. 18)

socialism in the United States Fairly minor political movement in the United States; at its height in 1912, it gained 6 percent of the vote for its presidential candidate. (Ch. 17)

"soft gold" Nickname used in the early modern period for animal furs, highly valued for their warmth and as symbols of elite status. (Ch. 14)

Songhay Empire Major Islamic state of West Africa that formed in the second half of the fifteenth century. (pron. song-GAH-ee) (Ch. 12)

Stalin, Joseph (1878–1953) Leader of the Soviet Union from the late 1920s until his death. (Ch. 20)

Stanton, Elizabeth Cady (1815–1902) Leading figure of the early women's rights movement in the United States. At the first Women's Rights Convention in Seneca Falls, New York, in 1848, she drafted a statement paraphrasing the Declaration of Independence, stating that men and women were created equal. (Ch. 16)

steam engine The great breakthrough of the Industrial Revolution, the coal-fired steam engine provided an almost limitless source of power and could be used to drive any number of machines as well as locomotives and ships; the introduction of the steam engine allowed a hitherto unimagined increase in productivity and made the Industrial Revolution possible. (Ch. 17)

Syrian civil war Conflict beginning in 2011 that generated over 12 million refugees and asylum seekers by mid-2016 and engaged both regional and world powers on various sides of the conflict. (Ch. 21)

systemic racism Racism that manifests in deeply rooted cultural and social attitudes and frequently finds expression in institutional practices. (Ch. 23)

Taiping Uprising Massive Chinese rebellion against the ruling Qing dynasty that devastated much of the country between 1850 and 1864; it was based on the millenarian teachings of Hong Xiuquan. (Ch. 19)

Taki Onqoy Literally, "dancing sickness"; a religious revival movement in central Peru in the 1560s whose members preached the imminent destruction of Christianity and of the Europeans and the restoration of an imagined Andean golden age. (Ch. 15)

Tanzimat Important reform measures undertaken in the Ottoman Empire beginning in 1839; the term "Tanzimat" means "reorganization." (pron. tahn-zee-MAHT) (Ch. 19)

Thirty Years' War Catholic-Protestant struggle (1618–1648) that was the culmination of European religious conflict, brought to an end by the Peace of Westphalia and an agreement that each state was sovereign, authorized to control religious affairs within its own territory. (Ch. 15)

Timbuktu A major commercial city of West African civilization and a noted center of Islamic scholarship and education by the sixteenth century. (Ch. 12)

Timur Turkic warrior, also known as Tamerlane, whose efforts to restore the Mongol Empire in the late fourteenth and early fifteenth centuries devastated parts of Persia, Russia, and India. His successors created a vibrant elite culture drawing on both Turkic and Persian elements, especially in the city of Samarkand. Timur's conquests represent the last major military success of Central Asian pastoral peoples. (Ch. 12)

Tokugawa Japan A period of internal peace in Japan (1600–1850) that prevented civil war but did not fully unify the country; led by military rulers, or shoguns, from the Tokugawa family, who established a "closed door" policy toward European encroachments. (Ch. 19)

total war War that requires each country involved to mobilize its entire population in the effort to defeat the enemy. (Ch. 20)

trading post empire Form of imperial dominance based on control of trade through military power rather than on control of peoples or territories. (Ch. 14)

transatlantic slave system Between 1500 and 1866, this trade in human beings took an estimated 12.5 million people from African societies, shipped them across the Atlantic in the Middle Passage, and deposited some 10.7 million of them in the Americas as enslaved people; approximately 1.8 million died during the transatlantic crossing. (Ch. 14)

transnational corporations Global businesses that produce goods or deliver services simultaneously in many countries; growing in number since the 1960s, some have more assets and power than many countries. (Ch. 22)

Treaty of Versailles The 1919 treaty that officially ended World War I; the immense penalties it placed on Germany are regarded as one of the causes of World War II. (Ch. 20)

Tupac Amaru Leader of a Native American rebellion in Peru in the early 1780s, claiming the last Inca emperor as an ancestor. (Ch. 16)

unequal treaties Series of nineteenth-century treaties in which China made major concessions to Western powers. (Ch. 19)

Vindication of the Rights of Woman Written in 1792 by Mary Wollstonecraft, this tract was one of the earliest expressions of feminist consciousness. (Ch. 16)

Vivekananda (1863–1902) Leading religious figure of nineteenth-century India; advocate of a revived Hinduism and its mission to reach out to the spiritually impoverished West. (Ch. 18)

Voltaire The pen name of François-Marie Arouet (1694–1778), a French writer whose work is often taken as a model of the Enlightenment's outlook; noted for his deism and his criticism of traditional religion. (Ch. 15)

Wahhabi Islam Major Islamic movement led by the Muslim theologian Muhammad Ibn Abd al-Wahhab (1703–1792) that advocated an austere lifestyle and strict adherence to the Islamic law; became an expansive state in central Arabia. (Ch. 15)

Wang Yangming Influential Ming thinker (1472–1529) who argued that anyone could achieve a virtuous life by introspection and contemplation, without the extended education and study of traditional Confucianism. (Ch. 15)

Warsaw Pact A military alliance between the Soviet Union and communist states in Eastern Europe, created in 1955 as a counterweight to NATO; expressed the tensions of the cold war in Europe. (Ch. 21)

Women's Department (USSR) A distinctive organization, known as Zhenotdel, within the Communist Party of the Soviet Union that worked to promote equality for women in the 1920s with conferences, publications, and education. (Ch. 22)

World Trade Organization (WTO) An international body now representing 164 nations and charged with negotiating the rules for global commerce and promoting free trade; its meetings have been the site of major anti-globalization protests since 1999. (Ch. 22)

World War I The "Great War" (1914–1918), in essence a European civil war with a global reach that was marked by massive casualties, trench warfare, and mobilization of entire populations. It triggered the Russian Revolution, led to widespread disillusionment among intellectuals, and rearranged the political map of Eastern Europe and the Middle East. (Ch. 20)

World War II in Asia A struggle to halt Japanese imperial expansion in Asia, fought by primarily Chinese and American forces. (Ch. 20)

World War II in Europe A struggle to halt German imperial expansion in Europe, fought by a coalition of allies that included Great Britain, the Soviet Union, and the United States. (Ch. 20)

yasak Tribute that Russian rulers demanded from the native peoples of Siberia, most often in the form of furs. (Ch. 13)

Young Ottomans Group of would-be reformers in the mid-nineteenth-century Ottoman Empire that included lower-level officials, military officers, and writers; they urged the extension of westernizing reforms to the political system. (Ch. 19)

Young Turks Movement of Turkish military and civilian elites that advocated a militantly secular public life and a Turkish national identity; came to power through a coup in 1908. (Ch. 19)

Zheng He Great Chinese admiral who commanded a huge fleet of ships in a series of voyages in the Indian Ocean that began in 1405. Intended to enroll distant peoples and states in the Chinese tribute system, those voyages ended abruptly in 1433 and led to no lasting Chinese imperial presence in the region. (pron. JUHNG-huh) (Ch. 12)

Index

A Note about the Index: Names of individuals are in **boldface.** Letters in parentheses following pages refer to the following:

(d) documents
(i) illustrations, including photographs and artifacts
(f) figures, including charts and graphs
(m) maps
(t) tables

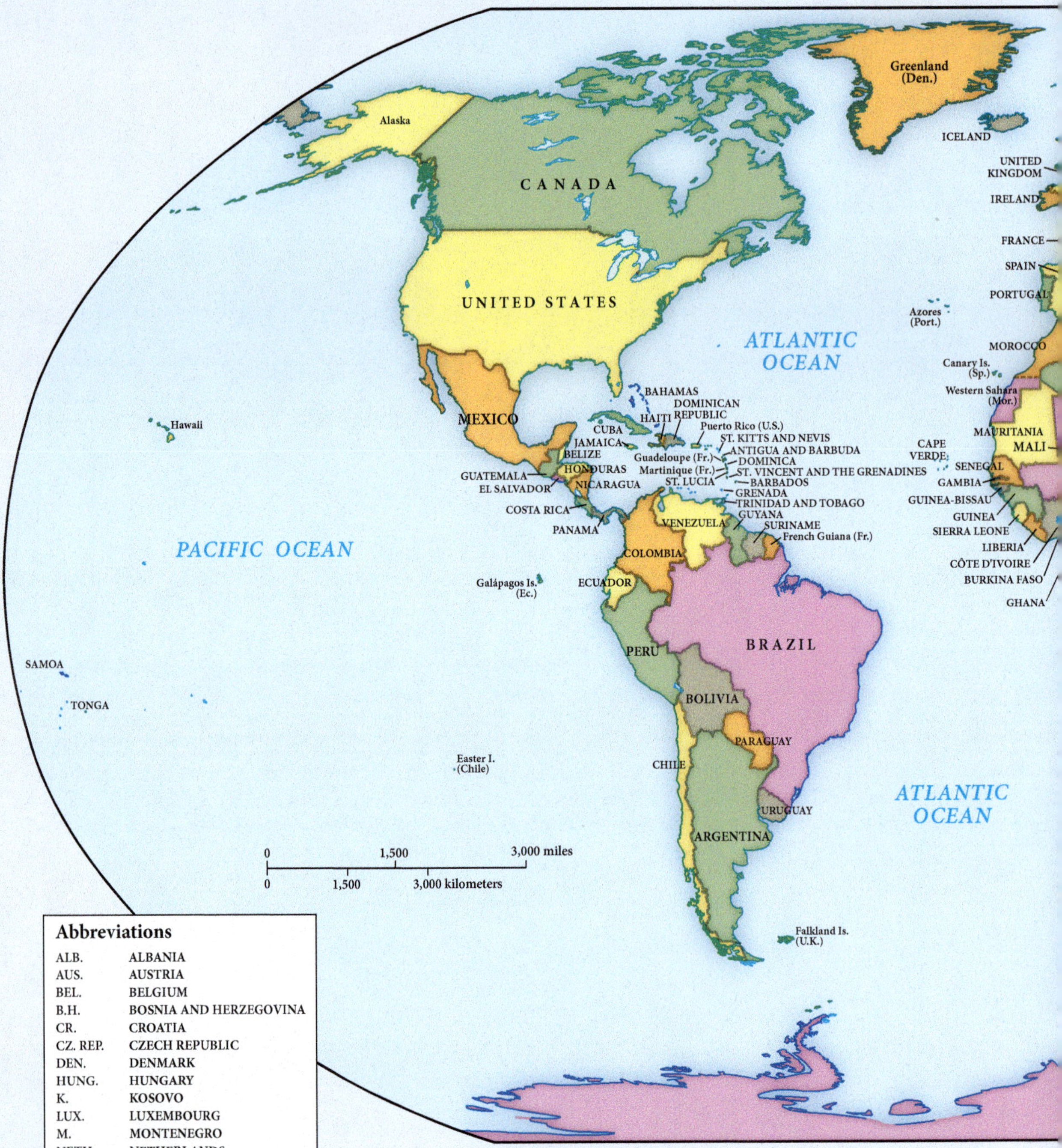

Abbreviations

ALB.	ALBANIA
AUS.	AUSTRIA
BEL.	BELGIUM
B.H.	BOSNIA AND HERZEGOVINA
CR.	CROATIA
CZ. REP.	CZECH REPUBLIC
DEN.	DENMARK
HUNG.	HUNGARY
K.	KOSOVO
LUX.	LUXEMBOURG
M.	MONTENEGRO
NETH.	NETHERLANDS
NO. MAC.	NORTH MACEDONIA
S.	SERBIA
SLK.	SLOVAKIA
SLN.	SLOVENIA
SWITZ.	SWITZERLAND

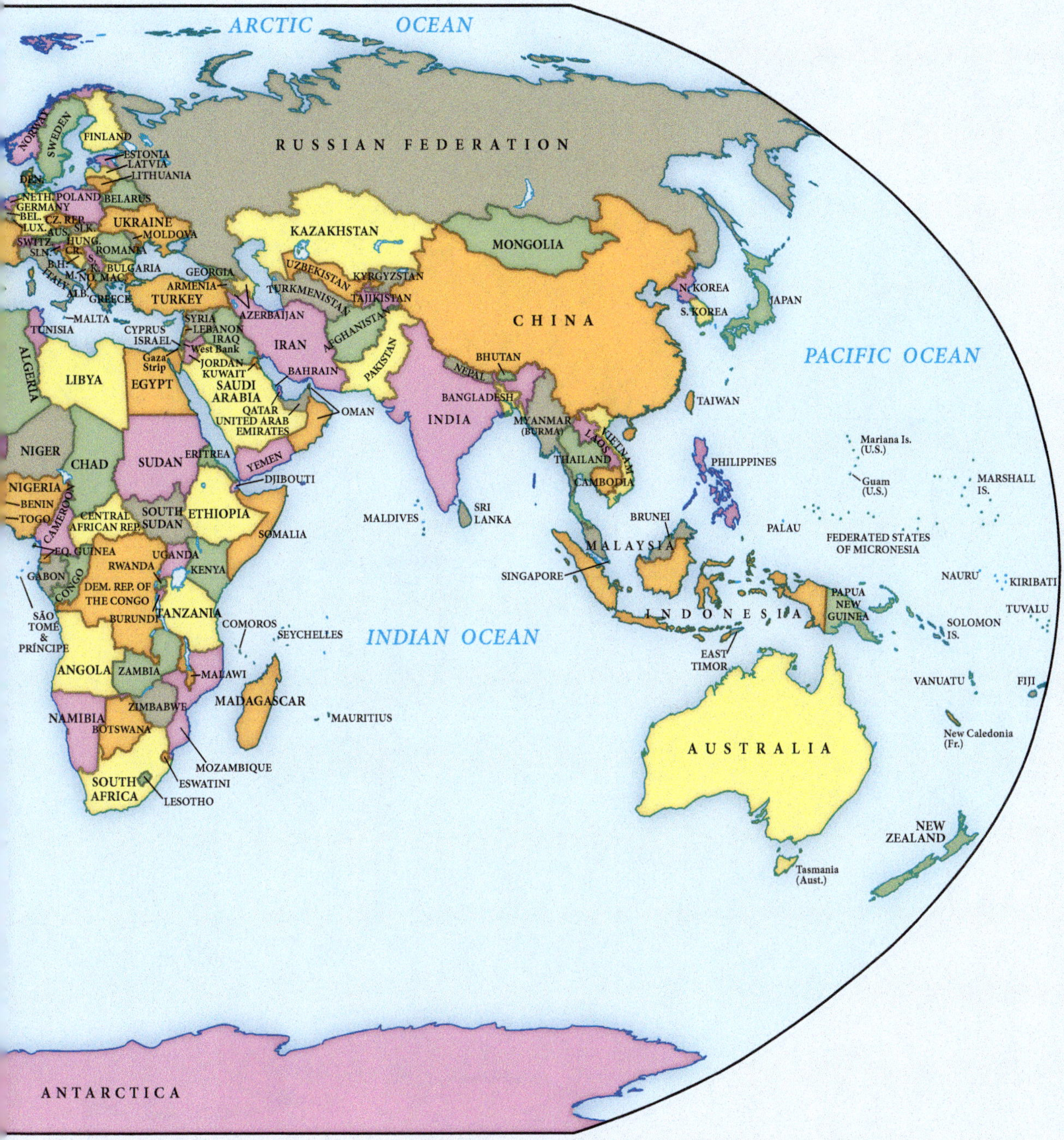

ARCTIC OCEAN
RUSSIAN FEDERATION
NORWAY
SWEDEN
FINLAND
ESTONIA
LATVIA
LITHUANIA
DEN.
NETH.
POLAND
BELARUS
GERMANY
BEL.
CZ. REP.
LUX.
AUS.
SLK.
UKRAINE
MOLDOVA
SWITZ.
HUNG.
SLN.
CR.
ROMANIA
B.H.
BULGARIA
M.
N.M.
MAC.
ITALY
ALB.
GREECE
GEORGIA
ARMENIA
TURKEY
AZERBAIJAN
KAZAKHSTAN
UZBEKISTAN
KYRGYZSTAN
TURKMENISTAN
TAJIKISTAN
MONGOLIA
N. KOREA
S. KOREA
JAPAN
CHINA
MALTA
TUNISIA
CYPRUS
SYRIA
LEBANON
ISRAEL
IRAQ
West Bank
IRAN
AFGHANISTAN
PAKISTAN
Gaza Strip
JORDAN
KUWAIT
BAHRAIN
ALGERIA
LIBYA
EGYPT
SAUDI ARABIA
QATAR
UNITED ARAB EMIRATES
OMAN
NEPAL
BHUTAN
BANGLADESH
INDIA
MYANMAR (BURMA)
LAOS
VIETNAM
THAILAND
CAMBODIA
TAIWAN
PHILIPPINES
PACIFIC OCEAN
NIGER
CHAD
SUDAN
ERITREA
YEMEN
DJIBOUTI
NIGERIA
BENIN
TOGO
CAMEROON
CENTRAL AFRICAN REP.
SOUTH SUDAN
ETHIOPIA
SOMALIA
EQ. GUINEA
UGANDA
GABON
CONGO
RWANDA
KENYA
DEM. REP. OF THE CONGO
BURUNDI
TANZANIA
SÃO TOMÉ & PRÍNCIPE
COMOROS
SEYCHELLES
ANGOLA
ZAMBIA
MALAWI
MADAGASCAR
NAMIBIA
ZIMBABWE
BOTSWANA
MAURITIUS
MOZAMBIQUE
SOUTH AFRICA
ESWATINI
LESOTHO
MALDIVES
SRI LANKA
INDIAN OCEAN
BRUNEI
MALAYSIA
SINGAPORE
INDONESIA
EAST TIMOR
PALAU
Mariana Is. (U.S.)
Guam (U.S.)
MARSHALL IS.
FEDERATED STATES OF MICRONESIA
NAURU
KIRIBATI
PAPUA NEW GUINEA
TUVALU
SOLOMON IS.
VANUATU
FIJI
New Caledonia (Fr.)
AUSTRALIA
NEW ZEALAND
Tasmania (Aust.)
ANTARCTICA

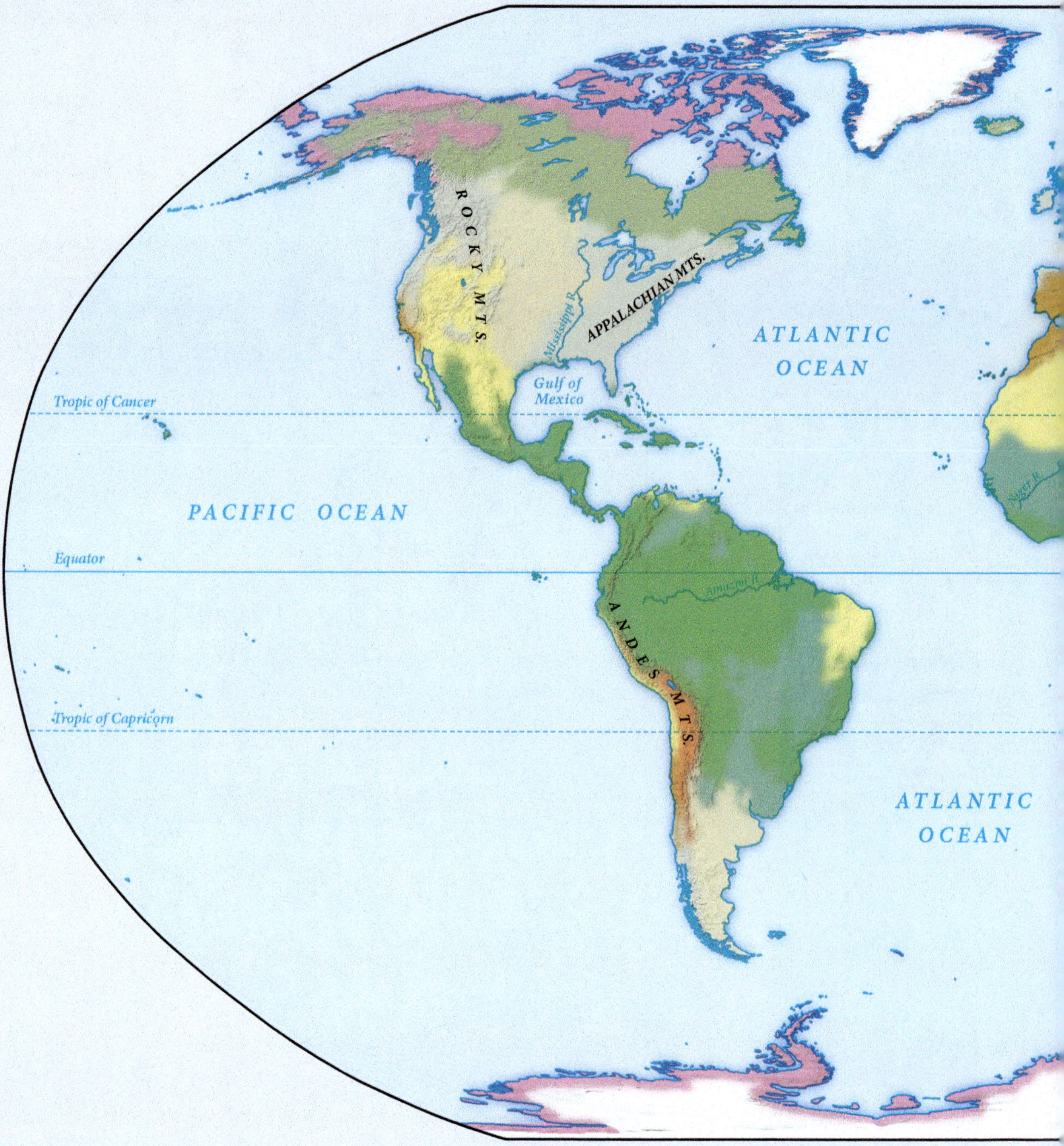
ROCKY MTS.
APPALACHIAN MTS.
Mississippi R.
ATLANTIC OCEAN
Gulf of Mexico
Tropic of Cancer
PACIFIC OCEAN
Equator
Amazon R.
Niger R.
ANDES MTS.
Tropic of Capricorn
ATLANTIC OCEAN

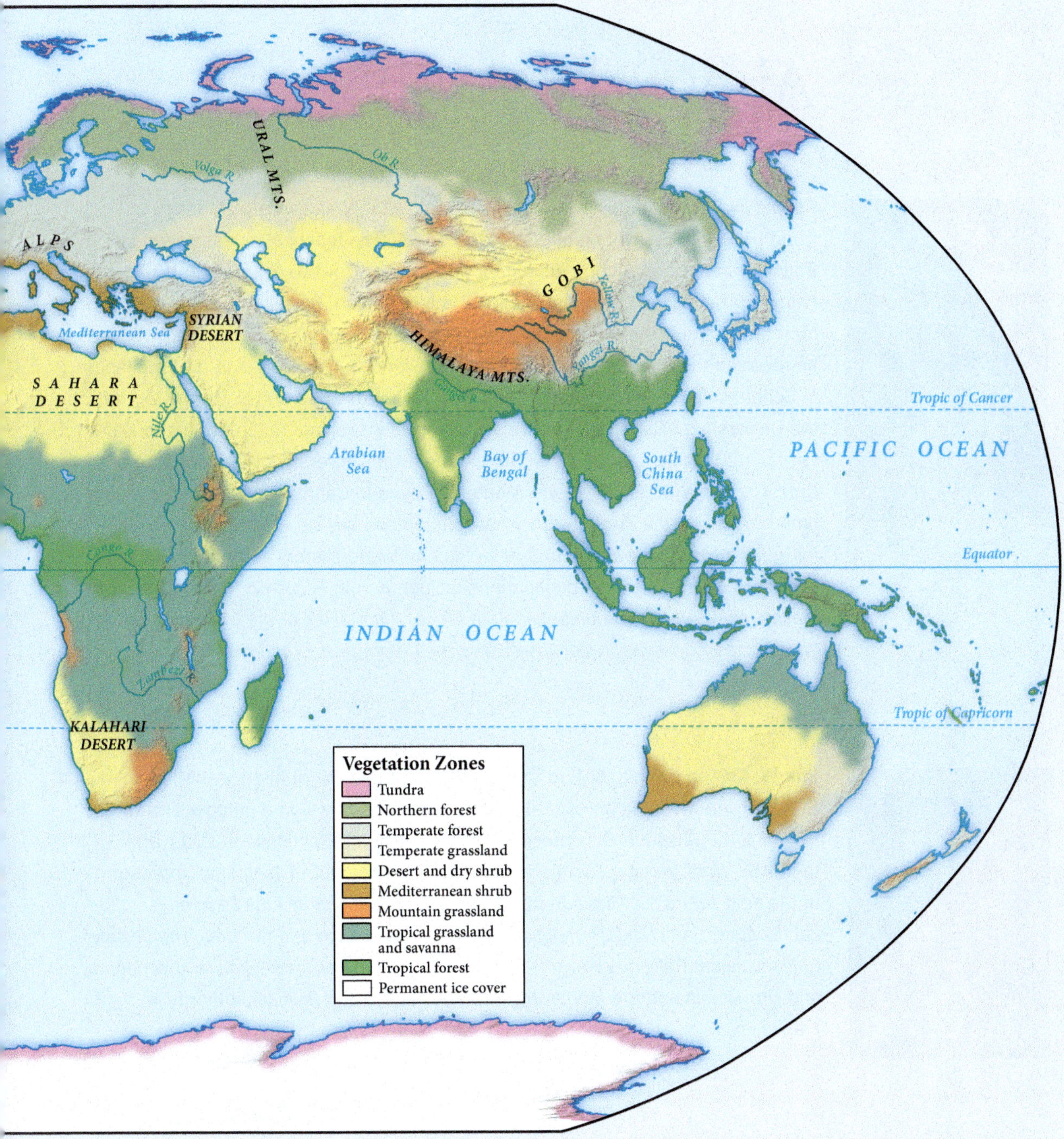

URAL MTS.
Volga R.
Ob R.
ALPS
GOBI
Yellow R.
Mediterranean Sea
SYRIAN DESERT
HIMALAYA MTS.
Yangzi R.
Ganges R.
SAHARA DESERT
Nile R.
Tropic of Cancer
Arabian Sea
Bay of Bengal
South China Sea
PACIFIC OCEAN
Congo R.
Equator
INDIAN OCEAN
Zambezi R.
KALAHARI DESERT
Tropic of Capricorn
Vegetation Zones
Tundra
Northern forest
Temperate forest
Temperate grassland
Desert and dry shrub
Mediterranean shrub
Mountain grassland
Tropical grassland and savanna
Tropical forest
Permanent ice cover

About the Authors

Jerry Burke

Robert W. Strayer (Ph.D., University of Wisconsin) brings wide experience in world history to the writing of *Ways of the World*. His teaching career began in Ethiopia, where he taught high school world history for two years as part of the Peace Corps. At the university level, he taught African, Soviet, and world history for many years at the College at Brockport: State University of New York, where he received the Chancellor's Awards for Excellence in Teaching and for Excellence in Scholarship. In 1998 he was visiting professor of world and Soviet history at the University of Canterbury in Christchurch, New Zealand. Since moving to California in 2002, he has taught world history at the University of California, Santa Cruz; California State University, Monterey Bay; and Cabrillo College. He is a longtime member of the World History Association and served on its Executive Committee. He has also participated in various AP World History gatherings, including two years as a reader. His publications include *Kenya: Focus on Nationalism, The Making of Mission Communities in East Africa, The Making of the Modern World, Why Did the Soviet Union Collapse?*, and *The Communist Experiment.*

Jesse Scheve/Missouri State University

Eric W. Nelson (D.Phil., Oxford University) is a professor of history at Missouri State University. He is an experienced teacher who has won a number of awards, including the Missouri Governor's Award for Teaching Excellence in 2011 and the CASE and Carnegie Foundation for the Advancement of Teaching Professor of the Year Award for Missouri in 2012. His publications include *Layered Landscapes: Early Modern Religious Space across Faiths and Cultures, The Legacy of Iconoclasm: Religious War and the Relic Landscape of Tours, Blois and Vendôme,* and *The Jesuits and the Monarchy: Catholic Reform and Political Authority in France.*